# The World Today Series®

Stryker-Post Publications
Harpers Ferry, WV
USA

# AFRICA

## by Charles H. Cutter

# 2005

## 40th EDITION

Next Publication Date, August 2006

**Charles H. Cutter . . .**

received his Ph.D. in Political Science from UCLA after taking his BA and MA degrees, also in Political Science, from the University of California, Berkeley. His post-doctoral work was done at Yale University in Art History. He has taught at UCLA, Yale (Morse College), Bristol University, England, and is presently Emeritus Professor of Humanities and Political Science at San Diego State University where he has taught courses ranging from Traditional African Political Systems to Political Change in Modern Africa and an introduction to African civilizations. Professor Cutter has been the recipient of Fulbright-Hays Foreign Language Fellowships to study Bamana and to conduct research in West Africa, as well as a fellowship from the American Council of Learned Societies to study African Art at Yale. He has published on both African art and political history and curated an exhibition of African Art for the San Diego Museum of Art.

First appearing as *Africa 1966,*
this annually revised book is published by

**Stryker–Post Publications**
P.O. Drawer 1200
Harpers Ferry, WV 25425
Telephones: 1–800–995–1400 (U.S.A. and Canada).
  Other: 1–304–535–2593
  Fax: 1–304–535–6513
  www.strykerpost.com
VISA–MASTERCARD–AMERICAN EXPRESS

International Standard Book Number: 1–887985–63–8

International Standard Serial Number: 0084–2281

Library of Congress Catalog Number 67–11537

Cover design by Filar Design

Cartographer: William L. Nelson

Typography by Barton Matheson Willse & Worthington
Baltimore, MD 21244

Printed in the United States of America
by United Book Press, Inc.
Baltimore, MD 21207

The World Today Series has thousands of subscribers across the U.S. and Canada. A sample list of users who annually rely on this most up-to-date material include:

Public library systems
Universities and colleges
High schools
Federal and state agencies
All branches of the armed forces & war colleges
National Geographic Society
National Democratic Institute
Agricultural Education Foundation
Exxon Corporation
Chevron Corporation
CNN

Photographs used to illustrate *The World Today Series* come from many sources, a great number from friends who travel worldwide. If you have taken any which you believe would enhance the visual impact and attractiveness of our books, do let us hear from you.

# CONTENTS

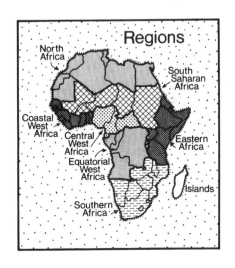

# ACKNOWLEDGMENTS

There are always many who have contributed in some way to the production of a book and this volume is no different. I wish to thank specifically the following: Connie Abell, Housseïni Abdou-Saleye, Rita Arendt, Avenir des Peuples des Forêts Tropicales-Université libre de Bruxelles, Jude Barnes, C.L. Beguelin, Beau Bennett, Gwen Benson, Barbara Blackmun, William P. Carl Fine Prints, Paul Carlson Partnership, Pat Crowell, Bill Davis, Ross Dunn, Ruth Evans, Haddush Fesseha, Isabelle Forter, Lance Fuchs, Galerie al Farahnick (Brussels), Christine Farrington, Mary Ellen "Tish" Grabski, Virginia Grady, Jose Manuel Hernández, Judi Iranyi, Powell Harrison, Beverly Ingram, David Johns, Joe Joyner, Bev Klein, Jinny Lambert, Sarah and Rodney McNabb, Taylor O'Connor, Cezar Ornatowski, Martin Ottenheimer, Sean Patrick, Joann Sandlin, Bianca Scotton, Carlos da Souza, Richard Styker, Theodore Trefon, Andy Trimlett, Fabien Violas, and Marian Zeldin.

To Lilla Sweatt, whose infinite patience and prodigious skill helped a writer through the mysteries of digital imagery, and to Jack Albrecht, whose extraordinary skills as a reference librarian I could always rely on, I wish to express my special thanks.

✳ ✳

**Of Time, Place, and Rhythms Eternal**

Photo by Jude Barnes

President Hu Jintao visits Gabon, February 2004

## Introduction

It was all so appropriate. Comrade Robert Mugabe celebrated the silver anniversary of Zimbabwe's independence in April 2005 with a 35-minute speech in the Chinese-built national sports stadium. While thousands listened (most were waiting for a soccer game to begin) and brand new Chinese jets and aged Russian ones streaked overhead, Mugabe castigated the West: "We have turned East," he told his audience, "where the sun rises, and given our back to the West, where the sun sets." The scene highlights the remarkably successful Chinese economic penetration of Africa, the full extent of which is relatively under appreciated.

In Zimbabwe, China administers hospice care to a mortally wounded economy. Inflation of over 600%, unemployment between 70% and 80%, and GDP contraction are the most obvious signs of a dying economy. The downward spiral began with willfully mad land policies that disrupted commercial farming. When notoriously rigged elections and a vile human rights record brought EU and American sanctions against Comrade Mugabe's regime, China stepped into the vacuum. Disregarding a Western arms embargo,

China supplied at least $240 million in military goods to Mugabe. Besides the modern jets, replacement for British models whose parts were embargoed, thousands of AK-47 assault rifles, riot gear, and mobile water canons—all useful in suppressing urban disturbances—were included. The Chinese also supplied radio-jamming equipment to thwart opposition broadcasts during the March parliamentary election.

Payment for these tools of regime maintenance comes from Zimbabwe's abundant natural resources—apparently future tobacco and gold sales have been mortgaged to this end. Special access has been provided Chinese firms in a number of sectors—mineral resources, energy, telecommunications, and construction—and cheap Chinese manufactures, shoes, clothing, and plastic items, for example, have driven local production from the market places of Zimbabwe. With a large parliamentary majority, Zimbabwe's governing party has recently introduced a constitutional amendment to nationalize all land, eliminating with a single legislative stroke the pesky commercial farmers who had used the courts to legitimize their land claims. It also frees up land to be given Chinese agro-business firms in

the desperate attempt to repay obligations and revitalize production. Zimbabwe has become, in short, an economic dependent of China.

Zimbabwe nicely illustrates the Chinese pattern for penetration: move to fill the void when Western (and sometimes Eastern) presence and influence wane; offer generous loans and credit arrangements to assist regime maintenance, regardless of how disreputable the regime may be ("We don't believe that human rights should stand above sovereignty," said the director of the African Studies Section of the Chinese Academy of Social Sciences); extract natural resources in payment; secure privileged access for Chinese corporations, both public and private, to other economic sectors; demand support for China's "One China" policy to integrate breakaway Taiwan into the mainland and generally support China's assertion of its Great Power status in various international arenas.

Although Zimbabwe represents Chinese strategy in its most concentrated form, the same pattern can be seen in Egypt, Sudan, Ethiopia, and more recently the Côte d'Ivoire. The strategy is the culmination of fifty years of evolving diplomacy and certainly the most expansive in-

# Africa Today

ternational pursuit of Chinese interests in centuries. Always preferring the long view, the Chinese like to say contact with Africa can be traced back to the 10th century BC, when trade between Egypt and China began. The two countries first established diplomatic relations in the 2nd century BC, but the most remarkable connection to Africa did not come until the early 15th century with the voyages of Zheng He. On the fifth of his seven epic voyages, the Ming Admiral of the Seas reached the east coast of Africa in ships that had no parallel in the West.

China's modern connection Africa begins with the Bandung Conference of 1955. The meeting gathered 29 African and Asian nations to oppose colonialism, promote economic and cultural cooperation, and define a non-aligned middle ground between post-war East and West. The five principles articulated at Bandung—mutual respect for territorial integrity and sovereignty, mutual non-aggression, non-interference in each other's internal affairs, equality and mutual benefit, and peaceful coexistence—remain the foundation of China's foreign policy today.

One year later the People's Republic established diplomatic relations with Egypt, the first with any African country. (In May 2006 the two countries will celebrate the 50th anniversary of relations by opening the Egyptian Chinese University, the first such undertaking in the region; the school plans to enroll 900 undergraduates for the 2006-07 academic year.) The first Chinese delegation to visit Africa arrived in March 1957 and since then there have been continuing high-level exchanges between African and Chinese leaders. More than 80 state leaders from over 50 countries have paid 120-plus visits to China. Since 1992 three Chinese presidents, Yang Shangkun, Jiang Zemin, and Hu Jintao, have made six official visits to the continent.

During the 1950s and 1960s, the Chinese relationship to Africa was highly ideological. The Bandung spirit was aggressively pursued. Liberation movements throughout the continent were actively supported; economic aid offered, and often-splashy showpiece construction built. During the 1960s, for example, China helped Zambia cope with Rhodesian trade sanctions by constructing a railway from Dar es Salam to Lusaka. The payoff came in 1971 when the People's Republic gained its legal claim to China's permanent seat on the UN Security Council with staunch African support.

Deng Xiaopeng's economic reforms of the 1980s gave new direction and greater impetus to Sino-African relations. Deng liberalized the Chinese economy and freed entrepreneurial energies that pro-

IMPORTANT NOTE:
In the chapters dealing with West Africa, these acronyms are frequently used:

**ECOWAS:** Economic Community of West African States
**ECOMOG:** Economic Community Monitoring Group

Gabon's resource riches: timber and oil

©Photographie Michel Hasson

vided the basis for surging economic development. To fuel continuing growth China has a nearly insatiable appetite for natural resources, but the basic economic quest is always clothed in standard political rhetoric redolent of the Bandung principles.

It is difficult to understand China's deep commitment to Africa without contemplating the needs of a growing economy. Until 1992, China was a net exporter of oil. In 1993 it imported 25,000 barrels per day (bbl/d). In 1996 the figure rose to 445,000 bbl/d, an eighteen-fold increase is just three years. Since then oil imports have grown exponentially. In 2003 China surpassed Japan to become the world's second largest consumer of petroleum products, importing 5.56 million bbl/d; its petroleum needs—to power vehicles, run machinery, make plastic, and most importantly, to fire power generation to compensate for severe electricity shortages—increase 20% annually. (In contrast, the U.S. uses about 20 million bbl/d, with a 2% annual use increase.) The International Energy Agency predicts that Chinese demand will continue to grow until 2030 when it will reach nearly 14 million bbl/d.

Given the expanding needs of its galloping economy, China has invested heavily in the development of African petroleum resources. China National Petroleum Corporation (CNPC) owns a 40% share of the Greater Nile Petroleum Operating Company, the Sudanese oil-producer. Located deep within southern Sudan, the oil fields around Benitu were distant from refinery and transport facilities, not to mention being subject to attacks by rebel forces. Though development there began only in 1996, the first cargo of Sudanese oil left the Red Sea oil

terminal in September 1999. China supplied the money and men (reportedly convict laborers) to build, extraordinarily rapidly, a 994-mile pipeline from the southern oil fields to the Red Sea. To protect construction and workers, China also supplied the Sudanese government with arms with which it effectively cleansed the producing areas of local inhabitants. In addition, CNPC built and operates the Khartoum Oil Refinery, suggesting the totalizing vision that drives Chinese investment in oil production. Sudan now accounts for 5% of all Chinese petroleum imports. That's a sufficiently large enough amount to make the government avoid any risk of supply destabilization: UN Security Council efforts to initiate sanctions against the Sudanese government to curtail its genocidal policies in Darfur have regularly been stymied by Chinese veto threats.

President Hu Jintao's 2004 trip to Africa (his first) brought him to three oil and gas producing states: Egypt (for historically symbolic reasons), Algeria (to confirm already-extensive relations in the petroleum sector and the continuing desire to purchase more oil and invest more extensively) and resource rich-Gabon, bordering the oil-boom developments in the Gulf of Guinea.

The visit to Gabon, Hu Jintao's only sub-Saharan stop, celebrated 30 years of diplomatic relations. Intensive economic relations did not begin until China's own economic liberalization in the 1980s; in 1986 a fishing venture was begun, and by 2004 some 100 Chinese vessels were engaged in industrial fishing operations off the Gabonese coast. Chinese fishing activities there were so extensive by 2003 that China opened its first overseas agency for

inspection of the country's ocean fishing fleet that year. Since 1974, Gabon's long-term President, Omar Bongo Ondimba, has maintained a regular dialogue with Chinese officials, making the trek to Beijing on nine separate occasions, perhaps a record for an African president.

The accords initialed by Hu Jintao and Omar Bongo Ondimba exemplified China's quest for natural resources and the types of assistance that could be offered an African state. Oil was the centerpiece of the agreements, despite the fact that Gabon's oil production is in decline. China Petroleum Company (Sinopec) signed a supply contract with Total Gabon, assuring delivery of one million tons of crude oil, while another agreement covered exploration, exploitation, and refining of off-shore oil, Gabon's great hope for future petroleum production. Under the memorandum Chinese firms will participate in engineering works, the construction of refineries and chemical plants; in exchange, China will transfer technology and training, particularly, one assumes, expertise China has gained in squeezing greater production from its own aging oil fields.

Besides oil, the Sino-Gabonese accords also covered mineral resources, a mutual interest of both parties. As oil revenues have declined, the Bongo government has pressed China and other investors to commit to development of its minerals sector. With rapid economic growth, China's large aluminum, copper and steel industries are dependent on imported raw materials. (China's imports of iron ore increased from 14 million tons in 1990 to 148 million in 2003.) Gabon is the world's number two producer of manganese (after South Africa), and China is already the metal's principal importer, but the new agreements focused on the country's untapped iron resources.

Huge reserves of iron, estimated at one billion tons, are located in the far north at Belinga, but the absence of adequate infrastructure to mine and move the ore has prevented development of the deposits. Given the Chinese economy's voracious appetite for raw materials, and state corporations unimpeded by the need to make a profit, one can understand the nature of China's commitment to the Belinga iron deposits. Development of the deposits will require construction of a hydroelectric dam on the Ivindo River to provide energy to operate mining equipment, two additional rail connections to the Transgabon railroad, and construction of a deep-water port at Santa Clara to ship the ore. It will be a huge undertaking, and in all likelihood, uneconomic, but exemplary of China's current economic and political strategy.

Gabon's President Omar Bongo Ondimba visits China, September 2004.

# Africa Today

Not covered by the new Sino-Gabonese accords is the existing trade in timber—unprocessed logs from Gabon's vast forests. As with petroleum and minerals, China has enormous needs in timber. After devastating Yangtze River floods in 1998, which resulted in more than 2,500 deaths and caused billions of dollars in damage, the government blamed over logging as the principal cause. It banned timber harvesting in the region and began a crackdown on illegal logging. The government now goes elsewhere for its lumber needs, and the forests of Gabon are one of its main sources. China buys some 65% of Gabon's annual 2.5 million cubic meters of mahogany exports. In 2003 it was also importing 1.5 million cubic meters of Okoumé, a soft wood used in making plywood.

China's lumber needs are huge, and growing. Construction, furniture making, and pulp mills are all nearly-insatiable consumers. Housing reform initiated in 1998 called for the construction of five billion square meters of new housing and two billion square meters of renovated housing by 2005. The reform (so markedly different from Soviet policy) was part of the government's urbanization policy—moving 300 million rural people into the cities and improving living spaces and quality of life in them. With the increased wealth consequent to development, Chinese citizens are replacing furniture at a faster rate and remodeling their homes, driving the demand for lumber even higher. The World Wildlife Federation (WWF) estimates that by 2010 China will be able to meet only half of its demand for industrial wood.

China is already the second biggest importer of logs in the world, entering 1.5 billion cubic meters in 2003, but various environmental groups estimate that anywhere from 44% to 50% of all the logs imported are illegally cut. In African states, where logging codes are ill defined and inadequately enforced, the percentage of illegal logging is higher. Estimates suggest at least 50% of Cameroon's logs, 70% of Gabon's, and up to 90% of the logs from Equatorial Guinea are illegally cut. Chinese demand has accelerated this predatory assault, and for some environmentalists China has become the main hub of a global network of trade in illegal timber.

What more can be expected? Certainly the needs of the Chinese economy will intensify competition for natural resources in Africa. Given sharp business practices by state-owned or state-subsidized firms, unimpeded by ethical-conduct legislation, moralistic NGOs, or profit-demanding stockholders, it is likely China Inc. will become Africa's primary export market for, and principal investor in, the continent's natural resources. With its own urbanization policies removing people from the countryside, China can also be expected to invest heavily in making African agriculture more productive and another potential export resource. It is also likely that once access to raw materials is secured, China will shape its foreign and military policies to protect that access. It is noteworthy, for example, that the marine fleet of the Chinese People's Army paid a friendly visit to Tanzania in July 2000, the first such visit to the East African coast in nearly 600 years—since the days of the Ming Admiral, Zheng He.

CHC
San Diego, CA
June 2005

# HISTORICAL BACKGROUND

**A Fanti Chief, Coastal Ghana**

Photo by Isabelle Forter

## PREHISTORIC AFRICA

Advances in archeology, population genetics and linguistics continue to flesh out our understanding of human evolution. Two things are most striking: we are all one human family and our ancestral home is Africa.

The greatest advances have come in biological sciences and the human genome has come to be a new archive for historians and prehistorians. Interpretation of these archival materials remains unsettled. One element of the human cell has its own DNA which escapes he reshuffling of genes in each generation. Inherited just through the mother's line, this material, called mitochondrial DNA, has allowed population geneticists to trace Homo sapien origins. Using this material Dr. Douglas Wallace and his colleagues at Emory University in Atlanta, Georgia, have identified the Vasikela Kung of the northwestern Kalahari desert as the population that lies nearest to the root of modern humans' origins.

Using the same DNA materials, Dr. Elizabeth Watson of Massey University in New Zealand indicates the Turkana people of Kenya show the greatest genetic diversity of any known human group. For Dr. Watson highest diversity is usually indicative of a species' place of origin. Regardless of the specific place of origin what is clear that Homo sapiens, modern humans, evolved in sub-Saharan Africa and, in a later split, migrated out of Africa some 50,000 years ago to populate the rest of the world. And this wasn't the first migration of hominids out of Africa.

Archeologists, like population geneticists, continue to add to our store of knowledge of human development. Only this year scientists digging in the former Russian republic of Georgia have discovered a 1.7 million-year-old hominid skull that shows clear linkages with African fossils. Tools found with the Georgian skulls resembled tools found in the Olduvai Gorge of Tanzania and dated at about 1.8 million years.

Migration routes of early hominids are also beginning to be discovered, allowing scientists to trace this incredible journey. A cave site in Zambia has revealed pigment and paint-grinding equipment that dates back 400,000 years, suggesting the ancestors of *Homo sapiens* were decorating themselves much earlier than ever thought. A recently discovered site along the Red Sea coast of Eritrea appears to be 125,000 years old and documents the utilization of marine resources—clams, crabs and oysters.

These are some of the more tantalizing discoveries that will form the basis of a fuller understanding of human birth and development in Africa. Existing archeological remains testify to the richness of African civilization.

1

# Historical Background

## EARLY CIVILIZATIONS OF THE NILE VALLEY AND MEDITERRANEAN SEA

The Nile Valley was settled and agricultural skills developed by 5,000 B.C. This population was able to form one of the first centrally organized societies of the western world by about 3,000 B.C., the beginning of the Egyptians. Under the control of the succession of kings (Phar-aohs), the social organization of the people permitted rapid evolution and development of writing, architecture, religion and the beginning of scientific thought.

The Egyptians' early religious efforts were varied; they conceived of a god represented by a variety of animal forms. Under the rule of the dynasties, these individual symbols were gradually discarded in favor of the obelisk (a tall, usually pointed four–sided structure with ornate carvings and frescoes which was used as a symbol of *Re*. It is probable that *Re* was associated with local gods which the people were accustomed to worship, but this concept of God led to the development of the first–known beliefs in life after death. The development of writing, first in hieroglyphics (illustrations portraying a variety of thoughts and concepts) and later in abstract symbols (an early "alphabet") in turn enabled the development of a highly stylized literature. A calendar of 365 days was adopted. The religious concept of life after death led in turn to invention of enbalming methods to preserve the human body after death. This further resulted in the combination of early geometry with architecture, which permitted the construction of obelisks and elaborate and immense pyramids, the burial tombs of the pharaohs.

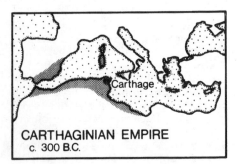

**CARTHAGINIAN EMPIRE**
c. 300 B.C.

The Egyptians under the pharaohs reached their period of greatest power in the 2nd millenium before the Christian era, and gradually declined in strength and organization until they were invaded by a succession of other Mediterranean powers—the Assyrians in the 7th century B.C., the Persians and finally the Greeks under Alexander in the 4th century, B.C. Phoenician traders on the northern coastline of the African continent combined over many centuries with the small number of other people of Middle East origin, emerging into a unified society known as Carthage in the 9th century B.C. in what is now Tunisia and part of Algeria. These aggressive people fought with the inhabitants of Sicily and Sardinia for about four hundred years, eventually winning control of the two islands after many changes in the fortunes of war in the 2nd century B.C. Carthaginian control was brief—the powerful Roman Empire was able to completely conquer Carthage by 122 B.C.

## EARLY CHRISTIAN ERA MOVEMENTS

There was a second but smaller immigration of people to Africa from some other land of the equatorial Indian Ocean and Far East–Indonesian area which probably occurred during the first millenium of the Christian era. These people, known as the Hovas, settled in the highlands of the island of Madagascar and possibly reached the East coast of Africa.

The Bantu and Sudanic groups expanded at a relatively rapid rate during the first millennium of the Christian era. There was an initial expansion of Bantu peoples into the eastern regions of Africa, into what is now Tanzania, Zambia and Zimbabwe.

The imposing stone constructions at Great Zimbabwe, located in the southwestern part of the nation now bearing that name, suggest a wealthy and privileged élite in control of a powerful state. The site was the capital of a Bantu kingdom that stretched from eastern Zimbabwe over parts of Botswana, Mozambique, and South Africa. The first known permanent settlement was established around the 11th century and building continued into the early 15th century. The large quantities of stone used to build on the site suggest control over considerable labor. The state's prosperity was based on trade in gold with Swahili speakers on the eastern African coasts.

Zimbabwe is the Anglicized version of the Shona word *Dzimbahwe*, meaning stone houses—later understood as graves, or dwellings, of chiefs. The significance must run far deeper. Built in a gentle val-

**Roman Imperial Ruins, Sabratha, Libya**　　　Photo by Pat Crowell

2

ley, it is believed that this was a sacred place where a person could communicate with his ancestors. Stone huts attached to portions of the ruins indicate that it later became a home for the living. Zimbabwe was abandoned in the early 19th century when fierce Zulu warriors destroyed the Shone confederation. The rituals which took place here are forever shrouded by the mists of time.

In succeeding centuries, the Bantu people emerged into rather powerful societies in what is now Uganda and the Congo River basin. A king of a Bantu state in Uganda who was deposed in 1966 claimed to be the 37th monarch in an uninterrupted rule of a single family. Since there was a lack of the written word during these early centuries, our knowledge of this history is dependent on oral sources. In many societies specialists, like the *griots* of West Africa, memorized the history and traditions of their peoples and passed them on to their sons. Spoken and sung, very much like the epics of Homer, these histories provided inspiration and identity for families and communities. Today, they remain an important source for historians attempting to reconstruct an African past.

The Bantu expansion southward continued at a relatively slow rate. As it pushed more deeply into the south it encountered Khoisan speaking pastoralists. When European sailing ships, mainly Dutch and English, began to make regular voyages around the Cape in the sixteenth century, they too encountered Khoisan pastoralists, eager to sell their surplus animals in exchange for iron, copper, tobacco, and beads.

## THE KINGDOM OF ETHIOPIA

By tradition, the Ethiopian kingdom dated back to a visit by the Queen of Sheba (a city in Yemen also known as Saba or Sabah) at the court of Solomon. Menelik I, son of Solomon and the Queen, founded the Ethiopian monarchy. There are other indications that the Ethiopians had progressed at a relatively early date in African history. Herodotus, a Greek writer of the 5th century B.C. described Ethiopia; Homer refers to the Ethiopians as a "blameless race" in his writing of about 800 B.C., but for the ancient Greeks, "Ethiopian" referred generally to "the most remote of men," most likely Nubians whose descendents live in modern Sudan, not present-day Ethiopia. There are forty-five references to Ethiopia in the Bible, but again, they point to the lands south of Egypt, Nubia, rather than the area of modern Ethiopia.

Not much is known of the history of Ethiopia at the beginning of the Christian era. The capital was moved from the an-

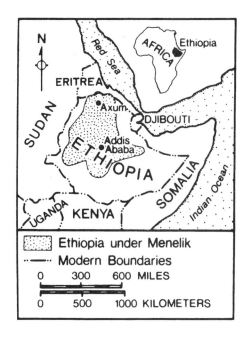

cient city of Axum to Addis Ababa and the distinctive Amharic language of the Ethiopians slowly evolved. The Christian Church in Ethiopia was established as a branch of the Coptic Christian Church headed by the Patriarch of Alexandria in Egypt. Contact with other Christians was later severed by the Islamic–Arab conquest of North Africa in the mid–10th century.

## THE SPREAD OF ISLAM

The teachings of Mohammed, a religious prophet of the neighboring Arabian peninsula, were the basis for the religion known as *Islam,* sometimes incorrectly referred to as *Mohammedanism.* The writings of Mohammed, together with his teachings, are gathered together in a book

known as the Koran. He envisioned his prophecy to be supplemental, or in addition to the other revelations, including those of Judaism and Christianity, of a single God. Preaching a belief in *Allah,* a single, all–powerful God, Mohammed was supposed to be the last prophet of God. He thought that there is a Last Judgment, a duty to donate to the poor, and, most important, there is an obligation to engage in a daily system of prayer.

A line of Islamic rulers established themselves in Damascus in Syria, and from that base other Muslim leaders conquered most of North Africa within a century, even going further to seize most of Spain.

Islam spread southward from the 8th century AD, converting most of the semi-arid regions south of the sands of the Sahara. Because of this contact with Islamic Arabs whose faith was based on a written text and who employed writing in their commercial transactions, we have much more extensive materials on which to build a history of this area. Al Umari, Ibn Khaldun and especially Ibn Battuta who visited the Mansa of Mali in the 14th century, have all left important materials to supplement local oral traditions.

## ARABS IN EAST AFRICA

From the 8th to the 10th centuries A.D. the Arabs penetrated the shoreline of East Africa in increasing numbers, establishing trading posts at Mogadishu (Somali Republic) and Mombasa (Kenya) and in what is now Mozambique. Ivory and African slaves were the basis of a brisk trade, as well as gold, shipped primarily to India. This continued in one form or another until control of the area was seized by European colonial powers in the last part of the 19th century.

## THE EARLY EMPIRES OF WEST AFRICA

A segment of people living in the area south of the Sahara gathered together in the first "empire" of West Africa in the 4th century A.D., eventually controlling a large area which is now part of Burkina Faso, southern Mali and eastern Senegal. The basis of this early group of people was a lively trade in gold and slaves with the nomadic people to the north. *Ghana,* as this empire is historically known, should not be confused with the modern state bearing that name. Its existence continued until it was conquered by the Islamic Berbers from the north in 1076, who converted the local people to their faith.

West Africa's history after Islam arrived in the sub–Sahara dry regions is one of conflict between various tribes and kingdoms, all located within the same general area. The Songhai Empire in western

The map legend reads:

Ethiopia under Menelik
Modern Boundaries
0    300    600 MILES
0    500    1000 KILOMETERS

# Historical Background

Niger, which had controlled the region since the 7th century, adopted Islam, as did the Mandingo Empire which arose in Mali. Initially, most of West Africa from about 1000 to 1200 A.D. was divided between the Songhai and Mandingo rulers, with the exception of areas closer to the coast in what are now parts of Guinea, Côte d'Ivoire, Ghana and Burkina Faso.

Trade with the Arabs to the north and east was lively for several centuries, with caravans linking Timbuktu, Gao (Mali), Kano (Nigeria) and the Lake Chad region with the Middle East by way of the Sudan and Egypt. The more affluent Islamic people journeyed on traditional pilgrimages to Mecca from this area of West Africa. Other trading was conducted with the Arab–Berber people of the North where Morocco, Algeria, Tunisia and Libya are now located.

The Mandingo rulers gradually acquired more territory at the expense of the neighboring ethnic groups after 1200 A.D. A brief domination by the Sosso people of Guinea, led by Sumanguru Kanté, was ended when the kingdoms of the savannah were rallied to overthrow Sosso's oppression in the early 13th century. The leader of this liberation struggle, Sundiata Keita, became the first of the Mansas or Emperors of Mali. Timbuktu, located in a remote part of what is now Mali, became a center of culture and progress fabled throughout West Africa, and was visited by many Arab merchants and travelers.

The Mandingo Empire disintegrated in the 15th century when Timbuktu was invaded and sacked by desert Tuaregs. A generation later, in 1468, the Songhai rulers were able in turn to expel the Tuaregs. The Songhai reached their greatest power in the following six decades, at a time when the first Portuguese explorers began to penetrate the area.

Several initially non–Muslim kingdoms arose along the southern coast of West Africa at about the same time the Islamic empires of the upper Niger River were powerful. The Fulani, also known as Peulh, established several states from what is now Senegal to Nigeria, occupying an area between the Muslim empires and the coastal lands, and gradually were converted to Islam. Closer to the coastline, the Mossi created two distinct states within what is now southern Burkina Faso and Ghana, also adopting Islam.

The Ashanti became established in what is now central Ghana, as did the Soso in Guinea, the Yorubas in Dahomey and southwestern Nigeria and the Ibos in southeastern Nigeria.

## EUROPEAN DISCOVERY AND EXPLORATION

The first exploration of the African coastline started early in the 15th century when Portuguese navigators reached Senegal, Guinea and the islands lying adjacent to the West African coast. By 1492 Fernão Poo reached the island off the coast of Cameroon which bore his name, translated into Spanish—Fernando Poo. Fifteen years later, Bartolomeu Dias, usually referred to in English as Bartholomew Diaz, was blown by a storm in a southerly direction to the bottom of the continent. Turning eastward, he became the first European to navigate around the Cape of Good Hope.

In 1497, shortly after Columbus' second voyage to America, Vasco da Gama sailed around the African cape in search of a way to India, using the primitive navigation information supplied by Diaz. He stopped at Mozambique, Mombasa and Malinda on the east coast of Africa, and was able to obtain the information necessary to proceed onward to India from the Arabs who were already established along the African coast.

With the arrival of increasing numbers of Portuguese vessels, quarrels with the Arab traders intensified. Francisco de Almeida was sent with a squadron to control Arab interference with Portuguese shipping; he took Mombasa in 1505 and ultimately demolished the Arab fleet in 1509, establishing Portuguese supremacy in the eastern coastal area of the continent.

In spite of this rather rapid navigational discovery, there was to be almost no penetration inland by the Europeans for more than three hundred years. With the exception of a Dutch settlement at the Cape of Good Hope, the sub–Sahara inland African regions remained the same dark, forbidding land that was first seen by the Portuguese. Following the precedent of the Arabs of East Africa, the Europeans started a lively West African trade in human cargo—slaves to perform the tasks of labor needed to colonize other parts of the world.

It was an easy task, with little exception, to acquire slaves along the so–called Gold and Ivory coasts of West Africa. Anchoring their slave ships in natural harbors, the Europeans negotiated with the chiefs of the more powerful ethnic groups that lived inland. When a suitable price (in terms of value, almost nothing) was agreed upon, the men and sometimes the women of a weaker neighboring tribe would be brought to the coast in bondage after a brief skirmish. They were delivered as promised to the slave traders. It was in this manner that black Africans, tempted by their desires for the wealth offered by the white slave traders, sold the bodies of other black Africans into slavery.

The Africans had no reluctance in this trade—they were doing no more than disposing of people that were a real or imagined threat to them, their families and their tribe.

Packed shoulder to shoulder in quarters on the slave ships that were so cramped no one could stand, the cargo of humans, regarded as animals, was transported across the sea, usually to the Western Hemisphere. Those unable to survive were dumped overboard at suitable intervals following their death. The remaining survivors were sold at a handsome profit compared to the sum paid for them along the African coastline—a profit possible

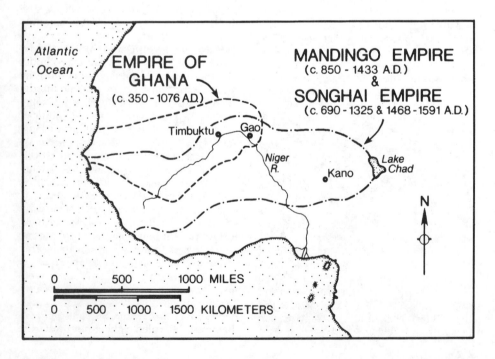

EMPIRE OF GHANA (c. 350 - 1076 A.D.)

MANDINGO EMPIRE (c. 850 - 1433 A.D.) & SONGHAI EMPIRE (c. 690 - 1325 & 1468 - 1591 A.D.)

Atlantic Ocean

Timbuktu • Gao

Niger R.

Kano •

Lake Chad

N

| 0 | 500 | 1000 MILES |

| 0 | 500 | 1000 | 1500 KILOMETERS |

**Royal Enclosure, 17th-Century, Gondar, Ethiopia**          Photo by Judi Iranyi

even if more than one–half of the ship's cargo died during the trip to the "new world." The fact that an individual slave had survived this journey was testimony to his hardiness and stamina as compared to his less fortunate brethren who had perished.

Arriving at a particular destination in the Western Hemisphere where he was sold, the slave was to begin a new and incredibly difficult life in a totally strange surrounding where he would be judged by his physical ability to perform long, long hours of hard manual labor.

### EARLY ETHIOPIAN–EUROPEAN CONTACT

In the late dark ages of Europe, a letter from a supposed Christian king of Africa received widespread acclaim as possibly being from an unknown people dating from Biblical times. Inspired by this, a Roman Catholic Pope dispatched several Dominican brothers in the 14th century to locate this Christian kingdom. The results of these efforts are not clear, but an Ethiopian emissary did reach Venice in 1402, arriving later at Lisbon and Rome. In turn, European kings and the Pope sent emissaries to Ethiopia, hoping to enlist help in the continuing "crusades" against the Islamic people of the Middle East and North Africa. This diplomatic effort continued unevenly for four centuries, and there was no other significant contact between this region of Africa and Europe during the passage of those years.

Increased penetration of Ethiopia by Europeans occurred in the 19th century. Although Ethiopia was not formally colonized by any European power, it became subject to a variety of "spheres of influence" of the British, French and Italians in the latter part of the century. The succession to the Ethiopian throne was irregular—every time a king died there was usually a two or three way contest for the throne. The somewhat weak character of the nation was further complicated by periodic skirmishes and quarrels over territory with the neighboring Sudanese who were led by religious–political figures with the title *Mahdi.* The Somalis to the east, who were Islamic, also claimed Ethiopian territory, sometimes with the assistance of the French or the Italians. The borders of the kingdom changed countless times during this period.

The modern history of the country begins with the reign of Emperor Menelik II, the first monarch to choose that name since the reign of the son of Solomon and Sheba. It was under the second Menelik that Ethiopia began to have regular contact with the outside world.

Although he was at first forced to acknowledge an Italian protectorate over Ethiopia, by 1896 he had consolidated his power sufficiently to send a military force which decisively defeated the Italians.

Lidj Yassu, the grandson of Menelik II succeeded to the throne in 1913, but was deposed in 1916. Zauditu, Menelik's daughter, was installed as Empress. Her cousin, Ras Tafari Makonnen ascended the throne in 1930, taking the name *Haile Selassie,* which means "the power of the Trinity" in Amharic.

### THE ARABS AND OTTOMAN TURKS IN NORTH AFRICA

The Arab–Berber rulers of North Africa who came to power with the spread of Islam were known first as the Almavorid and subsequently the Almohad dynasty. Initially these Muslim kingdoms were characterized by a centralized power, but in the 13th to the 16th centuries there was gradual division into countless numbers of local rulers. Just as Christianity had split into numberless sects, so also had Islam been divided. Although the internal unity of the Arabs diminished, they were usually able to unite against non–Arabs on the infrequent occasions when outsiders threatened their territory.

The Muslim rulers of the Turkish Ottoman Empire gained control of most of Egypt and Libya at the beginning of the 16th century; their power in this area was not absolute since both regions quickly became no more than tribute–paying vassal states of the Empire. The Ottoman rulers were almost continuously occupied in wars with Europe and had insufficient resources to bring North Africa directly within the Empire as was done in Syria and Iraq. It was not long before most of North Africa was within the Ottoman sphere.

With the exception of Egypt, the remainder of North Africa continued under the loose control of the Ottoman Empire until World War I. Egypt remained under the Ottomans until the invasion by Napoleon in 1798. The Turks sent Mohammed Ali from an Ottoman military family (probably of Albanian origin) as commander of forces opposing the French; together with the British under Lord Nelson, they were finally able to expel the invaders in the summer of 1799.

Mohammed Ali quickly established his personal rule in Egypt as an Ottoman *Pasha.* Although he and his successors were able to avoid absolute domination by the Ottoman rulers, in reality Egypt continued to be a tributary vassal of the Empire for about 75 years until the British influence became paramount.

Khedive Ismail, grandson of Mohammed Ali, ruled as king but under the

# Historical Background

authority of the Sultan and Caliphs of the Empire; he had received a European education for several years. The Suez Canal was under construction principally in order to provide the British with a shorter route to their possessions in India and the Far East, although the construction effort was in the name of a cooperative effort of most of the European nations and Egypt. In anticipation of the revenues expected from the canal which opened in 1869, Ismail borrowed large sums of money at extremely high interest rates from European banks. When he was unable to repay the loans on schedule, the British used this as a pretext to assert their authority in Egypt, initially with Egyptian cooperation, in order to bring areas bordering the Red Sea waterway and in the Sudan under control.

By 1876 Khedive Ismail had been forced to sell all Egyptian shares in the Suez Canal, and Egypt was placed under the supervision of British and French financial controllers. This is considered the start of the colonial period in Egypt; although the Khedives continued to be the nominal power, they were little more than the instrumentality through which the British ruled.

## EUROPEAN SETTLERS IN SOUTH AFRICA
### The Dutch at the Cape of Good Hope

Holland, seeking a food and fuel station for its ships sailing to the Dutch East Indies, established a small station on the Cape in 1652. A fort was constructed to guard against the Hottentots and Bushmen found in small numbers in the area. This outpost developed rapidly, with the outlying farms worked by slaves brought from the East.

There was a slow expansion of this Dutch community into the interior, though such was not actively pursued by the Dutch East India Company. A substantial number of Huguenot religious refugees from France arrived in 1688, adopting the Dutch social patterns. Further settlement of the interior by the Dutch *Burghers* continued for the next hundred years, since there was little opposition to their desire for additional farmland. It was not until the Dutch had penetrated 200 miles to the northeast that they first encountered the Bantu people who were then in a process of migration from the southeast lake region of Africa. Bitter frontier warfare between the two groups of migratory people continued for the next seventy–five years, with large numbers of casualties on both sides.

The British took possession of Cape Town in 1795 in the name of the Prince of Orange, who then reigned in Holland and in England when his nation was overrun by the French. The British handed the area over to the Batavian Republic, a puppet state of France, in 1803 (all of this was a product of shifting alliances in Europe involving Napoleon's activities). But in 1806 the British returned; the Cape Colony was officially ceded to it in 1814 and it became a Crown Colony. A substantial migration of British settlers arrived in the succeeding 30 years, which by 1834 caused widespread unrest among the Dutch farmers of the Eastern Cape, who resented British rule.

Led by men of courage like Andries Pretorius, for whom Pretoria is named, the Voortrekkers, or pioneers, journeyed in covered wagons to the northeast, overcoming severe hardships and fighting the fierce Bantu tribesmen. In 1839 they founded a new republic called Natal, but were later pushed even further into the interior by the arrival of British military forces. Crossing the Drakensburg (Dragon Mountains), they went into the Orange Free State and Transvaal. In each area, a Boer republic was proclaimed. Thus, toward the end of the 19th century, there were two Boer republics and two British colonies in what is now the Republic of South Africa. Discovery of a huge 84 carat diamond on the banks of the Orange River by an African shepherd boy in 1869 set off the South African diamond rush. Fortune hunters from all over the world flocked to South Africa. In 1886 the world's largest goldfields were discovered on the Witwatersrand, adding to the influx of non-Boers. With these discoveries South Africa was transformed. From an economic backwater it became a major supplier of precious minerals to the world economy.

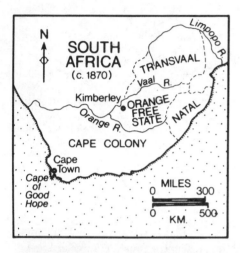

The Imperial Family of Ethiopia, 1930

Nigeria dances for Queen Elizabeth and Prince Philip, 1956

# The Colonial Period

## THE PORTUGUESE
### Coastal West Africa: Portuguese Guinea

Although the Portuguese explored the coastline of Guinea as early as 1446, the area remained a slave trading coastal region for about the next 450 years. Portuguese control of the area occurred only because it was permitted by the other, more aggressive colonial powers. This was somewhat poor territory and literally what was left after the French and British had colonized West Africa.

The final boundaries were delineated in 1905, after both Britain and France had appropriated parts of Portuguese Guinea. Penetration into the interior was negligible until about 1912; in recent years the Portuguese had only sporadic control of the region, which was still theoretically a part of European Portugal. It was declared independent on September 10, 1974.

### Equatorial West Africa: Angola, Cabinda, São Tomé, Príncipe

Angola was first explored in 1482 by Diego Cao of Portugal, who found this region of Africa controlled by the Bacongo people, led by a mighty King of the Congo. A scattering of Portuguese immigrants arrived during the following decades, but they were restricted to the coastal areas by the native Africans as a result of a series of bloody clashes. The King was overthrown, but later reestablished by the Portuguese in 1570.

During the 17th and 18th centuries, Angola was the prime source for slaves deported to Brazil to work the huge coffee plantations in that Portuguese Latin American colony. Also, an infamous penal colony was established in Angola.

During the late 19th and early 20th centuries, a multitude of treaties between Portugal and the British, French, Belgians and Germans gradually fixed the boundaries of Angola and Cabinda. The colony was given a form of internal autonomy in 1914, but this was strictly under White minority rule.

There were periodic uprisings in the 20th century, and in general, Portugal had almost exclusively favored the Portuguese immigrants and their descendants. In a flurry of civil war, accompanied by Cuban assistance for a Soviet–backed group, Angola, after formally being granted independence, became a Marxist state (see Angola).

Economic development under the Portuguese consisted of agriculture in the form of coffee and cotton production and mineral extraction based on diamonds in northeast Angola.

Cabinda is a part of Angola; it is a small enclave north of the Congo River. São Tomé is a tropical island devoted to cocoa production; it is inhabited by a uniform group of people of mixed, but predominantly African ancestry. There also was a small commercial element of Portuguese immigrants, most of whom left following the wars after independence. Príncipe is a small and poor island barely supporting the handful of descendants of freed slaves. These islands became independent on July 5, 1975 as The Democratic Republic of São Tomé and Príncipe.

### Southern Africa: Mozambique (Moçambique)

The Portuguese presence along the coast of Mozambique dates back to the voyage of Vasco da Gama in 1498. He found a number of trading posts that had been established by the Arabs, who offered little resistance to Portuguese construction of settlements and forts during the next century. These stations were intended more as an aid to Portuguese efforts in India and the Far East and were little more than stopping places for commercial vessels bound to and coming from those areas.

Shortly after Africa was partitioned at the Berlin Conference of 1885, both the French and Germans recognized Portuguese supremacy in Mozambique and elsewhere; Britain, preoccupied with its own colonial ambitions, ignored the Portuguese. Five years later, after expanding into neighboring Nyasaland (now Malawi), the British reached an agreement recognizing Portuguese claims. At the same time, the Mozambique Company was chartered to manage and invest in the colony, backed by substantial amounts of British capital. A massive uprising of Africans at the close of the 19th century hampered economic development in Mozambique. An early attempt was made in 1907 to establish a legislative council with membership restricted to White settlers in the colony.

As a result of the German defeat in World War II, the Portuguese added a small piece of German East Africa to Mozambique. The colonial period was relatively eventless between the two world wars. Railroad lines were extended initially from Beira to Nyasaland (Malawi), Southern Rhodesia (Zimbabwe), Northern Rhodesia (Zambia) and as far as the southeastern province of Katanga (Shaba) in the Belgian Congo, now DR Congo.

Portugal resisted attempts on the part of the native African majority to obtain independence during the postwar period. Following a liberal–army revolution in Portugal itself, this colony was granted independence in mid–1975 (see Mozambique).

## THE BRITISH
### Coastal West Africa: (The) Gambia

The claimant to the throne of Portugal granted English merchants, in exchange for an undisclosed sum of money, the

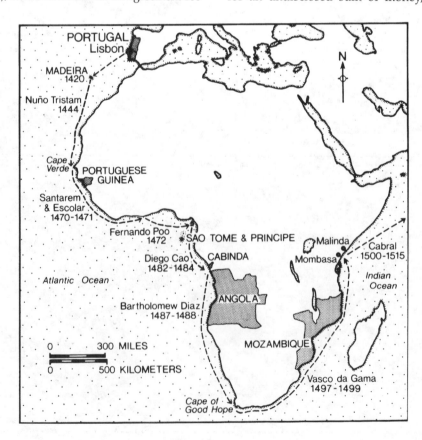

exclusive right to trade with the people along the Gambia River.

Queen Elizabeth I confirmed this sale by granting letters patent to English businessmen, and in 1618 James I granted a charter to the Royal Adventurers of England, giving the company trade franchises in Gambia and in the Gold Coast.

At the same time the British merchants were developing trade in the river area, French interests were expanding in Senegal, and the Gambia River was the best route to the interior of Senegal. Hence, an intense rivalry arose between the two nations in this area of colonial Africa. Their disputes were partially resolved by the Treaty of Versailles in 1783 which granted Gambia to the British, but reserved for the French a small enclave across the water from Bathurst.

There had been little exploration or penetration up the river to the interior until after 1860 when British explorers went inland and negotiated treaties with the local chief to obtain additional territory. The city of Bathurst remained a separate entity for the next two decades, sometimes administered from Sierra Leone, otherwise governed as a separate colony.

The present boundaries of The Gambia were delineated by a British–French agreement in 1889. Although the exportation of slaves had been prohibited, it was not until 1906 that the local practice of slavery within Gambia was abolished by British decree.

From the turn of the century until after World War II, there were few significant historical events in Gambia. Periodic efforts of the French to acquire control of the area were unsuccessful. With the exception of Bathurst, no Europeans lived in Gambia.

During World War II, Gambia not only served as an important naval base for military convoys, but contributed soldiers who fought valiantly in the Burma campaign of General Stilwell against the Japanese. The postwar period saw the birth of nationalist sentiment in Gambia. The Governor–General granted increasing powers of self government to the Africans of the country and established an advisory council.

In the late 1950's, Gambian leadership gathered into four political parties: the Progressive Peoples Party; the United Party; the Democratic Congress Alliance; and the Gambian Congress Party. The leaders of these groups actually had few differences, except with regard to possible association or federation with Senegal.

In general elections held in 1962, the Progressive Peoples Party gained 18 of the 32 popularly elected seats of Parliament. Prior to that time, Pierre Sarr N'jie, leader of the United Party, had been Chief Minister. David K. Jawara was selected Premier when his Progressive Peoples Party received support from the single delegate of the Gambia Congress Party.

Through subsequent defections, the United Party of N'jie lost five members to the organization of Jawara. An assembly of tribal leaders were selected by the Governor–General with the advice of the Prime Minister, but they had no vote. Thus, the National Assembly's membership totaled 38.

Internal self–government was granted to The Gambia in 1963, followed by explorations of the possibility of union with Senegal. A U.N. recommendation for unity between the two was turned down.

### Coastal West Africa: Sierra Leone

The people of the European mercantile powers, particularly in England, had felt increasing antipathy toward the principle of slavery by the end of the 18th century after the American Revolution. A Society for the Abolition of Slavery was formed under the leadership of Granville Sharp, which planned to establish a colony in Sierra Leone for the slaves that were to be set free. In 1788, the Temne King, Naimbana and his subordinate chiefs, sold a portion of the coastal area of Sierra Leone to the Society, which was then settled initially by a group of 300 Africans freed as a reward for their service in the British armed forces in the battles of the American Revolution, joined by some former Jamaican slaves. The diminutive settlement was administered by the Sierra Leone Company and was immediately burdened by the task of fending off attacks from neighboring groups and French warships.

There was little growth—the burden of defense, development and settlement proved to be severe for the Company, and in 1808 Sierra Leone was taken over by the British as a Crown Colony. The English Parliament had abolished slave trade in 1807. Freetown, the name of the Company settlement, became a base for a squadron of ships which sailed the shores of West Africa searching for and intercepting the privateer slave ships. The first slave ship found was quickly condemned in 1808; its human cargo, so recently abducted from other African areas, was released at Freetown. As further slave ships were captured in the succeeding years, thousands of Africans of great diversity in origin were released, most of whom elected to remain in Sierra Leone, settling largely in the areas closest to the coast.

The period of the 19th century was one of gradual development by the British in Sierra Leone, with the establishment of a flourishing trade, schools, a college and Christian church missions. The former slaves, called *Creoles,* isolated from their native peoples and traditions, adopted many English customs which prevail today among their descendants, now numbering more than 125,000. In 1896 a British protectorate was established over the territory, which by then had definite boundaries with the adjacent French territories as a result of treaties signed in 1861.

The roads to democracy and independence were ones of peaceful development of responsibility and unity among the Creoles and the inland groups, with the first elections for local office being held in 1924. Sir Milton Margai, a Creole leader, was appointed to successive offices in 1954 and the following years, becoming the first Prime Minister in 1960.

### Coastal West Africa: Ghana (Gold Coast)

The Portuguese intially landed in Ghana as early as 1470; they were followed in

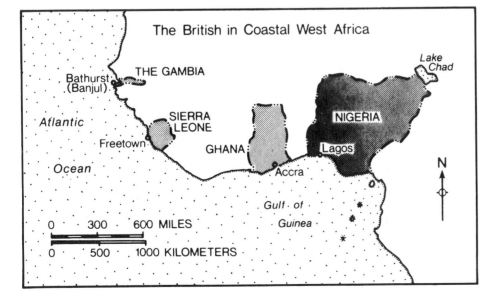

The British in Coastal West Africa

# The Colonial Period

1553 by an English arrival on the shores of what was then known as the Gold Coast. Seeking gold, ivory and spices, the Portuguese built a castle which now stands in ruins on the coast. English, Danish, Dutch, German and Portuguese commercial interests controlled ports on the Gulf of Guinea during the next 250 years. By 1750, only the English, Dutch and Danes remained.

Great Britain assumed control of English commercial settlements in 1821, negotiating treaties with the local chiefs in the southern areas in 1844. Shortly thereafter, the Danes and Dutch ceded their interests to the British.

It was necessary for the English forces to fight a long series of battles against the Asante of the interior; there were four major campaigns in which the British subdued them: 1824–27, 1873–74, 1893–94 and 1895–96. It was only in 1901 that colonial authority spread through the entire country. After seizing Togoland (Togo) from the Germans during World War I, the British administered it from Accra. With the exception of the commercial activity in the south coastal area, there was little economic development during the colonial period.

Following World War II, there was a sharp rise of nationalism among the Africans of higher education in Gold Coast, as the colony was called. The United Gold Coast Convention, led by J.B. Danquah, exerted continuous pressure for autonomy and independence.

Political developments quickly came to revolve around one person: Kwame Nkrumah. After receiving college educations in the United States and Great Britain, obtaining several degrees in advanced courses of study, he returned to the Gold Coast from England in 1947. As Secretary of the UGCC, he assisted in promoting riots and strikes in early 1948. Both he and Danquah were exiled to a remote northern village by the British Governor. The British accused Nkrumah of being a communist.

Under continuing pressure, the British in 1949 promulgated a new constitution and released the exiled leaders. Nkrumah, restless under the leadership of Danquah, formed his own political party, the Convention Peoples Party (CPP). Further civil disobedience under Nkrumah's leadership resulted in his arrest, conviction and sentence to a two–year jail term. Constitutional reforms in 1951 provided for election of a greater number of Africans to a legislative council and Nkrumah was freed from prison to head the new government.

A new constitution of 1954 established a cabinet composed entirely of African representatives. The subsequent elections

**Kwame Nkrumah**

again resulted in a majority for the *CPP*. Two years later, Nkrumah, as Prime Minister, demanded independence. The British, not convinced that this was the will of the people, held new elections in 1956, which perpetuated the majority of the *CPP* (71 out of 104 seats). Independence was declared in 1957.

### Central West Africa: Nigeria

The Portuguese were also the first explorers to land at Nigeria in 1472. For the next 300 years, traders from all nations called briefly in Nigeria, but there was no settlement. The principal purpose of their visits was to obtain human cargo to work in the colonies of the Western Hemisphere. The hundreds of Nigerian tribes periodically attacked each other, and the victor carried off the defeated to be sold into slavery for never more than $10.00 each. Transported across the ocean, they brought prices of up to $300.00. Close to 70% died in the slave ships. Slavery was not outlawed internally in Nigeria until 1901. There was a slow penetration of the British into the interior of Nigeria following the Napoleonic wars. The colony of Lagos was founded in 1862. Twenty–three years later, the Niger River Delta was established as a British Protectorate and British influence in Nigeria was formally recognized at the conference of European powers at Berlin in 1885. The British continued to expand in Nigeria through the Royal Niger Company, but in 1900 the territory came under the control of the British Colonial Office.

The people of northern Nigeria were believers in Islam; the Hausa and Fulani, as they are known, were feudally governed

by a variety of rulers known as Emirs (also spelled Amirs).

Even after penetrating into areas of Nigeria, the British had difficulty in controlling the people; there were widespread disturbances and revolts in southern Nigeria in 1904 and an uprising in the Sokoto region of northern Nigeria in 1906.

It was not until 1914 that northern Nigeria was fully brought under control, at which time the Colony and Protectorate of Nigeria was formally established. Shortly after World War I, African legislators were included in the Council governing Lagos and southern Nigeria. The British enlarged tin mines on the Jos Plateau and improved the roads, schools and port facilities of Nigeria during the succeeding decades. Following World War II, the Colonial Office adopted successive constitutions which expanded African participation in Nigerian administration on a representative, federal basis. Three political parties evolved on a regional basis: the Nigerian Peoples Congress (North), the National Convention of Nigerian Citizens (Southeast) and the Nigerian National Democratic Party (Southwest). The latter two of these parties pressed energetically for full independence, but the Nigerian Peoples Congress advocated a lesser nationalistic outlook because it feared domination by a combination of the other two parties.

Discussions were held in London in 1957, at which time there were demands by 15 ethnic groups that they become individual and independent nations within the territory of Nigeria. The British resisted these demands and established a central parliamentary government with many powers reserved to the individual provinces; independence was granted in 1960.

### Central West Africa: Cameroons

The British had early colonial ambitions in Cameroon and dispatched an emissary to negotiate treaties with the local chieftain in 1884. He arrived on the coast five days too late—the German representative had already concluded agreements with the coastal people, and Cameroon was to remain a German colony until 1916.

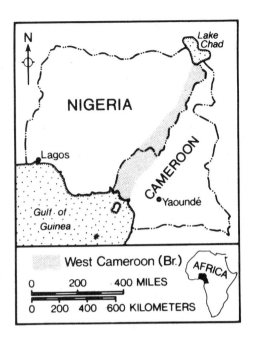

An extensive campaign was waged by the British and French against the German forces in Cameroon during the first world war. The fighting ended with the surrender of the Germans in 1916 (in Cameroon) and under the Treaty of Versailles Britain was awarded the smaller West Cameroon territory and France obtained East Cameroon. The fact that there were two colonies where there had been one gave rise to the plural name *Cameroons* for the area, creating confusion which persists even after they were again joined together in 1961.

The British held a mandate over its part from the League of Nations and subsequently under a trusteeship from the United Nations. Because of the language difference between the colonial powers of the two countries, there was wide divergence of opinion among the people of West Cameroon as to the political future of the territory in the late 1950's. The British conducted a plebiscite under UN supervision in 1961 to determine whether the people of West Cameroon desired to become a part of the English–speaking Nigeria to the northwest, or to join the French–speaking East Cameroon in a federation.

Rather than conduct the plebiscite on the basis of all votes cast in the entire territory, it was decided to count the votes of the northern and southern portions separately. The people of the North voted to become part of Nigeria, which was effected, and the people in the South voted for the federation with the former French Cameroon. The voting procedure was strongly opposed by East Cameroon, considerable opinion existing to the effect that the vote should have been counted as a

whole. Had this been done, no part of West Cameroon would have become a part of Nigeria.

———— • ————

The difference in language brought to West Africa by the British and the French has been the basis of post–independence problems. Almost uniformly, the official and commercial language of each area is that of its former colonial ruler. English–speaking Gambia should logically be a part of Senegal where French is spoken; Ghana is an English language nation surrounded by French–speaking nations, and many Ghanians, in the ethnic sense of the word, live in neighboring former French areas.

There also remains an economic pattern which is based on former colonial status; almost every nation of West Africa is economically tied to either France or Britain. Fluctuations and devaluations in currency, trade restrictions and the political problems associated with the European Common Market have all served to prevent a genuinely free flow of commerce among the present–day African nations.

## South Africa

Since the period of partial British control of what is now the Republic of South Africa was brief and hotly contested by the *Afrikaaners* of Dutch ancestry, the history of the colonial period appears in the section on South Africa. There were, however, three territories in the area over which exclusive British control was continuous: Botswana (called Bechuanaland), pronounced Beh–*kwa*–na–land), Lesotho (called Basutoland, pronounced Ba–*soo*–toe–land) and Swaziland (pronounced Swah–zee–land). During the colonial period, which ended in 1967–1968, all three were economically dependent upon what is now the Republic of South Africa even though they were colonies of Great Britain.

## Southern Africa: Botswana (formerly Bechuanaland)

The Tswana, as the majority of the people of Botswana are called, remained split into hundreds of tribes and communities until Khama I, Chief of the powerful Bamangwato tribe, consolidated them into a loosely constituted group in the last half of the 19th century.

As the *Boers* of South Africa were pushed northward from the Cape by the British, they attempted to penetrate into what is now Botswana, and battles erupted between the two peoples. Khama I, a Christianized native, appealed to the Brit-

ish for assistance, and the country was proclaimed to be under British protection.

Khama I reigned over the loosely united country until his death at the age of 93 in 1923, and was succeeded by his son, Sekgoma, who died three years later in 1926.

The British did little more than maintain peace in Bechuanaland during the period of the protectorate, although in later years they provided an annual grant to assist the colony's economy. In 1920 they set up two advisory councils—one for the native African people and one for the European settlers and their descendants who had come in small number to the area. Later, in 1934, they established a constitution which granted authority to the local chieftains and native courts.

The native rule of the Bamangwato passed to Seretse Khama, then the four–year–old son of Sekgoma, under the regency of Tshekedi Khama, brother of the dead ruler. The British had difficulty in controlling Tshekedi—at one time he was deposed as regent for a short time after having had a Britisher flogged.

Seretse Khama left for England in 1945 to pursue higher education; while studying law he met a young English woman, Ruth Williams, and married her. This interracial marriage of 1949 infuriated the white population of South Africa, and the embarrassed British Government removed Seretse Khama from office and forced him to remain in England until 1956.

After obtaining a renunciation of his chieftainship, the British permitted him to return to Bechuanaland in 1956 as "Mr. Khama." Many of the lesser chiefs opposed his return, as did his uncle, Tshekedi. The British established a Legislative Council in 1958 composed of 35 members equally divided between the races to advise and consent to the acts of the British High Commissioner, who was also executive authority in Swaziland, Basutoland and Ambassador of Great Britain to South Africa. Tshekedi was removed as Regent–Chief in 1959; the avowed purpose of establishing the Council was to prepare Bechuanaland for independence.

Political parties emerged rapidly after the first Council meetings—K.T. Motsete formed the Bechuanaland People's Party in 1960, demanding immediate independence and removal of political power from the White settlers. The British tacitly permitted Seretse Khama to enter politics because of his popularity, which had grown since his return from exile. He formed the Bechuanaland Democratic Party, with membership from both races, and advocated a policy of non–racism in government, a move toward internal self–government by 1965 and independence as soon thereafter as possible.

# The Colonial Period

The British reviewed the status of Bechuanaland in 1963 and established a new constitution in consultation with the representatives of the political parties. The first elections in 1965 under the new system were won by Khama's Democratic Party and he was named Prime Minister. Further negotiations led to an agreement for full independence which became effective on September 20, 1966; Bechuanaland took the name Botswana—land of the Tswana.

## Southern Africa: Lesotho (formerly Basutoland)

The people of what is now Lesotho, although composed almost of what are now referred to as South Sotho people, were organized in a multitude of sub–groups and tribes in the early 19th century. Raids from neighboring Zulus and Matabeles had depleted their number, and the remainder were gathered together in a loosely united kingdom by Moshoeshoe I, a chieftain from the northern region of Lesotho. The land was mountainous, hilly and generally regarded as unsuited for farming by *Boer* descendants of the original settlers of South Africa who had been driven from the Cape region into the interior of South Africa by British pressures.

But pressures for more land led to a twelve year war between the Whites of the Orange Free State and the Sothos between 1856 and 1868 which weakened the latter; they lost a substantial portion of their territory, still referred to as the "Conquered Territory." Facing total defeat, the Sothos appealed to the British for protection in 1868. The land area of the protectorate was poorly defined; the British resisted further *Boer* expansion, but had difficulty establishing control in what was considered a remote (from the Cape) land.

Basutoland, as it was then called, was annexed to the British Cape Colony in 1871, an act which was resented by the Basutos at the time because the English were just as eager for expansion in southern Africa as were the *Boers*. The unstable union was plagued by disturbances within Basutoland; the British, faced with a state of near–anarchy among the people, placed the colony directly under the control of Her Majesty's Government in 1884.

The British High Commissioners spent most of their time in Basutoland settling tribal differences and determining who was Paramount Chief—since the reign of Moshoeshoe I the land had been governed by about twenty–two lesser chiefs, who were in turn superior to approximately 2,000 minor chieftains. Little was done to improve and modernize the lives of the people living in the remote wilderness of the highlands.

Seretse Khama and his wife shortly before Botswana's independence

The Basutoland Council was informally constituted in 1903 to provide direction in internal matters, and it was recognized officially by the British in 1910 as a legislative body to be consulted on internal affairs of the colony. The Council requested further reform in 1955 in order that its decisions might be conclusive on all internal questions. After a period of negotiation a revised constitution was adopted in 1959, to take effect the following year, which granted the wishes of the Legislative Council.

Pressures for total independence slowly gathered momentum, and Britain decided on a course of action in early 1965. Elections were held in April of that year to determine the popular will with respect to leadership of the colony. The Basutoland National Party of then–moderate Chief Leabua Jonathan gained 31 of the 60 parliamentary seats. The opposition party, the Panafricanist Congress Party, led by Ntsu Mokhele, a leftist, received 25 seats, and the right–wing Maramatlou Freedom Party, which supported the aspirations for power of Moshoeshoe II, hereditary Paramount Chieftain, won 4 seats. One delegate from the Maramatlou party defected to the National Party shortly after the election.

Although Chief Leabua Jonathan, who conducted his campaign from a helicopter provided by the Republic of South Africa, had received a minority of 44% of the popular vote, he negotiated for independence with the British in London.

An independence agreement was reached on June 18, 1966 whereby Basutoland was to become independent and was to be called *Lesotho,* indicating the lowlands of the Sotho—the area they traditionally occupied.

## Southern Africa: Swaziland

The Swazis came to their present territory during one of the many Bantu migrations. In the 18th century, Zulu raids into their country forced the tribal chieftain of Mawati to seek British assistance through the Agent General in Natal, who mediated a peaceful relationship between the two groups. For a time, the Transvaal Republic (now a province of South Africa) protected and administered Swaziland. After the *Boer War* (see the Republic of South Africa), control of the territory passed to the British.

In 1907, administration of Swaziland was charged to the British High Commissioner for South Africa. A proclamation was issued in 1944 by the Commissioner

# The Colonial Period

ing decades. Salisbury emerged as a cosmopolitan and large city by the end of World War II, which was the beginning of a period of migration of more thousands of White Europeans—principally British—to Rhodesia.

The African people of Rhodesia became increasingly restless after 1960 as many colonies of Africa were granted independence under African leadership, but the resulting limited political effort was unsuccessful because of the power of the White minority which was firmly established. Southern Rhodesia was joined with Northern Rhodesia (Zambia) and Nyasaland (Malawi) into the Federation of Rhodesia and Nyasaland in 1953, but this crumbled because of the overwhelming opposition of the African majorities in what are now Zambia and Malawi. Although there were earlier visits by traders and missionaries, the first significant penetration of Malawi was by the intrepid Scotch missionary, Dr. David Livingstone, on September 15, 1859. For almost 15 years he devoted his life to exploration of southeastern Africa and teaching Christianity to the native people. Formal annexation of the area occurred in 1883 when a representative of the British government accredited to the kings and chief of central Africa appeared and negotiated treaties with them. In reality, this was no more than an effort to exclude Portugal and Germany from the area. The British energetically and successfully ended slave trade of Arab raiders.

During the colonial period, particularly after the discovery of gold and diamonds in South Africa and copper in Rhodesia (Northern), the men usually spent several years working in the mines of those territories, bringing their limited wages back home to Nyasaland, as the area was then called. Because of this, and the prevalence of the Christian faith among the people, there was no rapid surge of nationalism. This changed in 1953 when Nyasaland was joined into the Federation of Rhodesia and Nyasaland—the Nyasas greatly feared the White supremacy movements that were strong in the other two members of the Federation. In an effort to suppress opposition, the British tried to arrest the chief of the Angoni tribe who advocated a passive resistance to the Federation. The attempted arrest was unsuccessful, but was the source of an even higher level of mistrust of the British and other White people by the Nyasas. There was a gradual transition to internal autonomy from 1961 to 1963 based upon elections in which the Malawi Congress Party of Dr. Hastings Kamuzu Banda won an overwhelming victory. The despised Federation was dissolved in 1963 and independence was granted the following year.

Southern Africa at the Outbreak of World War I

■ British Possessions
▨ British Commonwealth Membership

which recognized the Paramount Chief and Council as native authority for internal matters.

The British agreed in 1967 that Swaziland was to be independent after September 6, 1968. Internal self–government was established in April 1967 and elections were held shortly thereafter. The Imbokodvo National Movement (also known as The Grindstone Movement), led by Prince Makhosini Dlamini, won all 24 seats in the National Assembly. King Sobhuza II ascended the throne at the time of independence. Dr. Ambrose Zwane, leader of the opposition Ngwane National Liberation Council, pressed charges that the elections were rigged before the Organization of African United and in the UN. Both organizations listened, but did nothing.

## Southern Africa: Rhodesia, Zambia, Malawi

A steady, but small procession of traders and missionaries of many European nations established themselves in Mozambique after the Portuguese in the 16th century. Actually, there was no colonial effort until almost four hundred years later. Diamonds and gold had been discovered in the former *Boer* states of South Africa, Transvaal and Orange Free State, both of which were coveted by the British. Transvaal had been successful in maintaining its independence. In an effort to

surround the people of Dutch ancestry, the British commissioned the British South Africa Company in 1889, giving it all rights to an area north of Transvaal without limit.

Under the leadership of Cecil Rhodes, Salisbury was founded in 1890 in what was then known as Mashonaland, inhabited by Matabele (Bantu) people. Leander Jameson, a close friend of Rhodes, was appointed administrator of the thinly–settled area which included what is now Zambia and the name Rhodesia was adopted in 1895.

Since the most valuable of the natural resources of this part of Africa were then believed to be only in South Africa, the settlement of Rhodesia was slow. For decades, Salisbury was a rural town with wooden sidewalks and was the only urban settlement in what was a vast agricultural area. In the early 20th century, Zambia was recognized as a distinct state called Northern Rhodesia; both areas were granted full internal autonomy in 1923, when Rhodesia was declared to be a Crown Colony instead of the property of the British South Africa Company.

The White Rhodesians were few in number, but steadily grew into an industrious, conservative society. The African people, with the exception of a few missionary efforts, were largely ignored, and restricted to the poorer lands in the ensu-

# The Colonial Period

### East Africa: Kenya, Uganda and Tanzania (Tanganyika and Zanzibar)

The first British efforts in East Africa occurred in 1823 when Admiral William Owen entered the coastal area, supposedly in an attempt to end the Arab slave trade that had been going on for centuries along the coast. In theory, the Sultan of Muscat on the Arabian coast was the ruler of the region, and his authority was exercised by a viceroy (Sayyid) on the island of Zanzibar. The British, using a combination of threats and treaties, gradually established their control about the turn of the century.

German exploration and annexation of Tanganyika and part of southern Uganda from 1878 to 1885, in turn, aroused the interest of the British in Kenya and Uganda. The Sultan of Zanzibar granted the British East Africa Company a 50–year lease of what is now Kenya in 1887; this in turn was changed to the East Africa Protectorate, governed by a Commissioner, by the British government in 1895.

The last quarter of the 19th century in the eastern region of Africa was turbulent. There were efforts by both the British and Germans to enter Uganda, which was divided into four semi–autonomous kingdoms—Buganda, Busoga, Butoro and Bunyoro, of which Buganda was the most powerful. King Mwanga of Buganda, who reigned from 1884 until he was captured and exiled in 1899, tried to play the British off against the Germans by alternating his allegiance. In addition to this swirl of activity on behalf of Germany and Great Britain, there were roving remnants of Arab slave traders and religious conflicts involving and between Catholic and Protestant missionaries and believers, as well as those of Islamic faith.

The borders of this region were adjusted countless times, and not generally along the lines of actual colonial power. By a process of bargaining and trading, accompanied by line–drawing, particularly in Berlin in 1885, the eventual boundaries of the German, British and Portuguese territories, as well as those of King Leopold of Belgium were fixed. The almost straight line that now separates Kenya and Tanzania cuts almost through the center of the territory inhabited historically by the Masai people.

The British encouraged immigration of White settlers to Kenya after the turn of the century, and they established immense plantations in the most select parts of the colony. The tribespeople of Kenya, particularly large numbers of the Kikuyu (referred to as "kooks" by the British) were relegated to the poorer, tsetse–fly infested farmlands. White immigrants entered Uganda only in very small numbers.

At the start of World War I, 300,000 British, South African and colonial Indian troops invaded German East Africa, renamed Tanganyika following the establishment of British control after the war. A force of slightly more than 200 German officers, commanding native troops numbering between 2,500 and 4,000 fended off the massive force for four years under the brilliant leadership of General Paul Von Lettow–Vorbeck.

After the war, the British sent the German settlers from Tanganyika, confiscating their lands; a small number were permitted to return within a few years. Kenya was completely dominated by the White farmers and a substantial number of Indians who were descendants of workers brought in to complete a railroad between Nairobi and Mombasa which had opened in 1895. Uganda was governed through the local kings, and the cultivation of cotton and coffee quickly rose to be the source of the leading exports, permitting Uganda to become the richest British colony in Africa.

Government in Kenya was through a variety of commissioners sent from Britain; it was at a relatively late date that local councils were permitted, and initially even these consisted of people appointed by the commissioners. The White farmers of Kenya requested a regional council for Kenya, Uganda and Tanganyika as early as 1926, but were turned down since it was felt that this was merely an effort of theirs to preserve and extend their power which excluded the African majority from sharing in government.

**Jomo Kenyatta**

Following World War II, the ability of the British to rule effectively in Kenya and Uganda sharply decreased. The population of Kenya was stratified into three groups: the rich, landowning White (a small minority), the Indian and Arab merchant class, and (at the bottom) the huge majority of Africans. The African population had doubled in 25 years, creating tremendous pressure for expansion into the lands exclusively held by White farmers. The White population, instead of recognizing the needs of the Africans, instituted progressively more strict and severe laws directed against the majority.

The restive Africans formed a terrorist organization, the *Mau Mau*, to achieve their goals. Dreadful brutality became commonplace. Not only did the *Mau Mau* seek the lives of the Whites, they mercilessly slaughtered those of their own people who were servile to and worked for the Whites. White retaliation was equally brutal. Jomo Kenyatta, the political leader of the majority of African people, educated in Europe, was arrested, tried and convicted for participating in the *Mau Mau* conspiracy. He was sentenced to seven years in jail. In 1957 Kenya erupted in a total state of civil anarchy. *Mau Mau* terrorism had spread into almost every area of the country. Africans suspected of participating in this secret society were shot on the spot by Whites. Even long–trusted house servants had by this time joined the secret organization.

It became increasingly apparent that in order to bring stability to Kenya, the British would have to accede to the demands of the *Mau Mau*. Most of the British farmers departed, and in 1960 an agreement

14

was reached in London which gave the Africans a majority in the Legislative Council.

Dissension and political quarrels among the Africans in Kenya retarded the goal of full independence. Kenyatta, released from jail, headed the Kenya–African National Union (KANU), which represented the larger tribes of the country. The Kenya African Democratic Union drew its support from the many smaller tribes. After prolonged discussion in London, a complicated constitution was adopted providing for a loose, federal system of government.

The election conducted in May 1963 resulted in an overwhelming victory for KANU. Under pressure from the majority, the constitution was amended to strengthen the authority of the central government. The British recognized the independence of Kenya in December 1963.

Uganda was not without disturbance during the postwar period, although not as bloody as that in Kenya. In 1953, with the intent of establishing a central government, the British Commissioner informed the Kabaka (King) of Buganda that there were to be reforms in administration which would undermine his authority. Edward Mutesa II, the Kabaka, adamantly refused to accept these regulations and he forthwith was dismissed as King and put on a plane for London. The Buganda people regarded this as nothing short of an outrage. The British had to constitute a form of martial law to control the people throughout Uganda, and the economy suffered a steep decline.

The British attempted to solve this state of affairs by proposing that the *Lukiko*, the Ugandan tribal assembly, be permitted to vote on whether a new king should be chosen; the Assembly would not listen to the proposal. Kabaka Edward Mutesa was subsequently returned and the British set up a ministerial system of government, increasing African membership in the Legislative Council. The United Kingdom of Uganda was granted full independence in October 1962.

The movement toward independence was relatively tranquil in Tanzania (Tanganyika). The British had received a mandate from the League of Nations to administer the former German colony. This continued under a U.N. trusteeship. A gradual development of internal self–government was undertaken by the British, starting with a Legislative Council appointed by the government in 1926. Subsequent elections were held in 1958 and again in 1960, the latter of which was won by the Tanganyikan African National Union of Julius Nyerere, who was President of Tanzania until 1985. He retired in that year, but is still a figure of power in

the country. Full independence was granted in December 1961.

## Northeast Africa: Egypt and the Sudan

During the first half of the 19th century, interest in European technology and education grew rapidly in Egypt, ruled by the Khedives (kings) nominally subject to the control of the Turkish Ottoman Empire's sultan. The basis for the construction of the Suez Canal lay in this interest, coupled with British and French desires for a shorter route to India and the Far East.

After negotiation with Khedive Ismail, European powers, working through their financial institutions, began construction of the canal, which was completed and opened amid great fanfare in 1869 with a multitude of European royalty present; they later heard the first performance of the opera *Aida*, by Giuseppe Verdi, erroneously said to have been written for the occasion. Egypt had been enriched by the demand for cotton created by the United States Civil War, but had also heavily borrowed at high interest rates to help finance the construction of the canal. From 1870 to 1883, the British succeeded in conquering most of the Sudan, penetrating as far as Uganda, supposedly in partnership with Egypt. The prime interest initially in this area was to end the oppressive slave trade that was firmly entrenched.

There was a financial crisis which compelled the Khedive to sell all of the Egyptian shares in the Suez Canal to Great Britain in 1876, giving the British a majority interest in the canal. Further financial

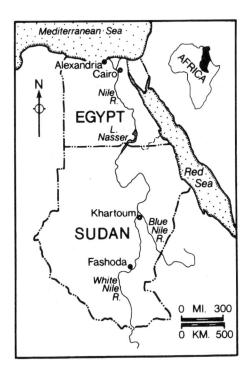

deficits and inability to repay European loans were the basis of increasing British control of Egypt. The Khedives rapidly became figurehead kings, totally subject to British control, which led to an early rise of Egyptian nationalist desires. An army revolt, coupled with a popular nationalist uprising was the excuse used to invade Egypt, and absolute British control of the region resulted.

Although the Khedives were retained as the nominal rulers, their power quickly became almost nonexistent in the face of growing pressures of the nationalist leaders. Eventually, a scheme of rule was devised under the so–called Organic Law which included a legislative council and cabinet with advisory powers. The Khedive was controlled by a "Resident and Consul–General" of the British; all high Egyptian ministers had a British "advisor."

In the Sudan, Mohammed Ahmed, a leader known as *Mahdi*, quickly achieved wide popularity following 1880—in addition to his political military support, he was regarded by his followers, the *dervishes*, as a modern–day prophet of Islam. By 1884, he had all but completely demolished British and Egyptian forces within the territory. An expedition sent by the British offered the *Mahdi* some concessions which were flatly rejected; the Mahdi immediately laid siege to Khartoum where General Charles Gordon and his forces were located.

After several months, the Mahdi entered the city and the British were slaughtered; General Gordon was impaled by a dervish spear. A relief force sent to help arrived in Khartoum three days later, but was greeted only by smoking rubble and the silent stench of death. Fearful of also being wiped out by the fanatical Sudanese, the rescue force beat a hasty retreat. The control of the Sudan remained with the Mahdi and his successor for ten years. The British, faced with the growing French expansion on the western side of the Nile River in the Sudan, sent a large force under General Sir Horatio Hubert Kitchener to reconquer the territory in 1896–1898. The Mahdi had died and the dervishes were disorganized; in the ensuing battle almost 10,000 Sudanese lost their lives and were only able to claim that of 50 British and Egyptians in return. One of the young lieutenants in the British force was none other than Winston Churchill, destined to lead Britain through World War II.

Kitchener was later entitled Lord Kitchener of Khartoum in recognition of his leadership. Entering Khartoum, he emptied the revered tomb of the original Mahdi and dumped the corpse into the river, and then quickly captured and killed the *Khalifa*, successor of the Mahdi.

# The Colonial Period

King Farouk at 16 in 1936

King Farouk at 32 in 1952

Kitchener marched rapidly southward, meeting the French at Fashoda (now Kodak) in an effort to reassert British power. The result was the Fashoda Crisis (discussed under *The French in Africa*) that was finally ended by agreement on areas of control which roughly defined the boundaries between what is now the Sudan, Central African Republic and Chad.

Great Britain and Egypt set up a joint administration of the Sudan; although they were nominally equal partners, the British were in fact the dominant power.

After World War I, the British had to institute increasingly harsh measures to maintain their control in Egypt and the so-called Anglo-Egyptian Sudan. At the start of World War I, the Ottomans in Turkey demonstrated sympathy for the German cause, and as a result, the British declared war against them. Although the Ottoman control in Egypt was little more than imaginary, the British used the war as a pretext to proclaim a protectorate status over Egypt, which aroused a great deal of local opposition. The Nationalist, or Wafd Party, quickly became dominant, opposing both the British and the Khedives.

A multitude of administrations under a semi-democratic constitution ruled following World War I. Ahmed Fuad, the Khedive, repeatedly dissolved nationalist governments and announced new elections, in all of which the nationalists scored tremendous victories and returned to power. The nationalist movement was not genuinely popular, however; its primary support came from the wealthy, land-owning *pashas* who had become established during the Ottoman era. The Protectorate status was withdrawn in 1922

and Egypt achieved internal autonomy as a result of Wafd efforts.

There were some efforts at economic development during the period between the two World Wars based upon the opening of dams along the Nile to partially control the age-old flood and drought cycle of the river. Constitutional reforms gave increasing power to the Egyptian *pashas*. The worldwide depression of the 1930's further lessened British control, and upon the death of King Fuad I in 1936, his handsome 16-year-old son, Farouk, came to power. Colorful and pleasure seeking, he was at first very popular. With the consent of the British and other European powers, Egypt became nominally independent in 1936 and was admitted to the League of Nations a year later. British military control was limited to the Suez Canal area.

The King dissolved the *Wafd* government in 1938, and the election that followed was a complete victory for the new pro-King party. Initially arming itself for World War II, Egypt maintained a passive neutrality during the conflict, although it was the scene of battles between the Allied and Axis powers.

Following World War II, the Egyptians sought to end the last vestiges of British domination. Weakened by the war, England was in no position to offer opposition to this demand. The picture was

further complicated by the presence of the newly-born Jewish state of Israel, carved out of a portion of Palestine, opposed by the Arabs, which led to a brief Egyptian-Israeli battle in 1948, won by the Israelis.

The Wafd Party again returned to power in 1950 after several changes of government reflecting the desires of the nationalists and unrest among the army leadership. Egypt demanded withdrawal of British troops from the Canal Zone and from the Sudan. Great Britain immediately retaliated with a plan for Sudanese independence; this appeared realistic in view of the traditional hatred for and distrust of Egyptians by the Sudanese. Events moved swiftly—the U.N. requested that Egypt lift its embargo forbidding use of the Suez Canal by ships bound for or coming from Israel. Egypt replied by abrogating its treaties with the British of 1899 and 1936 and the British navy attacked Port Said and landed forces in the area. Riots erupted in Cairo and there were two rapid changes of government. King Farouk, having grown fat and dissipated at the age of 32, was overthrown and exiled by the military in July 1952; a new era began in Egypt which is now generally thought of as the beginning of true independence in the modern age.

Prior to the defeat of Farouk, the British offered the Sudan a plan of internal self-government which was condemned by Egypt. The colonial government was able to work out a compromise arrangement with the military *junta* that succeeded Farouk, which provided that the Sudanese should decide whether they were to be independent or part of a federation with Egypt. In 1953 an overwhelming number of the Sudanese voted for independence, which was granted in 1956.

## THE FRENCH IN AFRICA
### North Africa: Algeria, Morocco and Tunisia

With the exception of Morocco, all of Arabic-speaking North Africa was at the turn of the 18th century in theory a part of the vast Ottoman Empire; the area consisted of a number of small principalities ruled by Turkish military men who had titles of *Bey* or *Dey*, depending upon the location. Commerce consisted of trade with regions to the south, and piracy of European shipping in the Mediterranean Sea.

The booty seized from the vessels consisted not only of cargo, but the crew as well, which was sold into slavery. After other nations had sent expeditionary forces against the Arab raiders, France sent a force into Algiers in 1830, deposing the Dey and seizing a few of the coastal towns. Another Dey was selected by the local people, who promptly marshaled attacks upon the French. Eventually the oc-

# The Colonial Period

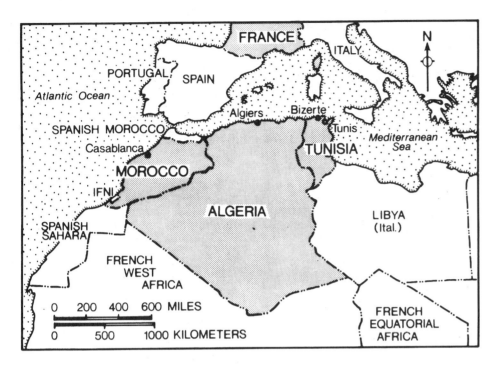

As was true with most colonial efforts, the French purpose in North Africa was primarily to enrich France. Although legally recognized as being in control of the area by 1910, actual control was much less than complete. During the entire colonial period from the 19th century until about 1960, the Arabs were almost in constant rebellion. Riff tribesmen of the Moroccan mountains and the Berber and Tuareg horsemen of southern Algeria never did accept French control. Arab unrest also came from the Muslim *Senussi* sect in neighboring Libya that spilled over into Tunisia which was populated by Italians as well as French immigrants.

Further complicating the peaceful colonization of North Africa, the immigrants to the area from France were principally military personnel and their families—they quickly developed a militant and conservative attitude as evidenced by their armed opposition to French efforts in the 1870's to placate the restless Arabs. Substantial numbers of Arabs went to France during the colonial period, but both in Africa and in France the two ethnic groups—French and Arab—resisted integration with vigor.

The French colonists assumed the dominant position in North Africa, both economically and in terms of status derived from education. Lower schools were provided for those of French ancestry, but with little exception, no comparable effort was made on behalf of the

cupying forces had to recognize the new Dey, Abd el–Kader. He engaged in sporadic warfare for fifteen years against the French, who relinquished to him their claim to interior lands initially, but later drove him into Morocco where other French forces invaded and captured him in 1847.

Although the French presence in the area now known as Algeria was initially military, efforts were made to settle colonists from France in the 1860's and 1870's when most of what is now Algeria was gradually brought under colonial control. In Tunisia, the French had economic competition from England and Italy. In return for control of Cyprus, the British acknowledged France's authority in Tunisia. Because of an outbreak of violence, a naval force seized Bizerte in 1881 and forced the *Bey* of Tunis to accept the status of a French protectorate over the area. The British, Italians, and Turks all protested, but France had the support of Germany in the move, given in exchange for French support of German colonial ambitions elsewhere in Africa.

Morocco initially escaped domination by a colonial nation, although the major powers had forced a treaty in 1880 which protected the rights of foreigners within the country. After a 13–year–old boy succeeded as Sultan in 1894, the internal conditions deteriorated, reducing Morocco to virtual anarchy by the turn of the century. In exchange for concessions in Libya, Italy relinquished any claim it might have had in Morocco and the British later also acknowledged French supremacy in 1904. A nominal French–Spanish control was established in 1906 after a visit to Morocco by German Kaiser Wilhelm II as evidence of a German interest; negotiations led to an acknowledgment of French domination of the country in 1909. This was given by Germany in exchange for some economic guarantees and a section of the French Congo, which became part of Germany's colony of Kameroun (now Cameroon).

**Habib Bourguiba celebrates Tunisian independence**

17

# The Colonial Period

Arabs. The local rulers were allowed to retain nominal powers, since it was actually easier to rule through them rather than try to depose them.

The earliest signs of Arab nationalism in the region occurred in Morocco in the 1930's, partially because of the world economic depression which had a severe effect on the economy of all North Africa which was based almost entirely on the agricultural production on farms of European immigrants and their descendants. This effort was the basis of continuing anti–French sentiment among the Arabs to which was added growing worldwide liberal–nationalistic ideals that were temporarily interrupted by World War II before making any progress.

Upon installation of a pro–German government under Marshal Henri–Phillipe Petain in France following the German invasion of that country in World War II, Algeria, Morocco and Tunisia were brought under the nominal authority of the Vichy (Vee–shee) government which he headed, named after a town in central France from which part of France was administered by his regime in 1940–1944. Although only a relatively insignificant number of French troops loyal to the Axis powers were stationed in the area, the Allies felt that it was necessary to establish Free French control in the area prior to invading Italy.

A combined American–British force invaded Morocco and Algeria on November 8, 1942, and three days later a cease–fire arranged with Admiral Jean François Darlan, the *Vichy* commander, led to Allied control of French North Africa within a short time, with Admiral Darlan achieving the post of Chief of State with Allied approval. Following his assassination shortly afterward, the Anglo–American command tried to install the aging General Henri Giraud as commander of French forces outside France in spite of the more energetic anti–Axis, anti–*Vichy* activities of the Free French led by the younger General Charles de Gaulle. His forces had conducted assaults in and from Brazzaville, French Congo. A brief German offensive in North Africa was repulsed by the Allies in May 1943.

The French were restored to continued colonial control of North Africa following World War II. Their rule was no more effective than the unstable and numerous French governments of mainland France. In Algeria, the conservative colonists *(colons)* of French ancestry completely dominated all phases of government, although Algeria was legally supposed to be an integral part of France. The Communist Party had been outlawed in Morocco, a colony, but this could not be done in Algeria since the communists

were not outlawed within France. The *National Liberation Front* quickly rose in power and spearheaded a revolt which started in late 1954 and lasted for seven years. This group was a leftist–socialist–communist Arab party, united in opposition to French colonial rule.

A last ditch effort of the Secret Army Organization (OAS), composed for the most part of French–descended Europeans, failed to stem the overwhelming tide of revolution in spite of cruel and terroristic anti–Arab measures in 1961. A cease–fire was finally negotiated in March 1962 and President Charles de Gaulle, who had promised the French to end the bloody conflict, recognized Algerian independence on July 3 of that year.

At the close of World War II, the Istiqlal Independence Party was formed in Morocco; it promptly issued a demand for independence which was refused. The party quickly gathered momentum with the tacit consent of the Alouite monarch, Sultan Mohammed V.

The willingness of this ruler to permit existence of the independence movement created great dissatisfaction among the French administrators. The French deposed him in 1953, sending him into exile, first on Corsica and then to Madagascar. Assisted by the Berber *Glaoui* (Sheikh) of Marakesh, the French placed Mohammed VI on the throne—a colorless, subservient member of the ruling family who was generally disliked by Moroccans.

Growing resentment led to severe rioting; terrorists struck swiftly, retreating to the safety of the hills and mountains to regather their forces, in the same manner as the formerly rebellious Riff tribesmen. The United States indicated great dissatisfaction with French policy, and in 1955, because of internal and external pressures, the French returned Mohammed V to the throne. Under the overwhelming influence of a strong and popular king and the independence party, Morocco ended its colonial status in 1956.

In Tunisia there was also a postwar surge of nationalism. A large middle class of well–educated people had emerged and backed this movement, led by an Arab lawyer educated in France, Habib Bourguiba. His New Constitution Party succeeded the older Constitution Party. Bourguiba's life during the French colonial period alternated between periods of exile and/or imprisonment and periods of nationalistic leadership. Exiled in 1934, he returned in 1936, was rearrested in 1938 and later was freed by the Germans in 1942. He again was arrested when the French returned, but escaped and went into exile. When he returned in 1952, he was arrested, and in 1954 was banished into exile.

By this time Tunisia was in a full state of insurrection requiring the presence of 70,000 French troops to attempt to control the colony. France granted internal autonomy to Tunisia in 1955 which also provided amnesty for all freedom fight-

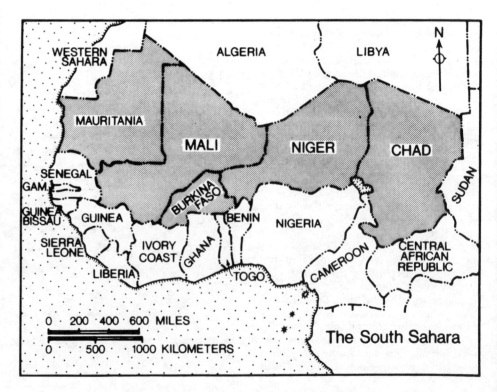

The South Sahara

ers. Bourguiba was permitted to return, and full independence was achieved on July 20, 1956.

## The South Sahara: Mauritania, Mali, Upper Volta (Burkina Faso), Niger, Chad.

Colonization of the southern Sahara region of Africa was a much slower process than in other areas of the continent because the almost uniformly arid land held little importance to the French, other than strategic. The only reasons for colonization were in order to connect other more valuable colonies together and to exclude other foreign colonial effort in the region.

At a meeting known as the Berlin Conference, arranged by Otto von Bismarck of Germany and the French foreign minister in 1884–1885, the major world and colonial powers officially decreed that African slavery was to be abolished and that there was to be free navigation of the major rivers of the continent. It was further decreed that colonial power in the area was to be based on presence and actual control. Unofficially, and more important, the representatives took a map of the continent and drew lines indicating areas of interest of the respective powers.

The maps of the continent at that time were uncertain—boundaries differed sometimes more than a thousand miles, depending on the map and the nationality of the cartographer. In their effort to connect the West African and Equatorial African colonies, the French, in 1896–98 sent an expedition under Jean Baptiste Marchand that pushed rapidly northeastward as far as Fashoda (later named Kodak) on the Nile River. At the same time, having defeated the Sudanese, supposedly on behalf of Egypt, British Lord Horatio Herbert Kitchener was leading his forces southward along the Nile from Omdurman, and a second British expedition was pushing north on the river from Uganda. Further complicating the picture was the imminent arrival of an Ethiopian army on the right bank of the Nile at Fashoda, accompanied by another group of French forces.

The result was the Fashoda Crisis in which the British and French were eyeball–to–eyeball on the brink of total war. However, France was preoccupied with a complicated political scandal involving top military figures in Paris (the Dreyfuss Affair) which had political and religious overtones. The French blinked first, ending the crisis with an agreement on the lines of French and British authority in the area, which approximately fixed the present eastern borders of Chad and the Central African Republic with the Sudan.

Although the major powers of the world recognized French authority in this barren land by the end of the 19th century, the nomadic people who lived in the south Sahara region refused fully to submit to foreign rule for several years afterwards. In the final analysis, France was compelled to rule this part of Africa through local tribal leaders who possessed a large measure of autonomy. This permitted nominal French control without large–scale military forces which would have been necessary for direct rule.

The region was administered as a whole; it was part of French West Africa. Mali, Niger, Chad and southern Algeria were also known as French Sudan, the French spelling of which was Soudan.

The lives of the people were hardly disturbed by colonial rule. There was virtually no immigration of Europeans such as occurred in North Africa; the only French presence was essentially military. Occasional revolts occurred which were contained, rather than defeated by the French.

Although there was some sporadic German penetration in World War II during the North African campaigns of 1942–43 in the Mali, Niger and Chad regions, the local people were not involved in the battles. Free French forces under General Jean LeClerc fought several engagements with the Germans in the northern Chad area. With little exception, there was no political movement toward independence from France following World War II in the south Sahara. Niger shared in the development of the Democratic African Rally Party, but in this respect was dominated by the members from the Ivory Coast under Félix Houphouet–Boigny. As a result of unrest of the Muslim Mossi people in what was then called Upper Coast, the area now constituting Upper Volta (Burkina Faso) was separated after World War II from Ivory Coast, taking the French name Haute Volta.

Following the election of Charles de Gaulle as President of France, the French Community was established in 1958—a plan whereby France's colonies in Africa were granted internal autonomy. This was an effort to satisfy independence movements in areas of French Africa outside the south Sahara. It proved to be unsatisfactory in many respects, not the least of which was continued opposition to French authority over foreign relations by a multitude of African nationalists within the Community. Because of this, France granted independence to the remaining south Sahara and West African colonies, numbering thirteen, in 1960. Thus, without any substantial internal effort to promote independence, the south Sahara region was freed of French authority (which in reality had never been firmly established).

## Coastal West and Equatorial Africa: Senegal, Guinea, Ivory Coast, Togo, Dahomey, East Cameroon, Central African Republic, Gabon, Congo.

France initially had no colonial ambitions along coastal Africa—scattered missionary stations were established in the 17th and 18th centuries and slave trade was also prevalent at the time. Following the abolition of slave trade in 1815, France maintained very small "factories" (trading posts) along the various parts of the coast.

Colonial interest quickened during the mid–19th century when the major European powers feared that one or another of them would obtain some valuable territory available to all nations, with a potential discovery of valuable metal ores and

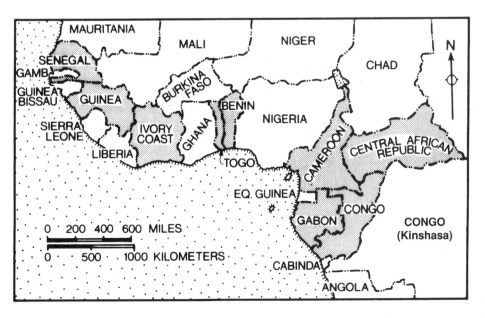

# The Colonial Period

**A Contemporary Artist Views the Black Elite that Emerges in the Colonial Period**
Photo by Judi Iranyi

gems. In reality, with the exception of widely scattered and exaggerated tales brought to Europe by occasional explorers, almost nothing was known of the interior coastal lands of West and Equatorial Africa.

Senegal was the first area of increased French activity—General Louis Faidherbe headed an armed force in 1854 that was immediately resisted by the natives and their Tukuler ruler, Hajk Omar, but it was gradually able to subdue most of the area. The most commercially important region of Senegal—the Gambia River Basin—had been seized by the British decades prior to the arrival of the French.

At about the same time a military mission was sent to Guinea, but because of the fierce resistance of the people of the region, penetration into the interior was slow. The Mandingo chieftain, Samory Toure, intially signed a treaty which permitted him to claim additional territory to the northwest. This peace was short-lived; further French military efforts were necessary in 1885–6, and a dire threat to the French was mounted when Toure united with the Tukuler people previously driven from Senegal into Mali.

The French offensive was on two fronts—north and east in Guinea and north and west in Ivory Coast, which finally resulted in the defeat of Toure in 1898. He was exiled to Gabon after his capture, where he died two years later. Penetration from southern Ivory Coast had also been slow. Although treaties were signed with the coastal chieftains of the Grand–Bassam and Assime regions, the Agnis and Baoules, two groups closely related to the warlike Ashanti people of Ghana to the west, offered fierce resistance to drives into the interior. Further north, the Mandingo people of Samory Toure and the Tukuler Africans prevented progress; Ivory Coast was not fully conquered by the French until about 1915.

As a result of a treaty signed with the French in 1851 by Ghezo, ruler of Abomey (Dahomey) a small commercial effort was initiated in that country. Coutonou was ceded as a trading post in 1868. The colonization of Dahomey was not uncontested—the Portuguese and British attempted to encourage inter–tribal rivalries in order to unseat the French from the coastal area, but without success.

Dahomey, with the exception of its narrow coastal strip, was left virtually untouched until 1890 when Benhazin, the last powerful king of Abomey, refused to sign additional treaties with France. Military occupation of Coutonou was ordered, swiftly followed by a violent uprising which continued with periodic interruptions until 1894, when Benhazin surrendered. The interior of Dahomey was slowly subdued during the following decades.

Togo was not gained by the French until World War I. The larger part of this former German colony was occupied by French troops in 1916; this control was converted into a mandate by the League of Nations, which divided the colony between France (East) and Britain (West). The British area was joined with the Gold Coast (Ghana). The East Cameroon region was also acquired from Germany in a similar fashion in 1916, also resulting in a League of Nations mandate.

Count Pierre Savorgnan De Brazza of France entered the northern side of the Congo River region of coastal Africa at about the same time that the British–American explorer Henry Stanley was claiming the southern side of the river region on behalf of King Leopold of Belgium in the first part of the 1880's. Both followed the same procedure of entering into so–called "treaties" with the various sub–chiefs of the once–mighty Kingdom of the Congo, a Bantu empire which once had extended from Gabon to Angola including an area several hundred miles inland from the coast. After exploring most of Congo (Brazzaville), De Brazza went into Gabon and established a small coastal outpost.

The area which now is the Central African Republic was not penetrated by the French until about 1889, when an outpost was established at Bangui, the present capital. The French named this territory Ubangi–Shari after its two principal rivers. It was not until after the turn of the century that effective French control was imposed on Congo, Gabon and the Central African Republic, all of which were combined in 1910 to form French Equatorial Africa, a distinctive administrative area. Upon receiving a mandate from the League of Nations over East Cameroon, a section of the former German colony (Kameroun) was made a part of French Equatorial Africa.

Mauritania, Senegal, Guinea, Ivory Coast, Dahomey, Mali, Upper Volta and Niger had been joined together as French West Africa in 1904; the entire territory was administered from Dakar, Senegal. The part of former German Togoland acquired after World War I was joined into this vast colony.

A variety of local councils were permitted by the French, giving the Africans a limited voice in their local affairs during the colonial period. European–style education was introduced, but never achieved widespread enrollment due to a shortage of trained teachers willing to live in Africa. Small numbers who did obtain secondary education usually went to France if they desired higher level studies.

Roads and railroads were constructed to the extent necessary to commercially develop this area of the continent, such as in Ivory Coast to permit export of agricultural products and in Gabon to support wood production.

After obtaining the necessary medical education, Dr. Albert Schweitzer, a world–renowned German philosopher and musician, received permission to establish a Protestant Christian medical mission and hospital at Lamborene in the interior of Gabon. He labored among the people, relieving the illness and misery of Africans regarded as little more than savages by the rest of the world—but whom he considered priceless human beings—from 1913 until his death in 1965. He adapted medical methods to harmonize with the customs of the Africans. The mission continues its work under the leadership of his daughter, who engages in fund–raising to support its activities.

Other than medical facilities provided principally for Europeans living in West and Equatorial Africa, almost none were established for the benefit of the African people during the colonial years, but there was some improvement in the post–World War II period. Boundaries were stabilized over a number of years by agreements with the British, Belgians and Liberians; the map of colonial Africa underwent no substantial change in West Africa after 1920.

The World Depression of 1929 and the following years had great impact in the coastal colonies of French West and Equa-

torial Africa, where agricultural products usually were the sole exports. The sharp drop in prices paid for foodstuffs meant a corresponding decrease of income, and accompanying lower living standards which had not really been much more than marginal.

When France fell to the overwhelming might of the German Nazi military machine, a puppet, pro–German administration was established in France— the *Vichy* government (1940), named for its location in central France. It quickly dispatched administrators and personnel to take control of French Africa; they were generally disliked by the French living in the colonies. Their policies tended in many cases to be openly racist and repressive. French General Charles de Gaulle led a force aided by British vessels which attempted to seize Dakar, Senegal in 1940, but it was repulsed. A month later, he was able to capture Douala, Cameroon; Brazzaville was also occupied and a powerful transmitter was erected in order to make daily Free French broadcasts which were received in distant areas.

Following World War II, colonial rule continued, but there was a rapid upsurge of nationalism among native Africans. France itself had been economically devastated by the war and only slowly recovered with great amounts of foreign assistance provided by the United States. Political extremism, both rightist and leftist (communist) was rampant, making orderly French government all but impossible. Félix Houphouet–Boigny, a nationalist leader in Ivory Coast, organized the Democratic African Rally (RDA) with associated parties in most of France's West African colonies; the allied party succeeded in electing almost all of the area's deputies to the Assembly in Paris between 1947 and 1950. The relatively small number of African delegates allowed by the constitution allied themselves with the communist deputies during this period in an effort to gain support for their nationalist viewpoint, but that allegiance was discontinued in 1950.

France was severely drained by the communist rebellion within its Indochinese colonies, including Vietnam, during the postwar period which ended in a military disaster for the French in 1954. Immediately, a second total rebellion was mounted by the Algerian National Liberation Front which resulted in devastating warfare within that colony for seven more years, with accompanying additional strain upon the French economy. Principally for those reasons, the French were in no position effectively to oppose nationalist demands of their African colonies.

The Overseas Reform Act (*Loi Cadre*) of 1956 gave the African colonies internal autonomy, leaving matters of defense and

foreign policy to France in an effort to quiet the demands for total independence. After Charles de Gaulle assumed almost absolute powers in France in 1958, he announced the creation of the French Community, the first step towards granting total independence to the colonies. Guinea, led by Sékou Touré, rejected the plan and that colony gained immediate independence.

Senegal and Mali were joined into the Federation of Mali in 1959 and France made some other minor changes, but granted full independence to all its remaining colonies in West and Equatorial Africa in 1960.

### East Africa: Madagascar, French Somaliland

The immense island of Madagascar was known to navigators since the 15th century, but there was no attempt at colonization. The Hindu Merina (Hova) people of Indonesian and Malaysian descent lived in the central highlands; persons of Arab and African heritage inhabited the coastal areas. There was only a brief period when the island was under single control during the 16th century, established by Sakalava (Arab) rulers.

The Merina kingdom became dominant in the 18th century under King Andrianampoinamerina (1787–1810); he and his successors alternately encouraged the French and British in their tentative efforts at colonization so that neither would gain the upper hand. Between 1775 and 1824, the island was a stronghold of marauding pirates, including John Avery, Captain Mission and William Kidd. The pirates even formed a republic called Libertalia, which was of brief duration.

Other nations of the world later established commercial relations with the Malagasy people; a treaty of peace, friendship and commerce between the United States and Madagascar was signed in 1881. During this period, British influence in the interior became strong. In 1869, Merina Queen Ranavolona I and her Court were converted to the English Protestant faith. French interests continued to dominate the coastline.

At the Berlin Conference of 1885, as a result of concession by the French to the British in other parts of Africa, Great Britain supported the establishment of a French Protectorate over Madagascar. This status led to the end of the Merina Kingdom. General Joseph Simon Galliene, the first French Governor, with the aid of French troops, unified the entire island.

The people—particularly the Merinas— had little use for French rule. In 1916 they rose unsuccessfully in bloody rebellion. The differences between the pro–French coastal inhabitants and those of the inte-

# The Colonial Period

**Leopold II of Belgium**

rior was expressed in this movement for independence which was limited to the people of the highlands. After the fall of France in World War II, Madagascar, first administered by the Vichy (pro–Nazi) government of France, was occupied in 1942 by the British to prevent possible Japanese seizure of the strategic island. The Free French gained control in 1943. By 1947, an independence movement had become overwhelming and there was a national uprising suppressed only after months of bitter fighting which resulted in the death of more than 10,000 people of the island.

Subsequent constitutional reform in France lessened the tensions in Madagascar, and led to the establishment of the Malagasy Republic within the French Community in 1958. The Republic became fully independent in 1960.

The tiny, sun–blistered colony of French Somaliland came into existence when treaties were signed with local chieftains in 1862. This colonization, as well as that of the British and Italians in the area, was to secure the regions south of the Suez Canal, then under construction, in order to prevent any disruption of shipping. The only asset of the territory was a deep, natural harbor facing the Gulf of Aden. At the turn of the century, a railroad from Addis Ababa, Ethiopia to Djibouti was completed and was thereafter the prime source of revenue. This colony achieved independence from France in June 1977

and is now known as the Republic of Djibouti.

## THE UNITED STATES OF AMERICA IN AFRICA
### See Liberia: History.

## KING LEOPOLD AND THE BELGIANS IN AFRICA
### The Belgian Congo, Ruanda-Urundi

The Belgian efforts at colonization in the Congo region of West Africa call to mind the name of one man: Henry Stanley. Following his birth in Wales, he migrated to the United States where he became an author, soldier and adventurer, fighting on both sides in the American Civil War. Seeking new adventure, he turned to Africa and went to locate the Scottish missionary, Dr. David Livingstone, who had disappeared while exploring central Africa. After locating Dr. Livingstone on the shores of Lake Tanganyika in 1871, he explored the lake regions of the continent and then proceeded westward to the Congo River region. It took him three years to traverse the length of the river; he arrived on the Atlantic coast in 1877 and departed for Europe.

Stanley was immediately summoned by King Leopold II of Belgium, who saw in this explorer a means to compete in the scramble for colonial territory in Africa. Stanley accepted the offer of employment and returned to the Congo, entering into treaties on behalf of King Leopold with the native chieftains. The curious thing about this colonization is that it was not on behalf of the Belgian nation—this was Leopold's personal project.

At the Berlin Conference of 1885 when great portions of Africa were divided between the European colonial powers, King Leopold had personally been awarded the area south of the Congo River as far as Portuguese possessions in the Angola region.

Although the area was referred to as "The Congo Free State," the years which followed were harsh. King Leopold desired wealth from the Congo and all policies in the territory were used toward that desire. Forced labor and torture were used to compel production of wealth; it is estimated that up to 8 million Africans lost their lives during the 23 years of Leopold's exploitation. By 1904, knowledge of these repressive conditions had become known in Europe and the United States; in response to pressure from Britain, Germany and the U.S., King Leopold sent a commission to investigate conditions. The report of the commission, issued in late 1905, indicated that the actions of Leopold's administrators were scandalously cruel and improper. Bowing to continued

international pressure, the Belgian parliament passed an act in 1908 annexing the Congo State of Belgium.

During the period at the turn of the century, there was friction between the British, French and King Leopold over control of the upper (southern) Nile area in the region near Lake Albert. As a result of a compromise, the Congo Free State received a small portion of territory known as the Lado enclave, which reverted to the Sudan (Anglo–Egyptian Sudan) at the death of Leopold in 1910. There were a variety of treaties between the several colonial powers that gradually and firmly demarcated the borders of the Congo region.

Under Leopold, the copper–rich Katanga (now Shaba) area had been opened up, and economic development based on that region's wealth proceeded forward under Belgian administrators. The general approach was that the native Africans should not be given too many privileges lest they become restless. Due to efficient administration, however, the per capita income rose to be one of the highest in colonial Africa.

Belgian forces moved to occupy the northwestern part of German East Africa at the start of World War I. This region, consisting of what is now Rwanda and Burundi, was then called Ruanda–Urundi and became a mandated territory assigned to Belgium in 1923; it was joined administratively with the Congo, which was given a wide degree of autonomy at the same time. Between the two world wars, Belgium made substantial capital investments in the Congo, including construction of railways connecting Kinshasa (then called Leopoldville) to the mineral wealth of Shaba (then called Katanga).

Nationalist pressures on the part of the native Africans mushroomed after World War II. Belgium, prostrated by the battles and German occupation of the war, was actually in no position to resist this movement. In a completely unexpected change, Belgium announced in January 1960 that it would grant independence to the Congo as of June 30th of the same year. It is highly probable that the Belgians hoped that a quick grant of independence would result in chaos to a degree that would justify continued colonial control. This hope, motivated by the desire for further wealth, was almost realized.

## THE SPANISH IN AFRICA
### Spanish Sahara, Spanish Guinea, Ifni, Ceuta, Melilla

The colonization and division of Africa between the major powers in the 19th century was during a period when Spain, having formerly been a powerful colonial nation, was in a state of decline. The result was that Spain succeeded in claiming

# The Colonial Period

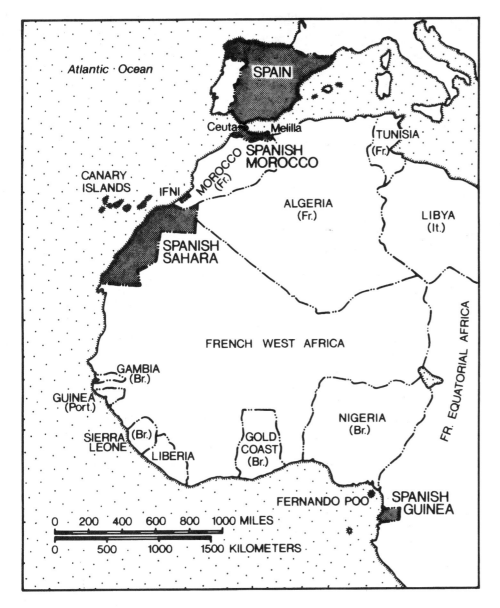

Poo, an island ceded to Spain by Portugal in 1778. There was no significant nationalist movement reported during the postwar period and no effort was made to prepare the colony for independence.

In the mid 1960's, Spain began to bring increasing pressure on the British to cede the Gibralter peninsula on the ground that it, lying at the entrance to the Mediterranean Sea, belonged to Spain by virtue of natural geography. In order to reinforce its arguments, Spain granted Spanish Guinea independence in 1968, giving little prior indication of its intention to do so.

## THE GERMANS IN AFRICA
### West Africa: Togo, Cameroon

Although there was some German missionary and trading activity on the coasts of Togo and Cameroon from 1845 onward, these areas also were open to religious and commercial efforts of the remaining European nations. In the rush to acquire colonies during the 1880's, Gustav Nachtigal negotiated treaties with the Ewe chiefs of the region at Togoville, located on the banks of Lake Togo. The most powerful of these was King Mlapa III.

During the thirty years that followed the announcement of a German protectorate in Togo, there was slow penetration into the interior. The borders with the surrounding colonies were adjusted several times by treaty. The rule of the German administrators was harsh and exploitive; there was no effort to provide any benefit to the people of the region, since the only interest was commercial. Large numbers of Togolese were jailed and forced to labor for the Germans. There was little regret when the British and French arrived early in World War I.

Spanish Sahara (also called Spanish Morocco, Rio de Oro), a barren desert area, and Spanish Guinea, a small section of oppressive jungle on the west coast at the Equator which included the island of Fernando Poo. The enclaves of Ifni, Ceuta and Melilla along the coast of Morocco were holdovers from the time when both Morocco and Spain were controlled by Moorish Arabs. The areas in which Spain was able to lay claim were available largely because of lack of interest in them on the part of other stronger colonial nations.

Although Spain was technically supposed to be in partnership with the French in Morocco during the colonial period, the actual control was by the French. Spain ceded its theoretical protectorate right to Morocco in 1956 when the French granted it independence; a small part of southern Morocco was relinquished in 1958. The enclave of Ifni was returned to Morocco in

1968; Ceuta and Melilla, coastal cities along the coast where Spain and Morocco are closest, remain under Spanish control with the tacit consent of the King of Morocco.

Wind–swept and arid, Spanish Sahara is inhabited by a handful of nomadic Berber–Bedouin tribesmen who had been left to themselves by the Spanish. There had been almost no interest in this area on the part of the rest of the world prior to 1966 when extensive and rich deposits of phosphate were located. After withstanding pressures from the UN, Morocco and Mauritania for a decade, Spain vacated the territory in 1976 (see Western Sahara).

Spanish Guinea, now the mainland portion of Equatorial Guinea, consisted of an undesirable, oppressively hot and humid area acquired at the Berlin Conference in 1885, which was joined administratively to form a single colony with Fernando

**Kaiser Wilhelm II of Germany**

# The Colonial Period

The territory was jointly administered for five years, but was then split into two areas with the British in a smaller, western portion and the remainder controlled by the French. The British area became part of what is now Ghana, formerly known as Gold Coast.

The Portuguese navigator, Fernao Poo (Fernando Po in Spanish) had explored the coast of Cameroon in 1472; the prolific shrimp in the River Wouri inspired the sailors to christen the river *Rio dos Cameroes*, meaning "River of Shrimp" in Portuguese. There was a variety of commercial activity during the 19th century pre–colonial period, a time when no single European nation dominated Cameroon. The British decided in 1884 to annex Cameroon and sent an emissary to sign treaties with the local inhabitants. He arrived five days too late—spurred by the rush for colonies, a German Consul had already visited Douala, the seaport, and obtained the signatures of the chieftains on treaties annexing Cameroon to Germany; the area was named Kameroun, a Germanization of the original Portuguese name.

The colonial rule of the Germans was similar to that in Togo—exploitive and often cruel. There was some penetration into the interior but control was not established in the northern regions by the Germans. Throughout the colony it became difficult to locate the tribal chieftains, who went into hiding to avoid possible punishment or being held hostage by the colonial administrators. In exchange for support of French claims in Morocco, Germany was granted about 100,000 square miles of Congo (Brazzaville).

Cameroon was the scene of an extensive campaign early in World War I. British and French forces wrested control from Germany, and by the terms of the Treaty of Versailles, Cameroon was split between the two powers. The land previously acquired from Congo (Brazzaville) was rejoined with that territory.

## South Africa: South–West Africa

The Germans first entered the region of South–West Africa in the 1840's in a strictly missionary effort, similar to British efforts in South Africa among the native Africans. This outpost, called the Bethany Mission, slowly expanded during the following decades, and numbers of Germans went into the interior from Walfish (Walvis, Walvisch) Bay. The German missionaries twice asked for the British to assume protection of the Bay area, and in 1877 this request was granted.

There was substantial German migration into South–West Africa during the last quarter of the 19th century. After

**Benito Mussolini**

quarreling with the British for several months, the Germans proclaimed a protectorate over the area in 1884; administration initially was by the German Colonial Company, but in 1892 South–West Africa came under the control of the German government.

The migrants to the area were principally farmers and herdsmen who occupied the scarce and choice lands suitable for cultivation and grazing. Discovery of mineral wealth led to further measures designed to exploit the wealth of the land for the benefit of the Germans. The Bantu Hereros, also known as Damaras,

rose in bloody revolt from 1904 to 1908, requiring 20,000 German troops to finally defeat them. Several thousand of these people fled to neighboring Botswana (then Bechuanaland) during the revolt.

Within a year of the start of World War I, a combined British and South African *Boer* army was able to defeat the German force of about 3,500 stationed in South–West Africa. The territory was assigned to the British–*Boer* Union of South Africa as a mandate by the Allied Council and later by the League of Nations.

## East Africa: Tanzania
## (German East Africa)

Initial exploration of the East African coast area occurred in 1860–1865 when Karl von der Decken entered the region, but it was not until 1884, when Karl Peters signed a series of treaties with native kings that the colonial effort actually started. The agreements provided for a sale of land to the Germans for a very small fraction of its probable value. The German status in the area was recognized at the Berlin Conference of 1885, and the German East Africa Company was created to administer the colony.

In the early colonial period, the Germans also acquired lands in adjacent Uganda and coastal Kenya by signing treaties in the former, and coercing the Arab viceroy in Zanzibar to surrender lands in the latter. These were given up by treaties to the British in exchange for a somewhat worthless island in the North Sea and other minor concessions; treaties were also entered into with King Leopold of Belgium and the Portuguese which

**Haile Selassie enters Addis Ababa in 1941**

fixed the border of German East Africa. Penetration into the interior was slow and difficult. The native Africans resisted the German movement; there was a violent uprising of the Muslim Arabs along the coast (1888–90), a revolt of the Wahehe (Wahaya) people (1891–93) and a combined Muslim–Angoni rebellion (1903–1905). The Angonis, a Bantu group related to the warlike Zulus of South Africa, were all but exterminated during this conflict, known as the Maji–Maji Rebellion, in which the Germans ruthlessly destroyed crops and villages, rendering a large area completely desolate.

In 1914, 300,000 British, South African *Boer* and Indian troops invaded German East Africa. A force of slightly more than 200 German officers, commanding native troops numbering between 2,500 and 4,000 fended off the massive attack for four years under the spirited and brilliant leadership of General Paul Von Lettow–Vorbeck.

With great effort, the allies slowly pushed Lettow–Vorbeck from German East Africa into Mozambique and Rhodesia. The Germans refused to stop fighting, and the battles ceased only when their commander was informed that the Armistice of November 11, 1918 had been signed, ending World War I, and providing for the evacuation of Germans from German East Africa.

The British received a mandate from the League of Nations to administer the former German colony, which was renamed Tanganyika. Substantial numbers of German immigrants who had established large, prosperous farms and plantations, were deported to Germany; a few were later permitted to return to the British colony.

A small, northwestern part of German East Africa which had been occupied by Belgian troops at the start of the war was mandated to Belgium in 1923; initially called Ruanda–Urundi, following independence it became the two nations of Rwanda and Burundi.

## THE SOUTH AFRICAN "MANDATE"
### Namibia (German South–West Africa, South–West Africa)

The Union of South Africa received a mandate from the League of Nations in 1919 over what had been German South–West Africa. After The UN came into existence, it exerted pressures to grant the people of Namibia their independence. Finally, on March 21, 1990, that goal was achieved (see Namibia, p. 148).

## THE ITALIANS IN AFRICA
### The Eastern Horn; Somalia, Ethiopia

In comparison to other European nations, Italian colonial efforts were rela-

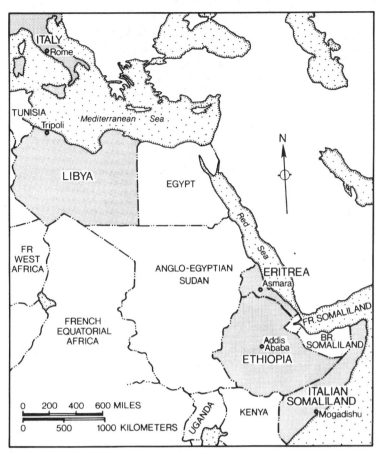

**The Italians in Africa**

tively weak and delayed because of the fact that Italy itself was not closely united as a nation. Following agreement among the stronger powers in 1885, the Italians signed treaties during the next four years with the three Muslim sultans in the "horn" region of East Africa. Although Italian Somaliland was acquired as a colony, full control was not established in the area until as late as 1927. The bleak, uniformly hot and dry region was considered to be valueless as a colony and the nomadic Cushites and Somalis who lived in the region, including part of Kenya and Ethiopia, were difficult to control.

British and French Somaliland, both areas somewhat more desirable, separated Somaliland from Eritrea, a semi–arid expanse given to the Italians by a lack of interest on the part of more powerful colonial nations. Benito Mussolini, the fascist dictator, came to power in Italy in 1922. He began to flex colonial muscles, eyeing with envy the vast territories taken without resistance by the rest of Europe in Africa and elsewhere.

From bases in Eritrea, Italian forces invaded ancient Ethiopia in 1936; Emperor Haile Selassie begged for assistance at the

League of Nations, but his plea fell on deaf ears. The fate of Ethiopia had been decided earlier in Paris, when the British and French gave the Italians wide authority over Ethiopia in an effort to appease Mussolini. The figurehead King of Italy proclaimed himself Emperor of Ethiopia, a title recognized at once by Austria and Germany and in 1938 by Great Britain and France.

Ethiopia was joined with Somaliland and Eritrea to form Italian East Africa; initially there was some effort at economic development and road building. However, an attempt was made to assassinate the Italian governor at Addis Ababa in 1937. A reign of terror followed, with widespread arrests and summary executions in an attempt to terrorize the population. Further unrest became intense, and by 1940 the Italians were besieged from within by Ethiopian terrorists and from without by British forces. Exactly five years after the first entry of Italian troops, Haile Selassie entered Addis Ababa at the head of a British–Ethiopian force and Italian rule was ended.

During the postwar period, a plan whereby Eritrea was to become a part of

# The Colonial Period

Ethiopia was promulgated at the UN; following its acceptance, the two were joined. The UN granted a trusteeship over Somalia to Italy in 1949; this area had been occupied by the British since the early years of World War II. The trusteeship provided for complete independence within ten years, which was achieved in 1960.

### North Africa: Libya

Although many Italian immigrants had settled in North Africa, particularly in Libya and Tunisia, there was no effort to colonize the area until the 20th century. The ambition had then been present for decades—when the British and French settled the Fashoda Crisis (see *The French in Africa*), the Italians protested since they did not share in the division of the Sahara region of the African continent. Using a short-term ultimatum to provoke a conflict, Italian forces invaded Libya in 1911 in an attempt to seize control from the Ottoman Turks. After taking a few coastal towns, a protectorate status was proclaimed by the Italians.

The Muslim *Sanusi* sect immediately organized a revolt that continued until about 1931 at various places within Libya. Because the Arab–Berber people were given only the poorest parts of the land in which to live, the people of Libya, through eventually subdued, continued to have a smoldering hatred for the Italians.

Italian rule was ended in the two years following 1940. Extensive campaigns were waged by the Allies throughout the land against the Nazis who had gained control of North Africa when it became apparent that Italy could not act with military authority in the area. The country, historically divided into three provinces of Cyrenaica, Tripolitania and Fezzan, was split between Allied powers at the end of World War II. Fezzan was occupied by the French, and the remaining two provinces were under British administration.

The question of Libya's status was submitted to the United Nations, which adopted a resolution providing for Libyan independence by the end of 1951.

Ethiopia's Emperor Haile Selassie aboard a U.S. warship with President Franklin D. Roosevelt, then on his way home from the 1945 conference in the Crimea.

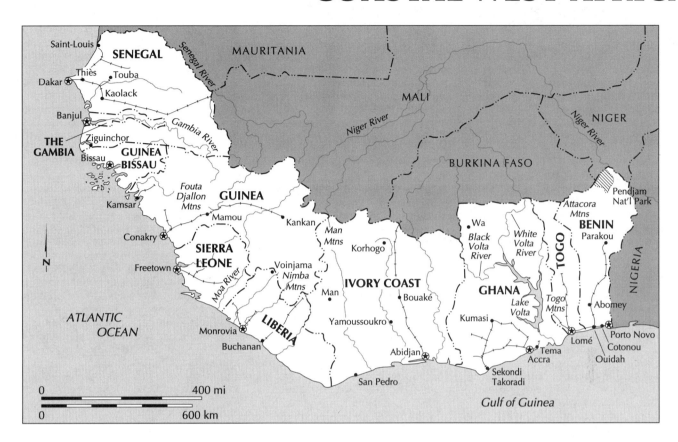

# The Republic of Benin

(pronounced ben–neen)

**Area:** 115,773 sq. km. = 44,483 sq. mi. (slightly larger than Tennessee).

**Population:** 7,460,025 (July 2005 est.)

**Capital City:** Porto Novo (Pop. 231,600, est.) (The main port is nearby Cotonou, the country's economic capital.)

**Climate:** Hot and humid in the South tempered by sea breezes; tropical in the North, with wet seasons in the South (mid-March to mid-July and mid-September to mid-November. Northern Benin historically had a single wet season (June-October) but more recently has tended to be touched by drought.

**Neighboring Countries:** Togo (West); Burkina Faso (Northwest); Niger (North); Nigeria (North, East).

**Official Language:** French.

**Other Principal Languages:** Fon, Adja, Yoruba, Bariba.

**Ethnic groups:** There are 42 distinct ethnic groups in Benin. The Fons, Adjas, Yorubas and Baribas are the largest, constituting more than half the population.

**Principal Religions:** Indigenous beliefs 50%, Christian 30%, Muslim 20%—estimated.

**Chief Commercial Products:** Cotton, crude oil, palm products, cocoa.

**GNI per capita:** $440 (2003)

**Currency** CFA Franc (African Financial Community).

**Former Colonial Status:** French Protectorate (1892–1960).

**Independence Date:** August 1, 1960.

**Chief of State:** Mathieu Kérékou, President

**National Flag:** A green vertical stripe at the staff with two horizontal stripes of yellow and red filling the remaining area

Benin lies in a small belt of land stretching from the warm waters of the Atlantic Ocean to a distance of 450 miles inland. The coastline is 78 miles wide, but in the North the width increases to over 200 miles.

The coastal area, with palm trees waving gently in the breezes from the ocean, is a region of picturesque lagoons and inlets. A narrow sandbar lies close to the entire coastline; the lagoons open to the sea in only two places.

A series of clay plateaus extend further inland for a distance of about 50 miles, terminating at the rocky foothills of the stretch of mountains which divides the North from the South. There usually has been abundant rainfall in this region, as well as along the coast, supporting dense vegetation in the areas not under cultivation.

Immediately south of the Attacora Mountains, which rise to a height of 2,300 feet, there is a swampy depression. From

# Benin

these mountains to the north, the land gently descends in a patchy forest with very little undergrowth, to the plains of the Niger River valley. Temperatures north of the mountains have a wider variation than is found in the rest of the country. The dry season from November to May has in recent years been transformed to a year–long drought, creating severe conditions for the people located in the area.

The Pendjam National Park, next to the borders of Burkina Faso and Niger, is a reserve to protect the country's dwindling numbers of wild game. It extends across the boundary into the two neighboring countries. Although hunting is not permitted within its limits, hunters pursue animals in the surrounding areas.

**History:** The record of shifting tides of migrant people in Benin extends back to the late 16th century. A group of people traveled west from the Mono River and settled near what is now the city of Allada, establishing a kingdom. After a war of succession to the throne in 1610, a young contender named Dacko went to Cana, near the present city of Abomey, and founded the Kingdom of Abomey, becoming its first ruler. This monarchy expanded gradually; Dacko's son conquered the lands belonging to a neighboring king named Dan. Angry with the aggressive invader, Dan is reported to have said "If I

don't surrender, you will go so far as to kill me and build over my corpse." Dan was beheaded, buried and a building was erected over his body. The former name of the country, Dahomey, comes from the two words *Dan Home* which literally means "on the belly of Dan." The Abomey Kingdom quickly became paramount over all other tribal rulers in the southern region. Their superior position continued for 350 years until the French abolished the monarchy.

Guézo, the ruler of Abomey from 1818 to 1858 signed a treaty of friendship and commerce with the French in 1851. His son, Glèlè, ceded the commercial city of Cotonou to the French 17 years later. For details of the colonial period, see *The French in Africa.*

Independence was achieved on August 1, 1960 and Hubert Maga was elected first president of the Republic of Dahomey in December. Part of the elite educated at the École William Ponty in Dakar, Maga had represented Dahomey in the French national assembly and was one of the few African politicians to hold a ministerial position in the French fourth republic, as secretary of state for labor from November 1957 to May 1958. A northerner, Maga was one of a triumvirate of nationalist politicians who shaped the early course of Dahomean politics. Caught between the rivalries of the two southern leaders, Sourou Migan Apithy and Justin Ahoma-

degbé, Maga was soon the target of southern political classes. Trade unions, historically powerful in the country, focused on his lavish spending to create the symbols of Dahomean sovereignty, especially a sumptuous presidential palace.

After a workers' strike and street demonstrations, Maga was overthrown in a military coup led by Colonel Christophe Soglo in October 1963. The coup ushered in a period of political instability in which military regimes restored authority to civilians, only to topple them once again. Maga, Ahomadegbé and Apithy circulated in and out of office with successive coups in 1965, 1967, and 1969. The military leader of the 1969 coup finally relinquished power to the three leaders collectively, creating Roman-style triumvirate in May 1970. With such tumult, the country came to be known as "the sick child of Africa."

The country's fifth *coup d'état* occurred in October 1972, when Commander Mathieu Kérékou ended the three-man Presidential Council, declaring "that authority of the State has disappeared everywhere." Many politicians were arrested and some were put to death. In an effort to widen his support, Kérékou announced a "program of national construction" and established the *National Council of the Revolution* in late 1973. A year later he announced Marxism-Leninism as the country's official doctrine and scientific socialism its way of development. On November 30, 1975, the name "Dahomey" was replaced by the more revolutionary "Peoples Republic of Benin," which became a single-party state controlled by the *Parti de la révolution populaire du Bénin* (PRPB: Revolutionary Party of the Benin People). Benin would be ruled by a Marxist military dictatorship for 17 years.

Foreign interests were nationalized. Although ties were established with the U.S.S.R., China, Cuba and North Korea, little assistance was forthcoming from those nations, aside from endless quantities of advice. These moves alienated western goodwill and resulted in lowered financial assistance.

With the PRPB the only legal party, the 196-member Revolutionary Assembly was its rubber stamp. Power was centralized in the hands of the party leader, Mathieu Kérékou, with state and party structures overlapping and merging. Kérékou was first elected to a three-year term as president in early 1980, then reelected to an extended five-year term in mid-1984 and yet again in 1989. All of this was of course achieved without opposition and with the massive "majorities" that characterize single-party regimes.

Kérékou's Marxist state was an economic disaster, and with the collapse of

**Water dwellers, Ganvie, Benin. The more elaborate house at left is that of the Chief of the Fons.**                    AP/Wide World Photo

**President Mathieu Kérékou**

communist regimes in Eastern Europe, Beninois felt increasingly free to speak out against a repressive regime. By June 1989 the regime was facing a severe financial crisis and growing social unrest characterized by an intensifying rhythm of strikes and demonstrations by civil servants and students. By the end of the year, the regime had adopted a structural adjustment program and the Revolutionary Party of the Benin People had abandoned Marxist-Leninist principles and accepted the separation of state and party.

The popular protests of 1989 led to a National Conference to discuss Benin's problems in early 1990. A good Marxist, Kérékou made public confession of his errors and submitted himself to popular will. In December 1990 the Beninois expressed that will: a new multi-party constitution was overwhelmingly (93.2%) adopted by referendum. "The People's Republic of Benin" became more simply the "Republic of Benin" and seventeen years of militaro-Marxist rule were ended.

A transitional parliament organized multiparty, democratic elections in 1991. Kérékou stood for election, but was defeated by Nicéphore Soglo, a French-educated economist with experience at the World Bank in Washington. In democratic Benin multiparty exuberance flourished, but with a multiplicity of parties, legislative majorities are difficult to obtain. Governance in such a situation is always a fragile affair, as President Soglo found out.

Soglo was not able to lessen Benin's economic woes despite a liberalization of Benin's economy. Privatization of state corporations drew the ire of unions and resistance slowed the pace of economic reform. The new president's style brought

him additional enemies. A flamboyant politician, Soglo frequently traveled abroad and installed far too many members of his family in government jobs. Ex-president Kérékou, chastened by electoral defeat, kept a low profile, lived austerely, found religion, and bided his time. At the first opportunity they had, the people, forgetting the miseries of his military dictatorship, returned Kérékou to office in March 1996.

In run-off elections, Kérékou gained the support of those opposed to President Soglo. He received 52.5% of the vote to Soglo's 47.51%. Once the election was won, the rewards had to be distributed. President Kérékou appointed the third-place finisher, Adrien Houngbédji, as prime minister, a post, curiously, that did not exist in the constitution. In that role Houngbédji would last only two years before returning to opposition.

President Kérékou's time in the political wilderness was transformative. Mao jackets were put aside, suit and tie donned, and a new nickname earned from his fellow citizens: The Chameleon. Economic liberalization, begun under Soglo, was continued. Since this involved privatization or closure of inefficient state enterprises and a downsizing of Benin's civil service, there was resistance. Strikes by public employees are continuing events in Benin and contribute to a climate of unrest.

Discussions on the merit pay plan for civil servants have gone nowhere, a characteristic feature of Beninois politics. In March 2002, some 32,000 civil servants went on strike, demanding wage hikes and the "immediate and unconditional withdrawal" of the government's merit promotions law. After three days of industrial action that brought the country to a virtual administrative standstill, the government backed down, agreeing to increase civil servants' pay and release back pay due them. It also agreed to rethink the promotions law.

Legislative elections in spring 1999 produced another slender majority in parliament—understandable when you realize that there have been at one time or another over 100 political parties in the country. When all the ballots had been counted, former President Soglo's Renaissance Benin (RB) party topped the list of about 10 opposition groups with 27 seats. In total the opposition won 43 out of 83 seats in the National Assembly, the slimmest of majorities.

Ultimately, as usual, the presidential party, being the party of power, has inducements with which to encourage opposition members to cross the aisle and enjoy the benefits of power. Where President Kérékou could not get a majority, he

could also issue a presidential decree to secure the same ends, another feature of Beninois politics.

Benin's reputation as a "laboratory of democracy" was severely tested by presidential elections in early 2001. In the primary, President Kérékou faced three challengers, including ex-President Soglo. In the first round, Kérékou received 47% of the vote while Soglo received about 29%. The third-place finisher, Adrien Houngbédji, President of the National Assembly, garnered 13% while Bruno Amoussou came in a distant fourth with a mere 4% of the ballots.

Without a clear majority, a runoff election was needed, but former President Soglo refused to run, citing a variety of irregularities that added up to massive fraud. The election was, he said, a "masquerade." The electoral commission went to the third-place finisher, Houngbédji, and was similarly rejected.

There being no alternative, Bruno Amoussou's name was placed on the ballot. A member of the Kérékou cabinet who had already asked his supporters to vote for the president in the runoffs, Amoussou did no campaigning and conceded the election before the ballots had been counted. Benin's electoral battle was won for lack of combatants. President Kérékou was reelected with 84% of the vote, cast by only 53% of eligible voters.

Local government elections—the first in Benin's history—were held in December 2002, and provided an opportunity for the opposition to test itself before parliamentary elections which would follow in March, 2003. (Citizenship in Benin requires a certain electoral stamina.) Results demonstrated a focus on "big men" and a regionalization of opposition strength. Nicéphore Sogolo's *Renaissance du Bénin* won 36 out of 45 seats on the Cotonou city council, allowing him to become mayor of the country's economic capital. The coalition of parties supporting President Kérékou, the *Union pour le Bénin du future* (UBF), won a paltry four seats. In Porto Novo, Adrien Houngbédji was elected mayor after his Democratic Renewal Party (PRD) swamped the presidential coalition, winning 27 out of 29 seats. Opposition parties also won in Parakou, the most populous city in the north and a traditional stronghold of President Kérékou.

Despite this penetration of the north, however, the opposition to President Kérékou remains a largely urban phenomenon. This was solidly proved in the March 2003 parliamentary elections. A total of 1,162 candidates representing 14 parties or party alliances competed for the National Assembly's 83 seats, but when all the ballots were counted, the UBF won an outright majority of 53. Soglo's *Renais-*

# Benin

*sance du Bénin* (RB), which could not overcome its own internal problems, captured only 15 seats—a humiliating loss of 12 members of parliament; Houngbédji's PRD, which had included RB dissidents on its electoral lists, took 11 seats—one more than it had in the previous assembly. The man who assembled the presidential alliance and organized its campaign was none other than Bruno Amoussou, now a minister of state in the Kérékou cabinet.

Given the new distribution of power, Houngbédji—who had helped elect president Kérékou in 1996 and once served as his prime minister—quickly asserted his claim to be the political chameleon of the day by defecting to the presidential alliance. Cynics were heard to mutter that one eye of the chameleon (whose careful observations are facilitated by eyes that move independently) was orbiting the presidential elections in 2006.

Benin's plethora of political parties—more than 120—may be significantly reduced by those elections. In an effort to make parties more meaningful and democracy more credible, new legislation requires parties to have a minimum of 10 founding members in each of the country's twelve administrative districts. Many will fail to attain that standard. To receive state subsidies, parties are also required to have a minimum of ten members of parliament, and if they fail to run candidates in two successive legislative elections they will lose their legal existence.

**Culture:** While Porto Novo is the official capital of the nation, most government offices and embassies are found twenty miles to the west at the port city of Cotonou (*Coo*–toe–new). This is Benin's chief commercial center and has in the past been a weekend resort for many foreigners, with excellent seafood.

Unfortunately, Cotonou, with a population of some 734,600 people, has become afflicted with some of the worst air pollution in West Africa, largely the product of gasoline engine exhaust. Its visibility is frequently zero, and the main culprit seems to be elderly used cars, but motorbikes also produce noxious exhaust. Drivers tend to believe that a vehicle uses less fuel when it's filled with oil, so there's a lot of burning oil to add to the pollution.

Adding to Cotonou's urban din and pollution are thousands of taxi motor bikes (72,000 in 2002) operated by young Beninois with no other job possibilities. Wearing bright yellow shirts, "zemidjans" [literally "take me quickly" in the local language] ferry passengers from place to place during the day. The more entrepreneurial owners rent their bikes for a more macabre evening service: transporting the bodies of the dead. For those families unable to afford standard mortuary charges, the motorbike hearse is an affordable alternative. The cadaver is placed on the bike, lashed to the driver and held by a family member as it is whisked to the family home for appropriate ceremonies.

With steady increases in the number of cars and motorbikes on the streets, the government faced increasing outcries for action. In late 2001 it ran a trial program to control exhausts and encourage owners to properly maintain their vehicles. Fines were administered, but ranged from around $13 for motorbikes to $47 for trucks. The program lasted for only 10 days.

A 2002 study for the West African Development Bank suggests the magnitude of the problem: in Cotonou 83 tons of carbon dioxide are emitted daily, 59% of which is generate by two-wheeled vehicles. An additional 36 tons of carbonic acid are also spewed into the atmosphere, 90% of which comes from two-wheelers.

The palace site of the Kings of Dahomey at Abomey has been on UNESCO's World Heritage list since 1985. The entire palatial site is vast, extending over approximately 108 acres. Each successive Dahomean king added to the site, making it a visual symbol of his obligation "to make Dahomey ever greater."

The palaces of King Guézo (1818-58) and his son King Glèlè (1858-89), with important relief sculptures that document the history and culture of the Dahomean kingdom, have undergone extensive restoration and conservation since 1992. They now house the Abomey Historical Museum, which contains three hundred years of royal history. Thrones, scepters, appliqué umbrellas and hammocks, state swords, royal vestments and commemorative altars called *asin* all form part of the museum's treasures.

Arguably the greatest expression of the kingdom's identity and ideology are the royal bas-reliefs of Abomey, lovingly restored with the aid of the Getty Conservation Institute and others. Each of the kings had a series of names; usually associated with a natural creature, these became the subject of palace reliefs. Proud Glèlè compared himself to a lion, while his father chose the buffalo. Near the coastal town of Ouidah modern artists have created concrete representations of these royal symbols, some of which have the sting of contemporary political relevance. One is a chameleon, the symbol of King Akaba (1685-1708)—who changed his policies to suit the situation. This may have helped him remain a contender for the kingship, for which he waited patiently (another quality of the chameleon) until he was about 60 years old.

**Economy:** It takes patience to see substantive action from Benin's political system or improvement in its economy. The

**Palace of the Dahomean Kings at Abomey**
Photo of Francesca Piqué, courtesy Getty Conservation Institute

30

lingering effects of its Marxist phase—a high degree of centralization and bureaucratization—lie heavily on economic development. Given a multiplicity of political parties and activist trade unions to protest anything that affects their interests, inertia and immobility characterize the political sphere and keep change in the economic sphere progressing at a chameleon's pace.

The economy remains dependent on cotton exports, as it was at independence. Eighty percent of export income comes from cotton, but falling world commodity prices in recent years have affected cotton production strongly. It declined from 415,000 tons in 2001-2002 to 220,000 tons in the 2003-2004 harvest season.

Given the importance of the cotton industry, it comes as no surprise that politics enter, almost always to the disadvantage of the farmer. One recent Minister of Rural Development encouraged the establishment of five new cotton-processing factories. Benin now has the capacity to process more than 650,000 metric tons of raw cotton, while producing less than 320,000 tons on average.

Along with Burkina Faso, Benin has been active in world trade discussions arguing the unfairness of subsidies granted cotton farmers in the United States and Europe. Agricultural subsidies to farmers in the developed world are estimated to have cost African producers $300 million dollars in revenue from 1999 to 2001.

Benin's port of Cotonou serves as a regional transit hub important for supplying landlocked Niger and Burkina Faso. Cargo handling at the port has been liberalized, and the Benin Port Authority (SOBEMAP) now competes with the Danish company Maersk. Given this newly competitive environment, the Autonomous Port of Cotonou (PAC) has registered increasing traffic and capacity. It has also benefited from political instability in neighboring Côte d'Ivoire as shippers have shunned the port of Abidjan. The only thing slowing growth in the use of port facilities is the endemic corruption that ramifies though every sector of port activity. Transaction costs have gotten so high businessmen look to neighboring ports as alternatives.

Corruption appears to be a national sport in Benin, and it is estimated that the state loses 25 percent of its receipts annually through fraud and corruption. World Bank officials estimate that only about 30 percent of international credits put at the government's disposal are actually utilized due to corruption and poor administrative practices. For the man on the Benin street everything can be bought,

from driver's licenses to diplomas. To get one what wants in Benin, one only needs to know how "to place a pebble on the dossier"—the local euphemism for corruption.

According to finance ministry figures, the state loses nearly $94 million a year through corruption, embezzlement and the misuse of public funds. The Minister of Justice claimed that corruption was rife "in the law courts, within the police, the gendarmeries, the private sector, and even strikes the Non-Governmental Organizations." Regional administration was, he said, similarly tainted.

In January 2004 twenty-seven Benin judges went on trial for corruption. They were only a part of nearly 100 court and finance ministry officials charged with stealing more than $15 million in state funds over a period of four years. By June 37 people were sentenced to between 30 months and five years for their part in the scandal. Suspended prison terms of between six and 30 months were given to 25 others, and the remaining 25 were acquitted.

When he returned to power in 1996 General Kérékou set up an ambitiously titled "public morality unit," vowing to stamp out corruption in the public sector. In July 1999 a presidential commission reported that more than $105 million had been misappropriated within Benin's civil service over the last three years.

Despite the fanfare, Beninois have remained skeptical about bringing the suspects to trial. None of Kérékou's earlier anti-corruption commissions have yielded any results. Trials for crimes related to fraud remain rare. Few investigations, in fact, are ever completed. The average citizen seems to have given up hope that top-level corruption will be reversed. New financial scandals seem to be uncovered daily.

Rampant corruption is one contributing factor in Benin's limited economic growth.

**Mud-relief sculpture of King Glèlè's "Jar of Unity."**

At three percent in 2004, economic growth is insufficient to keep up with population growth. On average, every Benin woman gives birth to 5.3 children.

Benin has benefited from China's thrust into Africa to expand its export markets for made-in-China goods, secure needed natural resources for booming industrialization and support for its reunification policy with Taiwan. In June 2004 the Chinese Vice-President, Zeng Qinghong, visited the country, insecting a variety of investments and technical assistance projects.

Since diplomatic relations between the two countries were established in 1972, Beijing has provided $135,323,000 in assistance and funding. The Cotonou Congress Palace was financed with an interest-free loan $ 22,244,879, while other projects include Cotonou's Friendship National Stadium and Lokossa Hospital. More than 10 Chinese medical teams have been sent to Benin and Beijing has also provided important technical assistance in rice-paddy cultivation.

**Future:** There is a palpable sense of disillusionment with a democracy in which economic benefits remain the privilege of a group of influential businessmen who have lent their support to President Kérékou. So too is there disillusionment with the political system itself, rendered meaningless in many eyes by the constant reassembling and realignment of parties and the ease with which a politician can be in opposition one day and the next be firmly embedded in the presidential camp. Heightened requirements to register as a party are a step in the right direction.

Those disillusioned look forward to the presidential elections in March 2006 as an opportunity to renew and rejuvenate an arthritic political class. President Kérékou is constitutionally prohibited from seeking another term of office and, at age 73, has made it clear he does not desire a third term. Nicéphore Soglo (born in 1934) is constitutionally prohibited from running for office by virtue of being over 70 years old. Adrien Houngbédji's party has already announced it will oppose any move to change these constitutional provisions, no doubt thinking its champion, only 61, is best situated to become Benin's next president.

"Everyone is preparing in their own way for the presidential elections of 2006," one Beninois told a UN Integrated Regional Information Networks reporter. "The men in power have been hoovering up money and transferring it abroad fraudulently and in massive quantities."

# The Republic of Cape Verde   (pronounced *Vair*–day)

**Mindelo, São Vicente. Cultural and intellectual capital of Cape Verde.**

**Area:** 4,030 sq. km = 1559 sq. mi. (slightly larger than Rhode Island). Ten rather mountainous islands and eight additional islets about 400 miles off the coast of Senegal.

**Population:** 418,224 (July 2005 est.)

**Capital City:** Praia (on São Tiago island.) Pop. 106.052 (2000 est.)

**Climate:** Temperate; warm, dry summer; precipitation meager and very erratic, producing prolonged droughts; harmattan winds from the Sahara can obscure visibility.

**Official Language:** Portuguese

**Other Languages:** Crioulo (a blend of Portuguese and West African words).

**Ethnic groups:** Creole (mulatto) 71%, African 28%, European 1%.

**Religions:** Roman Catholic (infused with indigenous beliefs); Protestant (mostly Church of the Nazarene).

**Principal Commercial Products:** Shoes, garments, fish, bananas, hides.

**GNI per capita:** $1,490 (2003)

**Currency:** Cape Verdean escudo

**Former Colonial Status:** Portuguese colony

**Independence Date:** 5 July 1975 (from Portugal).

**President Pedro Pires**

**Chief of State:** President Pedro Pires (since March 2001).

**National Flag:** Three horizontal bands of light blue (top, double width), white (with a horizontal red stripe in the middle third), and light blue; a circle of 10 yellow five-pointed stars is centered on the hoist end of the red stripe and extends into the upper and lower blue bands.

Cape Verde, 729 miles west of Senegal, is the Western end of the drought prone Sahel. Rain falls, if at all, only two or three months a year, and lack of rainfall shapes the archipelago's precarious economic existence. Its history is dominated by the years of famine and drought, with 1747 still referred to as the worst recorded. At nearly 10,000 feet, the Pico do Fogo volcano is the archipelago's most imposing landmark. Still active, the volcano last erupted in 1995.

**History:** Cape Verde had no indigenous people. It was settled by Portuguese, Jews, and Africans in the fifteenth century; they mingled, creating a Creole culture. A little over 400,000 Cape Verdeans live on the islands of the archipelago. More than 500,000 more live in the eastern United States, primarily in Rhode Island and Massachusetts.

Under the leadership of Amilcar Cabral, the struggle to free Cape Verde from Portuguese colonial rule began in the early 1960s. Cabral's mother was from Guinea-Bissau and the nationalist party he created, the African Party for the Independence of Guinea-Bissau and Cape Verde (PAIGC), fought to liberate and unite both

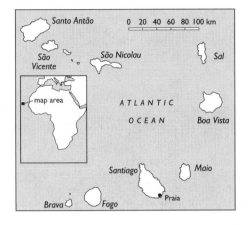

**Former Prime Minister Carlos Veiga**

colonies. Cabral saw neither. He was assassinated in early 1973 and the colonies were granted independence in 1975 under the leadership of Aristides Pereira.

Efforts continued to unite Cape Verde and Guinea-Bissau, but following the 1980 *coup d'état* in Guinea-Bissau, which resulted in the overthrow of Luis Cabral by Nino Vieira, union was no longer possible. In Cape Verde, the governing party renamed itself the *Partido Africano da Independencia de Cabo Verde*, or PAICV.

Pereira's authoritarian rule lasted until multiparty elections in 1991. These were won by the *Movimento para a Democracia* (MPD) led by Antonio Mascarenhas. President Mascarenhas was reelected in 1996 without much opposition or participation. Only about 40% of the electorate managed to turn out.

The electoral rivalries of the PAICV and MPD continue to divide the community of Cape Verdean immigrants in America. As expected in color-conscious America, the community is also divided over conceptions of race and color. Lighter-skinned, longer-established Cape Verdeans frequently refer to themselves as Portuguese. Others live in the black community and identify themselves as black.

This division of the community has worked against a collective response to elevated levels of youth unemployment, crime, and urban violence. At least 300 Cape Verdeans, children of immigrant families and mostly in their early 20s, have been deported to Cape Verde in the 1990s. They were convicted of certain felonies and fell under provisions of a 1996 law that required the U.S. Immigration and Natural Service to deport convicted felons. In impoverished Cape Verde they have few prospects and often resort to a life a crime.

Cape Verde grants voting rights to anyone born in the islands, so many Cape Verdean emigrants participated in the parliamentary and presidential elections of 2001. Absentee ballots are not employed in the process. Instead, polling places are set up in community centers wherever a concentration of islanders lives. There were nine official polling places in Massachusetts, Rhode Island, and Connecticut for this cycle of elections.

Based largely on diaspora support, the PAICV, which had governed the islands for the first fifteen years after independence, re-captured political power by winning 39 out of 72 parliamentary seats in January 2002 elections. The MPD won 31 seats, and an alliance of three opposition parties captured the remaining two seats.

The two parties faced each other again in the February presidential elections. Former Prime Minister Carlos Veiga represented the MPD, while Cape Verde's first head of government, Pedro Pires, led the PAICV, with three other candidates on the ballot.

The run-off pitted the two former prime ministers against each other: Veiga, a Lisbon-educated lawyer against the ex-guerrilla fighter Pedro Pires. The balloting was so close that results were not official until March. Once the Supreme Court had heard a number of electoral challenges, the National Electoral Commission announced a winner: Pedro Pires by a mere twelve votes.

The PAICV now controls both the executive and legislative branches, but because financial legislation sometimes requires a two-thirds majority, the party faces an opposition possessed of a formidable political weapon with which to force moderation. When the constitutional court declared parts of the 2002/2003 budget unconstitutional because it had not received a two-thirds majority, the government began to talk about amending the constitution. That too requires a two-thirds majority: cooperative understanding between the country's two major parties remains a necessity.

Municipal elections in March 2004 suggested a slight shift of voter sentiment to the opposition MPD. The party won nine of the archipelago's 17 municipalities and backed winning slates in two others. The PAICV won only six city halls, one less than they had in 2000.

**Culture:** Cape Verde has always been a cultural crossroads. Islanders speak Crioulo, a mix of Portuguese and West African languages, and Prime Minister Jose Maria Neves has promised to make Crioulo the Cape Verdean official language in 2005.

The islands' rich musical heritage reflects their isolation and poverty, and their synthesis of intersecting cultures. For generations the islands sent their men abroad to work, manning, in the nineteenth century, the ships of the American whaling fleet. Longing and loneliness characterize the most famous Cape Verdean musical form, the *morna*. It combines the sadness and longing of the Portuguese *fado* melodic line with a quickness of rhythm that is distinctly African.

The singers of *morna* sing of *"saudade,"* a Portuguese word meaning longing and yearning, homesickness and nostalgia. It is the haunting sadness of an island people driven to leave by poverty, but always looking back to home and loved ones. One of the greatest Cape Verdean singers is Cesaria Evora. Her recordings are perennially near the top of World Music charts and her live performances have captivated an international audience.

HIV/AIDS has made its appearance in Cape Verde and the government is taking action to curb its spread. The National AIDS Control Program (NACP) freely distributes condoms in the country, but they seem not to have been adopted with enthusiasm. The NACP director has vigorously condemned the irresponsibility of those who refuse to use condoms.

The International Narcotics Control Board (INCB) has identified Cape Verde as a transit point for the shipment of cocaine from South America to Europe. In July 2004 Cape Verde authorities seized over 400 pounds of the substance, lending substance to the INCB's observation of increased drug trafficking by sea, especially in Western Africa.

**Economy:** Cape Verde has extremely limited natural resources. An archipelago of ten larger islands, only nine of which are habitable, and eight smaller islets, Cape Verde has little land to cultivate. Only 20% of the land can be used for agriculture. Cape Verde is subject to persistent periods of drought, interrupted by torrential rains and floods that erode what useful land is available. Although 70% of the population

# Cape Verde

lives in rural areas, agriculture contributes only about 6.6% of GDP. (Some 74.5% of GDP is provided by the service sector.)

Beans and maize are the most important foodstuffs grown, but production fluctuates with climatic conditions. Other crops include bananas, sweet potatoes, yams, manioc, pumpkins, sugarcane, coffee, and groundnuts, but the country must import nearly 90% of its food. This results in a large trade deficit. During years of drought and failed crops, the country is dependent on the good will of the international community in supplying food to its most vulnerable citizens.

After attaining power in 1991, the MPD government reversed the socialist policies of its predecessor and liberalized the economy. The state is now less an agent of intervention. Prices and exchange rates have been freed from government control and a privatization program is selling off state corporations. These policies have encouraged foreign investors, donors, and lenders.

Because of the country's high rate of unskilled workers—30%-40% of the population—investors are able to take advantage of low-wage employment. Given a relatively high unemployment rate of 21%, the government is open to almost any job-creation opportunities.

Responsible economic policies have been duly recognized by lenders and have helped ease the burdens of Cape Verde's debt—totaling $415 million in 2002. In April 2002 the IMF extended a low-interest $11 million loan to the country. It is the first step in securing financial support from other multilateral lenders. The credit agreement will help eradicate internal debt, the servicing of which has been one of the main burdens on the state budget.

The World Bank has recorded an uneven growth rate over the past three years. GDP growth was a solid 6.8% in 2000, but by 2001 the macroeconomic situation had deteriorated and the reform agenda had stalled in the run-up to the elections of that year. The growth rate fell to 3.3% in 2001, lower than predicted, following the events of September 11, 2001 and the slowdown in the world economy. In 2002, it rose again to 4.3%, and the Central Bank is forecasting growth of 5% in 2005, a prediction that will probably prove optimistic.

What growth there is has been largely powered by development in the tourism sector. With an abundance of good quality beaches, coupled with a sunny climate, tourism has strong growth potential. The government recognizes this and has encouraged foreign investment in the industry. At the end of December 2004 the Portuguese Sacramento Campos Group announced it was re-launching plans to build Cape Verde's largest tourist complex on the resort island of Santiago. The Santiago Golf Resort, located about ten miles from Praia, will have five hotels, hundreds of villas, a marina, and shopping malls in addition to the golf course. Initial estimates peg the project at $715 million and it is expected to create 4,000 jobs. Avelino Bonifecio, the islands' economy minister has said that Chinese businessmen are also considering building a hotel on Santiago.

Tourism-fueled growth in Cape Verde is assymetrical. It mostly benefits Praia, the capital, the port city of Mindelo, on São Vicente, and the island of Sal, where Cape Verde's main international airport is located. Elsewhere poverty has increased, especially in the rural areas of Fogo, Brava and Santo Antão. Recent surveys by the National Institute of Statistics indicate that in 2002 36% of Cape Verdeans are living in official poverty, an increase from 30 percent in 1989.

Remittances sent home by expatriates are extremely important to the Cape Verdean economy. An estimated 20% of the GDP is derived from this source, and no visit of a Cape Verdean president to the United States is complete without a stop in Massachusetts and Rhode Island, where the wealthiest of the Cape Verdean diaspora reside.

Desperate for investment capital, the government looks to all potential sources, and this has provided an opening for Chinese investment. The minister of economy has signed an agreement with a Chinese company that assures cement production in the community of Santa Cruz. China will also build a dam for the municipality of Santiago, estimated to cost about $25 million.

At the same time, the government is also firming its ties to the European Union. The Cape Verdean escudo was once tied to the Portuguese escudo, but with the introduction of the Euro, it is now linked to the new currency. The government appears to be lobbying to adopt the Euro as its national currency, in much the same way the microstates of Andorra, Monaco, San Marino and the Vatican have adopted the currency.

Oil exploration is expected to start this year, with the Brazilian energy company Petrobas, and the Angolan state oil firm Sonangol mentioned as possible partners.

To round out this picture of eclectic internationalism it should be noted that the United States military is preparing to train a rapid intervention unit for Cape Verde.

**The Future:** The country's future is very limited by climate and geography. The government's privatization program should bring badly needed revenue to the treasury. Tourism and fishing look like the most promising areas of development.

**Coastline, Santo Antao**

# The Republic of Côte d'Ivoire

The government established the French form of *Ivory Coast* as the country's official designation, pronounced *Coat deev–whar*.

Our Lady of Peace, Yamoussukro—the world's largest Christian church.

**Area:** 323,750 sq. km. = 125,000 sq. mi. (somewhat larger than New Mexico).
**Population:** 17,298,040 (July 2005 est.)
**Capital City:** Yamoussoukro, the birthplace of former President Félix Houphouët-Boigny, is the political and administrative capital with a population of 130,000. Most government departments remain in the former capital of Abidjan (pop. 3.5 million), which is the major center for economic activities.
**Climate:** Tropically hot and humid in the South, with two wet seasons (March–July and October–November). Warm and less humid in the North with a single wet season (May–October).
**Neighboring Countries:** Liberia, Guinea (West); Mali, Burkina Faso (Upper Volta–North); Ghana (East).
**Official Language:** French.
**Other Principal Languages:** Anyi, Attié, Baulé, Bété, Dan, Guéré, Guro, Jula, and Sénoufo.
**Ethnic Groups:** More than sixty ethnic groups. Prominently, Baulé (15%), Sénoufo (10%), Bété (6%), Lagoon peoples (5%), Agni (Anyi-3%), and a Mandé cluster of groups, including Jula, Bambara, and Malinké (17%). Non-Ivoirian Africans, Lebanese, Asians, and Europeans composed nearly 27% of population before the recent disturbances.
**Principal Religions:** Muslim 60%, Christian 22%, and indigenous 18% (some of these are also numbered among the Christians and Muslims).

**Chief Commercial Products:** Cocoa, coffee, tropical woods, petroleum, cotton, bananas, pineapples, palm oil, and fish.
**GNI per capita:** $660 (2003)
**Currency:** CFA Franc (African Financial Community).
**Former Colonial Status:** French Colony (1839–1960).
**Independence Date:** August 7, 1960.
**Chief of State**: Laurant Gbagbo, after disputed elections, October 2000.
**National Flag:** Three vertical stripes of orange, white and green.

The Republic of Côte d'Ivoire occupies an area in the center of the south coast of the west African bulge. The coast, warmed by the waters of the Gulf of Guinea, is 340 miles long; from the border of Ghana for a distance of 185 miles to the west, it is flat and sandy, with many inland lagoons. The remainder of the coast towards Liberia has numerous sharp rocks and is higher. The surf along the entire shore line is quite heavy, steadily pounding the sand and boulders. Dense forests and jungles spread their green foliage further inland, covering almost 40% of the country. Tall niagou, samba and mahogany trees struggle against each other for precious sunlight, crowding smaller trees and undergrowth.

Approximately midway to the north, the trees gradually become thinner and are succeeded by low scrub trees, grasses and brush vegetation. This in turn gives way in the extreme northern area to a semi-arid climate, which has in the past supported grasslands, occasionally interrupted by taller growth. With the African drought of the past decade, this northern region has become increasingly desolate.

The country is almost entirely level—only the Man Mountains in the area closest to Liberia and Guinea relieve the monotony of the plains.

The southern and central portions of the country have traditionally received ample rainfall and have a high humidity. Temperatures are warm in the North, with less (or hardly any) rainfall.

**History:** Artifacts discovered in Côte d'Ivoire suggest that a Neolithic civilization flourished there in prehistoric ages. Not much is known of the history of this country prior to the 14th century.

At the time of the arrival of the first Europeans, there were three strong kingdoms, the Krinjabo and Bettie in the North and Boundoukou in the East. There were, besides the three major kingdoms, more than 50 other small tribal groups which had little contact with each other.

The severity of the surf and the forbidding appearance of the land discouraged early European exploration. For greater detail on early history and the colonial period, see *Historical Background* and *The French in Africa*. When full independence was gained by Côte d'Ivoire on August 7, 1960, Félix Houphouët-Boigny (*Fay*-lix *Who*-fway *Bwa*-nyee) became its first president. He was well-prepared for the tasks which faced him.

A Baulé, with ancestors including a line of chiefs, he attended the prestigious École William Ponty in Dakar, Senegal. The school brought together the very best students from each of the French West African colonies for advanced education that would prepare them for positions in the colonial civil service or French commercial enterprises. Houphouët-Boigny was trained as a *médecin africain*. Perhaps even more important for future political developments, Ponty created an educated elite which would ultimately bring the various colonies of the French West Africa to independence. The friendships they made at Ponty were crucial for that development.

Houphouët-Boigny traveled the colony extensively as a rural doctor and in 1940 inherited large-coffee producing tracts of land from his father, a wealthy planter and chief. Using modern techniques, he was able to expand their output, becoming a very wealthy man in a relatively short time. By the 1940s he was acknowledged as leader of disgruntled African planters and founded the African Agricul-

# Côte d'Ivoire

tural Union in 1944. The group fought colonial policies that favored French planters and worked to end forced labor of Africans on white-owned plantations.

He formed the *Parti démocratique de la Côte d'Ivoire* (PDCI) in 1945, mobilized African planters, and was elected a deputy to the French National Assembly in 1945 and again in 1946. In the Assembly, Houphouët initially affiliated with the French Communist Party. After long and persistent harassment by colonial officials, he broke with the Communists in 1950 and began to cooperate with the French. In West Africa his PDCI was part of the *Rassemblement démocratique africain* (RDA: Democratic African Rally), a Federation-wide party.

In 1958, when General de Gaulle offered the possibility of immediate independence to France's colonies, Houphouët instead campaigned vigorously for self-government within the Franco-African Community. He was an equally vigorous opponent of any large federation of independent states, refusing to see Côte d'Ivoire's wealth used to subsidize French West Africa's poorer states.

Félix Houphouët-Boigny became prime minister of the Côte d'Ivoire in 1959 and in 1960 was elected the first president of the independent state. He was the architect of Côte d'Ivoire's rise from colonial backwater to relatively wealthy republic.

His political base remained with the African planting class, and economic development reflected their interests. Commercial export of coffee and cocoa was encouraged and facilitated by development of roads. The port of San Pedro in the southwest was built to facilitate exports of the two crops. To work the plantations, migrant workers from Côte d'Ivoire's over-populated and underdeveloped north were encouraged to travel south. Similarly, migrant labor from Mali, and what is now Burkina Faso, was encouraged to travel to the plantations. Land ownership and even citizenship were made possible for the newcomers.

For thirty years the PDCI remained the country's sole political party, and Houphouët-Boigny governed by crafting an alliance between Akan-speaking southerners and largely Muslim northerners. When young northerners complained of unemployment and uneven regional development in the 1970s, a flurry of projects were started in the north, but by the early 1990s northern resentments and frustrations could no longer be so easily bought off.

As elsewhere in Africa, waves of sentiment for multiparty democracy were felt in Côte d'Ivoire in the late 1980s. In response to popular demand, and a bit of pressure from the World Bank, free forma-

tion of political parties was permitted for the first time during the 1990 elections. One of the most critical voices was that of Laurent Gbagbo, a member of the minor-

**President Laurent Gbagbo**

ity Bété community and former history professor who founded the *Front Populaire Ivoirien* (FPI) in 1990 and ran for president against Houphouët. Gbagbo's FPI gave expression to the frustrations felt by those who had long suffered under a government dominated by Akans. Ominously for the future, Gbagbo charged that Houphouët's power was based on the vote of "foreigners."

Côte d'Ivoire's founding father died in December 1993 and was succeeded by his protégé—another Baulé-speaker—Henri Konan Bédié. Less confident and politically skilled than Houphouët, Bédié seemed not to understand the basic pragmatism by which Houphouët had ruled, winning over opponents through co-optation and cooperation, consensus and compromise. As tough economic restructuring began to be implemented, a scapegoat had to be found. It would be Côte d'Ivoire's "foreigners," and more specifically, northerners.

Northern resentments built up. Northerners felt they were not receiving a fair return for political support and economic contributions given over the years. They received fewer political appointments, and economic development of the region was stinted. They were too frequently hassled when trying to obtain national identity cards and complained of being treated not like citizens, but as foreigners. Their answer was to split from the PDCI.

The *Rassemblement des républicains* (RDR: Republican Rally), based mainly in the north, was founded in September 1994 only a few months after Houphouët-

Boigny's death. Its leader was Houphouët's prime minister and rival with Konan Bédié as his successor, Alassane Ouattara.

Faced with an increasingly desperate economic situation and deprived of the PDCI's traditional northern support, Konan Bédié resorted to the baser instincts of his countrymen. "Foreigners" were stigmatized; a populist Ivorian ethnonationalism was generated. It was not the first time the regime had diverted attention from its problems by arguing the colony's wealth was exploited by foreigners. Dahomeans had been the object of attack in 1958, but now it was the turn of Burkinabé and Malian migrant laborers. It was easy, by extension, to include Bédié's lapsed allies—northern Muslims.

First articulated by Bédié in an August 1995 speech to the PDCI faithful, the concept of Ivorian identity—*Ivoirité* in French—became central to political discourse in the country and was used to justify what developed into violent xenophobia.

A program of "Ivoirization" was instituted in 1996, a direct reversal of the open borders policy of the country when plantation labor was needed. Now, to officially be a citizen, one had to prove his or her parents and grandparents were born in Côte d'Ivoire. Strict nationality rules for presidential candidates were introduced into the Ivorian electoral code.

Alassane Ouattara, once a prime minister under Houphouët-Boigny, was effectively prevented from running in 1995 because of these rules. He later accepted appointment as IMF deputy director. When, in April 1998, he announced that he would not seek reappointment and would be available to serve his country, the controversy re-emerged with a vengeance. One PDCI leader accused him of being a foreigner. "We must close ranks," he told a party audience, "and not let ourselves be distracted by provocations of messiahs coming from other lands."

The virulence of attacks on Ouattara suggested the nervousness and even paranoia of the political class. He was both a northerner and Muslim, the "other" for the Akan-speaking Christian core of PDCI support. Like his predecessor Houphouët-Boigny, President Bédié was a Christian politician in a country increasingly turning to Islam.

Raw statistics describe a situation ripe for xenophobic reaction: Côte d'Ivoire has an estimated three million people officially described as "residents of foreign nationality." Another two million are residents of foreign origin—migrant workers and their descendents, largely Muslim. In short, some 30% of the population could be demagogically defined as "foreign."

# Côte d'Ivoire

Bédié's campaign to promote Ivorian nationalism produced increasing hostility directed at foreigners and ethnic minorities. Smoldering resentment against "foreigners," particularly in the South, erupted in ethnic pogroms in several communities. Anti-ethnic riots and continuing political demonstrations took place against a background of deteriorating economic conditions. Particularly affected was the cocoa industry after the European Union agreed to allow chocolate manufacturers to use less cocoa butter in their confections.

Economic problems fueled political tension throughout 1999 as the country approached its presidential election. The government responded to its critics with a repression that indicated an intolerance of dissent. Opposition leaders were imprisoned and street demonstrations prohibited. The campaign against Ouattara became more and more personal. When one judge ruled that Ouattara qualified as a presidential candidate, the justice ministry forced that judge to resign and replaced him with a jurist who ruled that Ouattara's identity papers were forged. In early December the government issued a warrant for Ouattara's arrest.

## The End of the First Republic

The country's cumulative crises were resolved on Christmas Eve, when General Robert Gueï, a former army chief of staff, assumed leadership of disgruntled soldiers demanding back wages and overthrew the Bédié government. France, with significant commercial interests at stake, 20,000 citizens actually resident in the country, and 550 soldiers stationed there, did not act to restore the *ancien régime*. The country at large seemed to greet the coup with an enormous sense of relief.

Military intervention did not, however, cool the political temperature. Quite the contrary. Since the Christmas Eve coup Côte d'Ivoire has been plagued by violence and instability. General Gueï moved with military dispatch. A new constitution was written, submitted to voters, and massively approved in July 2000, but it carried into the Second Republic the fertile seeds of division cultivated in the First: Presidential candidates were required to have two Ivorian parents. Bédié's "*Ivoirité*," aimed specifically at his most feared opponent and ultimately anti-Northern, anti-Muslim, and divisive, was given formal constitutional recognition.

Presidential elections were organized for October, and nineteen people submitted the requisite candidacy papers. Fourteen were declared ineligible by a Supreme Court. Included among the disqualified were representatives of the largest opposition parties—Émile Constant Bombet (PDCI) and Alassane Ouattara, (RDR). Muslims were pointedly excluded. At best, the remaining five candidates, Robert Gueï among them, represented no more than 15% of Côte d'Ivoire's diverse population.

The campaign came down to a battle between General Gueï and Laurent Gbagbo, the former history professor who, as the leader of the *Front Populaire Ivoirien* (FPI), had opposed the governing PDCI since 1990. Security forces engaged in bloody assaults against northerners, judged by dress and religion to be opponents of General Gueï. When the electoral commission proclaimed Gueï the winner in October elections, Gbagbo called out his supporters to protest. People took to the streets in massive demonstrations. The general fled and Laurent Gbagbo proclaimed himself winner and president.

Attacks against "foreigners" did not end. The new regime, like it predecessors, found the ethno-nationalism of "*Ivoirité*" politically useful and played to its supporters' basest instincts. The worst such incident occurred at the Abidjan suburb of Yopougon. There gendarmes slaughtered 57 individuals and dumped them in a mass grave. Their only crime was to be Muslim or have a "northern" name.

Once installed as president, Laurant Gbagbo refused all suggestions that the election be rerun despite its dubious legitimacy—not only were the major candidates excluded, but 62% of registered voters boycotted it. He also failed, disastrously, to curtail state-sponsored ethnic violence, and even appeared to encourage it.

In December 2000 legislative elections were organized, and now a Gbagbo court, echoing Konan Bédié's, excluded Alassane Ouattara (a one-time ally of Gbagbo) from even running for the National Assembly. Demonstrations followed and many thought the country was on the verge of civil war. The RDR boycotted the election with such success that in some northern areas absolutely no one turned up at the polling stations. Only 33% of registered voters summoned courage or interest enough to vote.

The FPI obtained 96 seats in the 225-seat Assembly—not enough to govern alone—with the former governing Ivory Coast Democratic Party (PDCI) garnering 94 seats. Twenty-two independents would act as swing votes between the contending factions.

Municipal elections in March 2001 were dominated by Ouattara's RDR, now participating on a nation-wide basis. By selecting candidates representative of local constituencies, the RDR gained control of all towns in the northern region and some of the largest southern cities, including Gagnoa, Laurent Gbagbo's birthplace. With these elections the RDR proved that it was indeed a national party and could be successful in a fair election.

## The Politics of Reconciliation

Desperate to end the turbulence that threatened its internal power and external support, the Gbagbo regime convened a National Reconciliation Forum in late 2001. The forum brought together around 700 participants representing political parties, religious communities, non-governmental organizations, human rights and other groups. Ultimately, Côte d'Ivoire's Big Four—Bédié, Gbagbo, Gueï, and Ouattara—attended. The forum dealt with the issues that had ripped and torn the fabric of Ivorian society: immigration and "foreign" workers, ethnic violence, political repression and the central issue of Alassane Ouattara's citizenship.

Ultimately regime behavior seemed little changed. Persecution and discrimination persisted, and nowhere was there a link to notions of justice. Instead there seemed to be a growing impunity that emboldened xenophobes and made life increasingly insecure for opponents of the regime. (In August 2001 eight gendarmes, for example, were charged with multiple murder in the Yopougon massacre, but were acquitted by a military tribunal for lack of evidence.)

These tensions exploded on September 19, 2002. Dissident divisions of the Ivorian army mutinied, allegedly over issues of pay and demobilization. In coordinated attacks, the mutineers took control of the northern city of Korhogo and the central city of Bouaké. There was fighting in Abidjan, the commercial capital, but loyalist troops retained control of the city. During the fighting the interior minister was killed and the minister of de-

**Alassane Ouattara**

# Côte d'Ivoire

fense attacked. The government claimed it was an attempted *coup d'état* and used the occasion to eliminate its enemies.

Troops in army fatigues murdered General Guéï—who had just withdrawn his party from the governing coalition and was suspected of planning a coup—along with his wife, aides, and other family members. A similar armed squad arrived at Alassane Ouattara's home, but forewarned, he and his wife escaped over a wall into the neighboring German Embassy. He was later given sanctuary in the French Embassy.

The army mutineers soon incorporated civilian elements, named themselves the *Mouvement patriotique de Côte d'Ivoire* (MPCI), and announced their complaints and policy demands: They were fighting a "dictatorship" that treated them like "slaves," as one spokesman put it. They demanded Laurent Gbagbo's resignation and a transitional government that would organize new presidential elections, open to all.

The beleaguered president lofted his flimsy legitimacy, but it was a banner to which few rallied. Despite defense agreements with the country, France chose to pursue a "neither...nor" policy—neither interference nor indifference. In practical terms that meant dispatch of troops to protect French citizens and evacuate them from Korhogo and Bouaké, both controlled by the rebels.

With no outsider willing to fight the rebels, president Gbagbo was forced to rely on his own ill-trained, underequipped, demoralized, and disorganized army. The effort to retake Bouaké was a humiliating failure. To prevent further deterioration, France secured a ceasefire and established a buffer zone between government and rebel forces. The country was effectively divided in half. Rabid anti-French sentiment became the order of the day.

Pathologically incapable of recognizing any responsibility for the chaos into which the country had sunk, the regime accused hostile neighbors (Burkina Faso and Liberia) of arming and aiding the rebels. Claiming a "legitimate right to self defense" the Gbabgo government began to acquire arms and men wherever it could. The usual Eastern Europeans showed up, as did Angolan armor. (Gbagbo had gained Angolan goodwill by breaking Côte d'Ivoire's connections with UNITA on becoming president.)

Much like the Hutu regime in Rwanda, the government whipped up ethno-nationalist fervor in the streets and on the airwaves. Muslims, "foreigners," and political opponents became the object of virulent attack, and none more so than Alassane Ouattara who was all three to his

detractors. The nadir was no doubt reached when one daily, *La National*, proposed a simple word game: by using the letters in the name Alassane Dramane Ouattara, wrote the author, one could spell out the words "Satan," "demon," "*meurtre* (murder)," and "torture."

The wages of hate were not long in being gathered. Mobs demanding Ouattara besieged the French Embassy and nearly broke in. In early October 2002, illustrating the psychological centrality of the Yopougon massacre and its subsequent impunity, MPCI rebels massacred dozens of gendarmes at Bouaké after a chilling reminder: "Remember Yopougon? Now it's your turn." (Members of the Ivoirian regular army kept in the same holding area were not harmed.) Death squads began to roam through Abidjan, selectively assassinating regime opponents and intimidating others into silence by kidnapping and torture. A UN report of February 2003 suggested the death squads were comprised of elements close to the government, the presidential guard, and a Bété tribal militia.

Less immediately lethal, but resonant with the darkest pages of recent history, Ivoirian equivalents of the Nazi Nuremberg laws began to be enacted. In Bonoua, only 30 miles from Abidjan, "foreigners" could not be allocated any stall at the local market, or land on which to build. They were also forbidden to work as transporters or to enter into a mixed marriage, and, in the language of the legislation, every family was "strictly forbidden to have recourse to any procedure to integrate a foreigner into our ranks."

As violence and fear intensified in the cities, the war in the countryside took on larger regional dimensions. Two new rebel groups located in Western Côte d'Ivoire announced themselves in November 2002—the *Mouvement populaire ivoirien du Grand Ouest* (MPIGO: Ivorian Popular Movement of the Greater West) and the *Mouvement pour la Justice et la Paix*

**Charles Blé Goudé, leader of the Young Patriots.**                    ©IRIN

(MJP). Both claimed to be fighting to avenge the murder of General Guéï and to remove Laurant Gbagbo. Both drew support from President Charles Taylor of Liberia and recruited from his reserve of mercenaries without borders—willing to fight anywhere, at any time, for any booty.

Unfortunately, the Liberians soon resembled some sorcerer's apprentice who could not or would not stop what he had been trained to do. After France had gathered all the various forces together and twisted arms to secure agreement on a government of national union in January 2003, the need for mercenary services diminished significantly. Convincing them to go home proved more difficult. A joint operation by rebels, the Ivory Coast army, and 900 French troops was organized to clear western areas of the Liberian fighters.

Such co-operation was made possible by the Marcoussis peace accords hammered out at the end of January in a Parisian suburb. Those agreements, extracted by forceps and imposed on a reluctant Laurant Gbagbo, created a government of national union which included ministers from the rebel groups (now called the "New Forces") and was headed by a consensus premier, Seydou Diarra, a northerner.

The Diarra government found itself regularly impeded. So fearful for their security were they, rebel ministers were hesitant to show up for the initial cabinet meetings in Yamassoukro. In Abidjan, the hardliners around Laurant Gbagbo organized public demonstrations of opposition and private acts of terror against those thought to support the New Forces. Foremost among these thuggish forces was the Alliance of Young Patriots headed by Charles Blé Goudé.

Though he has periodically sworn to uphold the Marcoussis agreement, President Gbagbo has consistently delayed, circumvented, and obstructed any constructive progress to a peaceful resolution of the tensions that divide his country. Frustrated with Gbagbo's failure to honor the Marcoussis accord, the rebels withdrew from the unity government in September 2003 and only returned in January 2004.

President Gbagbo was received by French President Chirac with all the dignity of a head of state in February 2004, and seemingly emboldened by the recognition, he became even more intransigent. By March even the PDCI had become fed up; it accused the president of "destabilizing the peace process" and withdrew its ministers from the government. When the opposition proposed to demonstrate against the president's actions, Gbagbo decreed a prohibition on demonstrations through the month of April. Undaunted, opposition parties organized a pacific

An anti-French mob. ©IRIN

march in Abidjan to support Marcoussis, and the president responded with brute force. The city was closed down. Helicopters surveilled the participants from above, while below defense and security forces crushed the demonstration in blood. A UN report said at least 120 people were killed by government security forces and their militia allies. When they had completed their work, President Gbagbo congratulated his forces.

The UN report called the deaths "indiscriminate killing of innocent civilians," and noted that individuals from northern Côte d'Ivoire and immigrants from Burkina Faso had been "specially targeted" even though these communities had "little or nothing to do with the march." Following the massacre, New Forces rebels and the four main opposition parties in parliament withdrew their 26 ministers from the government of "national reconciliation" and broke off dialogue with President Gbagbo. He, in turn, chose to deepen the crisis by firing three opposition ministers (including two New Forces figures) and replacing them with members of his own Front Populaire Ivoirien party (FPI).

The government also continued to buy arms and hire mercenaries; by November it decided the time had come to crush the rebellion by military force. Aerial raids were launched against the five rebel strongholds in the north and west. During the last, on November 6, a government plane bombed a French military installation in Bouake, killing nine French soldiers and one American civilian. France retaliated by destroying virtually the entire Ivoirian air force. Anti-French mobs rioted in Abidjan, largely targeting their mayhem and violence at French property and personnel: shops were fired, women raped, and men beaten.

To protect their compatriots, French forces secured the Abidjan airport, while angry voices throughout the city fanned ultranationalist and anti-French sentiments. Young Patriots, told the French intended to remove President Gbagbo from office, surrounded the principal sources of regime power: the Presidential Palace and the national radio and television station. In the chaos at least 20 and perhaps as many as 60 Ivoirians were killed.

The UN Security Council issued an immediate arms embargo and gave leaders one month to get the peace process back on track or face a travel ban and freeze on their personal assets. The usually listless African Union enlisted President Mbeki of South Africa to lead an African mediation effort. Rather than immediately summoning the parties to Pretoria, Mbeki went himself to the Cote d'Ivoire, talked with contending forces, and against all odds, extracted minimal agreement and concession. The April 2005 Pretoria Agreement which emerged from discussions declared the war to be ended, reiterated previous accords, and perhaps most importantly, reaffirmed a determination to organize presidential elections in October 2005.

President Mbeki dealt deftly with the central issue of those elections: the candidacy of Alassane Ouattara. The truculent and intransigent Laurent Gbagbo was pressured to abandon his demand for a constitutional referendum on the topic, and in late April he announced that he was invoking "exceptional measures" to suspend the normal rules for the next election. "As a consequence," he told his television audience, "Mr. Alassane Dramane Ouattara can, if he wants, present his candidature in the presidential election of October 2005."

In May Ouattara and Henri Konan Bédié ended their long political feud to join forces against a common enemy, Laurent Gbagbo. The RDR and PDCI (plus two smaller opposition parties) created a new opposition coalition: *le Rassemblement des Houphouëtistes pour la démocratie et la paix* (RHDP: Rally of Houphouëtistes for Democracy and Peace). Each of the parties will field its own candidate in the presidential election, and, with the expectation that there is no way President Gbagbo can gain a majority in the first round of a fair poll, they agreed to unite behind a single contender in any run-off. "Fair" of course is the operative word.

For the cynical (and practical) there is little likelihood free, fair, or nationwide elections can be held in October. Though heavy weapons have been drawn back from the front lines, the country remains divided. Nationwide voter registration will be conducted by the National Institute of Statistics (controlled by a close

Gbagbo ally) instead of the Independent Election Commission and will prove a continuing source of controversy. Ominously, more than 10,000 militia members remain armed and dangerous, posing an ever-serious threat of xenophobic terror against "foreigners" to disrupt the electoral process. The Brussels-based International Crisis Group could well be prophetic: Their most recent report on the Côte d'Ivoire was titled "The Worst May Be Yet to Come."

**Culture:** Côte d'Ivoire's population is an ethnic mosaic consisting of some sixty groups, roughly divided into four linguistic families—Akan, Kru, Mandé and Voltaic—having distinct characteristics and regional identifications. Akan speakers dominate the southeast, and the most prominent subgroup, the Baulé, have also settled in savanna regions of central Côte d'Ivoire. Catholic missionaries were first active in the southeast, bringing mission education and literacy, which provided access to employment in the colonial civil service. From that position of privilege, Akan speakers came to dominate Ivoirian politics. Both presidents Houphouët-Boigny and Bédié were Baulé.

The southwestern region is dominated by Kru-speaking peoples. Though Protestant missionaries were active in the southwest, most peoples there practice indigenous religions. Laurent Gbagbo comes from one of the Kru subgroups, the Bété. Southern Mandé speakers are found in the western regions, and General Gueï belonged to the Yacouba subgroup. "Northerners" are almost equally split between Northern Mandé speakers and Voltaic speakers like the Sénoufo. The Northern Mandé include Malinké and Jula (or Dyula), traditionally long-distance traders. Alassane Ouattara hails from this group.

While Southern Mandé practice a variety of indigenous religions and Christianity, Northern Mandé are almost all Muslims and members of their merchant class have settled in most of the major cities of the south. There they have become influential enough to dominate the local politics of several southern cities.

Abidjan, the former capital city, is located on lagoons inland from the coast. The city now has a population of 3.5 million—the equivalent of the population of the entire country at independence in 1960. The city is home to most of the 7,000 to 8,000 French citizens who still remain in the country. Down from a population of 60,000 in 1978, today's expatriates live in a state of tension and fear, the objects of hostility and attack.

Much of the fear and tension is generated by a steady stream of anti-French invective spewed by Laurant Gbagbo's sup-

# Côte d'Ivoire

porters and applauded at the highest leadership levels. Many of the radical anti-French rhetoric comes from the ranks of the powerful student union—*Fédération étudiante et scolaire de Côte d'Ivoire* (Fesci). Organized into the Association of Young Patriots by the former Fesci leader, Charles Blé Goudé, they have become the regime's storm troopers. Known as "the general of the young," (and to his friends as "the machete") Blé Goudé tools around Abidjan (surrounded by his Kalashnikov-bearing body guards) in army fatigues, sleeveless tee-shirt, and baseball cap—an incarnation of the rejection of Marcoussis and what he calls "the dictates of Paris."

There is more than symbolism to the young man. He sees himself as the youth movement's ideologue and has begun to formulate the notion that decolonization has not yet ended and will only do so with the departure of the last Frenchman. Another of the anti-French rejectionists, Sansan Kouao, told one public gathering that "We are capable of doing to them [the French] what the Iraqis have done to the Americans"—a sentiment applauded by Simone Gbagbo, Côte d'Ivoire's First Lady.

**Economy:** Côte d'Ivoire's economy is heavily dependent on agriculture. Cocoa coffee, and timber are its principal exports. Together, they produce about 70% of total export earning and contribute 40% of GDP. Côte d'Ivoire is the world's largest cocoa producer, representing about 40% of the world's cocoa output. There are some 620,000 cocoa and coffee farmers out of a population of 16 million, and another three million people depend directly on the commodities for their livelihoods.

A young cocoa tree

©IRIN

Simone Gbagbo, First Lady

The country's cocoa and coffee industries were roiled by a series of negative events well before the civil war that began in September 2002. Commodity prices were regularly falling, and the state marketing board, which offered some guarantee of price stability to farmers, was liberalized in 1999. Unfortunately, liberalization took place just as world prices were dropping and a decade-long planting binge had helped to increase cocoa production. Prices plunged even further when the EU voted to allow "chocolate" to be sold with up to five per cent vegetable fat substituting for cocoa butter.

One consequence of the reliance on earnings from cocoa, coffee and palm oil, is that vast areas of tropical rainforest have been destroyed to create commodity plantations. Dependent on migrant labor, cocoa plantations, particularly in the Western region, have been the scene of vicious anti-foreign pograms. Many of the migrants, often from Burkina Faso and Mali, had lived in the region for years and had even bought property. Hyped up by the government xenophobic rhetoric, locals have chased thousands of northerners from their homes, lands, and livelihoods.

With the country currently divided, the Gbagbo government controls the cocoa-producing areas, the source of most of the regime's revenues. There is virtually no transparency, but donor-nation diplomats estimate that as much as 20% of those revenues are siphoned off to buy arms for the regime.

The principal economic resource for the New Forces government in the north is the region's cotton industry. A number of factors have compromised the industry's productivity. Planters and co-operatives have not yet been paid by processors, which as dissuaded many from replanting their fields. The absence of banks in the north impedes the transfer of funds, and cotton processors find it difficult to finance cotton shipments. With the division of the country, transportation costs have risen 40%. As a consequence, stocks accumulate at the factories and run the risk of deteriorating.

**The Future:** Fear remains very real for most Ivoirians, especially those singled out by ethno-nationalist hate speech. The xenophobic passions whipped up by former president Bédié have proved useful to the Gbagbo regime, and the impunity it has granted the perpetrators makes the pessimistic most uncomfortable with its genocidal possibilities.

# The Republic of The Gambia

**Mothers lined up for food**

Photo by Ken Brown

**Area:** 10,463 sq. km. = 4,005 sq. mi. (Connecticut is 1/5 larger).

**Population:** 1,593,256 (July 2005 est.)

**Capital City:** Banjul (Pop. 240,000. 1996 est.)

**Climate:** Subtropically warm with a wet summer (May–October) and a dry and somewhat cooler season (November–April).

**Neighboring Countries:** The Gambia is enclosed on three sides by Senegal.

**Official Language:** English.

**Other Principal Languages:** Fulfulde, Jola, Mandinka, Soninke, and Wolof.

**Ethnic Groups:** African 99% (Mandinka 42%, Fula 18%, Wolof 16%, Jola 10%, Serahuli 9%, other 4%), non-African 1%.

**Principal Religions:** Muslim 90%, Christian 9%, indigenous beliefs 1%.

**Chief Commercial Products:** Peanuts and peanut products, fish, cotton lint, and palm kernels.

**GNI per capita:** $310 (2003)

**Currency:** 1 Dalasi (D) = 100 Butut

**Former Colonial Status:** British Colony (1816–1965).

**Independence Date:** February 18, 1965.

**Chief of State:** Capt. Yahya Jammeh, President (1994).

**National Flag:** Three horizontal stripes of red, blue, and green; thin white lines separate the stripes. Symbolically, the blue stripe (Gambia River) is between the red and green stripes (sun shining on the river as it flows through the fertile land).

The Gambia has the smallest area of any independent nation on the African mainland. Slicing thinly into the northwest coast of Africa and facing the tropical waters of the Atlantic Ocean, this country lies within an area smaller than Jamaica. It was named *The* Gambia by the government to avoid confusion with Zambia.

The Gambia is a finger like projection into the territory of southern Senegal by which, except for the seacoast, it is surrounded. The Gambia River is navigable by ocean going vessels for 150 miles inland; smaller ships can traverse its entire length. The estuary contains one of the finest natural harbors in Africa.

The entire territory is low lying, never exceeding a height of 120 feet. On each side of the broad river, thick swamps contain mangrove trees which can reach heights of up to 100 feet. Further inland from the river is a region of swamps and river flats. This swampy belt is succeeded by round hills and rolling plateaus with thick growths of grass and periodic clumps of trees. There is ample rainfall for cultivation in this long and narrow nation, seldom more than 20 miles in width.

**History:** The first written descriptions of The Gambia come from Portuguese mariners who visited the area about the same time Columbus reached the West Indies. By 1500 the lower river area had become a regular port of call for traders seeking gold and slaves. For details of early and colonial history, see *The British in Africa* and *The French in Africa*.

Conferences between the British colonial rulers and The Gambia in 1964 led to full independence on February 18, 1965; David K. Jawara was installed as the first Prime Minister. The Gambia elected to become a republic within the British Commonwealth in 1970 at which time Prime Minister Jawara became President.

Elections held in April 1977 (the first in ten years) resulted in a continuation of control by the People's Progressive Party led by President Jawara, who was elected to a five-year term. In mid-1981, while he was in London attending the wedding of Prince Charles, a force of leftists attempted to overthrow the government. Elections held in May 1982 resulted in a legislature dominated by the PPP, which won 27 of 36 seats.

Presidential elections in 1987 were contested by two other parties competing with the PPP, but despite this, President Jawara was reelected by a comfortable 59% of the vote. President Jawara initially announced that he would not stand for reelection, but in early 1992 he changed his mind, and moved the elections from March to February. The outcome was not unexpected—he won 59% of the vote; his party elected 25 of the 36 members in the legislature.

Unrest had been bubbling just below the surface for a decade, and finally erupted decisively in mid-1994 when Lt. Yahya Jammeh staged a *coup*. The basic problem was army personnel who had not been paid while rampant government corruption was obvious. Jammeh established a five-man ruling council. A referendum was held approving the new constitution. Jammeh resigned his commission and was elected president in September 1996.

Parliamentary elections in January 1997 were contested by Jammeh's party, the Alliance for Patriotic Reorientation and Construction (APRC), the United Democratic Party (UDP) led by Ousainou Darboe, the People's Democratic Organization for Independence and Socialism (PDOIS), the National Reconciliation Party (NRP) and five independents. The APRC, organized to contest every seat, won more than a two-thirds majority—33 seats. The UDP won seven, the NRP two and the PDOIS one. The elections were controversial and most observers thought them neither fair nor free.

Given its origins in a military coup and fraudulent elections, it is little surprising that the regime is authoritarian and oppressive. President Jammeh dominates the country and controls the instruments of force and fear. He holds the ministry of defense portfolio through which he com-

41

# The Gambia

mands the army. The National Intelligence Agency reports directly to him. Oppositional activity is closely watched and the main opposition group, the United Democratic Party (UDP) is frequently denied permission to hold public rallies. Members of the UDP have been arrested and regularly accuse the police of torture. Members of parliament are prohibited from criticizing the president and denied the right of discussing any matter impending in the courts.

The media is equally subject to abuse and control. In 2003 *The Independent* newspaper came under particular attack; staffers received death threats, its editor-in-chief detained by the National Intelligence Agency following publication of an article critical of President Jammeh, and its premises were set ablaze by three unidentified men. In May 2004, President Jemmeh took to the airwaves to excoriate journalists who failed to register with the National Media Commission (NMC). "We believe in giving each fool a long rope to hang themselves (sic)," he said. If they failed to register in the remaining three months of grace, he warned, "[t]hey will either register or stop writing or go to hell."

Critical journalism in The Gambia is a life and death profession. In December 2004, Deyda Hydara, the editor of *The Point* newspaper and one of the country's leading journalists, was brutally murdered, shot three times in the head after he had been sharply critical of newly passed press laws. One made all press offenses, including libel, punishable by imprisonment—six months for the first offense and three years for repeat offenders. In order to continue publishing, media proprietors were required to prove they could pay the hefty new penalties created by the law if they published such material; owners are required to sign a bond worth $17,000 and use their homes as collateral. In addition they are required to purchase operating licenses five times as expensive as before.

The government also uses more brute force against its citizens. The APRC has traditionally used its youth wings, trained by Libyans, as its storm troopers, breaking up opposition rallies, bullying and beating hapless candidates and opposition supporters. At a UDP meeting in June 2000, things got out of hand and one APRC supporter was killed. The UDP leader, Ousainou Darboe, and some 20 of his followers were promptly arrested and charged with murder. Though most have been acquitted, the trial of Darboe, long-postponed, has yet to be resolved.

President Jammeh won another five-year term in October 2001 elections, beating the UDP's Ousainou Darboe, with a

margin of 53%, just enough to avoid a runoff. The election, described as "relatively free and fair" by observers, was not without its quaint charms. Voters indicated their preference by dropping a marble into the drum of their chosen candidate. The marble struck a bell inside the drum—to ensure that multiple voting could be detected. Bicycles were banned from the vicinity of polling stations to avoid confusion with their bells.

President Jammeh celebrated his victory by firing several civil servants from the finance ministry, customs and excise department, police force, Gambia International Airlines and social security services for alleged disloyalty. The dismissals came after an explicit campaign threat: "You are supposed to be loyal to the ruling party as civil servants and not opposition forces," Jammeh warned. "Anybody who does not cherish my party will not be working with us. I am ready to sack all opposition sympathizers in my government." After heavy lobbying, most were reinstated, but fear had been made reality.

Legislative elections in January 2002 resulted in a total triumph for Jammeh's ruling APRC after the UDP withdrew, claiming manipulation of the voter lists. Non-APRC candidates won only three seats in the 53-member legislature. One result of the contest was a split in the UDP. The party's former propaganda secretary, Lamin Waa Juwara, accused Ousainou Darboe of misappropriating party funds and wrongly congratulating Jammeh before the official declaration of election results. After openly calling for Darboe's resignation, Juwara was expelled from the UDP and formed his own party—the National Democratic Action Movement (NDAM).

As NDAM leader, Juwara became one of the regime's most vigorous opponents, regularly arrested and detained by security forces. In February 2004 he was sentenced to six months in jail for "uttering seditious words"—that is, calling for popular demonstrations to protest the continuing decline of the Gambia's currency, worsening economic conditions, and endemic regime corruption.

Corruption remains a serious problem, and President Jammeh proclaimed "Operation No Compromise" in October 2003. The biggest fish caught in the operation's net so far was Baba Jobe, the former majority leader in the National Assembly. In March 2004, Jobe was sentenced to more than nine years in prison and ordered to reimburse the government $3 million for economic crimes. Given a broad mandate, the anti-corruption commission is examining assets of active and retired ministers and senior military officials in what the government claims is the

first time a sitting African government has probed itself.

The next president election is scheduled for Fall 2006 and there is nothing to prevent President Jammeh from running to succeed himself. Parliamentary elections are scheduled for 2007.

**Culture:** The Gambia's population is 90% Muslim and female circumcision is widespread, practiced by varying numbers of Mandinka, Serahuli, Fula, Wolof, and Jola peoples. An estimated 80% of Gambian women have had their clitoris surgically removed. A variety of women's groups have been organized to ban female genital mutilation (FGM), but they receive no support from President Jammeh. In January 1999 Jammeh called those working to eliminate FGM "enemies of Islam" who sought to undermine the religion and African culture. (It should be noted that the Gambian vice president, Mrs. Isatou Njie Saidy, who is also minister of health and women's affairs, is among the staunch campaigners against FGM.)

The President's Koranic understanding may be a bit shaky. A 1998 meeting of religious leaders agreed that "neither Islam nor Christianity permits the destruction of any part of a healthy human organ." For these leaders, FGM was "a brutal form of violence, whose existence predates both Christianity and Islam. Religious principals have been distorted and used by those with selfish interests, to mutilate and subjugate women."

Divisions within the Islamic community have been fostered by President Jammeh himself. As elsewhere in West Africa, Islam in Gambia has been traditionally flexible, accommodating a variety of indigenous practices. Having condemned traditional religious leaders, both Christian and Muslim, for supporting the Jawara regime, the young Lt. Jammeh reached out to young Islamist clerics, educated in Saudi Arabia in Wahhabist fundamentalism. Upon returning to The

Capt. Yahya Jammeh

Gambia, they grew their beards, donned long white robes, and followed the more rigid practices of Islam and opposed the accommodationist Islam practiced by the majority of Gambians.

The young president solidified his alliance with the fundamentalists by building a mosque on State House grounds and staffing it with one of the Wahhabis, Imam Fatty. Following the events of September 11, 2001, the president's relationship with the Islamists has cooled. In July 2003, speaking on the ninth anniversary of the coup which brought him to power, the president directed his criticism to what he called "the criminal elements of Islam" who believe "that it is the long beard that will take you to heaven." "God will not judge you, by your long beards," he proclaimed. "God will judge you by what you do. You are a disgrace to Islam."

**Economy:** The Gambia's economy is agriculturally based and largely dependent on groundnut export earnings. Seventy to eighty per cent of the country's workforce is engaged in farming; of generally low productivity, Gambian farmers contribute less than 30% of GDP. About 60% of all cultivated land is planted in groundnuts (peanuts). Their export provides nearly 85% of all export earnings.

The groundnut sector has been in turmoil since February 1999 when the government closed down the main groundnut company. With insufficient funds to pay farmers fully, the government has seen them sell their produce across the border in Senegal where they receive lower prices, but immediate payment. Despite the importance of the agricultural sector, it has not received enough government investment to make it more productive.

A once-promising tourism industry is on the verge of collapse. The post-September 11 decline in travel is partially responsible, but the industry was in trouble well before that. Tourists, harassed by unemployed locals known as "bumsters" and solicited for drugs or sex, have turned their backs on The Gambia. (The country has developed such a reputation as transit point for the drug trade that fresh vegetable growers have seen their produce rot on the tarmac because flights from the Gambia are not accepted.)

Gambia's budget runs regular deficits and to make up some of the shortfall, massive tax increases were introduced to generate operating revenues in 2004. A variety of professions (mechanics, carpenters, hair-dressers, welders, butchers, masons, cattle dealers, tailors, and mobile foreign exchange dealers) have been asked to pay around $90 to $313 in income taxes. Buyers of imported water and soft drinks found the beverages newly taxed, though mosquito nets remained tax free.

Under increasing economic pressures, everyday Gambians increasingly see the regime as corrupt and self-serving. President Jammeh, whose salary was about $100 per month when he overthrew the government in 1994, has boasted on national radio and television that he will never be poor, his children will never be poor and his children's children will never be poor. He now owns a zoo, for which he imports expensive exotic animals from around the world, an expensive mansion in his home village, and reportedly a personal airline. The goods President Yahya Jammeh imports into the country are duty free. The exemption is limited, says the government, to goods he imports for his official use, but is bitterly protested. Dele-

gates to an October 2002 tax workshop demanded its revocation, calling it "discriminatory and self-serving by a president who professes passionate interest for the national cause."

The country's accumulated debt is enormous—$629 million as of 2003—and debt servicing consumes about a third of the budget. For the cynical, the government's vaunted anti-corruption campaigns are only intended to distract the citizenry from the country's economic decline. For the more positively minded, the debt reflects the transformation effected by the Jammeh regime. In ten years it has created a national university, increased access to education, especially for girls, built four new hospitals, paved hundreds of kilometers of roads and introduced national television. The country is nevertheless ranked 155 out of 177 on the UN's 2004 *Human Development Index*. President Jammeh has announced that oil had been discovered in commercial quantities in Gambia's offshore waters. Exploration licenses have been offered to bid and the first round offers were due in April 2005.

**The Future:** The Gambia remains a military dictatorship despite its democratic trappings. One should expect neither media nor opposition to flourish in this environment, for the regime is fundamentally unaccountable and will continue its repressions with virtual impunity. The only saving grace for Gambians has traditionally been the fact that their country is so poor in resources. In this case poverty promotes accountability, for the government is dependent on tax revenues, and to get these, it must moderate its worst instincts. If oil is indeed just over the horizon, however, even that regime restraint will be ended.

# The Republic of Ghana

**Coastal humidity creates a palpable atmosphere.**

Photo by Bianca Scotton

**Area:** 238,537 sq. km = 92,100 sq. mi. (Oregon is slightly larger).

**Population:** 21,029,853 (July 2005 est.)

**Capital City:** Accra (metropolitan area pop. 3 million estimated; pronounced Ah–Krah).

**Climate:** Hot and humid in the southwest; warm and less humid in the north. Ghana has a wet season (May–September) and a dry season (October–April).

**Neighboring Countries:** Ivory Coast (West); Burkina Faso (Upper Volta—West, North); Togo (East).

**Official Language:** English.

**Other Principal Languages:** Akan, Moshi-Dagomba, Ewe, and Ga.

**Ethnic Groups:** Akan 44%, Moshi-Dagomba 16%, Ewe 13%, Ga 8%, European and other 0.2%.

**Principal Religions:** Christian 43%, Indigenous beliefs 38%, Muslim 16%, other 3%. These are hazardous estimates at best.

**Chief Commercial Products:** Gold, cocoa, timber, tuna, bauxite, aluminum, manganese ore, and diamonds.

**GNI per capita:** $320 (2003)

**Currency:** 1 New Cedi (C) = 100 Pesewas

**Former Colonial Status:** British Colony (1821–1957).

**Independence Date:** March 6, 1957.

**Chief of State:** John Agyekum Kufuor, President.

**National Flag:** Three horizontal stripes of red, yellow and green with a five–pointed black star in the center of the yellow stripe.

Ghana is situated in the center of Africa's Gulf of Guinea coast, with a 334–mile–long shore washed by the Gulf's warm waters. The coastline is irregular, interrupted by streams and lagoons covered with strand and mangrove growth. In the eastern inland coastal area, the terrain consists of scrub and grassland, interrupted by clumps of bushes and small trees. Inland from the western coast there is an area of rainforest supporting dense growths of trees towering to heights of 200 feet.

Some 175 miles north from the sea, dense vegetation gives way to grassland areas with less rainfall and shorter, more sparsely distributed trees. The harmattan, a dry wind from the Sahara, penetrates from November to April. Humidity drops during this season, and both grasses and trees turn yellow; the trees lose their foliage within a few weeks. Temperatures in this region are high since there is no cooling breeze from the sea. In the extreme North, rainfall rapidly diminishes and becomes virtually nonexistent. Northern Ghana has suffered significant desertification in the past few years. There are no true mountains in Ghana—the highest elevation is 2,900 feet in the part closest to the eastern boundary.

**History:** Ghanaian oral traditions refer to migrations from the North, and it is probable that these legends relate to the travels of people from the Niger River area in the 10th–15th centuries A.D. The name Ghana is derived from a powerful kingdom believed to have been centered some 200 miles north of Bamako (now the capital of Mali).

After independence, granted in 1957, President Kwame Nkrumah (Kwah-mi N-kroo-mah) rapidly transformed the government into a dictatorship patterned after various communist nations. His Convention People's Party (CPP) became the instrument of all political thought, and the government was supposed to be the servant of the party. Nkrumah acquired the power to jail people for ten years without trial, and the press was rigidly censored. In spite of these repressive measures, he initially was an immensely popular figure, celebrated for having brought an end to colonial rule.

Establishing close ties with China and the Soviet Union, Nkrumah regularly accused the Western nations of "neo-colonialism." He bolstered his image with titles such as the "lion," "giant" and "prophet" of Africa. Rich by African standards, Ghana began its independence with a relatively full treasury. This permitted Nkrumah to borrow huge sums of money from abroad which were then squandered on lavish projects, prestigious but non-productive. Agricultural improvement and industrial development were largely ignored. A certain national pride might have been achieved, but the economic situation became increasingly difficult. When he was deposed in 1966, it became apparent that he had left Ghana in an economic shambles.

Army officers seized power while Nkrumah was visiting China and North Vietnam early that year. A Liberation Council was formed, Nkrumah sympathizers were arrested, and almost 1,200 political prisoners were released from jails. Communist technical and political personnel were quickly expelled. Nkrumah went to Guinea, where his personal friend, Sékou Touré, bestowed on him the honor of titular head of state. He died there in 1972.

Successive governments, military and civilian, were unable to solve the problems of soaring inflation, dishonesty in government, unemployment and all the ills accompanying a nation deeply indebted. In 1979 Flight Lt. Jerry Rawlings, with a group of young officers, took over the government and oversaw elections for a new civilian government. That government lasted only until New Year's Eve,

1981, when Lt. Rawlings again appeared on the scene and deposed the elected chief executive.

The new military leaders pledged to provide stable democracy. Rawlings, head of a seven-man Council, suspended the constitution, abolished all of Ghana's six political parties, accused the previous government of failing to provide for the needs of the people, and called upon the citizens to become actively involved in "the decision-making process."

The new government, on the surface, appeared to have turned radical—Rawlings, a bit of a moralist, was an unabashed admirer of Libya's Colonel Gadhafi. Following the Libyan model, plans were made to install "popular committees" which would, in theory, manage all aspects of the lives of Ghanaians. "People's Defense Committees" briefly mushroomed in city neighborhoods, in rural villages, and industry. Their stated purpose was to act as watchdogs against corruption and black market dealings.

Little seemed to halt the country's economic decline. Economic hardship added fuel to the fires of dissent and led to an about-face by Rawlings in 1987-88. A bloated and costly bureaucracy was downscaled—some 45,000 civil servants were fired—foreign investment was encouraged, and a less revolutionary rhetorical style was adopted. Encouraged by these and other moves to put Ghana's economy in order, the International Monetary Fund and the World Bank re-engaged with the country.

Bowing to international pressures, Lt. Rawlings allowed a multiparty system to develop in the early 1990s. Preparatory to elections scheduled for November 1992, he resigned from the air force (as required by new election laws) and ran for president as a civilian. He won with 60% of the vote, becoming the first of Africa's military rulers to don the dress of democracy.

President Rawlings and his National Democratic Council (NDC) won another mandate in 1996. Rawlings won the presidential race handily, taking 57.4 % of the vote, while his nearest rival, John Kufuor, heading the Great Alliance, consisting of the New Patriotic Party (NPP) and the People's Convention Party, won a respectable 39.6%. In legislative elections the NDC won 132 seats, an absolute parliamentary majority. Despite huge majorities in parliament and loads of international goodwill, Rawlings and the NDC were unable to revitalize the Ghanaian economy.

By the time the elections of 2000 rolled around the economy was in full decline, worsened by the reluctance of the Rawlings government to take hard decisions in an election year. Prices of Ghana's major exports, gold and cocoa, had declined, and petroleum prices had soared. Interest rates were nearly 50% and inflation soared to 60%. Unemployment hovered at 50% while the value of Ghana's currency, the cedi, had collapsed.

In 1981, before Rawlings took power, the cedi had been worth 2.75 to the dollar; by 2000 it took 6,800 to buy a single dollar. Per capita income in 1981 was $410; by 2000, it had dropped to $360. Growth was predicted to be a miserable 1%. People were suffering, and the party that had governed for so long was similarly made to suffer on election day.

Constitutionally prohibited from seeking a third term, Rawlings handpicked his vice-president, John Evans Atta-Mills, to be his successor. The NPP nominated John Kufuor, an Oxford-trained lawyer, businessman and long a conservative opponent of the regime. A Roman Catholic from the country's influential Asante tribe, Kufuor campaigned on a platform of "positive change."

Though marred by violence, the vote count was generally fair. The NPP won 100 of the 200 parliamentary seats. Its presidential candidate, Kufuor, nearly won a first ballot victory, taking a lead of 48.44% to John Atta-Mills' 44.8%. In the run-off, all five minor candidates threw their support to Kufuor, who won with an impressive 57%. When Vice-President Mills telephoned his concession speech, Ghanaians sighed in collective relief: Ghana had successfully achieved a democratic transfer of power.

The transition has not been without its problems and tensions. President Kufuor must regularly deal with the perceived threat that former president Rawlings poses. A man who twice led successful coups and an inveterate rabble-rouser, Rawlings has never played the role of leader of a loyal opposition. He remains a mountain of unveiled opposition whose rumblings usually disturb the locals and whose occasional eruptions produce a flow a molten rhetoric that can be genuinely frightening, given his reputation for creating chaos and instability. In August 2002, speaking in Kumasi, the heartland of Kufuor support, the ex-president called for "positive defiance" and reminded his audience that "We don't have to wait for the next election to prevent the rot." Justifying what many saw as a hankering for a coup to topple the NPP government, Rawlings accused it of lying and called it "the worst government the country has ever had." Relations between Rawlings and Kufuor remain cold at best, hostile at worst.

Ghanaians needed little prodding to understand how hyperbolic the comment was. After sitting for 18 months and hearing about 4,000 petitions, Ghana's National Reconciliation Council (NRC) submitted its report on human rights abuses during "periods of unconstitutional rule" in October 2004. The Rawlings years of unauthorized rule (1979; 1981–1993) featured prominently in the hearings, serving only to erode his claims of moral legitimacy and diminish his self-defined legacy.

Much like its South African model, the commission's mandate was to discover the truth about past abuses and help those who suffered deal with their pain and move on. It also sought to help the abusers come to terms with the experience and obtain forgiveness. The NDC, Rawlings' former governing party, saw less reconciliation than a witch-hunt of former leaders and officials. It was not a position that seemed to have much sympathy. (For those who want the details, the Commission has its own website: www.nrcghana.org.)

President Kufuor's style is less high-pitched than that Ghanaians had become accustomed to, and his mild-mannered directness may ultimately be more effective. He marked the end of his first year in office by holding an unprecedented public question-and-answer session. Dubbed the "people's assembly," the event featured Kufuor and his entire cabinet hearing complaints and answering questions posed by a capacity audience which filled Accra's international conference center. The assemblies have now become regular.

Similar efforts have been made to involve the Ghanaian diaspora. President Kufuor has held "Peoples' Assemblies" with a cross section of Ghanaian expatriates. Policies were explained, questions answered and thanks offered. (Bank of Ghana figures show diaspora remittances have topped the one billion dollar mark.) Government ministers have also traveled abroad to inform and listen to expatriate communities, marking a distinct change in relations between those who govern

**President John Agyekum Kufuor**

# Ghana

**Hon. Kofi Annan**

and those who are governed. It's a change that can only be called the "Kufuor style."

President Kufuor's government remained focused on repairing the economic damage caused by years of divisive and corrupt rule. In so doing, they have not been afraid to take political risks. Always sensitive, fuel prices were doubled; despite some grumbling, the move seemed to have been understood and accepted.

The December 2004 elections were a reprise of 2000's match up of the NPP's Kufuor and John Atta-Mills of the NDC. With strong world prices for cocoa and gold pushing Ghana's economic growth to over five percent a year and with substantial debt reduction from the World Bank and major Western donors, economic basics favored the incumbent. Some 83.2% of eligible voters turned out and President Kufuor won a solid 52.75% against his main rival, John Atta Mills, who won a respectable 44.32% of the vote. Observers all agreed the election was free and fair, an important consolidation of democracy for the country. Indeed, parliamentary elections saw many MPs, including ministers, lose their seats. President Kufuor's NPP garnered 129 seats in the 230-member house, while Atta Mills's NDC took 88; the remaining seats were distributed among smaller parties, including the once-dominant CPP which won only four seats in parliament.

**Culture:** Traditional kingdoms continue to flourish in Ghana, and their rulers exercise influence inside and outside the country. In spring 1999, Ghanaians mourned the loss of the greatest of their traditional kings, the Asantahene, paramount chief of the Asante Federation, Otumfuo Opoku Ware II. "A great tree has been uprooted," said his memorialists.

The Asantahene died at age 79, having occupied the Golden Stool of the Asante for 30 years. He was buried in the full splendor of traditional ceremonies that affirmed the importance of an enduring African culture.

The regency was assured by the Queen Mother, an all-important figure among matrilineal Asante, and after a suitable mourning period, the new Asantahene was named. Nana Kwaku Duah, a London-trained accountant and business executive, aged 48, asserted the long continuity of his office in his official name. As Asantahene he will be known as Osei Tutu II, after the first Asante king. Thousands watched as the new king was carried through the streets of Kumasi, surrounded by bodyguards wielding staffs made of gold. His coronation, an "enstoolment" among the Asante, took place on the Golden Stool. The stool is believed to have descended from Heaven in a cloud of white dust and to have landed on the lap of Osei Tutu I. Asantes believe it incarnates the soul of the Asante nation.

Teshi, one of Accra's suburbs has become a major point of attraction for tourists as the home of some of Ghana's most brilliant fantasy coffin makers. Coffins made in the form of fish, hens, roosters, leopards, lions, or elephants are readily available. Patrons of the funerary artists often want to bury loved ones in something that reflects their life or work. Hammers, mobile phones, canoes or cocoa beans and even Coca-Cola bottles are possible.

**Economy:** At the time of independence, Ghana was the world's leading cocoa exporter. Its economic prospects were excellent. When Kwame Nkrumah and his Convention People's Party came to power, they sought economic development through rapid industrialization, directed and funded through the state. Investment funds were largely derived from accumulated surpluses of the Cocoa Marketing Board. The state enterprises created at this time rarely proved profitable. State budgets went into deficit, which could not be covered by cocoa surpluses since cocoa prices were slipping precipitously on world markets. A huge accumulated debt was Nkrumah's legacy to his political heirs.

Desperation drove the Rawlings government to work out an Economic Recovery Program with the guidance of the IMF and the World Bank in 1983. Fiscal discipline was restored, better tax collection implemented, and by 1986 the budget showed a surplus. A second phase of the recovery program began in 1986 with structural adjustments. Cuts were made in a bloated civil service. A new investment code created to encourage foreign investment and privatization of state enterprises was actively pursued.

When multiparty democracy was returned in 1992, however, Ghana fell off the straight-and-narrow path it had followed under a military regime. As an inducement to civil service voters to support his party, Rawlings granted large public employee pay raises. He won the election, but five years worth of surpluses disappeared, inflation was fueled, and domestic debt increased.

In launching his re-election campaign, President Kufuor could point to increased economic growth, reduced inflation, interest rates and government borrowing, as

**University of Ghana, Legon**

well as a stabilized cedi, the national currency. The achievements came through tough political choices that imposed austerity and caused hardship. Utility rates were increased, school fees raised, and costly gasoline subsidies eliminated. Gas now costs about $2.40 a gallon, pricey for urban commuters. To soften the blow, the government purchased several hundred buses from Italy, Holland and China to provide more public transportation. It also raised the minimum wage by 26% — to $1.05 a day. (Senior government officials were excluded from the wage increase.) The economy recorded a growth of 5.2% in 2003, and exceeded 2004 predictions to achieve growth of 5.8%. Similar growth for 2005 is predicted.

Impressed, the World Bank has supported, under the enhanced Heavily Indebted Poor Countries (HIPC) initiative, a $3.7 billion debt reduction package for Ghana. Debt servicing was reduced by some $200 million, and the money saved has been invested in various aspects of the Ghana Poverty Reduction Strategy (GPRS). Among other things, the strategy aims at increasing production and promoting sustainable livelihoods among Ghana's desperately poor farmers.

Agriculture is the main sector of the economy, accounting for 35% of GDP and employing over 55% of the working population in 2003. Despite its generally dwindling fortunes, cocoa remains the county's biggest industry. Production in 2003-2004 harvest year was an exceptional 734,699 tons, the highest production in the history of the cocoa industry; the crop produced about $1.2 billion in export revenues. Nearly three million acres are planted in cocoa, worked by some 700,000 farmers. Most of the holdings are small, which contributes to Ghanaian cocoa's reputation for high quality. (The smallholder takes the time to sort bad nuts from the cocoa and more carefully tends the fermentation and drying process than occurs in large-scale production.) In more average years Ghana harvests between 350,000 to 400,000 tons of cocoa, less than a third of what Ivory Coast, the world's leading producer, grows.

Gold vies cocoa as the country's biggest foreign exchange earner thanks to a liberalized mining code. Ghana produces around 2.2 million ounces of gold annually, making it Africa's second largest gold producer after South Africa. The income represents about 45% of the country's foreign exchange revenues and was expected to amount to $929 million in 2004. To encourage foreign investment, the government has recently decided to open protected forest reserves to mining companies. The six companies receiving mining licenses (for gold and bauxite) have committed themselves to invest over $2 billion. Government ministers toured some of the reserves and met with local communities to help them make a decision. Desperate for amenities and secure jobs, many local residents favored the mines.

President Kufuor takes a personal role in government efforts to diversify and develop the economy. A test project, the President's Special Initiative (PSI) is being used to rejuvenate cotton production. The initiative seeks to modernize and increase cotton production in the rural areas, increasing jobs and local incomes. Simultaneously, another PSI has been launched to supply the cotton for garment and textile manufacture in urban areas, increasing jobs and incomes there.

A similar PSI has been launched to boost cassava production to industrial levels. The crop was chosen because it is easy to cultivate and highly labor-intensive, offering potential for job creation. In the cassava PSI about 1,500 farmers from nine communities cultivated 5,500 acres harvested in March 2003. Important to the PSI is adding value to the basic agricultural production. After harvesting, the cassava will be processed into starch for export in a new factory owned by the farmers. Cassava starch is used in the paper, textile, food, pharmaceutical, oil drilling and petrochemical industries. Currently, Ghana produces eight million metric tons of cassava annually; the government believes this can easily be doubled.

Timber, fishing and tourism all offer potential development opportunities. Although Ghana has an estimated 16.5 million barrels of recoverable oil reserves, that recovery is not yet commercially viable.

**Future:** Under the Kufuor government, Ghanaians have found a new confidence. The country remains deeply impoverished, and any progress in terms of economic development is dependent on political stability. December's presidential election represents a consolidation of democracy that should assure the political stability Ghana needs to make further economic advances.

**A traditional family compound**

Photo by Isabelle Forter

# The Republic of Guinea (pronounced *Gih*–nee)

Guinean family outside traditional thatch hut.

**Area:** 245,857 sq. km. = 95,000 sq. mi. (about the size of Oregon).

**Population:** 9,467,866 (July 2005 est.)

**Capital City:** Conakry (Pop. two million, estimated).

**Climate:** In the extreme Southeast and Southwest there are small hot and humid areas of jungle with two rainy seasons (May–July and September–November). The climate gradually changes the terrain to a warm, semiarid region in the North with a single rainy season (April–October).

**Neighboring Countries:** Guinea Bissau (West); Senegal, Mali (North); Ivory Coast (East); Liberia, Sierra Leone (Southeast).

**Official Language:** French.

**Other Principal Languages:** Baga, Dan, Fuuta Jalon, Kissi, Malinke, Maninka, Mano, and Susu.

**Ethnic groups:** Peuhl 40%, Malinke 30%, Soussou 20%, smaller tribes 10%.

**Principal Religions:** Muslim 85%, Christian 8%, indigenous beliefs 7%.

**Chief Commercial Products:** Bauxite, alumina, diamonds, gold, coffee, fish, and agricultural products.

**GNI per capita:** $430 (2003)

**Currency:** Guinea Franc.

**Former Colonial Status:** French Colony (1894–1958).

**Independence Date:** October 2, 1958.

**Chief of State:** Col. Lansana Conté, President.

**National Flag:** Vertical stripes of red, yellow and green.

Facing southwest on the Atlantic Ocean in the western bulge of Africa, Guinea has an irregular, but level coastline. Immediately inland there is a gently rolling area, covered with dense vegetation in the more southern coastal area. Grassy plains, interspersed with trees, are found in the north coastal region.

Further inland the landscape slowly rises in a series of flat plains and table mountains. The Fouta Djallon mountains rise to heights of 6,000 feet in central Guinea and are the source of three large West African rivers: the Niger, the Gambia and the Senegal.

Further to the northeast, the land slowly descends to a flat grassland which has greater variation in temperatures than the more humid coastal area. These grasslands attain a rich, green color towards the end of March, and vegetation grows rapidly in the ensuing rainy season, which lasts until November.

In southeast Guinea the terrain becomes somewhat higher, containing dense forests with a pattern of rain quite similar to that of the plains land. As the dry season commences in the latter part of November, the leaves of the trees turn into a panorama of brilliant colors, not because of cold weather, but because of the lack of moisture. This is the equivalent of "winter" in Guinea, and it is not until April that the landscape is again green.

**History:** Guinea was dominated from the 10th to the 15th centuries by the great West African kingdoms. The vast empires of Ghana, Mali and Songhai successively occupied the country during the period. Earlier migrations of people to Guinea remained during the period of these kingdoms. The nomadic Fulani (also known as Peulhs), the agricultural Mandingos, Malinkes and Soussous had established themselves in times unknown and continue to inhabit this area. For details of early and colonial history, see *Historical Background* and *The French in Africa*.

In the 1958 constitution of the French Fifth Republic, General Charles De Gaulle inserted a provision giving to France's colonies the choice of full independence or autonomy within the French Community. Under the leadership of the young trade unionist, Ahmed Sékou Touré, Guinea opted to become fully independent—the only French colony to make that choice—and it was proclaimed a nation on October 2, 1958.

Ahmed Sékou Touré became the country's first president, and, deeply imbued with Marxist-Leninist thought, he created a single party dictatorship. The Democratic Party of Guinea (PDG) was the sole political force in the country. Sékou Touré was its Secretary-General. Membership in the party was said to be as many as 2 million, organized into thousands of local committees. Elections were a mere formality, for the party expressed the will of the people. Opposition was considered tantamount to treason, and critics suffered grievously. The brutality of Touré's repression increased as his paranoia increased; it reached a peak in October 1971 when thousands were killed.

Sékou Touré's one-man rule ended in a Cleveland hospital where he died on March 26, 1984. Prime Minister Louis Lansana Beavogui, immediately took control of the government, and a 40-day mourning period was proclaimed. The party's 14-member political bureau was scheduled to meet to choose Touré's successor when a group of young military officers, disgusted with what they called a "bloody and ruthless dictatorship," took over the country on April 3, 1984.

A Military Committee for National Redressment (CMRN) was established and immediately began to release some political prisoners from Conakry's notorious Camp Boiro. More than 50,000 people disappeared, or were assassinated at the camp according to the Association of Child Victims of Camp Boiro.

Both the PDG and the constitution were suspended. Some 250 political prisoners were given radio time to relate their experiences and bear witness against the Touré regime. The new government was initially led by Col. Lansana Conté, president, and Col. Diarra Traoré, prime minister, but rivalry soon led to the latter's demotion in December 1984.

Dissatisfied, Traoré and others attempted a coup in July 1985 while President Conté was in Lomé (Togo) at a conference. The president returned to Guinea and had no difficulty in restoring control. Some 30 people involved in the attempt were summarily executed, including Traoré. The whole affair had tribal overtones.

After Sékou Touré's death, Guinea embarked on a more liberal economic course. A $2.3 million loan was negotiated with France, which had given Touré the cold shoulder after Guinea opted for independence. The International Monetary Fund granted a line of credit to begin reconstructing a potentially wealthy African nation. Programs were undertaken to cut the hugely inflated government bureaucracy (87,000 people) and to sell several government–owned enterprises—products of Touré's socialist economic policies—to the private sector.

Guinea's human rights conditions did not improve with a change of regimes. Military trials in 1986–7 of about 200 officials of the Touré regime resulted in 60 death sentences, 21 of them *in absentia*. Some of the accused were presumed to be already dead. The purpose was to instill fear, particularly in urban areas, where government popularity had plunged because of severe economic conditions. Amnesty International described "arbitrary arrests, torture, deaths in detention and death penalty" as "common currency" in Guinea.

Bowing to the winds of change following the collapse of Eastern European communism, the CMRN secured referendum approval of a new constitution in late 1990. It mandated a multi-party system and limited the president to two consecutive terms. The multi-party system was installed in April 1992. Though many parties have been formed, the opposition has been unable to break the stranglehold of President Conté's Party of Unity and Progress (PUP).

President Conté himself took office in 1994 after multiparty elections in 1993, deemed an "electoral masquerade" and "a comedy" by the opposition. He barely survived a military mutiny in 1996 when army units rebelled, demanding higher pay. They burned down the presidential palace, looted shops and led the president off to an army base. Fifty people were killed in the incident. President Conté was forced to sign a five-point accord with the mutineers before being returned to power.

Whatever modicum of liberalism he had died with the coup.

Amnesty, apparently, was not part of the agreement. Long-delayed trials began in early 1998 and exposed confessions extracted by torture and ethnic bias against soldiers not of the president's Soussou group. Stiff sentences of 20 years' hard labor were handed down on participants. Later the army was subjected to a major purge, mostly of President Conté's presumed ethnic enemies. (Under Sékou Touré the Peulh ethnic group was singled out for persecution; under Lansana Conté it tended to be the Malinké.)

The Soussou make up only 15% to 20% of the population, but dominate the machinery of repression—the ministries of the interior, police, and security; they also dominate the PUP. Risen to power by a coup, terrified by another, President Conté often exhibits a bunker mentality, viewing other ethnic groups with the greatest of suspicion and withdrawing to the safety of his own.

Presidential elections in December 1998 demonstrated the sharpness of ethnic division in Guinea. Conté faced four opponents, three of whom concluded an electoral alliance aimed at stopping president Conté from winning on the first ballot. Linked together within the Coordination of Democratic Opposition (CODEM) were the Malinké Alpha Condé, the Peulh Mamadou Ba, and Jean-Marie Doré of one of the smaller ethnic groups. If the alliance could force the president into a second ballot, all agreed to support his opponent. It was to no avail in a situation where the election is controlled by the regime in power. In dubious balloting, Conté was officially given a first-round victory of 56.12% by the Ministry of the Interior. Ba

**President Conté**

won a quarter of the vote and Alpha Condé slightly less than 17%.

Two days after his victory, President Conté had his rival Alpha Condé arrested—despite his status as a member of parliament—and charged with state security offenses. These included allegedly recruiting mercenaries to overthrow the Conté regime. Riots broke out in the principal Malinké communities and several people were killed. In Conakry, women bared their breasts—a traditional sign of mourning—in protest; they were arrested for assaulting public modesty. Fourteen leading members of the Malinké opposition, including members of parliament, were arrested, charged with threatening public order, found guilty and jailed.

President Conté conducted a major purge of the army in March 1999, sacking the armed forces chief of staff, Col. Oumar Soumah and 30 other officers in connection with the 1996 army mutiny.

A repressive regime creates enemies everywhere. Opponents who have fled the country represent a continuing threat, and in the fall of 2000 the Liberian leader Charles Taylor—a man who never forgets or forgives an enemy—focused his full attention on Guinea, making use of enemies of the regime both internal and external.

As things seemed to calm in neighboring Sierra Leone, RUF fighters there, dependent on Taylor, launched border raids on several northern Guinean towns. As usual with RUF engagements, death, plunder and devastation ensued, but their surprising military sophistication was attributed to training offered by Guinean officers, some of the mutineers of 1996 who had fled Guinea.

The two countries stood at the brink of war by September 2000. President Taylor demanded that Guinea expel Liberian dissidents—ULIMO-K members—harbored and trained there. President Conté accused Guinea's huge refugee population of ingratitude and of facilitating rebel infiltration. His countrymen responded by breaking up refugee camps and savaging their inhabitants.

In April 2001, President Conté significantly raised the ante for potential internal violence. On the occasion of the 17th anniversary of the army's seizure of power, Conté told assembled soldiers: "If you meet people with weapons who do not belong to the military, you must simply annihilate them. That is what I am saying, and it is an order that you must execute, if you are good citizens. There must not be a second army. You must fight them."

It was in this atmosphere of rising violence that the long-delayed trial of Alpha Condé finally concluded. In September 2000 an emergency session of a State Se-

# Guinea

**The Guinean coastline**                    ©Photographie Michel Hasson

curity Court convicted him of sedition and sentenced him to five years in prison. Condé himself was kept in virtual isolation, denied audience with his lawyers and family members.

The deplorable nature of Guinean justice made Condé a focal point of regime criticism nationally and internationally. President Wade of Senegal offered asylum and encouraged his release, but a regime fearful, threatened, and paranoid showed neither flexibility nor mercy. President Conté, faced with cumulative pressures, finally relented and granted Condé a presidential pardon in May 2001.

Guinea should have held parliamentary elections in November 2000, but with the multifaceted crisis facing it the government postponed them indefinitely. The government did, however, organize a referendum in November 2001 to amend the constitution to permit President Conté a third term. Official results indicated 87% of Guinea's four million registered voters dutifully trooped to the polls and 98% of them approved the referendum. The results are highly suspect since the opposition had organized a boycott of the election. Their figures indicated that fewer than 20% of registered voters actually took part.

Long-postponed parliamentary elections were held in June 2002, and this time the opposition was hopelessly divided. The parties of long-time opponents Mamadou Ba and Alpha Condé joined with those of two defectors from the presiden-

tial camp—Conté's former Prime Minister, Sidya Touré, and the former Speaker of the National Assembly, El-Hadji Biro Diallo—to form the Front for Democratic Change (FRAD). FRAD opted to boycott the election, while other opponents engaged the *Parti de l'unité et du progrès* (PUP), Guinea's governing party. The result was a crushing victory for PUP—90 of 114 seats.

Constitutional limitations now eliminated, President Conté, reportedly extremely ill from diabetes and heart problems, once again stood (not necessarily an appropriate verb in this case) for election in December 2003. He did well, despite being rarely seen on the campaign trail: ninety-five percent of the total vote. The actual vote was small, having been boycotted by all the major political parties.

Even before the elections there were signs of restiveness within the army. In early November, speaking on the occasion of the army's 45th anniversary, President Conté issued a warning to those planning a coup: "If any of you here think you are capable of becoming president," he told his uniformed audience, "then form a political party, make yourself candidate and face the electorate." By the end of the month dozens of junior army officers and soldiers had been arrested in a series of swoops on army barracks and private homes throughout the country.

In early January 2005, shots were fired at a presidential convoy in what the security minister characterized as an assassi-

nation attempt. The 70-year-old president was unhurt, but one of his bodyguards was seriously injured. The regime's security apparatus cracked down heavily. More than 1,000 persons were arrested and detained, but the culprits seem not to have been found. In May the chief prosecutor of Sierra Leone's war crimes tribunal identified Charles Taylor, Liberia's ex-president, as the man behind the attack.

**Culture:** There are more than 16 distinct ethnic groups within the country, the great majority of which profess Islam as religion. Despite the efforts of the former ruling party, traditional values have survived. Female circumcision is still practiced in Guinea, although it was officially banned in 1984. Prior to 1998 an estimated 90% of Guinean women were circumcised. The circumcisers, older, well-respect women in their communities, were professionals; their skills had been handed down from mother to daughter for generations. During the summer season, when schools were not in session, a circumciser would perform as many as 380 operations on young girls 8 to 15 years of age.

In November 1999 there was a symbolic breakthrough in the campaign against these cultural practices. Several hundred women who performed the operation handed in their ceremonial knives in the eastern town of Kouroussa. The campaign to abolish the practice continues, led by women, many of whom were once practitioners. In many locations didactic plays, using the traditional songs and dances of the circumcision ceremony itself, explain the issue and dramatize the consequences of FGM to a largely illiterate audience.

The World Bank reports that the campaign has contributed to reducing the number of new circumcisions to roughly 20% of young girls nationwide. Some 450 practitioners have left the field. Much of this is a result of a World Bank-funded project to provide circumcisers with training in alternative sources of livelihood and access to small business start-up funds.

**Economy:** Guinea is a land rich in natural resources—bauxite, iron, gold, and diamonds—and the water to produce the energy needed to process and convert those raw materials. The Senegal, Gambia, and Niger Rivers all flow from Guinea's mountains. Its land could produce a rich bounty of agricultural goods, but despite its mighty potential, Guinea's agriculture languishes, a hangover from the days of socialist collectives that stifled any initiative. Ports, roads, and schools—the central aspects of the economy's infrastructure—are deficient. Only a third of the population is literate, and life expectancy barely exceeds 46 years.

Guinea's non-development has its origins in the Marxist economic thinking of the Touré years. State-led development has proved an abject failure. With about one-third of the world's bauxite reserves—the principal ore used in making aluminum—government planners, fixated on modernization through industrialization, transformed Guinea from an exporter of agricultural products into a major bauxite exporter. That meant that Guinea ultimately had to import food to feed its citizens.

Other state enterprises created bloated bureaucracies whose salaries devoured any profits from bauxite. With little money to invest productively, there was neither growth nor development. Smuggling flourished and the government lost tax revenues as the clandestine economy grew. As its revenues declined, the government was less able to provide health and social services and the country's infrastructure deteriorated. In 1996 President Conté restructured his government to emphasize economic reform.

The vast bulk of its population is engaged in subsistence agriculture, and in many ways Guinea is a vast garden. A broad range of products can be grown year round, watered by abundant rains: Rice, tomatoes, onions, coffee, cocoa, bananas, and melons all flourish. Despite this, however, Guinea is not self-sufficient in food and must import most everything. Agricultural productivity remains low, and distribution, given dilapidated roads and bridges, is weak. Conakry consumers often pay dearly for mangos while they rot in the countryside. Traditional farming generates only around 24% of GDP while employing around 67% of the population.

Guinea's economy is dominated by its mining sector. Mining generates about 30% of GDP, while bauxite, alumina, gold, and diamonds produce about 90% of export revenues. Bauxite, a basic element in making aluminum via alumina, is the biggest element of the mining sector, accounting itself for nearly 80% of foreign exchange earnings. Guinea possesses an estimated 18 billion tons of bauxite reserves, representing about a third of world reserves. The *Companie des Bauxites de Guinée* (CBG)—a joint venture between the government and several North American, European and Australian firms—produces 14.5 million tons of bauxite annually, making Guinea the world's second largest producer after Australia. Processing the raw bauxite into alumina—and adding value to it—is only getting off the ground.

Guinea's number two bauxite company, the *Société des Bauxites de Kindia* (SBK), was established primarily to supply bauxite to the Nikolaeyev alumina refinery in Ukraine. It produces about 2 million tons of bauxite a year. In April 2001, Russian Aluminium (RusAl), the world's No. 2 aluminum producer, announced it would take over management responsibilities of SBK. It proposed to spend $40 million over the next three years upgrading and expanding SBK's mining activities.

The deal was part of a series of agreements signed by Presidents Conté and Putin of Russia. Among other things, Conté was shopping for weapons following incursions by Sierra Leonean and Liberian rebels. President Conté very much wants to develop Guinea's fleet of combat helicopters and upgrade the country's existing Soviet-made tanks and aircraft.

RusAl also received a concession to develop bauxite deposits at Dian-Dian. With one billion tons of high-quality bauxite ore, the Dian-Dian deposit is one of the world's largest. The concession lies close to the mine of *Compagnie de Bauxites de Kindia*, which RusAl already manages. The project is estimated to take seven years to build and cost $1.73 billion. When completed, the complex will have the capacity to produce 11 million tons of bauxite and 1.2 million tons of alumina annually. RusAl also plans to buy the aluminum smelter at Friguia, which it already co-manages with Guinea's government.

The Russian company has plans to increase the annual capacity of the Friguia alumina refinery from 700,000 tons to 1.4 million tons by 2008. The Friguia Alumina refinery badly needs upgrading. Built in 1958, has been under RusAl's control since December 2002. It annually produces two million tons of bauxite and 700,000 tons of alumina.

The Aluminum Corporation of China (Chalco) has been trying for years to gain access to Guinea's bauxite and alumina resources. It has evinced interest in the Frigia alumina refinery, which Conakry is thinking about selling.

Gold and diamond mining are both growing. Historically most famously associated with gold (the region gave its name to Britain's first gold coin), Guinea produced 400,000 oz. in 2001. Commercial diamond production in 1999, with a high proportion of gem-quality stones, was 21,908 carats. Overall, Guinea is estimated to have 25 to 30 millions of carats yet to be mined. In July 2004 it was announced that a young Guinean miner had found a huge 182-carat diamond (the size of a computer mouse) in the Banankoro region southeast of Conakry.

Despite a wealth of natural resources, Guinea's economic situation has consistently deteriorated since 2003. GDP has slowed from 4.2% in 2002 to 1.2% in 2003, with predictions of only 2.6% growth in 2004. That's simply insufficient even to keep up with population growth, estimated at 3% annually; in other words, Guinea's citizens are getting poorer every year. Finding poor performance and management, the World Bank halted loan disbursements to the country in early 2004, and the government, unable to pay its bills, resorted to the printing press to turn out more Guinean francs. The inflation rate rose to 15% in 2003 and was expected to reach 20% in 2004.

When the government raised highly-subsidized fuel prices 70%, drivers garaged their vehicles and users of public transportation took to their feet. Daily long lines of workers streaming into the capital on foot were a sign of the economy's implosion. A less-than-scientific opinion poll conducted by aminata.com, a Guinean site, found 26% of its respondents were eating only once a day; the number of families eating less than two kilos of rice a day rose to 44% from 20%. On the UN's 2004 *Human Development Index* Guinea ranked 160 out of 177 countries listed.

**The Future:** As poverty increases and public services deteriorate—water and electricity distribution are traditionally erratic—one should expect increased social tensions. Labor unions have already been vociferous, and in September 2004 soldiers had to be sent to the university campus in Faranah, central Guinea, to put down two days of destructive demonstrations by students protesting against poor living conditions and the high price of rice. An ill and aging president seems incapable of making the decisions to extricate the country from its present morass.

There is no agreed upon succession scenario should President Conté die. The opposition remains divided and implacably hostile to the regime. Army intervention seems likely, and almost reasonable, in the circumstances.

# The Republic of Guinea–Bissau

A quiet area near Bissau

**Area:** 36,260 sq. km. = 14,000 sq. mi. (the size of Connecticut and Massachusetts; includes the Bijago Archipelago).

**Population:** 1,416,027 (July 2005 est.)

**Capital City:** Bissau (Pop. 170,000, estimated (pronounced Bee–*sow*).

**Climate:** Very warm and humid with a wet season from May to October and a drier period from November to June.

**Neighboring Countries:** Senegal (North); Guinea (Southeast).

**Official Languages:** Portuguese

**Other Principal Languages:** Balanta, Crioulo (the lingua franca in much of Guinea-Bissau), Fulfulde, Mandinka, Mandyak, Papel.

**Ethnic groups:** Balanta 30%, Fula 20%, Manjaca 14%, Mandinga 13%, Papel 7%, European and mulatto less than 1%.

**Principal Religions:** Indigenous beliefs 50%, Muslim 45%, and Christian 5%.

**Chief Commercial Products:** Cashews 95%, fish, peanuts, palm kernels, and sawn lumber.

**GNI per capita:** $140 (2003)

**Currency:** CFA franc (as of 1 May 1997)

**Former Colonial Status:** Portuguese Colony (1885–1974). During this period, the area was considered by the Portuguese to be an integral part of European Portugal.

**Independence Date:** September 10, 1974 (The date on which Portugal recognized independence; unilateral declaration of independence was on September 24, 1973).

**Chief of State:** Interim President Henrique Pereira Rosa, since 28 September 2003.

**National Flag:** Three stripes—red, vertical nearest the staff upon which there is a centered, black star and two horizontal stripes of yellow (top) and green (bottom).

Bordering on the waters of the Atlantic, most of Guinea–Bissau is a swampy coastal lowland with about sixty small islands lying close to the shoreline. On its eastern and southern borders it is protected by the Foutah Djallon mountains of Guinea. The level land, coupled with more than adequate rainfall, contributes large quantities of produce with less labor than is found in most areas of Africa.

**History:** The Balanta people are probably the oldest inhabitants of Guinea–Bissau, joined only during the last millennium by Mandinga and pastoral Fula (Peulh) people. Early settlers were iron-using agriculturalists, skilled in rice growing and marine salt production. At a later period the region fell within the larger sphere of the Mali Empire, and contact with Europe was initiated by the Portuguese in the fifteenth century. The Portuguese used Guinea as the base for colonizing the Cape Verde Islands, importing slave labor to work in the island plantations.

The armed struggle against Portuguese colonial rule began in 1961 under the leadership of Amilcar Cabral and the *Partido Africano da Independência da Guiné e Cabo Verde* (PAIGC: African Independence Party of Guinea and Cape Verde). Because of this rebellion, Portugal had to maintain some 35,000 troops in the territory, half of whom were African, to oppose some 10,000 rebels who operated in traditional guerrilla fashion: an administrative or military post would be attacked, and the rebels would then melt into the dense

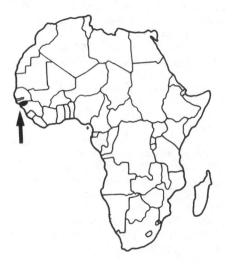

rainforests. Portuguese forces controlled only the coastal urban enclaves. Rebels dominated the interior and established basic schools and services to govern the area. Their support came from Soviet and Chinese arms and Cuban trainers all located in neighboring Guinea.

Cabral was assassinated in early 1973 in Conakry, where the PAIGC had established its headquarters. He was succeeded as head of PAIGC by his brother, Luís. By 1974 the liberation struggle had reached military stalemate, draining men, material, and morale from colonial Portugal. Disgruntled Portuguese army officers overthrew the Lisbon dictatorship and quickly negotiated independence with the country's colonies.

Guinea–Bissau's independence was recognized on Sept. 10, 1974, and the Portuguese were gone within a month. Amilcar Cabral's Cape Verdean half-brother, Luís de Almeida Cabral, became independent Guinea–Bissau's first president. The PAIGC was proclaimed the country's only party, and Guinea–Bissau was organized along Marxist-Leninist lines. As economic conditions worsened and a socialist economy proved inadequate to the tasks of growth and development, discontent set in, exacerbated by dominance of party, government and army by a *mestizo* intellectual minority representing a mere 2% of the population. Political dissent was ruthlessly suppressed; the Cabral regime killed thousands of its enemies. In 1980 a rival war veteran and member of the Papel minority, Joao Bernardo Vieira (known as "Nino"), seized power

Within the resistance movement there had always been tension between the Creole leadership from Cape Verde and the less educated indigenous mainlanders, but the anti-colonial struggle helped unite the factions. After the Vieira coup, however, union was no longer possible. In Cape Verde, the governing party renamed itself the *Partido Africano da Independência de Cabo Verde,* or PAICV, severing the party links between mainland and islands.

General Veira was elected to a term of five years as president in 1984 and again in 1989. Marxist rhetoric all but vanished as Vieira sought to re-establish ties with Portugal and the West. By 1992, however, Guinea was still a single-party state, and only grudgingly did the government open political space to multiparty competition. Elections scheduled for 1992 were repeatedly postponed, attracting considerable criticism. They were finally held in July 1994, and president Vieira and his party triumphed in the country's first multi–party contest, but not without accusations of election fraud. International observers termed the contest a fair one.

After 24 years in power the PAIGC grew complacent, divided, and directionless. In June 1997 the sixth party congress was paralyzed by conflicts between two major party factions—one led by its President "Nino" Vieira, and another led by a former prime minister, Manuel Saturnino da Costa, the party's national secretary. President Vieira's removal of da Costa as prime minister set him at odds with major PAIGC factions. Fateful for the president, those factions came to control parliament and would ultimately be responsible for his own removal.

Latent hostilities within the political class broke into open conflict with President Vieira's sacking of the Army Chief of Staff, Ansumané Mané, in June 1998. Mané was charged with insufficient control of cross-border arms trafficking. The army rose in revolt to support its popular leader and soon controlled most of the capital city. President Vieira called upon Senegal and Guinea for assistance against the rebels, but foreign troops were not enough to crush a popular rebellion.

The army and its civilian supporters controlled the countryside and a good portion of the capital, now largely destroyed and abandoned by most of its inhabitants. A bloody impasse resulted, only ending in May 1999 when the army once again rebelled as Senegalese and Guinean troops withdrew. President Vieira was driven from the burning executive palace to seek ultimate sanctuary in Portuguese exile.

Parliament drafted a new constitution and set multiparty elections for both parliament and president. The new constitution, approved in July 1999, seemed to settle long-term tensions about Cape Verdean leadership and domination of the revolutionary struggle in Guinea–Bissau. One constitutional provision stipulated that high-level state positions may be held only by citizens with both parents of national origin.

Elections were held in November and January, and the leading contenders for the presidency, Malam Bacai Sanhá and Kumba Ialá, both emerged out of the PAIGC. Sanhá, the parliamentary speaker and leader of one of the anti-Vieira factions in parliament, had been made interim president when Vieira fled to Portugal. His opponent was the product of missionary education, sent to Portugal where he studied philosophy at the University of Lisbon. On his return to Guinea–Bissau, Ialá taught at the national lycée and worked as a PAIGC militant. He ultimately became disaffected and left the party, going into opposition. In 1994 he courageously ran against Vieira in presidential election.

With 12 presidential candidates in the field, Ialá and Sanhá were thrown into a

January 2000 runoff. The result was a decisive victory for Kumba Ialá who won 72% of the ballots. With the defeat of Malam Bacai Sanhá, a quarter century of PAIGC domination came to an end.

The new president was a Balanta (the country's largest ethnic group), and never appeared in public without the bright red bonnet of a senior Balanta initiate. For many the bonnet symbolized his ethnic identity and his rejection of imported colonial religions (Islam and Christianity). He made it very clear that he believed the Balanta had provided the bulk of fighting men who brought the country to independence and that they had been treated unjustly by the previous regime. This sense of ethnic identity and grievance led to accusations that he favored Balanta over others in civil and military appointments and heightened ethnic tensions within the country.

In the legislative elections that followed, the PAIGC also did poorly, arriving in third place with only 24 seats. Ialá's Party for Social Renewal (PRS) and the Guinea–Bissau Resistance party (RGB) were the principal victors, but neither achieved a parliamentary majority. The PRS won 38 and the RGB claimed 28 seats. Five other parties shared the remaining 12 positions. The PAIGC refused to join in a grand coalition, choosing instead to become the principal opposition.

In February 2000, the PRS and the RGB formed a coalition government, and President Ialá set about the enormous task of recreating Guinea–Bissau. Political coalition did not produce stability, however, for the most sensitive issue facing the country was left unresolved: the relationship of army and junta to the new civilian government.

Long-simmering tensions between state and army culminated in November when General Mané canceled army promotions made by the president, declared himself

**Interim President
Henrique Pereira Rosa**

# Guinea–Bissau

army chief of staff, and once again plunged the country into turmoil.

The PAIGC and other opposition parties welcomed Mané's declaration, but the rebellion was short-lived. The general was tracked down and killed in a shootout with loyalist troops. When the general's widow was presented with her husband's body in a coffin—not part of Muslim burial practice—rumors circulated that he had been beaten to death. Thousands accompanied his remains to their final resting place shouting "Allahu Akbar" and calling for justice in Guinea–Bissau. With the general's death sectarian identity was added to the already combustible mix of ethnic rivalries.

Rid of the one man who had done so much to keep him from governing in peace, President Ialá did little to ease political tensions and secure stability in the country. His leadership proved unpredictable, impulsive, and erratic, producing a full-blown institutional crisis in a country whose institutions were already fragile. At odds with a parliament in which no party had a majority, President Ialá ran through five prime ministers and changed ministers so rapidly some embassies just gave up on maintaining a current cabinet list. He also dismissed judges and appointed their successors without consulting the National Assembly—raising serious questions about the independence of the judiciary—and threatened to fire the bulk of the civil service.

In November 2002 he peremptorily dissolved parliament (which had voted a new constitution curtailing presidential powers) and ruled by decree. Opponents were harassed and jailed, newspapers were shuttered, and radio stations silenced. The opposition took to the streets, accusing Ialá of trying to turn the country into a dictatorship.

Virtually bankrupt, the government had no money to pay its employees; soldiers were given bags of rice instead of paychecks. Unpaid for months, civil servants engaged in an endless series of public sector strikes. President Ialá's support from within the country and from the international community rapidly eroded, and Secretary-General Kofi Annan described the situation to the UN Security Council in increasingly bleak terms.

To end the paralysis that gripped the country, pressure was brought to bear on Ialá to hold new parliamentary elections, which he initially announced for February 2003. After much protest about the impossibility of having free, fair, and open elections on such short notice, the elections were several times postponed and ultimately set for October 2004.

In early September the Prime Minister remarked that the country would face

**Former president Kumba Ialá campaigns again in the presidential election of June 2005.**                    ©IRIN

troubles if President Ialá's Party for Social Renewal didn't win the October elections, and army leaders, who had already warned the President their restless troops needed to be paid, were galvanized. In the early hours of September 14, they acted. In less than a half hour, without firing a shot, President Ialá was deposed. A 32-member Military Committee of the Restoration of Constitutional Order and Democracy (CMROCD) set about its tasks amid international criticism and national relief.

Things moved rapidly. The army chief of staff, General Verissimo Seabra Correia, announced he would act as interim president until new elections could be held, and explained the army had acted because "we were in a country with no constitution, no judiciary, no parliament—a crazy country in other words." Under pressure from presidents Obasanjo of Nigeria and Wade of Senegal, he soon agreed to the appointment of a civilian president. A 17-member ad-hoc commission headed by Bissau's highly-respected Roman Catholic Bishop chose a politically unaffiliated Creole businessman close to the church, Henrique Pereira Rosa, as interim president. It only grudgingly accepted Antonio Arthur Sanhá, General Secretary of the PRS, as Prime Minister when the army insisted.

The ad-hoc commission also recommended creation of a Transitional National Council (TNC)—a broad-based council of civilian and military representatives that would act as a nominated legislature until parliamentary elections could be held. By the end of September the new government was sworn in, and the TNC, consisting of 56 members

headed by General Seabra Correia, was put in place.

National Assembly elections were held in March 2004, and 75% of Guinea–Bissau's 603,000 registered voters cast their ballots in what observers described as a free and fair election. The PAIGC did well, winning 45 seats, but not a majority, in the 102-member legislature; eleven other parties and three electoral coalitions had opposed the PAIGC. The PRS, still dominated by the shadowy presence of the erratic Kumba Ialá, came in second with 35 seats, followed by the United Social Democratic Party (PUSD) with 17.

In May, parliament appointed the PAIGC's Carlos Gomes Junior, a businessmen who is reportedly the richest man in Guinea–Bissau, as prime minister. His selection represented the political ascendancy of Creoles, culturally more westernized and better educated than other groups within the PAIGC, and his cabinet appointments emphasized the selection of men with advanced technical expertise and skill, something considered a handicap during the days of Kumba Ialá.

Civilian technical expertise proved incapable of controlling military militancy. A contingent of soldiers who had served as UN peacekeepers in Liberia mutinied in October, demanding back wages and benefits and improved living conditions. The mutiny resulted in the brutal murder of head of the armed forces, General Seabra Correia, and several others; to observers, their deaths had clear ethnic overtones: those killed were Papels and their killers were Balanta.

Having decapitated military leadership, the mutineers bullied the government into proposing an amnesty for actions extending back to the military coup of 1980 and imposed their choice of new military commanders. General Tagme Na Wai, a former guerilla fighter who fought in the PAIGC's war of liberation against Portuguese rule, was appointed armed forces chief of staff. A Balanta, Na Wai has little formal education and does not speak Portuguese, Guinea–Bissau's official language.

Prime Minister Gomes has had to work without a parliamentary majority and with a disunited PAIGC. One parliamentary faction, closer to former President Vieira than Prime Minister Gomes, is led by the PAIGC vice-president, Aristides Gomes and Cipriano Cassamá. By January 2005, factional rivalries resulted in Gomes suspending Cassamá from all the party's governing organs.

Mid-June presidential elections are meant to end the country's transitional period, but the lead up to them has seen an unsettling radicalization of Guinea–Bissau's political life. Supporters of former President Nino Vieira have gathered thousands of signatures urging him to run for election, while the PRS has formally designated Kumba Ialá its candidate. Both are banned from political office until 2008, but in applying for the law's suspension, Ialá, told reporters that "No law can ban my candidacy," and he threatened to seize power if the courts prevented him from running. In May Ialá, Guinea–Bissau's one-man destabilization force, withdrew his resignation, proclaimed himself thereby once again president, and with a few followers briefly occupied the presidential palace in May. The army remained loyal to the government and the June 19 elections were to proceed.

**Culture:** The Balantas tend to live by subsistence agricultural in the coastal lowlands; the Mandingas and Fulani of the interior place greater emphasis on the ownership of livestock. Contact between the Portuguese and the Africans was minimal during the colonial period; almost no educational facilities were provided for Africans. A tiny handful of Africans lived as *assimilados*, speaking Portuguese and adopting European customs. Cape Verde Creoles long dominated the business scene in Bissau and always assumed a higher position on the social scale than darker-skinned mainlanders. This was the cause of smoldering resentment.

The Guinean filmmaker, Flora Gomez, won the Prize of the City of Ouagadougou in the 2003 FESPCO for his film "Nha Fala" (My Voice). Gomez initially studied filmmaking in Cuba, and then trained in Senegal (1972-1974) to make newsreels. "Nha Fala" tells the story of Vita, a young 20-year old who leaves Bissau for Paris. She promises her mother to obey an old tradition that forbids women to sing, or be cursed, but meets and falls in love with a young musician, Peter. The prize was worth two million CFA francs. In U.S. dollars, it's less impressive: $3,364.

**Economy:** Guinea–Bissau is one of the poorest and least developed countries in the world, ranking 172nd out of 177 on the UN's *Human Development Index* for 2004. Its social statistics (2001) make depressing reading: 126 out of every 1,000 infants die at birth; life expectancy is barely 45 years. Illiteracy is a whopping 60%, rising to 75% for females. More than 88% of the population lives below the poverty line—less than one dollar a day.

An economy already in crisis was devastated by the civil war. Roads and bridges were left a shamble. The government remains the country's largest employer, but cash-strapped, it has regularly fallen behind in its salary obligations The country now depends largely on foreign assistance, accounting for 55% of its budgetary revenues.

Guinea–Bissau is burdened with a huge external debt, once estimated at around one billion dollars. Its enrolment in the Highly Indebted Poor Countries (HIPC) program brought that total down and significantly reduced the country's debt service expenses. In December 2000, a World Bank and IMF debt-relief package totaling $790 million was granted, alleviating some 85% of the country's total debt. The IMF promised to cover 100% of debt repayment in 2001/02 to ease the post-conflict transition. In May 2001, however, aid was suspended after nearly $15 million mysteriously disappeared into some black hole of corruption.

Under normal circumstances Guinea–Bissau's economy is heavily dependent on exports of cashews and timber and the sale of fishing licenses. Agriculture provides jobs for 82% of the population and generates about 69% of GDP and 93% of exports. Subsistence farming and animal husbandry presently dominate the sector. Only 9% of total land area is successfully cultivated; inland areas are largely savannah, useful for livestock rearing, while coastal areas consist of forest and mangrove swamps. The main food crop is paddy rice, which is grown on nearly 20% of all cultivated land. Efforts to expand out-of-season rice production through irrigation have produced a deadly side affect: malaria.

With Chinese assistance, irrigated rice fields were developed at Contuboel, about 100 miles east of Bissau. The paddies stretch over 660 acres and their luxuriant vegetation and ample water provide an ideal breeding place for the mosquitoes. The village has experienced a surge of malaria cases, swamping its clinic with suffering patients.

Cashew nuts account for between 80-90% of Guinea–Bissau's exports, most of which are shipped to India for processing. Guinea–Bissau is currently ranked as the world's sixth-largest producer of cashews. The government predicts a 2005 harvest of 100,000 to 105,000 tons of raw nuts, slightly higher than in 2004. It has set the minimum price at 250 CFA francs a kilo, about 50 US cents, and is requiring that all nuts sold be paid in cash. In 2004 many farmers bartered their cashews for rice from Senegalese traders, resulting in some 7,000 tons of the nuts being exported to the world market via Senegal. Imaginatively, the government has announced plans to build a series of small thermal plants around the country that would use the dried waste of the cashew fruit to produce electricity.

Areas for potential development are fishing, mining and timber. Coastal fishing resources are extremely rich, but subject to over-exploitation. Guinea–Bissau currently sells the right to fish in its 200-mile Exclusive Economic Zone, and industrial fishing trawlers, rapacious and damaging to the stock of fish, take their catch home for processing. Guinea–Bissau signed a new fishing agreement with the EU in March 2001 worth around $45 million.

Phosphate deposits have been discovered near Farim by Champion Resources of Canada, but as of spring 2003 the company was still looking for financing for the project. Seismic surveys in the country's offshore areas have been encouraging, with an estimated offshore oil production potential of seven million tons a year.

**The Future:** Difficult at best. The country desperately needs political stability to regain the confidence of international donors and investors. Factional division within the country's main political parties has led to increasing radicalization, and the army still sees itself an active, and privileged, political force. Neither is a recipe for stability or democracy.

# The Republic of Liberia

**A child soldier wearing a teddy-bear backpack aims his rifle**

**Area:** 111,370 sq. km = 43,000 sq. mi. (Pennsylvania is slightly larger).

**Population:** 3,482,211 (July 2005 est.)

**Capital City:** Monrovia

**Climate:** Warm and humid, with a wet season (April–November) and a drier season (December–May).

**Neighboring Countries:** Sierra Leone (West); Guinea (North); Côte d'Ivoire (Northeast, East).

**Official Language:** English.

**Other Principal Languages:** Over thirty, including Bassa, Dan, Gola, Grebo, Kisi, Kpelle, Krahn, Loma, Mano, Manya, Vai.

**Ethnic groups:** Kpelle, Bassa, Gio, Kru, Grebo, Mano, Krahn, Gola, Gbandi, Loma, Kissi, Vai, and Bella, Americo-Liberians 2.5% (descendants of immigrants from the US who had been slaves).

**Principal Religions:** Traditional 70%, Muslim 20%, and Christian 10%.

**Chief Commercial Products:** Diamonds, iron ore, rubber, timber, and coffee.

**GNI per capita:** $130 (2003)

**Currency:** Liberian Dollar.

**Former Colonial Status:** Liberia has traditionally been an area of United States development.

**Independence Date:** July 26, 1847.

**Chief of State:** Interim President Gyude Bryant (since 14 October 2003)

**National Flag:** Eleven horizontal stripes of red and white, with a single white star on a blue rectangle in the upper left–hand corner.

Liberia is located on the southern part of the west coast of Africa, facing the warm equatorial waters of the Gulf of Guinea. It is within the tropical region of Africa and as such, has a warm, humid climate. Its forest areas are thickly carpeted with roots, dead leaves and debris, which are quickly made a part of the earth by the rapid rate of decay. From the floor of the jungle, shrubs and small trees entangled with vines rise from 40 to more than 100 feet. Interspersed with this thick growth are the so–called crown trees, which bear foliage only at immense heights, having trunks up to twelve feet in width. The coastal area of Liberia, receiving the most rainfall, is dotted with lagoons, tidal creeks and marshes. Further inland the terrain rises slowly to a level of 1000 feet in a series of plateaus obscured by the dense undergrowth. Low mountains rise occasionally throughout the country, sel-

dom reaching a height of more than 3,000 feet, with the exception of the Nimba and Wale mountains, which are 4,500 feet high.

Six rivers flow from the interior southwest to the Gulf of Guinea; they are not navigable for more than a few miles inland and are bounded by level land suitable for cultivation.

# Liberia

During the eight-month rainy season, hardly a day passes without an inch or more of rainfall, including sharp thunderstorms intermingled with a steady, tedious downpour.

**History:** Kru, Gola and other ethnic groups had lived for countless centuries in Liberia before the arrival of Europeans. Portuguese mariners were the first to describe the Liberian coast and identify its commercially valuable products in the fifteenth century. The area came to be called the Grain Coast because of the grains of the Melegueta pepper, as valuable as gold to a Europe cut off from the Asian spice trade as a consequence of Ottoman conquests.

Easily reached by the ships of slave traders plying the south Atlantic, local chiefs along the Grain Coast willingly sold conquered peoples to them. The market for field labor on the plantations of the southern colonies of America and in the West Indies was immense. Traders often took only the men for heavy work, leaving the women and children to fend for themselves.

The origins of Liberia took vague shape as early as 1691 when the Virginia legislature passed a law requiring that any slave owner granting freedom arrange passage out of the colony within half a year. Where they went was not spelled out, but there was a growing feeling that it was dangerous to allow slaves and freed Africans to mingle.

More than a century passed before Virginia lawmakers once again considered the problems caused by slavery. The 1789 slave revolt in Haiti had sent a chill through plantation owners. Thomas Jefferson expressed the view that there should be a plan for colonizing blacks, and the Virginia legislature requested President James Monroe to obtain land outside the United States, preferably in Africa, for this purpose. The idea of a colonization project developed.

The American Colonization Society was founded in 1816. Its object was to transport freeborn blacks and emancipated slaves to Africa. In Henry Clay's words, such colonization would "draw...off" free blacks, lest they incite a slave rebellion. Remote Africa offered an ideal place to send such potential troublemakers.

In 1818 representatives of the American Colonization Society visited the Grain Coast of West Africa. After several failed attempts to secure land for the colonization project, the Society finally signed an agreement with local chiefs granting it possession of Cape Mesurado in 1821. The first American freed slaves landed in 1822.

By 1830 the tiny colonization effort had grown to a thousand people. This new "land of liberty" was named Liberia, from the Latin root for "free." The colony continued to expand, and its trade increased because the settlers preferred American food, which had to be brought in by ship.

The settlers united in 1839 to form the Commonwealth of Liberia under a governor appointed by the American Colonization Society. In 1847 the Free and Independent Republic of Liberia was proclaimed by Governor Joseph Roberts, a freeborn black man who hailed from Virginia. The new nation was recognized within a short time by the European powers, but not by the United States until 1862.

Life for the descendants of the freed slaves was harsh. This was a hostile land—a difficult place in which to survive, though the tribes of the interior were not particularly aggressive. Liberia's economic and political elite of Americo-Liberians remained pretty much in the coastal communities. The government could not exert effective authority for more than 20 miles inland. It was not until the 1930s that there was any real penetration of the interior by the Americo-Liberians.

The state ran up a huge debt, and in 1909 President Theodore Roosevelt appointed a commission to investigate Liberia's finances. The bailout plan involved a loan raised by international bankers, guaranteed by the state's customs revenues. The customs receivership, administered by British, French, German and American officials, brought some stability to Liberia's finances, but the country's financial reorganization was scuttled by World War I. Revenues dropped and the financial situation deteriorated.

When the Firestone Tire and Rubber Company secured a concession of one million acres to establish a rubber plantation in 1926, the Liberian government arranged a loan through the company to consolidate its debts. The loan helped to stabilize the country's finances, but the

**Liberia–Counties**

57

# Liberia

administration of its customs and internal revenue was placed in the hands of an American advisor. The government was not able to liquidate its external debt until 1952—the first time since it took its first loan in 1871.

Liberia's special relationship with the United States was intensified with the coming of World War II. With most Asian sources of rubber cut off by the Japanese occupation, Liberia was virtually the only source of natural rubber available to the allies. A defense agreement signed in 1942 brought vast infrastructure developments to Liberia. Strategic roads were constructed, along with an international airport and deepwater harbor at Monrovia, Liberia's capital city named after President James Monroe. The American dollar was declared legal tender in 1943.

William V. S. Tubman (b. 1895) was elected to a four–year term of office as president in 1944. Ultimately he would be elected to seven successive terms. Although a descendent of American immigrants, Tubman grew up in poverty, peripheral to the core of the Americo-Liberian elite. A self-made man, he studied the law after work and passed his bar examination at age 23. He joined the True Whig Party, the Americo-Liberian political machine that controlled Liberia economically and politically, and held a variety of public offices. At 35 he was elected to the Liberian Senate, where he became a bit of a gadfly opposing the Americo-Liberian establishment.

To remove the pesky critic, the True Whig leadership booted him "upstairs" with an appointment as an associate justice of the Liberian Supreme Court. From here Tubman unexpectedly announced his candidacy for President in 1943, successfully campaigned and won easily. He

would dominate Liberian politics for the next 28 years, dying in office in 1971.

Tubman realized the True Whig Party's continued hold on power depended on extending its reach beyond its Americo-Liberian constituency. He was the first president to appoint "country people"— that is indigenous Africans—to high positions. Efforts were made to establish linkages with traditional authorities in the hinterland, and one chief remembered the impact of Tubman's policies—and articulated the cultural gulf that separated coastal and hinterland peoples: "President Tubman really turned this country around. We tribesmen can now mix up with the civilized people freely and nobody is looking down on us. We can now eat at the same table, shake hands and dance with the civilized men and women."

Foreign investment under Tubman led to uneven development, with the hinterlands almost always receiving only crumbs and leftovers. This only exacerbated tensions between the Americo-Liberian elite and indigenous Liberians.

When President Tubman died in 1971 his vice-president, William Tolbert, succeeded him. Tolbert was the first Liberian president to speak an interior tribal language, and he attempted to follow through on Tubman's efforts to incorporate indigenous Liberians. For his efforts to expand educational opportunities and bring interior peoples into the elitist government, President Tolbert was criticized by Americo-Liberians for having "let peasants into the kitchen."

By 1979, long-term inequalities, rural poverty, and economic mismanagement had brought the country to a crisis point. When rice supplies dropped because growers found it more profitable to work as laborers on the large rubber plantations, the government proposed the price be raised from $22 to $26 per hundred pounds to encourage greater production. Since rice is the staple food of the people, the plan touched off populist riots in Monrovia; there was widespread looting. About 50 people were killed and another 500 injured.

Ninety percent of the businesses in the capital were either partially or totally destroyed, with damage said to be about $50 million. President Tolbert imposed a curfew on the city, and Congress granted him emergency powers, but these proved too late to stem the tide of rebellion. Enemies of the establishment surfaced, and on April 12, 1980, a group of non–commissioned officers led by Master Sergeant Samuel K. Doe stormed the Executive Mansion, assassinated President Tolbert (and disemboweled him), seized power and set up a People's Redemption Council (PRC).

Doe and his fellow non–commissioned officers represented a variety of back-country peoples who had traditionally been excluded from power by Americo–Liberians. Members of indigenous ethnic groups could achieve NCO status in the army, but Americo–Liberians, dominated most of the upper ranks. Doe was a member of the Krahn people, while his two principal partners, Thomas Quiwonkpa and Weh Syen, were Gio and Kru respectively. Ten days later the PRC organized the public execution of thirteen high officials of the deposed government. Its birth in blood continued to characterize the Doe regime.

Rivalries soon brought bloody death within the ruling junta. Weh Syen and four others were executed for plotting to kill Head of State Doe a year later. A coup involving Thomas Quiwonkpa, commander of the Armed Forces of Liberia (AFL) was discovered in November 1983. Granted clemency by Doe, he returned to his home base, only to flee the country when it was obvious his life was in danger.

During the same year Charles Taylor, who was serving as deputy minister of commerce in the Doe government, was charged with corruption. Among other things, he had ordered $1 million worth of bulldozers, which never arrived. The money was stashed in American bank accounts, and when he fled Liberia for his life, Taylor headed straight to the U.S. Arrested and jailed, he managed to hack saw his way out and made his way back to Africa. In 1988 Taylor, still a fugitive from American justice, was reportedly supported and trained by Moamer al-Qadhafi at a Libyan terrorist base.

Doe set about transforming himself into a civilian ruler, to pacify potential donors who might have any qualms about people who shoot their way into office. A new constitution was approved in July 1984, and in October 1985, general elections were held to implement its provisions. Doe, now head of the National Democratic Party of Liberia (NDPL) was elected president. The NDPL claimed victory by a slender margin: 50.9%, but the election was seen as utterly fraudulent by most observers. Under President Doe Krahns were given most of the authority in the military and the most significant posts in government. Ethnic rivalry intensified as a consequence.

Successive U.S. administrations poured over $400 million into President Doe's eager hands. Liberia became an important listening post and staging base for CIA operations in central and southern Africa, but by 1987 most of the money couldn't be accounted for, and the U.S. was forced to send in the auditors. It was an impossible mission; Doe simply refused to cooperate.

**M/Sgt. Samuel K. Doe**

**Interim President Gyude Bryant**
Photo by Getty Images/Stephen Chernin

Shortly after the 1985 presidential elections, Thomas Quiwonkpa, the former army commander, returned to Liberia via Sierra Leone and staged a coup against President Doe. It failed. Quiwonkpa was apprehended, killed, and dismembered. According to some reports (and a recurring theme in the Liberian tragedy), part of his body was consumed by his executioners. A nationwide pogrom against Quiwonkpa's Gio people and the closely related Mano ensued. Execution, flogging, castration, dismemberment and rape became all too common as Liberia sank into bloody civil strife.

Liberia's civil war broke out in earnest in December 1989 when Charles Taylor led an invasion of insurgents from Côte d'Ivoire. They called themselves the National Patriotic Front of Liberia (NPFL) and received support from Libya, Burkina Faso, Côte d'Ivoire and Liberians living abroad. From Libya they received training and money. Col. Qadhafi supported any group that would undermine American interests, and by now, America was deeply invested in Liberia. The Ivoirian president, Houphouët–Boigny, apparently condoned and the French ambassador winked. For Houphouët–Boigny the support was personal. A step–daughter had been married to A.B. Tolbert, murdered by the Doe regime like his father, the Liberian president. Burkina Faso was at the time caught up in the excitement of leftist ideology, generously funded by Libya. The Burkinabé president, Blaise Compaoré, also needed to buff his revolutionary credentials. These had been seriously damaged by Compaoré having been implicated in the 1987 murder of his predecessor, Burkina Faso's

charismatic young revolutionary, Thomas Sankara.

Mano and Gio youth flocked to Taylor's NPFL to avenge the sufferings of their people. General disgust with Doe rallied others, and soon Taylor's forces had overrun most of the country. Control of rich diamond-producing areas supported the rebellion. The violence was grim, the brutality bestial.

The scale of operations favored a breakup of the Front as local warlords sought to control territory and resources. By August 1990 anarchy prevailed and other West African states decided to intervene militarily to spare the nation. The military force they created was called ECOMOG, standing for the ECOWAS Monitoring Group. Charles Taylor would long remember the ECOMOG intervention, thinking it cheated him of total victory.

One of Taylor's principal aides, Prince (a relatively common Liberian first name, having nothing to do with royal filiation) Yormie Johnson, broke up the National Patriotic Front when he formed his own rebel force, called the Independent National Patriotic Front of Liberia (INPFL). In September 1990 Johnson's forces captured President Doe when he left the besieged Executive Mansion to meet with the head of ECOMOG. He was cruelly tortured, mutilated and executed—and the violence preserved on videotape.

Other rebel groups formed around local leaders. The United Liberation Movement of Liberia (ULIMO) was organized by Alhaji Kromah in March 1991, but later fragmented along ethnic lines. ULIMO-K was Kromah's Mandingo faction, and ULIMO-J organized around Roosevelt Johnson and his Krahn supporters. Destructive violence continued, unabated. Nigeria decided it could no longer sustain the Liberian effort and announced its withdrawal effective April 1, 1994, but the U.S. intervened to persuade Nigeria to postpone departure.

By mid-1995 even Monrovia had become a wasteland in which teenage rebels cruised the streets with loaded automatic weapons and medium artillery. When rebel factions began ambushing ECOWAS forces, Nigeria's military ruler, Sani Abacha, had had enough. Faction leaders were summoned to Abuja, disarmament ordered, an election date set, and an interim ruler—Ruth Sando Perry, who had been a senator during the Doe period—appointed.

Multiparty elections were finally held in July 1997 and Charles Taylor emerged victorious. Seventy-five per cent of the Liberian electorate placed their desires for peace in the hands of the man most responsible for the devastating civil war.

**Charles Taylor**

His National Patriotic Party (NPP) won an absolute majority in both houses of the legislature.

The extent of the destruction that took place in Liberia was staggering. More than 5% of the population was killed, and more than half a million Liberians fled the country. Almost 50% of those remaining were displaced from their home villages.

Under Charles Taylor Liberia took on the appearance of a security state. Security agencies, loyal only to president Taylor, were everywhere. The army (AFL), once dominated by President Doe's Krahn, was marginalized and its members reduced to begging for money on street corners or pleading at the defense ministry for their unpaid salaries. In effect, the AFL was replaced by militiamen, often little more than bodyguards for President Taylor, kept loyal by regular payments in rice and dollars.

The Special Security Service (SSS), large and heavily armed, was little more than another name for the presidential guard, responsible for presidential security, i.e. dealing with the president's enemies. The president's son, Charles Taylor, Jr., headed up the widely-feared Anti-Terrorist Unit (ATU)—some 2,000 men, including, in addition to Liberians, men from Gambia, Burkina Faso, and Guinea.

Power under Charles Taylor was personal and arbitrary, and occasionally just bizarre. In May 1999 President Taylor sacked almost his entire cabinet because they failed to attend a church service as he had ordered. More often power was simply coercive and frequently brutal. Most of the main faction leaders of the civil war went into exile, fearful for their lives had they remained in the country. State security forces—especially the Anti-Terrorism

# Liberia

Unit were flagrant abusers of human rights.

Not content with maintaining internal power through repression, President Taylor sought a larger regional role by destabilizing his neighbors. He was the principal patron of the remarkably vicious RUF in Sierra Leone, offering training, weapons, staging grounds for attacks and safe haven for retreat. The effort was paid for by Sierra Leone diamonds mined by the rebels, from which President Taylor exacted a share. Global Witness, a British NGO, also accused President Taylor of benefiting personally from assisting al-Qaeda agents convert banked assets into more liquid and movable diamonds.

The UN Security Council sought to limit Taylor's destabilizing machinations, and voted unanimously to impose sanctions on all diamond exports in March

2001. Taylor and other officials were subject to travel restrictions, and the council reiterated its 1995 arms embargo on Liberia. This proved as effective as a colander holding water.

To pay for its arms shipments, the Taylor government diverted money from the Liberian International Ship and Corporate Registry (LISCR). More than 2,000 ships fly the Liberian flag. The U.S.-based LISCR administers the country's maritime registry and normally transmits about $18 million to the Liberian government—a sum that represented about 25% of the country's annual revenues.

The Taylor government justified its illegal arms purchases by the insurgency it faced at home. Having underwritten rebel groups in Sierra Leone and Guinea, Charles Taylor's mischief turned back on its creator. Rebels seeking the overthrow

of his regime came together in a loose coalition calling itself Liberians United for Reconciliation and Democracy (LURD). LURD recruited from a variety of movements—like ULIMO-K and ULIMO-J, and even dissidents from Taylor's own NPFL. The only thing that united the rebels was a common antipathy for Charles Taylor. For his part, Taylor (correctly) accused Guinea of aiding and abetting his enemies.

As the rebel forces became more threatening President Taylor increased his arm purchases, little impeded by the paper ferocity of UN sanctions. Global Witness's March 2003 report, *The Usual Suspects: Liberia's Weapons and Mercenaries in Côte d'Ivoire and Sierra Leone*, documented how shipments of eastern European arms regularly entered Liberia, transiting through Nigeria and Libya. Arms-bearing ships ar-

**Liberian Refugees**

rived at Liberian ports controlled by timber companies closely associated with the Taylor regime, and poured their lethal cargoes into the civil strife.

President Taylor's support of two rebel groups in western Côte d'Ivoire (MPIGO: *Mouvement populaire ivoirien du grand ouest*, and MJP: *Mouvement pour la Justice et la Paix*) also boomeranged. In April 2003 a new rebel group, the Movement for Democracy in Liberia (MODEL)—financed by Côte d'Ivoire's president, Laurent Gbagbo—began to harass Liberian government forces from the southeast.

By June it was clear the Taylor regime was rapidly unraveling. While MODEL forces attacked from the south, fighters from main rebel group (LURD) swept south in an attempt to capture the capital. Peace talks aimed at ending the two-pronged rebellion were organized in Ghana, but were overshadowed by President Taylor's indictment by the Sierra Leone Special War Crimes Court. A ceasefire agreement was reached, but proved short-lived as rebels pressed their advantage, demanding President Taylor's resignation and departure as the price of peace.

Fighting intensified and fatalities mounted. ECOWAS agreed to supply peacekeepers and Nigerian troops arrived in August. His options reduced to nil, President Taylor resigned and flew away to exile in Nigeria, handing over the government to his vice-president and old companion in arms, Moses Blah. U.S. forces, which had remained at sea, just over the horizon, finally entered Liberia. In Ghana, rebels and representatives of the former Taylor regime signed an agreement formally declaring a ceasefire and end to Liberia's civil war on 18 August. The Accra Accord set the interim arrangements under which Liberia currently operates, and with guns quieted, the UN began what would become its largest peacekeeping mission, some 14,000 troops.

As interim president, the Accra conferees chose a politically neutral figure: Gyude Bryant, a little-known businessman who was not seen as having ties to either the former government or the rebels. Sworn in as head of state in mid-October, Bryant is hemmed in by a power-sharing arrangement involving former rebels, and representatives of civil society and the former government.

A new 76-member national assembly has been created, consisting of 12 members each from the former government and the two rebel groups; 18 members have been chosen by Liberian political parties, and seven more from civil society and special interest groups. The remaining 15 members were chosen to represent each of Liberia's 15 counties. The interim transitional government's task will be to rebuild a nation destroyed by 14 years of brutal civil war and organize elections for a new government scheduled to take power in October 2005.

The United Nations Mission in Liberia (UNMIL) was assigned the arduous task of disarming combatants. In theory, 15,000 UN peacekeepers would fan out through the country and effect disarmament of factional belligerents. By May 2005 over a hundred thousand fighters had been demobilized and disarmed. Each demobilized fighter qualifies for a cash settlement—about $300—and education or training to provide jobs skills in post-conflict Liberia. There have been persistent reports of individuals who never fought in the civil war signing up just to claim these benefits. Fewer than one in three registering for demobilization have actually handed in a gun, and many of these were crude hunting guns, known locally as "single barrels."

The international community has pledged $520 million for Liberia's reconstruction, and the United States has pledged $200 million for reforming the security sector. Thirty-five million dollars were earmarked for recruiting and training a new 4,000-man "state-of-the-art" army. DynCorp International, a privately-owned security company headquartered in Reston Virginia, has been hired to do the work.

Meanwhile, the cause of such costly woes, Charles Taylor, resides in comfortable exile in Calabar, Nigeria, maintaining contact with his followers by cell phone. He has been indicted by the war crimes tribunal in Sierra Leone for crimes against humanity involving his role in arming and training the notorious Revolutionary United Front (RUF). In May 2005, the court's chief prosecutor accused Taylor of being behind January's attempted assassination of the Guinean president, Lansana Conte. "He has also mobilized his network of warlords and cronies to keep West Africa in turmoil," the prosecutor said.

There is mounting determination to see Taylor stand trial. President Obasanjo will be under mounting pressure to hand him over to judicial authorities. But little action is expected before Liberia's presidential elections next October.

There will there be no war crimes tribunal in Liberia during the transitional period. Interim-president Bryant, working with a power-sharing government that includes all the factions whose fighting destroyed Liberia, has explicitly ruled out such a judicial undertaking.

A culture of corruption—Charles Taylor's most enduring legacy to Liberia—continues to plague the country. The government is frequently unable properly to account for its funds, and the National Transitional Legislative Assembly (NTLA) has been shaken by charges and counter charges of financial malpractice. In February 2005 a World Bank mission bluntly told the government it had to crack down harder on corruption and show greater transparency in its finances if it expected donors to come to the country's aid.

The political season leading to the October 2005 presidential and parliamentary elections has already begun. Some eighteen parties have been registered and an equal number await approval. Over 45 people have announced their intention to run for the presidency.

**Culture:** Before the revolution of Samuel Doe, there was a basic divergence of cultural traditions in Liberia. The descendants of freed slaves living in the coastal regions were for the most part urban, Christian people. English was the language of choice and they preferred American styles in dress. They particularly valued formal attire, including tuxedos and top hats—notwithstanding the close, tropical climate. That is a way of life destroyed by the strife that has engulfed Liberia since 1980.

Monrovia, the capital city, still suffers the effects of destructive civil conflict. Its power system was knocked out in 1990 and there is little prospect of an early restart for the city's main electricity supply. In its place, the sound of thousands of private generators fills the evening air. The war also stopped the flow of water from the city's taps, and residents are dependent on polluted wells, expensive truck-delivered purified water, or jerry cans of water sold from handcarts on the city streets. Water distribution pipes are so old, rusted, and broken they will have to be ripped up and replaced in order to supply drinking water to residents; the cost will be huge.

**Economy:** Liberia's 14-year civil war pretty much destroyed its economy. GDP dropped 25% to 50% of its prewar levels, and per capita income sank to $140—the very bottom of the UN's *Human Development Index* for 2002. (In 2003 and 2004 there was insufficient data to rank the country.) Since the Accra Accords of August 2003, however, there has been some economic improvement; after a decline of 31% in 2003, the country's GDP rose by 2% in 2004.

Prior to 1990 the economy was primarily based on iron ore, rubber, timber, diamond and gold exports. With substantial investments in rich iron ore deposits, Liberia was once world's fifth largest exporter, but war completely disrupted the industry.

# Liberia

Before the war the rubber industry generated over $100 million annually in export earnings. Some 50,000 people earned their living through the industry. The Firestone rubber plantation, roughly 188 square miles containing 8 million rubber trees and 670 miles of roads, was the largest rubber plantation in the world. It has yet to recover fully from war damages. Many of its trees were over tapped by looters and will have to be cut down and replanted. It takes seven years for a rubber tree to mature and be ready for tapping.

In February 2005 the transitional government extended Firestone's land concession for 36 years as part of its efforts to revitalize the economy. For its part, Firestone indicated it planned to invest more that $100 million in the rubber industry. Among other things, the company planned to give 600,000 rubber stumps to small-scale farmers to help them replant their plantations.

In 2000 Liberia recorded exports of $61.6 million, led by rubber and timber. The figures represented a 23% increase over 1999 and illustrated the feverish logging activity in Liberia's forests. Like much of Liberia's economic activity, the timber industry was dominated by Charles Taylor. Global Witness examined the importance of timber for President Taylor and concluded it was more financially valuable to him and his security forces than was the diamond trade.

Taylor awarded a huge logging concession—more than 3.5 million acres—to the Oriental Timber Company (OTC) headed by one of his intimates, Gus van Kouwenhoven. OTC also has been given a virtual monopoly over the country's transport. It controlled the port of Buchanan to which logging trucks delivered their cargo and then picked up illegal arms shipments. Roads built and maintained for timber extraction were conveniently used for weapons movement within Liberia and ultimate shipment to those forces of destabilization President Taylor unleashed on Côte d'Ivoire, Guinea or Sierra Leone. (In March 2005 Dutch authorities arrested van Kouwenhoven, provisionally charging him with war crimes and breaking the arms embargo against Liberia.)

With some 170 timber companies operating in Liberia, logging was being done at such an unsustainable rate that it threatened to devastate the Liberian rainforest within the decade. In December 2003 the United Nations Environment Program (UNEP) reported that the country's forest cover had been reduced from 38 percent to 31 percent as a result of uncontrolled logging. In the UN Security Council, France and China, the two principal buyers of Liberian timber, vetoed an embargo on Liberia's "logs of war" until May 2003, an action which contributed to unfettered logging activity.

Liberia's "flag of convenience" ship registry was long a honey pot for the Taylor regime. The registry is second only to Panama's, and includes more than 2,000 vessels. (Thirty-five per cent of the world's tanker fleet and a large number of cruise ships are also covered by the Liberian flag.) Fees brought in about $18 million annually, and helped to pay for President Taylor's arms purchases.

As part of its anti-terrorism campaign, the U.S. government signed an accord with Liberia in February 2004 which allows the U.S. Navy to board Liberian flagged vessels in international waters to inspect for unconventional weapons. The agreement was the first of its kind and resulted from fears that terrorist networks would use ships to attack the American economy.

**Future:** Difficult. Civil conflict has killed more than 200,000 people and displaced at least half the prewar population of 2.5 million. The legacy of war is appalling. Child soldiers, given drugs to fortify their fighting resolve, pose difficult social problems. Medical experts estimate that up to 70 percent of all combatants continue to use drugs and many have become addicts. Unless a place in society (care, support and education) is found for these former combatants, violence could reignite at any moment.

Ominously, the flow of drugs into Liberia is basically unimpeded. Law enforcement agencies seem unable or unwilling to stop the smuggling of illegal substances. Liberia is believed to have become a transit point for drug trafficking throughout the region.

Infrastructure and services have collapsed. Roads are everywhere more potholes than surface. There is no effective sanitation service; safe drinking water is often difficult to come by, and electricity supplies outside the capital are nonexistent. Schools have few teachers, and health-care facilities lack basic essentials. Reconstruction of Liberia will cost every penny of the $520 million pledged by donors.

Whether these reconstruction funds will actually get to their intended projects is open to question. Members of the transitional government seem to have spent more of their energies on securing the biggest share of the "elephant's meat"—jobs, perquisites, and the opportunity for lucrative reconstruction contracts—than anything else. Corruption is rife and acts dissuasively on donor generosity.

This rush for spoils results from the fragility of power: both LURD and MODEL are subject to internal factional disruption and have backers (Lansana Conté and Laurent Gbagbo) whose own grasp of power may be uncertain. Guinea's President Conté remains in poor health, and Laurent Gbagbo's duplicitous ways in Côte d'Ivoire have increased instability in that country. It is uncertain what would happen to either group should its sponsor pass from the scene.

# The Republic of Senegal

Presidential palace

**Area:** 196,840 sq.km. = 76,000 sq. mi. (about the size of Nebraska).

**Population:** 11,126,832 (July 2005 est.)

**Capital City:** Dakar (pop. 3.5 million estimated).

**Climate:** Warm and dry in the North; warmer and more humid in the South, with usually a wet season (July–October) and a dry season (November–June).

**Neighboring Countries:** The Gambia is a finger–like projection extending eastward from the Atlantic coast to the interior; Mauritania (North); Mali (East); Guinea–Bissau, Guinea (South).

**Official Language:** French.

**Other Principal Languages:** Over 30. Prominently: Bambara, Pulaar (Peul), Diola (Jola), Malinké, Serere, Soninké, and Wolof, spoken by about 75% of the population.

**Ethnic groups:** Wolof 43.3%, Peul 23.8%, Serer 14.7%, Diola 3.7%, Mandinka 3%, Soninké 1.1%, European and Lebanese 1%, other 9.4%.

**Principal Religions:** Muslim 92%, indigenous beliefs 6%, Christian 2% (mostly Roman Catholic).

**Chief Commercial Products:** Fish, ground nuts (peanuts), petroleum products, phosphates, and cotton.

**GNI per capita:** $550 (2003)

**Currency:** CFA Franc

**Former Colonial Status:** French Colony, a part of French West Africa (1895–1960). French commercial interests were active in Senegal prior to the formation of French West Africa.

**Independence Date:** June 20, 1960.

**Chief of State:** Abdoulaye Wade, President, since March 2000.

**National Flag:** Three vertical stripes of green, yellow and red, with a green star on the middle yellow stripe.

The Republic of Senegal, the westernmost portion of Africa, lies in a transitional zone between the steaming jungles of the Gold–Ivory Coast to the south and the endless, dry Sahara to the north. Its unique position has made it a true "crossroads" of the world—between Europe and Latin America, the United States and the Near and Far East, and finally, between South Africa and the European and American continents.

This is a flat, rolling plains country with characteristic grasslands and low tree vegetation. In the Southwest there is a small area of jungle and the coastline is often marsh or swampland. There are no high mountains in Senegal, but there are four large rivers flowing in parallel courses from east to west. These rivers are navigable to a substantial distance inland from the Atlantic, particularly during the wet season.

The strong winds from the Sahara usher in the traditional dry season each November. This wind of dry months, called the *harmattan* by the people, occasionally rises to almost torrential velocity, producing severe dust and sandstorms. All too frequently, the wind is year–around, creating severe drought problems and intrusion of the Sahara at the rate of about four miles per year.

**History:** Early migrations of peoples from the East were long-established in the country by the time of the first European explorations in the fifteenth century. Paleolithic and Neolithic artifacts have been found near Dakar, and early copper and iron objects have been found elsewhere.

# Senegal

Berbers from the north established a Muslim monastery in the Senegal River region in the eleventh century, converted local populations to Islam, and began a military expansion that ultimately resulted in the conquest of both Ghana and Morocco and the invasion of Spain.

By the sixteenth century Wolof peoples were organized into four competing states: Jolof, Walo, Cayor and Baol. The region was strongly influenced by Islamic revival movements from the later seventeenth century well into the nineteenth.

Inching their way down the African coast under the inspiration of Prince Henry—known as "The Navigator"—Portuguese mariners reached the Senegal Coast around 1444; they established trading posts at the mouth of the Senegal River, on the island of Gorée, and at Rufisque.

Under later French rule, the trading sites of St. Louis, Gorée, Dakar and Rufisque were granted special political rights. Regardless of race, inhabitants of the "Four Communes," as they were called, were French citizens with the right to elect a representative to parliament in Paris. Initially these representatives were French or mulattos, but in 1914 electors chose the first African, Blaise Diagne, as the Communes' Deputy to the National Assembly. Diagne was given the rank of governor-general to assist in recruiting African soldiers to aid France in World War I. Some 200,000 were eventually recruited from all of French West Africa.

African citizens of the Four Communes lost their privileges during World War II when France was occupied by German forces. With the creation of the Fourth French Republic, Senegal's two socialist deputies, Lamine Guèye and Léopold Sédar Senghor, worked to restore and extend these rights of full French citizenship. Senghor, a brilliant student who achieved the highest academic degrees in the French

Senegal's first president, Hon.
Léopold Sédar Senghor

language, taught the language in French lycées and was essentially the grammarian responsible for the language of the Fourth Republic's constitution, led Senegal to complete independence in 1960.

Senghor (b. 1906) dominated Senegalese politics for the first two decades of the country's independent existence. An internationally proclaimed poet, Senghor combined a humanist orientation with refined political skills. A Roman Catholic in an overwhelmingly Muslim country, he collaborated with the grand *marabouts*, leaders of Senegal's major Islamic brotherhoods, and maintained close ties with the former colonial ruler, France. A Serer, he led a predominantly Wolof nation. Under his leadership Senegal developed a more tolerant and pluralist state than most other African states.

In the early period, his Progressive Senegalese Union (UPS) ruled as a single dominant party, but in 1976 Senghor authorized opposition parties. Despite greater political openness, the additional parties had little electoral success; President Senghor was overwhelmingly reelected in 1978 to another five–year term.

In perhaps the most orderly transfer of power seen to that point in Africa, the aging president resigned his office on December 31, 1980, and turned it over to his able prime minister, Abdou Diouf, who completed his predecessor's term of office. In February 1983 President Diouf rolled up an impressive victory in democratic elections; both he and the Socialist Party (PS) received more than 80% of the vote. Seven other parties competed in the contest.

Opposition to the Diouf administration centered around Abdoulaye Wade's Senegalese Democratic Party (PDS), the principal opposition party in the 1983 and 1988 elections. President Diouf won handily in both these contests, and after brief but bitter opposition following the 1988 elections, Wade and three other opposition leaders joined the socialists in a coalition government; this lasted until 1992 when they resigned, complaining they had been influential on only trivial issues.

The resignation allowed Wade to compete in early 1993 elections free of administrative ties, but because the opposition remained deeply divided, Diouf and the PS continued to dominate Senegalese political life.

Presidential elections in February 2000 featured eight candidates, but only four had any reasonable expectations of electoral success. The two principal candidates were familiar opponents. President Diouf was the standard bearer of the PS and the long-time opposition leader Abdoulaye Wade represented the *Parti Démocratique Sénégalais* (PDS).

**President Abdoulaye Wade**

After forty years in power, the PS had become increasingly dysfunctional as a political family. Two PS defectors, both one-time party heavyweights, entered strong candidacies, made stronger by their ability to criticize Diouf and the PS from inside knowledge. Djibo Leity Kâ, representing the Union for Democratic Renewal (URD), had been part of the PS leadership until he lost favor in 1998. Moustapha Niasse, a former foreign minister, enjoyed an international reputation and access to considerable campaign financing.

At 73 years of age, Abdoulaye Wade was the grand old man of Senegalese opposition, but the darling of the young. His campaign stops drew enthusiastic crowds. Change was in the air and "*Sopi*," the Wolof word for change, was the chant of the crowds. If elected, he promised, he would organize a referendum to dissolve the national assembly and change the constitution.

Change, indeed, was what the Senegalese voters wanted. With a host of international observers watching, the usual mechanisms of electoral manipulation were put aside. Dramatically, President Diouf failed to obtain a majority in the first round of voting. In the runoff, Wade won 58.5% of the vote. Diouf graciously admitted defeat and announced his retirement from politics. (He is now the Secretary-General of La Francophonie, largely the international organization of former French colonies and protectorates, basically equivalent to the Commonwealth.)

President Wade quickly drafted a new, more democratic constitution. Among a number of important changes, presidential terms were reduced to five years from seven. The Senate, an ineffective retirement home for faded PS politicians, was abolished and the National Assembly reduced from 140 members to 120. The president was granted the right to dissolve the Assembly (dominated by the PS) after two years of existence. The right to form opposition parties was entrenched; the prime minister's duties were enhanced and the judiciary given more independence. For the first time women were given equal property rights with men.

In early January 2001, 94% of Senegalese approved the new constitution. Elections to choose the members of the new National Assembly were held at the end of April, and a coalition of 40 pro-Wade parties calling itself "Sopi" swept the field, winning 90 of 120 seats. The landslide victory gave President Wade a free hand to effect the changes his constituents demanded.

The victory also highlighted the fragile nature of Wade's coalition. Relations between President Wade and Moustapha Niasse, his first premier, had already deteriorated. In the April 2001 legislative elections, Niasse's Alliance of Progressive Forces (APF) campaigned independently, won eleven seats—just ahead of the former ruling *Parti Socialiste*—and became the official opposition.

On September 26, 2002 Senegal experienced great national tragedy when the Joola, a ferryboat run by the Senegalese military and carrying three times as many passengers as allowed, capsized in the Atlantic off the coast of Gambia while making its way from Zinguinchor to Dakar. The tragedy came just ahead of the end of school holidays, and many of those who drowned were the best and brightest of Casamance's students returning to their academic work in the capital. In the final assessment, 1,863 died—more than the Titanic; only 64 were rescued. The vast majority of them were from Zinguinchor, the regional capital—a terrible toll for a sleepy county seat of only 200,000 people: In Casamance they still speak of a "lost generation."

The Joola sinking also took a political toll. Both the transportation and armed forces ministers resigned, and the country's navy chief was fired. After her initial dismissal of government responsibility for the accident, Prime Minister Boye was also replaced by President Wade. Her cabinet was dissolved and the president appointed a new premier—Idrissa Seck, a close aide of the president who had a strong background in both business and politics.

The shades of the Joola continue to overhang Senegalese political life. The government agreed to set aside an indemnity fund of some $34 million to compensate the victims' families, but distribution is slow and the process has become mired in controversy. President Wade has used the accident to mobilize his civil servants and fellow citizens to higher standards of behavior. Attributing the accident to "slackness, irresponsibility and greed," he called for "an examination of conscience conducted lucidly, courageously and impartially."

Personal behavioral change is probably not what most of his supporters envisioned in the notion of "*sopi*," and neither bureaucrats nor citizens have become less lax or more responsible. Public transportation buses remain dangerously overloaded with passengers, for example, while the drivers of private *cars rapides* (minbus taxis) can squeak by safety inspections with a small bribe. Nor has civic-mindedness overtaken Dakar's citizenry, who continue to ignore waste receptacles and toss their garbage on city streets. (Where the state does not enforce its regulations, there is little incentive for citizens to accord themselves by its rules.)

## Casamance

The Movement of Democratic Forces of Casamance (MFDC) has been intermittently fighting some 20 years for the region's independence. Located south of The Gambia, the province has long thought of itself as exploited, virtually colonized by northerners. Unlike most north/south conflicts in Africa, the struggle in Casamance does not pit an Islamic north against an animist south because most of the region's people are Muslims, including a slight majority of the dominant ethnic group, the Diola. Instead, the conflict is economic.

Casamance produces peanuts, like the rest of Senegal, but also has rich fishing grounds off its coast and has over the years become a tourist Mecca for Europeans. It produces cotton for northern factories, and its forests provide charcoal for Dakar. Coastal waters hold the promise of petroleum yet to be found. Despite the region's wealth, however, Casamançais have seen few benefits. They question where the money has gone and deplore the degradation of the region's resources. For them, Dakar represents "northern domination" and "Senegalese neo-colonialism."

Industrialized fishing fleets are depleting coastal waters, and forests are shrinking rapidly. They note that traditional rice cultivation, based on natural inundation, was destroyed by the importation of cheap foreign rice. At the same time they point out huge investments in the north to create a rice industry based on much more expensive damming and irrigation. Insufficient development of roads has hampered the marketing of local fruits and vegetables; Casamançais oranges and mangos rot on the ground. Currently, one of the most productive crops is "*yamba*," the local name of cannabis. Driven by a huge demand in Dakar, *yamba* has become one of the principal sources for rebel financing; dismantling criminal gangs involved in the *yamba* trade will be one of the major tasks facing the government following any peace agreement.

One factor complicating settlement over the years has been the division of the MFDC into two factions, one loyal to the Abbé Augustin Diamacoune Senghor, the group's president, and the other to Sidi Badji, founder of the armed wing. Following the death of Sidi Badji in May 2003, the military wing's hard-line leadership continued periodic attacks on government and civilian targets despite efforts by the political wing to end the conflict. The struggle has resulted in thousands of deaths and shattered the region's economy.

The rebels have long been able to replenish their arms supply with weapons smuggled from Guinea-Bissau and paid for by the rebels' cannabis profits. Because of this, Senegal has worked to maintain good relations with the Bissau govern-

**The Caliph of the Mourides**

**The Caliph of the Tijanis**

# Senegal

**Waiting for the evening catch.**

ment. The two countries signed agreements on sharing future offshore oil discoveries, and are working to reduce arms supplies reaching the rebels.

By December 2004 the conflict's intensities had abated sufficiently that the government could sign a peace accord with Abbé Diamacoune Senghor in which the rebels renounced armed struggle and agreed to open "serious negotiations" with the government. Dampening the enthusiasm of the moment was the absence of three MFDC factions.

**Culture:** Dakar, the busy seaport and capital of Senegal, has been a pole of attraction for visitors the world over. The city has grown by leaps and bounds, however, and its beauty subject to the problems of urban congestion.

With more than three million inhabitants Dakar can boast a cyber café on nearly every corner in the center city, but its transportation system is paralyzed by rush hour gridlock that rivals Lagos. Urban transport is one of President Wade's first and most demanding problems. Dakar's buses are known for air pollution. The city's drivers are noted for bad manners and frayed tempers. Rubbish collection, too, tests the patience of those living in the capital.

Wielding great influence in this Muslim nation are the Sufi orders, or "brotherhoods," which characterize Senegal's Islamic culture. The orders—two major ones and several smaller—are hierarchically organized around several religious lineages. Disciples are organized into associations and owe both loyalty and labor to their *marabouts* (pronounced *mara boos*) or spiritual guides.

The most numerous of these is the *Tijaniyya* order, divided into several branches. Smaller but more cohesive is the *Mouride (Moo*–reed) order, which owns the largest peanut plantations and is generally considered the most influential. Each has its own spiritual leader, or *Caliph General* (pronounced *Hah*–leaf). The authority of this high office is transmitted through family dynasties that formed after the deaths of the orders' founders.

With a rich and vital cultural life, Senegal is famed for its writers, filmmakers and musicians. Senegal's founding president, the poet and philosopher Léopold Senghor, died in December 2001 at the age of 95. Along with Aimé Césaire of Martinique and Léon G. Damas of French Guyana, Senghor was one of the originators in the 1930s and '40s of the concept of *Négritude*, a notion celebrating the authenticity of African values and the contribution they make to what he called the "civilization of the universal."

Negritude spoke to young Africans, encouraging pride in African culture and protesting the notion that an African's value came exclusively through assimilation to Western culture. "Let us report present at the rebirth of the World," he wrote in his poem *Prayer to Masks*, "like the yeast which white flour needs. For who would teach rhythm to a dead world of machines and guns?"

In 1984 the poet and man of letters was elected to membership in the *Académie française*, France's most prestigious cultural society. Founded in 1635 by Cardinal Richelieu, the French Academy is limited in membership to 40 members, known as the 40 immortals. Senghor was its first black member.

At age 81, Ousmane Sembene is Senegal's most distinguished filmmaker and the most significant force in the history of African filmmaking. His ninth feature-length film, *Moolaade* (Protection), opened in the Fall of 2004. It deals with the very current subject of female genital mutilation (FGM). Starting with *Mandabi* in 1968, Sembene has worked not only with all-African crews, but in indigenous languages. *Moolaade* employs Bambara in an exploration of conflicting African traditions: the "purification" ceremony of genital mutilation and the right of the individual to seek protection (*moolaade*) from a neighbor. When an FGM opponent offers sanctuary to four young girls fleeing the ceremony, the rhythms of village life are violently disrupted.

**Economy:** Senegal's economy has been dependent upon the production of peanuts for the past three decades; production now exceeds well over one million metric tons a year, made possible by improved methods of cultivation and development of plantations to replace smaller farms. Though surpassed by other exports in terms revenue, groundnuts (as peanuts are referred to outside the U.S.) remain the most important source of employment in Senegal. Forty per cent of cultivated land is now used for peanut production. Overall the agricultural sector represents only 18% of Senegal's GDP, but employs 70% of the country's work force.

Under pressure from the IMF, the process of commercializing Senegal's peanut production is changing rapidly, leaving farmers confused, frustrated, and, in some cases, unpaid. The state-owned company responsible for purchasing and processing most of Senegal's groundnuts, was scheduled for privatization in 2003. Its subsidiary company, responsible for collection and transportation of the groundnuts, has already been dissolved. This has left farmers dependent on private transportation operators and costs determined by the market.

Structural reform in the peanut industry, troublesome as it may be, demonstrates Senegal's commitment to improved economic performance. Until 1994, Senegal's performance was mediocre, but since the devaluation of the CFA Franc in 1994 and adherence to vigorous structural reform programs, economic growth has averaged about 5.3% from 1996 to 2000. When he was elected in 2000, President Wade set out to create annual growth rates of 7% or more, but though there is improvement, economic growth has not been spectacular.

GDP grew in 2001 by 5.7%, but slowed considerably in 2002—down to 2.4% after poorly organized groundnut collection in the spring and sparse rains in the summer. It reached 6.5% in 2003 and is predicted to be around 6% in 2004, despite crop damage by locusts. The story for 2005 is likely to be the same—GDP growth of around 6.4%.

Rice is Senegal's favorite food. The Senegalese eat their way through some 900,000 tons of it every year, but only produce 200,000 tons locally. Rice imports cost a staggering $110 million—about 2.2% of the country's GDP. To reduce rice imports President Wade is trying to persuade his countrymen to eat maize, a grain with more protein than rice and that can be grown more widely. With government encouragement, maize production is rising—from 85,779 tons in 2002 to a remarkable 521,000 tons in 2003.

Since the CFA devaluation in 1994, fishing has become Senegal's principal revenue earner. Nutrient-rich cold waters off the Senegalese coast have made an extremely rich fishing area, but since the arrival of foreign trawlers, particularly from the EU, fish stocks have crashed. Several hundred trawlers from Spain, the Netherlands, Portugal and other EU nations have badly over fished the area. EU trawlers already have an annual catch of 100,000 tons, and biologists warn that fish stocks are at a critical point. Senegal's agreement with the EU expired in 2001, and faced with Morocco's refusal to renew its agreement, the EU pressured Senegal to increase fishing quotas by an unconscionable 61%.

After nine rounds of negotiations a new four-year agreement was signed in June 2002. Overall fishing quotas on species living near the seabed were decreased 20%, but remained the same for tuna vessels and ships fishing near the surface with long lines. Annual compensation paid Senegal increased to $17.9 million from $13.4 million, with some 18% of that set aside for conservation measures and strengthening the Senegalese fishing sector. The EU also agreed to a two-month biological rest to help fish stocks recuperate and a reduction on operational fishing zones for European vessels.

Overall, it should be noted, 80% of Senegal's fish catch is produced by artisanal (or semi-industrial) fishing. Given the demand, more and more fish are being caught for export and many farmers are turning to fishing as a means of escaping the uncertainty to living off the land. Artisanal fishing has seen spectacular growth, passing from 130,000 tons landed in 1980 to 350,000 in 2000. About 60% of the fish supplied to factories that process it for export comes from artisanal fishermen.

In the past few years Senegal's tourism sector has developed strongly and has become the second most important earner of foreign exchange after fish. Its touristic resources—miles of beautiful beaches, a rich culture, and important historical sites like St. Louis and the island of Gorée—remain relatively unexploited.

According to official figures, Senegal received just under 700,000 visitors in 2003. The government would like to reorient the tourist industry to higher-end traffic, which would entail banishing the backpacking tourist. The advantage: It estimates tourist receipts would double without doubling the number of visitors. In 2002 the government set a goal to 1.5 million tourists by 2010.

One bright economic note is the interest a number of independent oil companies have shown in Senegal's off-shore prospects. ROC (Australia) has invested heavily in three blocks known as the Casamance blocks. The concession covers over 8,000 sq. km. and lies north of two oil discoveries made by Houston-based Vanco oil company. Until commercially viable discoveries are made and begin pumping, however, Senegal remains a country without major natural resources and desperately poor.

Basic social statistics reveal the magnitude of the challenges facing President Wade. Per capita income is $550 and life expectancy at birth is 52.3 years. The rate of illiteracy for women is 70% and for men 52%. The fertility rate (births per woman) is five, but infant mortality is 79 per 1,000 births; 139 out of 1,000 children will die by the age of five. In 2000 the country slipped into the category of Least Developed Countries. It ranks 157 out of 177 on the UN's *Human Development Report* for 2004. The depth of poverty in Senegal (and its attendant human misery) is best expressed in a single figure: 57% of the population lives on less than two dollars a day.

The government's biggest economic concern is unemployment. In 2001, 48% of all Senegalese were without work. Every year an additional 100,000 young people leave school and enter the job market, but with a lackluster economy, they find no jobs. Many spend their time standing line for a visa at the Embassies of France, the United States or Italy.

President Wade has actively promoted democracy and economic liberalism in Africa. Both are key to future investment, essential to future economic growth and jobs. He has also actively encouraged diaspora Senegalese to invest in their homeland. Immigrant remittances annually amount to about 5% of GNP—more than the earnings from the fishing sector.

**The Future:** Given the expectations raised by his election, the burdens on President Wade are enormous. The economy is sluggish at best, and the critically important peanut industry is suffering. The even more important fishing industry is threatened by an exhaustion of its resources, and peace in Casamance seems fragile at best.

Legislative and presidential elections are scheduled for 2006 and 2007. Already the opposition has begun a process of coalition building. Much of the original "Sopi" coalition has pealed away. President Wade's critics accuse him of capriciousness, having reshuffled his government so often he's had more prime ministers—four so far—than Senegal has had presidents.

**Presidents Wade and Bush following their speeches on Gorée Island, July 2003.**

Photo courtesy U.S. State Department

# The Republic of Sierra Leone (pronounced See-*air*-uh Lee *own*)

**Panoramic View of Freetown**

**Area:** 72,326 sq. km. = 27,900 sq. mi. (slightly larger than West Virginia)

**Population:** 6,017,643 (July 2005 est.)

**Capital City:** Freetown (Pop. 530,000, estimated).

**Climate:** Equatorial, very warm and humid.

**Neighboring Countries:** Guinea (North and Northwest); Liberia (Southeast).

**Official Language:** English (regular use limited to literate minority).

**Other Principal Languages:** Mende (principal vernacular in the south), Temne (principal vernacular in the north), Krio (English-based Creole, a lingua franca and a first language for 10% of the population but understood by 95%.

**Ethnic groups:** 20 native African tribes 90% (Temne 30%, Mende 30%, other 30%), Creole 10% (descendants of freed Jamaican slaves who were settled in the Freetown area in the late-eighteenth century, refugees from Liberia's recent civil war), small numbers of Europeans, Lebanese, Pakistanis, and Indians.

**Principal Religions:** Muslim 60%, indigenous beliefs 30%, Christian 10%.

**Chief Commercial Products:** Diamonds, rutile, cocoa, coffee, and fish.

**GNI per capita:** $150 (2003)

**Currency:** Leone.

**Former Colonial Status:** British Colony (1808–1961)

**Independence Date:** April 19, 1961.

**Chief of State:** Ahmad Tejan Kabbah, President.

**National Flag:** Three equal horizontal stripes of green, white and blue.

Sierra Leone lies on the west coast of Africa that extends westward into the Atlantic above the equator. Its climate is almost identical with that of the Congo River basin to the southeast—hot, rainy and oppressively humid. The Freetown area along the seacoast receives 150 inches of rain each year, and the relative humidity seldom drops below 80%. The coastal belt, averaging sixty miles in width, is a region of dense mangrove swamps quite similar to the Florida Everglades.

Stretches of wooded hill country rise from the coastal belt to gently rolling plateaus in the North. Mountains tower to heights of 6,000 feet in the southeast area near the Moa River. Although there is a nominally dry season from November to April, heavy rains, especially in July, August and September, contribute to the dense, jungle growth characteristic of portions of Sierra Leone. This compact green vegetation contains the many species of the rain forest, but few of the hoofed animals of the African plains.

**History:** Coastal Sierra Leone was thinly populated by the Sherbro, Temne, and Limba peoples who had probably lived in

# Sierra Leone

the area for thousands of years by the time the Portuguese explorer, Pedro de Cintra, visited the coastal area in 1460. Impressed by the beauty of the mountains of the southeast, he named the territory Sierra Leone—"Lion Mountains." Already established by this time were Mande-speaking peoples who settled inland. Islam was introduced by Muslim traders and took root initially in the north, but later spread throughout the area.

Freetown, the capital, started out as a place of refuge for freed slaves resettled from British colonies like Nova Scotia and Jamaica. Much like Americo-Liberians, these resettled former slaves formed a culture separate from hinterland peoples. They were English-speaking and Christian, and this cultural identity was reinforced after Britain outlawed the slave trade in 1807 and took over the Freetown settlement as a naval base in 1808. British ships patrolling the Atlantic would capture slaving ships and return them to the Freetown base where the captives would be liberated. Between 1807 and 1864 more than 50,000 captives had been resettled. They were a heterogeneous lot, coming from all over western Africa.

With British encouragement they were turned into a more homogenous Christian community, known as Creoles (or Krios), by the efforts of Protestant missionaries and the black pastors of Freetown churches. Coastal Creoles had privileged access to European education in the Sierra Leone colony. Fourah Bay College was founded by the Church Missionary Society to train teachers and missionaries, and ultimately it became the most important educational institution in the country. Creoles prospered, entered the professions, and qualified as doctors and lawyers, becoming an educated elite.

British influence gradually extended inland from the coastline, and in 1895 a protectorate was proclaimed over the colony's hinterland. In the protectorate, the British preference for indirect rule prevailed. Local chiefs ruled under the direction of district commissioners. It was not a system that encouraged the transformation of tradition. In general, the protectorate lagged behind the colony in social and economic development.

World War II gave rise to much nationalist ferment, and following the war Britain began the process that would lead to independence. The privileged status of Sierra Leone's Creole elite was not entrenched. In the constitution of 1951, the notion of majority rule, which privileged hinterland peoples, prevailed. The first government elected under it was led by Milton Margai of the Sierra Leone People's Party (SLPP)—basically a protectorate party.

Following achievement of independence in 1961, the parliamentary government was controlled by the SLPP, led initially by Sir Milton and, after his death in 1964, by his brother, Sir Albert Margai. Elections held in 1967 were hotly contested by a rival party, the All People's Congress (APC), led by Siaka Stevens. Interior peoples supported the SLPP and the coastal Creoles favored the APC. A pre–election attempt of Margai to outlaw the APC failed. Early returns indicated that the APC had captured 32 seats in the parliament to 28 for the SLPP. Governor General Sir Henry Josiah Lightfoot Boston (a Creole) quickly gave the oath of office to Siaka Stevens, making him prime minister. The military arrested both Stevens and Boston ten minutes later.

A National Reformation Council, established by the officers, continued in power until April 1968, when privates and non-commissioned officers mutinied, imprisoned their officers, and restored parliamentary rule under Stevens and the APC. He ruled with increasing repression, using the army to subdue hinterland supporters of the SLPP.

In 1978 Stevens proposed a constitutional referendum to create a single-party state, and the regime generated a huge majority—97.1%—in its favor. Stevens was sworn in for a seven-year term under the new constitution and rejoiced in the voters' rejection of " . . . the worn-out, multiparty (system) . . . inherited from our colonial master, Britain."

Much of Sierra Leone's current civil strife began during Siaka Stevens' repressive single-party rule. The notorious Internal Security Unit, or groups of unemployed urban youth, fed with drugs and promises of employment, were used to terrorize and intimidate regime opponents. Corruption was institutionalized and Stevens and his cronies looted state resources. The economy declined; the tax based virtually disappeared, and what remained of the economy went underground. The state's ability to supply services collapsed. Rural Sierra Leone was increasingly isolated from the capital (the railroad linking Freetown to the hinterland was dismantled in the 1970s and no roads replaced it) and spiraled into abject poverty.

As his term of office was drawing to an end in 1985, the elderly Stevens designated Army Chief Maj. General Joseph Momah his successor. Momah sought to continue Stevens' single-party, authoritarian rule.

Faced with the economic chaos that was Stevens' legacy, President Momah turned to international lenders. Austerity measures insisted on by the IMF lowered the standard of living even more and raised

**Captain Valentine Strasser**

social tensions even higher. Subsidies of rice and fuel were gradually reduced while anger increased. Government corruption became pathological. When workers were forced to appear personally to pick up their pay in cash, it turned out that 75% of those listed as employees didn't exist.

A rebel insurgency led by Foday Sankoh, aided by Moamer al-Qadhafi and Charles Taylor's National Patriotic Front of Liberia, broke out in 1991. It found willing recruits in the communities of southeastern Sierra Leone that had suffered much from the corruption of the APC regime. Increasingly Momah had no control over corruption, government, or insurgency. His poor prosecution of the war against Sankoh's Revolutionary United Front (RUF) and failure to support his troops in that effort led junior officers, under Captain Valentine Strasser, to take power in April 1992.

Under Strasser, then 26 years old, the situation continued to disintegrate. Senior officers lost control over their troops and being a soldier became regarded as a license to murder and steal. His administration collapsed and an army colleague, Brigadier Julius Bio, replaced him on January 16, 1996.

Faced with economic and political chaos, Bio agreed to hold elections to restore civilian rule. As testimony to Sierra Leone's fragmented political culture, 13 parties competed and six managed to elect members to the House of Representatives. The largest number, 27, came from the SLPP, followed by 17 seats for the United National People's Party (UNPP).

The SLPP's Ahmad Tejan Kabbah and the UNPP's John Karefa-Smart topped the field of ten presidential contenders, and in the runoff election Kabbah was declared the victor with 59.5% of the vote. A former UN official, he slowly built confidence in his leadership to the extent that in late 1996 the RUF agreed to discontinue its re-

# Sierra Leone

bellion and surrender all arms. A promising beginning ended in May 1997 when the army revolted over unpaid wages, threatened cutbacks in their rice rations, and possible reductions in force. President Kabbah fled his capital, and an Armed Forces Revolutionary Council (AFRC) was installed to govern Sierra Leone. The country descended into anarchy.

Soldiers looted indiscriminately and within days were joined by fighters of the rebel front hungry for a share of the spoils. Their common experience was poverty, and they expressed their sense of injustice in robbery and mayhem.

ECOWAS foreign ministers met in Conakry in late June to see if they could negotiate a return to civilian rule, but diplomacy with the AFRC failed. The army and its allies seemed more interested in plunder than peace. The West African states decided to intervene militarily.

Warfare would be waged for nearly ten months, involving three major components. ECOWAS forces, army mutineers and their guerrilla rebel allies, and groups of traditional hunter societies called Kamajors, loyal to the deposed Kabbah. Reportedly armed and trained by private security companies guarding Sierra Leone's diamond mines, the Kamajors became a major element in the ensuing struggles.

In February 1998 ECOWAS forces (dominated by Nigerian troops) drove the military junta from Freetown. President Kabbah was triumphantly returned in March to his war-ravaged capital. Mutineers and rebels had stolen anything of value. Schools and Fourah Bay University were stripped; foreign embassies were sacked before the mutineers withdrew to the countryside where their depredations continued with murderous intensity. Opponents of the AFRC, local supporters of President Kabbah, and members of the Kamajor hunting groups were singled out for particularly venomous reprisals.

Kabbah's ECOWAS-supported government exercised only a tenuous control over the country. In early January 1999 the rebels launched a brutal attack on the capital itself. The cruelty one had come to associate with the rebels seemed to reach new heights. Random killing, mutilation, and rape were horrifically widespread. After nine days of intense fighting, the rebels, who had come close to capturing the city, withdrew. A fifth of all the capital's buildings were destroyed.

Under intense pressure from the international community an accord between government and rebels was signed in July 1999 in Lome, Togo. Its content could not give heart to humanitarians. Violence, fear, and intimidation received their reward. RUF leader Foday Sankoh was put in charge of Sierra Leone's diamond pro-

**President Ahmad Tejan Kabbah**

duction, and Major Johnny Koroma, head of the Armed Forces Revolutionary Council (AFRC) that overthrew President Kabbah, was named Chairman of the Commission for the Consolidation of Peace. For those who elaborated, directed, and implemented a brutal policy of rape, mayhem, murder, and maiming, amnesty would be granted.

Unfortunately, UN peacekeepers received little cooperation from RUF leaders. Few rebels turned in their arms, and peacekeepers were not permitted to enter areas controlled by the RUF. Rebel diamond production continued and was easily filtered out through The Gambia, Burkina Faso or Liberia.

In May 2000, when the Nigerian-led ECOWAS peacekeeping force announced its departure, the rebels attacked, held several hundred UN peacekeepers captive, and advanced on Freetown. Britain's Tony Blair, seeing the moral necessity of action, intervened militarily, saving the capital and Kabbah's government.

Three things changed the Sierra Leone situation. First, the British intervention effectively prevented the RUF from taking Freetown, and thus the country. Second, Foday Sankoh, the RUF leader, was captured and imprisoned in May 2000. Third, the international pressure on Charles Taylor, the Liberian president, to end his support of the rebels was consistently ratcheted upwards. The rebels signed a ceasefire in November 2000 and slowly began to disarm. By January 2002 45,000 combatants had handed over their weapons, and UN peacekeepers declared the war over.

President Kabbah's term of office expired in March 2001, but was prorogued by parliament. With stability restored, the long-postponed presidential elections were held in May 2002. Given an opportunity to choose their leader freely and safely, a remarkable 80% of registered voters turned out. There were nine candidates. Given the credit for bringing in the British and restoring peace by his fellow citizens, Ahmad Tejan Kabbah won a stunning 70.6% of the popular vote, eliminating the need for a run-off with his nearest rival. Alimany Paolo Bangura, the candidate of the RUF, was supported by only 1.7% of Sierra Leone's voters.

As of mid-2005, one can be guardedly optimistic about this Lazarus of states, returned from the dead. The United Nations Mission in Sierra Leone (UNAMSIL) has completed the demobilization of more than 70,000 combatants. The overall security situation appears to be generally stable, and UNAMSIL, which peaked in 2001 with a total of 17,500 military personnel, is gradually being phased out. In February 2005 the contingent had been reduced to 3,622, and it will likely drop to around 3,500 in July when the mission's mandate expires. Given the many problems that remain before achieving long-term stability, an extension of UNAMSIL's mandate is likely.

From 2001 to July 2004 the UN completed the repatriation of more than 179,000 Sierra Leonean refugees, largely from Liberia and Guinea; 92,000 more returned on their own. (Some 66,000 Liberian refugees, most of them quartered in eight camps in the southern and eastern parts of the country, are scheduled to be repatriated to a newly stabilizing Liberia between 2004 and 2006.)

The training and equipping of security forces continues, largely underwritten by the United Kingdom. By mid-2005 a total of 9,500 police personnel are expected to be available. Some 900 officers have already been trained in basic computer skills, 75 in fingerprinting techniques, and 100 in file management; an additional 121 officers have qualified as trainers. Three thousand of the new police recruits have been given special human rights training. Police barracks have been built in several provincial locations, and responsibility for domestic security is increasingly being handed over to the Sierra Leone police.

Similarly, strenuous efforts have been made to train and equip the armed forces, but serious problems remain. Hugely inflated, the army needs to be downsized, but this has caused resentment and resistance. While senior military officers acknowledge the primary role of the police in maintaining law and order throughout the country, there is widespread frustration in army ranks about not being assigned a more prominent role in state security. Perhaps most worrying is a continuing public mistrust about the troops' loyalty to the government.

Sierra Leone's Truth and Reconciliation Commission (TRC), appointed in May 2002, submitted its final report in October 2004. The main report weight in, quite literally, at 1,500 pages, with a 3,500-page annex, bearing the testimonies of over 8,000 who had been brutalized by the country's 11-year civil war. Only ten copies were distributed.

The commissioners coldly dissected the causes of the conflict and concluded that the country's political conflicts were all about power and the benefits it conferred. "Tragically," said the commissioners, "these characteristics persist today in Sierra Leone." Corruption, which had been one of elements initially prompting Foday Sankoh's rebellion, remained pervasive in their eyes, and if not curtailed, it would sap the country of its life force and provide grounds for further conflict.

The TRC also recommended a vast series of reparations, humanely seeking justice for every category of war victim: the wounded, the sexually exploited, the widows and orphans. For adult amputees and the victims of sexual violence, the commission recommended monthly pensions and free physical and mental health care for the rest of their lives. For child amputees, war wounded and victims of sexual violence, it recommended access to free education until senior secondary level. Given the expense involved, however, it is unlikely the government will ever be able to translate the report into working policy.

Even the prospect of symbolic compensation to war victims through the Special War Crimes Court for Sierra Leone seems limited. Established by the UN Security Council to try those who bore the greatest responsibility for human rights abuses during the civil war, the court has managed to produce only 13 indictments. Two of these, Foday Sankoh and his deputy Sam "Mosquito" Bockerie, have died, and two others—the military junta leader Johnny Koroma (in flight) and the former Liberian president, Charles Taylor, indicted as bearing the greatest responsibility for war crimes and crimes against humanity committed during the war, but living in comfortable exile in Nigeria—are beyond the court's authority.

So far nine militia leaders and commanders are in the court's custody. Among them is Sam Hinga Norman, once Sierra Leone's Minister of Internal Affairs and the former leader of the pro-government militia known as "Kamajors." Norman, who helped defeat the Revolutionary United Front (RUF) rebels, has withdrawn all cooperation with the court, a model of behavior since emulated by the other defendants. As a consequence, the court seemed to have reached a stalemate.

Despite statistical economic growth, the general populace has seen little improvement in its life circumstances. Sierra Leone ranks at the very bottom—number 177—on the UN's *Human Development Index* for 2004. Fifty-seven percent of its population lives in abject poverty, earning less than a dollar a day, three-quarters of those between the ages of 18 and 35 are unemployed, and life expectancy is a mere 34.5 years.

Already, however, the political class is looking towards the presidential election in 2007. President Kabbah's SLPP is deeply divided over the potential candidacy of Vice-President Solomon Berewa. He is disliked by many party stalwarts as an opportunist and newcomer, and whispered allegations abound that he has received kickbacks from the contracts granted from his office. They allegedly go directly to a fund that will finance his campaign in 2007. President Kabbah, who is 73 years old, has denied any plans to resign and ease the path for Mr. Berewa.

**Culture:** The population is made up of some 18 different ethnic groups, each exhibiting similar cultural features. These include governmental systems based on chieftaincies and patrilineal descent, secret societies, and subsistence agriculture. The Mende, found in the east and south, and the Temne, in the north, are the two largest groups and constitute about 60% of the population. Creoles, descendants of freed blacks who arrived in the 19th century, live mainly in Freetown and the western region. There has been much intermarriage between groups and eleven years of civil war displaced massive numbers of people from their traditional home areas.

Paramount chiefs are the traditional rulers of Sierra Leone, especially in the provincial areas. There are 149 paramount chieftaincies in the country and 63 of the incumbents died during the 11-year civil war. Elections to replace them were held in early 2003. In thirteen of the districts there were strong protests and threats of violence where the elections had been politicized. In each, the SLPP was accused of selecting candidates who were party supporters rather than representatives of the traditional ruling houses.

**Economy:** Since the end of conflict in January 2002, the Kabbah government has struggled to regain control over the country's territory and economy, based on agriculture and mining. The bulk of the population is engaged in subsistence farming, with plantation agriculture significant only in certain parts of the country.

The entire sector was seriously disrupted during the civil war. Overall, agriculture traditionally contributed 50% of GDP and employed between 65% and 80% of the population. The most important commercial crops are cocoa and coffee, and the government's goal is to revitalize these and assure food security by boosting domestic production of rice. (Sierra Leone exported rice until the 1980s, but since then has been an importer of the grain.)

Mining has long been the major bulwark of Sierra Leone's economy, with ru-

**Hills and streets of Freetown**          Photo courtesy U.S. Embassy, Freetown

# Sierra Leone

tile (an important source of titanium) and diamonds the principal source of government revenues. Sierra Rutile Ltd. (SRL), the world's largest producer of natural rutile until it was closed for security reasons in 1995, was the country's largest taxpayer, private sector employer and foreign export earner. With U.S. and EU financial backing, SRL plans to restart production in 2005.

Sierra Leone's alluvial diamond fields lie in areas once controlled by the rebels. The bulk of RUF diamond production was smuggled to Liberia where it was converted to cash with which to buy arms. Arms were sourced in Ukraine or other eastern European states and supplied to the rebels through Liberian or Burkinabé connivance, with Liberia's president reportedly profiting handsomely as middleman in these operations. The international community branded these war diamonds as "blood" or "conflict" diamonds, and ultimately banned their sale.

Under a sysem of the international controls aimed at ending the illicit trade in "conflict diamonds," the value of Sierra Leone's official diamond exports has increased signficantly, from $76 million in 2003 to $127 in 2004. The total value of the country's annual diamond production, however, is estimated at between $250 million and $300 million. The diffrence is smuggled out of the country to finance a variety of (usually) illicit activities.

Sierra Leone's diamond trade, legal and illegal, is controlled by the large Lebanese trading community which dominates the country's commercial sector. In 2004, one Lebanese company, owned by a Sierra Leonean-born Lebanese trader, exported almost half of all officially certified diamonds.

Because of capitalist investment required, deep mining of diamonds buried in kimberlite pipes is insignificant compared to alluvial (surface) mining. Only one industrial mining company has undertaken the task, and kimberlite diamonds represented only 11% of official exports in 2004. Still, the easily accessible alluvial deposits had to come from some-

where, and it is likely deep mining operations will be undertaken once peace and stability are assured.

The country's external debt is huge—$1.6 billion in 2003—but the IMF and World Bank are providing debt relief under the Heavily Indebted Poor Country (HIPC) initiative. At least 60% of the government's budget is funded by grants and loans from international financial institutions. Few foreign companies have ventured back into the country, with the notable exception of Chinese concerns. Tolerant of high risk, and aggressive in seeking economic advantage due the first in, Chinese businesses can been seen in virtually every sector of Sierra Leone's economy. One particular point of attraction: tantalizing evidence of offshore oil deposits.

**The Future:** There is more to be optimistic about in Sierra Leone than there has been for years. Corruption and popular disillusionment with the pace of progress will temper that optimism and challenge the government.

**Alluvial diamond mining**

Photo courtesy U.S. Embassy, Freetown

# The Republic of Togo

Lying almost in the center of the Gold and Ivory coasts, Togo is a long, narrow country stretching 360 miles from the blue Atlantic into the interior. This small nation is only thirty–one miles wide at the coast and 100 miles in width at its broadest point. As is common to this region of Africa, the climate of Togo is predominantly hot and humid on the coast with a drier and slightly cooler region in the North. Picturesque Lake Togo, with quiet, fresh water, is located in the central coast region, a center of modern recreational facilities. The central section is traversed by the Togo Mountains and is succeeded in the North by a level territory of farms.

**History:** Togo's archeological record remains to be explored in detail. Pre-colonial history is based on oral traditions, passed on verbally through many generations. These indicate that in the 15th to 17th centuries Ewe clans from Nigeria and the Ane from Ghana and Ivory Coast settled in the region which was already occupied by Kwa and Voltaic peoples.

Togo is Coastal West Africa's only German colony, and German missionaries arrived as early as 1847, followed soon by German traders. With such interests to protect, the German government sent out agents to induce coastal chiefs to accept a German protectorate, which was recognized by European states in 1885.

At the outbreak of World War I, British and French troops invaded Togo from their respective neighboring colonies, Gold Coast and Dahomey. German forces surrendered unconditionally, and Britain and France occupied separate areas of the territory. Germany renounced its colonial territories in the Treaty of Versailles, which concluded the war. In 1922 the newly created League of Nations charged France and Britain with the administration of their respective spheres of occupation as part of the League Mandate system.

In 1956 a UN-sponsored plebiscite allowed the people of British Togoland to vote on joining the Gold Coast, which was rapidly approaching independence. The two were united and became independent as Ghana in 1957. French Togoland became an autonomous republic within the French Union in 1956 and achieved its independence in 1960.

Pre–independence elections installed Nicholas Grunitzky of the Togo Progressive Party (TPP) as premier. Advocating independence, the Togo Unity Party (TUP), led by Sylvanus Olympio, defeated Grunitsky's TPP in 1958 elections, and Olympio went on to become Togo's first president when the country became independent in 1960. Olympio was not a native of Togo, having been brought to Africa from Brazil by his father when he

**A balanced conversation in Lomé**

AP/Wide World Photo

**Area:** 56,950 sq. km. = 21,988 sq. mi. (Half of Mississippi, vertically).

**Population:** 5,681,519 (July 2005 est.)

**Capital City:** Lomé (pop. 900,000 est. in 2000.)

**Climate:** Warm, humid and tropical.

**Neighboring Countries:** Ghana (West); Burkina Faso (Upper Volta, North); Benin (East).

**Official Language:** French (the language of commerce).

**Other Principal Languages:** Ewe and Mina (the two major African languages in the south), Kabye (sometimes spelled Kabiye) and Dagomba (the two major African languages in the north), and Gourmanché, also spoken in the north.

**Ethnic groups:** Over thirty, among the most prominent the Ewe, Mina, and Kabre. 99%; European and Syrian-Lebanese less than 1%.

**Principal Religions:** Indigenous beliefs 70%, Christian 20%, and Muslim 10%.

**Chief Commercial Products:** Phosphates, cotton, coffee, and cocoa.

**GNI per capita:** $310 (2003)

**Currency:** CFA Franc (no longer tied to the French franc).

**Former Colonial Status:** German Colony (1885–1916), French Colony (1916–1960).

**Independence Date:** April 27, 1960.

**Chief of State:** President Faure Essozima Gnassingbé, President, since disputed elections of 24 April 2005.

**National Flag:** Green, yellow, green, yellow equal horizontal stripes. A red square at the staff top half with a superimposed white five–pointed star.

# Togo

was a small child. He spoke several foreign languages as well as Ewe, the predominant language of southern Togo.

Olympio was assassinated in early 1963 outside the U.S. Embassy in Lomé where he had been seeking refuge. Grunitzky returned later and was named prime minister by Sgt. Gnassingbé Eyadéma, who was in the group that killed Olympio. A new constitution was adopted, and four political parties participated in elections held in 1963, which were officially won by Grunitzky's Togo Progressive Party; he became president.

Dissatisfied with a general lack of progress, which he attributed to the bickering of politicians, Gnassingbé Eyadéma, now a Lt. Colonel, seized power in 1967 and abolished all parties. He later formed the Rassemblement du Peuple Togolaise (RPT) and ran in 1972 as the sole candidate for president, receiving about 90% of the vote in a "yes" or "no" contest.

President Eyadéma and the military governed Togo for more than thirty years. For more than three decades assassination, torture, and routine abuse of civil liberties and human rights have characterized the regime. Gilchrist Olympio, the son of assassinated president Sylvanus Olympio, was almost killed in a 1993 assassination attempt after he emerged as a potential rival to President Eyadéma. He retreated to exile in France, fearing he would not survive in Togo. The 1993 election was a sham—as many dead people as live ones voted.

The mid-summer presidential elections of 1998 were prepared with care. A new constitutional court created to hear any election disputes was filled with Eyadéma supporters. A new communications authority was established to oversee the media. It too was controlled by Eyadéma appointees. A new electoral code was passed, giving responsibility for organizing and supervising the elections to the ministry of the interior. The preparation of new electoral rolls was advanced, catching the opposition unawares. Of course, they were uninvolved in the Code's preparation. Finally, in March 1998 the elections, originally scheduled for August, were advanced to June. Surprise, the president-general knew, is a tactical-element.

To the surprise of none, the election proved that dinosaurs live, sustained by a DNA of fraud. Eyadéma was re-elected by a modest 52.13% of the votes cast, just enough to avoid a runoff election. Immediately prior to announcement of election results, the head of the electoral commission resigned, saying she had received telephone calls threatening her life. Four other members of the commission also resigned. Eyadéma's principal rival, Gilchrist Olympio, was allotted a generous

34.1% of the ballots by the interior ministry, which ran the election.

Opposition protests were met with tear gas grenades. Olympio said his own calculations showed he won 59% of the vote and vowed to use all peaceful, legitimate, and constitutional means to have the results annulled, all of which, of course, were of no avail. The president-general, who had already served 31 years as head of state, became Africa's longest serving leader and second only to Fidel Castro in longevity of rule.

The spring 1999 legislative elections did not rise much above the level of electoral farce either. The opposition boycotted, and candidates of Eyadéma's RPT won 79

**President Eyadéma**

of 81 parliamentary seats. The interior ministry claimed that over 66% of registered voters participated; the opposition claimed the figure didn't pass 10%. The European Union, which had suspended economic cooperation with Togo after 1993's electoral farce, called for an "internal dialogue" between the opposition and the regime, but the positions of each seemed so entrenched that dialogue appeared to be only a distant possibility.

In May 1999 Amnesty International described Togo as a "state of terror," characterized by executions and extra-judicial executions perpetrated by authorities throughout the political crisis from 1993 to 1998. Hundreds had been killed in the days leading up to the 1998 elections alone. Evidence gathered from Togolese and Beninois fishermen indicated that manacled opponents had been thrown into the sea from Togolese air force planes.

The Togolese army, on which President-General Eyadéma's repression relies, consists of 9,450 men, more than one for every 560 citizens. The army, like the other forces of order, is largely recruited in the

North, President-General Eyadéma's region of origin. Four new brigadier-generals were appointed in early 1998, and all of them were, like Eyadéma, northerners. Of the nine Togolese generals, five, including the president, are of the same ethnicity (Kabye). The elite Presidential Guard is led by President Eyadéma's son, Colonel Ernest Gnassingbé, while another son, Commandant Rock Gnassingbé, leads a motorized division.

President-General Eyadéma's brutal repression and cavalier attitudes toward democratic processes left Togo in a permanent political and economic crisis. Only in 1999 were there signs that the president-general was willing to compromise with his opponents, and then, only after years of economic sanctions had taken their toll. "National reconciliation" discussions took place in July under the authority of four facilitators appointed by the EU and La Francophonie, the French equivalent of the Commonwealth. On a visit to West Africa President Jacques Chirac of France forcefully announced that only national reconciliation would enable the EU to resume its aid.

After conversations with the president-general, Chirac himself announced that Eyadéma would step down at the end of his presidential term in 2003, respecting the constitution by not presenting himself for a third term. The president-general announced he would dissolve the contested National Assembly and call new parliamentary elections in March 2000. He also agreed to the creation of an independent electoral commission. All parties present affixed their signatures to what was called the Lomé Framework Agreement.

Opposition intransigence, however, scuttled much of the facilitators' effort. Gilchrist Olympio, fearing for his life, refused to participate in the Lomé reconciliation talks for security reasons. Internal opponents of the regime found numerous details to quibble and complain over. In exasperation, the four "facilitators" sent their recommendations directly to the National Assembly, which approved a new election code in March. When the legislature amended the proposed code, the opposition once again objected and withdrew from reconciliation discussions. The elections of 2000 never took place.

On the eve of President Chirac's visit, the Benin League for the Defense of Human Rights confirmed Amnesty International's charges that hundreds had been summarily executed and their bodies dumped into the sea in the run-up to 1998's presidential elections. The League reported finding more than 100 bodies in coastal villages. Some were headless, handcuffed, or riddled with bullets. They were, said the League, "pushed from low-

# Togo

flying planes and helicopters coming during the night from Togo."

From the Togolese government there was much bluster and bravado about legal action against Amnesty International. Later it emerged that the government had hired witnesses to perjure themselves at hearings and journalists to write articles questioning the facts and motivations of those who presented them.

By June 2000 a joint commission between the United Nations and the OAU was set up to investigate the allegations of state-sponsored massacres, no doubt much to the embarrassment of President Eyadéma who had begun serving a term as OAU chairman. Shortly before the commission of inquiry was to release its report in February 2001, the government's disinformation machine was cranked up. Amnesty International was accused of accepting a bribe of $500,000 from Gilchrist Olympio to prepare its "highly negative human rights reports" about Togo.

When the inquiry team released the results of its investigation, it made clear its belief that individuals linked to Togolese security forces, working in cooperation with the Togolese police and allied militias, had indeed carried out summary executions of the government's political opponents. It was not the first embarrassment with which the president-general had had to deal.

The Fowler Report to the UN Security Council of March 2000 had identified Eyadéma as one of those facilitating the continuing arms supply of Jonas Savimbi's UNITA forces in Angola. A follow-up experts report issued in December accused Togolese authorities of accepting "blood diamonds'" from Savimbi in exchange for illegal arms and fuel shipments.

European mediators left Togo at the end of January 2001, admitting that their efforts had "ended in failure." Obstructions and delays have continued to undermine new elections. The National Independent Electoral Commission (CENI), composed of ten members each from the government and opposition groups, set parliamentary elections for October 14, 2001. But in early August the CENI announced yet another postponement, to March 2002.

As the March 2002 elections approached, President-General Eyadéma's government returned to its traditional suppression of civil liberties. Freedom of expression in all its forms was curtailed. Yaovi Agboyibo, the former head of Togo's Bar Association, was jailed in August 2001 for having accused the Prime Minister Agbéyomé Kodjo of "complicity with criminals" while heading the Lomé Port Authority. Two call-in radio talk shows, which gave citizens an opportu-

**President Faure Gnassingbé**

nity to voice their opinions, were suspended for broadcasting "defamatory" programs.

In February, the government rushed a series of self-serving amendments to the elections code to the legislature, which, having no opposition members, passed them unanimously. Under the changes, presidential candidates are required to have lived in Togo continuously for twelve months immediately preceding an election. This would of course eliminate Gilchrist Olympio, living in neighboring Ghana for his own safety. Under new provisions, the Independent National Electoral Commission's membership is cut in half, from twenty to ten members. Street demonstrations against the new code ensued, undissuaded by contingents of anti-riot police.

The March elections were once again postponed, this time to October. To prepare the groundwork for these, President-General Eyadéma unilaterally declared the National Electoral Commission dysfunctional and appointed a new panel of seven judges.

Togolese voters went to the polls in late October 2002, but there was little choice. Most opposition parties boycotted the election (and here the story gets drearily repetitive), calling it an "electoral farce." Unsurprisingly, President Eyadéma's Rally of the Togolese People (RPT) won 72 of 81 seats. In December the RPT used its majority to amend Togo's constitution, allowing President-General Eyadéma to seek, once again, re-election.

That legal nicety dispatched, the engine of state proceeded along its usual paths to insure an Eyadema victory. Opposition figures were intimidated, arrested and tortured. Opposition marches and meetings were forbidden, and any expression of critical opinion was punished, all un-

der the cover of law. With recent modifications, the Togolese press code allows journalists to be sent to jail for one to five years for defaming the President of the Republic; radio or newspaper publications can be suspended for one to three months, and the Minister of the Interior can seize a newspaper by simple decree for "publication of news contrary to reality."

As presidential elections approached, the opposition, always prone to creating coalitions of unity, marched in disarray. Gilchrist Olympio's *Union des Forces du Changement* (UFC), Togo's main opposition party, withdrew from the umbrella group known as the *Coalition des Forces Démocratiques* (CFD) to nominate Olympio as their candidate for the presidency, only to have his candidacy banned for technical irregularities in his nomination papers. Unable to agree on a single nominee, the eight remaining CFD parties decided to present individual candidates.

The governing Togolese People's Rally (RPT) did the obvious and nominated President-General Eyadéma as its candidate, while the UFC nominated its deputy leader, the 75-year old Emmanuel Bob-Akitani, a retired mining engineer who essentially ran as a proxy for Gilchrist Olympio. Four other opposition candidates managed to weave their way through the intricacies of the electoral code and find a place on the June 2003 ballot.

When the less-than-surprising final results were announced, President-General Eyadéma won 57.22 percent of the votes cast. The UFC's Emmanuel Bob-Akitani came second with 34.14 percent, while the remaining votes were shared by the four other opposition candidates. Togo's on-going political crisis and economic stagnation appeared likely to extend for another five years, but providence intervened and President-General Eyadéma died in early February 2005; thirty-eight years of dictatorial rule were ended.

The army quickly closed the borders, keeping the President's constitutional successor, the speaker of the Assembly, out of the country and installing a presidential son, Faure Essozima Gnassingbé, as president. The National Assembly, filled with ruling-party placemen, gave political cover by amending the constitution to permit the succession. Togo's streets filled with protesters and the international community waxed indignant—as only it can when dealing with a small and insignificant country. The AU roused itself from somnolence to denounce the action and ECOWAS imposed sanctions; Faure Gnassingbé resigned, promising elections in 60 days.

# Togo

The opposition actually managed some semblance of unity, nominating the UFC's elderly Emmanuel Akitani Bob, who everyone understood to be the stand-in for Gilchrist Olympio. With its skills at electroral fraud honed in past elections, the Togolese People's Rally (RPT) generated a victory for its nominee: 60.15% of the vote to Faure Gnassingbé, with 38.25% for the opposition. Mass protests ensued; in the capital gangs of opposition supporters erected burning barricades and pelted vehicles, but the army stepped in, bloodily, and crushed the insurrection. Thousands—at least 30,000—fled to Ghana or Benin.

West African diplomats and leaders desperately sought to cobble together an agreement between contending forces to form a government of national unity well before the next legislative elections, scheduled for late 2005.

**Culture:** The people of the populous southern coast area are better educated and economically better off than those of the sparsely settled North. The Ewe people have dominated the cultural life in Togo and extend beyond its borders well into Ghana to the west. There are few communities that lack educational facilities within the Ewe country. Although a few of this group continue the animist customs of their past, most are Christians, widely employed and leading modern, urban lives. In spite of this, the literacy rate of Togo ranges from an estimated 74% for men to 45% for women.

The Koutammakou landscape in northeastern Togo, which extends into neighboring Benin, was made a UNESCO World Heritage site in 2004. Home to the Batammariba people, the landscape is characterized by distinctive architecture: many two-story tower-houses and granaries that are almost spherical above a cylindrical base. The World Heritage designation called Koutammakou "an outstanding example of a system of traditional setlement that is still living and dynamic."

**Economy:** The Togolese economy is mainly dependent on subsistence agriculture, which accounts for 41% of the GDP and 75% of jobs. Combined exports of commercial crops like cotton, cocoa, and coffee, account for nearly 40% of total export earnings.

Cotton is Togo's most important commercial crop. More than 230,000 Togolese earn their living from cotton, but their livelihoods are always subject to fluctuating weather and world prices.

The mining sector accounts for more than one-third of export earnings; phosphate mining is the most significant element of the sector, contributing 26% to 28% of export earnings—vying with cotton for primacy of place. Togo is the world's fifth largest exporter of calcium phosphate and possesses large reserves, estimated at over 150 million tons of high-grade ore.

Togo generates only 30 per cent of its own electricity needs. For the rest it depends on electricity supplied by Ghana's Akosombo Dam. In 1998 waterlevels at the dam fell precipitously, and electricity rationing had to be introduced. To rectify its power insufficiencies, Togo is participating in the West African Pipeline Project to distribute Nigerian natural gas to Benin, Togo, and Ghana for the generation of electricity. The pipe, measuring 18 inches in diameter with a daily capacity of 400 million cubic feet, will stretch some 382 miles along the Gulf of Guinea coast, running mostly underwater. Deliveries are not expected to begin before the end of 2006.

Togo continues to suffer economic malaise, largely caused by its continuing political crisis. Dependent on foreign aid for economic development, Togo has been largely cut off from international investment since death and violence marred its transition to democracy in 1991. The absence of aid and investment explains Togo's low growth rates and the failure of the Eyadéma regime to develop the economy. Over the past twenty years per capita income shrank by 50%. As the economy shrank, an informal—and increasingly criminalized—economy developed. Illegal weapons and drugs, money laundering, human trafficking, and smuggling of all types came to dominant the country's trade. Togo is now considered one of the world's drug trafficking hubs.

One bright note for the economy: Togo is about to become an oil producer. Hunt Oil Company, which owns a huge concession covering all of Togo's offshore, has confirmed off-shore reserves with two drillings. A joint venture oil production agreement was signed in October 2002 between the government, Hunt Oil, and Malaysia's Petronas Carigali. Many believe the oil project hardened the ambition of President-General Eyadéma to continue in office and keep the office in the family.

Lomé has the deepest water of West Africa's ports and has picked up business with shippers frustrated by delays at container ports in Abidjan and Lagos. As a consequence, a new $100 million container handling facility is planned. The facility would be capable of unloading 200 to 250 containers an hour, much faster than existing facilities at the region's other ports. The port has already benefited from the troubles in neighboring Côte d'Ivoire that closed the port of Abidjan and forced shippers in Burkina Faso and Mali to use alternatives.

**The Future:** Tense, unstable, and uncertain. Faure Gnassingbé, politically inexperienced, is dependent on both the army and the RPT, but both institutions are themselves dependent on the young president's ability to convince the international community and his fellow citizens of his sincerity to move Togo forward.

# CENTRAL WEST AFRICA

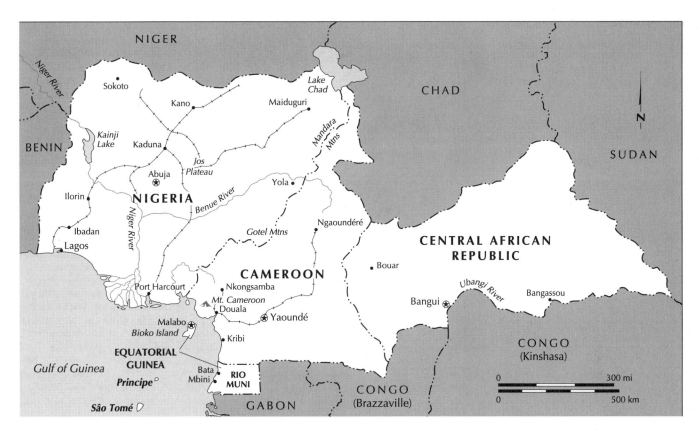

# The Republic of Cameroon

**Area:** 475,400 sq. km = 183,552 sq. mi. (Size of California and 1/4 of Oregon).

**Population:** 16,380,005 (July 2005 est.)

**Capital City:** Yaoundé (pop. 900,000, estimated; pronounced Yah-oon-*deh*).

**Climate:** Hot and humid in the South, progressively becoming drier to the inland north; arid in the Lake Chad area.

**Neighboring Countries:** Nigeria (Northwest); Chad (Northeast); Central African Republic (East); Congo, Gabon, Equatorial Guinea (South).

**Official Languages:** French (East Cameroon) and English (West Cameroon).

**Other Principal Languages:** There 24 major African language groups, involving more than 275 separate languages. Prominent are Akoose, Bafia, Bafut, Bakoko, Bakundu, Bamileke, Bamun, Basaa, Beti, Bulu, Duala, Eton, Fang, Fe'fe', Fufulde, Gbaya, Kanuri, Kenyang, Kom, Lamnso', Limbum, Mafa, Makaa, Masana, Mbo, Medumba, Mungaka, Musugu, Ngiemboon, Ngembe, Tupuri, Yemba. Cameroon Pidgin, an English-based Creole language is spoken primarily in the Southwest and Northern provinces and has become a widespread lingua franca in Cameroon, spoken as a second language by more than half the population.

**Ethnic groups:** Cameroon Highlanders (Bamilike, Bamoun) 31%, Equatorial Bantu (Beti) 19%, Kirdi 11%, Fulani 10%, Northwestern Bantu 8%, Eastern Nigritic 7%, other African 13%, non-African less than 1%.

**Principal Religions:** Christianity (about 53%), traditional beliefs (about 25%), Islam (about 22%).

**Chief Commercial Products:** Crude oil and petroleum products, lumber, cocoa beans, aluminum, coffee, and cotton.

**GNI per capita:** $640 (2003)

**Currency:** CFA Franc

**Former Colonial Status:** German Colony (1884–1916), British Colony in West Cameroon (1916–1961); French Colony is East Cameroon (1916–1960).

**Independence Date:** January 1, 1960 (East Cameroon); October 1, 1961 (West Cameroon independence and federation with East Cameroon).

**Chief of State:** Paul Biya, President (since 1982).

**National Flag:** Three vertical stripes of green, red and yellow with a yellow star in the red stripe.

This land of contrasts, containing almost every species of flora and fauna of tropical Africa and numerous varieties of wild game, stretches north from the Atlantic in a "hinge" position between West and Central Africa. From the Polynesian—like beaches, washed by the waters of the Bight of Biafra, there rise towering mountains which proceed directly north into West Cameroon. Mount Cameroon, the tallest peak in western Africa, towering almost 14,000 feet high, is an active volcano located close to the seacoast. The southern part of Cameroon, extending eastward in a horizontal line, is characterized by a low coastal basin with equatorial forests. In the more north–central part of the country there is a series of grassy plateaus whose heights reach 4,500 feet, but in the extreme northern Lake Chad region, the dry climate supports only seasonal grazing and nomadic herding, culminating in a marshland.

**History:** Archeological evidence suggests that Cameroon has been occupied for at least 50,000 years. Originally populated by pygmies, who are now found only in small numbers along the southern border, Cameroon was successively invaded by other groups. There is evidence of early state-building societies, the most important of which is Sao, centered in the Lake Chad area. In 1472, a Portuguese explorer, Fernão do Poo (Fernando Po in Spanish) arrived on the coast of what is now Cameroon.

Once part of the German colonial empire, Kamerun, as it was then called, was stripped from Germany by the Treaty of

# Cameroon

Versailles ending World War I. The former colony was made a mandate of the League of Nations in 1922, and administrative responsibilities for the mandate were shared by Britain and France. Modern Cameroon results from the merger of the French and a portion of the English areas. France granted independence to East Cameroon on January 1, 1960; the British relinquished West Cameroon on October 1, 1961, and there was a reunification of the two Cameroons.

Under the leadership of Ahmadou Ahidjo and his *Union nationale camerounaise* (UNC) a federal constitution, which enshrined a single-party system, was adopted. President Ahmadou Ahidjo (from East Cameroon) and Vice President John Foncha (from West Cameroon) received 97.5% of the vote in 1970 elections. Constitutional reforms in 1972 eliminated the state government of the two regions, but guaranteed continuation of the French language in the East and English in the West.

Legislative elections were held in 1978, and presidential elections in 1980 confirmed the dominance of President Ahidjo and the UNC. He was elected to a fifth five-year term, and all candidates for parliament were from the UNC. During his long rule, power was centralized in the capital, and in Ahidjo's hands. The regime was authoritarian and repressive and justified its suppression of civil and human rights by a need to contain ethnic division.

President Ahidjo suddenly resigned on November 6, 1982, handing over power to his prime minister, Paul Biya, who completed Ahidjo's term of office. The former president was said to be exhausted, but he retained his leadership of the UNC, the country's sole political party. Two centers of power, party and state, could not co-exist for long. Biya soon ousted Ahidjo from party leadership and sent him into exile. In January 1984 elections, President Biya, a Christian from the south, was elected in his own right to a five-year term of office by a margin of 99.98%. With this mandate, Biya set about consolidating his own power.

To eliminate potential competition the constitution was amended to remove the office of prime minister. To emphasize the unitary nature of the state, most of whose powers he held personally, Biya had the country's name changed from the "United Republic of Cameroon" to simply the "Republic of Cameroon."

In early April 1984, Biya's Republican Guard mutinied. Fierce fighting erupted in Yaoundé—members of the Republican Guard, composed mostly of Islamic northerners, waged a pitched battle with regular army units. After the rebellion was snuffed out, Biya announced that it had

**President Paul Biya**

been on behalf of the exiled Ahidjo. The official number of deaths was "about 70," but the actual number was probably close to 1,500. Within weeks, 35 were tried and summarily executed. Ahidjo was tried in absentia and condemned to death for complicity in the plot.

A year later, to demonstrate his "New Deal" policies, President Biya renamed the country's sole legal party the Cameroon People's Democratic Movement (RDPC). To add democratic content to the newly renamed party, 324 candidates were approved to contest 180 seats in the legislative elections of April 1988. Given a choice, voters sent a number of aging political lions into retirement. The result was a National Assembly with younger members. The president was reelected with a 98.75% majority. Having received the mandate he sought, Biya announced wide–ranging programs to deal with Cameroon's economic crisis.

Structural adjustments and budget cuts were needed. Biya agreed to downsize the bureaucracy and cut government expenditures. Belt-tightening hurt and resentments rose. To accommodate demands for greater democracy following political changes in Eastern Europe, Biya approved a multi–party system in 1990.

Opposition parties proliferated. Some 48 contested the legislative elections in March 1992, but fractured, the opposition stood little change against the RDCP. The ruling party won 88 of 180 seats in the National Assembly. The principal opposition party was the National Union for Democracy and Progress (UNDP), which elected 68 members to parliament. Sixteen opposition parties boycotted the election, including that of popular English–speaker John Fru Ndi—the Social Democratic Front.

The presidential election was advanced from the spring of 1993 to October 1992 to catch the divided opposition unprepared, and its conduct was marred by massive fraud, irregularities, and unfairness. The state–owned television, for example, gave

two-and-a-half hours of time to Biya, but only 16 minutes to the opposition.

The same pattern prevailed in the 1997 legislative elections, with the RDCP increasing its legislative majority to 109 of 180 seats. John Fru Ndi's Social Democratic Front captured 43 seats to become the principal opposition party. As usual, widespread intimidation and fraud were reported.

October 1997 Presidential elections were virtually meaningless. President Biya refused to allow an independent electoral commission to organize them, and the main opposition parties refused participation. Most citizens treated it as a non-event, but the government reported that 60% of registered voters participated and gave 80% of their votes to Biya.

Political power in Cameroon is concentrated in the office of president. The president appoints the cabinet, which serves at his pleasure. He names judges, generals and governors, district administrators and the heads of state corporations. Parliament, dominated by President Biya's Cameroon People's Democratic Movement (RDPC), consistently defers to the legislative program submitted by the government.

Unsurprisingly, Biya's control has been used to increase presidential powers. Constitutional amendments in 1996, for example, increased the presidential term to seven years. In general, presidential power is maintained through active repression of the political opposition, especially in election years.

The government closely controls the electoral process, which is administered through the Ministry of Territorial Administration. Members of oppositional ethnic groups and those living in areas dominated by the opposition are effectively prevented from registering to vote. The government operates almost all broadcast media (a small private Catholic station rebroadcasts programs from Vatican Radio), and coverage of opposition activity is underwhelming. Print media, of small circulation and limited to urban distribution, are tightly circumscribed by criminal libel laws.

Tensions continue in the Anglophone areas of Cameroon, which feel marginalized by Cameroon's Francophone majority. Separatist demonstrations in the western regions are regular occurrences. So is their repression by state security forces. Northern resentments, going back to the events of 1984, persist. Among many there is a sense of being discriminated against and excluded from a fair share of national riches.

Legislative elections were held in June 2002, and in advance President Biya effected a major revitalization of the RDPC.

Banning tribal chiefs from standing for party posts, Biya also urged party activists not to be swayed by candidates willing to buy themselves into power. In a March 2002 party voting, some seventy per cent of grassroots RDPC leaders were replaced. Party barons lost to young men and women, suggesting the party was reinvigorating itself with a bit of new blood.

The June elections resulted in a crushing victory for the RDPC, which took 149 of the 180 seats. John Fru Ndi's Social Democratic Front (SDF), driven by internal conflicts, won only 22, but remained the principal opposition party. The loss, in percentage terms, was even greater for the Union nationale pour la Démocratie et le Progrès (UNDP), which went from four seats to one.

The RDPC victory, worthy of a single-party state, may have been achieved by means typically associated with those regimes. A Roman Catholic NGO monitoring the election reported numerous irregularities, including phony polling places, and Douala's Cardinal, Christian Tumi, called them "obviously and intentionally" mismanaged.

In assembling his cabinet, President Biya seemed to have an eye on presidential elections in 2004, enlarging it to nearly 50 to include every relevant region and ethnicity. In this cabinet of national union, even the UNDP, which had been reduced to a single parliamentary seat, was given two cabinet portfolios.

In the delicate ethnic and regional balancing necessary in the Cameroonian government, prime ministers are traditionally English-speakers, and Biya reappointed his Anglophone premier, Mafany Musonge, who holds an engineering degree from Stanford University. (Cameroon's third most important office, the speakership of the National Assembly, is traditionally held by a northerner.)

Premier Musonge acted as Biya's campaign manager in the October 2004 presidential elections. After 22 years in power, President Biya had little opposition and the voters had little enthusiasm. John Fru Ndi of the SDF and Adamou Ndam Njoya, representing a coalition of opposition parties, provided minimum challenge. The Interior Ministry announced a landslide for Biya—75% of the vote with 80% of those eligible voting. Few gave much credence to the figures. Symptomatically, only 4.6 million of an estimated eight million people over the age of 20 who were qualified to vote actually got their names on electoral registers.

Cardinal Tumi expressed the sentiment of many: people had lost confidence in the government's ability to hold a fair and impartial election. All of them since independence, he forcefully declared, had been "surrounded by fraud." A Commonwealth observer group said the election "lacked the necessary credibility," and expressed concern that so many young people had failed to vote because they felt alienated from the political process.

To suggest change, President Biya appointed new Prime Minister, Ephraïm Inoni. Like his predecessor, the new Prime Minister is an English speaker from the South West, with degrees from the National School of Administration and an American MBA.

Cameroon faces border tension with several neighbors. With Nigeria, there have been disputes over the Lake Chad basin area and tensions over the Bakassi peninsula, a 400-square mile swamp-infested area of southwest Cameroon thought to hold significant oil reserves. Both countries submitted their Bakassi claims to the International Court of Justice (ICJ) and in October 2002, the court decided in favor of Cameroon. With little compliance action by late April 2005, the United Nations office for West Africa (UNOWA) accused Nigeria of deliberate delay in demarcating the official border separating the two countries. Nigeria has, however, turned over 32 villages in the Lake Chad area

In the parched northern region, Cameroon's plans for irrigated agriculture brought it into conflict with both Nigeria and Chad. Nigeria has threatened to bring the country back to the ICJ over disputes involving development projects on the Benue River. Chad has threatened similar action over irrigation and rice production projects on the Logone River. Even the border with the Central African Republic has seen several incidents of incursion.

**Culture:** For two years in a row in the late 1990s Cameroon topped Transparency International's list of countries perceived as being corrupt. Stung by its classification as the world's most corrupt state and with its consequent investor mistrust and diplomatic chastening, President Biya's government lumbered into an anti-corruption campaign. Progress was slow; by 2004, Transparency ranked Cameroon as the sixth most corrupt country in the world. More than 50% of all Cameroonians survey admitted to paying a bride in 2003, the highest figure anywhere in the world.

So commonplace are corrupt acts that Cameroonians, like the proverbial Eskimo describing snow, have elaborated a rich vocabulary to describe them. Magouiller means "to scheme," pistonner le dossier "to pull strings;" bien parler is to "do what you have to," while engraisser la patte is to "grease someone's palm."

Prime Minister Inoni has become the terror of the bureaucratic classes. Unannounced visits to ministries have resulted in those absent being sacked. Ministry doors are locked to ensure promptness; those who dally risk being fired. The names of 73 top civil servants accused of embezzling public funds were published in early 2005 to highlight the anticorruption campaign, and in March, 500 more were accused of either awarding themselves extra money or claiming salaries for "non-existent" workers. The government estimated the scam cost the government one million dollars a month.

In October 2001 the Cameroonian writer Mongo Beti died. "Mongo Beti" was the pseudonym under which Alexandre Biyidi-Awale published some twenty novels, most of them politically engaged. He denounced imperialism and Western exploitation of Africa, but reserved some of his most biting barbs for the African elite who aided that exploitation. He once labeled President Biya an "ectoplasm" and a "zombie." His funeral was held amidst the more or less total indifference of the Cameroonian political class.

**Traditional fishing**

Photo by E. Dounais
Courtesy of APFT-ULB

# Cameroon

**Economy:** Cameroon's economy was traditionally based on agriculture until the discovery of oil in the 1970s, but oil production peaked in 1985 at 158,000 barrels a day (bbl/d). Cameroon's crude oil output had been predicted to fall to between 50,000 and 60,000 bbl/d by 2005 as productive fields are exhausted.

If no major oil fields are discovered, current major oil fields will be depleted by 2010. In 2002 the government revised its petroleum laws to provide greater investment incentives and subsequently there has been new exploration in all three of its major petroleum basins.

The most significant oil development in Cameroon is the oil export pipeline from neighboring Chad. Peak production from Chad's Doba fields is projected to be around 225,000 to 250,000 bb/d. Crude oil from some 315 wells is transported through a 650-mile pipeline to an offshore marine terminal near Kribi, Cameroon.

The World Bank, despite stiff opposition from environmentalists, supplied 3% of the financing for the $3.5 billion pipeline project, and a consortium of major oil companies—ExxonMobil, Petronas (the Malaysian National Oil Company) and Chevron undertook the project. The pipeline was the largest single investment project in sub-Saharan Africa and was completed in July 2003, one year ahead of schedule. Oil began to flow in October 2003. For the next 25 years some 900 million barrels of oil will flow south from Doba.

Aside from oil, the country's main revenue earners are timber, cotton, cocoa and aluminum (mostly produced from bauxite imported from Guinea). Together, they account for 78% of export receipts. Cameroon is the world's fifth largest cocoa producer, and cocoa provides about 40% of its exports. Still, declining world market prices have resulted in reduced production. In several areas parts of cocoa plantations have been destroyed to pave way for food crops such as tomato, vegetables and plantain.

The palm oil sector has suffered decreased production because of aging palm plantations, 37% of which are more than 25 years old. In 2003 there was a deficit of some 60,000 tons, a short fall which hiked prices for homemakers and left industries dependent on it, like soap manufacturers, running at only 35% of their capacity. Malaysian investors are looking at the sector as an area of opportunity.

About 40% of Cameroon's land is forested, but the forests are disappearing rapidly because of irresponsible logging activity. Logging concessions are awarded by a bidding system. The winner is traditionally not the highest bidder, but the company prepared to offer the highest financial inducements to officials.

Senior political and military figures have become participants in the sector. In 2000, for example, three concessions were allocated to *Ingénierie Forestière*, a company connected to the son of President Biya.

Cameroon is now the largest producer of logs in Africa. It currently exports more than three million cubic meters of wood, but in January 1999 the government announced it would stop issuing export permits for raw timber. Forest preservation was less the goal than the encouragement of the local saw-milling industry. The government hopes to increase exports of processed sawn wood and veneers.

Friends of the Earth-Cameroon has estimated that half the timber logged in the country is illegally cut, costing the state around $2.7 million a year in lost revenues. Some suggestion of the illegal trade comes from comparing declared exports to European countries with declared imports. In 1998, for example, Cameroon declared 57,038 cubic meters of timber destined for Portugal, while Portuguese figures for the same year indicated imports of 91,111 cubic meters.

Cameroon qualified for $2 billion in debt relief under the Highly Indebted Poor Countries program in late 2000, but was cutoff from program benefits in August 2003 after an IMF mission found "considerable deterioration in Cameroonian public finances in 2003-2004." As of 2003, the country's debt total stood at nearly $9.2 billion.

There is a significant and growing Chinese presence in Cameroon. From as early as 1983, with the Lagdo hydroelectric dam on the Benue River, China has made major infrastructure contributions. Following President Biya's 2003 trip to China, the China International Water & Electrical Corporation offered to build several dams to supply the National Electricity Company. Most recently a Chinese consortium, China Road and Bridge Corporation, won the contract to repair the dilapidated roads in and around Douala, the business capital.

Notable have been the Chinese efforts in the medical field: the Yaounde Gynecological and Obstetric hospital, as well as hospitals in Guidir, Mbalmayo, and private clinics throughout the country have been built by the Chinese. The 110–bed Buea District Hospital was rehabilitated by Chinese architects and turned over to the government in February 2004. Chinese herbal medicine is increasingly popular and every major town seems to have at least one traditional Chinese clinic.

The Yaounde Conference Center is Chinese built, and China provided an interest-free loan to build the Yaounde Sports Complex. In 2004 Chinese gymnastics experts provided two-months of intense lessons in choreographic movement to youth and sports coaches, and a Chinese Language Training Center was established in 1996. Since then it has trained 500 students from 15 African countries in Chinese language and culture.

President Biya has made three trips to China and the Peoples' Republic is now Cameroon's fifth-ranked trading partner. Chinese goods are massively available in Cameroonian markets, and one poultry producer, Xiongshi Feed Company, threatens to dominate the national market for fresh chickens and has the capacity to export its birds to neighboring countries. Increasing cooperation in Cameroon's oil sector is a mutual goal.

**The Future:** Economic growth is insufficient to mask the repressive nature of the political system. The regime's electoral manipulations have increasingly alienated voters, especially the young.

**Rainforest logs reach the sea**

Photo by G. Philippart de Foy
Courtesy APFT-ULB

# The Central African Republic

**Diverse fauna, a tourism potential**

**Area:** 626,780 sq. km. = 242,000 sq. mi. (slightly smaller than Texas).

**Population:** 3,799,897 (July 2005 est.)

**Capital City:** Bangui (Pop 690,000, estimated; pronounced Ban–*ghe*).

**Climate:** Temperate, with a rainy season (June to October) and a dry season (November to May).

**Neighboring Countries:** The two Congos (South); Cameroon (West); Chad (Northwest); Sudan (Northeast and East).

**Official Language:** French.

**Other Principal Languages:** Sangho (lingua franca and national language), Arabic, Hausa, Swahili.

**Ethnic groups:** Baya 34%, Banda 27%, Sara 10%, Mandjia 21%, Mboum 4%, M'Baka 4%, Europeans 6,500 (including 3,600 French).

**Principal Religions:** Indigenous beliefs 24%, Protestant 25%, Roman Catholic 25%, Muslim 15%, and other 11%. Note: animistic beliefs and practices strongly influence the Christian majority.

**Chief Commercial Products:** Diamonds, timber, cotton, coffee, tobacco.

**GNI per capita:** $260 (2003)

**Currency:** CFA Franc

**Former Colonial Status:** French Colony (1894–1960).

**Independence Date:** August 11, 1960.

**Chief of State:** General François Bozizé (by military action, March 15, 2003)

**National Flag:** Four horizontal stripes (from top to bottom) of blue, white, green and yellow, divided by a red stripe down the middle, with a yellow star on the left hand side of the blue stripe.

Located in almost the exact center of Africa, the Central African Republic is a vast, rolling plateau rising 2,000 to 2,500 feet above sea level. Lying more than 300 miles from the sea, this sun–drenched land of agricultural and forest products found its original wealth in ivory from its once large herds of massive elephants. Prolific groups of wild animals roam the land today, making it one of the most zoologically interesting areas of Africa.

There is a small area of forest in the southwest which is rapidly succeeded by the rolling plateaus of the plains, rising gently to the mountains of the northeast. Heavy rainstorms occur almost daily during the wet season from June to October, seldom permitting the ground to become dry. November is the start of the dry season when the leaves of the trees turn to brilliant hues because of lack of moisture. In the following weeks the leaves fall, and the grass, having grown to the height of more than five feet, turns tinder dry. Fire becomes a great danger as the drought continues.

The Ubangi River flows along a good portion of the southern border, then plunges south to join the waters of the mighty Congo.

**History:** Humans have inhabited the area for at least 8,000 years, as polished flint and quartz tools testify. Huge stone megaliths near Bouar date back 2,500 years and suggest a relatively large-scale society with specialized labor. A wide variety of Niger-Congo and Nilo-Saharan languages suggest widespread migrations into the area, dating back to the 10th century. For details of earlier and colonial history, see *Historical Background* and *The French in Africa*.

The Central African Republic's independence is intimately associated with the work of a Catholic priest, Barthélémy Boganda. The first African Catholic priest in Ubangui-Chari, as the colony was then known, Boganda represented the territory in the French National Assembly in 1946. His nationalist sentiments developed rapidly, and he left the priesthood and formed his own political party, the *Mouvement pour l'Évolution Sociale de l'Afrique Noire* (MESAN) in 1949. Responsible for the country's name (*la République Centrafricain*), its flag, national anthem and motto, Boganda profoundly influenced CAR's early history. Immensely popular, he was re-elected deputy in 1951 and 1956.

Boganda was among those African nationalists who opposed the balkanization of the former French Federations into independent states, but when his federal notions received little support, he returned to Ubangui-Chari to work for its eventual independence.

Independence came on August 11, 1960, and the territory took the name Central African Republic. Boganda did not see the fruit of his labors. He died in a plane crash in March 1959. The void was filled by David Dacko, who became CAR's first president. Dacko soon created a single-party state and established close relations with the communist Chinese. The influx of Chinese technical and diplomatic personnel aroused the resentment of the military, which ousted Dacko on the night of December 31–January 1, 1966. General Jean-Bédel Bokassa assumed power, abolished the constitution, dissolved the legislature and centralized the administration in his appointed cabinet. Power seemed to be infectious for Bokassa.

In late 1976 a new constitution created the Central African Empire. In late 1977 in sweltering Bangui, a crowd of over 3,000 guests witnessed Jean-Bédel Bokassa place a 2,000-diamond encrusted crown on his head and proclaim himself Emperor Bokassa I. The spectacle was said to have cost well over $22 million in this land-locked country where the average per capita annual income was $120.

Opposition to Bokassa hardened at home and abroad. While visiting Libya in September 1979, he was overthrown by his cousin and advisor, former president

# Central African Republic

David Dacko. With the support of French armed forces, Dacko reestablished the Republic, but the CAR continued to be plagued by corrupt, inept government. Elections held in 1981 were clouded by charges of fraud, and when Army Chief of Staff General André Kolingba demanded President Dacko's resignation four months later, he quickly received it.

General Kolingba operated a virtual military dictatorship for the next decade. The new constitution of 1986 provided him a single-party state and a six-year term as president. He organized a new political party, the *Rassemblement démocratique centrafricain* (RDC), and in parliamentary elections, held in 1987, all candidates for the National Assembly had to belong to the presidential party. There was little to restrain Kolingba's exercise of power.

The presidential elections of 1986 took place shortly after the unexpected return of CAR's former Emperor, Jean-Bédel Bokassa who had fled virtual house arrest in France. Bokassa was put on trial, charged with murder and a variety of other crimes, the lurid details of which prompted international news coverage. After several months of intermittent action, the trial concluded in 1988 with Bokassa's guilt and death sentence. President Kolingba commuted the sentence to life in prison and later shortened even this. The former Emperor died of natural causes in 1996.

By the early 1990s the citizens of the CAR had little to show for a decade of President Kolingba's authoritarian rule. Civil rights were severely restricted, human rights were systematically abused, the economy had deteriorated, and the treasury was empty.

Strikes and work stoppages by government employees, unpaid for months, eventuated in riots. In April 1991, Kolingba, under heavy pressure, promised to allow political opposition. The newly responsive National Assembly revised the constitution to transform the country into a multiparty democracy in July. President-General Kolingba, fearing he had lost control of things, proposed a "Grand National Debate" (GND) to discuss democratic transformation.

The opposition would have none of it, and when the GND was about to open, in August 1992, members of the United Democratic Forces—a coalition of fourteen opposition parties—protested, demanding a genuine national conference to bring democracy to the country. President-General Kolingba sent in the troops. Soldiers attacked the marchers with tear gas, then plowed into the crowd swinging their rifle butts. One opposition leader was savagely beaten and later died of his wounds.

The situation continued to deteriorate. Elections were scheduled and then postponed. The opposition split. In May 1993 Kolingba's presidential guard mutinied, demanding its back wages. It was the first time the armed forces had rebelled against the regime, but it would not be the last.

In the late 1993 elections, Kolingba came in dead last. Ange-Félix Patassé of the *Movement for the Liberation of the Centrafrican People* (MLPC) beat out David Dacko to become president. Twelve years of military rule were ended, but President Patassé faced an empty treasury, a disgruntled civil service, an unpaid army, and a deeply divided country.

Years of military dictatorship had elevated army power and prestige. Soldiers were little prepared to see these cut back, as President Patassé had to do. In April 1996, when the government could not find sufficient funds to pay them, the troops mutinied. French troops crushed the mutiny and Patassé came up with money and promised amnesty, but soldiers mutinied a second time in May, after accusing Patassé of violating the amnesty by arresting some of the April mutineers. In November troops mutinied yet again, escalating their demands to include the President's resignation.

The demand highlighted the regional and ethnic conflicts that beset the country. The mutineers were southerners, mostly members of the Yakoma tribe of ex-President Kolingba. Patassé is a northerner, a member the Baya tribe.

Mali's highly respected former military ruler, Amadou Toumani Touré, was invited to mediate. The Bangui Accords he brokered involved amnesties for mutineers, a government of national unity, and the deployment of African peace-keepers to replace French troops. The Accords were signed in January 1997, but did not restore peace.

The Inter-African Surveillance Mission for the Bangui Accords (MISAB) was barely in place before it faced another mutiny in June. French and Chadian troops responded with a "muscular offensive" against the mutineers, whacking them soundly into another cease-fire in early July 1997. French troops withdrew in mid-April, 1998 and were replaced by the UN Mission in the Central African Republic (MINURCA).

Legislative elections in November and December 1998 did little to build a climate of trust. In the first round, President Patassé's MLPC had a slight lead, winning 26 seats to the opposition's 17. For the second round, fourteen opposition parties signed an electoral pact to support the best-placed candidate against those of the MLPC. The results were inconclusive. The MLPC and its allies held 51 seats; the opposition, were it to be united, held 53. Seven independents were elected, making them the focal point of everyone's attention. "Discussions" with the independents went on, and, suddenly, there were defections to President Patassé's coalition. The defector was "bought," said the opposition spokesman. "We have a majority," said the president as he proceeded to appoint a prime minister.

This was the political climate that preceded the September 1999 presidential elections. The opposition could not agree on a single candidate to confront President Patassé, so ten names appeared on the presidential ballot. The most prominent candidates were former presidents David Dacko and André Kolingba. The opposition found much to complain about and rejected the results even before the election was held.

Hopes that Patassé would be forced into a runoff election were dashed. Some

**General Kolingba**

**Former President Patassé**

56% of registered voters went to the polls and the president won by a razor slim majority: 51.6%. General Kolingba received 19.3% of the votes and David Dacko came in third with 11.1%. Observers declared the election free and fair. Any irregularities, they said, were not of a kind to affect the overall result.

The election brought no stability. Desperately poor, the Central African Republic teetered on the brink of implosion. Unable to pay civil servants their salaries, students their stipends, or retirees their pensions, the government faced an on-going series of protests and demonstrations. A near-permanent strike of government workers began in November 2000 when demonstrators set up barricades and burned tires in the capital before being dispersed by security forces. They demanded nearly 30 months of back wages.

CAR represents a worst-case scenario for the abjectly poor state: economic crisis exacerbates political tensions and facilitates social disintegration. Crime in the capital and banditry in the countryside increased. The state had little capacity to project its authority beyond the Bangui city limits, and armed banditry reached insurrectional proportions, threatening the state's authority in the provinces. Bandits raped, robbed, and murdered at will, disrupting trade between nearby Chad and the Cameroonian port of Douala, the CAR's main outlet to the sea.

In May 2001 the troublesome General Kolingba instigated a *coup d'état* against the Patassé government, but the attempt was repressed by the intervention of Libyan troops and several hundred *Mouvement de libération du Congo* (MLC) troops of Jean-Pierre Bemba, who crossed the Ubangui River from their northern Congolese bases. Mop-up operations, little sensitive to human rights concerns, focused on General Kolingba's minority Yakoma tribesmen, heightening ethnic tensions.

With some justification, the regime turned increasingly paranoid. Patassé fired his defense, interior, security, and disarmament ministers in August, and in October the army chief of staff, General François Bozizé was sacked.

Bozizé fled to neighboring Chad in November after an attempt to arrest him led to five days of fighting between his supporters and troops loyal to the government. In March 2002, the government put some 680 people on trial for involvement in the May 28, 2001 coup attempt—600 of them had already fled the country. General Kolingba, his two sons, and around 20 others from his Yakoma ethnic group, were sentenced to death, *in absentia*.

As the country deteriorated socially and economically, only foreign arms kept President Patassé in power. Forces loyal to General Bozizé left their Chadian refuge and invaded Bangui's northern suburbs in October 2002. After ten days of destructive fighting, Bozizé's soldiers were driven out with the help of Libyan and Congolese forces. For Bangui's suffering citizenry, salvation was nearly as bad as rebel assault: Undisciplined, Bemba's MLC troops raped and robbed the very people they were supposed to defend, further alienating them from President Patassé. It was the fifth coup attempt the CAR president had survived. He would not survive the sixth.

Soldiers loyal to General Bozizé left their Chadian sanctuary in March 2003 and completed the work they had begun the previous October. Bangui fell to the rebels in a day. There was almost no one left willing to defend the Patassé regime. The president himself was out of the country, and Libyan troops had been withdrawn the previous December in favor of a peacekeeping contingent supplied by the Economic and Monetary Community of Central African States, known by its French acronym CEMAC.

General Bozizé returned from Paris and was greeted as a liberator by Bangui crowds. (The international community clucked about the use of force, but there were no calls to return the deposed Patassé to office.) Reportedly a thoughtful and deeply religious man, the general showed himself tough, generous, and moral in his initial pronouncements. "Thieves and other looters," he said, "will henceforth be considered military targets." The violence and looting in Bangui, particularly against figures of the former regime, ended quickly. Beginning the process of national reconciliation, Bozizé amnestied all those who had plotted the overthrow of President Patassé in May 2001. To head a transitional government of national unity, he called upon the Mr. Clean of CAR politics, Abel Goumba.

**General François Bozizé, President**

Nearly 77 years old, Goumba was a companion from the early days of Barthélémy Boganda, the Republic's founder. A man of principle, Goumba had opposed each of the Republic's four presidents (Dacko, Bokassa, Kolingba and Patassé). At the time of his appointment he was the leader of the Patriotic Front for Progress (FPP) party and head of a 12-member coalition of opposition parties.

The new regime's most pressing problem was the restoration of security. Achieving this in the capital was the easier task. Once done, Bangui's citizens felt free to "walk anywhere, even late at night, without worrying about getting shot or robbed," as one local put it. Outside the capital, however, the government still works to reassert its authority. In January 2004, after receiving vehicles and equipment from China, France, Morocco, and Sudan, the army sent 1,000 troops into the southwestern region—where most of the country's mines are located—to restore order. In April a specially trained Mixed Intervention Battalion was dispatched to the northern provinces to fight banditry.

In many cases it was difficult to determine who the "bandits" were. Some were Chadian mercenaries hired to support Bozizé's invasion who had not yet been sufficiently paid for their services. Others were unemployed soldiers loyal to former president Patassé or his defense minister Jean-Jacques Demafouth, while still others were simply opportunistic highway robbers who set up road blocks, plundered travelers, and held the more prosperous for ransom. In late April 2004 President Bozizé agreed to pay the Chadian fighters the local equivalent of $1,000 to encourage their return home.

Some of the money may have come from a $2 million interest-free loan given by China to help chronically cash-short Bangui deal with unpaid civil servants. In

# Central African Republic

late July the IMF and World Bank finally came through with emergency post-conflict aid, the first time the institutions had provided funding since October 2002. The financing helped the regime push forward with its other central task, the restoration of democracy.

Voter registration began in September 2004, and voters overwhelmingly approved a new constitution in December. The transitional constitutional court approved only five of fifteen individuals who submitted their candidacy papers to run for president. Among the approved were François Bozizé, who declared himself an independent candidate, his vice-president Abel Goumba, former president Andre Kolingba, and two others. The court disqualified all candidates from the MLPC, the country's former ruling party. After considerable public outcry, President-General Bozizé allowed three of these—Jean-Paul Ngoupandé, Martin Ziguélé, and Charles Massi—to seek the presidency. He told a radio audience the move was designed to preserve national peace and international donor support for the electoral process. It was legitimized, he told his listeners, by Article 22 of the new constitution which allowed the president to ensure "the regular functioning of the public powers and continuity of the state."

When the ballots from the March 2005 election were counted, Bozizé topped the poll. With only 42.97% of the vote, he was forced into a run-off with the MLPC candidate, former Prime Minister Martin Ziguélé, who received 23.53%. In run-off elections 64.23% of the electorate opted to continue the president-general in office. His rival received 35.77% of the vote.

**Culture:** HIV/AIDS is well established in the Central African Republic. The government officially estimates some 300,000 people out of the 3.5 million population are affected. At a July 1999 seminar the Minister of Health observed that every citizen had already lost at least one family member because of AIDS.

Researchers have noted a disturbing phenomenon in the CAR's AIDS epidemic—the presence of elevated HIV/AIDS rates among the best-educated sectors of the population. AIDS was the principal cause of death among teachers, for example, between 1996 and 1998. "It's a profession," said one researcher, "where one is more exposed to easy sexual relations."

One expert called the official figures of a 10–15% infection rate "too timid." Based on a recent sample of 2,059 persons, he estimated the infection rate closer to 24%.

**Economy:** CAR's economic situation remains precarious. President Bozizé inherited an economy in shambles. Mismanagement since Bokassa and continuing civil strife have led to general economic deterioration and deepening poverty for most citizens. Average annual income has fallen from $380 in 1990 to $260 in 2003. In 2003 the economy shrank by 7.3% and the country's basic economic indicators were no better than they were in 1997.

President Patassé opted for a patrimonial blend of state and private resources; much of CAR's wealth found its way into the hands of his friends and family. Central African Republic is now one of the ten poorest countries in the world—ranked 169 of 177 on the UN's *Human Development Index* for 2004. According to one UN report, more than two-thirds of the population lives on less than a dollar a day.

Civil conflict has devastated the economy. Most of the private and public buildings that were damaged, destroyed or looted have not been repaired. In June 2004 the Chinese government donated $4 million in material and equipment, including some 20,000 sheets of corrugated iron to rebuild military barracks, plus computers, furniture and bicycles to equip offices during the 2005 elections.

Salary arrears, always a problem in CAR, have reappeared. China once again helped bail the government out of difficult circumstances with a $2-million interest-free loan in March 2004 to pay civil servants. Major reconstruction financing will not be forthcoming until democracy and security prevail.

Agriculture and forestry are the mainstays of economy, accounting for 54.8% of GNP in 2002 and employing 66% of the workforce. Subsistence farming dominates, with farmers growing cassavas, yams, bananas, sorghum, millet, and rice. Cotton and coffee are cash crops, grown for export, but prices for both commodities have declined on world markets. The effect has been to reduce income, acreage, and production.

After producing 50,000 to 60,000 tons of cotton in the 1970s, the country produced only 15,000 tons in 2000. Civil conflict, banditry, and insecurity in the countryside have made it impossible for cotton farmers to sell their crops for three years. Coffee is grown in several regions of the country and covers over 138,000 acres, mostly in the southwest. Ninety percent of coffee growing is done on small plantations, often less than an acre in size, with relatively low yields. Some 300,000 to 400,000 families gain their livelihood from coffee production, but like cotton farmers, they have had difficulty getting their

crops to market given the prevailing insecurity in the countryside.

The country has significant forestry potential, with over 60 commercially viable trees. Development of the sector is hampered by high transportation costs and delivery problems that can add 60% to production costs. (Because it is landlocked, CAR must send its logs down river via Brazzaville to Pointe-Noire, or by road to Douala in Cameroon.)

Log exports dropped 32% in 2003, but much of the decline can be attributed to the government's suspension of the timber cutting and selling permits "to fight against the mafia that is crippling the sector." The forestry ministry predicts 2004 production levels should recover to more or less equal those of 2002.

Diamonds have traditionally contributed half of CAR's foreign earnings, but production is affected by political instability. An estimated 80,000 small-scale miners recover about 500,000 carats each year, over half of which are of gem quality. Diamond exports account for about 54% of the nation's export earnings. From export taxes, the government earns between three and four million dollars annually, but smuggling remains a significant problem, reducing government revenues from diamond sales.

As signs of stability have begun to emerge, interest in the sector has increased. DeBeers signed an exploration contract covering some 35,000 sq. km in June 2004, and Energem Resources (formerly DiamondWorks) has resumed its operations in the country. The group's six mining concessions, covering 11, 577 sq. km, resumed in May 2004.

With a resource-hungry economy China is keenly interested in CAR. When President Bozizé met with Chinese President Hu Jintao in August 2004, the Chinese leader made this clear, saying China was interested in exploring cooperation in the oil, diamond, iron ore, and timber sectors. With plans to build new nuclear power plants, China is also interested in CAR's uranium deposits at Bakouma.

There is considerable evidence that the oil basin currently being pumped in southern Chad extends across the border into the Central African Republic and China's national oil company, Sinopec is reportedly seeking concessions in the area. Given the Peoples Republic's continuing generosity (Bangui's new sports stadium is Chinese built) it is likely Chinese companies will gain significant access to CAR's natural resources in the coming years.

**Future:** Still precarious, but there is more optimism than there has been for years.

# The Republic of Equatorial Guinea

**Selling yoghurt**

Photo by Cayuela Serrano
Courtesy: APFT-ULB

**Area:** 28,051 sq. km = 10,830 sq. mi. (slightly larger than Vermont).
**Population:** 535,881 (July 2005 est.)
**Capital City:** Malabo (on Bioko Island, pop. 58,000, est. 1998).
**Climate:** Tropically hot and humid.
**Neighboring Countries:** Cameroon (North); Gabon (East and South). The island portion of the country lies some twenty miles off the west coast of Cameroon.
**Official Languages:** Spanish and French.
**Other Principal Languages:** Fang, Bubi, Ibo, and Pidgin English.
**Ethnic groups:** Bioko (primarily Bubi, some Fernandinos), Rio Muni (primarily Fang), Europeans less than 1,000, mostly Spanish.
**Principal Religions:** Most people are nominally Roman Catholic; traditional tribal beliefs are intermingled with their Christian faith.
**Chief Commercial Products:** Petroleum, timber, and cocoa.
**GNI per capita:** $930 (2003)
**Currency:** CFA Franc
**Former Colonial Status:** Spanish Colony (island, 1778–1968, mainland 1885–1968).
**Independence Date:** October 12, 1968.

**Chief of State:** Brig.-Gen. Teodoro Obiang Nguema Mbasogo, President (Pronounced Tay–oh–dor–oh Oh–be–ang N–gway–mah M–bah–so–go).
**National Flag:** Three horizontal stripes of green, white and red, with a blue aquamarine isosceles triangle next to the staff. Centered in the white stripe is the coat of arms: six yellow six-pointed stars (representing the mainland and five offshore islands) above a gray shield bearing a silk-cotton tree and below which is a scroll with the motto UNIDAD, PAZ, JUSTICIA (Unity, Peace, Justice)

Note: Between 1974 and the present, geographic place names have been changed from Spanish to African and then to *other* African designations and back to Spanish. The island, first known as Fernando Po, was renamed by the late president in his own honor. It then was designated *Bioko* after an early king of the region. The mainland, formerly Rio Muni, became Mbini, but it is now again generally called Rio Muni.

On the protected shoreline of mainland Equatorial Guinea, hot and humid Rio Muni, the narrow white sandy beach quickly gives way to thick growth of interior rain forest, where immense ebony, mahogany and oak trees crowd each other to bask in the sun. It is uniformly hot and oppressive. Few roads penetrate into the interior, but the land is thick with streams which are the home of giant frogs (as long as three feet and weighing up to six pounds!) which perch motionless on the spray–drenched rocks, their tongues darting out to catch unwary insects.

The scenic Island of Bioko is large and was productive until the 1970s, being the source of one of the best varieties of cocoa in the world. Production was on large plantations; contract labor from Nigeria was imported, but almost all fled during the brutalities of the Macías Nguema regime. Ships from many nations called at the port, and the international airport was the base from which relief supplies were flown into strife–torn Nigeria in the early 1970s.

**History:** Little is known of the pre-colonial period of this remote part of Africa; the Fang and other Bantu people settled thinly in Rio Muni and the Bubis settled on Bioko. Bioko island (formerly Fernando Po) was sighted by the Portuguese mariner, Fernão do Pó, probably in 1472. The Treaty of Tordesillas of 1494, by which the Pope settled territorial claims between Spain and Portugal stemming from the discovery of the New World, gave the Portuguese exclusive rights in Africa. In 1778 they ceded Fernando Po, along with rights over the neighboring coastal areas, to Spain as a source for slave labor in Spain's New World possessions.

In the nineteenth century Fernando Po was used by the British navy in its efforts to suppress the slave trade. Many of the freed slaves were settled on the island and the British assumed responsibility for its

# Equatorial Guinea

administration. The island was abandoned for this purpose when the British shifted their operations to Sierra Leone in 1843. Spain reoccupied the island in 1844 and by 1879 was using it as a penal settlement for Cubans considered too dangerous to be kept on that island. Economic development only began after the Spanish-American war of 1898, when Fernando Po and its neighboring coastal enclave became Spain's last significant tropical colony. The two provinces were collectively known as Spanish Guinea.

The provinces were made internally self-governing in 1963, and their name was changed to Equatorial Guinea. Spain granted independence to Equatorial Guinea in 1968. In UN-supervised elections mainland Fang outnumbered the more educated Bubi of Fernando Po, and their candidate, Francisco Macías Nguema, became the country's first president.

Almost immediately Macías Nguema's paranoid style became apparent. Prominent political figures were arrested and executed on grounds they were plotting his overthrow. Family members were installed in key government posts, but they remained under close surveillance. Cocoa plantations were nationalized, and the economy spiraled downward. In 1972 Macías Nguema's hand–picked National Assembly named him "President for Life." He assumed absolute personal power in 1973 and had the island of Fernando Po renamed in his honor. Titles were collected: in addition to "President for Life," Macías Nguema was also "Grand Master of Education, Science and Culture."

As his paranoia increased, life became more and more grim for the citizenry. Death squads formed by the "Macias Youth" roamed the countryside, raping, looting and killing. Mass executions were held while loudspeakers blared a recording of "Those Were the Days, My Friend." Others were buried up to their necks—to be eaten alive by insects. Educated Guineans, mostly Bubi, were specially targeted for slaughter.

A militant atheist, Macías Nguema was especially venomous towards Christians. He ordered his picture to hang beside the altar of every church in the country and compelled priests and pastors to recite the slogan "All for Macias" at every service. The World Council of Churches branded him a "modern Caligula." One island visitor called the country "the concentration camp of Africa—a cottage-industry Dachau."

By 1979, when he was overthrown, Macías Nguema is believed to have murdered 50,000 Guineans. Another 100,000, one-third of the country's population, had been driven into exile. Among the dead were two-thirds of the last elected national assembly and 10 of the 12 original cabinet ministers. Guinea's small educated class had been virtually eliminated through death or flight.

In the summer of 1979 Macías Nguema was overthrown by his nephew, and deputy defense minister, Lt. Col. Teodoro Obiang Nguema Mbasogo. Any joy at Macías Nguema's fall was restrained. Lt. Colonel Obiang Nguema had been one of the principal architects of the Macías reign of terror, and human rights groups had long accused him of personal involvement in a number of killings.

His governance of the country has been repressive and dictatorial. Until 1993 he operated through a single party, the Democratic Party of Equatorial Guinea (PDGE), and concentrated political power in his own hands. Economic power was concentrated in the hands of the Nguema clan.

Although multiparty elections were introduced in 1993, nothing approaching democracy exists in Equatorial Guinea. President Obiang was elected to a seven-year term in 1996 in a contest dominated by fraud and intimidation. The government and 14 opposition groups signed a national pact in April 1997 agreeing to the basic conditions for future legislative elections. One month later, however, the government announced that a plot to overthrow the president had been uncovered. This set off another wave of political repression. Relations with Spain deteriorated when Spain granted asylum to Severo Moto, leader of the *Partido del Progreso de Guinea Ecuatorial* (PPGE) and alleged leader of the so-called coup.

In pique, Obiang made French the official language of this former Spanish colony. In May Severo Moto, along with eleven others, was tried *in absentia* for treason, found guilty and sentenced to 101 years imprisonment. The PPGE was banned in June, indicating just how quickly the opposition can be dispatched in Equatorial Guinea.

A new separatist group emerged in January 1998, attacking three police posts and killing several people. It identified itself as the Movement for Self-determination for the Island of Bioko (MAIB) and demanded independence for the island's indigenous population of Bubi peoples, marginalized and excluded from the country's political and economic life by the mainland Fang. Mass arrests followed. Fifteen Bubi were condemned to death by a military court. The sentence was reduced in September, by presidential grace, to life imprisonment after an outpouring of international protest.

March 1999 legislative elections could be called farcical were it not for the thuggish brutality of the Obiang Nguema regime. Opposition candidates were threatened, arbitrarily arrested, and prevented from campaigning. For the election itself, additional polling places were set up in schools, barracks and state-owned enterprises, close to the governing party's adherents. Alliances between parties were prohibited. On election day armed soldiers or other security agents stood inside polling areas. Voters were often forced to cast their ballots publicly. Unsurprisingly the PDGE won seventy-five of eighty parliamentary seats. Appeals to the National Electoral Commission would be unavailing. Its chairman was also the minister of the interior, in charge of all those police and security agents.

The European Union and most other bodies who had been requested to send observers refused to sanction any of this by their presence. Little wonder Freedom House lists Equatorial Guinea among "the worst of the worst", in its 2005 report on the world's most repressive societies.

The government strictly controls freedom of speech and press. Press laws authorize government censorship of all publications, and the Ministry of Information can require pre-publication approval of article content. Self-censorship is the better part of valor. All electronic media are censured. The ruling party controls the country's main publications, radio and television. It owns and operates Radio Malabo, the most widely heard station. Only in 1998 did the government allow the country's first private domestic radio station, Radio Ansonga, but that is owned by the Minister of Waters and Forests, Fishing and Environment, Teodoro ("Teodorino") Obiang Nguema, the president's eldest son.

State and family are closely conjoined in Equatorial Guinea. The president's second son, Gabriel Mbegha Obiang Lima, is state secretary for oil, while his brother-in-law, Teodoro Biyogo Nsue, once Equa-

**President Obiang Nguema Mbasogo**

torial Guinea's ambassador to the UN, now manages family/country interests in the U.S., including a $300 to $500 million bank account. The state security apparatus is dominated by his closest relatives, for this is a task, says the president, that cannot be confided in strangers: "I must be able to count on loyal people." (For his personal protection, Obiang relies on a contingent of Moroccan troops!)

His brother Armengol Ondo Nguema (same mother, same father, as he is wont to say) is Director General of National Security and one of the most feared men in the country. Another brother, Antonio Mba Nguema, is also part of the security service, as is his son-in-law, Julian Ondo Nkumu.

It is the state security apparatus that is most responsible for Equatorial Guinea's appalling human rights record. The U.S. State Department's *Human Rights Practices Report* (2004) notes the routine use of torture to coerce confessions, gang rape of female prisoners and forced labor from prisoners as part of Equatorial Guinea's security and penal system. Because of Guinea's sleazy human rights record the U.S. has kept President Obiang at arms length. Despite requests to meet with them, neither the American president nor Secretary of State has met privately with him. American relations with the country are handled at the assistant-secretary level.

In the lead up to presidential elections in late 2002 regime critics were subjected to the usual harassment, repression and torture; the country's four main opposition parties withdrew, saying the balloting was so rigged there was no way there could be a fair election. With well over 90% of the votes, Teodoro Obiang Nguema Mbasogo was re-elected to another seven-year term as president. The constitution places no limits on the number of terms a president may serve.

In early 2004 it appeared someone was attempting to hasten the President's departure from office. Rumors of an impending coup had circulated for weeks in Malabo, but they were given substance in early March when 15 mercenaries were arrested in the country and another 64, allegedly on their way, were taken off a plane in Zimbabwe. The government hastily pointed fingers at its *bête noire*, Severo Moto, head of the opposition Progress Party, funded by what the Minister of Information called "enemies and multinational companies." *The Economist* magazine claimed to have documents linking Armengol Ondo Nguema, the president's brother and secret service chief, and the mercenary leader, Nick du Toit.

Indeed, dissention within the clan Nguema is very real. Reportedly seriously ill with prostate cancer, President Obiang

has sought to assure the presidential succession by his eldest son, "Teodorino" Obiang Nguema, a young man whose flamboyant lifestyle has captivated the Western press, but whose trenchant criticisms of his uncles, the generals, has fostered bitter enmity in them and cordial dislike within the army. The younger Obiang has accused them of control and expropriation both the economy and the apparatus of the state and deliberately absented himself from the country in protest. In a deeply patriarchal society questions of age are important, and the generals detest the thought of taking orders from one junior to them.

Equatorial Guinea's opposition thought the whole brouhaha is just another attempt by the regime to divert attention from forthcoming elections, and certainly it did.

Parliamentary seats had been increased in September 2003—to 100 from 80—to allow the "democratic opposition" to be represented in the legislature, but almost all the candidates of the two main opposition parties were rejected on technical grounds.

The PDGE and its electoral coalition took 98 out of 100 seats in parliament and 237 municipal councillors out of 244. The main opposition Convergence for Social Democracy (CPSD) got two seats in parliament and only seven on local municipal councils. Thus does democracy flourish in the "Kuwait of Africa."

**Culture:** The oil economy means the people of Rio Muni no longer live in rural

solitude. Four–wheel-drive vehicles tooling along the faded elegance of Spanish colonial boulevards suggest the ruling elite has begun to enjoy the economic fruits of political power. The dispossessed must suffer through daily water and power cutoffs and drinking water regularly polluted by drainage water, mainly because of broken pipes.

The use of marijuana is widespread and traditional. Referred to as the "sacred weed of the people" and once used only in traditional ceremonies, marijuana has found its way into every level of Equatorial Guinean society. The plants are grown locally between cassava plants or banana trees, and on the streets of Malabo a poor man's joint can be had for 100 CFA francs (about 20 US cents.). The drug provides, for the poor, escape from worsening poverty amid the riches of an oil boom. "We can neither go to school nor to work and people think we are thieves," said a young unemployed woman. Another of Malabo's poor said he and his companions "take refuge in marijuana. At least it helps us to take a less aggressive view of life." Perhaps. A senior police officer was less sanguine. Most young smokers, he thought, "turn into dangerous delinquents. Under the influence of the sacred weed, they do not hesitate to use machetes, knives, and guns to carry out armed robberies." The process has already been seen in places like Liberia and Sierra Leone.

**Economy:** The export of cocoa and coffee had been the traditional backbone of the

**Traditional short-hoe farming**

Photo by N. Cayuela Serrano
Courtesy of APFT-ULB

# Equatorial Guinea

nation's economy, but under Macías Nguema the plantations were nationalized and destroyed. In the 1960s nearly 98,000 acres were devoted to cocoa production, mostly on Bioko Island; by the 1980s, only 7,400 acres remained in production. Annual yields fell from 38,000 metric tons to a low of 4,500 tons. Coffee production similarly collapsed. About 8,500 metric tons, most of it grown by African farmers on small plots in Rio Muni, were produced in 1968. By the late 1980s production had fallen to 1,000 tons.

There are few incentives for farmers to continue cocoa cultivation. The Equatorial Guinea Institute for Agricultural Promotion (*INPAGE*), which buys and sells farm produce on behalf of the state, offers farmers significantly less for their produce than farmers earn in nearby Cameroon. Little wonder, then, that workers are increasingly abandoning plantations to seek jobs in the burgeoning oil sector.

Equatorial Guinea's reversal of economic fortune began in the 1990s with the discovery of oil in the Gulf of Guinea. By 2004 oil production averaged 350,000 barrels per day (bbl/d). Equatorial Guinea has overtaken Gabon to become sub-Saharan Africa's third biggest oil producer (after Nigeria and Angola). Oil, with proven reserves of 1.1 billion barrels, accounts for about 80% of GDP.

There are also reserves of some 7 trillion cubic feet of gas. Marathon Oil Company has started site work to construct a liquefied natural gas (LNG) facility on Bioko Island; it will supply 3.4 million tons of LNG when completed in late 2007.

People have begun to refer to the country as "Africa's Kuwait." The economy has grown (at least statistically) with enormous rapidity as a consequence of its oil income. Real gross domestic product (GDP) growth was estimated at 65% in 2001, up from the 16.9% growth in 2000, and barely missing the whopping 71.2% GDP growth of 1997. As the oil industry matures, however, growth rates slow. Real GDP growth in 2003 was 14.2% and 21.2% in 2004.

With escalating international oil prices the country will earn hundreds of millions, with a population of just over half a million. There are few signs of the oil dividend trickling down to the common citizenry, and the World Bank has been uncharacteristically blunt, saying that oil revenue has had "no impact on Equatorial Guinea's dismal social indicators." Health-care spending for example, has *declined* from 6% to just over 1% of the budget. Malabo, the capital, suffers from chronic water shortages.

How much money has come in, where it's deposited, and how it's being spent are all unclear. President Obiang has told the IMF these statistics are state secrets. In January 2003 the *Los Angeles Times* lifted one small corner of the veil that conceals state patrimonialism. According to its investigations Equatorial Guinea kept an account with Riggs Bank in Washington DC where international oil companies directly deposited at least $300 million. The account was controlled exclusively by President Obiang. As he told a reporter for the *New Statesman,* "I am the one who arranges things in this country because in Africa there are a lot of problems of corruption…I'm 100 per cent sure of all the oil revenue because the one who signs is me."

The revelations set off a series of probes. July 2004 hearings before the Senate Permanent Subcommittee On Investigations found around $700 million in Obiang-controlled bank accounts at Riggs Bank. The sums led careless bankers to disregard reporting requirements and even facilitate money laundering by helping to set up offshore companies. Evidence indicated the presidential clan had a large slice of anything that produced income in the country. Investigations by the FBI and the Securities and Exchange Commission continue.

Should there be any question about the president's omnipotence, the state radio has described him as "like God in heaven," who has "all power over men and things." In the July 2003 Fang-language broadcast, a presidential aide also noted that the president "can decide to kill without anyone calling him to account and without going to hell because it is God himself, with whom he is in permanent contact, and who gives him his strength."

The U.S. has attached great importance to developing Equatorial Guinea's oil sector to lessen its dependence on Middle Eastern suppliers. Washington's new enthusiasm for the country can be seen in the State Department's approval for Military Professional Resources Inc. (MPRI)—a private firm run by Pentagon retirees out of Alexandria, Va.—to help the government develop a coast guard to protect its offshore oil fields. Those are being operated by American firms like ExxonMobil, ChevronTexaco, and Amerada Hess.

Collectively American companies have invested some six billion dollars in the country and more than 3,000 U.S. oil workers are manning the pumps. With 28 days on the job and 28 days off, the expatriate staff now has the luxury of direct flights between Houston and Malabo. Given increased American presence in the country, the U.S. reopened its embassy in Malabo in October 2003.

Developments in the petroleum sector have far overshadowed the other important resource for the country's ruling clan: timber. Initially small scale, logging operations exploded around 1994 when huge Asian transnationals moved in. By the mid-1990s there were more than 20 logging companies exploiting the rain forest on concessions reportedly owned by President Obiang. Forestry became the second most important economic sector after oil, but aggressive logging threatened the approximately 3.2 million acres of forestland in mainland Equatorial Guinea with overharvesting.

In June 2000, the World Wildlife Fund (WWF) and the Washington-based World Resources Institute (WRI) released a long suppressed report condemning destructive logging practices by largely Asian firms, mainly from Malaysia, Indonesia, Korea, and Hong Kong. The authors were so disturbed by what they saw that they recommended a complete moratorium on logging in eleven countries, one of which was Equatorial Guinea.

Oil revenues have only allowed the Obiang regime to enrich and further entrench itself. As it had controlled jobs in the bureaucracy, awarding them to its faithful supporters, the clan Nguema controls access to the new, high-paying jobs of the oil industry. The best jobs are reserved for the PDGE faithful.

**The Future:** The Nguema clan intends to stay in power as long as possible. The best the opposition can hope for from the new oil wealth is that the presence of hundreds of foreigners might restrain regime repression. Tensions within the clan, particularly focused on President Obiang Nguema's eldest son, could easily explode in bloody violence as the abortive March 2004 coup suggests.

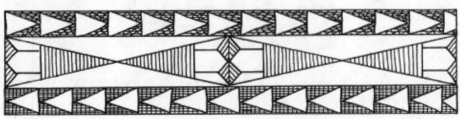

Tire advertisement does not help this traffic jam in Lagos

AP/Wide World Photo

**Area:** 924,630 sq. km. = 357,000 sq. mi. (the size of the traditional southern states east of the Mississippi River, omitting Florida).

**Population:** 128,771,988 (July 2005 est.)

**Capital City:** Abuja (Pop. 850,000, estimated).

**Climate:** Hot and humid in the coastal belt and southern interior; hot and less humid in the central plains regions; semi–arid to arid and hot in the extreme north.

**Neighboring Countries:** Benin (West); Niger, Chad (North); Cameroon (East).

**Official Language:** English.

**Other Principal Languages:** There over 450 languages spoken. Prominent are Edo, Fulani, Hausa, Ibibio, Igbo, Ijo, Kanuri, Nupe, Tiv, and Yoruba.

**Ethnic groups:** Prominent are the Hausa, Fulani, Yoruba, Ibo, Ijaw, Kanuri, Ibibio, and Tiv.

**Principal Religions:** Muslim 50%, Christian 40%, indigenous beliefs 10%.

**Chief Commercial Products:** Petroleum and petroleum products 95%, cocoa, rubber.

**GNI per capita:** $320 (2003)

**Currency:** 1 Naira (N) = 100 kobo

**Former Colonial Status:** British Colony (1914–1960).

**Independence Date:** October 1, 1960.

**Chief of State:** Olusegun Obasanjo, elected February 27, 1999.

**National Flag:** Three vertical stripes of green, white and green.

Nigeria, the fourteenth largest country on the African continent with the largest population of any African nation, lies facing the Gulf of Guinea on the southern coast of West Africa. From the warm waters of the ocean the land has a flat appearance; there is a belt of dense swamp and towering mangrove trees 10 to 15 miles wide. This marshy coastal area resembles the bayous of Louisiana, particularly in the delta of the Niger River.

Further inland, there is a region 50 to 100 miles wide where the vegetation is thick green tropical forest rising from more stable ground. The trees of this warm and humid area reach heights of 200 feet where vines entwine all growth. This forest area and the coast receive up to 150 inches of rainfall per year.

The land rises slowly in a series of foothills to the Jos Plateau, reaching altitudes up to 1,000 feet. Tall grasses grow rapidly between widely spaced trees. The dry season, from October to April, evaporates moisture from the ground, hardening the earth so that when the spring rains come, the soil erodes into the rivers.

There is a semi–arid to arid region in the extreme north, close of Lake Chad and Niger. This is the transition zone lying between the Sahara Desert and the green forests and jungles of the South, receiving 25 inches or less of rain per year. In the last decade, the "or less" has been the rule. This area is threatened by the expansion southward of the great desert.

During the dry season, particularly in December and January, the *harmattan*, the hot wind blowing from the desert, penetrates to the Gulf of Guinea, lowering the humidity and raising dust storms in the interior.

**History:** Some of the most important archeological work in Africa has been done in Nigeria, producing evidence of human habitation that goes back thousands of years. The oldest evidence of a widespread organized society is associated with the Nok culture (c. 500 BC–200 AD).

Yoruba peoples were established in the southern coastal region by the eleventh century, and by the fourteenth and fifteenth centuries the Yoruba empire was a regional power. Hausa kingdoms were gradually formed after the twelfth century in the North and began to undergo conversion to Islam by the fourteenth century. Fulani (Peulh) nomadic herdsmen became rulers in the Hausa regions of the North as a consequence of an Islamic reformist jihad in the late 19th century. In the densely forested southeast region Ibo peoples organized themselves in small-scale political units centuries before the arrival of the first Europeans.

The British annexed coastal Lagos in 1861 as part of its continuing efforts to

# Nigeria

suppress the slave trade, but treasury parsimony made them unwilling to incur the costs of maintaining an administration in Nigeria. To keep costs down Lagos was first administered from Sierra Leone. Only in 1886 did Lagos become a separate colony. Later, two other protectorates were declared, one over the Oil Rivers and the other over the Lagos hinterland. In 1894 both entities were merged into the Niger Coast Protectorate.

In the north the first British High Commissioner, Frederick Lugard, set about controlling the Fulani emirs. Some were deposed, some defeated in battle, and others collaborated, but by 1903 Lugard's conquest of the emirates was complete. Though defeated, the emirates were not dismantled. To spare the British treasury administrative costs, Lugard developed a policy of "indirect rule," relying on existing administrative structures of the emirates. Much of the North's traditional feudal structure was thus maintained. In 1914 northern and southern administrative areas were consolidated into Nigeria, and the difficult tasks of balancing regional interests and identities would dominate Nigerian colonial history.

In the colony's 1947 constitution, the British introduced a federal system of government which entrenched the dominant interests of the colony's three major regions: the northern and mainly Muslim Hausa and Fulanis, the predominantly Catholic Ibo in the east, and the Anglican and Muslim Yoruba in the west. When Nigeria became independent in 1960, regional differences were inevitable. Much of the nationalist agitation that had culminated in independence had come from southerners, better educated and more progressive through longer contact with European missionaries and traders.

Balancing regional tensions is a leitmotif in Nigerian history and politics. When Nigeria became a federal republic in 1963, its president was the distinguished nationalist, Nnamdi Azikiwe, an Ibo. The federal prime minister was a northerner, Sir Abubakar Tafewa Balewa. An initial harmony was entirely superficial. Symptomatically, efforts to conduct a census and publish its results—which would determine the allocation of resources to the various regions on the basis of their populations—only fueled regional and ethnic tensions. Elections in 1965 only exacerbated tensions and exposed deep-seated corruption within the system.

Resentment against northern domination of the federal system resulted in a bloody *coup d'état* in January 1966. It would be the first of the military interventions that would characterize Nigerian political life. Led by Major-General Johnson Aguiyi-Ironsi, an Ibo, the coup resulted in the brutal murder of the most prominent northern politicians, including Prime Minister Balewa and the Sarduana of Sokoto. Southerners, especially Ibos, who, because of their educational achievements had been employed and posted throughout Nigeria, became the object of bloody reprisals in the north. Ibo families fearing for their lives began a mass exodus to the eastern region.

General Ironsi was killed in a counter-coup in July and was replaced by neither a northerner nor a southerner, but a man of the Middle Belt, Lieutenant-Colonel Yakubu Gowon. Conferences to settle the conflict were unproductive. With the leadership of Colonel Odumegwu Ojukwu, an Ibo, three eastern states seceded from the federation in 1967 to form the independent Republic of Biafra.

From 1967 to 1970 Nigeria was consumed by civil war. The world took note when images of starving Biafran children, their bellies swollen in starvation and their hair turned orange by Kwashiorkor—the Ghanaian word for protein deficiency—became nightly features on the televised news. The war ended abruptly in 1970 when Ojukwu fled and Biafrans surrendered. Estimates for the death toll during the war range between 500,000 and 2 million.

The early seventies were dominated by efforts to rebuild the nation's economy, severely damaged by the war, and to reintegrate the eastern region into the federal system. Some of this work was facilitated by the oil boom of the period. As a consequence of its oil production, Nigeria became one of Africa's wealthiest states, but in many ways, oil has been as much a curse as a boon.

As the country increased its dependence on petroleum, it suffered from price fluctuations—boom in the seventies, bust in the early eighties when the price of oil plummeted. Investments in the energy sector diverted money from the development of the agricultural sector, just as petroleum-related jobs drew thousands from their fields. The vast income derived from oil only intensified regional discontent. Producing areas suffered environmental degradation and felt as though "their" resources were siphoned off to the central government, from which they received few benefits. Oil income also encouraged lavish construction projects and provided endless possibilities for corruption.

The construction of the new federal capital city at Abuja was a classic example of Nigerian corruption. By the mid-1980s half-completed government buildings and luxury hotels were everywhere, replete with poor quality, design, workmanship and materials. Transfer of governmental bureaus from

**President Shehu Shagari (from 1979 through 1983)**

overcrowded Lagos to Abuja took much longer than expected.

In 1975 General Gowon was overthrown and replaced by Brigadier Murtala Ramat Mohammed who began the process of moving the federal capital to Abuja. Caught in a Lagos traffic jam, Mohammed was assassinated in a 1976 coup attempt. His replacement, Lieutenant-General Olusegun Obasanjo, led the effort to introduce a new, American-style presidential constitution. Elections under the new constitution brought a northerner, Alhaji Shehu Shagari, to power in 1979.

Oil revenues, which peaked in 1980, provided prosperity that drew attention away from regional and ethnic tensions. By 1983, an election year, income from oil had dropped by half. The government responded to popular pressures and expelled more than one million foreigners, mostly Ghanaians, saying they had overstayed their visas and were taking jobs from Nigerians. The act proved popular in Nigeria, and the northern coalition reelected President Shagari in an election deeply flawed by irregularities.

Corruption under the civilian government was endemic, massive, and economically debilitating. The military, disgusted with rampant corruption, took power under the leadership of General Ibrahim Babangida. After 25 years of turbulence and corruption, a wide variety of Nigerians— intellectuals, the press, businessmen and even former politicians—supported Babangida. The new government instituted military tribunals for officials suspected of corruption and offered public executions of violent criminals as proof of moral rigor.

General Babangida's government was under heavy external and internal pressure to return power to civilians by the beginning of the 1990s. Suspicious of any proliferation of parties, Babangida decreed that there be only two parties. One, the Social Democratic Party, was to be "a little" to the left; the other, the National

**Northern Nigeria's ancient Muslim city of Kano at the edge of the Sahara**   AP/Wide World Photo

Republican Convention, was to be "a little" to the right. Such was the military mind at work, simplifying the complex and making choice easier.

Elections were held in June 1993, but were annulled when preliminary results showed victory by Chief Moshood Abiola, a super-rich Yoruba businessman who also happened to be a Muslim with good connections with some northern politicians. Soon thereafter President Babangida resigned from office, and Chief Ernest Shonekan was appointed head of the Interim National Government. The interim was brief. On 17 November Defense Minister Sani Abacha staged yet another coup. With Abacha, Nigeria entered one of its darkest periods.

Infinitely corrupt and sadistically brutal, Abacha flaunted both civil and human rights, and violently suppressed the opposition. Political parties were outlawed, their candidates silenced, and labor strikes promptly abolished; state, local and federal government offices were seized. When Abiola proclaimed himself

president in 1994, Abacha had him arrested and imprisoned. Abacha, of course, promised to restore civilian rule.

The military government worked through local, traditional rulers to maintain control of Nigeria, particularly in the oil-producing regions. In 1994 Nigerian playwright Ken Saro–Wiwa and eight other activists from the Ogoni people of Rivers State decided to dramatize the regional inequalities from which their people suffered. They claimed that the Ogoniland environment was being ruined. Four traditional Ogoni leaders were gunned down, and the government charged Saro–Wiwa and his cohorts with the murders. A trial, held in secret, by a court selected by Abacha, followed. Death sentences for all nine men were inevitable, and despite international protest, they were carried out.

It was clear that General Abacha was planning to run for the Nigerian presidency later in 1998. Relative success in Liberia and Sierra Leone, though terribly expensive, had given a temporary boost

to his reputation as a regional leader. As of April, all five legally permitted parties had asked Abacha to be their candidate. In effect this meant that the presidential election was now a referendum: Abacha or not?

The Abacha era came to an abrupt end in June 1998 when the dictator suddenly died. General Abdusalam Abubakar, chief of the defense staff, succeeded him as head of state and effected a transition to civilian rule. Political detainees were released, including General Obasanjo who had been detained since 1995 as a suspect in an anti-Abacha coup. Chief Abiola, in detention since 1994, suddenly collapsed on July 7. All efforts to save his life failed. His death eliminated a major problem for General Abubakar and facilitated the relatively smooth transition to civilian rule in May 1999.

Elections for a civilian government were organized and successfully carried out. Northern power brokers—the Kaduna mafia—agreed to a shift in power that would bring a southerner to the pres-

# Nigeria

**A Nok Sculpture from Nigeria's earliest great civilization**
Photo Courtesy Galerie al Farahnick, Brussels

idential office for the first time. For the presidency, two Yoruba opposed each other. Olu Falae, a former finance minister, was the standard bearer of the progressive Alliance for Democracy and the more conservative All People's Party (APP). Olusegun Obasanjo, the only military man actually to hand back the reins of government to civilians, represented the centrist People's Democratic Party (PDP). Obasanjo, who clearly had the backing of northern politicians and the army, won 62.8% of the vote to Falae's 37.2%. The PDP also won a clear majority in both houses of parliament.

President Obasanjo's first term was characterized by years of crisis-to-crisis management. The return to democracy placed extraordinary demands on the government. Freed from 15 years of iron-fisted military rule, Nigerians erupted in what appeared at times a volcanic expression of grievance, complaint and demand, often descending into ethnic, regional or sectarian conflicts—most of which went back to the very origin and creation of the state.

At the heart of all current controversies are the nature and definition, if not the existence, of the Nigerian state: What should be the balance of resources and power between the central government and individual states?

## Regional and Sectarian Tensions

Regional tensions persist in both north and south. In the south, crisis is sited in the Niger Delta area, source of Nigeria's wealth, but an area in which the processes of extracting that wealth have created an ecological hell. Since 1986, between two and three million barrels of oil have been spilled on the land and creeks of the Delta region, killing the soil and polluting the waters, depriving local inhabitants of their traditional means of livelihood. Every day eight million cubic feet of natural gas are flared, adding deadly illumination to the processes of extractive destruction.

Despite its generation of fabulous wealth, the Niger Delta area remains one of Nigeria's poorest and least developed regions. For residents there is a near total absence of schools, drinking water, electricity, and medical care. A crescendo of regional complaint has been raised, demanding a greater share of petroleum profits. The most intractable of demands came from young members of the Ijaw community, probably the fourth largest group in Nigeria.

On December 11, 1998, some 5,000 members of the Ijaw Youth Council (IJC) from the Delta region had met in Kaiama, Bayelsa State, and passed what has become known as the Kaiama Declaration. The declaration gave vent to their frustrations with the leadership of an older generation that had achieved so little in terms of communal and environmental improvement. "We are tired," the resolution said, "of gas flaring, oil spillages, [and] blowouts. . ." In many ways it amounted to a declaration of secession from a Federal Nigeria. The IJC declared that it ceased to recognize all decrees "enacted without our participation and consent."

The Declaration went on to claim ownership of all natural resources found in Ijaw territory and demanded that the oil companies stop exploration and exploitation activities. Oil workers were given an ultimatum to vacate Ijaw land or face the consequences. The deadline for cessation of activities and withdrawal of personnel was set for 30 December. Then, the Declaration said, "Ijaw youths in all communities in all Ijaw clans in the Niger Delta will take steps to implement these resolutions. . ."

To ease tensions, the government agreed to implement a constitutional provision that allocates 13% of oil revenue to each oil-producing region. But the legislation creating a Niger Delta Development Commission (NDDC)—caught in a dispute between legislature and executive—was long delayed, and the basic question of whether the provision covered both off-shore and on-shore oil production proved difficult to resolve. (Non-oil-producing states opposed inclusion of offshore production, realizing it would reduce their revenues.) Legislation basically abolishing the distinction was finally signed into law in February 2004.

Funding of the NDDC remains controversial. By law, the Federal government was to contribute 15% of its oil revenues, the state governments 10% of theirs, and oil producing companies 3% of their budgets to the commission. Oil-producing states have refused to contribute, saying the federal legislature could not statutorily allocate monies constitutionally granted to the states, while both the Fed-

**President Olusegun Obasanjo**

**Natural gas storage sphere, Escravos Project**　　　Photo courtesty Chevron

eral government and companies have been slow to fulfill their allotments.

Three years into its existence, the NDDC's work is equally controversial. Critics charge lack of transparency, bloated contract awards and general shoddiness. President Obasanjo has expressed disappointment with the commission's handling of its funds and is seeking amendments to reduce the Federal contribution—from 15 percent to ten—as well as a "downward review" in the oil companies' contribution. Tellingly, he has criticized the commission for not even having a youth directorate to deal with the interests of restive young people.

Ethnic violence, amounting to a virtual rebellion by militant Ijaw youth, surged in 2003, forcing oil companies like Chevron-Texaco and Royal Dutch Shell to evacuate the region and the Federal government to establish a heavy security presence in the regional center of Warri. Tensions persist and will only intensify as politicians jockey for attention and influence among the region's powerful local tribes, youth groups, and militias in the lead up to the 2007 presidential elections.

The Obasanjo government faced its greatest crisis after the governor of an obscure northern state decided to implement Sharia law for the state's Muslim population. Sharia imposes a variety of harsh and in many ways brutal punishments. At independence Nigeria's legal system had incorporated aspects of Islamic, Western and customary law. Customary law applied to land and marriage matters in parts of the Christian and animist south, for example, while Islamic law applied strictly to personal matters, not criminal matters in the North.

Under Sharia law some states have banned prostitution, gambling and the consumption of alcohol, while others have introduced single-sex schools and taxis. Sentences include death by stoning for adultery or sodomy, amputation of limbs for stealing, and public flogging for premarital sex or drinking alcohol in public. The introduction of Sharia as applied to criminal matters by the northern states—now some twelve in number—has resulted in destructive sectarian and communal riots in some areas and is an on-going source of tension.

Nigeria's minister of justice has raised the issue to a constitutional level. In letters to the governors of the northern states that had adopted Muslim law, he described Sharia penalties as unconstitutional. "A Muslim," he wrote, "should not be subjected to a punishment more severe than would be imposed on other Nigerians for the same offense. Equality before the law means that Muslims should not be discriminated against."

At some point the relationship between Nigeria's secular federal constitution and the states' sectarian legal codes will have to be resolved. When Dubem Onyia, a junior foreign minister, was asked by reporters why President Obasanjo did not challenge Sharia in court, his response was both blunt and ominous: "Anyone who wants to destroy this country should keep asking questions like that."

The state already faces security challenges from militant Islamists. In December 2003, some 200 members of the militant *Al Sunna wal Jamma* sect, which seeks to establish a strict Islamic state, attacked police stations in two small towns of Yobe state in the far northeast, killing two policemen and seizing arms and ammunition before trying to occupy the state capital, Damaturu. A combined force of soldiers and police suppressed the insurrection after several days of skirmishes in which some 18 people were killed. Many of the militants, inspired by the Taliban and allegedly funded with Saudi money, were arrested.

President Obasanjo ran for re-election in April 2003, facing nominees from twenty political parties. In practical terms, his principal opponent was another retired general and former president, Muhammadu Buhari, nominated by the All Nigeria People's Party (ANPP), the renamed APP.

As the governing party, the People's Democratic Party (PDP) had significant advantages, and these advantages were reflected in election results. The PDP won majorities in both houses of parliament, the bulk of state governorships (27 out of 36), and its presidential candidate, Olusegun Obasanjo, roundly defeated the

ANPP's Buhari—62% to 32%. The remaining votes were shared by the 18 other opposition candidates.

The election was far from perfect and monitors reported instances of ballot stuffing, multiple voting and outright forgery of results. Bitterness remains. An ANPP challenge to election results is still in court and a coalition of opposition parties, the Conference of Nigerian Political Parties (CNPP), planned mass protests on the first anniversary of the election. Warned by the State Security Service that a demonstration would jeopardize national security, the coalition postponed the protest. A presidential spokeswoman accused the opposition of "overheating the system," adding that those who did this "should be regarded as an enemy of Nigeria."

Even before this (and perhaps explaining the heavy-handed response), a palpable sense of unease characterized the country. In early April 2004 a number of Nigerian military officers were arrested following what were termed "serious breeches of security." President Obasanjo went so far as to urge his people to protect civilian rule from "unpatriotic elements" in his Easter address to the nation. "The future of this country," he told his audience, "clearly lies in our continued adherence to democratic principles." This will be tested as the 2007 presidential elections, in which President Obasanjo cannot succeed himself, approach.

**Culture:** Nigerians pride themselves on being, in many ways, the "biggest" and the "best." Nigeria is the most populous country in Africa. The ruling PDP is the largest political party in Africa and the Nigerian Television Authority is the largest television network in Africa. It can also claim to have the largest number of universities in Africa, but the educational system, from primary through university, is a shambles.

According to USAID, only 60% of those eligible are enrolled in primary school and nearly half of these eventually drop out before completing primary education; of those who complete sixth grade, only 40% are functionally literate. At Nigeria's once-proud universities, the curriculum is outdated and sorely in need of updating, while facilities are in a state of rapid decay. None of this is surprising. The government's budgetary allocation for education has fallen steeply from 11.2% in 1999, to 1.83% in 2003. UNESCO recommends an allocation of 26% of a country's annual budget to education, but given competing priorities, there is no way the government will reach this level for years, if at all. (With a GDP of $58.4 billion in 2003, Nigeria is a classic example of the "paradox

# Nigeria

of poverty." Vast oil wealth has been translated into neither development nor improved living conditions for the bulk of its huge population. On the UN's *Human Development Index* for 2004, Nigeria ranked 151 out of 177 states, just two steps above Haiti!)

The country's health statistics were not improved by events in Northern Nigeria. There, obscurantist religion and politics collided with lethal impact in 2003. Claiming that polio vaccines were contaminated and may be responsible for the spread of AIDS, Muslim clerics in four Northern states—Bauchi, Kano, Kaduna, and Zamfara—forced a halt in the World Health Organization's program to eliminate the crippling disease in Nigeria. WHO reported that 40% of new cases of polio in 2003 were in Nigeria; and by 2005 the agency had tracked cases directly traceable to the Nigerian strain of the virus in sixteen countries—all the way to Indonesia.

In September 2003 Nigeria became the third African country (after South Africa and Algeria) to have a presence in outer space when a Nigerian satellite was launched from the Plesetsk Cosmodrome in Russia. The satellite is designed to survey things like deforestation and water resources where ground observation would be laborious and difficult. While prestigious and generating a lot of media coverage, the satellite did raise some eyebrows and questions: in a country where more than 80 million people live in abject poverty, is a space venture an appropriate expenditure of limited resources?

**Economy:** Nigeria's economy was radically transformed by the advent of oil production. From an agricultural economy, deriving 65% of foreign exchange earnings from food exports, Nigeria moved to become a major oil-exporting nation. The petroleum industry, centered on the Delta region of the Niger River, dominates Nigeria's economy. It accounts for nearly 95% of foreign exchange earnings, 80% of federal government revenues, and a whopping 40% to 45% of GDP.

Nigeria contains an estimated 35.2 billion barrels of oil reserves—most of them along the Niger River Delta. In 2004 the country was pumping an average of 2.5 million barrels of oil a day (bbl/d). Royal Dutch/Shell is the biggest company in the oil patch, accounting for nearly half of Nigeria's total oil production; other major players are the American firms Exxon-Mobil and ChevronTexaco, the Italian company ENI/Agip, and France's Total-FinaElf.

With extensive offshore exploration, the country hopes to increase its reserves to 40 billion barrels by 2010. Work towards

this goal has been stymied by the inability of the state-owned Nigerian National Petroleum Company to come up with the capital to fulfill its joint venture contracts with private oil firms. That Nigeria lacks investment capital while pumping more than two million bbl/d suggests the pervasive nature of Nigerian corruption and its deadly impact on economic growth.

Of the 145 countries ranked on Transparency International's *Corruption Perception Index* for 2004, Nigeria is ranked 144th, barely above Bangladesh and Haiti which were tied for last place as the world's most corrupt nations. Pervasive corruption, coupled with colossal economic mismanagement and excessive dependence on oil, are largely responsible for the country's poor economic performance and appalling poverty. GDP per capita, at $320 today, is well below the $370 Nigeria achieved in 1985. Some 66% of the population lives below the poverty line of a dollar a day, compared to only 43% in 1985. Actually, that's an improvement over the Abacha years when 87% of the population lived on less than a dollar a day.

Oil production has been sporadically interrupted by local protest and ethnic violence in the Delta region. Sabotage, occupation of oil facilities, hostage taking and kidnapping were all employed by local activists. In the run up to the 2003 elections ethnic conflict between Itsekiris and Ijaws over local government boundaries compelled major oil firms like Chevron and Shell to shut down their operations in the area. At the height of the troubles Nigeria's oil exports were cut by more than 840,000 bbl/d—more than 40% of normal

production. Over the past five years Nigeria is estimated to have lost $6.8 billion in oil and gas revenues because of the continuing crisis in the Delta region.

For the young Ijaw militants, this was altogether positive, a successful implementation of the Kaiama Declaration. Closing down the oil companies was a blessing—people could breathe fresh air and drink clean water; fewer would die, they argued. For them Shell was a criminal organization, the major enemy of Delta peoples, a company whose operations killed more than 10% of the people before they attained the age of 20.

In May 2005 ChevronTexaco admitted its aid program to local communities was proving "inadequate, expensive and divisive." Over the past decade the company had donated $129 million in aid, but this had only fuelled local tensions and created opportunities for corruption. "Violent, incessant inter-and-intra ethnic conflicts," said the company, "have left many of the development projects funded by the company destroyed, not to count the many lives and property lost." The findings were similar to those of Shell, and both companies have decided to eliminate cash grants and work with regional councils to devise projects locals want.

Shell and other oil producers have suffered staggering daily losses from organized thievery, or "bunkering," by lethally-armed criminal networks. Illegal oil bunkering would appear to be Nigeria's most profitable private business. Estimates of daily losses vary widely. The governor of Delta state has said that thieves steal 300,000 barrels of Nigerian crude every day. Shell alone has reported

**National Mosque—Abuja**

losing 100,000 barrels a day. If one assumes a price of $15 to $20 a barrel—it is illegal after all—the thieves are earning between $2-6 million daily. Working with the tacit support of local and foreign business mafias and abetted by powerful local military or political "godfathers," these criminal networks are important sources of funding for local militias and fueling the Delta's destabilizing arms race.

There are also huge environmental impacts from bunkering. In 2003 there 582 recorded pipeline vandalizations. Most of these were puncturing to steal oil, but after puncturing the pipelines, the thieves leave them leaking. The resultant spills have damaged wetlands, forests, and farmlands; they are also linked to the deadly fires that occur when local villagers attempt to scoop up the leaked oil. Pipeline fires have claimed more than 2,000 lives in the past six years.

Under-equipped and overwhelmed by the magnitude of bunkering, the government has only recently stepped up patrols of the Niger Delta, aided by seven ships donated by the United States. Anglo-Dutch Shell, which suffers so much from illegal bunkering, has proposed a system of chemical analysis that would let investigators determine the country of origin of any oil suspected of being stolen. All of this may be too little, too late. The criminalization of Nigeria's oil industry may have transcended the state's capacity to control its most important resource.

Nigeria is moving to diversify and decrease its dependence on oil. Natural gas, closely associated with oil, will ultimately replace it as the backbone of Nigeria's economy. The move to gas production comes from the government's desire to curb flaring, the simple burning off of gas associated with oil drilling and pumping. Seventy-five per cent of all associated gas is currently flared, making Nigeria one of the world's worst heat polluters. Under environmentalist pressure, the government has worked to reduce flaring and in December 2004 announced reductions of 30%. Official policy calls for elimination of all flaring by 2008.

Nigeria's proven gas reserves are put at about 176 trillion cubic feet, the ninth largest in the world. The Chevron project at Escravos, opened in 1997 for domestic and international markets; it will ultimately export natural gas to energy-starved Benin, Togo, and Ghana through the 400-mile West African Gas Pipeline (WAGP). The pipeline promises to make natural gas the basis of industrial development throughout coastal West Africa and help integrate the economies of the West African states.

Gas production in Nigeria faces the same problems of order and stability as the oil industry. Only 30% of Nigeria's gas reserves are offshore. Another 30% are in swamplands, and the rest are on dry land where production is vulnerable to escalating violence.

An even greater priority for the government is its privatization program. Action has been sluggish because it's hard to give up statist thinking and even harder to give up potential sources of political patronage. Nigeria has more than 1,500 state–owned enterprises (SOEs), and they cost the country more than $2 billion annually. Most are over-staffed, inefficient and make do with obsolete machinery. State corporations also provided huge patronage possibilities and were the basis of much of the power wielded by the old élites. There were more than 4,000 directors and executives of the largest corporations appointed by the president.

Movement on privatization—selling off an abundance of SOEs—is essential for a variety of reasons, the least important of which is money gained through the sales. In a post-military Nigeria, the control exercised by the federal government will need to be decentralized. The state can no longer afford to subsidize inefficient corporations when regions and local communities demand a share of scarce resources for their own development; privatization will help redress the balance between center and periphery. If handled properly, privatization could make a greater contribution to job creation and poverty elimination than continued donor support. Thus far, privatization has been slow and troubled.

Nigeria remains an important hub in the international illicit drug trade that seems to expand wherever Nigerians go. When ECOMOG forces were sent to Liberia, Monrovia's port became an important drug distribution point. When a Nigerian peacekeeping force went to Sierra Leone, the first thing that happened was that the Freetown airport became a drug trafficking platform. Nigerian drug trafficking rings are a worldwide phenomenon. One was identified working the Philippines in 1995. In the same year, Cambodian law enforcement authorities claimed that most drug traffickers in that country were from Nigeria or Ghana. Traffickers have a preference for repatriation of their profits, and the consequence of this has been the growth of elaborate money-laundering schemes. Outright fraudulent schemes, usually involving the alleged transfer of funds, also tumble creatively from the minds of Nigerian criminals. So extensive are these schemes that the American Secret Service maintains a separate Nigerian fraud squad in metropolitan Washington.

**The Future:** Over-reliance on the oil sector poses enormous problems for economic development. Nigeria is Africa's largest recipient of foreign direct investment, but 85% of this has gone to the hydrocarbons sector. President Obasanjo is keenly aware of the damage oil-reliance has done to the agricultural sector. Shortly after his election he announced that agriculture would be the main thrust of his administration. He indicated state governments would also be encouraged to do more in terms of agricultural development to guarantee more employment. Patience is counseled. To turn the Nigerian behemoth will take time. Lots of it.

**Oba Erediauna II, ruler of the Benin Kingdom**  Photo by Barbara Blackmun

# The Democratic Republic of São Tomé and Príncipe

(pronounced Sow Toe–*may* and *Preen–see*–pay)

São Tomé's volcanic shoreline

**Land:** 1001sq. km.=385 sq. mi. São Tomé is 275 miles off the coast of The Gabon; Príncipe is 125 miles off mainland Equatorial Guinea. Both lie just north of the Equator. (About one-third the size of Rhode Island).

**Population:** 187,410 (July 2005 est.)

**Capital City:** São Tomé

**Climate:** Tropical; hot, humid; one rainy season (October to May).

**Official Language:** Portuguese

**Other Principal Languages:** Crioulo

**Ethnic groups:** Mestico, Angolares (descendants of Angolan slaves), Forros (descendants of freed slaves), *Servicais* (contract laborers from Angola, Mozambique, and Cape Verde), Tongas (children of *servicais* born on the islands), and Europeans (primarily Portuguese).

**Principal Religions:** Roman Catholic, Evangelical Protestant, and Seventh-day Adventist.

**Chief Commercial Products:** Cocoa, copra, coffee, palm, and oil.

**GNI per capita:** $320 (2003)

**Currency:** Dobra (Db)

**Independence Date:** 12 July 1975 (from Portugal).

**Chief of State:** Fradique Melo Bandiera de Menezes (since July 2001).

**National Flag:** Three horizontal bands of green (top), yellow (double width), and green with two black five-pointed stars placed side by side in the center of the yellow band and a red isosceles triangle based on the hoist side; uses the popular pan-African colors of Ethiopia.

São Tomé and Príncipe form an archipelago of two main islands and several associated islets lying just north of the Equator. Of volcanic origins, the islands have fertile central highlands from which numerous fast flowing streams carry soil to the ocean. Tropical rainforests cover 75% of the land area and shelter flora and fauna similar to that found on mainland Equatorial Guinea.

**History:** Portuguese navigators discovered the uninhabited islands in the late 15th century. By the mid-16th century slaves had been imported, and the islands had become a major exporter of sugar. A slave-based plantation economy characterized the islands well into the 20th century based, after the decline of sugar exports, on coffee and finally cocoa.

The rich volcanic soils proved well-suited to cocoa trees, and by 1908 São Tomé had become the world's largest producer of coco. The crop was grown on extensive plantations called *rocas*—owned by Portuguese companies or absentee landlords—that occupied all productive farmland. The *rocas* system inevitably led to abusive treatment of African farm workers, and the history of the islands is filled with slave revolts and resistance to labor demands.

Local dissatisfaction with working conditions on the plantations led to an outbreak of riots in 1953. In what became known as the "Batepa Massacre," over 1,000 *forros* (the descendants of freed slaves) were shot by Portuguese troops for refusing to work the *rocas*. The massacre is seen as the beginning of the nationalist movement in the islands.

A Committee for the Liberation of São Tomé and Príncipe was created in exile in 1960. It changed its name to the Movement for the Liberation of São Tomé and Príncipe (MLSTP) in 1972. Unlike its counterpart in Guinea-Bissau, the MLSTP never mounted a guerrilla campaign against the Portuguese.

Following the overthrow of the Salazar dictatorship in 1974, African troops in São Tomé mutinied, and the new government agreed to hand over power to the MLSTP in 1975. Independence was granted on July 12, 1975. Most Portuguese had already departed, taking skills and capital with them. At independence, the Portuguese legacy was a 90% illiteracy rate, few skilled workers, and abandoned plantations.

At independence the MLSTP became the nation's sole political party and ruled with little tolerance for opposition for 15 years. Its leader, Manuel Pinto da Costa, assumed the new nation's presidency, and Miguel Trovoada, another founder of the MLSTP, was elected prime minister.

To cope with the country's disastrous economic inheritance, President Pinto da Costa turned to Marxist-Leninist models of political and economic organization. Most plantations were nationalized, and no one was allowed to own more than 247 acres. The single ruling party largely absorbed the country's organizational life. Social control and surveillance were organized through a series of people's militias set up in workplaces and villages.

When cocoa prices collapsed in the mid-1980s, the economy was severely damaged. Popular dissatisfaction led to a process of liberalization, and multiparty democracy was introduced in 1990. Constitutional reforms included the direct election of the president, and Miguel Trovoada, whom Pinto da Costa had accused of complicity in a coup plot and had jailed from 1979 to 1981, returned from exile to battle his old comrade-in-arms for the presidency. Running as an independent, Trovoada won. He survived a coup attempt in 1995 and went on to win re-election to a second five-year term in 1996 against his old foe, Manuel Pinto da Costa. The country's political and economic crisis continued.

In November 1998 legislative elections the MLSTP, in alliance with the Social Democratic Party (PSD), won an absolute majority 31 of 55 seats in the National Assembly. President Trovoada's Independent Democratic Alliance (ADI: *Accao Democratica Independente*) became the official opposition. São Tomé's politics remain bitter, personal and contentious.

The government continued to face serious social agitation in the late 1990s.

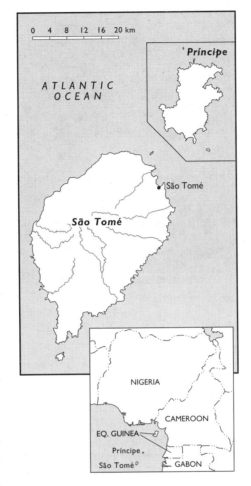

Workers saw their own conditions deteriorating while rumors of a huge oil bonanza were rife. Civil servants, including doctors and teachers, regularly struck to protest their salaries and working conditions. In July 1999, president Trovoada admitted that salaries and pensions were inadequate.

More darkly, he sent a warning to the government: "São Tomé's oil cannot be a matter for political colleagues, friends and relatives. Its revenue should benefit citizens and the population as a whole." With remarkable candor Trovoada accused "a number of citizens and political leaders of eagerly getting themselves into positions to reap fabulous personal benefits." The battle lines were sharply drawn for the next president election.

The July 2001 election results came as a surprise to many. The best known name—former president Manuel Pinto da Costa—went down to a humiliating defeat, unable to get enough votes to force a run-off election. Fradique de Menezes, a wealthy businessman, was elected president with 56.31% of the vote. Pinto da Costa received only 38.73%, with the remaining ballots distributed among three minor candidates.

For most San Toméans, Pinto da Costa resurrected memories of authoritarian single-party rule and disastrous Marxist Leninist economic policies under the MLSTP. Fradique de Menezes interjected an entrepreneurial dynamism into the campaign. Where da Costa spoke of a fair distribution of oil and gas revenues, de Menezes said he would encourage their investment in agriculture, the mainstay of the country's economy.

In addition to wanting abandoned agricultural concerns to be rehabilitated, de Menezes presented a thoughtful analysis of the country's problems and prospects. He wanted, he said, "to dynamize" the country. That would mean reducing the huge bureaucracy created by the MLSTP and finding good managers for the public sector. "We have made lots of mistakes in our 26 years of independence," he said. "We have destroyed what little we inherited from the colonial era. Does it make any sense that there should be only one hospital in the entire country?"

Stalemate between the new president and the MLSTP majority in parliament made cohabitation impossible. The National Assembly was dissolved and legislative elections held in March 2002. The political kaleidoscope shifted slightly, but in the end things remained pretty much the same. The ADI went through an internal crisis, divided between supporters of ex-president Trovoada's son Patrice, and the party's secretary-general, Carlos Neves. President de Menezes backed the formation of the Democratic Movement of Forces for Change (MDFM), which attracted a number of ADI dissidents and joined with the only other party to hold seats in the National Assembly—the *Partido da Convergencia Democratica* (PCD). Patrice Trovoada, wealthy and ambitious, linked up five parties to create an opposition alliance, Ue-Kedadji (Light of Day).

Since party platforms were largely similar, voters could make few sharp distinctions; the election resulted in a virtual tie, the MLSTP winning 24 seats and the MDFM/PCD 23. Ue-Kedadji took the remaining eight seats. President de Menezes, who had hoped for a parliamentary majority, was forced to accept a coalition national unity government.

São Tomé has a semi-presidential political system that combines aspects of both presidential and parliamentary systems. It is the president who nominates the Prime Minister, who must be approved by the National Assembly. It is a recipe for institutional conflict, with both executive and legislature vying for primacy. Tensions between president and Assembly are regular, persistent and potentially destabilizing. They spiked in early 2003 as President de Menezes dealt with the sen-

# São Tomé and Príncipe

sitive issues surrounding São Tomé's oil future and its relationship with the Colossus to the North, Nigeria.

Finding three oil contracts signed by the Trovoada government grossly unfair, de Menezes decided to reject them and demand renegotiation. The president was also engaged in delicate negotiations with Nigeria over disputed boundaries, critical because of potentially vast oil resources located in the disputed territories. Since the negotiations were being handled by the president and his natural resources minister, Rafael Branco, almost exclusively, the institutional jealousy of the Assembly was roused. (Once the boundary dispute was settled valuable exploration rights would be sold off, a honey pot to which legislative factions did not want to be denied access.)

Legislation was introduced to amend the constitution and reduce the power of the presidency. Among other things, the president's ability to negotiate international treaties would be limited. Terming the proposed reforms a "palace coup," President de Menezes vetoed the amendment package and dissolved the Assembly. Mediators managed to soothe ruffled feathers. The dissolution was withdrawn and the Assembly agreed to a national referendum on the constitutional amendments before the end of the President's term of office.

Relations with Nigeria pit a São Toméan David against the Nigerian Goliath. The resources are utterly asymmetrical, with Nigeria having 800 times the population. To resolve the boundary dispute, President de Menezes deftly lined up a number of backers. Membership in the community of Lusophone (Portuguese-speaking) states gave access to the experience of East Timor, renegotiating its oil contracts with Australia. More importantly, it brought the weight of countervailing influence from West Africa's other petroleum giant, Angola. Finally, he mobilized support in the United States, stressing São Tomé's democratic credentials, (relative) stability, and strategic location in an oil producing area that could easily replace a hostile, dangerous, and unstable Middle East. It worked.

The Americans pressured Nigeria to give up efforts to station a force of two hundred soldiers in São Tomé. Three questionable oil contracts were successfully renegotiated, and, once those impediments had been cleared away, the boundary settlement was finalized.

Despite successful conclusion of the boundary and contract issues, political tensions between the president and his critics persisted, fanning social discontent as the bulk of the population saw no improvement in their life circumstances. On

**President Fradique de Menezes**
Photo by AFP/Andre Kosters

July 16, 2003, soldiers staged a *coup d'état*, seizing key sites and arresting government ministers. (President de Menezes himself was in Nigeria at the time.) The coup was mounted by local soldiers (grievances about living conditions, salary arrears, obsolete equipment, and government corruption) and members of a small, shadowy, and marginal political party, the *Frente Democrata Crista* (FDC: Christian Democratic Front).

Universally condemned, the coup ended within a week. The putschists and President de Menezes signed an agreement with international negotiators led by Nigeria. President de Menezes was reinstated, but agreed to greater transparency in oil negotiations and greater respect for the separation of powers between the presidency and parliament. Parliament unanimously approved a general amnesty for the junta, while Nigeria, South Africa and the United States agreed to assist the government in setting the tone for national reconciliation—in effect, taking on the role of guarantors of the country's stability.

By March 2004 political tensions between president and parliament reached crisis proportions over the development of São Tomé's oil resources. Prime Minister Maria das Neves (MLSTP) demanded the resignations of her ministers of natural resources and foreign affairs, both of whom she accused to negotiating petroleum agreements without her knowledge. Both ministers were members of the president's Democratic Movement of Forces for Change (MDFM) party, and when the two other MDFM ministers resigned in solidarity the Prime Minister's three-party coalition government was reduced to two parties and a very slim majority in parliament.

After months of rivalry, Menezes dismissed das Neves in September when her name was raised in a corruption scandal. Damião Vaz d'Almeida, a former labor minister, was asked to form a government and managed to cobble together a coalition of MLSTP and ADI ministers. The anti-corruption investigations by São Tomé's Attorney General are rippling through the country's political class with greater speed since the Assembly finally lifted parliamentary immunity from a number of its members, including two former prime ministers (Maria das Neves and Posser da Costa) in February 2005.

Faced with persistent corruption, the imminence of oil revenues, and intense pressure from the IMF, São Tomé's National Assembly enacted a remarkable legal framework for the management of oil revenues in August 2004. A national petroleum fund is to be set up, with strict transparency and accountability mechanisms: transfers of money will require the signatures of the president, prime minister, central bank governor and other senior finance officials. Two annual audits of the fund must be carried out, one by the national Court of Accounts and the other by an international accounting firm. At least 65% of annual oil revenues must be devoted to health, education and infrastructure projects, and a separate 5% will go to the island of Príncipe, the smaller and poorer of the country's two major components.

**Culture:** Wilder than Cape Verde and closer to Europe than the Caribbean, São Tomé and Príncipe represent a relatively unspoiled paradise for tourists. Clean beaches, a stunning Blue Lagoon, rain forest and mountains with the Obo Natural Park are all available to the intrepid. These would appear to be few: in 1998 there were only some 2,000 visitors to the islands.

The climate is equatorial, and to avoid oppressive humidity it's best to arrive during the driest and coolest months—from June to September. Roads are few, and any serious tourism requires four-wheel drive vehicles.

São Tomé, the capital, has a wealth of down-at-the-heels colonial architecture. The city's atmosphere is unrushed and unhurried. Blackouts are frequent, adding to the somnambulant mood. For many the best cup of coffee in the world comes from local beans.

**Economy:** The country has been traditionally dependent on the export of cocoa. In 1975 Portuguese plantation farmers held 90% of all cultivated land on the islands. After independence, with a regime in the thrall of Stalinist economic thinking, the cocoa plantations were collectivized. Production collapsed and the plantations deteriorated. From exports of 11,400 tons of cocoa in 1900, production plummeted to 4,000 in 1996.

São Tomé's dependence on cocoa has been virtually total, and it suffers greatly from the fluction of cocoa prices on world markets. Any fall in prices is especially disastrous for small producers, many of whom are forced into debt. The islands have consequently faced vertiginous inflation and high unemployment.

Diversification is essential, and the government is exploring a variety of options. Sweet peppers and flowers, which have a high value on the international market, are seen as viable alternatives. Fishing agreements bring in some revenue to the national treasury. Commercial timber operations are mostly geared to local usage, though the bark of cinchona trees is commercially harvested for quinine production.

The most important potential for São Tomé lies in its oil prospects. President de Menezes has successfully lifted the burden of onerous industry contracts, worst of which goes back to 1997 when one of the minnows of the industry, Louisiana-based Environmental Remediation Holding Corporation (ERHC), secured a contract which gave it enormous control over the country's oil development. After a new contract was initialed São Tomé and Nigeria signed a settlement of their boundary dispute.

The settlement creates a Joint Development Zone (JDZ) out of the area of overlapping claims. The two states will jointly develop the JDZ and share the resources on a split of 60% for Nigeria and 40% for São Tomé. (Reserves in the JDZ are estimated at six billion barrels.) In February 2005 the two signed the first agreement for exploration in the JDZ with a consortium headed by ChevronTexaco and ExxonMobil. The signature bonus was nearly $125 million.

Actual oil production is many years off. While São Tomé awaits discovery and production from the JSZ, Nigeria is to provide it with 10,000 barrels of crude oil daily, thus providing an oil dividend income before actual production begins.

Until oil investment and production revenues begin to flow, São Tomé will remain largely dependent on foreign aid. Its budget is chronically in deficit and the country's enormous debt of $364 million (2002) is one of the highest per capita in the world. Foreign aid, mostly supplied by Taiwan, France, and Portugal, presently accounts for about 80% of GDP and covers 95% of public investment. That represents one of the highest per capita aid rates in the world—$239.4 per person (2003). The World Bank and IMF have agreed to help reduce the country debt obligations through the Highly Indebted Poor Countries Initiative.

Sao Tome is central to the U.S. strategy for ensuring security of oil supplies from the Gulf of Guinea. In early 2004 it agreed to finance an $800,000 viability study for expanding São Tomé and Príncipe's international airport and building a deep-water port. The islands are an ideal location for monitoring satellite observations of the Gulf of Guinea.

**The Future:** President de Menezes has shrewdly exploited the shift in American interests following the terrorism of September 11, 2001. Strategically located in the rich oil fields of West Africa, São Tomé may yet prove that oil income can alleviate crushing mass poverty rather than provide elite enrichment.

São Tomé's rain forest

# EQUATORIAL WEST AFRICA

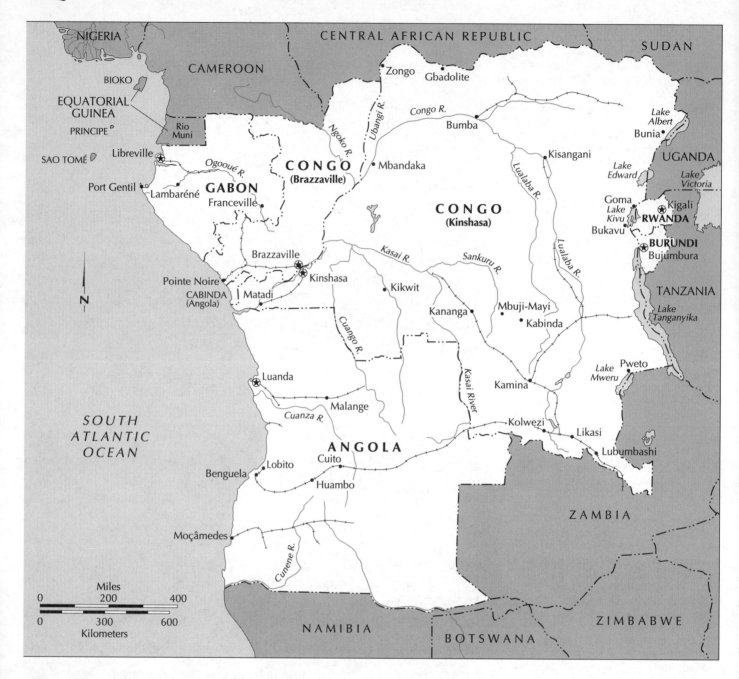

## The Republic of Angola

**Area:** 1,245,790 sq. km. = 481,000 sq. mi. (about four times the size of New Mexico).

**Population:** 11,190,786 (July 2005 est.).

**Capital City:** Luanda (Pop. 4 million, est.).

**Climate:** Moist and warm in the North, dryer and hot in the large, central plateau area; arid, semi–desert in the South.

**Neighboring Countries:** Congo–Kinshasa (North); Namibia (South); Zambia (Southeast).

**Official Language:** Portuguese.

**Other Principal Languages:** Over forty African languages, including Tchokwe, Kikongo, Kwanyama, Mbundu, Nyaneka, and Umbundu.

**Ethnic groups:** Ovimbundu 37%, Kimbundu 25%, Bakongo 13%, Mestico (mixed European and Native African) 2%, European 1%, and other 22%.

**Principal Religions:** Indigenous beliefs 47%, Roman Catholic 38%, Protestant 15% (1998 est.).

**Chief Commercial Products:** Crude oil 90%, diamonds, refined petroleum products, gas, coffee, sisal, fish and fish products, timber, cotton.

**GNI per capita:** $740 (2003)

**National Flag:** Two horizontal stripes of equal width, red and black, upon which is centered a 5–pointed yellow star, halfway surrounded by a wheel and crossed by a machete.

**Currency:** Kwanza.

**Former Colonial Status:** Portuguese Colony until November 11, 1975; actual control passed in early 1975.

**Independence Date:** November 11, 1975.

**Chief of State:** José Eduardo dos Santos, President.

For most of its sprawling area, Angola is a high, grassy plateau land ranging from 3,000 to 4,000 feet above sea level, dotted by occasional trees and brush—barely enough to withstand the scorching heat of the day. The coastal belt, home to about 20% of the population, is from 15 to 60 miles wide, stretching from the tropical mouth of the mighty Congo River, down to the palm-lined central beaches, and then on to the reddish sands of the Namib Desert in the extreme south.

Lofty mountains drive eastward, splitting the country in half until the terrain gradually levels out, dipping first northeast into the hot, steaming rain forest of Zaïre's river basin and then southeast to isolated, semi–arid land. The mountains are the source of rivers, which fan out in all directions.

The Cuanza River, Angola's largest, twists north for 600 miles in a wavering half–circle and then drains into the Atlantic below cosmopolitan Luanda. The Cunene's cold waters gush south down the mountains, slow as they pass through the plains, become sluggish in the silent desert, then lazily turn westward and are caught by the huge Cunene Dam, which regulates its flow as it forms the 175–mile border with Namibia to the ocean. Another river, in the northeast, offers unique drama.

Meandering aimlessly across the sun–parched grasslands, the Lucala unexpectedly reaches a wide, curved rock shelf where the placid waters suddenly plunge into a 350–foot gorge, sending up a heavy spray–mist which transforms the immediate area into a lush oasis, rich with dark mosses and tropical foliage—the Duque de Bragança Falls—a truly spectacular sight. Again docile, the river moves across the flat land and joins the waters of the larger Cuanza.

Cutting across otherwise unspoiled country teeming with wildlife is the Benguela Railroad. Its tracks have clattered to the tune of millions of tons of rich copper ore shipped from the vast mines in Zaïre and Zambia to coastal Benguela and then to Lobito, Angola's principal port. Due to guerrilla activities, the line has not been in regular use since 1975 except in the coastal region.

**History:** The Bushmen were probably the first inhabitants of Angola during the late Stone Age; they were driven southward by a Bantu migration, which was to occupy most of Africa below the Sahara Desert. This region constituted the southernmost part of the once–mighty Kingdom of the Kongo—a loose confederation of Bantu peoples dominated by the Bakongo prior to the arrival of European explorers. For details of early and colonial

**The consequences of civil war: massive destruction of infrastructure**

©IRIN

history, see *Historical Background* and *The Portuguese in Africa*.

Portugal's colonial policies generated increasing resistance and resentment by the 1950s. Assimilation had produced a small group of educated Angolans, mostly *mestiços*, who recognized there was no equality of treatment for an African, even if assimilated. In the countryside, the settlement of white farmers and use of forced labor embittered the rural peasantry.

Anti-colonial, nationalist sentiment first coalesced in Luanda, the capital, with the formation of the Popular Movement for the Liberation of Angola (MPLA) in 1956. The heart of the movement was a multiracial core of leftist urban intellectuals. Its ethnic core resided in the Mbundu people of Luanda and the surrounding area. As of 1962, the group was headed by Agostinho Neto, an assimilated Mbundu physician.

The MPLA's greatest rival in the early years was the National Front for the Liberation of Angola (FNLA). Led by Holden Roberto, FNLA began as a spokesman for ethnic interests of Angola's northern Bakongo peoples, but by 1958 it expanded its goals to independence for all Angola. A national liberation army was created, and young Angolans were sent to North Africa to train with Algerian forces engaged in their own nationalist struggle. A Revolutionary Government of Angola in Exile (GRAE), headquartered in Leopoldville, was also created and claimed sole representation of the interests of the Angolan people.

A falling out between Holden Roberto and his foreign minister in the GRAE,

Jonas Savimbi, led to the creation of the National Union for the Total Independence of Angola (UNITA) in 1964. The group's membership was rooted in Angola's largest ethnic group, the Ovimbundu, peasant farmers who dominated the fertile central highlands. In 1965 Savimbi (who earned a doctorate in political science from the University of Lausanne, Switzerland) and several of his followers went to China where they received military training and became disciples of Maoism. Like its rivals, UNITA claimed to be the sole representative of the Angolan people.

Angola's march to independence centered on these three military-political groups. They had one common enemy, Portugal, but differing nationalist visions. Each was specifically rooted in the geographical and ethnic reality of Angola and drew on different sources of external support that intensified rivalries, both personal and ideological. At a time of intense ideological competition internationally, each of the groups ultimately became an extension of Cold War rivalries between East and West.

With its Marxist-Leninist orientation, the MPLA attracted the support of the international left. Its military cadres received training in Eastern Europe and Cuba. Recently independent African states with similar left-leaning inclinations provided sympathetic support. Soviet arms transited through Tanzania and Zambia to supply its forces.

The nationalist struggles in its African colonies drained Portugal's will and re-

# Angola

sources. Some 11,000 Portuguese soldiers had been killed by 1974, and on April 25 of that year disgruntled military officers overthrew the Portuguese government and began the process leading to decolonization. Angola's transition to independence was difficult. A transitional government involving all three nationalist groups was created, but Portuguese settlers resisted and rioted. Rivalries between the three nationalist groups intensified. External aid and intervention increased.

The United States supported the pro-Western FNLA when it seemed the strongest of the groups, but it later shifted its support to UNITA. The Soviet Union responded with increased arms deliveries to the MPLA, and Cuba sent military instructors and combat troops. OAU negotiators brought Neto, Roberto, and Savimbi together in June 1975 to produce a draft constitution for independent Angola, but soon afterwards the transitional government collapsed. The FNLA and UNITA withdrew, and, recognizing their military weakness individually against the MPLA army, united and declared war against the MPLA. Group rivalry turned into civil war.

In support of the FNLA-UNITA alliance, South Africa, which had already worked with Portugal fighting nationalist guerrillas in Angola, and SWAPO guerillas fighting for the independence of South West Africa from Angolan bases, sent in an invasion force to protect hydroelectric facilities on the Cunene River in August 1975. A larger South African-led force invaded Angola in October. Six provincial capitals were occupied, and the invaders came within 62 miles of Luanda.

The combat this threat, the MPLA received a massive increase in Soviet military aid, while Cuba poured thousands of troops into the country; the military balance tipped in its favor. South African support of the FNLA and UNITA tainted both groups. Portugal granted independence amid the chaos of civil war on November 11, 1975, marking the end of four hundred years of Portuguese colonial rule.

The MPLA, in control of the capital, proclaimed the People's Republic of Angola. A rival "Democratic People's Republic of Angola" was proclaimed by the FNLA-UNITA alliance, but it was clear the MPLA, backed by some 10,000 to 12,000 Cuban troops, had emerged on top. International recognition followed, and the MPLA moved to create a Marxist-Leninist single-party state. Agostinho Neto served as both MPLA secretary-general and president of Angola. With Cuban assistance the FNLA was defeated militarily, leaving only one rival to dispute the MPLA government's legitimacy, Jonas Savimbi's UNITA.

President Neto died following an operation on September 10, 1979 and was succeeded by his foreign minister, José Eduardo dos Santos. Angola faced continuing instability from internal and external elements. UNITA continued armed resistance to the MPLA government. The presence of SWAPO guerilla bases brought frequent South African incursions, and this resulted in clashes between Cuban and South African troops.

The linked external problems were resolved in a grand diplomatic solution of 1988. South Africa agreed to the independence of South West Africa, while Cuba and South Africa jointly agreed to withdraw their troops from Angola. There remained only the irksome presence of Jonas Savimbi and UNITA.

Negotiations between the two nationalist rivals resulted in a June 1991 ceasefire. The lull in military conflict prepared the way for political conflict. Angola's single party constitution was amended to permit multiparty elections, and these were scheduled for September 1992. President dos Santos won a plurality of votes on the first ballot, but UNITA refused to accept the results, claiming widespread fraud. Within a few days UNITA resumed the civil war. UNITA supporters were chased from Luanda, and the second round of elections was never held.

Full-scale fighting continued until a peace accord was signed in Lusaka in November 1994. The Lusaka Protocol called for demilitarization of UNITA and the creation of a national army integrating UNITA elements into the Angola Armed Forces. It also called for a government of national unity and the extension of state administration to areas formerly under

**Dr. Jonas Savimbi of UNITA**

UNITA control. Neither side seemed genuinely committed to the peace accord. Indeed, the government was never committed to anything less than the total destruction of UNITA and the elimination of its leader, Jonas Savimbi.

Localized fighting continued throughout 1995 and 1996 despite the Lusaka Protocol. The year 1995 was marked by a major UN effort to bring peace to Angola. Under funded and understaffed, the multinational "peace-keeping" force could hardly observe activity throughout the country, but it did begin to implement the Lusaka provisions.

By April 1998 virtually all the Lusaka provisions had been implemented. UNITA had turned over almost all of the territory under its control to government administration; its soldiers, for the most part, were disarmed, and its propaganda radio shut down. For its part, the Angolan government recognized UNITA as an unarmed political party with the right to organize and campaign throughout the country. Savimbi was officially recognized as the main opposition leader with rights to hold regular consultations with President dos Santos, access to government media and the right to visit Angolan embassies abroad. For his personal safety, Savimbi was permitted a bodyguard of 400 men, ultimately to be reduced to 150. UNITA's participation in a Government of National Reconciliation (GURN) was made real with the inclusion of 70 deputies in parliament and the grant of seven ministerial portfolios in the unity government. What seemed a successful implementation of the Lusaka Accord was entirely superficial. In September 1997 the MPLA government suspended UNITA's ministers, vice-ministers, and parliamentarians, threatening GURN's existence. The government also mounted an effort to destroy UNITA as a political party by inducing a number of UNITA figures participating in GURN to break with Savimbi and form a new party. UNITA-Renovado, as it was called, deposed Savimbi as president was recognized by the government as the authentic "interlocutor for national reconciliation."

In the countryside, far from the probing eyes of reporters of UN monitoring teams, the Angola National Police (ANP) pursued another systematic approach to UNITA's destruction. Party leadership and grassroots structures were targeted. UNITA administrators, party officials and even persons merely accused of collaborating with UNITA were simply murdered.

After UNITA closed its radio station as part of the Lusaka agreement, the government filled the airwaves with what Western diplomats referred to as "fabricated news reports of UNITA atrocities." London's *Economist* reported that the propaganda campaign had become so virulent that both the UN and the Americans had issued statements denouncing the use of "false information" and "provocative rhetoric." The government's intent was clear: to create an atmosphere of fear and justify a renewal of hostilities against its foe.

## Mobutu's Fall and Its Consequences

Angola aggressively aided and exploited the collapse of the Mobutu regime in Zaïre as part of its campaign to destroy UNITA. It intervened militarily in the two Congos to destroy support and supply for Savimbi. Mobutu, who had long aided UNITA, was an obvious target; Angolan troops were sent to assist his opponent, Laurent Kabila. President Lissouba of Congo (Brazzaville) had also aided UNITA, so when civil war erupted between Lissouba and ex-president Sassou-Nguesso, Angolan planes bombed the capital and helped dispatch Lissouba to unhappy exile. Troops were also sent into Congo-Brazzaville to ferret out UNITA bases from which attacks on Cabinda had been made.

If the MPLA government was willing to use its armies against sovereign states, it was clear they would once again be used against UNITA. At the MPLA party congress in December 1998 President dos Santos made that clear, bluntly saying "the only way to achieve peace in Angola is through the political and military neutralization of UNITA and its president." The campaign, it appeared, would be directed by dos Santos himself.

He restructured his cabinet, dismissed the prime minister and assumed his powers, as well as those of the supreme command of the armed forces. He also moved to consolidate his personal power in the party as well as the state.

By spring 1999 both the government and UNITA had restocked their weapons and engaged in feints and tests of each other's capabilities. With no peace to observe, the UN withdrew, its $2.2-billion mission having expired in utter failure. The dos Santos government was free to pursue unlimited war against its foe.

Having spent a half a billion dollars on new armament, the Angolan army kept UNITA forces on the run once the war began. UNITA's central highland cities were captured and its forces fragmented and dispersed. The government obtained permission from its close ally, Namibia, to pursue fleeing rebels into Namibian territory.

By 2001 the government had eliminated UNITA's capacity to conduct conventional warfare, but was incapable of destroying the group. UNITA forces melted into the

**President José Eduardo dos Santos**

landscape and resorted to traditional guerilla tactics. Having failed to destroy its enemy militarily, the MPLA government found itself faced with growing demands for some negotiated settlement from civil society.

Over the years Angola's civil society had grown larger, stronger, and bold enough to condemn the government's war that had destroyed the country but not the enemy. Increasingly vociferous church groups and humanitarian organizations lead the way. Military destruction remained the preferred option for the government, however, which continued to buy arms wherever it could.

Possessed of overwhelming superiority in weaponry, the Angolan army pursued its UNITA foe relentlessly throughout 2001, shrinking Jonas Savimbi's sphere of operations to the province of Moxico, a vast under-populated region bordering Zambia. It adopted a scorched earth policy in the province, removing any civilians that might have aided the rebels. A number of Savimbi's leading officers were captured and the army penetrated his security network. The end came on 22 February 2002. Savimbi was pursued, cornered and killed. After more than thirty years of guerilla warfare, the government's *bête noire* was dead.

Within six weeks of Savimbi's death, UNITA's military commander signed a ceasefire. Parliament facilitated things by voting a blanket amnesty covering "all civilians and soldiers, Angolan or foreign, who committed crimes against the security of the Angolan state." The civil war, which had devastated Angola for some 27 years, left more than 500,000 dead, 100,000 maimed, 100,000 orphaned, and 3.1 million—roughly a quarter of the population—displaced by the fighting. In the last year of the war alone the government's scorched earth policies had forced 400,000 more people to flee their homes. The war has also left a legacy of anti-personnel

land mines—12 to15 million of them, more than one for every man, woman and child in the country; an estimated 70,000 to 200,000 people have lost limbs to them.

Interim leadership of UNITA fell to its secretary-general, Paulo Lukamba—better known as General Gato. General Lukamba would provide temporary leadership until a party congress could sort out issues of leadership and reconciliation of the various UNITA factions and wings.

Jonas Savimbi's death dramatically transformed Angola's political landscape. President dos Santos announced in August 2001 that he would not contest the next presidential election, and would work on his legacy—the reconstruction of Angola. There was much to be done.

The economy is a shambles. GDP is down 48% over the past 25 years. Infrastructure outside of Luanda, the capital, is virtually non-existent and the state's capacity to deliver services minimal. The state's vast oil wealth has not contributed one iota to the improvement of lives outside the capital. Angola ranks 166th out of 177 states assessed by the UN Development Program (2004). Some 60% to 70% of the population lives below the poverty line, and access to health services is abysmal: there are only eight physicians per 100,000 people. Infant mortality is extraordinarily high: 154 out of every 1,000 die at birth; 260 out of 1,000 children will die before the age of five. Life expectancy is only 46.7 years. Together, war and corruption have led to this sorry state of affairs. Together, they are the real legacy of José Eduardo dos Santos.

The government and UNITA are working towards creating a post-Savimbi Angola. The two have agreed (amongst themselves and without consultation of others) to a new constitution. Under its provisions, considerable authority would be concentrated in the presidency. The president will name and can remove the prime minister. He will also appoint provincial governors, but appointments will be made from nominations of the party that receives the majority of votes in the province. The two parties also agreed on a single-chamber parliament, though a consultative body incorporating traditional leaders and local officials may yet emerge.

President dos Santos has not moved to secure approval of the new constitution, a deliberate inaction, charges the opposition, to avoid holding elections. Indeed, in March 2004 the MPLA unveiled a list of 14 preconditions for elections and made it quite clear there was no way elections could be held before 2006. Financing the poll is not an issue: the EU has agreed to fund the country's first general election since 1992.

# Angola

**Working to rebuild a bridge.**                                    ©IRIN

There is little to suggest the MPLA is interested in changing much in Angola. Its main goal is to maintain control and keep the opposition down. In February 2003, for example, the Catholic radio station, Radio Ecclesia, was attacked for practicing what the Minister of Information called "antenna terrorism." The party has also refused to disband its civilian militias, armed by the government during the civil war, and seems to turn a blind eye when militia thugs intimidate UNITA organizers in the provinces. UNITA's new leader, Isaïas Samakuva (chosen by a party congress in June 2003) has charged the MPLA is "set on returning to the time of a one-party state."

Given its Marxist origins and Stalinist orientation, the MPLA does find change a difficult prospect. At the party's fifth national congress in December 2003 José Eduardo dos Santos was unanimously reelected party president; there was no alternative candidate and voting was done publicly, by a show of hands. One notable innovation: the party now has a vice-president—Pitra Neto—to assist the aging party leader coordinate administrative tasks assigned by the party's politburo and central committee. Freed from administrative burdens, dos Santos now has more time to prepare a presidential campaign, a distinct possibility raised when a party spokesman noted "the question of the candidacy of citizen José Eduardo dos Santos is an open question within the party."

Electoral laws approved in April 2005 suggest the MPLA's unwillingness to share power or lose control. A new National Electoral Commission that would organize the 2006 elections has 11 members, nearly two-thirds of them appointed by President Dos Santos.

The MPLA's desire to maintain and impose its power is also manifest in its policy toward armed rebellion in Cabinda. Having militarily defeated UNITA, it seems committed to do the same to the armed rebellion in Cabinda.

## Cabinda

In April 2001 the former president of Portugal, Mario Soares, commented on the continuing struggle for self-determination in Cabinda. The nearly 30-year liberation struggle was, said Soares, "no internal Angolan affair." "Anyone who supports self-determination," he added, "cannot deny the right of a population to discuss the issue, and when this reaches the pitch it has in Cabinda, it moves out of the realm of domestic politics."

The speech was occasioned by kidnappings of Portuguese workers by various elements of the *Frente de Libertação do Enclava de Cabinda* (FLEC)—the Liberation Front for the Cabinda Enclave. Abducted to focus international attention on FLEC's demands for self-determination, some of the captured workers had been held for nearly a year when Soares spoke.

With an area of just a bit more than 2,800 sq. miles, the Cabinda enclave is completely separated from Angola by a narrow stretch of land on either side of the Congo River. It exists as a consequence of colonial power politics. Leopold II, the brash and entrepreneurial Belgian King, wanted access to the sea for the Congo Free State, his personal fief in the heart of Africa. The Portuguese government, possessed of little capacity to protest, was pressured into making the concession.

The enclave contains around 250,000 Cabindans, most of whom would probably prefer independence if given a chance. It produces nearly 70% of Angola's oil from its offshore wells. Like the people of the Niger Delta, Cabindans feel exploited, abused, and short-changed. Cabinda reportedly receives 10% of the taxes paid by the oil companies—Chevron is the dominant player on the Cabinda fields—but FLEC has long argued this is insufficient. It's not an argument that finds much sympathy in Luanda.

Cabindan separatism stems from several sources. Ethnically and linguistically, Cabindans are more closely akin to the peoples of southwestern Congo. Historically, the enclave was administered separately by the Portuguese until 1956, and this provided a clear sense of distinctness from Angola. "In our souls, we don't feel we are Angolans, we are Cabindans," said one FLEC leader.

There is also a sense of historical exclusion. Cabindan interests were not represented in discussions between mainstream nationalist groups and Portugal that resulted in independence. The feeling then, and now, was that the enclave was simply arbitrarily annexed to Angola at independence. Even the more recent Lusaka agreement was restricted to the MPLA government and UNITA and ignored FLEC's troublesome demands.

For years the dos Santos regime failed, as with UNITA, to eliminate the various FLEC factions. (One reason for Angola's military advance into the two Congos was to eliminate the support and refuge both UNITA *and* FLEC groups found there.) With Jonas Savimbi's death, however, the Angolan army launched a massive offensive against FLEC forces. There were no official figures, but journalists and NGOs estimated the number of troops involved at anywhere from 10,000 to 35,000 soldiers. (Cabinda's total population is only around 220,000.)

To deal with the separatists, the army adopted a scorched-earth policy, where destroyed villages, summary executions, rape, and torture featured prominently. It has managed to capture the secessionist's forest strongholds and controls the area through force and violence. In December 2004, Human Rights Watch reported that the army had "arbitrarily detained and tortured civilians with impunity."

The army of occupation is a visible and heavy presence, a reminder that there is yet no peace. Despite divisions and small size, the FLEC forces have always had the support of Cabindans. The army may not be shooting for the moment, but it is still there. So are the problems that gave rise to the secession: Only 10,000 Cabindans have wage-paying jobs. Unemployment is estimated at 70%. There is only one hospital for the entire province—220 beds—and Cabindans, inhabitants to Angola's richest oil province, have to queue up for gasoline. (Angola's only refinery is at Luanda, and gasoline, in insufficient quantities, is shipped by boat to Cabinda.) Most consumer goods have to be imported from Congo-Brazzaville, at exorbitant prices.

Given the savagery of repression and its resultant insecurity, there are signs Cabindans may be willing to set aside their demands for independence temporarily. Father Jorge Congo, an outspoken priest and human rights campaigner, noted that independence was no longer peoples' principal concern. Now, he said, they were more concerned with personal safety and survival. In February 2005 tens of thousands rallied in Cabinda city to support self-rule for the province.

**Culture:** Until 1974 there were two cultures in Angola—the approximately 300,000 Europeans, mostly Portuguese, who were the businessmen and farmers, and that of the original inhabitants of the land. The latter lived a marginal existence in the cities and in the hinterland, working as laborers in the factories and fields of Angola. A small group of these lived as *assimilados*—they adopted European customs, the Portuguese language and passed an educational test. They now are the leadership of the MPLA.

Between the MPLA and UNITA leadership lies the chasm of culture and history and race. UNITA emerged as a factor in the liberation struggle from the perception that the Popular Movement for the Liberation of Angola was dominated by mixed-race intellectuals from the coastal cities. Historically the Luandan elites had looked down on countryside folk as inept and inferior. Jonas Savimbi sought to exploit and mobilize those differences.

UNITA is based on the highland Ovimbundu people. It has always claimed to represent "real Africans," "sons of the soil," "living in the bush" against a better-educated, wealthy, cosmopolitan urban elite. As almost living proof of the cultural division, President dos Santos left Luanda to visit the rest of the country only once in seven years, during a brief campaign

Children receiving food aid at San'Antionia school, Benguela ©IRIN

swing. Savimbi's populist nationalism, with potential appeal to the dispossessed masses living in the squalor of squatter shacks on the outskirts of Luanda, was deeply threatening to the status and perks of that urban elite.

It is almost impossible to describe the devastation produced by more than 30 years of continuous conflict. Everything needs to be reconstructed: bridges, streets and roads, communications systems, airstrips, hospitals, and schools. Hundreds of thousands of people live in shantytowns of utmost squalor and misery on the outskirts of the capital.

Luanda now has four million inhabitants, but only about 20,000 of them have running water or modern toilets. The government could easily afford to build a sewage treatment plant and pipe drinking water from nearby rivers to the city. In the absence of such services, millions of Luanda's poor pay up to 10,000 times more for drinking water than the elite, who merely open a tap.

Contrasts between wealth and poverty are overwhelming. The capital's streets are filled with potholes and jammed with traffic, with a lot of expensive imported cars costing more than $50,000. On the

# Angola

north side of town people swarm over accumulated garbage at the city dump, looking for any scrap of food that can be eaten. On the south side suburb of Futango Angola's elite lives and plays. Across the bay at Mussulo, they can take a speedboat and dine at air-conditioned restaurants serving up grilled lobster for $100 a plate.

With the bulk of government resources devoted to defeating its armed opponents (military spending was 21.2% of GDP in 2000) or corruptly siphoned off to private coffers, Angola's health system, which might provide some alleviation of peoples' misery, has totally collapsed over the years. In an unusually frank report, *Medecins Sans Frontières* (MSF: Doctors without Borders) reported that Angolan authorities displayed "a striking lack of interest in the health of their population." The report, issued in November 2000, deemed government spending on the health system "inconsequential" and its provision of drugs and medical supplies "completely insufficient." The government had made a clear choice: let humanitarian agencies fund health; let the government fund war. The consequence was equally clear: the Angolan population benefited not a jot from the wealth of its land.

**Economy:** Just what is the reality of Angola's great wealth? The country is presently the second most productive oil state in sub-Saharan Africa. New offshore discoveries seem to be announced daily. Angola produced an average 902,000 barrels per day (bbl/d) in 2003, and the government has predicted production levels of 1.6 million bbl/d in 2005. It is expected to be producing two million bbl/d by 2008. Oil income accounts for some 90% of the state's revenues and over 40% of its GDP. The United States imports about 40% of Angola's oil, and following a push to secure oil supplies China now imports around 30% of Angolan production.

The government also produces about $850 million in diamonds every year, and Angola is the world's fourth largest diamond producer. As government forces took back more of the diamond producing areas from UNITA, recorded diamond production rose, and in 2002 the government opened the country's biggest mine: the Camafuca mine in northeastern Angola will produce gems worth roughly $4.7 million a month and contains reserves worth about $4.7 billion.

Since the end of the civil war, however, Angola has seen a massive influx of foreigners seeking to take advantage of the country's diamond resources. To control illegal mining activities, the government conducted a series of raids from December 2003 through April 2004. Police and soldiers destroyed miners huts, seized firearms, generators, sieves, scales and satellite phones. Amid stories of rampant torture and abuse, the government admitted it had expelled 11,000 people, largely Congolese, to end "exploitation of economic resources."

Despite the abundance of natural-resource wealth, Angola usually runs huge budgetary deficits, and the country is a major debtor, having accumulated an estimated $10.9 billion in debts by the end of 2003. One fourth of state spending goes to meeting foreign debt payments. Inflation was a galloping 1,650% in 1996, slowed to a mere canter of 91% in 1998, only to rise to 325% in 2000, a jump occasioned by increased defense expenditures. By 2003 it had subsided to a mere 98%. Final figures for 2004 showed a drop to a 50% inflation rate, and in 2005 inflation was 45%. Domestic savings are impossible in these circumstances.

War, of course, is only excuse and justification. Equally contributory is an Olympian corruption that provides a comfortable life for President dos Santos, his family and supporters. (The President's eldest daughter, Isabel, is widely reported to have extensive holdings in both oil and mining operations. Many of the Angolan generals own or have shares in the numerous security firms that are essential to business, especially the diamond business.) They have enriched themselves through their government connections while three quarters of the country's population lives on less than $1 a day. Symptomatically, Transparency International's 2004 *Corruption Perceptions Index* ranks Angola very near the bottom—the fifth most corrupt government in the world.

The books of the national oil company, Sonangol, are virtual state secrets in an authoritarian state where transparency has no value. A Swiss judge elicited from the former President of Elf-Gabon the revelation that oil companies had paid hidden commissions—"bonuses" in "petrospeak"—of more than a billion dollars to secure Angolan exploration permits in 1998. Much of it disappears off the books. An IMF report gave a five-year total (1997-2001) for money unaccounted for in state finances of $4.36 billion. Another IMF report indicated that more than $900 million had gone missing in 2003 alone.

With the IMF refusing to sanction loans until some degree of transparency and accountability has been achieved, Angola has largely turned to Chinese loans to fund reconstruction and rehabilitation projects. The lines of credit or loans are large (two billion dollars alone in March 2004), generous (interest-free), and repaid in oil, desperately needed by China's burgeoning economy. At the conclusion of an official visit in February 2005 by Chinese Vice Premier Zeng Peiyan, the two governments announced plans to develop a joint oil exploration project in Angola's offshore fields, an agreement for "the long term supply of oil" to China, and development of a new refinery.

A Chinese presence is everywhere visible in Angola. Chinese companies are building a new finance ministry, a new justice ministry, and rehabilitating Angolan railroads, among others. It is unlikely the influx of Chinese capital will make much of an improvement in the daily lives of most Angolans. Well over half the working age population is unemployed, but contracts provide that Chinese companies get 70%, leaving only 30% for local firms. An influx of about four million Chinese citizens is expected during the application of the March 2004 line of credit.

Many economists fear that many of the projects will become expensive white elephants that the government will be unable to maintain. Neither loans nor contracts are subject to transparency or accountability requirements, thus subject to predation by a venal governing class.

**The Future:** With Jonas Savimbi dead the government no longer has an excuse for the miserable conditions in which Angolans live. Accounting for income, reining in spending and curbing corruption are all prerequisites for alleviating Angola's poverty. Each will come slowly, for they are all dependent on transparency, and little in its conduct thus far has suggested a willingness on the government's part to be transparent about much of anything. There are far too many vested interests to be protected.

The possibility of the MPLA organizing "free, fair and transparent" elections seems equally remote. The timing and conduct of any election will accord with the MPLA's need to maintain itself in power. At the moment it looks as though one means of doing this could be the buying off of UNITA. With enough perquisites and power, UNITA could comfortably subside into a pattern of bipolar condominium with the MPLA, to the exclusion of other political forces and the detriment of Angola's social development.

# The Republic of Burundi

Aerial view of Bujumbura and the northernmost extent of Lake Tanganyika

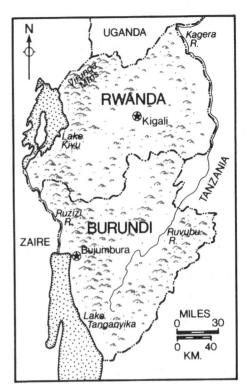

**Area:** 28,490 sq. km. = 11,000 sq. mi. (slightly larger than Maryland).

**Population:** 6,370,609 (July 2005 est.)

**Capital City:** Bujumbura (Pop. 186,000, estimated).

**Climate:** Temperate, with an alternating wet season (October–April) and dry season (May–December).

**Neighboring Countries:** Rwanda (North); Tanzania (East): Congo-Kinshasa (West).

**Official Languages:** French, KiRundi.

**Other Principal Language:** KiSwahili.

**Ethnic groups:** Hutu 85%, Tutsi 14%, Twa (Pygmy) 1%, Europeans 3,000, and South Asians 2,000.

**Principal Religions:** Christian 67% (Roman Catholic 62%, Protestant 5%), indigenous beliefs 32%, and Muslim 1%.

**Chief Commercial Products:** Coffee, tea, cotton and hides.

**GNI per capita:** $100 (2003)

**Currency:** Burundi Franc.

**Former Colonial Status:** Part of German East Africa (1899–1917); occupied by Belgian troops (1916), Belgian trust territory under League of Nations and United Nations (1923–1962).

**Independence Date:** July 1, 1962.

**Chief of State:** Domitien Ndayizeye (a Hutu), President (since April 2003).

**National Flag:** Divided by a white diagonal cross into red panels (top and bottom) and green panels (hoist side and outer side) with a white disk superimposed at the center bearing three red six-pointed stars outlined in green arranged in a triangular design (one star above, two stars below).

A cool, pleasant land of mountains and plateaus, the Republic of Burundi was known as Urundi before its independence; it was the southern portion of Ruanda–Urundi. Burundi is situated in the highlands of central Africa, and though only two degrees below the Equator, the climate is tempered by altitude. Fabled Lake Tanganyika, the longest fresh water lake in the world, separates Burundi and the Democratic Republic of the Congo. This amazing body of water is more than 2,500 feet above sea level on the surface, yet its floor reaches a depth of about 2,000 feet below sea level. The lake abounds in fish, hippopotami, crocodiles and other native species.

Eons ago a great strip of land between parallel faults in the earth sank to great depths, forming the basin of the Red Sea and continuing into the land mass of east and central Africa. This unique land fea-

ture is known as the Great Rift Valley, an area of grassy, upland plains. The wet season has characteristic daily downpours with intermittent clear, sunny weather. Almost no rain falls during the five–month dry season.

**History:** Tradition indicates the Twa (Pygmies) were the first inhabitants of this region. Around 1300 Hutu people settled the region, imposing their language and culture on the Twa. Later Tutsi settlers establish themselves as feudal rulers—a tiny elite dominating the great bulk of the population. In 1890 the Tutsi kingdom of Urundi and neighboring Ruanda (Rwanda) were incorporated into German East Africa. During World War I Belgians occupied the area, and in 1923 Belgium was granted a League of Nations mandate to administer Ruanda-Urundi. For details of early and colonial history, see *Historical Background, The Germans in Africa* and *The Belgians in Africa.*

In the great wave of decolonization that began in the 1960s, Urundi was separated from Ruanda-Urundi and became a constitutional monarchy in 1962. The Kingdom of Burundi was given independence as a monarchy under Mwami (King) Mwambutsa IV, but even at birth, the country was characterized by instability. In the lead up to independence, legislative elections had resulted in a victory for the Union for National Progress (UPRONA), whose leader was Prince Rwagasore, the

# Burundi

**Former President Pierre Buyoya**

eldest son of Mwami Mwambutsa. UP-RONA was a Tutsi-Hutu coalition party, but was dominated by Tutsi nobles of the *Ganwa* clan. Prince Rwagasore's assassination in October 1961 ushered in a period of political instability that characterizes Burundi to this day.

In 1963 ethnic violence forced thousands of Hutus to flee into Tanzania. Political violence erupted again in January 1965 when a Tutsi gunman killed the Hutu prime minister, Pierre Ngendandumwe. Following legislative elections in May of that year, in which Hutu had won 23 out of 33 seats in the National Assembly, Mwami Mwambutsa refused to appoint a Hutu prime minister, preferring to appoint his private secretary, Léopold Biha, and keep power centered in the crown. This prompted a coup attempt by Hutu policemen. Prime Minister Biha was seriously wounded by gunfire, Mwambutsa departed for Switzerland, 76 Hutu leaders were executed and the defense minister, Michel Micombero, was given absolute power.

Mwambutsa made a half–hearted effort to return to his kingdom, but was ousted by his son, Ntare, in July 1966. A few months later when the youthful King was out of the country, Micombero proclaimed himself president of the first Republic of Burundi in November. He had the support of the Bahima clan of the Tutsi, traditionally jealous of Ganwa power.

Restless Hutus living in exile in Tanzania plotted revolution with the aid of that country in mid–1972. Emboldened by drugs and assurances of invincibility from local folk priests, they mounted a swift campaign. The plot involved Mwami

Ntare, but after being put under house arrest, he was later killed "while escaping." About 2,000 Tutsis were mercilessly slaughtered; they responded with a genocidal blood bath that took the lives of more than 200,000 Hutus within six weeks—about 5% of the population. Worst of all, the April-May killings were directed against educated Hutus. A second wave of Hutus poured over the Tanzanian border in May 1973.

The 1972 events generated distrust and hatred in both Tutsi and Hutu communities; they lie at the heart of Burundi's problems today. They also became a source of tension within the Tutsi minority. Ultimately this led to the 1976 overthrow of Micombero in a military coup led by Col. Jean-Baptiste Bagaza, who initiated the Second Republic.

In 1980, Bagaza commenced a series of anti–Catholic Church measures; by 1987 more than 450 foreign priests had been expelled as he sought to bring the Church more thoroughly under the control of the state. He viewed the Church as an instrument of potential Hutu rebellion. Belgian Catholic priests were frequently Flemish, with their own sense of ethnic and linguistic identity and persecution by French-speaking Walloons in Belgium. As such they had a strong sense of identity with and sympathy for oppressed Hutu.

The crisis in Church-state relations provoked yet again another military coup. Bagaza was ousted by a fellow clansman, Pierre Buyoya, in September 1987, and the Third Republic was declared. The new leader quickly welcomed back the expelled Catholics despite the suspicions of right–wing Tutsis. Buyoya introduced several progressive measures to deal with ethnic resentment. Efforts were made to achieve ethnic parity within the government, and a national commission was created to seek ways of strengthening national unity. Ideas developed in the capital, however, did not always translate well in the provinces. There Tutsi civil servants continued to discriminate against Hutu citizens.

Another outburst of ethnic hatred was not long in coming. Provoked by local officials and encouraged by Rwanda-based exiles, Hutus in the northern provinces killed some 500 Tutsis in August 1988. In the backlash some 20,000 people were killed, most of them Hutu. Thousands more fled to Rwanda.

President Buyoya secured ratification of a new multiparty constitution in March 1992. It explicitly prohibited political organizations that advocated "tribalism, divisionism, or violence" and stipulated that all political parties must include both Hutu and Tutsi representatives. In the June 1993 elections that followed—the

country's first free, democratic elections—Melchiore Ndadye, a Hutu, defeated Pierre Buyoya to be elected president. He ruled only briefly, assassinated in October by paratroopers loyal to former President Bagaza. This set off the inevitable round of recriminatory ethnic slaughter. Since then Burundi has been gripped by a cycle of terror and counter-terror referred to as *la crise*—the crisis. The conflict has claimed the lives of an estimated 200,000 people

Amid the violence Burundi's parliament finally chose Cyprien Ntaryamira, a moderate Hutu, as president. Ntaryamira took office in February 1994, but just a few months later President Ntaryamira was killed in the same plane crash that killed Rwanda's president and set off the genocide of that year. Amid general agreement that the security situation did not permit another round of elections, parliament eventually appointed another moderate Hutu, Sylvestre Ntibantunganya to the presidency.

Communal tensions were not eased. Rogue elements of the army, controlled by Tutsis, and extremist Hutu militias engaged in nearly daily atrocities against civilians. In November 1995 Burundi and its neighbors agreed to a regional peace initiative. Former Tanzanian President, Julius Nyerere, was designated as mediator between the various factions.

Mediation only seemed to intensify hostilities. Fearful and frustrated, the army intervened in July 1996. President Ntibantunganya went into hiding and Major Pierre Buyoya seized power, for a second time. Burundi's neighbors united to impose economic sanctions on the country in an effort to force a restoration of democracy. As with many such efforts, the goal was not achieved and the consequences were disastrous. The economy further deteriorated, malnutrition rates soared, and the atrocities continued; sanctions could not stop the flow of arms into Burundi.

Given the continuing security threat, the government decided to create a group of resettlement centers that would gather rural and isolated communities, mostly Hutu, into more controllable and protected camps. This involved relocating more than 800,000 people—about 12% of the population—into 58 camps whose conditions were appalling by the most generous of appraisals. In one there were only 25 latrines for 5,000 inhabitants. The Hutu opposition called them "concentration camps," and the international community condemned them. Before being dismantled the prospect of resettlement camps set off another wave of refugees fleeing to camps in Tanzania.

In June 1998 a Transitional Constitutional Act (TCA) designed to pave the way for the Tutsi–led government to share power with the mainly Hutu opposition was signed into law. The TCA transformed the structure of Burundi's government. Parliament was enlarged by 57 new seats to make government more representative. The government appointed 27 members from Burundi's civil society; small parties not heretofore represented appointed nine of the new members, and the Hutu opposition party, *Front pour la démocratie au Burundi* (FRODEBU), designated the remaining 21 seats.

With these power-sharing reforms as background, seventeen delegations gathered in Arusha, Tanzania, to begin peace discussions. The most militant of the Hutu rebel groups, the Forces for the Defense of Democracy (FDD) and the hard-line *Party for the Liberation of the Hutu People-National Liberation Forces* (PALIPEHUTU-FNL) were excluded from the talks. Progress, which was sluggish at best, was brought to a halt by the death of the mediator, Julius Nyerere, in October 1999.

Africa's most distinguished ex-president, Nelson Mandela, was prevailed upon to take on the role of mediator and assumed his duties in February 2000. His presence brought the klieg lights of publicity to previously obscure discussions. His moral stature allowed him publicly to chastise all parties. His international prestige and contacts allowed him to proffer the carrot of aid to reconstruct a devastated country.

Nineteen parties signed the Arusha Peace and Reconciliation Agreement in August 2000, but key issues—including the leadership of the transitional period and agreement for a cease-fire—remained unresolved, and both the FDD and the FNL increased military activity against President Buyoya's government.

The Burundian National Assembly ratified the Arusha Accord in early December. Shortly afterwards an international donors' conference in Paris agreed to provide $440 million for reconstruction programs. The Transitional Government's (TG) leadership was settled in July 2001: President Buyoya would lead the first half of the three-year transition, with Domitien Ndayizeye of the main Hutu opposition party, FRODEBU, as vice-president. In the second half of the transition, Burundi would have a Hutu president and a Tutsi vice-president.

Transitional institutions displayed carefully modulated ethnic balances required to gain acceptance. Fourteen of the 26 transitional cabinet positions were allotted to Hutus and 12 to Tutsis, who kept the key posts of defense, foreign affairs and finance. Ministries of the interior and of public security went to Hutus. In the National Assembly, 60% of seats were as-

**President Domitien Ndayizeye**
Photo by AFP/Peter Busomoke

signed to Hutu parties, 40% to Tutsis. A protection force of South African troops was created to act as bodyguards of some 27 Burundian leaders.

Negotiation with the rebel movements was always difficult, given their tendency to separate into factions and wings (more by personality than policy), but by late 2002 it began to look as though the long negotiations were at last fruitful. The FLN faction of Alain Mugabarabona and the FDD faction of Jean-Bosco Ndayikengurukiye signed a ceasefire in October. Shortly after in December, President Buyoya and Pierre Nkurunziza, head of the principal FDD faction, signed an historic ceasefire (the first since 1993) in Arusha. Only the hard-line PALIPEHUTU-FNL rebels refused any ceasefire discussions.

As scheduled, President Buyoya relinquished office in April 2003, and was succeeded by his Hutu vice-president, Domitien Ndayizeye, the FRODEBU leader. The new Tutsi vice-president was Alphonse Kadege, head of Buyoya's *Union pour le progrès national* (UPRONA); the appointment symbolized the continuing consensus between UPRONA and FRODEBU. Important for Tutsi security fears, the new vice-president was given new rights: any new security texts would require the signatures of both the president and vice-president.

The whole structure of the transitional government remained fragile. Agathon Rwasa's PALIPEHUTU-FNL refused to join the peace process, rejected the transitional government entirely, and showed its strength by periodically assaulting the outskirts of Bujumbura. Increasingly isolated, the group seemed to offer an olive branch to the government by announcing a unilateral cease-fire in April 2004. Fighting broke out the very next day, however, with both sides accusing the other of firing the first shot.

Mistrust and low-level intermittent fighting continued. The fighting has left the country in ruins—exsanguinated, indebted, and fearful. Around 1.2 million people have been internally displaced; more than 300,000 people have been killed and about 15% of Burundi's children have been orphaned.

Regional leaders have kept the pressure up for Burundians to work out their differences through the new power-sharing institutions. The most sensitive issue is the reconstruction of the army. The old army is to be dismantled and a new army is to be created, made up of 50% government forces and 50% Hutu rebels. For Tutsis, the army is the bulwark of their security. For Hutus, it is the instrument of their oppression. Reconciling the two has been a task fraught with hazards and stumbling blocks, but for the first time in Burundi's history, the army's senior officer corps is open to members of the Hutu majority.

In August 2004 the transition process suffered a major set back when nearly 160 Congolese Tutsi living in a refugee camp at Gatumba (near Bujumbura) were shot, hacked to death with machetes, or burnt alive inside their homes by Hutu rebels. Palipehutu-FNL claimed responsibility (though eyewitnesses identified Congolese Mayi-Mayi and former Rwandan army and Interahamwe elements), and regional authorities quickly branded the group as "terrorists."

Regional and international pressure was maintained on participants to implement transitional agreements, and President Ndayizeye scheduled a referendum on a new constitution for the country in late December, but this was postponed until late February 2005. The text affirmed Burundi's sharing of power by ethnic quota: In the National Assembly 60% of the seats went to Hutus and 40% to Tutsis, with three seats reserved for Twa representation. Allocation of government positions followed with same distribution pattern: 60% for Hutu and 40% for Tutsi, while Senate membership was equally distributed between the two ethnicities with three seats reserved for Twa. Some 91.2% of the country's three million registered voters approved the text.

Wrangling over cabinet appointments continues (Tutsi parties pressured the president to reject the Tutsi nominee of the Hutu majority to be interior minister, for example), and presidential elections were postponed until August 2005. Even the Palipehutu-FNL rebels seem to see things moving to normalcy: in April 2005 the group once again indicated it was willing to stop fighting government troops and enter into "serious negotiations" with the interim government. In another positive sign, the UN High Commissioner for Ref-

# Burundi

ugees has said the agency expects to repatriate up to 150,000 Burundian refugees by the end of 2005.

The United Nations Operation in Burundi (ONUB) currently has 5,400 peacekeepers on the ground (with an additional 200 military observers and 120 police officers) to help protect Burundi's fragile political gains. Financing the operation is daunting; for the initial twelve months costs were estimated at $418 million, and the UN expects to spend $296 million during 2005-2006.

**Culture:** Burundi's Twa people, less than one per cent of the population, are almost politically invisible. None occupies an important post in the Burundi government. The highest position occupied by a Twa is that of Member of Parliament, and until the new constitution, there was only one. In local administration there are no Twa zone heads, no commune administrators or provincial governor. The only administrative position held by a Twa is that of a *nyum-bakumi*—leader of a set of 10 households—for other Twa people.

The scourge of AIDS has reached tiny Burundi thanks to war, dislocation and poverty. There are around 250,000 HIV positive people in the country, and some 25,000 Burundians die of AIDS annually. The most affected group is people aged between 15 and 49 years, the most productive section of society. Rural and urban areas have different HIV prevalence rates, with 20% and 7.5%, respectively.

**Economy:** Agriculture is the mainstay of Burundi's economy, representing about 50% of GDP. Most cultivated land is devoted to subsistence crops—mainly cas-

**Pierre Nkurunziza, CNDD-FDD leader**
©IRIN

sava, bananas, and sweet potatoes, but widespread violence has driven many farmers from their fields. Cattle rearing is also an important source of food, as was fishing on Lake Tanganyika until it was banned by the government as a security measure to prevent rebel infiltration.

The main cash crop is coffee, more than 90% of which is higher quality *arabica*. Coffee exports account for over 95% of Burundi's foreign exchange revenues. With such heavy reliance on a single crop, the economy is seesawed by fluctuations in world coffee prices. In 2002 the cost of producing the crop was higher than its sales price. As a consequence, the govern-

ment's budget went into deficit and public expenses were curtailed.

The IMF long refused to give money to Burundi, claiming that it was only used to purchase arms, but a national teachers strike led some western governments (primarily France and Belgium) to urge support during the transitional period, lest the peace process be jeopardized. In January 2004, the IMF approved a $104 million arrangement to support the country's economic reform program over the next three years.

Conflict and sanctions have devastated the economy. Burundi is one of the poorest countries in the world, ranking 173rd out of 177 countries on the UN's *Human Development Index* for 2004. Its economy is estimated to have contracted by 25% over the past five years. GDP per capita has fallen from $180 in 1993 to $100 in 2003, and about 68% of the population now survives on less than one dollar a day.

Burundi carries an accumulated external debt of $1.2 billion (2002), but satisfactory economic performance (i.e. continuation of the government's privatization and liberalization policies) could make it eligible for the IMF's Highly Indebted Poor Country (HIPC) initiative. This would cut debt significantly and add thirty to forty million dollars to the government's budget for poverty alleviation.

**The Future:** Burundi's future is closely linked to developments in the Congo. As long as places of refuge exist there, armed rebel forces have little incentive to sign a ceasefire. Reconstruction of the country will be enormously expensive, and Burundi will remain dependent on international goodwill for years to come.

# The Republic of Rwanda (pronounced Roo–*wahn*–dah)

**The Murambi Genocide Memorial**

Photo by Ruth Evans

**Area:** 28,900 sq. km. = 11,158 sq. mi. (slightly larger than Maryland).

**Population:** 8,440,820 (July 2005 est.)

**Capital City:** Kigali (pop. 600,000, 2000 est.)

**Climate:** Temperate, with dry seasons (January–February, June–September) and wet seasons (March–May, October–December).

**Neighboring Countries:** Congo-Kinshasa (West); Uganda (Northeast); Tanzania (East); Burundi (South).

**Official Languages:** English, French, and KiNyarwanda.

**Other Principal Languages:** KiSwahili

**Ethnic groups:** Hutu 80%, Tutsi 19%, Twa (Pygmy) 1%. These are rough estimates; it is impossible to establish Rwanda's ethnic makeup accurately because the government has forbidden ethnic monitoring and has removed ethnicity from Rwandans identity documents.

**Principal Religions:** Roman Catholic 65%, Protestant 9%, Muslim 1%, indigenous beliefs and other 25%.

**Chief Commercial Products:** Coffee, tea, hides, and tin ore.

**GNI per capita:** $220 (2003)

**Currency:** Rwanda Franc.

**Former Colonial Status:** Part of German East Africa (1899–1916); occupied by Belgian troops (1916); Belgian trust territory under the League of Nations and the United Nations (1923–1962).

**Independence Date:** July 1, 1962.

**Chief of State:** Paul Kagame, President.

**National Flag:** Three horizontal stripes. On top sky blue, with a full sun of 24 yellow rays in the top right-hand corner. In the middle, a yellow stripe and on the bottom a green stripe, each half the width of the upper blue stripe.

Rwanda, once called the "African Switzerland," is a land lying in the eastern lake region of Africa, composed for the most part of a gently rolling hilly plateau land. Sharp volcanic peaks rise to towering heights in the West on the border of Lake Kivu. Another mountain range lies to the northwest, topped by Mt. Karisimbi, at a height of 13,520 feet.

Rwanda has a mild and temperate climate—the temperature seldom rises above 80°F during the daytime and the nights are always cool, with frost in the highlands and the mountains.

Centuries ago the Virunga volcanoes, some of which are still active, dammed up a section of the Great Western Rift Valley, creating Lake Kivu. This lake drains into Lake Tanganyika to the south through the waters of the Ruzizi River. Volcanic activity thus diverted water which previously flowed northward to the Nile River, forcing it to flow westward to the Atlantic through the immense Congo River.

**History:** As is true in Burundi to the south, the original inhabitants of Rwanda were the Twa, a pygmy hunting and gathering people. The Twa were followed by the Hutu who established themselves as farmers. In the 14th century the pastoral Tutsi appeared and imposed their domi-

111

# Rwanda

nance over the mass of Hutu agricultural-ists by military power. The Hutu were re-duced to serfdom, each choosing a Tutsi lord protector who gave them the use (but not ownership) of cattle, the most impor-tant status symbol and source of wealth among the Tutsi. In the 15th century a Tutsi kingdom was founded near Kigali, which by the late 19th century had rounded out its borders to become a uni-fied state whose Mwami (king) ruled through a centralized military bureau-cracy. Local chiefs and military captains received tribute from Hutu communities.

In 1890 the Tutsi kingdoms of Ruanda (Rwanda) and neighboring Urundi were incorporated into German East Africa. During World War I Belgians occupied the area, and in 1923 Belgium was granted a League of Nations mandate to adminis-ter Ruanda–Urundi. It administered the mandate through existing Tutsi political structures. As a consequence, the Tutsi remained a privileged and dominant mi-nority after World War II. For details of early and colonial history, see *Historical Background*, *The Germans in Africa* and *The Belgians in Africa*.

In 1957, at the close of the colonial pe-riod, restless Hutu, weary of their serf-dom, began to organize and articulate a political program. They demanded a voice equal to their numbers and rose in revolt in 1959.

The 1959 revolution produced a civil war between Hutu and Tutsi. *Mwami* Kigeri V was forced into exile, along with thousands of other Tutsi. Hundreds of Tutsi were killed. With the success of the "Hutu Revolution," the monarchy was abolished and communal elections were scheduled for 1960. Conducted under Belgian supervision, they resulted in a tri-umph for the *Parti du Mouvement de l'Emancipation du Peuple Hutu*—PARME-HUTU. Rwanda was declared a republic in January 1961 and became independent the next year under the leadership of Gré-goire Kayibanda, Rwanda's first presi-dent. Ethnic clashes erupted again in 1963, driving more Tutsi into exile.

Under Kayibanda, opposition parties were gradually eliminated, and PARME-HUTU was the only party to present can-didates for the elections of 1965. The party was routinely returned to office in 1969.

Renewed strife between the Hutus and the Tutsi minority occurred in March 1973 following ethnic violence in neighboring Burundi. Kayibanda was criticized for be-ing too lenient with the Tutsi, whose eth-nic confreres were slaughtering thousands of Hutus in Burundi. At the same time re-gional tensions between northern and southern Hutus intensified. Suspecting his Defense Minister Juvenal Habyarimana—the lone northerner in the Cabinet—of dis-

loyalty, Kayibanda ordered him arrested. This resulted in a military coup by Gen-eral Habyarimana on July 5, 1973, and a reordering of Rwandan politics. Power was shifted from civilians to *militaires*, and from Hutu of central Rwanda to those from the northern provinces.

In 1975 President-General Habyari-mana founded his own party, the *Mouve-ment Révolutionaire National pour le Développement* (MRND), assumed the party chairmanship, and so melded state and party hierarchies that one was indis-tinguishable from the other, down to the lowest level of administration. The regime increasingly discriminated against both Tutsi and Hutu not from the north-west. Within this privileged group there emerged an inner circle of friends and rel-atives of the president-general and his wife; the fruits of association with the presidential circle were great economic and political power. The *akazu*, or "little house," as this group was known, shared a Hutu supremacist ideology.

By 1990 Habyarimana and MRND were facing increasing opposition from other Hutu factions. On October first of that year the Rwanda Patriotic Front (RPF), made up of the children of Tutsi refugees who had fled the country during the ear-lier Hutu revolution, attacked the country from Uganda. President Habyarimana used the invasion as an excuse to arrest thousands of his opponents, Tutsi and Hutu.

Under pressure from internal oppo-nents, the international community, and

RPF invasion, Habyarimana finally agreed to a new constitution and the notion of multiparty elections in June 1991. The MRND was given a superficial facelift—renamed the *Mouvement Républicain Na-tional pour la Démocratie et le Développement* (MRND). In April 1992 a transitional gov-ernment, which included the opposition, was formed. For the first time the MRND became a minority party in the govern-ment, holding only 9 of 19 ministerial port-folios. Crucially, however, it maintained its control over local administration.

The new government opened negotia-tions with the RPF. The result, known as the Arusha Accords, provided for the sharing of military and civilian power be-tween the RPF, opposition parties, and the MRND. If implemented, this would have meant demobilization for many in Habya-rimana's army and a significant loss of power, privilege, and profit for the Hab-yarimana inner circle.

To prevent such a loss, the regime re-sorted to the last defense of the fearful: ethnic division and incitement to violence. Tutsi were collectively stigmatized as ac-complices of the RPF as were Hutu oppo-nents, especially if they did not hail from the northwest provinces. Hutu opposition parties were successfully divided, each hiving off a wing that supported the gov-ernment. Hutu party youth wings, the most notorious of which was the MRND's *Interahamwe*, were organized and given military training. Lists of persons to be eliminated were prepared, and arms were distributed to Hutu civilians by local ad-ministrations, controlled by the MRND. The regime would need only a spark to ig-nite the whole machine of destruction.

Fighting in Burundi following the as-sassination of its democratically-elected Hutu president was a major factor in ig-

**Former President Bizimungu**

**President Paul Kagame**

niting the Rwandan genocide of April 1994. Tutsis from Burundi poured into Rwanda by the tens of thousands. Clandestine and government radio stations in both nations fueled the flames of hatred ("You [Tutsis] are cockroaches! We will kill you!").

The Rwandan genocide started in early April 1994 when a plane carrying President Habyarimana and the Hutu president of Burundi was shot down while landing at Kigali airport. The enraged presidential guard embarked on barbaric slaughter of anyone considered the president's enemy—all Tutsi and any Hutu moderate. There is as yet no definitive forensic investigation of the crash. It is most probable that disgruntled Hutu military personnel were the perpetrators.

Upon Habyarimana's death, members of his inner circle took control of the state and turned it into an instrument of genocide to maintain their power. The holocaust unleashed was horrifying in its dimensions. Conducted through the armed forces and the *Interahamwe* militia, the slaughter took upwards of 937,000 people over a 13–week period. Seventy–five percent of the country's Tutsi population was killed, most of them in the first five weeks. At the slaughter's peak five people per minute were being killed.

Once the slaughter began, Western countries acted timidly and ineffectively, allowing the regime to consolidate its position and continue the genocide. The magisterial Human Rights Watch report, *Leave None to Tell the Story*, is devastating in its condemnation of Western govern-

ments. "The Americans were interested in saving money, the Belgians were interested in saving face, and the French were interested in saving their ally, the genocidal government," said the report's chief author. "All of that took priority over saving lives."

The Rwanda Patriotic Front (RPF) army, made up of diaspora Tutsi who had lived in Uganda and had been an important part of Yoweri Museveni's efforts to topple the government there, took the capital of Kigali in July. Protected by a French "humanitarian" intervention, the Rwandan army and militias (trained and armed by the French) fled to Zaïre, along with thousands of Hutu who now feared for their lives. Hutu militants took over the refugee camps and turned them into training grounds for yet another round of ethnic confrontation. The Tutsi search for security in this situation dominated every action of the RPF coalition government established by General Paul Kagame.

When President Mobutu proved incapable or unwilling to control Hutu extremists in Zaïre, the RPF intervened and supported a successful rebellion against Mobutu. Laurent Kabila was installed in his place in 1997, and a year later, when Kabila himself had failed in his commitments to Rwandan security, a second intervention was undertaken, this time in support of Congolese Tutsi, called Banyamulenge, and other groups disenchanted with Kabila. Rwandan military activity in the Congo was not without criticism, including charges of smuggling, corruption, and human rights abuses.

In April 2000 parliament elected Vice President and Minister of Defense Paul Kagame Rwanda's first Tutsi president. In his inaugural address, Kagame called upon diaspora Rwandans to return home to rebuild the country. He also justified the presence of Rwandan troops in the Congo as central to Rwanda's security concerns: Hutu *génocidaires* were sheltering in the Congo where they had been given arms and were allowed to carry out military training. Their only goal was to kill Rwandan citizens and destroy what had been reconstructed.

Following those guidelines, Rwandan military action focused on *Interahamwe* elements armed and employed by the Kabila government. Fighting in Katanga resulted in a crushing defeat for the DRC government and it allies defending Pweto in early December 2000. Congo's then army chief of staff, Joseph Kabila, had to beat a humiliating retreat, abandoning his helicopter to escape the rout by ferryboat.

Pweto marked a high water mark for Rwandan arms and suggested the difficulty of its position before the international community. Hundreds of *Intera-*

*hamwe* escaped across the border into Zambia, but the army held back from pursuing and destroying them, fearful of international reaction.

The Clinton administration, perhaps driven by the guilt of inaction during Rwanda's genocide in 1994, was lavish in praise and generous in support of the RPF government. Emergency military aid amounting to $75 million had been dispatched soon after the RPF had installed itself in Kigali. The Bush administration, in contrast, seemed more concerned about Rwandan militarism and its penetration deep into the Congo.

President Kagame made it quite clear that withdrawal of his troops from the Congo would only come "after a solution is found to the genocide suspects who are still in the Congo, who wish to continue in a genocidal policy." Kigali considers the arrest and trial of the worst genocide perpetrators critically important for stability and for creating the conditions necessary to ensure the genocide never again occurs. "If we do arrest the top guys," said one senior official, "we know the rest will give up. If we do not, the threat of another genocide will remain."

The government's priority of priorities is thus the arrest and trial of those Hutu strategists who conspired to create and implement the plan to destroy the Tutsi people. One example is Felicien Kabuga, described as "a mastermind behind the genocide." He was Rwanda's richest man, possessed of tea estates, transport companies and a variety of shops and factories. Part of the *akazu*—the Hutu elite that controlled wealth and power in Rwanda under President Habyarimana—Kabuga used his wealth to create *Radio Télévision Libre des Mille Collines* (RTLM), the most vile of the anti-Tutsi propaganda machines. He also used his wealth to import vast numbers of machetes to arm the *génocidaires*.

Kabuga remains at large, after a failed attempt (January 2003) to capture him in Kenya where his money apparently bought safety from the most heinous of crimes. Thousands of unrepentant Hutu extremists still shelter in the Congo; to Rwandans, they remain an omnipresent threat. In April 2005 the government signed cooperation agreements with police agencies in ten East Africa countries. Besides cooperation in eradicating illegal drugs and crime, the agreements will facilitate the transfer of criminals who flee to other countries to escape justice. The Rwandan government hopes the accords will help apprehend genocide perpetrators like Kabuga.

The International Criminal Tribunal for Rwanda (ICTR), which was created to try the genocide masterminds, has faced a va-

# Rwanda

**Ankole cattle grazing on the hills of Rwanda.**

riety of difficulties which have slowed its actions. As of spring 2004, only eighteen convictions had been secured, but since then efforts have been made to the expedite genocide trials. Fifteen dossiers of suspects still at large were handed over to Rwandan judicial authorities, and a fourth courtroom was added in March 2005.

Domestically, President Kagame's principal goal is national reconciliation, without which there can be no peace, development, stability or progress. A National Unity and Reconciliation Commission was created. The previous mandatory national identity card, which bore the owner's ethnic identification has been abolished. "Solidarity camps" re-educate both Hutu fighters returning from the Congo to seek re-integration into the Rwandan army and young Hutus who were arrested and imprisoned as child participants in the genocide of 1994. The re-education program is designed to facilitate the two national objectives of justice and reconciliation.

New national symbols—anthem, flag and coat-of-arms—were created in 2001. The new flag has a golden sun with 24 rays on a field of green, yellow and blue. President Kagame said the colors stood for prosperity, wealth, peace and happiness. Where the old national anthem lauded the supremacy of Rwanda's Hutu majority, the new praises Rwanda's natural beauty and refers to its people simply as Rwandans. It was composed by a group of jailed Hutus awaiting trial on charges of genocide.

More than 120,000 prisoners were jailed for crimes arising from the 1994 genocide and kept in appalling conditions of incarceration. To break the judicial logjam, the government passed two pieces of legislation. One defines four categories of criminality, and the other creates a system of grassroots justice—traditional village courts called *gacaca*.

Under the new judicial legislation, only category one criminals—masterminds of the genocide—would be tried in the regular court system. All others would be brought before *gacaca* courts—ten villagers elected to hear and pass judgment.

Suspects would have to confront relatives, their own and those of their victims, a process that might, it is hoped, provide catharsis and reconciliation. Those who had participated in the genocidal events of 1994 as children and have passed through a solidarity camp were expected to bear witness against those who had ordered and directed their murderous activities.

Truth-telling is at the heart of the child-participant's re-education, and truth, perhaps more than justice, is the goal of the *gacaca* system. Rwanda's minister of justice has described the system succinctly: "We've already seen in group trials that when people are brought together in a commune they do tell the truth. We take them to where the crime was committed, everyone comes, including witnesses, and they are charged there. The suspect fears to lie because everyone knows what happened."

The *gacaca* system has its flaws, but it has its roots in traditional processes of reconciliation and may represent the best solution for a practical problem. The *gacaca* trials began in February 2005, but already several have been marred by a resurgence of violence. When a woman and her husband who were due to testify in one trial outside Kigali were hacked to death by unidentified people, most other witnesses refused to testify. Incidents in Gikongoro and Butare provinces were similar: genocide survivors have been murdered and others intimidated into fearful withdrawal of their witness.

As the trials began former Rwandan Army (Hutu) fighters apparently sneaked back into the country from their DRC-Congo bases and sought to recruit Hutu civilians into rebel ranks. Fear was created by telling the credulous the government was planning to kill them all. Rather than face *gacaca* proceedings, many fled across the borders to Burundi (which moved inland) or Uganda (which repatriated them).

In post-genocide Rwanda political life has been circumscribed. Given the experience of ethnic parties that fulminated group hatred, parties are prohibited from mentioning any ethnic affiliation. In local elections there was no party campaigning: candidates stood as individuals, not representatives of parties.

Forming a political party in these circumstances is a risky business. Former President Bizimungu, a Hutu who was the symbol of national reconciliation in the early post-genocide years, spent nearly one and a half years in jail after attempting to form his own political party—the Democratic Renewal Party (PDR). In his trial, which concluded in June 2004, Bizimungu was sentenced to 15 years in jail for embezzlement, inciting violence, and "associating the criminals." By taking on such a high-profile individual, the government made abundantly clear its policies of reconciliation and unity would tolerate nothing that even hinted at "divisionism"—political language and appeal based on ethnic identity.

The Rwandan parliament adopted a new constitution on April 23, 2003. The constitution creates a semi-presidential regime, with a president elected by universal suffrage for a seven-year term (once renewable) and a bicameral parliament. Only 53 deputies of the 80-member National Assembly are elected by universal suffrage; the rest are designated in the name of their social category: 24 women, two youth, and one handicapped person.

The 26-member Senate is chosen indirectly. Local officials in each of Rwanda's 12 provinces select a senator and the President of the Republic nominates eight; political parties appoint four, while colleges and universities elect the remaining two. Senators serve for a non-renewable eight-year period.

One interesting (but potentially awkward) constitutional innovation attests to a desire to diffuse political power and emphasize unity in governance: the president, prime minister, and president of the National Assembly must all belong to a different political party. To prevent the dangerous hate mongering that facilitated genocide, political parties are strictly limited; they are not permitted to hold public meetings outside of electoral periods, and are strictly forbidden to make any reference, in any manner, to ethnic, religious, regional or clan differences. Several parties were forced to change their statutes and names: the *Parti démocrate islamique,* for example, became the *Parti démocrate idéal,* while the *Parti démocrate chrétien* (Christian) became the *Parti démocrate centriste.*

Eight political parties were registered to participate in the presidential and legislative elections that followed approval of the constitution. As the candidate of the Rwanda Patriotic Front, Paul Kagame won an overwhelming victory in August 2003 elections: 95% of the electorate supported the man who had ended Rwanda's genocidal regime and restored significant security to the country.

His nearest opponent was Faustin Twagiramungu, a moderate Hutu. Twagiramungu had opposed President Habyarimana and helped revive the Republican Democratic Movement (MDR) of Grégoire Kayibanda, Rwanda's first president. He barely escaped assassination when the genocide began, and became prime minister in the transitional government of July 1994. The former prime minister received only 3.6% of the votes cast.

The election was hardly perfect. Twagiramungu complained that he had not been permitted to campaign freely and his supporters had been intimidated. The Belgian Foreign Minister, Louis Michel, was more diplomatic, regretting that the "optimal conditions for a free and fair election had not been entirely met." On balance it was clear the great bulk of the population, overwhelmingly Hutu, had given a vote of confidence to Kagame's efforts to date.

The RPF confirmed its dominance in the legislative elections that followed, winning 73.78% of the total votes cast. That gave the party 33 of the 53 directly-elected seats in the National Assembly. The *Parti social démocrate* followed with seven seats, and the *Parti libéral* with six; the *Parti démocrate centriste* won three seats, and *Parti démocrate idéal* two. The *Parti socialiste rwandais* and *Union démocratique du peuple rwandais* each won a single seat.

In April 2004, the tenth anniversary of the genocide, President Kagame inaugurated a national genocide museum on one of Kigali's many hills; it stands atop five concrete tombs containing hundreds of coffins filled with the remains of an estimate 250,000 people killed in and around Kigali.

In the presence of presidents Thabo Mbeki of South Africa, Yoweri Museveni of Uganda and Mwai Kibaki of Kenya, as well as the Belgian prime minister, Guy Verhofstadt, Kagame spoke movingly of the events a decade before: "It was a deliberate, calculated, cold blooded and the architects were keen to kill, rape, rob, ravage and inflict pain and agony. This was a result of distorted ideology that preached death and hatred."

"We are prepared," he added, " that what happened here should never happen again not only in Rwanda but anywhere in the world."

The ceremonies of remembrance also displayed Rwanda's profound contempt for the shameful role of France in the decade-old events. In biting and undiplomatic language, President Kagame detailed French activities in Rwanda: "Their role is self-evident," he said, going on to accuse them of arming and training government soldiers and militias and of being aware the extremists intended to commit genocide.

France also provide an escape route to Zaïre for Hutu extremists as the RPF neared Kigali. It evacuated 394 regime officials by air, including President Habyarimana's widow, who was reportedly deeply implicated in planning the genocide. Unlike Belgium, France has yet to apologize for its actions in Rwanda. In April 2005 the French Ambassador offered the most circumscribed of apologies: to the Rwandan employees of the Kigali Embassy who had been "abandoned to their fate" when the genocide began."

President Kagame's outrage seemed a response to an investigative report by a French judge looking into the downing of the Habyarimana plane in 1994. His conclusion, leaked to the Parisian daily *Le Monde* shortly before the tenth anniversary ceremonies, relied on regime dissidents and Kagame opponents who had long repeated the story: it was Kagame himself had given direct orders for the rocket attack on the plane.

Though it might prefer historical amnesia, France will not easily escape reflection on Rwanda. Patrick de Saint-Exupéry, a leading journalist with the French daily *Le Figaro,* has published a searing indictment of French actions in Rwanda: *l'Inavouable, la France au Rwanda,* Paris: Editions Les Arènes, 2004. In February 2005 French lawyers lodged six formal complaints with a military tribunal on behalf of genocide victims. The complaints allege complicity in the genocide on the part of French soldiers. They are designed to raise public awareness of France's role in the events of 1994.

**Culture:** More than 90% of the people of Rwanda are agricultural, rural folk, living in homesteads scattered on Rwanda's densely crowded hills. Houses are set within enclosures surrounded by cultivated fields. In addition to growing crops, most farmers also raise small livestock—goats, chickens and rabbits. Only a few wealthy individuals have one or a few cattle. This pattern of family enclosures provides Rwandans with much valued privacy. Living close to their fields also allows farmers to better protect their crops from theft. Although most Rwandans are Christian, particularly among the Hutus, almost half retain traditional beliefs. Relations between the Rwandan government and the Catholic Church remain strained given the participation of clergy in genocide activities. Two priests have already been sentenced to death for participation in the genocide. Many Rwandans lost faith in their church, and though it is still a predominantly Catholic country, Rwanda's fastest growing religion is Islam.

HIV/AIDS has become Rwanda's new genocide. The virus was already working its way into Rwandan society by 1990, but the genocide contributed to its explosive growth. The mass rape of Tutsi women was an integral part of the planned genocide. Radio propaganda taunted Hutus with a mythology of Tutsi women: they were taller, more beautiful, arrogant and threateningly dangerous because of their sexual wiles. They had to be tasted and humiliated before being killed. According to the UN, at least 250,000 women were raped in Rwanda in 1994; more than two-thirds of the rape survivors are HIV-positive.

In July 2001 Rwanda's National Commission for the Struggle Against AIDS indicated that an HIV-infected baby is born every six hours. Twenty to thirty percent of pregnant women have been found HIV-positive, and 40,000 to 50,000 babies are born HIV-inflected every year. At least 10% of the Rwandan population is believed to be HIV-positive.

There are several vectors through which Rwanda's silent death is spread. One consequence of 1994's genocide was that with so many men killed, female survivors were prepared to share husbands in order to have a family. The practice of sharing men, known as *"kwinjira,"* is widespread in rural areas. Health officials say that it represents the greatest challenge to their efforts to combat the spread of AIDS.

Kigale's street children, most of them AIDS orphans, have been found to be precociously active sexually in a recent Johns Hopkins survey. Thirty-five percent of the young children aged between 6-10 were already sexually active. Between 11-14 years of age 47.4% were active, while 81% at 15 and above fell into the sexually active category. The survey concluded that its interviewees were a "high risk population characterized by early sexual experimentation, multiple sex partners, unprotected sex, drug use and poor nutrition."

# Rwanda

**Economy:** Often described as the land of a thousand hills, Rwanda is a country whose economy is largely based on subsistence agriculture. For the past several years, it has been engaged in a process of economic reconstruction following the genocide of 1994 which effectively cut Rwanda's GDP in half. Roads, bridges, and whole sectors of the economy were destroyed. Thanks to several years of relative stability, the GDP has grown annually, showing a healthy 6% growth rate in 2001 and 9.4% in 2002. Growth is fueled by a booming construction industry (buildings seem to be popping up on every corner in Kigale) and increasing agricultural production.

Agriculture employs more than 90% of the population and contributes about 44% of GDP. Rwanda's most important exports are coffee and tea, which bring about 80% to 90% of export revenues. Tea production is strategically important to the country's economic development. Over the past 30 years it has grown consistently and now occupies 27,000 farmers and 30,000 workers. It is also the country's second most important export, representing 36% of total export earnings. The government plans to privatize nine tea estates and expects tea production will increase significantly. In addition to coffee and tea, Rwanda also exports over 54 tons of flowers to European countries annually, making them the third largest export commodity.

Local production of foodstuffs is insufficient for consumption needs, so most food is imported from neighboring countries. Rwanda traditionally imported between 8,000 and 10,000 liters of milk each day from Uganda, but in 1999 the cross border trade was banned for health reasons. Relations between the two countries were strained until July 2001, when Rwanda lifted the ban to increase milk supplies to both urban and rural populations.

There are plans to redevelop the dairy industry by importing some 3,000 cows from Germany, but few have yet been purchased. In June 2002 a U.S-based NGO, Heifer Project International sent 170 pregnant Jersey heifers to Rwanda to improve food security and boost farm incomes. The shipment was part of a program to provide about 500 head of dairy cattle to enhance crossbreeding and increase milk production.

The government's biggest economic problem, apart from security costs, remains the integration of more than two million refugees returning home. Housing and jobs are of critical importance. Some have been living as refugees since 1959. So many returnees did not speak French that the government was compelled to make English an official language. There are political as well as economic tensions between those who returned and those who stayed and survived the genocide. Survivors complain that returnees, with considerably more capital, are favored and privileged.

Rwanda is a heavily indebted poor country (HIPC) with a total debt of $1.435 billion as of 2003; its budget remains heavily dependent on foreign aid. A new investment code and a liberalization of the economy have encouraged direct foreign investment, which increased from $2.7 million in 2002 to $4.6 million in 2003. China has long been a significant investor in infrastructure projects, helping to build critical roads in a country without railways or navigable rivers. In May 2000, Chinese authorities agreed to fund a feasibility study for a rail link between Kigali and Northern Tanzania.

China has offered economic cooperation in agriculture (rice plantations and irrigation projects), energy (training in solar energy technology), and education. It has helped reestablish the Rwandan cement industry, while Chinese firms have rehabilitated the National Stadium and built the Kigali Conference Center. President Kagame last visited China in 2001 to celebrate 30 years of diplomatic relations.

**Future:** Though vastly improved, security remains a concern. Pockets of Hutu extremists still shelter in the neighboring Congo, and President Kagame's November 2004 threat to invade in order to suppress them seems to have focused the attention of both the Kabila government and UN peacekeepers to the issue. In the run up to elections in the Congo, Rwanda will experience considerable verbal hostility generated by demagogic politicians

Already one of the most densely populated countries on the continent, Rwanda faces increased demographic pressure with population growing at nearly 3% annually. Land use and allocation issues loom large.

**President George W. Bush meets with President Paul Kagame of Rwanda in the Oval Office Tuesday, March 4, 2003.**

Photo courtesy The White House

# The Democratic Republic of the Congo

**A poster of former President (of Zaïre) Mobutu Sese Seko burns**

AP/Wide World Photo

Note: This country has been known as Belgian Congo, Congo (Leopoldville), the Democratic Republic of the Congo, Zaïre, and most recently, Democratic Republic of the Congo.

**Area:** 2,345,410 sq km = 905,562.8 sq. mi. (slightly less than one-fourth the size of the U.S.).

**Population:** 60,085,804 (July 2005 est.)

**Capital City:** Kinshasa (pop. 6.55 million)

**Climate:** Warm and humid tropical weather in the western and central areas, temperate in the eastern highlands.

**Neighboring Countries:** Congo (North, West); Central African Republic, Sudan (North); Uganda, Rwanda, Burundi and Tanzania (East); Zambia and Angola (South).

**Official Language:** French.

**Other Principal Languages:** Over 200 African languages are spoken. Most prominent are the Alur, Bembe, Chokwe, Fuliiru, Hunde, Kituba (a creole based on the KiKongo dialect spoken in Manianga area of the lower Congo River), Kinyarwanda, KiKongo, Lega, Lingala (a lingua franca trade language), Luba, Lugbara, Mangbetu, Mongo, Nandi, Ndo, Ngbaka, Phende, Sanga, Shi, Songe, Swahili, Tetela, and Zande.

**Ethnic groups:** Over 200 African ethnic groups of which the majority are Bantu; the four largest peoples—Mongo, Luba, Kongo and the Mangbetu-Azande make up about 45% of the population.

**Principal Religions:** Roman Catholic 50%, Protestant 20%, Kimbanguist 10%, Muslim 10%, other sects and traditional beliefs 10%.

**Chief Commercial Products:** Diamonds, copper, coffee, cobalt, and crude oil.

**GNI per capita:** $100 (2003)

**Currency:** Congolese franc (CF)

**Former Colonial Status:** Personal possession of King Leopold II of Belgium (1885–1907); Belgian Colony (1907–1960).

**Independence Date:** June 30, 1960.

**Chief of State:** Joseph Kabila, President (appointed 25 January 2001).

**National Flag:** A plain blue field upon which is centered a large gold star, with a line of six small stars at the pole.

The deep green region of the Congo has intrigued explorers, adventurers and writers for centuries, becoming one of the popular stereotypes of Africa in the western mind. Dark rain forests abounding in game adjoin huge mining developments

117

# Congo (Kinshasa)

and vast plantations, some of which have been broken down into smaller farms. The very size of the Congo—as large as Western Europe—is one of its most distinctive features. Even more interesting, this huge nation has only a 25–mile–long coastline which allows it to "breathe" on the South Atlantic Ocean.

There are three distinctive features of this land mass: the immense river basin of the Congo and its tributaries, tropically hot and humid; the rich mining areas are located in the eastern sector and the upland plains in the northeast and southeast with tall, rippling grasses and snow–capped mountains rising to almost 17,000 feet in the East near the Equator. The eastern lake region, which includes Lake Kivu and the western shores of Lakes Tanganyika, Mweru, Albert and Edward, is unsurpassed in scenic beauty and abounds in wildlife.

Tributaries of the great Congo River flow from these lakes into the Lualaba River, which in turn becomes the Congo after it reaches 4° south latitude. From this point, the Congo surges in a wide, island–dotted course through the tropical forests, joined by its other tributaries. Three hundred miles inland from the Atlantic, at Malebo Pool (near bustling Kinshasa), the river widens into a lake, continuing on to the sea with a width of up to ten miles. The river is navigable for the most part and widely used in commerce, interrupted only by cataracts at Malebo Falls (formerly Stanley Falls) and below Kinshasa. Railway by–passes have been constructed at these cataracts to maintain the continuity of commerce.

**History:** Before the arrival of European explorers, the mighty Kingdom of the Kongo included not only the present–day Democratic Republic of the Congo, but portions of what is now Angola and west equatorial Africa. First contact by Europeans was established in 1482 by Portuguese navigator Diego Cao. Early Portuguese penetration was not significant, though it did result indirectly in the consecration of the first Black bishop by the Roman Catholic Church in 1520. Until the middle of the 19th century, this area remained unknown to the western world.

More became known as a consequence of 1874–77 explorations by the English journalist, Henry Morton Stanley, who navigated the Congo River to the Atlantic Ocean. Stanley was shortly thereafter hired by King Leopold II of Belgium to establish the king's authority in the Congo basin. Following the Berlin Conference of 1884-5, which recognized the king's claim to the basin, the area was colonized by Leopold as the Congo Free State. The Congo Free State was Leopold's personal fief, brutally exploited for personal profit. By 1907 international outrage at Leopold's abuses could no longer be denied or suppressed, and the Free State was taken over by the Belgian government, which renamed it the Belgian Congo. For details of early and colonial history, see *Historical Background* and *King Leopold and the Belgians in Africa.*

Belgian rule tended to be characterized by control through compulsion. There was little effort made prior to independence to prepare the people of the Congo for self–rule. When local government reforms in 1957 first presented an opportunity for political participation, Congolese *évolués*—the colony's miniscule educated elite—responded quickly. Bakongo *évolués* formed the *Alliance des Bakongo* (ABAKO) based in Léopoldville (now Kinshasa). Though ethnically based, ABAKO first articulated the demand for Congolese independence, and under the leadership of Joseph Kasavubu became a forceful voice of anticolonial protest.

Once started, nationalist sentiments gathered enthusiastic followings. The most important multiethnic grouping dedicated to the Congo's national unity was the Congolese National Movement (MNC). With Patrice Lumumba at its head, the MNC became the most militant advocate of the colony's independence. When French Congo, across the river, was offered independence by President Charles de Gaulle in 1958, there was increased pressure on Belgium to grant independence to its colony. An impending threat of independence, coupled with tumbling world copper prices, led to a withdrawal of foreign capital from the country in the late 1950s, weakening the economy and creating widespread unemployment.

In January 1959 the Belgian administration's decision to cancel an ABAKO meeting in Léopoldville led to violent urban protests. Virtually the entire African population of the city took to the streets, and protest soon turned into looting. When finally suppressed, the Léopoldville riots officially resulted in 47 Congolese dead; in reality, many more were probably killed. Shock, sadness and fear gripped the administration, and the timetable for independence was advanced.

In this turbulent atmosphere, Belgium summoned African leaders to Brussels in early 1960 and announced that independence would become effective on June 30th. A multitude of new parties sprang up, almost overnight. The intense political activity served as a forewarning to thousands of Europeans, who began to leave the Congo in droves. In parliamentary elections Lumumba's MNC won the greatest number of seats, but not enough to govern without coalition partners. After ten days of bargaining behind closed doors, Lumumba announced a 37–member cabinet, containing officials from no fewer than 16 parties. When independence was formally declared, Patrice Lumumba became prime minister and Joseph Kasavubu president of the renamed Democratic Republic of the Congo.

The situation quickly deteriorated into lawlessness, rebellion, anarchy, revolt, and secession. Disintegration began when the *Force Publique*, Congo's army, mutinied on 5 July, immediately followed by the intervention of Belgian paratroopers sent to protect the lives of Belgian citizens. Hundreds of whites were mercilessly slaughtered and others beaten and tortured. The Congolese government was incapable of action, incapacitated by a lethal power struggle between Lumumba and Kasavubu, each of whom dismissed the other. Almost simultaneously Katanga, Congo's richest province, declared itself independent on 11 July under the leader-

President Kasavubu (center) and Premier Lumumba confer with Belgian army chief, 1960

# Congo (Kinshasa)

The forests of Kivu

## Mobutu in Power

Conditions remained unstable in the eastern Congo even after former Prime Minister Tshombe's exile and ultimate house arrest in Algeria. But General Mobutu maintained the loyalty of the army and skillfully played ethnic and political factions against each other to consolidate his control. Pressured by the U.S. and other foreign powers to hold elections, he created the *Mouvement Populaire de la Révolution* (Popular Movement for the Revolution; MPR) and was elected unopposed as president in 1970.

In 1971 Mobutu elaborated a campaign of cultural nationalism or "authenticity." He renamed the country Zaïre and himself Mobutu Sese Seko, donning a leopard skin cap as the symbol of his status and power as an African chief. Katanga became Shaba and the river Congo became the river Zaïre. Zaïriois, the citizens of the newly renamed country, were required to adopt African names.

The constitution was revised in 1974 to contain "Mobutuism", which embodied the president's thoughts and teachings. It became the required curriculum even in Zaïre's Catholic schools. Most plantations and farms owned by foreigners were nationalized, and all mineral ores had to be refined within Zaïre, even though there were insufficient facilities to perform the task.

Infrastructure deteriorated rapidly as the MPR-state and its ideology of Mobutism proved inadequate to the tasks of national integration and governance. Increasingly the state was held together by little more than a web of client-patron relations sustained by state resources. The regime gave rise to the term "kleptocracy"—rule by thieves.

Relative peace and stability prevailed until 1977 and 1978 when Katangan rebels, based in Angola, launched a series of invasions into Shaba (ex-Katanga). The rebels had to be driven out with the aid of foreign troops—French, Belgian and Moroccan. Elections in 1977 resulted in another victory for Mobutu and his party. The legislature, however, became meaningless as Mobutu increasingly ruled by decree. Despite this, foreign aid continued to pour in on the theory that Zaïre was a bastion against communism. From 1965 to 1991 Zaïre received more than $1.5 billion in U.S. economic and military aid. While he was still favored by the U.S., Jonas Savimbi and UNITA received much of their assistance through Zaïre.

Realizing that his personal security and future were clouded, Mobutu summoned Israeli military personnel to train a Presidential Guard in 1982. They performed well, and the elite guard slowly became the only coherent and capable force in Za-

ship of Moïse Tshombe. On 12 July Tshombe and Kasavuvu jointly appealed to the UN for assistance in restoring order.

The arrival of the UN Peacekeeping force only increased the friction between President Kasavubu and Prime Minister Lumumba. Lumumba demanded that UN forces suppress the Katangese secession, by force if necessary, and Kasavubu categorically refused the idea. In September Lumumba turned to the Soviet Union for assistance in sending Congolese troops to Katanga, introducing cold-war politics into the Congo crisis. Amid further provincial secessions and increased violence, Army Chief of Staff Col. Joseph Mobutu announced on 14 September that the army would henceforth govern in association with a caretaker government headed by President Kasavubu.

Kasavubu decided to eliminate his rival, Lumumba, once and for all. The army captured the charismatic leader in December, and Kasavubu turned him over to the self–proclaimed President of Katanga, Moïse Tshombe. Lumumba was shortly

thereafter killed, with Belgian complicity and probably American foreknowledge.

Even though Kasavubu's sacrifice of Lumumba to the Katanga secessionists was intended to facilitate the breakaway province's return to a united Congo, the Katangan secession continued until early 1963 when Tshombe gave in to the central government. UN troops withdrew in midyear, and unrest and rebellion in the provinces continued as the central government was unable to assert its authority. From January to August 1964 rural insurgency engulfed five of Congo's 21 provinces, and in desperation President Kasavubu appointed Moïse Tshombe as premier. Ironically, the defeated secessionist used foreign mercenaries and Belgian paratroopers to put down secession and assert the central government's authority over a unified state. He got no word of thanks from President Kasavubu, who, frightened and envious of Tshombe's growing popularity, fired him as premier, whereupon Colonel Joseph Désiré Mobutu took center stage and ousted the president in late 1965.

# Congo (Kinshasa)

merged the two governments in 1994. A High Council of the Republic-Parliament of Transition (HCR-PT) was created with the resilient Mobutu as head of state. The HCR-PT repeatedly scheduled presidential and legislative elections over the next two years, but they were never to take place.

By now, Zaïre's economy was barely functional. So much of the state's resources had been siphoned away into Mobutu's patronage network that capital investment was impossible. Several copper mines of Shaba, for example, had been flooded and idle for years. The Mobutu regime had become the mirror image of Leopold II's—personal, arbitrary, and venal.

In 1996 Mobutu traveled to Switzerland for extensive treatment of prostate cancer. While there, a Rwandan-backed rebel force captured much of eastern Zaïre as the ethnic tensions in neighboring Rwanda suddenly engulfed Zaïre. Hutu militia forces (the *Interahamwe* driven from Rwanda in 1994) had attacked Rwanda from their Zaïre refugee camps. Despite repeated requests, the Mobutu government had done nothing to curb their violence, which quickly turned even more malign when Hutu forces linked up with remnants of the Zaïrian armed forces (FAZ) to attack local Tutsi, the Banyamulenge, in eastern Zaïre. To prevent another genocide, Rwanda and its allies, particularly Uganda, invaded Zaïre.

### Laurent Kabila

Plucked from obscurity to provide a non-Tutsi face to the insurgency was the semi-retired roly-poly professional revolutionary Laurent Kabila. A Luba from Katanga, he had been long engaged in the anti-Mobutu struggle, but always in secondary roles.

When Che Guevara, the charismatic Cuban revolutionary who was looking for further fertile fields to ply his trade, arrived in eastern Zaïre he ran across Kabila and provided a withering critique of his revolutionary potential. Despite being "the best of the Congolese leaders," Kabila was seen as "too addicted to drink and women." Reluctant to engage in any actual fighting, Kabila seemed to take his best shots across the bar. He was available when the call to leadership came.

Once the insurgency began, there was little effective resistance. The Zaïrian army fled in terror before the onslaught; they had little loyalty except to themselves. The only thing that impeded Kabila's *Alliance des Forces Démocratiques pour la Libération du Congo-Zaïre* (AFDL) was the fact that there were no roads or bridges, just rutted, frequently flooded, and muddy areas that allowed trucks to pass irregularly. Because of these conditions, it

ïre. The remaining armed forces were expected to make their way by theft and corruption. Government workers were unpaid and were expected to survive the same way. Bribery and corruption became coping mechanisms for government workers. While workers scrambled to keep alive, President Mobutu became one of the richest men in the world. In 1992, according to the World Bank, 64.7% of Zaïre's budget was reserved for Mobutu's "discretionary spending."

When Zaïre defaulted on Belgian loans in 1989, foreign aid was severely cut. Since the eastern Euroepan model had begun to collapse around the same time, Zaïre was no longer a necessary bastion against communism. Development programs were cancelled and the economy deteriorated even further. Pressure mounted to open up the political system.

In April 1990 President Mobutu agreed to end the ban on opposition parties and appointed a transitional government. Liberalization of the regime was, of course, illusory. May student protests at the University of Lumumbashi (ex-Elizabethville) were brutally suppressed. Anywhere from 50 to 150 students were killed, according to Amnesty International.

When soldiers threatened to rebel over unpaid wages, the government resorted to printing more money—in higher denominations as inflation mounted—or gave them free reign to pillage and loot. In September 1991 they rioted and devastated Kinshasa. Some two thousand French and Belgian troops had to be ferried in to evacuate 20,000 foreign nationals from the city. Increasingly the president absented himself from his capital, seeking refuge in the sumptuous comfort of a fortress-palace constructed at Gbadolite in northwest Zaïre. All the while conditions in the country continued to deteriorate.

Finally, after many promises and more avoidances, Mobutu capitulated to the holding of a Sovereign National Conference in 1992. Over 2,000 representatives from various political parties and civil society attended. The conference took its "sovereign" power seriously and elected Étienne Tshisekedi, leader of the *Union pour la Démocratie et le Progrès Social* (UDPS) as prime minister.

By the end of the year Mobutu had created a rival government with its own prime minister. Rival pro- and anti-Mobutu governments created a stalemate that was only broken when a compromise

**Mobutu Sese Seko**

took until May 1997 for the insurgent army to reach Kinshasa.

Laurent Kabila proclaimed himself president and took the oath of office on May 31, 1997. He promised democracy, but said elections could not be held for two years because of the need to bring order to the country. To fit with its new aspirations, the country was once again renamed. Mobutu's Zaïre became, again, the Democratic Republic of the Congo (DRC). Laurent Kabila spent most of 1997–98 consolidating his power.

By August 1998, it had become apparent that Kabila was little more than a mini–Mobutu. The security demands of Rwanda and Uganda were still unmet, Hutu rebels still posed threats from bases in the Congo, and enemies of the Museveni regime scampered back and forth across the border, doing damage to Ugandan citizens. Inside the Congo Banyamulenge Tutsi had little sense they would be incorporated into any national dialogue, and it became evident that Kabila was moving to place relatives and members of his own ethnic group in the most important positions of power. Nepotism was accompanied by its sister vice, corruption.

When Kabila moved to sack his Rwandan military advisors and send them packing—the very people responsible for elevating him to presidential status—the crisis of confidence came to a head. A second rebellion arose in the East no sooner than the plane bearing the exiled advisors landed. A brilliant tactical flight to the West brought rebel forces close to the doors of Kinshasa and for a moment it looked as though the regime were doomed. A fearful Kabila called upon his fellow authoritarians in Angola and Zimbabwe. Both presidents Dos Santos and Mugabe responded with interventionist forces. The western threat was ended and military action focused on the Eastern Front.

The Second Rebellion developed into Africa's first continental war. Besides Angola and Zimbabwe, Namibia, Chad, Sudan and Libya came to the support of the Kabila government. Rwanda and Uganda supported local Congolese rebel factions. By mid–1999 the Democratic Republic of the Congo had been, *de facto*, partitioned. The rebel coalition controlled the eastern third of the country. Laurent Kabila remained in office by virtue of foreign arms, and it was difficult to talk of the central government exercising control over its territory.

Having enjoyed initial military success, the rebel forces opposing him soon fell to bickering among themselves. The principal rebel group, the *Rassemblement Congolais pour la Démocratie* (RCD) split in two. Rwanda and Uganda, themselves divided on the best way to fight the war, supported different rebel factions. Yet a third rebel faction emerged under the leadership of Jean-Pierre Bemba, the leader of the *Mouvement pour la Libération Congolaise* (MLC). Backed by Uganda, Bemba took charge of the rebellion's northern front. Rwanda and Uganda themselves engaged in heated fighting around Kisangani on at least two occasions.

### The Lusaka Agreement

War and peace continued, intermittently bringing hope and despair to everyday Congolese. Peace prospects seemed hopeful in the summer of 1999 as warring states gathered in Zambia's capital, Lusaka. Conditions for ending the war were defined and a precise timetable was set, a sign of the terminal optimism of conference participants.

Within 24 hours of the signing, hostilities were to cease. A Joint Military Commission (JMC), consisting of two representatives of each belligerent party, under a neutral chairman designated by the OAU, would oversee implementation of the accord until the deployment of a UN peacekeeping force.

To ensure compliance, the international force would collect weapons from civilians and supervise the withdrawal of all foreign troops. The agreement also envisioned tracking down and disarming armed groups, screening for mass killers and war criminals, and ultimately the handing over of suspected *génocidaires* to the International Criminal Tribunal for Rwanda (ICTR) in Arusha, Tanzania. (The "armed groups" were fundamentally the rebel oppositions destabilizing Rwanda, Uganda, and Burundi, along with Angola's principal *bête noir*: Jonas Savimbi's UNITA.)

Forty-five days after signing the Lusaka agreement, the DRC government, the *Rassemblement Congolais pour la Démocratie*

(RCD), the *Mouvement de Libération Congolais* (MLC), unarmed opposition groups and Congolese civil society were to begin open political negotiations leading to the creation of a new political dispensation for the Congo.

On paper the plan looked excellent, but political reality and diplomatic brilliance are hardly the same. President Kabila signed the Lusaka ceasefire agreement to avoid losing the war. Quibble, protest, rejection, and delay provided time to rebuild his forces, but additional Chinese arms and North Korean training were of little avail.

In February 2000 the Security Council approved a paltry Congo peacekeeping force of some 500, backed by about 1000 soldiers. The 500 could hardly monitor a cease-fire only reluctantly and intermittently observed in a country the size of Western Europe. The year 2000, unsurprisingly, was punctuated by regular violations of the cease-fire and dramatic successes of the rebel alliance

### Kabila's Military Failures

In August 2000 President Laurent Kabila announced that his government would no longer observe the Lusaka accord because Congo was occupied by Uganda and Rwanda. In October the Congolese army (FAC) and its allies attacked Rwandan and rebel forces on the southern Katangan Front. The attack was intended to open a corridor for Burundian Hutu rebels—members of the *Forces de la Défense de la Démocratie* (FDD)—to infiltrate Burundi. Burundi was always considered the weakest link in the anti-Kabila alliance. If it could be destabilized, the government would have to withdraw its troops from the Congo.

The government coalition was initially successful, but its lines were overextended. Roads were in such miserable shape the Zimbabwean heavy artillery could not be resupplied. When the Rwandan Patriotic Army (RPA) and its allies counter-attacked, Kabila's troops fell back precipitously. The government's military failure was completed in early December when Rwandan troops and their RCD-Goma allies captured the strategic southeastern city of Pweto, a critical gateway to the riches of Katanga province, Kabila's homeland.

At least 200 of Pweto's defenders—Rwandan Hutu *Interahamwe*, Burundian Hutu rebels, and members of FAC—were killed. Those not killed, up to 10,000 including a full battalion of Zimbabwean soldiers, fled across the border into Zambia.

Material losses to Kabila's allies at Pweto were equally staggering. Zimbabwe lost a MIG jet-fighter, shot down

# Congo (Kinshasa)

**Former President Laurent Kabila**

by a Rwandan surface-to-air missile, and a huge store of equipment. With the capture of Pweto and the scattering of its defenders, the road to Congo's second-biggest city, Lubumbashi, lay open.

The rout of Kabila's forces prompted a debate within the Rwandan government. Some thought the victory should be exploited to destroy the Interahamwe in Katanga completely, and some even argued for tracking them down in Zambia. The diplomatically attuned successfully argued the backlash against such a move would simply be too costly. Indeed, Pweto was the high-water mark of Rwandan arms in the Congo; other events were soon to tip the balance towards more peaceful solutions.

### Laurent Kabila Assassinated

Many in Kinshasa had the feeling the Kabila regime had entered its final stages by September. In his regular search for plots, conspiracies, and opposition, President Kabila ultimately turned on his initial supporters.

One of those was Anselme Masasu, a founding leader of the AFDL. Masasu had commanded the army of child soldiers (*kadogos*) from Eastern Congo that swept into Kinshasa in the wake of Kabila's victory. In October he was reported to have made subversive comments at a meeting of some 1,200 *kadogos* and was subsequently arrested and tortured, along with many others of eastern origin. Some 47 were executed in the presence of President Kabila, who allegedly killed several himself. Anselme Masasu and eight of his companions were reportedly sent to Katanga where they were murdered on 27 November.

Masasu's murder resonated strongly among the *kadogos*, and its rumor was a factor in their massive desertion at the battle of Pweto. Others plotted more direct action to avenge the murder of their commander—the assassination of Laurent Kabila.

Kabila was assassinated on 16 January 2001, forty years, to the day, after the murder of Patrice Lumumba. According to the official version, he was shot by one of his own *kadogo* bodyguards, Rachidi Kasereka, who was, in turn, shot to death by Kabila's aide-de-camp, Col. Eddy Kapend.

Col. Kapend and around 80 others were accused of plotting Kabila's death and were sent before a special military tribunal. Lawyers had little or no contact with them and little capacity to prepare their defenses. In January 2003 Kapend, and 29 others were convicted of plotting and killing Kabila and sentenced to death.

The consequences of Kabila's death were significant for the Congo. Laurent's son, Joseph Kabila, elevated to the presidency by his father's inner circle and their Angolan and Zimbabwean backers, reached out for international understanding and support. With that in hand, he quickly reversed many of his father's decisions blocking implementation of the Lusaka agreement.

### Joseph Kabila

Joseph Kabila had long enjoyed the confidence of his father, alternating military assignments with more confidential missions on his father's behalf. Quiet, direct and frank, Joseph is stylistically very different from his father. He rejected the "Marble Palace," built by Mobutu and favored by his father, and worked from the OAU's Kinshasa headquarters. Educated in Tanzania and Uganda, Kabila reportedly feels more comfortable speaking English than French. When elevated to the presidency he was serving as the army chief of staff. He was 29 years old, Africa's youngest president.

With the guidance of Sir Ketumile Masire, the OAU facilitator, participants in the Inter-Congolese Dialogue reached an agreement in the South African resort of Sun City in Spring 2002. Nearly four hundred delegates, representing the government, rebel factions, opposition parties, and civil society, met to thrash out plans to end conflict and begin reconstruction of the Congo.

Follow-up meetings led to the withdrawal of Rwandan and most Ugandan and Zimbabwean troops by early November, and in December 2002, dialogue participants signed an agreement in Pretoria to share power in a transitional government. By March 2003 a transitional constitution had been hammered out, and, more

**President Joseph Kabila**

sensitively, an agreement on future control of the armed forces was signed in late June.

Under the agreements, President Kabila will lead the transitional government, assisted by four vice-presidents—one each from the present government, the two main rebel groups, and the unarmed opposition—in a two-year transitional authority. The new cabinet is expansively scaled: 35 ministers and 25 deputy ministers—certainly large enough to reduce the unemployment rate among politicians.

The new vice-presidents include Jean-Pierre Bemba, the leader of the *Mouvement de libération du Congo*; Abdoulaye Yerodia Ndombasi, a long-time Kabila ally; Arthur Z'Ahidi Ngoma, a long-time opposition politician who represents the unarmed political opposition, and RCD-Goma's secretary-general, Azarias Ruberwa. Each vice-president was to oversee a cluster of ministries, while ministerial appointments, governorships, ambassadorial assignments, and commands of military regions were shared among the signatories to the various agreements.

Despite the progress and the optimism it has generated, peace remains precarious in the DRC; its benefits have yet to trickle down to the average citizen and tensions are rising. In Kinshasa, the "one plus four" formula (one president, four vice-presidents) proved little workable: neither the president nor anyone else seemed to be coordinating action. The Independent Electoral Commission was not voted into existence until mid-April 2004, and conditions in the country argued against its ability to conduct a census and register voters in any short time. Roads are so awful, for example, that it takes nine hours to travel a little more than 62 miles from Kinshasa.

Life in the capital itself is often unstable: armed attackers assaulted several military and civilian installations in March

# Congo (Kinshasa)

Bridge repair in the eastern province.

©Paul Carlson Foundation

2004. In the provinces, active fighting continues in the northeast, in both North and South Kivu. The whole of the territory is awash in guns and ethnic hostilities in many places have only intensified. The UN Mission in the Congo (MONUC) has failed to disarm or stabilize the region and has itself become the target of local militias in Ituri.

Elements of the former Rwandan army, now ironically calling themselves "Democratic Forces for the Liberation of Rwanda" (FDLR), and remnants of the genocidal *Interahamwe* still operate in the Kivus, posing security issues for neighboring Rwanda and a justification for intervention. The UN estimates there are 8,000 to 10,000 Rwandan rebels in the Congo, and recent recruiting among the children of Hutu refugees may have increased their ranks. The DRC Armed Forces (FARDC) have increased their pressure on the Rwandan fighters, but much of it has been more rhetorical than real: In early May 2004 the regional military commander identified them as "evil forces operating in our country" and asked the citizenry to provide information that would enable the FARDC to "neutralize" them.

Work on creating new unified national army (combining government and rebel forces) that might help the government project its authority in the provinces is painfully slow. Belgium and France are training a mixed brigade of some 3,500 troops, but there are serious doubts about its deployment to the Eastern provinces.

Lacking logistical support, it would be routed by the rebels. Worse, there are fears the troops would simple sell their weapons to the ethnic militias or *Interahamwe* forces active in the area. What minimal order that can be maintained results from the presence of UN peacekeepers, but MONUC forces are slightly less than 17,000, spread relatively thinly, and in constant demand as new hot spots flare up.

In May 2005 a contingent had to be sent to Mbuji-Mayi in Kasai-Oriental to protect MONUC personnel and installations after riots broke out protesting delays in Congo's promised elections. At least four people died in the turmoil, triggered by Etienne Tshisekedi's call for his UDPS supporters to make the provincial capital a "dead city" of strikes and stayaways. Security forces moved in after UDPS faithful razed the offices of their political rivals—President Kabila's People's Party for Reconstruction and Democracy (PPRD) and Jean-Pierre Bemba's MLC.

The events came shortly after one positive sign of visible progress in the fragile transitional process: the National Assembly and Senate had passed a new constitution. In it, presidential powers are limited, and a president can serve a maximum of two five-year terms. The minimum age for presidential candidates was set at 30, allowing Joseph Kabila, now 33, to run for office. Strikingly, and perhaps the most hopeful sign, the new constitution recognizes as citizens all ethnic groups present at independence in 1960. That grants citizenship to the thousands of Rwandans, Hutu and Tutsi, whose presence has so long been so contentious.

The text must now be approved in a national referendum to be held within six months. After that the transitional process should, if all goes well, end with presidential and parliamentary elections.

**Culture:** Kinshasa, Congo's capital, remains a testament to the Congolese capacity to suffer and endure. A hugely swollen population escaping the devastation of war, estimated now to be near seven million, survives cut off from the city's traditional sources of food. Half of Kinshasa's food supply was lost when rebels captured fertile Equateur province and controlled the river that once carried food to the capital. Virtually every available parcel of ground in the city is planted with foodstuffs to supplement the meager food supply.

The consequences are heart rending. The majority of *Kinois* (the city's inhabitants) have had to content themselves with a single, frugal, daily meal, usually eaten at night so they can go to sleep with a full stomach. Parents have fasted for two or three days to provide food for their children, but malnutrition grows and with it, an increase in childhood disease and death. The New York-based International Rescue Committee estimates the total number of lives claimed by the Congo war now approaches three million—most of them from malnutrition and disease.

As living conditions deteriorated in the Congo, there was a proliferation of religious sects, particularly in Kinshasa. Church sources indicate there are as many as 400 different sects in the capital, some of them violent. Many have been inspired by full-gospel, born-again Christian evangelical groups. The "Army of Heaven," whose 40 members briefly destabilized a city of seven million people in March 2004, was totally unknown before the attacks.

**Economy:** At the time of independence, this was one of the potentially richest nations in the world, with vast deposits of natural resources. The Congo contains 80% of the world's cobalt (essential in hi-tech and defense production), 10% of its copper, and one-third of its diamonds. There are also considerable reserves of gold, uranium and manganese. But government corruption, mismanagement, and profligacy destroyed Congo's economy. War has only furthered the collapse.

A statistical description of the Congo today is appalling. The country is $10.56 billion in debt (2003). More than 70% of the population lives in absolute poverty and

# Congo (Kinshasa)

85% is unemployed. Industry operates at a mere 25% of capacity, and there is a tax base of less than one million people in a country of more than 60 million. Its GDP rose by a modest 5.6% in 2003, having fallen by 2% in 2001, and 11.3% in 2000. The social impact of economic collapse can be seen in two additional statistics: life expectancy is only 45 years, and infant mortality is very high: 129 per thousand. (The average for sub-Saharan Africa is 105.)

Production in all key sectors has declined dramatically. The mining sector has imploded. *La Général des Carrières et des Mines* (Gécamines), once the crown jewel of the Congo mining industry, is in near-terminal decline. State-owned Gécamines' production has fallen drastically since the late 1980s, and today it is estimated to be producing at a mere 10% of its capacity. Deeply in debt, the company requires $150 million just to revive production. To reach its maximum output will require an investment of $1 billion. The government has begun to sell off some of the more productive parts of the mining giant rousing the ire of its labor unions, but even that could not restore economic health so precipitously had productivity fallen.

A new Mining Code and healthy privatization may yet revive Congolese mining. London-based America Mineral Fields (AMF) has high hopes for its Kolwezi copper-cobalt tailings project. AMF, which owns 83% of the project, is currently seeking some $300 million to finance it. Kolwezi essentially involves reclamation and treatment of stockpiled leftovers from earlier Gécamines operations—113 million tons of copper tailings. These are rich in both copper and cobalt and AMF hopes to begin operations in 2005, producing 42,000 tons of copper and 7,000 tons of co-

balt annually. For the company's CEO, "The Kolwezi project has the potential to become the world's largest and lowest cost cobalt producer."

Congo is the world's third-largest exporter of diamonds, and in the past ten years diamonds have replaced copper as Congo's major source of foreign exchange. Diamond exports—mostly of industrial-quality diamonds—account for about 70% of the DRC's total export revenues. The state-owned diamond mining company, MIBA (*Compagnie Minière de Bakwanga*) like Gécamines, a traditional government cash cow, fell on hard times during Congo's prolonged instability.

In 2000 the company produced around 4,600,000 carats, which was 75% lower than in 1999. By the end of October 2002, MIBA production had risen to 5.6 million carats. The Congolese government owns 80% of MIBA shares.

Total Congolese diamond exports rose in 2004 (8.6% in quantity and 12.5% in value) and will probably reach record proportions as some degree of stability returns to the country. Output reached 29.4 million carats (most produced by artisanal mining) worth $723 million for the year.

Civil conflict provided an opportunity for combatants on both sides to exploit Congolese natural resources to pay their war-making expenses. Congo's deputy-minister of mines estimated that the illegal exportation of the country's diamonds resulted in the loss of some $800 million a year. Much of the recent increase in diamond exports reflects tightening up on smuggling operations.

Recognizing the progress made by the government in its economic reform efforts, the IMF and World Bank designated Congo a beneficiary of debt relief under provisions of the Heavily Indebted Poor Countries (HIPC) initiative in July 2003. Noting positive economic growth in 2002 and a significant drop in inflation, the two institutions said relief would reduce the country's external debt by up to 80%. This would come over the next 25 years in the form of sweeping cuts in debt service payments and forgiveness of past payments arrears.

If debt relief is a sign of confidence on the part of the Bretton Woods institutions, private business is far more skeptical and cautious about investing in the DRC. President Kabila toured Europe in early 2004 to drum up investments, but came up disappointingly short. Belgian companies made it clear that some $650 million in debt owed Congolese and Belgian companies had to be reimbursed. Among other conditions posited, they asked that the tax on new capital investments be reduced from 5% to 1%, and for more aggressive

efforts to make the informal sector pay its taxes, thus lifting the burden from existing companies who saw themselves as easy targets to be harassed by Congolese tax administrators.

In general, existing conditions in the DRC—political tension in the capital and insecurity in the provinces—do not encourage investment.

**The Future:** Relationships within the transitional government will become increasingly tense as the prospect of elections approaches. President Kabila, who controls the security agencies, has refused to permit ministers from leaving the capital without authorization, and one RDC minister resigned over the issue. A RDC spokesman threw fuel on the fire by accusing President Kabila of trying to regain the powers he had lost in Pretoria to restore a new dictatorship.

President Kabila's deliberate exclusion of Etienne Tshisekedi, one of the country's most popular political leaders, from any role in the transitional government has already proved its downside with the deadly riots in Mbuji-Mayi and conditions are not likely to improve. Despite laws which compel the state media to cover political parties equally, Tshisekedi's Union for Democracy and Social Progress (UDPS) finds it difficult to be heard on Congo's airwaves (particularly in the provinces), while the president's party—the People's Party for Reconstruction and Development (PPRD), which is already campaigning for an elected Kabila presidency—can use the media whenever it wants.

There is no way elections will be held before 2006, which will add to frustration and tension. The EU, which as agreed to finance them, seems fearful that Kabila, like is predecessors, will postpone, delay, and sabotage the electoral calendar. Its public pressure on the president to maintain the schedule has been notable, but if the elections are not well prepared, with adequate census and registration, their results simply will not be accepted.

Congo's economic problems remain enormous. President Kabila needs an estimated $8 million a month just to supply fuel to his unhappy country. The conflict zone of the Kivus is a humanitarian disaster, with a reported 1,000 people a day dying. There is little infrastructure to link the regions to Kinshasa, so any plans for a centralized state will simply repeat the failures of the past. Political reconstruction might best look at a variety of federal arrangements. Economic reconstruction of the Congo will require billions. The country will be dependent on outsiders for decades to come.

**Market transport in the eastern region: the Tsjugoudu, a hand-crafted bicycle made almost entirely of wood and capable of carrying up to 400 pounds of produce to market.** Photo by Theodore Trefon

# The Republic of Congo

**The hazards of the highway**

Photo by G. Philippart de Foy
Courtesy APFT-ULB

**Area:** 349,650 sq. km = 135,000 sq. mi. (twice the size of Missouri).

**Population:** 3,039,126 (July 2005 est.)

**Capital City:** Brazzaville (Pop. 850,000, estimated).

**Climate:** Tropically hot and humid.

**Neighboring Countries:** Gabon (West); Cameroon (Northwest); Central African Republic (North); Democratic Republic of the Congo (East, South).

**Official Language:** French.

**Other Principal Languages:** Lingala and Munoukutuba (a Kikongo-based creole); both are lingua franca trade languages. Many local languages and dialects (of which Kikongo has the most users).

**Ethnic groups:** Kongo 48%, Sangha 20%, M'Bochi 12%, Teke 17%, Europeans NA%; note—Europeans estimated at 8,500, mostly French, before the 1997 civil war; maybe half of that in 1998, following the widespread destruction of foreign businesses in 1997.

**Principal Religions:** Christian 50%, animist 48%, Muslim 2%.

**Chief Commercial Products:** Oil, wood products and timber, potash, palm oil, cocoa, bananas, peanuts.

**GNI per capita:** $640 (2003)

**Currency:** CFA Franc (no longer tied to the French franc).

**Former Colonial Status:** French Congo (1883–1910); one of the four territories of French Equatorial Africa (1910–1960).

**Independence Date:** August 15, 1960.

**Chief of State:** Denis Sassou-Nguesso, President (since January 1998).

**National Flag:** Diagonal green, yellow, and red stripes; the yellow is narrower dividing the two fields.

This lush, green land of ancient tradition lies immediately to the north of the great Congo River. Formerly a part of French Equatorial Africa, the country has the same general geographical features as Congo (Kinshasa) to the south.

As early as the fifteenth and sixteenth centuries, this land was part of the great Kongo Kingdom. Its present day boundaries, as is so often the case in Africa, are based upon arbitrary determinations of 19th century European powers rather than on cultural and physical reality.

A low–lying, treeless plain extends forty miles from the coast to the interior, succeeded by a mountainous region parallel to the coastline known as the Mayombe Escarpment. This is a region of sharply rising mountain ridges covered with jungle and dense growth. Continuing further, the Niari River Valley, an important agricultural area, extends to the east, and to the north lies The Pool, a region of treeless hills and a succession of grassy plains, covering some 50,000 square miles. Part of the Congo River Basin lies in the extreme northeast, a region of dense jungle and all but impassable plains. The climate is uniform and equatorial—hot and humid all year.

**History:** As in the neighboring country of Congo (Kinshasa), oral tradition conveys the story of the mighty Kingdom of the Kongo, probably founded in the 14th century. It was not until 1482 that the first European, the Portuguese navigator Diogo Cao, explored the coastal areas. Colonization of the area started through the efforts of Pierre Savorgnan de Brazza in the 1880s. An Italian count and later French citizen and naval officer, de Brazza signed treaties of protection with a number of African chiefs, founded the city of Brazzaville, and governed the area from 1886 to 1897.

When horrific reports of abuse of African workers by companies holding concessions in the colony became insistent enough to require action, de Brazza was sent to investigate in 1905. Two years later France restricted the use of forced labor by concessionaires. In 1910 the French joined Moyen-Congo (Middle Congo), as the colony was known, with three others to form French Equatorial Africa (FEA). Brazzaville served as the capital of FEA. For additional details of early and colonial history, see *Historical Background* and *The French in Africa*.

Under the leadership of Félix Éboué, a black colonial administrator, French Equatorial Africa rallied to General Charles de Gaulle during World War II. A grateful de Gaulle made Éboué governor-general of FEA, and honored the federation's capital by gathering colonial administrators for the Brazzaville Conference of 1944 to discuss postwar colonial reforms.

Following World War II Congo was given a territorial assembly and representation in the French parliament, which increased both political awareness and activity in the colony. With General de Gaulle's Fifth French Republic, Congo became an autonomous republic within the Franco-African Community in 1958 and opted for full independence in 1960.

The Abbé Fulbert Youlou, a catholic priest instrumental in charting the course toward independence, was installed as president in 1960. His party, *Union Démocratique pour la Défense des Intérêts Africains* (UDDIA) drew its strength from southern peoples who had benefited most from colonial education and opportunity. The party advocated private ownership and close ties with France, but corruption, incompetence, massive labor unrest, and lack of French support led to a coup and Youlou's ouster in 1963. In typically French fashion, the three-day revolution was referred to as the "Trois Glorieuses"—mimicking the Parisian events of 1830.

His successor, Alphonse Massamba-Débat, took inspiration from French Marxism, creating the National Revolutionary Movement (MNR) as the country's single party. Congo became a "people's republic" complete with red flag, the *Interna-*

# Congo (Brazzaville)

*tional* as its anthem, and disastrous economic policies for the next twenty-five years. Continuing north-south regional tension and administrative incapacity led the military to replace Massamba-Débat with Major Marien Ngouabi in 1968.

Ngouabi maintained the socialist line, insisting that Marxism was a "universal science." He renamed the country the People's Republic of the Congo and replaced the MRN with the Congolese Labor Party (PCT) as the country's sole political party. With Ngouabi, a northerner, power shifted away from traditional power centers in the south. In highly politicized Brazzaville and other southern cities, opposition soon developed among both student and labor groups.

President Ngouabi was assassinated in March 1977; a military tribunal was hastily convened, which quickly accused and convicted Massambat-Débat of being behind the killing. He was executed and an 11-man military committee took control. Ngouabi's military successor, Col. Joachim Yhombi-Opango, lasted two years before he was at odds with the PCT. In 1979 he handed over the presidency to the PCT, which selected Col. Denis Sassou-Nguesso as his successor.

More politically attuned than his predecessors, Sassou-Nguesso maintained a delicate political balance among the leading political groups—the army, the trade unions, and Marxist intellectuals. Despite being the representative of the PCT's more militant wing, Sassou-Nguesso moderated the regime's Marxist rhetoric and established better relations with Western countries. With the fall of the Berlin Wall, Sassou-Nguesso would begin the task of dismantling Congolese Marxism.

Required membership of government officials in the PCT was dropped in 1990, and a new constitution establishing a multiparty system was drafted. Dropped was the word "People's" from the country's official name. Adopted by referendum in March 1992, the constitution provided for a new set of multiparty elections. Ultimately, 14 political parties participated. The *Union Panafricaine pour la Démocratie Sociale* (UPADS), led by Pascal Lissouba (Massamba-Débat's, prime minister), won 39 of the 125 assembly seats. In August Lissouba was elected president, defeating Sassou-Nguesso.

Former president Sassou-Nguesso was granted amnesty for any acts committed during his years in office. Neither graceful defeat nor political retreat seemed to rest easily on his personality.

The legislative elections of 1992 had been inconclusive, and the coalition government which resulted lasted only until late 1992. New elections, highly disputed, were held. President Lissouba's party won a razor-thin majority of 65 out of 125 seats in the National Assembly. A period of shaky parliamentary government ensued.

Political opponents organized private militias to oppose the government and President Lissouba deemed it best to create his personal militia, avoiding any reliance on the national army. Each of the militias had its own distinctive, colorful, and threatening name. Bernard Kolélas, the charismatic mayor of Brazzaville, had the "Ninjas." Sassou-Nguesso's were "Cobras," and President Lissouba's, trained by Israelis, were "Zulus." After Lissouba appointed Kolélas Prime Minister in 1997 and moved to eliminate Sassou-Nguesso's militia, bloody and destructive conflict broke out in Brazzaville.

To combat his foes, President Lissouba recruited Israeli mercenaries to train his militiamen, but as the "Cobras" gained strength, he ordered more than $60 million in arms—a dozen shipments of helicopters, rockets, missiles and bombs. (The attack helicopters were Russian, while most of the light weapons were Iranian.)

Desperate for cash, Lissouba began discussions with an American oil company, and promptly lost the support of the French who refused to aid him against the forces of ex-president Sassou-Nguesso. Lissouba later charged that Sassou-Nguesso was supported by money coming from France's state oil giant Elf. Sassou-Nguesso also received interventionist support of Angolan forces. (Under Lissouba, Congo had become a launching pad for Cabindan rebels and a place through which Jonas Savimbi could sell the diamonds used to finance UNITA's war against the Angolan government.)

In the battle of the warlords Brazzaville was bombed and targeted by mortars, laid waste by internecine strife. Lissouba lost and fled into bitter exile. Elf returned to its damaged skyscraper office building and offered to contribute significantly to the rebuilding of Brazzaville. Angolan forces seemed to be a permanent presence in the Congo.

Denis Sassou-Nguesso's bloody conquest of Brazzaville did not end Congo's civil conflict. The civil war continued in the south throughout most of 1999. Pointe-Noire, Congo's economic capital, was virtually cut off from the rest of the country. Water and electricity supplies were disrupted by rebel activity. Some 800,000 people in the south were dislocated, many fleeing to the forest to escape the depredations of the rebels, the government, and its allies. Supported by Angolan troops and helicopter gun ships, as well as by remnants of the Hutu *Interahamwe* and a few Chadian and DR Congo fighters, government troops turned the tide of battle against the rebels by mid-year—not without compiling an absolutely horrific human rights record.

By the end of 1999, offers of amnesty and integration into government security forces in exchange for disarmament had secured cease-fire agreements with major militia commanders. Following the ceasefire, a "national dialogue," carefully managed by President Sassou-Nguesso, brought together representatives of the government, the internal and external opposition, plus other political groups and civic organizations.

The process was mediated by Sassou-Nguesso's son-in-law, President Omar Bongo of Gabon, and delegates focused on producing a draft constitution and preparing follow-up elections. There was little, if any, opportunity to address the causes that led to the Congolese conflict in the first place. Although billed as "all-inclusive," the national convention carefully excluded former President Pascal Lissouba and his last prime minister, Bernard Kolélas. Having been sentenced to death (*in absentia*) by Congolese judicial authorities, the two men were, said the government, not eligible to take part in the deliberations.

The draft constitution that emerged was tailored to the style and personality of Denis Sassou-Nguesso, featuring a strong presidential regime. The president of the republic, elected for a seven-year term—with one renewable mandate—would wield exclusive executive power, extensively. He would, for example, appoint the prime minister and could not be impeached by parliament; he could also reject its legislation and rule by decree.

In January 2002 the new constitution was approved by referendum—84% of those voting, according to government figures. Despite the calls by opposition parties to boycott the vote, the govern-

**President Sassou–Nguesso**

126

ment announced that 78% of all registered voters participated in the balloting. (Massive support was needed by Sassou-Nguesso to legitimize his assumption of power through brutal force of arms.)

With Lissouba and Kolélas excluded, and the principal remaining opposition candidate withdrawing at the last minute, the presidential election was held in March 2002. To no one's surprise, Denis Sassou-Nguesso was the victor—garnering 89.4% of the vote. None of the six other candidates won as much as 3% of the vote. Reports of low voter-turnout not withstanding, the interior minister released little-credible figures indicating 74.7% of the electorate had participated in the poll.

With a resurgence of militia violence in the south—remnants of the Kolélas' Ninjas now operating under the leadership of Rev. Frédéric Bitsangou, better known as Pasteur Ntoumi—legislative elections scheduled for April 2002 were postponed to May. When the National Assembly races were over, the president's PCT had won 53 seats and the *Forces démocratiques unies* (FDU: United Democratic Forces)—a coalition of parties supporting him—30, a clear majority in the 153-member house.

The elections brought neither stability nor security. Pasteur Ntoumi's Ninjas continued their depredations in the pool area and even managed to attack the vital rail link between Brazzaville and Pointe-Noire and bring commercial traffic to a standstill. In conducting its campaign against the rebels, the Congolese army seemed oblivious to both professionalism and human rights.

In March 2003 Ninja rebels and the government signed an agreement to end the crisis in the Pool region. Pasteur Ntoumi agreed to end hostilities, disarm his fighters, and help the state to re-establish its authority in the area. In return, the government agreed to extend amnesty to the Ninjas and reintegrate some of their members into the national army.

The disarmament, demobilization and reintegration program (DDR)—administered by the UN Development Program and financed by the EU—has made only halting and minimal progress. According to government figures, more than 42,000 small arms still circulate within the country and some 37,000 former fighters still await a return to civilian life. As a consequence, urban life remains insecure.

That the government's commitment to the peace accord was disingenuous seemed obvious when it asked Pasteur Ntoumi for a list of 250 rebels to be integrated into the armed forces. The rebel leader rejected the proposal, calling the government's quota "a drop in the ocean" and claiming to have 50,000 fighters un-

der his control. In reaction, he indicated he would only disarm his militiamen when the government opened up political space, forming a government of national unity in which his *Conseil national de la résistance* (CNR) could take part.

The Ninjas still await integration into the military or assistance returning to civilian life. They pose a continuing security threat, especially in the Pool region. In early 2005 Pasteur Ntoumi launched a drive to recover all guns to improve security in the area, but he made it clear this was not part of the DDR process. "From now on guns will no longer circulate in Vindza and indeed, in all of the Pool, " he said. "We will be collecting our stockpiled weapons and we will see how we can work with the government."

**Culture:** Tribal patterns dominate the social life of the Republic of Congo. Although discrimination is legally prohibited, tens of thousands of indigenous Pygmy people, living largely in the northern forest regions, enjoy less than equal treatment at the hands of their Bantu neighbors. Many have Bantu patrons to whom they are obligated in perpetuity.

The Congo's most important human rights organization, the *Observatoire congolais des droits de l'homme* (OCDH), has criticized the government for failing to issue the indigenous pygmies identity cards or register their births. It has also documented significant numbers of indigenous women who have been victims of rape by Bantu men. According to the *Observatoire* spokesman, there were also cases of gang rapes, and "even of rapes perpetrated in police offices by the very people charged with protecting the population."

AIDS has made its appearance in Congo, traveling in the wake of civil disturbance and disruption. According to armed forces health officials, AIDS is the number one cause of death in the Congolese armed forces. According to the director of the First Military Zone's health service, Colonel Prosper Kinzonzi, AIDS accounted for more than 60 percent of army deaths during the period 1989-1993. This was the equivalent of three companies of men during the period. The colonel attributed this mortal toll to prostitution and the sexual violence committed by soldiers while participating in the conflicts that have devastated Congo. Fourteen percent of Congolese servicemen have tested HIV-positive.

Nationally, government figures indicate 4.2% of the population is HIV positive. Infection rates are higher in the southern provinces (Pointe-Noire has a rate of 5%, while Brazzaville's is 3.3%) and among women (4.7%, as opposed to 3.8% for men).

Unlike some of its neighbors, Congo has a relatively strong tradition of urbanization. One sixth of the population has traditionally lived in the two principal cities, Brazzaville and Pointe-Noire. As a consequence, the country has one of the highest literacy rates in Black Africa, estimated at nearly 83%, though female literacy is generally lower—about 77%. Also related to this urban tradition is the relatively high percentage of Christians in the population—mostly Roman Catholic—and the early development of labor unions.

**Economy:** The object of armed struggle in Congo is the state's oil revenue, about 78% of state income and 95% of all its export earnings. In 2003 production averaged 247,000 bbl/d, making the country sub-Saharan Africa's fourth largest producer—after Nigeria, Angola, and Equatorial Guinea. The oil sector dominates the economy, representing 67% of GDP. Mostly conducted offshore, the sector was virtually untouched by the events of the civil war. The rest of the economy was severely damaged by those events.

Some 20,000 people were killed in the various phases of the war, and 800,000 people were displaced. Half of Congo's agricultural output was destroyed, particularly in the south where the richest agricultural land is located. Some 75% of the country's livestock was also destroyed. Congo's highly urbanized population, especially in Brazzaville, has felt the impact deeply. Since 1997, the percentage of the urban population below the poverty line has increased from 30% to 73% (2001). Half the population is unemployed, and life expectancy has fallen from 53 to 51.7 years (2003).

Reduced conflict has allowed the government to reopen railroad service between Brazzaville and Pointe-Noire and dredge the port of Pointe-Noire, the only deep-water port on Africa's western coastline south of Dakar. Since 1987, when it was last thoroughly dredged, the port had silted up and lost some six feet of depth.

The government has invested some $30 million in repairing the Congo-Ocean railroad linking Brazzaville and Pointe-Noire. As part of its commitment to the IMF, the government has announced plans to privatize the railroad.

Reopening the Congo River, the railroad, and the port, all significantly benefit the timber industry—after oil, Congo's most important source of income. There are two main areas of commercially exploitable forests in Congo. In the south forests cover more than 11 million acres, and by 1995, nearly 10 million acres were held as logging concessions. In the more isolated north there are some 22 million acres of commercially useful forests, but

# Congo (Brazzaville)

exploitation here was much slower given transport difficulties.

During the war when river and rail traffic was curtailed, loggers in the north had to ship their timber by road via Cameroon to Douala, adding considerably to their costs. Normally they would have floated logs down river to the main river port of Brazzaville and then on to Pointe-Noire by train. In October 2003 local officials in the southwest accused Chinese and Malaysian companies of violating state regulations and over-logging their concessions. The Chinese firm Man Faï Taï issued a categorical denial, asserting that though logging was "highly industrialized," the firm was "far from maximal production in the Congo." Hardly a reassuring comment.

Congo's small mining sector is dominated by developments in magnesium. (Used in automotive parts, high purity magnesium alloys allow manufacturers to decrease the body weight of their cars and improve fuel efficiency.) A Canadian magnesium mining company, Magnesium Alloys Corporation (MAC), plans to begin annual production of 60,000 tons of magnesium metal and high purity magnesium alloys by 2005. The facility is located on the Kouilou River, 30 miles north of Pointe-Noire. MAC expects to power the plant with electricity purchased from the rehabilitated Inga hydroelectric project in the DRC.

The reality of Congo's diamond resources is totally uncertain, especially after the country was suspended in mid-2004 from participation in the Kimberley Process Certification Scheme, designed to keep illicit diamonds from the market. At best around 50,000 carats are produced annually, almost exclusively by individual miners. When the country's annual exportation figures of three to five million carats could not be explained to a visiting Kimberley mission, Congo's participation was suspended, and the mission concluded that its entire production was illicit.

Given the terrible damage inflicted by years of civil war, investors are hesitant about placing money in the Congo. The country's biggest problem is finding the resources to repair infrastructure and productive capacity—estimated at nearly $2 billion. China has managed to penetrate Congo's oil sector, long a French preserve, by granting loans through its Export-Import Bank that are paid back in oil. In 2003, for example, it advanced $238 million—85% of total estimated costs—to build a hydroelectric dam at Imboulou, some 133 miles north of Brazzaville, where the Congo and Kasai rivers meet. The city has long suffered chronic power shortages; Imboulou will generate 120 MW, more than doubling the country's installed capacity and reducing Brazzaville's dependency on electricity supplied by its neighbor, the Democratic Republic of the Congo (DRC).

Built by a consortium of two Chinese firms, Imboulou is estimated to be completed in 2009. The government expects the project to create 900 permanent jobs and 2000 temporary ones. A paved construction road is expected to produce additional economic benefits from improved access to the region.

Government deficits over the years have created a huge total debt of $8.4 billion (2003). Some 46% of the projected 2001 budget was absorbed by debt servicing, and the government is actively working with the IMF and other lenders to reduce this enormous burden.

Agreement with the IMF has been difficult given what the institution sees as a lack of transparency in the operations of the *Société nationale des pétroles du Congo* (SNPC), Congo's national oil company, and continuing budgetary deficits. The government did not help its image for financial restraint when the president hired 3,450 new civil servants in 2004, adding to an already-bloated 70,000 government employees.

Nevertheless, following publication of audits of both SNPC and the government's oil revenues, the IMF expressed "guarded optimism" about Congo's economic and political situation and cautiously extended some $84 million in funding in December 2004. World Bank directors simultaneously approved a $30 million credit from the International Development Association.

Whether or not additional funding will be forthcoming is questionable. In January 2005 President Sassou-Nguesso ousted his finance minister, Roger Andely, in a cabinet reshuffle. Andely had almost single-handedly been responsible for the transparency in oil accounts that led to IMF funding.

**The Future:** Militarization of Congolese society with its pervasive violence poses an ongoing threat to future stability. It is unlikely the government will be able to integrate all former militia members into its security services. It is equally unlikely these youth, unskilled except in the ways of violence, will take easily to employment in "civic improvement" activities like rebuilding police stations destroyed in the war. Given the government's financial problems, it will be strapped to find funding for even those projects that might be attractive to former militiamen.

# The Republic of Gabon (pronounced Gah–bonh)

**Gabonese school children chasing soap bubbles**

Photo by Marian Zeldin

**Area:** 264,180 sq. km. = 102,000 sq. mi. (about the size of Colorado).

**Population:** 1,389,201 (July 2005 est.)

**Capital City:** Libreville (pop. 600,000)

**Climate:** Hot and humid. Although there is almost no rain from June to September, the humidity remains quite high. Rainfall in the remaining months totals more than 100 inches per year.

**Neighboring Countries:** Equatorial Guinea (Northwest); Cameroon (North); Congo (East, South).

**Official Language:** French.

**Other Principal Languages:** Around 40. Prominently: Mbere, Myene, Fang (a widely used *lingua franca*), Njebi, Punu, Sira, and Teke.

**Principal Religions:** Christian 55%–75%, Muslim less than 1%, and animist.

**Ethnic groups:** Prominently: Fang, Eshira, Bapounou, Bateke; about 6,000 French.

**Chief Commercial Products:** Crude oil 81%, timber 12%, manganese 5%, and uranium (1996).

**GNI per capita:** $3,580 (2003)

**Currency:** CFA Franc

**Former Colonial Status:** French Colony (1903–1960).

**Independence Date:** August 17, 1960.

**Chief of State:** Omar Bongo Ondimba, President (since 1967).

**National Flag:** A tri–color, with horizontal stripes of green, golden yellow and royal blue.

Lying astride the Equator on the west coast of Africa, Gabon is a land of hot and humid rainforest with a heavy rainfall. The coastal lowlands from 20 to 120 miles in depth receive up to 150 inches of rain per year. A series of densely forested plateaus rise further inland, spreading from the northeast to the southeast of the country with altitudes from 1,000 to 2,000 feet. The remainder of the land is covered by gentle, round mountains extending to heights of 5,200 feet.

**History:** Little is known of the various Bantu peoples who migrated into the area before the arrival of Portuguese mariners in the 1470s. They named the territory "gabão"—after being struck by how the Komo River estuary looked like a type of Portuguese coat called a "gabão." The coast became a center of the slave trade until efforts to suppress it in the nineteenth century. Between 1839 and 1841 local rulers signed away their sovereignty

in treaties of protection with France, providing the basis for further interior exploration. Protestant and Catholic missionaries established educational centers in the coastal area, and in 1849 a small group of freed slaves was settled on the coast. The settlement was called "Libreville" (free town) and ultimately became the colony's capital.

# Gabon

French authority in the hinterland was established largely as a consequence of the expeditions of Pierre Savorgnan de Brazza in the 1870s and 1880s. In 1886 the area was attached to the French Congo under Brazza's governorship and in 1910 became one of the four constituent colonies of French Equatorial Africa. As in Moyen-Congo, France sought to develop the colony through private companies, and it granted monopoly concessions to exploit the colony's resources. Abusive labor practices provoked much resistance and formed the basis of anti-colonial sentiment.

Between the two world wars missionary schools created an educated elite of young Africans who would lead the country into independence. Under the constitution of France's Fifth Republic, Gabon achieved self-government in 1958 and full independence in 1960 under President Léon Mba.

At independence there were two major political parties—Mba's Gabon Democratic Bloc (BDG) and the Social Democratic Union of Gabon, led by J.H. Aubame. Efforts by President Mba to eliminate his rival and institute a single-party state led to a rebellion of young military officers in February 1964. They deposed the president, but French troops intervened the next day and reinstated Mba. When Mba died in 1967, he was succeeded by Vice President Albert Bongo, who took over the one-party state.

In 1973 Bongo was re-elected president. He announced that he was renouncing Roman Catholicism and adopting Islam, changing his name from Albert–Bernard

**President Omar Bongo**

to El–Hadj Omar. Bongo's single party regime was authoritarian, quick to suppress the slightest sign of opposition, completely deaf to appeals for multiparty democracy, and utterly corrupt.

Declining oil prices in the 1980s brought on an economic downturn and increased political unrest. Much of this was orchestrated by the Movement of National Renewal (*Mouvement de Redressement Nationale*; MORENA), an illegal opposition group that highlighted the regime's deficiencies in governance and civil liberties. In 1990 budgetary belt-tightening—a consequence of austerities imposed by structural adjustment programs—set off street demonstrations by students and workers.

Shaken, Bongo at first rejected the notion of multiparty democracy, but quickly

reversed his position. Opposition parties were legalized, but in parliamentary elections held in September and October the government demonstrated its reluctance to have its fate determined by voters. In what would become a reoccurring scenario, the election was manipulated and the opposition decried its fraudulence.

In the December 1993 presidential elections Bongo was re-elected by a modest 51% majority. His principal opponent was Father Paul Mba Abessole of the National Rally of Woodcutters (*Rassemblement National des Bûcherons*; RNB), but ten other candidates effectively diluted opposition voting. Complaints about electoral irregularities continued months afterwards.

Gabon held another disputed presidential election in December 1998. President Bongo was again opposed by the mayor of Libreville, Paul Mba Abessole, leading the RNB, and Pierre Mamboundou of the High Resistance Council (*Haut conseil de la résistance*; HCR). The Ministry of the Interior announced final results: Bongo 66.55% and elected on the first ballot; Mamboundou, said the ministry, won 16.54% and Abessole collected 13.41%.

Observers noted the ministry had managed to add another 30,000 voters to the electoral lists a mere 48 hours before the election. Voters in precincts known to favor the opposition discovered that their polling place had been transferred to another site, usually at some distance. The regime even managed to hire its own election observers—long time friends of President Bongo in French legal circles. They dutifully reported that all was well.

Washington, Paris and Geneva investigations have revealed the nature and extent of President Bongo's personal enrichment from Gabon's oil production. A U.S. Senate investigation has named him as one of a "rogues' gallery" of foreign leaders who have funneled millions through American banks. In Switzerland an investigative judge developed testimony on the practice of offering "bonuses" to leaders of oil producing states to secure exploration permits. Money—a minimum of $100 million—went into at least three accounts belonging to Bongo, but held in another name.

In October 2000, the Gabonese parliament offered protection to the president by amending the constitution to give former heads of state immunity from legal prosecution for any act committed in the performance of their official duties.

Legislative elections in December 2001 were yet another disaster. Opposition parties threatened to boycott when the electoral commission announced that the electoral rolls contained 778,000 eligible voters—nearly 75% of the country's population. Clean-up reduced the number to

**Oil storage at Port Gentil**

a little less than 600,000, but 80% of those preferred to stay home rather than go to the polls on election day.

So mismanaged were the elections that the courts invalidated ten percent of them, including one in which the winning candidate carried ballots from polling place to counting center. It didn't matter. Bongo's ruling Gabonese Democratic Party (PDG) went into the election holding 90 of 120 seats and emerged with almost the same number. Some 24 parties put up candidates, but only eight could be considered oppositional. Even President Bongo's traditional rival, Paul Mba Abessole, broke with opposition calls to boycott the election.

Since becoming mayor of Libreville, Abessole had become an apostle of "convivial opposition," and the RNB participated in December's legislative elections with a clear eye to the future. Their reward came in January 2002 when Bongo called for an "opening" of the government. Four members of the opposition were included in the new cabinet. Abessole was given the portfolio charged with human rights (all the more powerful ministries were tightly controlled by the Bongo clique). A year later he added the agriculture ministry and the newly created post of third deputy prime minister to his portfolio.

Control of state resources has allowed President Bongo to fund and co-opt the opposition for years, and the regular migration from opposition to presidential supporter seemed to have eroded public confidence in both the political system and individual politicians. Massive absenteeism has characterized recent elections. The turnout in the December 2002 local elections was so dismal that the opposition called for their annulment. One election official put it quite simply: "I don't know if the Gabonese have lost their sense of patriotism," he said, "but it's clear that they don't believe in elections any more."

Parliament amended the constitution in July 2003 to repeal a two-term limit for the head of state. Already in power for 37 years, President Bongo can now run in the December 2005 presidential elections. Taking nothing for granted, parliament also amended the constitution to reduce the electoral process to a single round of voting: the candidate with the most votes on the first ballot, regardless of how few, will be declared the victor. The provisions seem to guarantee lifetime tenure for President Bongo. More than 30 of Gabon's 35 political parties have already signed on to support the President should be choose to run.

**Culture:** The majority of Gabon's people live in cities and larger towns. Most of the interior is densely forested and minimally populated. Libreville, the capital city, contains over a third of the population of the entire state.

Situated on a strategically located peninsula, Libreville has experienced rapid growth. With a population of nearly 600,000, the city is dependent on imported food and is ranked as the fourth most expensive city in the world to live in, more costly than London, Paris or Geneva. The poor of Libreville, seeking food and firewood in the surrounding area, contribute to enormous environmental pressures building up on the peninsula.

Over 60% of the population is literate. Two institutions of higher learning, Omar Bongo University (OBU) in Libreville and the Masuku University of Science and Technology at Franceville in the east, together enroll some 11,000 students in somewhat difficult circumstances. Built in the prosperous 1970s, OBU was designed to accommodate 3,000 students, but currently enrolls 9,000. There are no current subscriptions for scientific journals, the most recent of which go back to the 1980s, and there are reportedly only twenty or so computers available.

**Economy:** Gabon is the richest of the sub-Saharan states because of oil, timber and mineral extraction. It is sub-Saharan Africa's fifth largest oil producer, and crude oil exports are the backbone of the economy. Oil contributes over 40% of GDP and represents 80% of total export revenues. Sixty percent of government revenue comes from the oil sector, and budgets are seriously affected by price fluctuations in the world market.

Oil production, however, is slowing as fields age and are exhausted. No major discoveries have been made in recent years, and oil production has not grown since the mid-1990s. At the moment, much hope rests on ultra-deepwater drilling. In November 2002 the Cabinet announced that oil production had fallen by a third over the past five years, cutting oil revenues in half.

Because of falling revenues, the 2002 budget had to be reduced as the government faced financial crisis. One critical aspect of the crisis is Gabon's huge accumulated debt—over $3.8 billion (2003). Debt servicing gobbled up nearly 50% of the 2002 budget (down from 67.4% in 2000). Civil service salaries constituted another 19% of the budget, leaving nothing for investment and little for social services.

The government is desperate to renegotiate its debt and to this end has sought assistance from the IMF. In April 2005 President Bongo indicated Gabon could reach an agreement with the Fund "if the ministry of Economy and Finance holds

**Maize cropping in the rainforest**

Photo by A. Binot
Courtesy of APFT–ULB

fast" on public spending. With a presidential election coming up in December one suspects "holding fast" will be more illusion than reality. The country is hardly a model of good governance and financial accountability. Conditions set by the IMF for assistance may require a degree of transparency the regime is reluctant to provide.

As Gabon has seen its oil production (which is onshore) decline, it has eyed offshore possibilities. In February 2003, Gabon asserted sovereignty over the island of Mbagne in Equatorial Guinea's Bay of Corisco. The islet had been a point of contention since 1972, but took on strategic importance with the discovery of vast oil reserves in Equatorial Guinea's waters. In July 2004 the two governments announced an agreement to establish a Joint Oil Zone around the island, but the details are yet to be worked out.

Gabon's forestry sector is the country's second largest industry and, after the civil service, the country's second largest employer. Thick forests cover 76% of the country, and exports of timber have risen in recent years. In 1957, less than 10% of Gabon's forests were allocated as logging concessions; today more than half have been designated for logging. There is concern that, like oil, this resource may be rapidly exhausted. The government's new forestry code envisions a network of national parks and President Bongo has indicated the government plans to devote 10% of the national territory to the development of protected forest areas.

Unfortunately, the code is ill defined and inadequately enforced. An estimated 70% of all logging in 2002 was illegal, and national goals of processing 75% of all

# Gabon

timber logged are a distant dream; less than 18% of Gabon's log production is processed before exportation. China is the principal buyer of Gabonese woods, taking some 65% of Gabon's annual 2.5 million cubic meters of mahogany exports. In 2003 it was also importing 1.5 million m3 of *Okoumé*, a softwood used in making plywood.

Gabon has become increasingly dependent on Chinese markets, and Chinese aid and cooperation loom large in Gabon's economic development. President Bongo has traveled to China nine times, and over the decades has met with Mao Tse-tung, Chou En-lai, and Deng Xiaoping. When China's present leader, Hu Jintao visited the African continent in February 2004, Gabon was his only sub-Saharan stop, after Algeria and Egypt, two other oil producing states. The visit celebrated 30 years of diplomatic rleations between the two countries, and resulted in a memorandum expressing their desire "to develop exploration, exploitation, refining and export activities of oil products."

As oil evenues decline, the Bongo government has pressed China and other investors to commit to development of its minerals sector. Gabon is the world's number two producer of manganese (after South Africa), and China is already the metal's principal importer. Huge reserves of iron, estimated at one billion tons, are located in the far north at Belinga, but the absence of adequate infrastructure to mine and move the ore has prevented development of the deposits. Given the Chinese economy's voracious need for raw materials and state corporations unimpeded by the need to make a profit, China's seemingly uneconomic commitment to Belinga may be understood. Development of Belinga will require construction of a hydroelectric dam on the Ivindo River to provide energy to operate mining equipment, two additional rail connections to the Transgabon railroad, and construction of a deep water port at Santa Clara to transport the ore.

China has already executed several high-profile projects in Gabon including hospitals in Franceville and Libreville and both the National Assembly and Senate buildings. A least 100 Chinese vessals are fishing off the Gabonese coast, enough to cause China to set up its first overseas inspection agency there in late 2002. China also provides a variety of interest free loans to the government. Their advantage is that they have none of the conditionalities demanded by Western lenders; their disadvantage, given the absence of transparency and accountability standards, is their susceptibility to corruption.

Politics and economy are very much family affairs in Gabon. The president's eldest son, Christian, is a former deputy Director-General of the National Timber Company (SNBG) and a principal voice in the company's privatization. SNBG holds a monopoly on the commercialization of the two most valuable timber species—*Okoumé* and *Ozigo*—and is owned by the state (51%) and forest companies (49%).

A deputy Director-General of the *Union Gabonaise de Banques*, Christian Bongo is also president of the Transgabon railroad's administrative council; the principal stockholders of the railroad are timber companies. Another presidential son, Ali, in addition to being Gabon's defense minister, is also chairman of the board of OPRAG, the country's port authority through which Gabon's principal natural resources—oil and timber—are shipped.

**The Future:** There is a huge disconnect between political class and citizenry in Gabon. As revenues diminish, budgets shrink, services evaporate and prices rise, that political class could be in for some very bumpy times.

The lagoon area near Port Gentil

# SOUTHERN AFRICA

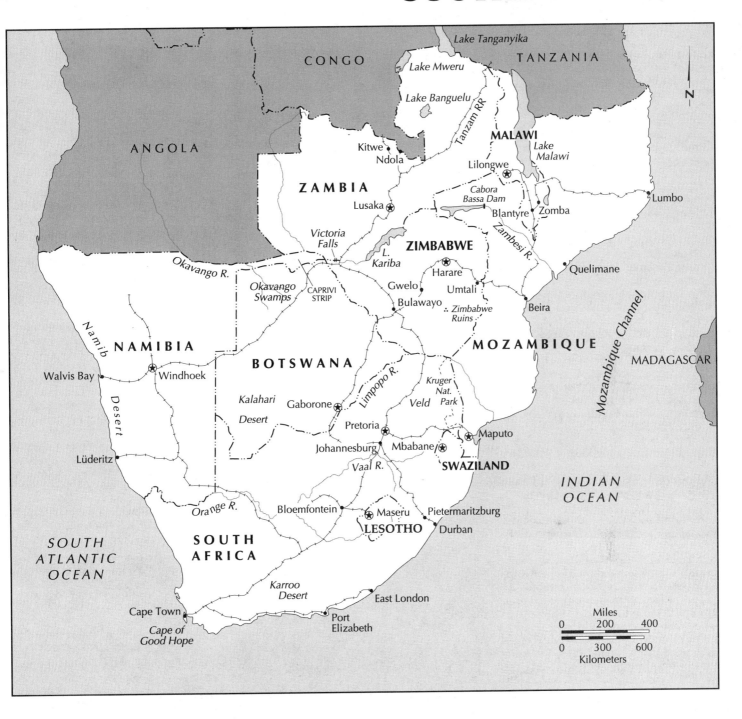

# The Republic of Botswana

**Area:** 569,800 sq. km = 220,000 sq. mi. (slightly larger than France).

**Population:** 1,640,115 (July 2005 est.)

**Capital City:** Gaborone (pronounced ha-bo-ro-neh), pop. 213,017 (2000).

**Climate:** Subtropical, with temperatures as high as 100°F. in the summer (November–April) and as low as 20°F. in winter (May–October). Rainfall varies from 25 inches per year in the North to 9 inches or less in the southern Kalahari Desert.

**Neighboring Countries:** Namibia (West and North); Zambia (North); Zimbabwe (Northeast); South Africa (South).

**Official Languages:** English, seTswana.

**Other Principal Languages:** Afrikaans, Herero, Kalanga, Kgalagadi, Kung and other Bushman languages, Mbukushu, Subia, Tswana, Yeye.

**Ethnic groups:** Tswana (or Setswana) 79%, Kalanga 11%, Basarwa 3%, other, including Kgalagadi and white 7%.

**Principal Religions:** Indigenous beliefs 50%, Christian 50%.

**Chief Commercial Products:** Diamonds 76%, copper, nickel 4%, and meat.

**GNI per capita:** $3,530 (2003)

**Currency:** 1 Pula = 100 Thebe

**Former Colonial Status:** British Protectorate (1885–1966).

**Independence Date:** September 30, 1966.

**Chief of State:** Festus Mogae, President (since April 1998).

**National Flag:** Five horizontal stripes of blue, white, black, white and blue.

Botswana is a large, landlocked country that lies in the transition zone between the dry deserts of South Africa and the forests of Angola. In the South, a vast area is covered by the shifting red sands of the Kalahari Desert, occasionally interrupted by limestone rock formations and clumps of grass and scrub brush at the few places where water is close to the land surface.

The change from desert to grassland is so gradual that it is hard to see where the first ceases and the latter begins. The growth becomes increasingly thicker and there are frequent patches of trees. Annual rainfall slowly increases until it reaches a level required to support farmland where the food and cattle of the nation are produced in non–drought years.

Vegetation becomes dense in the North and the land turns into the marshland in the Okavango Swamp, fed by the Okavango River flowing from the low mountains of Angola. There is no exit to the ocean for these waters. The country's elevation, averaging 3,300 feet, modifies its subtropical climate.

**History:** The original inhabitants of Botswana were the San people (Bushmen). Bantu peoples of central and east Africa migrated into the area in the 16th century; during the following centuries, intermarriage and population growth of the Bantus reduced the number of pure Bushmen to a handful.

The Tswana remained split into hundreds of tribes and clans until they gathered together under Khama III, Chief of the powerful Bamangwato tribe; this was a loose federation which emerged in the last half of the 19th century. For details of pre–independence history, see *Historical Background, The British in Africa* and *The Republic of South Africa.*

After gaining independence on September 30, 1966, the pre–independence government continued in office. Elections since then have resulted in substantial majorities in the Legislative Assembly for the Botswana Democratic Party (BDP). There are three other small political parties which actively compete in the free elections, but they have yet to dislodge the BDP from its political primacy.

The chiefs of the eight largest tribes are permanent members of the House of Chiefs and are joined by seven other sub-chiefs. The National Assembly consists of 57 directly elected representatives (four additional seats are nominated by the President), but it cannot act upon matters concerning internal tribal affairs without first submitting a draft to the House of Chiefs.

Elections in October 1979 resulted in a resounding victory for President Sir Seretse Khama (who had been re-elected chief executive since independence), with almost 60% of the voters turning out at the polls. He was to have served for another five years, but the president died in June 1980; Vice President Quett K.J. Masire was installed to fill out his term and was re-elected in September 1984. Khama's eldest son, Ian Seretse Khama, was installed in May 1979 as Paramount Chief of the Bamangwato, the largest of the Twsana-speaking tribes; he also served as Commander of the Botswana Defense Force until 1998.

For eighteen years President Masire maintained the multiparty traditions of democratic Botswana and exercised a conservative fiscal restraint on the use of the country's riches, producing 16 years of budget surpluses and large foreign reserves. After his initial election as President in 1984, he led his BDP to successive electoral victories in 1989 and 1994.

With a broadly diverse constituency—civil servants, trade unionists, business people, cattle ranchers, and rural traditionalists—the BDP is subject to internal factionalism. As two party factions vied for party control before the 1999 elections, President Masire decided to retire to avoid an open split in the party. He secured passage of legislation providing for the automatic succession of Botswana's vice president and in November 1997 announced his retirement, effective in six months. On April 1, 1998, he was succeeded by his Vice-President and Finance Minister, Festus Mogae.

Almost simultaneously, Lieutenant-General Ian Seretse Khama resigned as

**The Okavango Delta**  Photo by Judi Iranyi

134

# Botswana

chief of the Botswana Defense Force. Having consulted with traditional Bamangwato leaders, he was given temporary release from his chieftaincy to pursue a career in politics. Moving swiftly to fill the vacant Vice Presidency, Mogae nominated General Khama to the position. With the popular Khama on his side, Mogae effectively closed off internal opposition to his leadership of the BDP.

President Masire's chosen successor, Mogae, an Oxford University graduate, was seen as a straight-talking, pragmatic, no-nonsense leader, capable of uniting and energizing a fractured and complacent BDP. In the fall 1999 parliamentary elections, Mogae's political wisdom in appointing Khama became manifest. The dashing young general campaigned vigorously, often flying about the country in military helicopters to galvanize party and electorate.

The Botswana Democratic Party's victory was abetted by a serious split in the opposition. In 1998, Botswana National Front (BNF) dissidents withdrew and formed the Botswana Congress Party (BCP). Separated, the two parties, along with the smaller Botswana Alliance Movement (BAM), contested the October 1999 parliamentary elections. Divided, the opposition was decimated. The BDP swept 33 of 40 elected seats, even winning four of eight urban seats traditionally occupied by the opposition.

In the October 2004 elections, little changed. The BDP, supported by its traditional rural base, took 44 of 57 directly elected seats in the National Assembly. Victory was again facilitated by opposition division: in most districts the BNF and the BCP put up rival candidates, allowing the Botswana Democratic Party to win several districts with a plurality of votes. The BNF won 12 seats and the BCP one. Despite its dominance in the legislature, the BDP won only 52% of the vote nationwide. The Opposition finds its greatest support in urban centers; in Gaborone, for example, the BNF won three of the five districts that cover the capital.

Botswana's president is chosen by the National Assembly following legislative elections and the BDP majority re-elected President Mogae to his second five-year term. The October elections also confirmed the political strength of Vice-President Ian Khama. Most of the BDP deputies are Khama loyalists, several of the new cabinet members have served in the Botswana Defense Force (which Khama once commanded), and President Mogae has indicated he will step down in March 2008 to make way for Khama to succeed him. This would give Khama 18 months as head of state before the next legislative elections in October 2009.

With political and economic chaos in neighboring Zimbabwe, Botswana has had to confront an influx of refugees. Border communities are particularly affected and resentments are high: "Our women can no longer gather firewood for fear of being raped," complained one traditional leader, "our houses are not safe any more, and even our livestock find their way across the border." Xenophobia seems to be rising with complaints about immigrants taking jobs from citizens and rising petty crime rates attributed to the refugees. An estimated 36,000 illegal immigrants were deported back to Zimbabwe in 2004.

Shortly after an outbreak of foot and mouth disease in the Zimbabwe border area, the government decided to build a thirteen-foot electric fence along the entire 310-mile border to keep out diseased cattle. The solar-powered fence, capable of delivering a 220-volt shock (nasty but not fatal), will be patrolled 24 hours a day by security forces. Due to become operational in June 2005, it will presumably also stem the flood of two-legged economic refugees.

**Culture:** One of the highest concentrations of rock art in the world is located at Tsodilo. There are over 4,500 paintings in less than four square miles. The site, classified by UNESCO as a World Heritage site, is frequently referred to as the "Louvre of the Desert."

The government's heavy-handed development plans for the San people of the Kalahari have drawn international attention. Most of Botswana's 50,000 San population has already been relocated into 63 resettlement villages, where, the government says, water, health and education services can be better provided. The re-

**A young Botswanan woman**
Photo by Joann Sandlin

settlement villages, miles from the traditional hunting grounds of the San, have been likened to American Indian reservations.

Botswana has one of the highest HIV/AIDS infection rates in Africa. Nearly 40% of sexually active adults are infected. These grim figures emerge even after an extensive government education campaign. Billboards, posters and bumper stickers in cities and villages throughout the country warn of the dangers of unprotected sex, with messages like "Don't let casual sex kill Botswana's future" and "Be wise, condomise." The government provides free distribution of condoms in all public institutions.

President Mogae has gone to extraordinary lengths to publicize the public health crisis. He mentions the HIV/AIDS crisis in nearly every speech in tough, unrelenting terms. In March 2001 he chillingly warned his countrymen that Botswana faced extinction if it failed to slow the spread of the deadly virus within the next five years, and in September 2002 he told an audience the epidemic posed a threat to every gain, economic or otherwise, the country had made since independence. He has tried to break the culture of silence and shame surrounding AIDS by personally revealing the results of his own HIV test (negative) and encouraging his ministers to do the same. As of January 1, 2004 HIV tests became automatic at government hospitals and clinics unless patients specifically decline them.

Botswana now has one of the most significant anti-HIV/AIDS campaigns in the world. It is funded by Microsoft's Bill Gates, while the international drug company, Merck, has pledged $50 million and provides an unlimited supply of antiretroviral medicines; some 35,000 Botswanans are being kept alive by anti-retroviral drugs

Despite these efforts, the virus continues to spread, with an estimated five new infections per hour and 75 deaths a day. (If there were a similar AIDS death rate in the U.S., 15,000 Americans a day would die.) There are more than 65,000 AIDS orphans and that figure is projected to double or triple by 2010. Life expectancy has dropped from over 65 to 38, while Botswanans spend their weekends at funerals.

**Economy:** Since independence Botswana's economy has shown impressive growth, averaging of 10% per year from 1976 through 1991. More recently it has shown signs of slowing down, with GDP growth not more than 5.4% in 2003.

Botswana's economy is diamonds. The country is the world's largest diamond producer, and they account for 70% of its

# Botswana

export earnings, 30% of its gross domestic product and more than half of all government revenues. All of this is generated by Debswana, a company equally owned by the government and De Beers of South Africa. The company produced 30 million carats of diamonds from its four mines in 2003, and the government granted De Beers a 25-year renewal of all four of its mining leases in December 2004.

All is not rosy, however. Given a general economic slowdown internationally, diamond revenues have slowed. One possibility of improving diamond revenues is to add value by cutting and polishing the gems locally. Internationally, the trade is dominated by low-wage India, which controls 95% of the market. Because of wage differentials De Beers has been reluctant to pursue local diamond transformation, but the Leviev Group, owned by the Israeli billionaire Lev Leviev is interested in establishing a polishing plant in Botswana. It has already built Africa's largest diamond cutting and polishing factory in neighboring Namibia.

Debswana faced wildcat strike action in late 2004. Nearly half its employees walked off their jobs to demand a 16% pay raise and a 24% bonus for 2004–05. They are already the highest paid workers in Botswana, and their benefits include free housing and transportation, subsidized water, power, and schooling, not to mention free medical insurance. After several hundred strikers were fired, the workers accepted the company's offer of a 10% salary increase and a one-time bonus of 10% in September.

Despite the economic dominance of diamonds, the bulk of Botswana's workforce is employed in agriculture, though the primary sector contributes only 2.4% of GDP. The national cattle herd is almost three million head and represents an important source of food, income and employment, either directly or indirectly through related industries (processing and canning meat products, hide tanning, shoes and other leather products).

The state-run Botswana Meat Commission (BMC) co-ordinates and processes meat production and has a statutory monopoly on the export of beef. Botswana has a quota 18,900 tons of beef for entry into the European Union, but because of erratic supply, it has never been able to meet the quota. European sales account for 90% of total exports. Two recent outbreaks of foot and mouth disease have led to a decline of exports to the European Union and other emerging markets. This has led to job losses as thousands of head of cattle were destroyed to control the disease.

The driving imperative of Botswana's government is diversification of the economy. Mining jobs account for only 3.6% of the country's workforce, and attempts to diversify into manufacturing have barely dented an unemployment rate estimated at 21%. Young, jobless voters have been the principal support of opposition parties, and the government has been unable to generate sufficient new jobs to absorb the 27,000 school leavers who enter the employment market each year.

The government welcomes diversification investment from any source, and China, which has already built hospitals, schools, and roads in the country, is a major potential investor. China has granted several African countries, including Botswana, "approved" status as a destination for its outbound tourists, and President Mogae has singled out tourism as a potential area for Chinese investment.

There is however growing resentment about the country's increasing Chinese presence from the grass roots. "They do not contribute anything to Botswana," said one critic. "They do not even rent our houses. They would rather plant shacks on the site. It is even difficult for them to attract and keep local talent because they underpay us and subject us to insults and racist slurs."

Botswana's era of annual budgetary surpluses is over. President Mogae had predicted a budget deficit of close to $400 million dollars for 2004, partly due to the high cost of government AIDS programs. Economists estimate Botswana's GDP growth rate will drop by 1.5%; within 25 years the country's economy will be 31% smaller than it would have been without the pandemic.

Tensions with neighboring Namibia have diminished. Their border dispute over an island in the Okavango River was settled in Botswana's favor by the International Court of Justice in December 1999, and the two countries have agreed on a border demarcation. Unresolved are tensions created by Namibian desires to pump water from the Okavango River to its parched capital, Windhoek. The river goes nowhere, but in good years it floods the vast Okavango delta in Northern Botswana, attracting millions of birds and animals which are the country's principal tourist attraction. Namibia's plans would threaten the delta, which accounts for 75% of Botswana's earnings from tourism, contributes 6% to its gross national product, and employs thousands.

**The Future:** President Mogae faces the hard task of dealing with the consequences of Botswana's superficially successful economic development: inequalities, unemployment and domination of the economy by a privileged few. Seemingly well-off, Botswana presents a paradox: despite rapid economic growth, its human development statistics have declined. Development has been uneven. Pockets of severe poverty persist in rural areas, the consequence of a contracting agricultural sector that was starved of investment and development while the mining sector was expanded.

The shadow of AIDS darkens everything.

**Botswana AIDS poster**      Photo by Judi Iranyi

# The Kingdom of Lesotho (pronounced (Leh–*su*–tu)

**Catholic Church, National University of Roma, Lesotho**

Photo by Joe Joyner

**Area:** 30,303 sq. km. = 11,700 sq. mi. (somewhat larger than Maryland).

**Population:** 1,867,035 (July 2005 est.).

**Capital City:** Maseru (150,000 est.1998)

**Climate:** Temperate. Summers hot, winters cool to cold; humidity generally low and evenings cool year round. Rainy season in summer, winters dry. Southern hemisphere seasons are reversed.

**Neighboring Countries:** Lesotho is completely surrounded by the Republic of South Africa.

**Official Languages:** Sesotho, English.

**Other Principal Languages:** Zulu, Xhosa.

**Ethnic groups:** Sotho 99.7%, Europeans Asians, and others, 0.3%.

**Principal Religions:** Christian 80%; the rest indigenous beliefs.

**Chief Commercial Products**: Manufactures 65% (clothing, footwear, road vehicles), wool and mohair 7%, food and live animals 7%.

**GNI per capita:** $590 (2003)

**Currency:** 1 Loti = 100 Lisenti. At par with South African Rand.

**Former Colonial Status:** British Protectorate (1868–1966).

**Chief of State:** King Letsie III.

**Head of Government:** Prime Minister Pakalitha Mosisili.

**Independence Date:** October 4, 1966.

**National Flag:** Divided diagonally from the lower pole side corner; the upper half is white, bearing the brown silhouette of a large shield with crossed spear and club; the lower half is a diagonal blue band with a green triangle in the corner.

Lying deep within the lofty peaks of the Drakensburg Mountains, Lesotho is the only nation of the world which is completely surrounded by another country. One–fourth of the land is relatively low—

from five to six thousand feet above sea level. The warm sun of Africa raises the temperatures in this agricultural region during the summer. The rest of the nation is made up of scenic highlands from 6,000 to 9,000 feet, with some peaks rising as high as 11,000 feet above sea level.

The snow–capped Drakensburg Mountains form a natural boundary between Lesotho and KwaZulu-Natal Province of the Republic of South Africa; they also provide water for the neighboring country. The mountain snows melt, and, augmented by gentle and usually uniform rainfall, the water flows into the small streams which unite to form the Orange and Tugela rivers, which flow into an otherwise somewhat dry South Africa.

The mountain scenery of Lesotho is comparable to the pastoral setting of Malawi and the mountainous parts of Kenya.

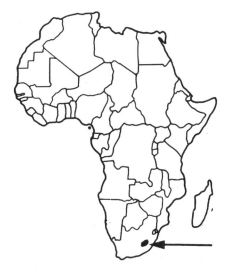

**History:** In times immemorial the Bushmen established a thinly populated society high in the mountains of Lesotho. The waves of Bantu migration from east and central Africa of the 17th century reached the country as did the Bafokeng, Maphetia and Baphuthi tribes, which settled among the Bushmen. The two ethnic groups intermarried during succeeding generations, and their descendants are a somewhat uniform people known as Basutos, or Basothos. For details of early and colonial history, see *Historical Background, The British in Africa* and The *Republic of South Africa*.

An independence agreement was reached in 1966 whereby the colony, called Basutoland, would become independent under Chief Leabua Jonathan. The royalists and left–wing representatives had walked out of the independence conference, and Jonathan signed the treaty. The Union Jack was finally lowered at Maseru on October 4, 1966.

Friction soon developed between Leabua Jonathan and King Moshoeshoe (pronounced Mo-*shway*-shway), the hereditary monarch. The King was placed under house arrest and several left-wing leaders who had participated in Maseru riots were jailed in 1966. Elections held in early 1970 pitted Chief Jonathan's Basotho National Party against the leftist Basotho Congress Party, led by Ntsu Mokhele. When Jonathan realized he was being defeated, he announced a state of emergency, arrested the opposition and took steps which led to the exile of the King. (After agreeing to stay out of politics, the King returned the following year.)

In late 1973, the BNP and Jonathan announced plans to make Lesotho a one-party state. Mokhele and his followers attempted a *coup* in early 1974 which failed. Reprisals were taken not only against the leadership (some of whom escaped to South Africa and Botswana) and members of the BCP, but villages suspected of harboring BCP followers were destroyed. A single-party state is rarely benevolent towards its opponents.

South Africa, charging that Lesotho was harboring members of the outlawed African National Congress (ANC), raided Maseru and other parts of the country in 1982-1983. Chief Jonathan denounced the move, charging that it was an effort on behalf of the Lesotho Liberation Army, the military wing of the BCP, and denied granting sanctuary to members of the ANC. Jonathan further alienated South Africa by visiting communist China, North Korea, Yugoslavia, Romania and Bulgaria in mid-1983. This also infuriated the Catholic clergy, who had strongly supported the government (Jonathan was Roman Catholic).

# Lesotho

Elections were not held after 1970, and there was no indication when they would be held until the BNP Congress in November 1984. In July 1985, Chief Jonathan announced that balloting would take place in September, but when no opposition candidates registered to run by the August 14 deadline, he declared there was no need for an election. The move was denounced as a farce. Increasingly leftist, Jonathan continued to develop the institutions of a single-party state. He formed a "Youth League of Chief Jonathan's Basotho National Party" and imported about 14 North Korean "advisers." This set the conservative element within the military on edge, given the Youth League's radical orientation.

South Africa continued to charge that Lesotho harbored members of the ANC and periodically closed the borders and conducted raids in Maseru to root the rebels out. Finally, on January 20, 1986 the Lesotho military acted, ousting Chief Jonathan. A Military Council was installed, headed by Major General Metsing Lekhanya, and the border re-opened. Pretoria (wink, wink) denied having anything to do with the *coup*.

The military government announced amnesty for all opposition leaders, including Ntsu Mokhele. The King, however, decreed that all political activity would cease for two years and set himself at opposition to the military. From 1987 increasing powers were wielded by the King—too many for the comfort of General Lekhanya, who sent him into exile in the spring of 1990.

To legitimize itself, the military installed the eldest son of the king, Prince Mohato Sereng Seeisa (King Letsie III) as monarch in late 1990. Military control was tenuous, and under pressure, parliamentary elections were held in 1993. The result gave the BCP all 65 seats in the National Assembly, and Ntsu Mokhele, now a centrist rather than a leftist, became Prime Minister. Moshoeshoe II was restored to the throne in January 1995, but died under mysterious circumstances in an auto accident in early 1996. He was succeeded by the crown prince.

In early 1997, factional attempts to oust Mokhele from BCP leadership failed, lacking support among party deputies in the legislature. Mokhele responded in July by leaving the BCP, taking a majority of 40 members of parliament with him and creating the Lesotho Congress for Democracy (LCD). The new formation then declared itself the government and took over the BCP's black, green and red colors. In February 1998, King Letsie dissolved the squabbling parliament to prepare for May elections.

**His Majesty King Letsie III**

When the election results were announced, the LCD had won 79 out of 80 parliamentary seats. Ntsu Mokhele having been sidelined from active politics by age and health, Pakalitha Mosisili was chosen Prime Minister. The opposition, stung by the magnitude of its defeat, could only imagine it the consequence of fraud. Protests were mounted and became virtually round-the-clock affairs. When the King's palace was blockaded by protesters, electoral experts from Botswana, South Africa and Zimbabwe, guarantors of Lesotho's democracy since 1994, were called in to examine the election.

The probe was completed in two weeks, but its publication was delayed, which only added fuel to the protesters' indignation. When finally released, the commission's report evinced "serious concerns" about the general election, but its overall conclusion, expressed in tortured prose and double negatives, was that "We cannot postulate that the result does not reflect the will of the Lesotho electorate."

Demonstrators closed down government offices in the capital, Maseru, locked the gates of parliament, and shut down the Lesotho Bank. In the midst of the demonstrations junior army officers mutinied, took their seniors prisoner and forced their resignation. Sensing a coup very much in the air, the government requested assistance from the Southern African Development Community (SADC).

South Africa and Botswana agreed to intervene to restore order in the kingdom. South Africa sent in an initial force of 600 soldiers on September 22, 1998, but was unprepared for stiff resistance from the Lesotho army. Botswana's forces, responsible for securing Maseru, were delayed, which had disastrous consequences for the city. Young Lesotho nationalists vented their rage at South Africa by looting, burning and destroying businesses known to be owned by South Africans.

The flames spread and much of the capital was reduced to ruins. About 60 people died in the events.

Negotiations produced an Interim Political Authority (IPA) which would steer the country to new elections. The IPA consisted of two members from each of Lesotho's 12 political parties, and was supposed to conclude its work in 18 months; it eventually took four years to produce a plan to which all parties agreed. In the final compromise, 80 Assembly seats would remain single-member districts with the remaining 40 distributed by proportional representation. Taking advantage of the new provisions (which offered strong representational possibilities), several of Lesotho's numerous minor parties—nineteen of them in all—registered to participate in the election.

The results of the election, held in May 2002, proved the disputed 1998 elections had been no fluke. Once again the LCD won a sweeping victory, taking 77 of the 120 seats for an absolute majority in parliament. The Lesotho People's Congress (LPC) secured 21 seats, and other opposition parties took the rest. Some 68% of Lesotho voters participated in the election, and observers were unanimous in declaring it free, fair, and transparent, undercutting the complaints of fraud issued by discontented losers.

**Culture:** The people of Lesotho have a very high rate of literacy—81%—in spite of the fact that they live, for the most part, in rural isolation: only 18% of the population is urbanized. Sheep and cattle raising occupy their daily lives among the scenic peaks and plateaus, but all is not idyllic. Deeply impoverished, Lesotho has few employment opportunities, and Basotho men regularly migrate to South Africa to find work. Mobility and prolonged residence away from families little conduce to chastity. The result has been an extremely high HIV/AIDS infection rate and consequent social and economic devastation.

United Nations Development Program statistics show that 31% of Lesotho's economically productive population (between the ages of 15 and 49) is infected. Women are the most vulnerable, and 52% of all pregnant women in urban areas have tested positive for HIV. According to government figures 75% of all new infections are found among girls. There are 73,000 AIDS orphans in the Kingdom and indications that child prostitution is at an all time high in Maseru, the capital. Life expectancy has dropped to 37.2 years (2003).

In January 2003 the Lesotho government began providing anti-retroviral drugs to combat mother-to-child HIV transmission at a number of pilot sites.

Boehringer Ingelheim, a multinational pharmaceutical company, is providing nevirapine at the test sites, free of charge, for five years.

**Economy:** Lesotho is completely surrounded by South Africa and, possessing no significant natural resources, is economically dependent on its larger neighbor. The agricultural sector represents 18.3% of GDP (2002) and employs 24% of the labor force. Approximately 85% of rural households are dependent on agriculture for their livelihoods, but only 9% of the country is suitable for agriculture; the rest is hills. As a result, large numbers of Basotho men traditionally leave to work in the mines of South Africa. At one time 70% of rural household income came from remittances sent by migrant workers.

Crop yields and livestock numbers have fallen since the 1970s due to drought, hailstorms, tornados, excessive rains and other uncharitable acts of nature. Disease, theft, and mismanagement have also diminished agricultural production; AIDS has only exacerbated the problem by weakening and killing those most capable of bring in the harvest.

The country usually does not produce enough food to feed its population, but for the past three years it has experienced devastating drought conditions. In March 2004 the World Food Program warned that hundreds of thousands of people would require international food assistance for a third consecutive year.

Cattle are still employed to do the bulk of ploughing, and stock theft has severely affected agricultural output. In its 2002-2003 budget the government allocated enough money to purchase a fleet of 50 tractors to increase agricultural output. As farmers are being resettled to make way for the Highlands Water Project, alternative crops like seed potatoes, giant garlic and paprika are being introduced to give them added income.

With the shrinking of mining jobs, many Basotho men were forced to return to Lesotho and face extended unemployment. From 1995 to 2001, the number of migrant mine workers employed in South Africa declined from 104,000 to an estimated 59,000. This steady decline in jobs has pushed Lesotho's unemployment rate to a staggering 40% to 45%. Remittances by emigrant workers, so critical to the Lesotho economy, have also plummeted. They once contributed about 67% of the country's GDP (1990), but declined to about 33% in 1996 and are much less today.

The Kingdom's principal revenues are now customs receipts from the Southern African Customs Union (SACU). In 2001 SACU payments constituted 47.3% of total revenue. Its second source comes from payments made for water produced by the Lesotho Highlands Water Project (LHWP)—Lesotho's "white gold."

With an elaborate series of dams, tunnels and canals, the LHWP diverts the waters of the Orange River, in the mountains of Lesotho, to drier industrial areas of South Africa. Estimated to cost around $4 billion, the project is one of Africa's biggest civil engineering undertakings. Once completed it will pump 79 cubic meters of water a second northwards to Johannesburg, Pretoria and the Witwatersrand industrial heartland. With the completion of Mohale Dam in June, 2002, the first phase of the project was nearly completed, but around 8,000 workers lost their jobs in the subsequent downsizing. The completion of Phase One was officially celebrated in March 2004.

The LHWP, it should be noted, represents one of the ironies of development projects. The Mohale dam will inundate Lesotho's most fertile land area, the only region which produces a food surplus. In supporting the project, the World Bank argued that earnings from water sales to South Africa would far exceed the value of Mohale valley crops.

Commencement of the LHWP's second phase, which would have provided desperately-needed employment opportunities, has been postponed indefinitely. Estimates for water demand in South Africa have been lowered, and it is unlikely the second phase will begin anywhere in the next ten years. This leaves Lesotho with a reservoir of trained and skilled workers available for (once again migratory) work elsewhere in southern Africa.

For some of these workers there is a possibility of employment on what is being called the Lesotho Lowlands Project (LLP)—a joint endeavor by Lesotho and South Africa to supply water (again through a network of dams and pipelines) to Maseru and the surrounding area, including some South African border towns. Construction on the project, if given a go-ahead, won't start until 2006, so there is no immediate relief in site for Lesotho's unemployed construction workers.

The water supplied by the LLP is needed to support Maseru's developing industrial base, particularly its clothing manufactures. As a consequence of the U.S. African Growth Opportunities Act (AGOA), East Asian textile firms rushed in to take advantage of cheap labor and reduced duties on African manufactured goods entering the U.S. The number of textile factories in Maseru rose significantly, and clothing manufacture became a key growth factor for Lesotho's economy. The factories could import fabric and export manufactured clothing items, and with AGOA, they could avoid a 17% duty on cotton goods and a 33% duty on synthetics. Textile manufacturers invested more than $100 million in Lesotho and created thousands of new jobs; the industry grew to be Lesotho's largest employer, with over 50,000 workers. By 2003 the industry represented 10.5% of Lesotho's GDP and was the country's biggest foreign exchange earner.

All this changed beginning in January 2005 when the end of worldwide textile quotas went into effect. Over the December holiday period six foreign-owned textile factories closed their doors, leaving 6,650 workers jobless. Even worse, the owners—from China, Taiwan, Mauritius and Malaysia—departed without informing or paying their employees.

The action was typical of the new textile factories whose labor practices had long been criticized by trade unions. Working conditions were described as "appalling," with poor wages and unduly long working hours. Many employees were required to work seven days a week with additional overtime to meet production targets, and failure to do so resulted in wage cuts.

The decline of the American dollar has also made it difficult for local manufacturers to sell. In 2002 garment factories had only to sell $56 worth of clothes to the United States to cover the monthly wages of a sewing machine operator. By 2005 a factory had to sell $109 worth of goods to cover the same salary. As a consequence of quota elimination and a collapsing dollar, up to 50,000 workers may lose their jobs.

**The Future:** Lesotho will maintain its reputation as Southern Africa's most unstable state. Despite massive poverty and unemployment—issues which demand unity for solution—tensions between the country's main political forces will persist. With seventeen registered political parties there is much to bicker about. Prospects for future stability are further diminished by internal struggles within both the Lesotho Congress for Democracy and the Basotho Congress Party.

# The Republic of Malawi

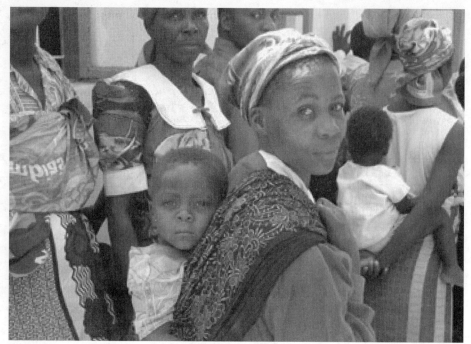

**Malawi mothers**  Photo by Sean Patrick

**Area:** 95,053 sq. km. = 36,700 sq. mi. (the size of Indiana).

**Population:** 12,158,924 (July 2005 est.)

**Capital City:** Lilongwe (Pop. 400,000 est. 1998). Blantyre in the country's commercial center and largest city, with over 500,000 people.

**Climate:** Hot in the low–lying extreme South; cool and temperate in the highlands with heavy rains (November–April); the amount of rainfall is related to the altitude.

**Neighboring Countries:** Mozambique (South, Southwest, Southeast); Zambia (Northwest); Tanzania (Northeast).

**Official Language:** English and Chichewa.

**Other Principal Languages:** Lomwe, Ngoni, NyakYusa-Ngonde, Nyanja, Sena, Tonga, Tumbuka, and Yao.

**Ethnic groups:** Chewa, Nyanja, Tumbuko, Yao, Lomwe, Sena, Tonga, Ngoni, Ngonde, Asian, and European.

**Principal Religions:** Protestant 55%, Roman Catholic 20%, Muslim 20%, traditional indigenous beliefs.

**Chief Commercial Products:** tobacco, tea, sugar, coffee, peanuts, and wood products.

**GNI per capita:** $170 (2003)

**Currency:** 1 Kwacha = 100 tambala

**Former Colonial Status:** British Colony (1883–1964).

**Independence Date:** July 6, 1964.

**Chief of State:** Dr. Bingu wa Mutharika, President (since May 2004).

**National Flag:** Three equal horizontal bands of black (top), red, and green with a radiant, rising, red sun centered in the black band.

Malawi, formerly known as Nyasaland, is a country of high mountains covered with lush, green foliage, interspersed with large, sparkling lakes and fertile plateaus. Situated on the western edge of the Rift Valley, Lake Nyasa (also known as Lake Malawi) spreads its long, deep waters over three–fourths of the eastern boundary of Malawi. The surface of this body of water is 1,500 feet above sea level; the water extends to a depth of 2,300, thus the floor of Lake Nyasa is over 700 feet below sea level. The lake pours into the River Shire, which flows southward to join the Zambesi River 250 miles away.

The countryside of Malawi has characteristic plateaus in the middle and on the top of steep mountains. For the most part, these are 3,000 to 4,000 feet above sea level, but rise as high as 8,000 feet in the North. Immediately south of Lake Nyasa are the Shire Highlands, gently rolling plateau country which is 3,000 feet high. From this green, almost level land, the mountain peaks of Zomba and Mlanje tower to heights of 7,000 and 10,000 feet, respectively.

The altitude modifies an otherwise equatorial climate. The summer, from November to April, is pleasantly warm with equatorial rains and sudden thunderstorms. Towards the end of March, the storms reach their peak, after which the rainfall rapidly diminishes. During the winter from May to September, wet mists float down from the highlands, invading the cool and dry reaches of the plateaus. There is almost no rainfall during these months.

For strikingly beautiful scenery, Malawi is almost unexcelled by any other nation on the African continent.

**History:** Before the waves of Bantu migration arrived many centuries ago, Malawi was probably very scantily settled. Restive Bantu peoples from the north expanded slowly southward from about the 10th century onward, sending successive waves of transients through this country on their journey to the south. Some stayed as permanent settlers, forming into distinct tribes based on common ancestry. For details of early and colonial history, see *Historical Background* and *The British in Africa*.

The Nyasaland African Congress (NAC) was formed in 1944 to give expression to African political aspirations, long-subordinated to the interests of European settlers. In 1953 Britain yielded to settler pressures to create a larger economic space, yoking Nyasaland with Northern and Southern Rhodesia in what was called the Central African Federation. The move prompted bitter opposition from Africans and the NAC gained popular support by mobilizing nationalist sentiment to oppose the Federation. One long-time opponent of British federation plans was Dr. Hastings Kamuzu Banda, an Edinburgh-trained medical practitioner. Even though working in Ghana, Banda had been active in the nationalist cause, and was finally persuaded to return to Nyasaland to lead the NAC. He did so in 1958.

As president of the Nyasaland African Congress, he toured the colony and effectively mobilized nationalist sentiment. Universal suffrage was demanded and disturbances ensued. Colonial authorities declared a state emergency in 1959 and jailed the troublesome Dr. Banda. As pressures built, Banda was released (1960), only to be invited, a few months later, to participate in discussions leading to a new constitution for Nyasaland. Under the new arrangements, Africans were granted a majority in the colony's Legislative

# Malawi

Council. Elections in 1961 gave Banda's Malawi Congress Party (MCP) 22 out of 28 seats, and Banda served as minister of natural resources and local government until becoming prime minister in 1963. In that year the Federation was dissolved and a year later, on July 6, 1964, Nyasaland became independent as Malawi.

In 1966 a new constitution made Malawi a single-party state under the MCP. Banda established himself as president-for-life in 1970. He ruled with autocratic firmness for 30 years, consistently (some would say ruthlessly) suppressing any opposition. During the 1980s, elections involved only MCP candidates, selected by Banda. Opposition figures died under very suspicious circumstances, and President Banda became increasingly authoritarian. Human rights violations, particularly those involving the MCP's Malawi Young Pioneers, which emerged as a paramilitary organization, became common. A cult of personality flourished around Banda.

Under external and internal pressures for political liberalization, the life-president grudgingly agreed to a referendum, which was held in 1993. He was stunned when 67% voted for multi-party democracy. Illness overtook the president in late 1993 when he had to go to Johannesburg for brain surgery. During his absence a presidential council was formed and the life presidency was abolished; the MCP's grip was ended; its youth group was officially disbanded, and a new constitution was adopted.

Malawi held multiparty elections in 1994 for the first time in three decades. The United Democratic Front (UDF), a new party whose political base lay in the densely populated south, emerged victorious. The UDF's candidate for president, Bakili Muluzi, received 47% of the vote to Banda's 34%. Muluzi's UDF also won an 83-seat plurality in the National Assembly, where it joined with independents and disaffected opposition members to create a working majority. The elections demonstrated a marked regional division within the country. The UDF dominated the south, while Banda's Malawi Congress Party took the center and the Alliance for Democracy (AFORD) the north.

In 1995 the new government tried Banda and his supporters for the 1983 murders of opposition leaders. Well into his 90s, Banda was totally deaf, senile, and too ill to attend the sessions. A seven-member court (controversially) acquitted all defendants in December. In early 1996 Banda addressed the nation on radio and apologized for any and all wrongs that might have occurred during his 30-year tenure. He died in November 1996, remembered for his leadership of the na-

**Dr. Bingu wa Mutharika, President**

tionalist struggle that gave Malawi independence.

Malawians also remembered him for thirty years of autocratic rule, quirky, almost Victorian, morality and a lavish life style. During his tenure in office he built two palaces, one of which cost 100 million U.S. dollars, while most Malawians lived in abject poverty.

For the presidential elections of May 1999, the MCP and AFORD formed an electoral coalition to oust President Muluzi. The MCP leader, Gwanda Chakuamba, was designated the alliance's presidential candidate, and AFORD leader Chakufwa Chihana was chosen for the vice-presidential slot, much to the annoyance of the MCP deputy leader, John Tembo.

President Muluzi was reelected with 52.4% of the vote to Gwanda Chakuamba's 45.2%, and his United Democratic Front won 93 seats in the National Assembly—less than a majority in the 192-seat house. The MCP won 66 seats and its AFORD ally picked up 29 seats. The opposition vigorously protested election irregularities and took their case to the courts, but found no support there. Efforts to boycott parliament failed to find unanimity within the opposition, and rancorous division dominated Malawi's politics.

The Malawi Congress Party was split by a sulfurous clash between Chakuamba and John Tembo, still smarting from being pushed aside as a vice-presidential candidate in the 1999 elections. The party suddenly had two leaders and two factions, with Tembo's faction opportunistically siding with the UDF in many parliamentary votes.

The ruling UDF fared little better. President Muluzi's interest in seeking a third term (which would require a constitutional amendment) angered some party leaders who split off to oppose a third

term. Critics of the president were ruthlessly dealt with. A senior cabinet minister, Brown Mpinganjira, was fired and kept busy in court responding to various charges brought by an implacably hostile government after he formed an opposition group, the National Democratic Alliance (NDA).

The third-term issue dominated political life for the next two years, dividing both the ruling party and opposition and rousing a storm of indignation in the country—led by the powerful religious lobby. Two attempts were made to amend the constitution to permit Muluzi to run for a third five-year term, but each failed and the president conceded defeat in March 2003, announcing he would not seek an additional term in office.

Punishment to those who had not supported third-term efforts was soon meted out. In early April Muluzi sacked his entire cabinet, getting rid of anyone who had not supported the constitutional amendment and anyone who might have shown an interest in running for the presidency. Leaving nothing to democratic uncertainty, Muluzi also designated his potential successor—a 68-year old economist, Bingu wa Mutharika. Dr. Mutharika had been serving as deputy governor of the Reserve Bank of Malawi before being appointed minister for the Department of Economics and Planning in Muluzi's new "national unity" cabinet.

President Muluzi's authoritarian style and thwarted ambitions polarized Malawi and divided the UDF. His choice of a political outsider as his successor prompted a host of party defections, including his vice-president Justin Malewezi. Malewezi and another UDF alumnus, ex-Foreign Minister Brown Mpinganjira both ran for the presidency in the May 2004 elections.

A deeply divided electorate produced a minority victory for wa Mutharika, the UDF/AFORD nominee, who won only 35% of the vote. His nearest rivals were John Tembo (MPC) with 27%, and Gwanda Chakuamba, who received 26% representing an opposition coalition of seven parties known as *Mgwirizano* (Unity). The election was not without its problems; observers stopped short of calling it both free and fair, and the opposition lodged a court challenge to the results.

In the new parliament, President wa Mutharika's UDF placed second, with only 49 seats. Opposition parties, led by the MCP, held 92 seats in the 193-member parliament; three of them—MCP, NDA, and the Unity Coalition—pledged not to take part in government. Opposition unity was short-lived: Gwanda Chakuamba, rallied to the government after his party was guaranteed three cabinet appointments.

# Malawi

Assumed to be little more than a Muluzi tool, President wa Mutharika soon proved to be his own man. Where the previous administration had handled the country's monumental corruption problem with kid gloves, Mutharika declared "zero tolerance." Comfortably feathered nests were rudely jolted. Relations with the UDF deteriorated completely, and in February 2005 Mutharika resigned from the party, accusing Muluzi of frustrating his anti-corruption campaign and of plotting assassinate him. Mutharika launched his own Democratic Progressive Party which drew support from independents and disgruntled members of the UDF.

A rueful Bakili Muluzi apologized to Malawi and the UDF for "imposing wa Mutharika on the country. I didn't know he would be accommodating dissenting views," he told a political rally in April 2005. Those "dissenting views" have resulted in at least five senior UDF figures facing criminal charges, including a former finance minister. Aggressive prosecution of the "thieves" of the previous decade has rallied support to a beleaguered president.

**Culture**: Malawi is one of the most densely populated countries in Africa, with an average population of 117 per sq. km. The shape of the country has tended to emphasize regional concentration of its various ethnic groups. This concentration has provided the basis of political support for the country's three main political parties. Chewas constitute 90% of the population of the central region; the Nyanja predominate in the south and the Tumbuka in the north. The UDF draws its strength from the south; the MCP is centrally based, and AFORD is strongest in the north.

Malawi has one of the highest HIV/AIDS infection rates in the world. Government figures indicate an estimated one million Malawians are HIV-positive and at least 70,000 people die of AIDS every year. Around 250 people are newly infected each day, and HIV/AIDS patients occupy at least 70% of Malawi's hospital beds. The country already has an estimated one million AIDS orphans. The disease has cut Malawi's life expectancy to just 37.5 years.

After years of silence, the country's political class has begun to speak out and highlight the issue. Ex-President Muluzi revealed that his own brother died of an AIDS-related disease and the NDA leader, Brown Mpingajira, disclosed that of eleven brothers and sisters, six have already perished because of HIV-related diseases. President Mutharika has called upon a million of his fellow citizens to undergo voluntary HIV/AIDS testing in 2005.

**Economy:** Malawi is desperately poor. With little in the way of mineral resources, its economy is agriculture-dependent; the sector supports nine out of ten Malawians, most of whom work as small-holders rather than on large plantations. Few smallholder farmers have access to productive land, a situation particularly difficult in the southern region where agriculture is dominated by large estates growing cash crops like tea and tobacco. Government policy under President Mutharika seeks to better support small-scale farmers.

Malawi's four major export crops—tobacco, tea, sugar and coffee—account for more than 90% of the country's export revenue. Per capita income is extremely low—$170—and Malawi is classified as one of the poorest countries in the world: 165th out of 177 on the UN's *Human Development Index* for 2004. Sixty-five percent of the population lives below the poverty line—less than one dollar per day. Economic growth is sluggish at best (estimated to reach 4.25% in 2004–05) and is limited by an annual population growth averaging 2%.

Landlocked, Malawi faces high transport bills—estimated as high as 40% of total import costs. The shortest and cheapest route to the sea for Malawi is the 48-mile rail link to Mozambique's port of Nacala. The track had fallen into disrepair during Mozambique's civil war (which ended in 1992) and western donors helped rehabilitate it.

Tobacco, which alone accounts for about 70% of export revenue, demonstrates many of the problems of economic development in Malawi. World prices have declined, and farmers earn barely enough to repay loans taken out for current crops. High interest rates and low exchange rates for the Kwacha combine to limit investment to boost production. Fertilizer is largely imported and a weak Kwacha makes its purchase prohibitive. Even if fields could be made more fertile there are international pressures to limit tobacco production. The World Health Organization's Framework Convention on Tobacco Control has already been signed by 168 countries.

Cannabis, known in the southern African region as "Malawi Gold," remains a big business despite police crackdowns. "It's so bad," said one police spokesman, "that we refuse to release figures indicating how much marijuana Malawi grows annually, in case the figures encourage even more people to grow the weed." Police action has only resulted in growers retreating to Malawi's inaccessible mountains where there are no roads.

The economic impact of Malawi's HIV/AIDS epidemic is significant. An estimated 5.8% of Malawi's farm labor force has died of AIDS, and a substantial number of farmers are too weak to work their farms fully. The government spends nearly $123,500 (outside its operating budget) to finance the funeral expenses of civil servants who die. HIV/AIDS is predicted to lower Malawi's GDP at least 10% by 2010.

Concerned with Malawi's endemic corruption and fiscal management the IMF stopped aid disbursements to the country in December 2000. (About a third of the country's annual budget was expected to disappear into the pockets of leading politicians and their clients.) The impact was critical: up to 80% of Malawi's development budget was funded by donors, and once the IMF had made its decision, most donors followed suit.

Under President Mutharika, the government has put its financial house in better order. An IMF mission in late 2004 was "encouraged by recent signs that Malawi's economy is strengthening." Donors are hesitantly re-opening their purse strings.

**The Future:** Despite "zero-tolerance" pervasive corruption will continue to brake development, and erratic government conduct will continue to frighten businessmen. Ongoing political bickering is likely to undermine the search for stability and raise doubts about the government's ability to address major social and economic problems.

**In Malawi the coffin maker is open 24 hours a day**     Photo by Ruth Evans

# The Republic of Mozambique (pronounced Moe–zam–*beek*)

**Electoral Remains**

**Area:** 786,762 sq. km. = 303,769 sq. mi. (twice the size of California).

**Population:** 19,406,703 (July 2005 est.)

**Capital City:** Maputo (pop. 1,100,000 est.)

**Climate:** Tropically hot and humid, modified somewhat in the mountain areas close to Lake Nyasa, the uplands bordering Zimbabwe and in coastline, cooled by ocean breezes.

**Neighboring Countries:** Tanzania (North); Malawi, Zambia (Northwest); Zimbabwe (West); South Africa, Swaziland (Southwest); Madagascar lies 300 to 600 miles off the coast.

**Official Language:** Portuguese.

**Other Principal Languages:** Over 30, including Chopi, Chwabo, Lomwe, Makhuwa, Makonde, Marendje, Nyanja, Ronga, Sena, Shona, Tsonga, and Tswa.

**Ethnic groups:** Indigenous tribal groups 99.66% (Shangaan, Chokwe, Manyika, Sena, Makua, and others), Europeans 0.06% Euro-Africans 0.2%, Indians 0.08%.

**Principal Religions:** Indigenous beliefs 50%, Christian 30%, and Muslim 20%

**Chief Commercial Products:** Aluminum, prawns and other fish, cotton, cashew nuts, timber, sugar and copra.

**GNI per capita:** $210 (2003)

**Currency:** 1 Metical (Mt) = 100 centavos

**Former Colonial Status:** Portugal claimed that Mozambique was an integral part of Portugal until September 7, 1974; a provisional government was decreed to wield power until formal independence.

**Independence Date:** June 25, 1975.

**Chief of State:** Armando Emilio Guebuza, President.

**National Flag:** Three equal horizontal bands of green (top), black, and yellow with a red isosceles triangle based on the pole side; the black band is edged in white; centered in the triangle is a yellow five-pointed star bearing a crossed rifle and hoe in black superimposed on an open white book.

The flat terrain of the coastline of Mozambique, filled with dense, tropical jungle in areas which are not cleared, gives way gradually to a series of plateaus and highlands which gently rise toward high mountains in the part closest to the western borders. Towering green peaks are located in the Lake Nyasa area, and the temperature is moderated by the altitude. Most of the intense agricultural production takes place in the coastal lowlands and surrounding plateaus.

**History:** Prior to the arrival of European explorers, Arab traders had established active trading posts along the coast of Mozambique, dealing principally in slaves and, to a much lesser degree, agricultural products. For details of earlier periods and colonial history, see *Historical Background* and *The Portuguese in Africa*.

Nationalist resistance to Portugal's particularly benighted colonialism was organized in 1962 by left-wing Mozambique exiles living in neighboring Tanzania. Under the leadership of Eduardo Mondlane they formed the Mozambique Liberation Front (*Frente de Libertação de Moçambique*: Frelimo) and began a guerrilla war against the Portuguese in 1964. Mondlane was assassinated in 1969, but the war effort was continued and expanded by his successor, Samora Machel.

Portugal poured some 70,000 troops into the colony to suppress the insurrec-

# Mozambique

tion, but by the early 1970s it could do little more than defend the cities. Frelimo controlled most of the countryside and drained Portuguese manpower, resources and will. Disgruntled army officers overthrew the Portuguese government in April 1974, and the new government granted Mozambique its independence a year later. Frelimo created a single-party state organized on Marxist-Leninist principles with Machel as president.

The Portuguese colonial legacy was appallingly meager. After more than 400 years of Portuguese presence, more than 90% of Mozambique's population was illiterate. For the entire country there were only 80 doctors and 100 high school teachers. The new government imposed socialist organization and planning, including large-scale nationalization, leading to a massive exodus of Portuguese colonists.

Over 100,000 left, taking with them the bulk of the country's administrative and managerial skills. What they could not take, they destroyed. Some drove tractors into the sea; others ripped plumbing out of buildings. Factories were destroyed; government files and business records were burned.

Some 4,000 commercial farms were abandoned, resulting in disastrous declines in export-crop production. Following Stalinist precedent, the Frelimo government collectivized agriculture. State farms were created; agricultural cooperatives and communal villages were organized. Major portions of export earnings were devoted to the purchase of farm equipment, but there weren't enough skilled mechanics to maintain them, nor enough income to buy spare parts. Costly farm machinery lay idle as Soviet theories of mechanized agriculture proved inadequate to African reality.

Created, for the most part, by Lusophone urban elites, the Frelimo government, like its colonial predecessor, based itself on the cities, especially the capital—renamed Maputo. It increasingly grew out of touch with the countryside. The government appointed village "presidents" loyal to Frelimo and discarded traditional chiefs. Government-set prices for food crops were kept low to placate Frelimo's urban constituency, but they offered peasant farmers no incentive to produce. Not unexpectedly, farmers returned to subsistence production.

By 1983 even the most starry-eyed Marxists had to admit that socialism as practiced was a miserable failure. Eighty percent of state resources had gone to state farms, but they represented only 10% of the country's agricultural sector and had proved costly failures. Given a shortage of trained manpower, basic record keeping and production reports were vir-

tually impossible. One major state farm operated 42,000 acres with one bookkeeper and a novice economist. State farms and enterprises sent false reports to the government because they had no facts to report. When the government made it a crime to submit false reports, it got none at all.

Overt opposition to Frelimo's policies coalesced with the aid of the white government of neighboring Rhodesia in 1976. Fearful of Mozambican aid to Robert Mugabe's rebel forces fighting to dislodge it, the Rhodesian government organized Mozambican dissidents into an opposition army which called itself the Mozambican National Resistance (*Resistência Nacional Moçambicana:* Renamo). When Mugabe's forces triumphed in Rhodesia, support of Renamo fell to the apartheid government of South Africa, equally terrified of black radicalism on its borders supporting its own black opposition, the African National Congress (ANC).

Rural, conservative, traditional, and speaking the indigenous languages of the illiterate populations of central and northern Mozambique—everything, in short, that Frelimo was not—Renamo was implacably opposed to the Leviathan state Frelimo sought to create. For some sixteen years it engaged the Frelimo government in bloody civil war, the objects of its wrath any and everything that symbolized the Frelimo state. Roads and rails, utility lines, schools, clinics and stores, farms and factories were all destroyed. The economy was brought to a standstill. Well over 100,000 were killed; more than a million were displaced.

Faced with civil war and a collapsed economy, Frelimo's Fourth Party Congress, held in 1983, began to shift the state away from inept centralized planning and forced social organization. President Machel, who once thundered to his audience that "Our country will be the grave of capitalism and exploitation," began to solicit western investors.

By 1984, the government sought to cut off its Renamo opponent by severing its ties with South Africa. A mutual agreement was reached at the border town of Nkomati: Mozambique would end sanctuary and support for ANC forces, and in exchange South Africa would end its military support for Renamo. Despite the Nkomati Accord, the South African army continued to aid and supply Renamo forces, and they, in turn, continued their depredations in Mozambique.

In October 1986 President Machel was killed when his plane, Russian built and piloted, crashed under mysterious circumstances shortly before landing in Maputo; suspicions of South African involvement have yet to be allayed. Frelimo's central committee met and elected Mozambique's foreign minister, Joachim Chissano, party chairman. As such, he automatically became president.

President Chissano, regarded as a moderate and the man who had convinced Samora Machel to make overtures to western capital, expanded Machel's tentative opening to the West. The end of the Cold War forced change on Mozambique's Marxists. With Chissano as party leader, Frelimo's Fifth Congress dramatically ended the party's official Marxist-

**At the Mozambique Zimbabwe border**    Photo by David Johns

144

# Mozambique

Leninist orientation in 1989. Chissano learned the language of Western democracy and economic liberalism. Multiparty elections became possible, and dutiful acquiescence to IMF economic reform policies was offered.

In October 1992, President Chissano and Afonso Dhlakama, Renamo's chief, signed a peace accord. Deep mutual suspicion, sixteen years of devastating civil war and diametrically opposed ideological visions separated the two. Frelimo has never accepted Renamo as a legitimate representative of those rejected and marginalized by its policies. To this day it still refers to Renamo as "bandits," but Mozambique has now seen two multiparty presidential and parliamentary elections.

The first electoral competition between the two antagonists came in 1994. Opposition to President Chissano came from Renamo and Dhlakama and ten other presidential candidates. The elections graphically showed the regional cleavage of Mozambique. Frelimo was popular in southern, more populated areas and of course swept the capital of Maputo. Chissano won slightly more than half the votes cast for president. Dhlakama ran strongly in the north—a thousand miles from Maputo—and central areas, winning 34% of presidential votes. Renamo ran ahead of its leader in parliamentary races, winning 112 of 250 seats in the Assembly of the Republic to Frelimo's 129.

Municipal elections in June 1998 were meant to implement Frelimo's decentralization policies. Instead, they displayed Frelimo's fundamental resistance to surrendering its control of local authorities. Frelimo proposed to devolve authority to only 33 larger cities already organized and dominated by executive councils appointed by, and totally integrated into, the structure of the Frelimo state.

Renamo, encouraging the power of traditional authorities in the rural areas, demanded official recognition of their role in local communities. This position was rejected by the government, and Renamo declared an election boycott. So successful was the call nationally that 85% of registered voters absented themselves from the polls. In 19 of the 33 constituencies allowed to elect municipal assemblies, Frelimo was the only party competing. In the northern cities of Nampula and Beira, abstention rates were 92% and 90%.

Nationally, parliamentary majorities allowed the Frelimo government to liberalize a state-dominated economy and become the darling of donors and international lending agencies. Development money poured into Mozambique. Growth rates were eye-popping, but the process was not without its downside as criminal

**Mozambique Provinces**

elements found expansion opportunities galore.

Mozambique has been in a state of tension since the December 1999 elections. According to official figures, President Chissano won a surprisingly close victory, winning 52.3% of the vote to Afonso Dhlakama's 47.7%. In elections for the 250-seat Assembly of the Republic, all minor parties received less than 5% of the vote and were completely shut out. Frelimo took 133 seats, Renamo 117. There were serious questions about the results. Indeed, some diplomatic observers suspected Dhlakama actually won. Mozambique's Supreme Court ultimately rejected, by a split vote, the request by Renamo and a coalition of smaller parties to invalidate the results.

The election crisis peaked in November 2000 when national protests against rigged elections went tragically awry in the northern community of Montepuez. Demonstrators converged on the police station and began to liberate arms and prisoners. Seven policemen were beaten to death after they had fired on the crowd; at least 18 demonstrators were shot to death. Nationally, over 40 people were killed in the demonstrations, most of them by police bullets.

The next day security forces began a dragnet to arrest Renamo leaders and sympathizers throughout the northern region. Hundreds were arrested. Most were

jailed in deplorable conditions of overcrowding. In Montepuez, 84 prisoners died in a single night from asphyxia. Record keeping was so bad the police had no idea of who had died. Their bodies were buried in a mass grave.

Almost before the bodies had been buried Mozambique received one additional shock: Carlos Cardoso, the country's most respected investigative journalist, was assassinated—gangland style. His exposés had revealed growing and pervasive corruption in the Frelimo state; his death highlighted the country's growing crime and criminality. Two years later, in November 2002, six individuals were tried for murder and complicity. The trial, broadcast live on radio and TV, was conducted in a high security prison in Maputo for safety reasons.

Testimony publicly confirmed the ramification of corruption through every level of the Frelimo state. At the heart of the conspiracy were two members of the rich, powerful, and politically well-connected Abdul Satar family. Cardoso was investigating how they defrauded a state-owned bank of $14 million, and the trial elicited allegations of international drug dealing, money laundering and customs fraud, all of which was abetted by corruption in various state administrative structures. (In June 2000, the Attorney General and six of his deputies were fired by President Chissano after a series of Cardoso articles accused them of accepting bribes from the Abdul Satars and of complicity in the fraud by losing documents and disorganizing the case file.)

One of the defendants—Anibal dos Santos Junior ("Anibalzinho"), the man responsible for organizing the assassination and hiring the gunmen—was tried *in absentia*, having "escaped" a high security prison in September 2002, shortly before the trial began. It was a release that could have only been authorized at the highest level, and Attorney General Joaquim Madeira called it "a body blow to our judicial system." The Minister of the Interior (in whose jurisdiction the prison system falls) was so complacent about the whole affair, he could only respond to a parliamentary question by a question of his own: "In what part of the world do prisoners not escape from jails?"

Trial testimony brought the Cardoso murder very close to President Chissano himself. Three of the defendants testified that Nyimpine Chissano, the president's eldest son (and business partner of the Abdul Satars) had paid for the assassination. The lead investigator confirmed that one of the defendants had "confessed in a number of conversations" that President Chissano's eldest son had ordered the assassination. When called before the court,

# Mozambique

**Armando Guebuza, President**

Nyimpine denied everything, but the trial judge, courageously persisting in the face of threats on his life, opened a dossier for further investigation of "others" who might be involved in the murder.

At the end of January 2003, all six were found guilty of the Cardoso murder and sentenced to jail for 23 to 28 years. Anibalzinho, captured in South Africa the day before the sentence was rendered, received the longest sentence. In addition to jail time, Judge Paulino ordered the defendants to pay restitution to the Cardoso family—four billion Meticais, about $175,000. The Mozambiquan press named him "personality of the year."

In December 2001 President Chissano announced that he would not run for a third term in 2004, setting off a political scramble between the party traditionalists (socialist hardliners who think President Chissano had gone too far in economic liberalization) and modernists (who want to go even further.) In June 2002, Frelimo's central committee overwhelmingly elected Armando Guebuza, head of Frelimo's parliamentary group, the party's secretary general and thus its candidate in the next presidential election.

A militant of the earliest Frelimo days, Guebuza rose through the ranks from guerrilla commander to general during the independence struggle and has the reputation of being a tough politician. At independence it was Guebuza who launched the "24/20" slogan that gave Portuguese settlers 24 hours to leave with only 20 pounds of baggage. He is also associated with the vaguely Stalinist forced removal program of 1983, where the urban unemployed were moved to sparsely populated northern rural areas.

With the fall of the Soviet Union Guebuza effected an ideological conversion, becoming a pro-Western, free-market liberal; in the process he became one of the country's richest men. He has extensive interests in a variety of sectors—banking, export-import, tourism, fishing, transport—and his business partners are frequently government colleagues or involved in state companies.

The revelations of the Cardoso trial badly damaged Frelimo's credibility and prestige. The very real concern is that the state has been captured by criminal elements. As one Frelimo legislator put it: "clearly the state has been highly infiltrated by organized crime." In urging officials to act promptly against corruption, he articulated the central dilemma facing Mozambique: "If the state does not control the bandits, the bandits will control it."

Municipal elections in November 2003 suggested Renamo was incapable of capitalizing on crime and corruption as political issues, at least at the local level. Voters in 33 municipalities showed little change of political loyalty: the south supported Frelimo and the north cast its lot with Renamo. Voter participation was dismally low; barely 24% of the electorate cast a ballot. Renamo did manage to capture two important cities in central and northern Mozambique—the port cities of Beira and Nampula.

Beira highlighted the country's asymmetrical development and the grievances in whose name Renamo speaks. The city has one of Mozambique highest AIDS rates (over 15% while the national infection rate is 12%), and its economy is a shamble with the collapse of the Beira Corridor, the transportation route linking the port to landlocked Zimbabwe.

December 2004 Presidential and parliamentary elections pitted Afonso Dhlakama as Renamo's standard bearer against Frelimo's Armando Guebuza. Far better organized and financed, Frelimo won massively. Guebuza took 63.74% of the vote and Dhlakama 31.74%. Frelimo captured nine of eleven provinces, winning 160 seats in the Assembly of the Republic, Mozambique's unicameral legislature; Renamo took the remaining 90 seats. Smaller parties were completely shut out.

No one was willing to call the election both free and fair. Renamo justifiably lodged complaints: in at least 100 polling stations in central and northern Mozambique (Renamo's traditional stronghold) official figures put the turnout at between 92% and 101%, almost all of which went to Frelimo candidates. The announcement of official results was delayed for more than two weeks, giving more than ample time to manipulate electoral computers. The voters themselves could have cared less: only 36% of those eligible actually took the time to vote, suggesting a general popular fatigue with the Frelimo state, the venality of its politicians, and its willingness to tolerate impunity for both the criminal and the corrupt.

One of a series of amendments to the constitution in November 2004—the first since the advent of multiparty politics in 1992—seemed to suggest a commitment to trackling potential corruption at the highest levels. Henceforth Mozambique's President will no longer be immune from prosecution; by a two-thirds majority, the Assembly can impeach a President "for crimes practiced in the exercise of his duties." Another amendment also took a step towards separating state and party: a new national anthem was enacted, replacing Frelimo's party anthem, which had functioned as the country's national song since independence.

**View of the Cabora Bassa Dam**

146

# Mozambique

**Culture:** Since the end of the civil war, Mozambique has become an important transit area for illicit drugs. Cocaine, for example, is shipped from Columbia to Brazil and then into Mozambique for redistribution to other parts of the world. Heroine is transported from Pakistan to Dubai, then to Tanzania, from whence it is shipped into Mozambique for international distribution. In 2001 it was estimated that more than one ton of cocaine and heroin passed through the country each month. According to one observer of the Mozambique scene, the value of the illegal drug trade passing through the country represented more than all legal foreign trade combined.

Corruption from high to low facilitates the traffic. Customs officials are bribed to enable entry and removal of the drugs; immigration officers provide identity and residence papers to the traffickers; police are bribed to turn a blind eye to the trade, and judicial officers are put on the payroll in case the traffickers are ever (rarely) brought to trial.

Attorney General Joaquim Madeira was the first AG to speak openly about corruption and propose ways of dealing with it. His annual reports to parliament have detailed the processes by which the entire judicial system, including attorneys and judges had failed. The police too have been subject to his withering criticism. "It is not possible to combat crime with policemen who are allies of the underworld or who derive benefits from it," he told parliament in his 2001 report.

In March 2005 the courts heard Attorney-General Madeira's libel suit against one of the Abdul Satars (Momade Assife), who had published an open letter in the weekly *Demos* accusing him of interfering in the Cardoso murder case to protect Nyimpine Chissano. To the consternation of journalists, the presiding judge closed the hearings to observers, disregarding a constitutional amendment that made criminal trials public. (Libel is a criminal, not civil offense in Mozambique.)

As the Cardoso case illustrated, criminal elements have so corrupted the police and judicial systems they can order the assassination of investigators and prosecutors with impunity. The greatest worry is that the magnitude of corrupt practices may have escaped the ability of parliament to control and monitor the state.

For a large number of Mozambicans, it is less a question of ability than desire to control corruption. When "Ethics Mozambique," an anti-corruption NGO, issued a study of corruption perceptions in 2000, 42% of the sample thought the government had no interest in tackling corruption. Over half the sample, 50.5%, thought the police had no interest in eradicating it,

and even more—58.8%—believed members of the government were involved.

**Economy:** The international community is determined to make Mozambique a showpiece of capitalist development. A darling of the donor community, 60% of Mozambique's budget is made up of foreign aid. What has the government done to warrant this support? Basically, it has created one of the most open economic regimes in Africa, aggressively pursued foreign investment, and actively dismantled the state-centered economy of its Marxist past. The consequence has been eye-popping economic growth figures, suggesting Mozambique has one of the most dynamic economies in southern Africa.

All is not steadily progressive, however. Mozambique's economy is fundamentally agricultural, with farming employing 80% of the working population. Given the absence of transport and transportation links, most farmers produce only enough for their own subsistence needs. They toil with the most rudimentary of techniques: only 7% of farmers use traction (animal or mechanical) and only 2% use fertilizers or pesticides. The typical farmer is usually a woman (with a baby on her back) who turns the soil with nothing more than a hoe.

More than 54% of Mozambique's nearly 18 million people continue to live in absolute poverty, the vast majority in rural areas distant from the economic success story of Maputo, the capital city. Industrial development has been privileged—to the detriment of agricultural development. From 34% of GDP in 1991, the agricultural sector has fallen to 26%; concomitantly, industry now represents 31% of GDP (2003).

Until the advent of its aluminum plant, Mozambique's biggest export earner had been prawns. In 2000, 9,729 tons of prawns were exported, earning $92.4 million. With other nations entering the market, competition has heightened and prices declined, leading to lower interest and catches. Overall earnings from assorted fisheries products declined. In 2000, Mozambique earned $138.3 million from fisheries exports. That declined to $130 million in 2001, with a further decline to $93.5 million a year later. Fisheries now contribute 4% of GDP.

Cotton and cashews were once Mozambique's two largest cash crops and the nation's largest foreign currency earners. Production of both crops fell dramatically during the civil war, and both are subject to the less than tender mercies of fluctuating demand and prices in the world market.

Cotton, mostly grown in northern Mozambique, involves about 200,000 peasant families. Collapsing market prices have

severely weakened production enthusiasm on the part of farmers, and the EU has granted economic assistance to help them shift to alternative crops. In 2001, 85,000 tons of cotton were produced in the country.

Mozambique was once the world's largest producer of cashews, but the stock of trees has been destroyed by war, ravaged by disease, and reduced in production as a consequence of aging. An estimated one million trees die or go out of production each year because of age, disease or neglect. On average only 300,000 have been planted annually to replace them. Current production has been around 50,000 tons a year, mostly grown in the northern province of Nampula. In the 2002/2003 season, the government's rejuvenation project began to pay off. Production increased to more than 65,000 tons. The production target for 2004 was 100,000 tons.

The cashew industry has also suffered from trade liberalization imposed by the World Bank and the International Monetary Fund (IMF), which forced most processing plants to close. The bulk of Mozambique's cashews are sold to India, and the government is seeking to convince Indian companies to take advantage of cheap labor and save transportation costs by opening their own processing plants in Mozambique.

Mozambique's once thriving sugar industry is also being revived. Thanks to rehabilitation efforts the country expects to produce 300,000 tons of sugar a year from 2003—a 200% increase over 2001 when 67,000 tons of sugar were produced.

Mozambique's preferential sugar quotas for exports to Europe, America, and SADC markets remain very low—about 30,000 tons, which receive special (higher) prices. The remaining 170,000 tons must be sold on the domestic market, or on the free sector of the world market, where prices have collapsed to $150 a ton. Sugar smuggled from Zimbabwe poses major price competition for domestic sales.

One huge mega-project suggests the country's economic vitality and potential—an aluminum smelter located at Maputo. A joint venture between British, Japanese and South African investors, Mozal represents an investment of $1.34 billion. The first aluminum was poured in July 2000, and Mozambique's first aluminum exports, 1,350 metric tons worth $2 million, were shipped in August. Mozal completed an extension project, doubling its annual capacity to 506,000 tons of aluminum ingots in April 2003.

The smelter has been a catalyst for Mozambique's development. Construction employment was almost 9,000 workers, 70% of them Mozambicans. More than 5,000 people have been trained in basic

# Mozambique

building skills, and when the plant is fully operational, it will employ a staff of 800, of whom 700 are local. Some sense of the scale of the Mozal project lies in its consumption of electricity. When fully operational the smelter will use twice as much electricity as the whole of Mozambique today. Another indicator of Mozal's impact on the economy: in 2002, 28% of all Mozambique's imports were destined for the Mozal expansion.

The South African energy company Sasol has won the rights to commercialize Mozambique's natural gas riches. The Pande and Temane gas fields give Sasol proven reserves of 2.8 trillion cubic feet—enough gas for 30 years. The company will construct a pipeline to carry the gas to Maputo and South Africa. Ownership of the pipeline will be shared: 50% by Sasol, with the governments of South Africa and Mozambique each holding a 25% share. In the future natural gas could easily vie with aluminum as Mozambique's most valuable export.

In northern Mozambique, Dublin-based Kenmare Resources has secured funding to produce titanium from heavy mineral sands. Rich in titanium dioxide, the sands do not require smelting to be upgraded, and the project will reputedly become one of the world's lowest cost titanium producers. Construction of the project, located some 185 miles south of the port of

Nacala, was scheduled to begin in 2003 with mining to begin in 2004. As with all major industrial projects in Mozambique, electricity is in short or non-existent supply. Kenmare will install a 105-mile line to bring electricity generated by Cabora Bassa dam.

Cabora Bassa, built in 1974 by Portugal on the Zambezi River, has an output of 3,700 mw, but is in ruinous financial circumstances. Owned by Portugal (85%) and Mozambique (15%), the operating company's largest client is the South African energy giant, Eskom, which pays a ridiculously low price for its electricity and has shown itself obstinate in renegotiating the purchase agreement. Mozambique is moving ahead with the controversial construction of yet another dam on the Zambezi, at Mepanda Uncua in central Tete province. Estimated cost of the project is $1.3 billion. The new dam is only 43 miles downstream from Cabora Bassa.

Years of upheaval and economic mismanagement left Mozambique heavily indebted. By 1999 its external debt was estimated at $7.7 billion, but the government's economic liberalization policies brought favorable reaction from the IMF. Mozambique qualified for the Fund's Highly Indebted Poor Country (HIPC) initiative, and by 2003 its debt had been reduced to a little more than $5 billion. In theory, monies saved in debt servicing

payments should go to poverty-alleviation programs.

Debt reduction and asymmetrical economic development have yet to improve the lives of most people. Life expectancy is deplorably low (41 years or less) and enfant mortality deplorably high (101 per thousand live births). Sixty percent of the population remains illiterate, well above the sub-Saharan average of 35%. At least the countryside is at peace and people are producing. That's a modicum of hope for the future.

**The Future:** All parties seem to have agreed to seek first economic improvement in Mozambique. The important thing will be the extent to which economic development makes a difference in the lives of average citizens. Thus far the evidence indicates it hasn't.

Major investments in human capital will be required if growth and development are to be sustained. Current aggregate adult literacy rates of 40% disguise severe gender differences: more than twice as many men are literate than women; low school enrollment also remains a challenge to development plans.

Development is highly unbalanced, with most centering in the southern regions, especially around Maputo. This disequilibrium, adding to northern poverty, will continue to fuel political tensions.

**Women trained and employed in the construction of the Mozal works**
Photo courtesy Mozal

148

**Christus Kirche (Lutheran), Windhoek**

Photo by Judi Iranyi

**Area:** 823,620 sq. km. = 318,000 sq. mi. (twice the size of California).

**Population:** 2,030,692 (July 2005 est.)

**Capital City:** Windhoek (Pop. 175,000, estimated).

**Climate:** Hot and dry except in the Caprivi Strip, which has more rainfall.

**Neighboring Countries:** Angola (North); South Africa (South); Botswana (East); Zambia (Northeast).

**Official Language:** English.

**Other Principal Languages:** Afrikaans common language of most of the population and about 60% of the white population, German 32%; indigenous languages: Oshivambo, Herero, Damara, Nama and Kavanga.

**Ethnic groups:** Black 86%, white 6.6%, mixed 7.4% About 50% of the population belong to the Ovambo people and 9% to the Kavangos people; other ethnic groups are: Herero 7%, Damara 7%, Nama 5%, Caprivian 4%, Bushmen 3%, Baster 2%, Tswana 0.5%.

**Principal Religions:** Christian 80% to 90% (Lutheran 50% at least, other Christian denominations 30%), native religions 10% to 20%.

**Chief Commercial Products:** Diamonds, copper, gold, zinc, lead, uranium; cattle, processed fish, and karakul skins.

**GNI per capita:** $1870 (2003)

**Currency:** Namibian Dollar

**Former Colonial Status:** The Republic of South Africa asserted control of the territory (as South–West Africa), claiming a mandate under the League of Nations continued since the formation of the United Nations. The UN passed a resolution in 1966 declaring South–West Africa to be under direct UN control and designated the area *Namibia* in 1968.

**Independence Date:** March 21, 1990.

**Chief of State:** Hifikepunye Pohamba, President

**National Flag:** Diagonal stripes of blue, red and green separated by thin white stripes. On the blue stripe, near the pole, is a golden sunburst.

The narrow white beach of Namibia is quickly replaced by a 60–mile–wide stretch of red–colored Namib Desert which runs the entire length of the coastline. The barren Kalahari Desert stretches along the north and eastern borders of the territory, occasionally interrupted by harsh formations of gray rock and thin scrub vegetation. The only rain in this region comes from torrential storms which occasionally gather—their rapid downpour is swallowed up quickly without leaving a trace of moisture.

The central area of Namibia is a vast plateau suited to pastoral raising of sheep and cattle. Here, there is somewhat more rain, which permits a thin forage to cover the soil. This region produces thousands of karakul sheep, the lambs of which are treasured for their shiny black, curly pelts used in fur coats.

**History:** In times unknown, Bushmen groups settled in what is now Namibia, followed by several Bantu tribes. Ovambos and Damara–Hereros became the most numerous groups. For details of early and pre–World War II colonial history, see *Historical Background* and *The British in Africa, The Germans in Africa* and *The South African Mandate.*

South Africa controlled the area under a mandate from the League of Nations after occupying it in 1915. After the United Nations was created, all previously mandated dependent territories came under its supervision. In most cases, the mandates were transformed into trusteeships requiring annual reports concerning the territory's development and progress towards eventual independence.

South Africa applied for "permission" to make South–West Africa part of that nation in 1946. The UN rejected the proposal, but offered South Africa a trusteeship. South Africa rejected the offer and moved to incorporate the land within its national boundaries regardless of UN protests. By 1949, certain South African laws had been extended to South–West Africa, and its white representatives sat in the South African parliament. The UN condemned South Africa for its failure to live up to the terms of the UN Charter, but this meant nothing in the absence of force.

During the 1960s nationalist sentiment and action coalesced in the South–West African People's Organization, or SWAPO. SWAPO sought majority rule and independence for the territory. While its political leaders headquartered in Dar es Salaam, Tanzania, SWAPO's fighters roamed the territory, recruiting volunteers, terrorizing black and white farmers, sabotaging public utilities and ambushing army patrols. South Africa reacted quickly. Hundreds of guerrillas were rounded up and jailed, including the group's leader, Herman Toivo ja Toivo; he was sentenced to 20 years imprisonment on Robben Island, South Africa, after being convicted of "crimes against state security" in 1968. Backed by surrounding black African nations committed to the struggle against

# Namibia

apartheid, SWAPO intensified its armed resistance.

By 1966 the UN decided once and for all to terminate the South African "mandate." It renamed the territory Namibia (derived from the name of the Namib Desert) and recognized SWAPO as the "representative" of the Namibian people. After considerable diplomatic pressure from the U.S., Canada, Britain, France and West Germany, South Africa agreed to peace discussions that would include SWAPO representatives.

The first talks in early 1978 ended in failure, and negotiations dragged on and on. The situation was further complicated by Angola's Marxist regime, which supported SWAPO and provided refuge for its guerilla fighters. South Africa, which was aiding UNITA rebels in their efforts to overthrow the Marxist regime in Luanda, invaded Angola in 1982–1984 to clean out SWAPO rebels. Clashes between South African forces and Cuban troops, present in the country since 1976, intensified the regional war.

In 1983, South Africa declared a "linkage" policy: South African troops in Angola would not be withdrawn until Cuban troops were first withdrawn. Angola and Cuba responded firmly: Cuban troops would only depart after South African forces had been withdrawn.

Inside Namibia SWAPO increasingly resorted to terrorist tactics, and government forces engaged in widespread atrocities in retaliation. SWAPO defectors and enemies also felt its wrath. Some 2,000 Namibians, some of whom had merely demanded more democracy within the movement, were accused of spying for South Africa and flung into crude prisons located in Angola. Many were "disappeared" with Stalinist efficiency.

By 1988 the external actors saw the Namibian situation as counter–productive to their own interests. A grand diplomatic solution was reached in December 1988. South Africa agreed to the independence of South–West Africa, while Cuba and South Africa jointly agreed to withdraw their troops from Angola. Free elections would be held for a national assembly that would draft a constitution leading to independence in April 1990.

After a brief transition period, elections for the constituent assembly were held with almost 98% of registered voters participating. SWAPO took 57% of the vote, just short of the two-thirds majority that would have given it free reign in writing a new constitution. The Democratic Turnhalle Alliance, a multiracial coalition of conservatives with white leadership, received 29% of the vote. In February 1990 the Constituent Assembly adopted a constitution that created a multiparty system, limited its executive president to two five-year terms, and enshrined a bill of rights. Distancing itself from its socialist background, SWAPO participants voted to include provisions that granted private ownership of property and affirmed a mixed economy where foreign investment would be encouraged. The collapse of the Soviet Union had diminished the allure of socialist utopias.

The Constituent Assembly converted itself into the National Assembly on February 16, 1990, and unanimously proceeded to elect Sam Nujoma Namibia's first president. Its first presidential election was held in December 1994, and Nujoma swept to triumphant victory, thrashing his DTA opponent, Mishake Muyongo, with nearly 70% of votes cast. SWAPO gained an overwhelming majority in parliament.

Nujoma's political dominance posed problems for SWAPO as it contemplated presidential elections in 1999. Despite the constitutional prohibition on more than two terms, Nujoma announced in April 1997, "I am still young and if the people of Namibia want me to continue making a contribution I will continue to do so." Dutiful and deferential to its leader, the 1997 SWAPO party congress recommended that the constitution be amended to permit the President to run for a third term.

SWAPO parliamentarians dutifully amended the constitution, but the move helped provoke a split in the party. Ben Ulenga, a former guerrilla, trade unionist and Namibian high commissioner (ambassador) in London, resigned from SWAPO, to form an opposition party, Congress of Democrats, and contested the 1999 elections.

Ulenga had impressive credentials as a candidate. His liberation struggle credentials were impeccable—wounded in combat and 15 years detention on Robben Island. His disillusionment with SWAPO began even before independence, when thousands of fighters disappeared without explanation in SWAPO detention camps. Nujoma's decision to seek a third term confirmed that disillusionment. Ulenga shocked the party with a scathing attack on Nujoma's autocratic rule, corruption, and the very idea of a third mandate for the president.

The Congress of Democrats was the first credible alternative to SWAPO to emerge, particularly in its traditional northern strongholds. Ulenga himself was also an Ovambo from the north, a center of SWAPO strength. The election was hard fought and not without the usual bullying tactics by SWAPO and its supporters. Ulenga accused his old party of corruption, arrogant leadership, and mismanagement of an economy struggling with a 35% jobless rate.

The opposition DTA was terminally wounded by the call of its long-time leader, Mishake Muyongo, for Caprivi's secession, and there was little hope the party could provide an effective challenge to SWAPO. The December election proved a smashing success for SWAPO; Nujoma obtained 76.8% of the vote, while Ulenga garnered only 10.5%. The DTA's Katuurike Kaura won 9.6%, and a fourth candidate trailed the field with a mere 3%.

In the National Assembly elections SWAPO increased its electoral support, winning 76% of the vote. Seats in the 72-member house are distributed proportionally. SWAPO was allocated 55 seats; the Congress of Democrats and the DTA were

**Weaver, Karakulia Center, Swakopmund**          Photo by Connie Abell

**The Namib Desert**                    Photo by Judi Iranyi

each allocated seven seats, while the United Democratic Front (UDF) got two and the small Monitor Action Group settled for one.

President Nujoma's authoritarian leadership style did not change, and this was affirmed with his single-handed commitment of Namibian armed forces in support of Laurent Kabila in the Congo. The actual number of troops committed, the number who died, or even the overall costs of the adventure remain shrouded in mystery. After his re-election, Nujoma also allowed Angolan troops to enter Namibian territory—without any reference to parliament—to search out and destroy bases and personnel of Jonas Savimbi's UNITA.

In late 1998 Nujoma faced secessionist agitation in the remote Caprivi. The Caprivi Strip, Namibia's panhandle, had long been a center of opposition. During the independence struggle South Africa stationed forces in Caprivi to fight SWAPO and received the collaboration of local peoples—a fact which hardly generated sympathy among SWAPO decision makers. As an opposition area, Caprivi was regularly shorted in the distribution of development funds. SWAPO believes that friends are rewarded, enemies deprived.

In November 2001, at age 72, President Nujoma announced that he would not be a candidate for office in 2004. He reaffirmed the position in May 2003, despite a plea from traditional chiefs (used to notions of life-time tenure in office) that he run for a fourth term. Nujoma maintained absolute control over the selection of his own successor. At SWAPO party meetings in August 2002, he made it abundantly

clear that no nominees other than his would be considered for top party jobs and successfully imposed his choices for party vice-president, secretary-general, and deputy secretary-general on the membership.

Nor would he tolerate factionalism to develop among those jockeying to become his successor. Neither of the two principal figures earlier bruited as possible successors, Prime Minister Hage Geingob or Hidipo Hamutenya, then Minister of Trade and Industry, were given top party posts. Prime Minister Geingob's political career was humiliatingly ended. He was removed from the party's politburo and demoted from the premiership to a secondary ministry, which he refused to accept. Geingob became the executive secretary of the Washington-based Global Coalition for Africa and resigned his parliamentary seat in February 2003.

In his waning years as Namibia's absolute ruler, President Nujoma resembled a lesser version of Zimbabwe's Robert Mugabe. Poorly educated (he was a shepherd and office cleaner before beginning his guerilla career), Nujoma has always admired the far better educated Mugabe and has often followed his lead, as Namibia's intervention in the Congo suggests. Like Mugabe, Nujoma raised the decibel level on the land issue.

In Namibia, whites—mainly Afrikaners and descendents of German settlers—make up only 6% of the population, but they own half the land. The government has opted for a voluntary system of land acquisition (willing buyer, willing seller), but seems frustrated with the pace of change. According to government figures, over 20 million Namibian dollars ($2.5

million) are being spent every year to buy farms for redistribution. By 2004, however, only some 124 farms had voluntarily changed hands, though redistribution to "landless peasants" may not fully describe the results. Government ministers, including Nujoma and his personally anointed nominee as SWAPO vice-president, Hifikepunye Pohamba, have purchased some of these.

Choosing SWAPO's presidential candidate was a bruising affair. President Nujoma made abundantly clear he was no lame duck, vigorously supporting his lands minister Hifikepunye Pohamba as the party's next presidential candidate. He had already secured Pohamba's election as SWAPO's vice president and simply destroyed others who might have sought the nomination. He peremptorily fired Hidipo Hamutenya, now his foreign minister, undercutting his support before SWAPO's party congress in May. Cowed before raw political power, most delegates dutifully voted for Pohamba. In the second round of balloting, he received 341 delegate votes—67%; Hamutenya received the support of a courageous 33%—167 ballots.

In the November 2004 elections, seven parties ran presidential candidates. But so overwhelming was the SWAPO juggernaut that even the most successful of Pohamba's opponents, Ben Ulenga representing the Congress of Democrats (CoD), could garner only a feeble 7.3%, less than he had received in 1999. Pohamba swept the polls with 76.4% of the vote, a testimony to SWAPO's control of the election machinery and its unwillingness to lose power. Protests were lodged and the High Court in Windhoek saw too many irregularities to approve the results. It ordered the Electoral Commission to recount the entire presidential election in ten days, but little changed. CoD, for example, was given precisely one additional vote.

In parliamentary elections SWAPO also secured 75% of the vote, winning 55 out of 72 seats in the National Assembly. The CoD became the leading opposition party with a paltry five seats, with four going to the DTA and three to the United Democratic Front; five additional seats went to other parties. SWAPO's dominance of Namibia's political institutions is unchallengeable. It will presumably use its power to speed up land redistribution, a favorite theme of President Pohamba. In March 2005 he warned that Namibia could face a "revolution" unless white farmers agreed to give up their land.

**Culture:** A small minority—some 50,000 whites—have enjoyed the wealth of Namibia, and the vast majority has been living, for the most part, in poverty, en-

# Namibia

gaging in herding livestock to support themselves. Namibia has 4,045 commercial farms—70% of them owned by whites.

According to government statistics, about 75 million acres are owned by whites and only 5.4 million by black farmers. Absentee landlords own a further 7.1 million acres. (The state itself owns 5.6 million acres of land.) The consequences of all this are obvious: The World Bank indicates that income distribution in Namibia "is one of the most unequal in the world." Indeed, the UN's *Human Development Report* for 2003 ranked Namibia as the country with the most unequal distribution of wealth in the world. (The figures are somewhat misleading since they include none of the oil-producing sheikdoms.)

HIV/AIDS has become a critical problem for Namibia. According to UNAIDS, Namibia is among the top five countries most afflicted by the virus—right up there with Botswana, Zimbabwe, Swaziland and Lesotho. The disease has spread with extraordinary speed—from an infection rate of 4% in 1992 to the present 22%. About 140,000 Namibians are living with HIV/AIDS, and in 2003 the disease accounted for more than 20% of all deaths in the country. The latest estimates indicate at least 120,000 children have already been orphaned by the disease, and life expectancy has dropped to 40.3 years (2003).

The education sector has been particularly hard hit by the epidemic. A study released by education authorities predicts that 20% of Namibia's total teaching staff of 18,000 could be lost to HIV/AIDS by 2010. At Katima Mulilo, at the far eastern end of the Caprivi Strip one in four are believed to be infected.

The budgetary implications of HIV/AIDS are significant. Government policy prohibits discrimination against anyone because he has HIV or AIDS. This has resulted in ever-increasing budgetary allocations to cover medical expenses for civil servants.

The government has targeted Namibia's gay and lesbian community for special condemnation and harassment. The minister of home affairs once urged police to "eliminate gays and lesbians from the face of Namibia," and President Nujoma has called gays and lesbians "unnatural," "ungodly," "un-African," and "idiots who should be condemned." While addressing University of Namibia students in March 2001, Nujoma asserted that Namibia allowed neither homosexuality or lesbianism. Police, he said, "are ordered to arrest you, and deport you and imprison you too." He continued by urging regional leaders to identify gays and lesbians in their communities so they could be arrested.

Nujoma freely employed his racialist and homophobic rhetoric in the 2004 presidential campaign, calling opposition leader Ben Ulenga "a coward and a homosexual without a vision who went to the white people to be taken from behind." Namibia's National Society of Human Rights reported that human rights in the country had "deteriorated dramatically" from July 2003 to July 2004, specifically citing the rise of hate speech against whites, sexual minorities, independent media, and opposition parties by the government.

**Economy:** Namibia's modern market sector produces most of its wealth; traditional subsistence agricultural sector supports most of its labor force. Principal exports are diamonds, and the Namibian economy depends greatly on Namdeb, its

**Hifikepunhye Pohamba, President**

largest mining company. Namdeb, jointly owned by the Namibian government and De Beers of South Africa, accounts for 10% of the country's GDP and 30% of its exports; it is the biggest tax payer and, apart from the government, the country's biggest employer.

Offshore diamond production in Namibia is growing at such a fast pace that marine output has already overtaken onshore production. Mining companies are flocking to Namibia's Atlantic coast to join the biggest underwater diamond rush the world has ever witnessed. An estimated three billion carats of diamonds—worth around $500 million—lie some 400 feet below the surface.

With at least a 40% unemployment rate, the government has cast about for any means of job creation in the diamond industry where technology has increasingly replaced human labor. One possibility of adding value to diamonds is cutting and polishing. DeBeers opened a polishing factory in 1999 and young Namibians

proved themselves the rivals of counterparts in traditional diamond-polishing centers like Tel Aviv, Antwerp and Johannesburg. While quality was high, cost-effectiveness was not, largely because of high labor costs reflecting strong Namibian labor unions. Polishing a diamond in Asia costs between $10 and $15; in Namibia it is almost double the cost. Worldwide, some 95% of all diamonds are polished in India. Given the economic disadvantages, DeBeers' interest in the project flagged.

This has not stopped the Leviev group, owned by the Israeli billionaire Lev Leviev, from opening Africa's largest diamond cutting factory in Namibia. Opened in 2004, the factory employs more than 200 young Namibians; 430 more are being trained in different cutting and polishing methods by some 67 overseas trainers. About a thousand diamonds a day are polished at the factory.

In parched Namibia, water is a central concern and a potential limitation on meeting the demands of economic development, urbanization, and population growth. Approximately 80% of the country consists of desert, arid and semi-arid land. Yearly rainfall averages roughly 12 inches, but ranges from less than 2 inches along the coast to more than 27 a year in the northwest and Caprivi Strip. The country's water consumption was estimated at 250 million cubic meters per year in 1990; by 2005 it is projected to increase to 400 million.

The government is constantly seeking new and alternative sources of water supply. This has meant maintaining the closest of ties with Angola and, to a lesser extent, Botswana. One of the most grandiose proposals is for a hydroelectric project on the Cunene River, shared with Angola, at Epupa. Initial estimates set the cost at $540 million, but controversy surrounding the project is enormous: a dam would eliminate a major scenic wonder—the Epupa Falls, displace more than 1,000 local inhabitants, destroy 380 square kilometers of grazing land and inundate 160 Himba graves and 95 cultural sites. Angola, which shares the river border and whose cooperation is necessary, has alternative site plans for hydroelectric development on the river.

The government, casting its ambitions more modestly, has unveiled initial plans for a smaller hydropower plant on the Okavango river. The Okavango river system originates in Angola, Namibia and Zimbabwe and terminates in the Okanvango Delta Swamps of Botswana. Lengthy discussions within the Okavango River Basin Water Commission (Okacom) will be required before any construction begins.

The government has previously laid covetously eyes on the waters of the Okavango. Following a devastating drought in 1996 the government proposed a 250-kilometre pipeline connecting the central area, especially the capital city of Windhoek, to the river. Windhoek is already one of the few capitals in the world to recycle and reuse 80% of its water. Plans to divert the Okavango waters pose a major problem: the river feeds into one of the most delicate and beautiful ecosystems in the world, the Okavango Delta, Botswana's premiere tourist attraction. Needless to say, Botswana is stiffly resistant.

Budgetary profligacy probably means there won't be enough capital for major investments such as these. The principal cause: ever-increasing spending on the state bureaucracy and its creature comforts. Described as a "high priority project" is a lavish new State House to accommodate the president. Like Louis XIV escaping the din and danger of Paris for Versailles, President Nujoma plans to construct a vast new presidential village on a mountainside south of Windhoek.

Inspired by a presidential visit to North Korea, the project includes a residence and office for the president, cabinet chambers, conference and banquet halls, and a guesthouse complex designed to accommodate six heads of state and their entourages. North Korean-built, the project has received a nearly $10 million grant from China and is expected to cost around $73 million before completion. In its 2003-2004 annual report Namibia's National Society of Human Rights criticized building the project while 600,000 Namibians were facing food shortages.

Other large building projects include an enlargement of the National Assembly chambers to accommodate joint sessions of the two houses of parliament, a new headquarters for the ministries of home affairs and labor, and a Heroes' Acre and Memorial Museum in Windhoek "to honor the fallen heroes of Namibia"—another inspiration from Nujoma's model, Robert Mugabe.

Namibia has a hugely bloated civil service—more than 77,000 workers in a country with a population of around 1.9 million people—which has expanded to accommodate the needs of the SWAPO faithful. Efforts to trim this fatty mass by funding early retirement schemes have yet to produce results. In the meantime the budget remains in deficit, and its debt stood at nearly $1.7 billion by early 2004.

**The Future:** In many ways SWAPO is still caught up in its identity as a liberation movement. It believes it legitimized itself in the independence struggle and is owed deference on that basis. The perquisites of victory, thus, are natural. Sweeping electoral majorities have produced delusions of grandeur and invincibility. Like his predecessor, President Pohamba seems to make little distinction between state and party, appointing the SWAPO Secretary-General as a Minister of State in his new cabinet.

Privilege and complacency have also provided fertile grounds for corruption. SWAPO membership has long been a means of personal advancement and, for many, becoming a politician has been seen as a way to get rich quickly. The need to maintain political solidarity means that many cases of suspected corruption have been swept under the rug.

Organized crime will also require increasing governmental effort. Namibia is a transit point between Southern Africa's most developed country, South Africa, and its least developed and most lawless one: Angola. Vehicles (automobiles and 4x4s) and consumer electronics stolen in South Africa find a ready market in Angola, paid for by illegal diamonds. In the opposite direction, cocaine is smuggled through Namibia to South Africa.

In addition to dealing with crime and corruption, the tasks facing the government are enormous. Unemployment is estimated at 40%. An estimated 25,000 school leavers enter the job market every year with few prospects of finding a job. The indirect costs of HIV/AIDS, added to the direct costs of medical care, have meant huge losses to the economy.

To meet the challenge of these problems, which require the mobilization of all available national energies, SWAPO will need to think of itself as less a liberation movement than a genuine political party, gathering and synthesizing a variety of societal demands. To hear those demands, it will have to create a more genuinely democratic environment.

Hifikepunye Pohamba has promised that his presidency would pick up where Nujoma left off. That's not an endorsement of change.

**Herero women in their finery**          Courtesy: CALTEX

# The Republic of South Africa

Modern, sophisticated Johannesburg at night

**Area**: 1,222,470 sq. km. = 472,000 sq. mi. (three times the size of California).

**Population:** 44,344,136 (July 2005 est.)

**Capital Cities**: Pretoria (now Tshwane) (administrative, pop. 1.1 million); Cape Town, (legislative, pop. 2.2 million); Bloemfontein (judicial, pop. 260,000).

**Climate:** Temperate and sunny. The eastern coastal belt is hot and humid, the western areas are dry and hot. Only high mountain peaks are covered with snow during winter.

**Neighboring Countries**: Namibia (Northwest); Botswana, Zimbabwe (North); Mozambique, Swaziland (Northeast); Lesotho is enclosed by South Africa.

**Official Languages:** 11 official languages, granted "parity of esteem" in the Constitution. They include Afrikaans, English, Ndebele, Pedi, Sotho, Swazi, Tsonga, Tswana, Venda, Xhosa, and Zulu.

**Other Principal Languages:** Fanagolo, a Zulu-based pidgin, widely used in towns and gold, diamond, coal, and copper mining areas. About 70% of the vocabulary comes from Zulu, 24% from English, 6% from Afrikaans. Also Tamil and Urdu, especially in KwaZulu-Natal.

**Ethnic groups**: Estimated 76 percent black Africans—Nguni (Zulu, Xhosa, Swazi, Ndebele), Sotho-Tswana, Venda, Tsonga-Shangaan, Khoisan; 13 percent whites—Afrikaners, British, other Europeans; 8.5 percent colored, 2.5 percent Indian.

**Principal Religions**: Christian 68% (includes most whites and Coloreds, about 60% of blacks and about 40% of Indians), Muslim 2%, Hindu 1.5% (60% of Indians), traditional and animistic 28.5%.

**Chief Commercial Products**: Gold, other minerals and metals, food, chemicals.

**GNI per capita:** $2,780 (2003)

**Currency**: Rand.

**Former Colonial Status**: Member of the British Commonwealth as the Union of South Africa (1910–1961). Previously, British authority in a colonial sense was sporadic in the Orange Free State and Transvaal.

**Independence Date**: 31 May 1910 (from UK).

**Chief of State**: Thabo Mbeki (pronounced Mm–*beh*–kee), since June 1999.

**National Flag:** From the pole, a black triangle separated by a thin gold stripe from thick green stripes which join to extend horizontally across the flag; there is a white stripe on either side of it separating the green from a field of red at the top and one of blue at the bottom.

Washed on the west by the South Atlantic and on the east by the Indian Ocean,

154

the Republic of South Africa occupies the southernmost part of the continent. This land of bright, sunny days and cool nights has a consistently uniform climate year around, with a mean annual temperature of slightly less than 60°F.

In the extreme southern Cape area, there is a period of rain between April and September, but the summer (December–May) is warm and dry. The western coast is washed by the cool Benguela Current originating in Antarctica, which produces a climate that supports a large colony of penguins on the shore line. Further inland to the north, after the interruptions of the Cedarburg, Swartberg and Louga Mountains, the land stretches forth in a vast, semi–arid region known as the Karroo Desert. This is not a true desert as encountered in the central Sahara, since the periodic light rainfall supports vegetation which provides food for many species of wildlife. Occasional sharp projections of volcanic rock stand prominently in an otherwise flat land.

The eastern coast along the warm Indian Ocean is hot and humid, supporting almost every type of wild game known to southern Africa. In modern times, this climate has fostered the growth of high intensity agriculture similar to that found in southern California. Multi–colored coral formations are prominantly displayed by the brilliant white sands of the beaches. The northwestern central territory, is a high plains land (veldt), stretching to the north from the scenic peaks of the Drakensburg Mountains. Receiving ample rainfall for the most part, its temperate climate supports rich farmland; the land also contains huge gold and diamond deposits.

The northeastern plains are lower than the high veldt to the south. Kruger National Park, on the eastern border, is visited by tourists from all over the world. Here, all game is preserved, and visitors are not permitted to get out of their autos, which proceed slowly along the road to enable their occupants to see and photograph the many species.

Actually, two–thirds of South Africa is desert, semi–desert, marginal cropland or urban. Altogether, only 12% is ideally suited for intensive cultivation.

**History:** Before the arrival of Dutch East India Company employees in 1652, South Africa was thinly populated by Bushmen and a very few pygmies. Bartholomew Diaz had reached the southern cape in 1486, six years before Columbus touched the West Indies. The rough, inhospitable appearance of the cape region attracted only free Dutch burghers, sent to grow grain and make wine to supply ships bound to and from Dutch East India possessions.

### Settlement

They were joined by French Huguenot refugee settlers at the close of the 17th century, fleeing religious persecution under Louis XIV. The two peoples gradually melded into a single society and gradually expanded in a northeast direction; cattle-raising was their principal undertaking. Because of the need for farm labor, slaves were introduced from West Africa and later from Asia. They were added to modest numbers of Hottentots working under conditions of virtual slavery. Large families were common among the pioneers, and the children born of the union of settlers and slaves became the ancestors of today's Cape Coloured population of South Africa.

As a consequence of competition between Dutch and English merchant capitalism, British interests ultimately came to dominate the Cape. Formal control was asserted in 1795 with the British initially acting under color of the authority of the exiled Dutch Prince of Orange. All pretense was abandoned in 1806 when Britain seized Cape Colony as a strategic base protecting its developing trade with India. Slave trade was abolished, creating labor shortages and setting the interests of Dutch farmers at odds with British colonial authority. British authority heralded the arrival of substantial numbers of British colonists, increasing competition for land.

The new settler farms and towns faced chronic shortages of labor since Britain had abolished the slave trade in 1807. Increasingly, Africans were enserfed to supply needed labor. When slavery was formally abolished in 1834, about 35,000 people were emancipated.

The Dutch, or Boer, farmers chafed under British authority, and to escape it, many went northeastward into what were Orange Free State and Natal. At the same time, numerous Bantu tribes from the north were occupying the area. Conflicts with the settlers were inevitable as white settlers became more numerous. Their numbers grew substantially during the period of the Great Trek which pushed north and east of the Orange River in 1835–42.

### Anglo-Boer Disputes

The Boers, Dutch-descended people, having migrated to escape British authority, preferred to live in isolated communities where their independence could thrive. Inevitably, they would come in conflict with the British. Over a period of years, various forms of government were tried by the British, the success of which

**Trekkers' Monument, Pretoria**

# South Africa

In Kruger National Park

was directly related to their ability to leave the Boers alone. Self-government was tried in Natal, Transvaal and the Orange Free State. Discovery of immense sources of wealth in diamonds (1867) and gold (1886) however, brought in hordes of fortune-seekers. The Boers actively disliked the new people, calling them outlanders, but the processes of transformation had begun; Boer isolation could no longer be maintained.

Towns sprang up virtually overnight as a result of the new mineral wealth. Johannesburg, laid out in 1886, soon had a population of more than 100,000, about half of whom were black. The Boer republics (Orange Free State and Transvaal) became linked to the world economy through their supply of precious minerals. Cecil Rhodes consolidated the diamond industry under a single producer—De Beers Consolidated Mines—in 1889, and became Prime Minister of Cape Colony in 1890.

President Paul Kruger, the Boer leader of Transvaal, correctly concluded that Rhodes was financing an anti-Boer movement among the outlanders. The first tangible act was the aborted raid (1895) led by Rhodes' lieutenant, Leander Starr Jameson, allegedly in support of an outlander uprising. In the fall out, Rhodes was ousted as prime minister and relations between the British and the Boers soured even more.

A minor dispute over voting rights of immigrants was the pretext for the Boer War of 1899–1902, but the area had become too valuable—following the discovery of gold in the Transvaal Highveld—to escape the ambit of British imperial control. By the end of the conflict the British

were hopelessly mired down. They had to build concentration camps for Boer women and children, some 25,000 of whom died of disease and neglect. (14,000 Africans died in separate camps.) Some 500,000 British troops were required to barely "win" over about 87,000 Boers, who knew the territory better and became effective guerrilla fighters. Although often thought of as a "white man's war," both sides employed Africans—at least 10,000 of them fought for the British. With both sides weary and weakened, Republican forces sued for peace. The signing of the Treaty of Vereeniging on 31 May 1902, recognized their military defeat: the Boers became British subjects. Left unresolved was the question of citizenship for Africans in post-conflict South Africa.

## The Union of South Africa

Principally in response to the pleas of General Jan Christiaan Smuts (Boer commander-in-chief of the Republican forces in the Cape Colony during the final months of the war), the British established the Union of South Africa in 1910, thereby granting self-government in Transvaal and Orange Free State. The constitution bound together the two former Boer republics with the British Cape Colony and Natal. An administrative capital was established at Pretoria (Transvaal), a legislative capital at Cape Town (Cape Colony) and a judicial seat at Bloemfontein (Orange Free State), an arrangement that still prevails.

At the same time, General Louis Botha and James Hertzog founded the South African Party. It was moderate, encompassing both English and Afrikaans speakers, stressing the equality of both, and pressing for independent status within the British Empire. Within a short time, however, Hertzog and the rural, conservative Boers split off to form the Nationalist Party (1914).

The Native Land Act was passed in 1913 that limited the areas in which Africans could own or occupy; it resulted (along with the land act of 1936) in 87% of the land being put under the control of South Africa's white minority. It also restricted the movement of Asians. Controversy over these restrictions led to the creation of the Native National Congress—the precursor of the African National Congress—and a civil rights campaign among the Indian population, then led by the young lawyer, Mohandas K. (Mahatma) Gandhi. The Native Land Act of 1913 was the beginning of legal separation of the races—apartheid—which would be more fully enacted into law after World War II.

## World Wars and the Interwar Period

South Africa joined in World War I, fighting the Germans in their African possessions (German S.W. Africa, German East Africa, now Namibia and Tanzania). Hertzog appeared at the Paris peace conference at the close of the conflict to demand independence for South Africa, but was ignored. Because no other logical power was in the region, South Africa was given a League of Nations mandate to control the former German colony of South West Africa in 1919. (This continued without interruption until 1990.) The British ultimately recognized the Union of South Africa as an independent nation within the British Commonwealth in 1931.

Until 1934 the government was controlled by either or both the South African Party (Smuts) and the Nationalist Party (Hertzog). When the two merged, adopting the name United South African Nationalist Party, conservative members of Hertzog's National party withdrew and maintained the old party name under the leadership of Daniel F. Malan. Since the turn of the century, anti-black sentiments had been slowly crystallizing; they would be exploited by Malan's National Party.

South Africa declared war on the Axis Powers of World War II, but its participation was minimal because of its distant location from the fighting. Further, there was a sizable Boer element in parliament which had no use for liberal English-speakers. During the opening years of World War II, this group expressed little regret at a possible defeat of England by Germany.

The end of the conflict was the end of the Hertzog-Smuts coalition which had been in power since 1934. As 1948 elections approached, the National Party, then led by Daniel F. Malan, campaigned on an openly racist platform, advocating that white South Africans insure their moral and financial future by enacting into law apartheid, the Dutch Boer word for "separate" (pronounced A-par-tate).

## Apartheid

Prime Minister Malan and the National Party wasted no time in their efforts to deliver the promises made during the 1948 campaign. Four major acts created the basic structure of apartheid. Within a year citizenship and other important rights for black Africans were curtailed or eliminated.

Perhaps the most fundamental law calculated to transform the country was the Group Areas Act of 1950 which placed race classification at the center of South African policy. Combined with earlier land acts, it strictly limited the areas in which a person was allowed to live based on race. Under the act's provisions an estimated 3.5 million black people were removed from lands they occupied.

The Group Areas Act essentially denied blacks any possibility of ownership based on their occupation of land. Thus, if a given tract was within a "white only" area, all that was necessary to oust a black person was proof that he wasn't white and therefore it was illegal for him to occupy the tract by living on it.

The Population Registration Act classified everyone living in South Africa by race at the time of their birth: black, white, Asiatic, Coloured, or other. This determination controlled almost every aspect of a person's future—where he lived, worked, went to school, wages, voting (if any), property ownership, etc., and became a foundation for the laws requiring that everyone have a passbook. In many cases, it was illegal for a person to simply be in a given area.

The Internal Security Act of 1982 granted virtual dictatorial powers to the government and abolished any semblance of civil rights which remained. It provided for the banning of organizations opposed to the state, made it illegal for individuals to belong to them, imposed involuntary censorship on the press, allowed detention without trial of persons suspected of terrorism, and imprisonment of anyone for 10 days without any charges.

To enforce apartheid laws, the police developed an intensive system of espionage—informants and control calculated to strike fear into the hearts of all. The use of informants was widespread, enabling police to arrest would-be criminals before their crime could even be attempted. Prison facilities were designed to further the ends of justice under apartheid. If the degree of proof of the guilt of an individual was dubious or flawed, he or she

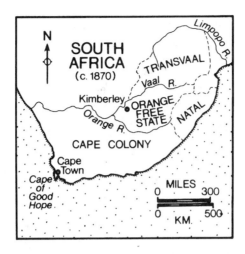

might well die in prison awaiting trial. "Slipped on the soap while taking a shower" . . . "fell downstairs" . . . "was assaulted" . . . "died while trying to escape" were all heard with frequency in South Africa if, indeed, anything was heard at all.

Before the days of compulsory censorship, newspapers were guided by the principles of "voluntary" censorship. At its most fundamental level, this simply meant that anything embarrassing to the state should not be published. If a newspaper violated this imperative too seriously or too often (elusive quantities), paper supplies, bank credit and often telephone service evaporated. Worst of all, no official at whom a finger could be pointed ever did anything illegal. Things just happened.

The Publication Bill unashamedly was directed at reporting of black activities in the press. It demanded that the media exercise "due care and responsibility concerning matters which can have the effect of stirring up feelings of hostility between different racial, ethnic, religious or cultural groups" in South Africa. True to the form of Boer religious conservatism, it professed to "avoid the spirit of permissiveness and moral decay sweeping the world and communications media in the country."

## The African National Congress

The African National Congress was initially formed in response to the Land Act of 1913. Passage of the act resulted in the expulsion of some people without adequate compensation from lands they and their ancestors had occupied for generations. The organization had little mass appeal prior to 1948 because of limited political awareness and limited economic strength. The group's leadership was generally conservative, hoping to deal with the white-dominated government in seeking redress for land seizures. After 1948,

with the advent of apartheid it became a militant force, openly sympathetic with communist thinking, and determined to oust the white minority from power and seize the economic wealth of the nation in the name of black power.

In the immediate post-war period, communist rhetoric and action terrified South Africa's government. It outlawed the South African Communist Party (SACP) in 1950 and ANC, under the leadership of Nelson Mandela, responded with a campaign of civil disobedience. Repression intensified, and in 1960 nearly seventy black demonstrators were killed in Sharpeville. (Another 180 Africans were wounded, most of whom were shot in the back as they were running away.) The ANC was promptly banned; in response, its military wing, Umkhonto we Sizwe (Spear of the Nation: MK), launched a sabotage campaign in 1961. Warrants were issued for the fugitive leadership of both the SACP and ANC in 1962.

After a year and a half as fugitive, Nelson Mandela was tried in 1964 (the Rivonia trial) and found guilty. The sentence: life imprisonment without possibility of parole. Mandela was sent to Robben Island prison, noted for its harsh conditions. The leadership not arrested remained underground, taking refuge in neighboring and nearby nations such as Zambia (the location of its headquarters), Mozambique, Tanzania and Botswana. From these exile posts they directed the affairs of the ANC.

During the 25 years after Mandela's trial the ANC grew steadily as the rigid racial separation and denial became far more onerous. (During the 1970s more

**General Jan Christiaan Smuts**

# South Africa

than three million people were forcibly re-settled in black "homelands.") Ironically, the ANC helped to found the Inkatha Freedom Party of the Zulus in 1974, feeling that the anti-apartheid movement ought to have some lawful presence in South Africa.

## ANC Lobbying in the U.S.

The ANC took its cause to the United States, enlisting the aid of the Congressional Black Caucus. Embargoes on trade with South Africa were also demanded, and, most importantly, economic sanctions against South Africa were aggressively pursued.

The sanctions enacted in September 1986 included (1) a ban on all investments and loans in South Africa, (2) a ban in the import of iron, steel and agricultural products as well as uranium, coal and textiles, (3) termination of South African airlines landing rights in the U.S., (4) exclusion of all South African bank deposits in the U.S., (5) a continued ban on the export of U.S. oil, arms or equipment connected with nuclear power, (6) approval of $40 million in aid to disadvantaged South Africans (technically, regardless of race) and finally a "request" that the ANC end its ties to the South African Communist Party, suspend its terrorist activity, and commit itself to a free and democratic future.

## Urban Overcrowding and Resulting Unrest

During the 1960s and onward, there was a continual influx into black town-ships which were located on the edge of every major and smaller city of South Africa; this was caused by starkly primitive conditions prevailing in rural areas and an influx of immigrants from surrounding African nations. South Africa tried to limit expansion of these urban slums by adopting an identity card (pass book) system intended to protect employed workers around the cities from competition by illegal immigrants. (These pass laws were not repealed until 1986.)

To take the population pressure off black townships, the government established African Bantustans (or "homelands") with the Promotion of Bantu Self-Government Act in 1959. The act originally created eight (later ten) separate black tribal and geographical units. (Bantustan affairs were run from Pretoria by the Bantu Administration and Development Department, known by its acronym, BAD.) The Bantustan lands were overcrowded and overgrazed. Industry and employment were next to non-existent; health and education were starved of resources. Indeed, the Bantustans were meant to reduce the government's burden to provide decent housing and services to its black "citizens" and neutralize black political power. Technically, all township residents were required to vote in the homeland from which they or their ancestors had come, or to which they had been assigned.

## Soweto

In 1953 the government had ordered that instruction in all high schools be 50% in Afrikaans and 50% in English, but not in the native language of the pupils—used during the first six years of a young person's schooling. This was to become a flashpoint between the apartheid regime and black students in Soweto in 1976.

Soweto, outside of the large city of Johannesburg, was one of the early black townships. It had a great many four-room houses built by the government, and on the surface appeared reasonably presentable. In reality, only about 15% of them had inside running water and toilet facilities. The great majority of the homes had 6 to 8 people crowded in very limited space with no heat.

As early as 1960 (Sharpeville) black citizens had demonstrated a capability and willingness to use firearms against the white police (which had, it should be noted, a substantial number of black officers also). The disturbance which is most widely remembered occurred in Soweto in mid-1976, and arose out of the 1953 language agreement.

That agreement had established a 50-50 use of English and Afrikaans in high school instruction, but this had gradually been ignored in favor of English only. This was eminently sensible—Afrikaans was and is a parochial language compared to English. This was, however, unacceptable to Boer nationalists. Boer members of the parliament, led by the arch-conservative, Dr. Andries Treurnicht, insisted on 50% Afrikaans in high school classrooms.

Soweto teachers spread the word of the new policy enforcement. Protests began

Durban Port

on 16 June and within hours a disturbance turned into a riot that lasted until the 24th; before it was over, 174 blacks (and two whites) were killed. There were 1,222 black casualties, contrasting sharply with 6 whites wounded. The riot was suppressed with excessive force, and President Pieter Botha retracted the demand that Afrikaans be used as a language of instruction.

The reaction to the Soweto riot was probably ill-advised, but the powerless have few weapons to express their anger: the decision was made to boycott schools. The slogan "liberation before education" became a watchword, but it proved to be costly. As black majority rule approached in 1994, it became evident that 18 years of school boycotts had left South Africa a generation of young illiterates.

### Black Homelands

A "solution" to racial problems for the government was adopted under President Vorster in the form of a Bantu Homelands Citizenship Act (1970). The Act made every black South African, irrespective of actual residence, a citizen of one of ten homelands, each designated for specific ethnic groups. As such, they were classified as "foreigners" and excluded from the South African body politic. Between 1960 and 1985 some 3.5 million blacks were forcibly evicted from their land under the homeland system.

Each homeland was granted internal self-government and when a homeland requested independence, it was to be granted. The first to take the plunge was the Xhosa area in southeast South Africa, Transkei, with about 3 million inhabitants (1976). The next occurred the following year when Bophuthatswana ("homeland of the Tswanas"), a nation in six separated areas with 2.1 million people, was granted self-rule; most of its parts lay to the north, bordering Botswana. Venda, with almost a half million, became independent in 1979 and Ciskei in 1981. No nation in the world recognized these creations as "independent."

The Black Homelands solution addressed only a portion of South Africa's social and economic impasse. More than 14 million black people lived in townships adjacent to the largest cities and industrial areas of South Africa; even the government classified them as "detribalized." But to express themselves politically, they were required to vote in the homeland to which they had been assigned (which had no role or vote in the government of South Africa) whether or not they had ever been physically present. The system of identity cards was used, in part, to determine who could live outside his or her "homeland."

**Rocktail Bay, Indian Ocean Northern Kwazulu-Natal**          Photo by Judi Iranyi

### Attempted Reforms

President Pieter Botha, as early as 1980, saw the need for additional reform and embarked on a wide-ranging series of measures that would have revolutionized the system of apartheid. He proposed elimination of the Group Areas Act, the Slums Act and the Community Development Act; the names sounded innocent, but the laws were essential tools of apartheid. Conservatives in the National Party, led by the intractable Andries Treurnicht, resisted any reform whatsoever. They persuaded the president to embark on a "new" approach that ultimately led to violence and change in South Africa.

The plan was an attempt to placate both international opinion and internal resistance by blacks to white rule. It was supposed to be the answer to the exclusion of blacks from any participation in government. Sometime in the mid-1970s a new constitutional scheme was concocted.

### A Three-House National Assembly ... (With No Blacks)

To appear to be as democratic as possible, the new constitution created a three-house National Assembly, with a large body restricted to white membership, and two smaller units to represent Coloureds and Indians, but no blacks. The latter were to be given control of the townships in which they were a majority.

In this way, the government felt, black leadership could be used to contain increasing unrest in the townships and, at the same time, satisfy the hunger for self-rule. The Boer leadership actually con-

vinced themselves that something was being given to the blacks of South Africa. The ANC correctly saw it as no more than just another chapter in the book of apartheid.

The new National Assembly had a 185-seat white parliament, a 92-seat one for Coloureds and a third for Asians (46 seats). The smaller houses had no powers except with respect to matters of concern to the minority they represented. The larger white parliament could veto any act of the other two. This three-tiered system of parliament, coupled with black "home rule" proved to be white South Africa's most costly and serious mistake, for it was instrumental in the downfall of white-controlled government.

The plan itself was unworkable, and quickly gave way to a government by oligarchy: the Presidential Council of about 60 members proposed all laws and the parliament became a rubber stamp. Even worse was black reaction: instead of seeing a half full glass, they saw only a half empty one. A fundamental decision was made in response to the measure—make South Africa ungovernable!

The ANC devised a two-pronged agenda to accomplish its aim of seizing control of South Africa (it did not envision doing its will through the ballot box until the early 1990s). First, using violence as a tool against non-Zulu black South Africans, an effort was made to coerce all persons, particularly within the townships, to become members of ANC or sympathizers with the cause it espoused. This was accomplished by making it danger-

# South Africa

ous not to fall within one of the two categories. Second, the ANC leadership recognized that Inkatha, led by Mangosuthu Gatsha Buthelezi, was a potential rival that had to be eliminated or at least controlled in the struggle for power that was to come. Both of these programs unleashed terrible violence, but the police were virtually helpless to deal with it because of its sheer magnitude.

The ANC ordered a boycott of all township elections. Those who participated, and assumed office in township governments, were dreadfully treated. They were regarded as subservient Uncle Toms, cooperating with the despised white-controlled government. They, and anyone cooperating with them, became acceptable targets of ANC and MK violence. The most grisly of deaths was from "necklacing"—having a tire filled with gasoline placed around one's neck and set light with a match. After violence rose to the level hoped for, the ANC and its sympathizers began to use the turmoil as justification for disinvestment and sanction programs against South Africa by foreign businesses.

In the decade 1984–1994, over 20,000 blacks were killed in South Africa, about half of them (11,000) were murdered after 1990 when Nelson Mandela was released from prison by the government. Of the total, about 1,500 were killed by South African Defense Forces. Ninety-four per cent of the horrific township violence was murder of blacks by blacks. The commission which developed those figures also concluded that of the black on black homicides, those killed were about 85% ANC members or supporters, or lived in ANC-controlled areas.

## Inkatha Freedom Party and Chief Buthelezi

By the early 1970s the ANC had been all but eliminated as an imminent threat by the white-controlled government of South Africa, and the organization was demoralized. The system of spies and informants which was developed by the South African Defense Forces made it dangerous to belong to the underground organization or to be a communist comrade-in-arms. In order to try to maintain some form of legal pressure against apartheid, the ANC leadership recognized the need to have a Zulu-based organization to bring pressure on the white government.

The Zulus live primarily in Natal province, and have traditionally never been friendly with the Xhosas, who are the core of the ANC, together with the Sothos and Tswanas. Thus, although they had no particular affinity for potential rivals, it was a matter of practicality for the ANC to encourage and assist the founding of the

Inkatha Freedom Party (IFP) in 1974. Its leader was and is Chief Mangosuthu Gatsha Buthelezi (Man-go-soo-too Gat-sha Boo-teh-lay-zee), a moderate leader, known for his ability to communicate with the white leadership, in spite of Inkatha's staunch opposition to apartheid.

Buthelezi believed that change in South Africa was possible, but also believed that if changes occurred in such a manner as to impoverish the country, they would be worthless. His attitudes largely reflected the lifestyles of most of the members of Inkatha, as well as most Zulu non-members.

Xhosas and Sothos tended to cluster with their families in shantytowns around large industrial and mining centers of South Africa, where children were raised in poverty and hardship. The Zulus, on the other hand, were the chief clientele of hostels—shelters for male workers with a minimum of comfort and convenience—where they lived for usually 27 out of 30 days. On days off, they went back home (where they had been sending their wages after expenses) to their wives and children. Living in this manner, their needs were minimal, their wages were comparatively high, and family tensions and quarrels were usually low level—since they didn't have time to escalate. Of equal importance, wives and children weren't exposed to the crime, violence, and deprivations of the townships.

In reaction to ANC efforts to destabilize South Africa with violence, National Party leadership sought and obtained an informal alliance with Inkatha to help combat rising violence. There is a substantial body of evidence that the Zulus were armed and trained by members of the South African Defense Force and the armed

forces. As this became evident to the MK leadership, efforts against Zulus were redoubled.

Among Zulu customs, the carrying of traditional weapons is important. They are uniquely associated with the passage from boyhood to manhood. Though not carried at all times, their presence certainly marks the bearer as a Zulu. For reasons that are not clear, an obscure South African judge in 1989 ruled that they were dangerous weapons in the eyes of the law, and therefore could not be carried in public. The government agreed, and told the Zulus they could not carry spears and axes as they had in the past. (When resorting to violence—usually considered by them to be defensive—Zulus used modern weaponry.)

Chief Buthelezi and his followers were shocked at the decision. He and Goodwill Zwelethini, King of the Zulus, denounced the measure in no uncertain terms. Together with conservative white South Africans, the chief began to speak with regularity of a black state seceding from South Africa under his leadership. A system of strong federalism was favored, creating the equivalent of states' rights. This attracted favorable interest among many white conservatives, who wanted to establish a "white homeland" in the event of a black-dominated government in South Africa.

## Exit President Botha, Enter President de Klerk

With the townships in revolt and South Africa in a state of emergency, Nelson Mandela wrote to then President Pieter W. Botha in 1988, urgently stating the two should confer about matters vital to the future of the nation. Although it was not

**Part of a large photomontage celebrating the development of freedom in South Africa**

Photo by Cezar Ornatowski

**South African Vineyards**

Photo by Christine Farrington

publicized, the conservative president met with Mandela.

President Botha suffered a stroke in January 1989, but after a brief recuperation, he announced in March that he would resume his duties as president. There was immediate opposition from the party leadership, which nominated Frederik W. de Klerk to run in September elections. Three weeks before the elections, an angry and frustrated Botha made a television broadcast denouncing de Klerk, the ANC and anyone else he thought to be hostile, and resigned his presidency.

### Nelson Mandela

Nelson Mandela, was born in Umtata (later within the homeland of Transkei) in 1918. When the ANC was banned in 1962, he went underground. Apprehended, he was charged under the anti-communist and anti-terrorism laws and was sentenced to life imprisonment without hope of parole. While in prison, he kept abreast of current matters in South Africa, including the turn to violence and terrorism that characterized the period of 1984–1989.

It was not until F.W. de Klerk became president in 1989, and had a chance to solidify his power base, that further contact was established between the government and Mandela. This ultimately led to his release from prison, along with Walter Sisulu and other ANC activists. President de Klerk had correctly concluded that continued detention of Mandela would be counter-productive—and that his chances for meaningful negotiations had greater probability if they were conducted with the older generation of ANC leaders. A reform program to dismantle apartheid was begun.

In February 1990 de Klerk ordered the release of Nelson Mandela, whose name by that time had become legendary. A peace accord was signed with the ANC and the state of emergency lifted. There was dancing and widespread celebrating in the townships. Mandela was almost immediately made Deputy President of the ANC, effectively transformed overnight from prisoner to head of the organization from which he had been removed almost 27 years previously. He walked a tight

wire astutely, keeping his base of followers mobilized, while negotiating with President de Klerk, traveling abroad in search of desperately needed funding, and acknowledging that the anti-apartheid rival, Inkatha, had to be given some sort of recognition. A year later, in 1991, international sanctions against South Africa were lifted, and the remaining apartheid laws repealed.

Mandela's conduct, viewed as too concessionary, infuriated the more radical members of the ANC who had been brought up on visions of black power, confrontation, and seizure of the state by bloody revolution. Some of his early statements played to that audience, but shocked white South Africans: "We have waited too long for our freedom. We can no longer wait. Now is the time to intensify the struggle on all fronts. To relax our efforts now would be a mistake which generations to come will not be able to forgive."

In the same speech, as if to confirm the worst fears of white South Africans, he insisted upon nationalization of South Afri-

# South Africa

can industries, in particular, the immense Anglo-American Mining Company—a multi-national consortium with worldwide interests as well as its diamond and gold mines in South Africa. In 1992, when he concluded that his advocacy of sanctions and disinvestment was the wrong policy, Mandela found that trying to turn away from these policies in order to attract investment to South Africa was far harder than he had imagined. His earlier position had laid the foundation for an atmosphere of suspicion and distrust.

Many had expected Mandela to be a dedicated, violent revolutionary, gripped by the misjudgments of an uninformed old age. He showed great astuteness and flexibility, increasingly committed to racial reconciliation. It is clear he understood the difference between a revolutionary movement and a political party charged with governing a country. It also became clear in all he did that he understood the necessities of politics in a South Africa about to change. Development of the country and improvement in the lives of its citizens would require, above all, the political stability that would give confidence and assurance to investors on whom that development largely depended.

The pressures under which Mandela survived were tremendous. He had to risk the disfavor of the militant wing of the ANC, conditioned by years of a struggle mentality and ideologically shaped by economic thinking which exulted the role of a highly centralized state. The tensions between Mandela's perceived need for moderation as a governing party, and the militants' more radical claims were constant and trying. In the case of his wife Winnie Mandela, they were even personal. After many months of pondering what to do about her, he finally opted to part ways, separating himself from a figure romanticized by some of the most youthful and radical elements of the party as "Mother of the Nation."

## Winnie Mandela

As an ANC activist, Winnie Mandela had been internally exiled for years. Violating her exile in 1986, she worked her way to Soweto, a black township outside of Johannesburg. A luxurious home, complete with swimming pool, had been built for her amid the two-room tarpaper and tin shanties of the town. There was a minor uproar of protest, so she did not immediately move in.

When she did, she formed "The Winnie Mandela Soccer Team," a gang of young thugs which proceeded to terrorize Soweto and other nearby black townships. Trials of real and imagined offenders took place in her home, where she often "presided." Sentences of beating and

death were meted out. A memorable incident occurred in 1988 when a 13-year-old boy was kidnapped from a Soweto Methodist Church shelter by the "team" and taken to Mandela's house. He was accused of being a police informer and was beaten severely, with Mandela herself reportedly taking part. Taken to a nearby field by the "team," he was murdered.

Acting through his lawyer from prison, Nelson Mandela ordered her to release three other kidnapped youths and to disband the "team." She was ousted from the ANC, losing her informal title "Mother of the Nation." A trial was held, interrupted by radical members of the ANC who threatened and actually kidnapped co-defendants and state witnesses, removing them from the country. After listening to her testimony the judge (there was no jury trial in South Africa) called her a "calm, composed, deliberate and unblushing liar." She was sentenced to six years in jail; an appeals court sustained the conviction in early June 1993 but, in a political decision, vacated the prison sentence.

Her trial was held after Nelson Mandela's release from prison; neither he nor the ANC leadership rallied to Winnie's defense. She was rebuffed in an effort to rejoin the ANC leadership by becoming president of the Women's Auxiliary. While her husband was trying to engage in meaningful negotiations with the white government, Winnie appealed to the militant sector of the ANC; they remembered her for her famous 1987 statement: "With

our matchboxes and our necklaces, we shall liberate!"

Under pressure from senior ANC officials, Mandela divorced his wife in early 1996. The reason: foreign investment was discouraged by her presence in any position of power. Ex-President Mandela now enjoys the company of his new wife, the widow of Samora Machel of Mozambique.

By April 2003 the political climate had changed to such a degree that a South African court could find Madikizela-Mandela guilty of 43 charges of fraud and 25 of bank theft and sentence her to jail. "The state's evidence is overwhelming," said the judge as he found her guilty of obtaining bank loans worth more than $120,000 in the name of bogus employees of the ANC Women's League, of which she was president. She was sentenced to five years in jail, but will serve a minimum of eight months there, the rest being completed in community service. Madikizela-Mandela resigned her parliamentary seat and positions in the ANC. The party did not place her on its list of candidates for the 2004 elections.

## The Repeal of Apartheid

President de Klerk and the National Party wasted no time in 1990–91 to repeal apartheid laws in South Africa. Black Africans were free to move about their country. One downside was an upsurge of crime. At night there was almost no one on the streets of the formerly bustling city

**Soweto Township** Photo by Judi Iranyi

of Johannesburg. Luxury hotels closed, re-opening several months later at bargain prices to attract customers. Fences and walls around homes in white suburbs grew higher. Prison bars at the windows, together with elaborate security systems became the order of the day. Purse snatch-ing and petty thievery were common. In rural areas and small towns it was no better:

Morale of the South African Defense Force and local police organizations de-scended to an all-time low. Turnover in personnel was high, resulting in a train-ing period of only six weeks. Recruits had to be constantly reminded they were a "le-gal" target for just about any gun-toting person, criminal or otherwise, who bore a grudge against the police in general or simply wanted to escape criminal respon-sibility for an act.

## Constitutional Negotiations

In 1991 the various competing elements in South Africa began meeting informally and later in conferences of CODESA—Congress for a Democratic South Africa. Prior to negotiations, several apartheid laws had been repealed and political ex-iles (often common criminals) numbering 50,000 were amnestied to return to South Africa. The talks were periodically in-terrupted by rising tides of violence, particularly between ANC and Inkatha supporters. Political sniping from the con-servatives led de Klerk to have a national referendum on his policies. His efforts were supported by 70% of whites, who thus for the first time voted to share power peacefully with the black majority.

The discussions were delicate, at times awkward. The ANC had to exercise cau-tion, because blacks distrusted the idea that whites would genuinely negotiate away their control of South Africa. Out-side the conference room, Mandela was careful to level gross insults at de Klerk calculated to reassure his own supporters that he wasn't giving in to white pres-sures. Inside the room, consensus was reached: (1) an interim government had to be elected to draw a permanent constitu-tion and to govern, and it (2) would have to provide minority (i.e. white) protection. Black power without limit was quietly discarded by the ANC senior leadership (but not its membership).

## A New Constitution

Agreement on the interim constitution was signed on November 17, 1993, the re-sult of months of painstaking negotia-tions. The substance of the document was a fundamental victory for the ANC. A transitional government of National Unity (GNU) was established to prepare for na-tional elections by universal suffrage.

The constitution provided for elections and specified that the 400-member Na-tional Assembly would not represent any specific constituency. They were to be cho-sen from lists prepared by each national party. The number of seats for each party would be based on the party's percentage of the total (national) vote. A Senate of 90 members would consist of 10 members se-lected by each of the nine states into which South Africa was to be divided. In effect this placed all power in the hands of the national parties.

After the constitution's adoption, plans proceeded for elections on April 26, 1994. The ANC, in anticipation of the elections, had started a registration drive the previ-ous March (1993). Thorny questions re-mained to be settled—who was a voter, what were the requirements or lack thereof, where and how would he or she vote?

## A Last Minute Accord

Because of increased political violence and apprehension over the imminent elections, President de Klerk declared a state of emergency in KwaZulu-Natal on March 31, 1994, which infuriated Chief Buthelezi and made him even more adamant. He demanded the constitution be amended to secure the position of King Goodwill Zwelithini and the historic Zulu kingdom. On April 5, 15,000 Zulus armed with spears and clubs marched through the town of Empangeni; the SADF forces considered them too danger-ous to disarm.

The election commission said balloting in KwaZulu would have to be postponed. Mandela rejected this, and international mediators, including Henry Kissinger from the U.S., finally secured a break-through on April 19th after two days of talks. The Zulus would, after all, partici-pate in the balloting, abandoning de-mands for amendment of the constitution. But there were guarantees as to the con-tinued status of the monarchy and the kingdom of KwaZulu-Natal.

The real nature of the settlement was not apparent until almost a month after the elections. More than a million acres of KwaZulu-Natal land was promised to Zwelithini. Buthelezi (jobless after the elections) would become Minister of Home Affairs in the expected new gov-ernment lead by Mandela.

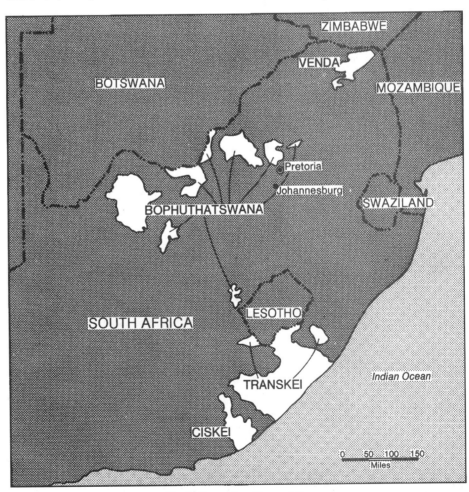

Black "homeland" republics

# South Africa

**President Thabo Mbeki**

## The Elections

Elaborate and painstaking preparations were made for the first popular balloting including all races in South Africa. The problem of illiteracy was immense—50%—so it was decided that the pictures of the leaders of each party would be listed above that choice on the ballot. Overcoming well-grounded fears, and waiting in line for hours on end, more than 70% of those registered voted.

## Other Political Parties and Groups

Other groups participating in the election included the Freedom Front (FF)—formed in March 1994. The Freedom Front was headed by former defense chief General Constand Viljoen whose less than right-wing approach appealed to many conservatives.

White conservatives formerly belonged exclusively to the Conservative Party (CP). Its principal objective was the creation of an all-white state by the interim constitution, a proposition that was never taken seriously. It refused to register as a political party for the elections.

The Democratic Party (DP) was the successor of two liberal parties popular among English speakers which opposed apartheid. It was headed by Tony Leon.

The Pan Africanist Congress (PAC) and its militant wing, the Azanian Peoples Army, was a radical black party which adopted a slogan "one settler [a white], one bullet."

The results, awaited with great suspense, were predicted before announced. The ANC demonstrated nationwide ap-

peal and secured a majority of Assembly seats. The National Party and the Inkatha Freedom Party found their support more localized in Western Cape Province and KwaZulu-Natal. The National Party did well among Coloured and Asiatic Indian voters. The Freedom Front did well in areas dominated by rural whites.

## The ANC in Power

Once in power the ANC demonstrated the balancing of ideology and practicality required by the responsibility of governance. Its initial budget envisioned a million new housing units and a million new jobs over a five-year period, without the necessity of new taxes.

The Restitution of Land Rights Act, a very controversial measure, was adopted in late 1994 and established a Land Claims Commission and a Land Claims Court. The act directs "balancing the desirability of remedying past human rights violations against . . . the need to avoid major social disruption."

South Africa's arms industry, condemned by liberals, was recognized as the moneymaker it was, and maintained. As a concession to liberal critics, arms exports would be limited, said the government, to nations using the arms for legitimate purposes and not for human rights violations. Since no known purchase order had ever been submitted with this as a justification for purchase, one was left to wonder how it would be implemented.

To the chagrin of those who preferred a state-controlled economy, foreign investment was encouraged and the government announced plans for a significant

**Chief Mangosuthu Buthelezi**

privatization of state-owned companies. The two policies were interrelated, for privatization was seen as a means of assuring the international business community that the state was moving towards a more liberal economy.

So great was President Mandela's moral authority that he could successfully say "No" to the more outrageous demands from various sectors of the liberation struggle. When the leader of former guerrilla forces threatened to return to armed struggle over problems arising from the integration of these forces into the South African army, Mandela warned against a "suicidal plot."

## Social Discontent

Tensions ran high among South Africa's black population. During the election campaign they were promised far, far more than could be realistically delivered. As the months wore on after the contest, their lives changed little. Symptoms of this malaise included a high crime rate, near-anarchy, corruption, squatting on land, moving into nearby homes after ousting the occupants, and illegal strikes.

All of this was strongly condemned by President Nelson Mandela in his February 1995 speech opening parliament. He criticized what he termed "a culture of entitlement," and accused blacks who "misread freedom to mean license." He condemned those guilty of murder of police officers, taking hostages, riots, looting and other crimes.

The Constitutional Commission completed its work in May 1996. One notable provision paves the way for the purchase and transfer of land back to black Africans. It calls, however, for market-based compensation, which the government cannot afford. The Senate was changed to a Provincial Council of premiers of the nine provinces and others chosen provincially. The South African constitution has a Bill of Rights that is far more liberal than that of the U.S., but essentially continues the structure of government without change—maintaining a strong central authority, with the powers of provinces and smaller areas being strictly limited.

## From Transition to Transformation

The ANC party congress chose Thabo Mbeki as party President in December 1997. President Mandela increasingly relinquished governmental affairs to Mbeki in preparation for the 1999 presidential elections.

Thabo Mbeki had long been groomed for leadership. Son of one of the principal ANC leaders, Govan Mbeki, Thabo was early marked for leadership by his father and his father's friend and colleague, Nelson Mandela. He left South Africa in 1962 for England where he studied economics at Sussex University; his Master's thesis was on small businesses in Ghana and Nigeria. Like his father Mbeki was a member of the Communist Party and in 1970 he went to Russia for military training. On his return to South Africa in 1990 he pragmatically resigned from the party.

Mbeki's brief biography captures the ambiguity of the man. Steeped in Marxism, he is also trained in Western economics. Nurtured in the idealism of a revolutionary movement and well-versed in its Stalinist organizational style, he is practical and pragmatic. The breadth of his intellectual background would be needed to hold together his coalition partners and to get a handle on a legacy of problems created by apartheid.

Mbeki's accession to power marked a change in tone and language in the ANC's relationship with South Africa's white minority. The shift was signaled by Nelson Mandela's valedictory speech to the 1997 ANC party conference. In this speech, reportedly prepared by Mbeki, President Mandela departed from the soothing rhetoric of multiracialism that had eased the transition to majority rule. Whites had "demonstrated consistently" a desire to cling to the privileges they enjoyed under apartheid, he said. Some were accused of being involved in a "counter-revolutionary conspiracy." It was vintage Marxist rhetoric, stylistically out of character, highly controversial, and an affront to those white South Africans who had long opposed apartheid.

**Clifton Beaches near Cape Town**            Photo by Rita Arendt

**King Goodwill Zwelethini**

During his first term as president, Mbeki would repeatedly return to the theme. "Racist" would become a potent political charge leveled against white critics of his policies. The term also had the added advantage of undermining black support of any such criticism. Thabo Mbeki's emphasis on race was one indication of how difficult the transition from liberation movement to political party would be for the ANC.

The ANC soon discovered being the party of power is quite different than being in opposition, and this has deeply affected its relationship with its traditional partners, the Congress of South African Trade Unions (COSATU) and the South African Communist Party (SACP). Membership in the three groups often overlaps. Leadership of the two partners is frequently co-opted and interlocks with ANC leadership. After the 1999 election, for example, COSATU had to replace four of its principal officers elevated to parliament by virtue of membership on the ANC lists.

COSATU's new president, Willy Madisha, developed his career in the teachers' union and the SACP. Its new general secretary, Zwelinzima Vavi, was a National Union of Mineworkers (NUM) organizer as well as a member of the SACP.

Both COSATU and the SACP remain deeply socialist in orientation. They were not part of the process that created a major piece of the government's economic legislation, GEAR (Growth, Employment and Redistribution), and both feared GEAR leaned much too much towards a liberal capitalist economy. Both seem to prefer nationalization to privatization. The collision of the three partners seems inevitable, though "unity of the movement," at least in the short term, trumps the obvious divisions among them.

Big election issues for the ANC in 1999 were jobs and crime. Unemployment was unofficially estimated at 50%, making it one of the country's most urgent problems. An estimated 4.7 million people were unemployed and looking for work. GEAR had set a goal of 252,000 new jobs for 1997, but this did not adequately take into account the continuing recession in mining where the industry had to cut 50,000 mining jobs.

### The 1999 Election

South Africa's second multiparty democratic election took place in early June 1999. Some 42 political parties participated. They ranged from God's People Party, dedicated to fighting Satan, to Keep it Straight and Simple (you work out the acronym). The ANC overwhelmed all comers, nearly winning a two-thirds majority with 266 seats. The National Party, burdened with the historical weight of apartheid and deprived of forceful leadership, fell to a fourth-place finish. Not even calling itself the New National Party (NNP) helped to slow its decline; it won only 28 seats in the legislature.

Its role as official opposition was assumed by the Democratic Party a distant second-place finisher with a mere 38 seats. The Democratic Party is the home of white liberals and has benefited from

# South Africa

**Penguins, Boulders Beach, False Bay**

Photo by Judi Iranyi

NNP defections, especially the Western Cape Province. Its leader, Tony Leon, was articulate and fiery as an orator. As leader of the opposition he provided some of the best and much-needed criticism of the ANC. Chief Buthelezi's IFP won 34 seats.

The only other party to win more than ten seats in the new parliament was the United Democratic Movement led by Bantu Holomisa, a former military general and former deputy to Nelson Mandela after the 1994 elections. Popular, but perhaps too honest for his own good, Holomisa was thrown out of the party in 1996 after accusing some of his government colleagues of corruption.

South African voters do not vote directly for their representatives and have no idea who will represent them because of South Africa's proportional representation system. Parties create national and provincial lists and individuals enter parliament in terms of their ranking on those lists, which represent much internal politicking. In 1999, for example, Winnie Madikizela-Mandela was number ten on the ANC national list, guaranteeing her a position in parliament.

In June 2000 the Democratic Party (DP), under the leadership of Tony Leon, merged with the New National Party (NNP) to form the Democratic Alliance (DA). In many ways it was a merger of fish and fowl. The DP had inherited South Africa's white-minority liberal tradition. The NNP was, of course, the recently re-baptized National Party, which had created and enforced apartheid for 46 years.

In many ways the merger seemed to represent a voluntary death for the NNP. Loathed by black Africans as the party of apartheid, the NNP had little to offer, and its cosmetic name change proved of little value in the last election. (It won less than 7% of the votes cast.)

The first test of the new Democratic Alliance came in the municipal elections of 2000. Six "megacities" with powerful mayors had been created, and the struggle for power in these localities was intense. When the final results were in, the DA did surprisingly well, picking up 22% of the vote. (In 1999 its constituent elements had won only 16%.)

The ANC focused its fiercest energies on Cape Town, South Africa's second largest city and a melting pot of white, black, and mixed races. It lost to the DA, which prevailed by a small margin. The question that remained was how long this awkward merger of DP and NNP would last.

According to the South African constitution, MPs lose their seats in parliament if their party is disbanded. It was therefore agreed that the NNP and DP would continue to exist in parliament until the 2004 national election. Such was not to be, however, for the alliance was shattered by

**Nelson Mandela**

166

between the ANC and the NNP could easily topple Inkatha's control of the KwaZulu-Natal provincial legislature. President Mbeki and the ANC quickly moved to use the new alliance to further strengthen their domination of South African political space.

Legislation was passed to permit "floor-crossing"—allowing a representative to change parties without the unpleasant democratic necessity of resigning from office and standing for re-election on a new party list. The opposition, with little more than a thin line of lawyers to defend themselves against the ANC juggernaut, challenged the legislation's legality and South Africa's Constitutional court gave them partial victory. Floor-crossing in the municipalities was permitted, but at the provincial and national levels the constitution had to be amended before members could change parties. With more than a two-thirds majority in parliament, this posed no impediment for the ANC and its NNP partner.

Constitutional amendments to permit party changes at the national and provincial levels were approved in February 2003. When the 15-day period in which lawmakers were permitted to change political identity ended on April 4, the South African political landscape had been recast. Nine members of parliament crossed over to the ANC, giving the party 275 seats in the 400-seat body—a two-thirds majority of its own.

Other black opposition parties were also affected. Bantu Holomisa's United Democratic Movement lost more than half of its seats in the National Assembly, emerging in the post-shuffle period with just four national representatives. Given its totalizing vision of politics, the ANC reportedly approached Holomisa to rejoin the party, but aside from promising coop-

**President de Klerk and Mr. Nelson Mandela (February 1990)**

leadership disputes in Western Cape Province at the end of 2001. Grasping to keep the party and his own political career alive, the NNP leader, Marthinus van Schalkwyk, withdrew from the DA, negotiated a new relationship with the ANC, and transformed the face of South African party politics.

For the ANC, the alliance was attractive because the governments of Cape Town and its province, from which it had been excluded, were now assumable. At a national level, the ANC's political partners, COSATU and SACP, seemed not to have been consulted on the new relationship, and some of their members expressed discomfort, adding to the strains within the triple alliance. Chief Buthelezi's IFP seemed to question its own relationship with the ANC, especially since an alliance

**Winnie Madikizela Mandela**

# South Africa

eration in foreign policy and security, Holomisa went no further.

## Mbeki and Transformation

Thabo Mbeki's presidency inaugurated a new phase in South African politics. From the transition years of Nelson Mandela, the system moved to transformation. Nelson Mandela had used his moral authority to convince his fellow Africans to accept the new political system. His moderation and restraint similarly convinced whites to support the new dispensation. A Truth and Reconciliation Commission sought to soothe the emotional pains on both sides of the racial divide. Acceptance and reconciliation seemingly gained, the new government moved to transform the legacy of injustice that characterizes contemporary South Africa. Symptomatic are four laws passed early in the year 2000: the Promotion of Access to Information Bill, the Promotion of Administrative Justice Bill, the Preferential Procurement Policy Framework and the Promotion of Equality and Prevention of Unfair Discrimination Bill.

Two of the bills give ordinary citizens the right to make the government—at all levels—accountable. The Promotion of Administrative Justice Bill forces government to create mechanisms to explain its decisions, such as cutting welfare grants to affected members of the public. In theory, bureaucrats will think before acting, realizing they may have to justify any action they take.

The Promotion of Access to Information Bill is a reaction to the secrecy with which the former white regime shrouded state affairs. The bill affirms a right of access to "any information held by a public or private body,"—subject to restrictions. It will not apply, for example, to the cabinet and its committees, to judicial functions, or to individual members of the national or provincial legislatures. Defense, security and foreign affairs information is also excluded.

The two remaining bills seek to transform apartheid's legacy of racial injustice. The Preferential Procurement Policy Framework Bill gives preferences in government contracts to companies that have actively hired workers disadvantaged on the basis of race, gender or disability. The program is probably better known to Americans as "affirmative action" and to South Africans as "positive discrimination."

The Promotion of Equality and Prevention of Unfair Discrimination Bill seeks nothing less than an end of discrimination. Its scope is vast. Discrimination is defined in the broadest possible terms and applied to seventeen prohibited areas: race, gender, sex, pregnancy, marital status, ethnic or social origin, color, sexual orientation, age, disability, religion, conscience, belief, culture, language and birth or any other recognized ground.

Effective implementation of such laws, each of extraordinary breadth, will depend on budgetary allocations necessary to set up guidelines, procedures and hearing venues—often specially charged courts. The ambiguities of provisions in the four laws suggest that years of legal wrangling can also be expected before full implementation is achieved. In the meantime the government has to deal with issues more pressing.

## Crime

South Africa is awash in a tidal wave of crime that threatens to sink the state's capacity to protect its citizens and diminish its international reputation. (One study found that violent crime was cited by 60% of emigrants as a reason for leaving South Africa. North African states vying against South Africa to hold the soccer World Cup finals repeatedly stressed its insecurity.)

Car theft has been one of the most common crimes in South Africa. Police statistics indicate there were 74,281 car thefts between January and September 2001. The worst of these result in violence, even murder. Johannesburg ranks as the world's carjacking capital. Located on Gauteng province, Johannesburg's vehicles all bear license plates with the initials GP. Local cynics persist in saying it means "Gangster Paradise." In 2003 the province had 9,371 car hijackings, an increase of 23.1%

According to Interpol statistics, South Africa's murder rate is one of the highest in the world. Neither high nor low are spared, a fact brought home to South Africans when the country's former first lady, Marike de Klerk, was found murdered in her Cape Town apartment in December 2001. In September 2002 police reported the murder rate had "stabilized," with 59 people a day being murdered. That's 21,535 a year. South Africa still remains one of the few countries in which one is more likely to be murdered than die in an automobile accident.

A year later the police for the first time released crime statistics based on incidents per 100,000 of the population, and immediately found themselves criticized for masking crime increases behind population increases. Even using the new format, South Africa's murder rate was exceptional: 47.4 murders per 100,000. In one area murder did not stabilize, indeed it increased: In the 2002–2003 reporting year, 150 police officials were murdered, an increase of 7.9%. The government's failure to deal with crime has had one positive effect: the money spent on private security services has soared—$185 million in 1990 to $2.1 billion in 2002.

Rape attacks are more than double the annual murder rate in South Africa, making it the rape capital of the world. The September 2002 statistics show six women were raped in South Africa every hour of every day—52,560 annually. A woman born in South Africa has a greater chance of being raped than learning how to read, while one in four girls faces the prospect of being raped before the age of 16. The new and improved reporting format of September 2003 shows rapes to have decreased by 5%. Some experts estimate that at least 60% of all rapes go unreported.

In its September 2004 statistics, the South African Police Service alleged that major crime was seeing a downturn: murder decreased by 1.7%, rape was down 5.7%, and car-jackings dropped by 20.2%. When critics challenged the findings, Thabo Mbeki himself critiqued the critics in one of his weekly newsletters. He was particularly vehement when condemning one feminist writer—Charlene Smith, an ANC activist and rape victim herself—whom he accused of saying "African traditions, indigenous religions and culture . . . institutionalize rape" and "inherently make every African man a potential rapist." She said no such thing, of course, but it reflects the mindset of the 1960s which shaped and continues to shape Mbeki's thinking.

Despite the president's protestations, South Africa appears to have deeply embedded cultural values that create a rape culture. In Johannesburg, which has the highest incidence of rape in South Africa, a survey conducted among 1,500 school children in Soweto township found that a quarter of all boys interviewed said that "jackrolling"—a South African term for recreational gang rape—was fun. Weaknesses in the criminal justice system also contribute to the culture of rape. Only about seven per cent of reported rapes result in convictions, leaving most rapists with little fear of punishment.

In 2001 and 2002 the South African public heard a continuing tale of horrific brutality as newspapers reported incident after incident of child and baby rape. A parliamentary debate on child abuse revealed a 400% increase in sexual violence against children in the previous decade. About 40% of the 52,000 reported rape cases in 2001 involved victims under 18 years of age. One plausible explanation for the increase of sexual violence against children may be the relatively widespread myth that sex with a virgin will cleanse a man of HIV or AIDS.

Charlene Smith, the journalist and rape victim who became an AIDS activist, argues that the virgin myth is widespread in every community of South Africa and spreading. In the Northern Province, the

**Providing improved services: building a water-treatment facility**

©IRIN

director of a rape intervention project made the disturbing observation that when one looked at the rapes that took place between 2000 and 2002, "it is predominantly children, and they are getting younger and younger."

## Education

Among the most important issues facing the Mbeki government are the distribution of social services, particularly education. The crisis in education has been ongoing, a consequence of apartheid policies on curriculum and funding, and the absence of a clear policy direction from the ANC government. President Mbeki has spoken often and with conviction of an African Renaissance. His new African century must produce doctors and engineers and scientists, but the education system has been a shambles. Its desperate state is symbolized by the results of the 2000 matriculation exams—only 48.9% passed. The results were a shock and a call to arms.

Since then, the government has poured money into schooling, effected change, and produced improved results. Matriculation exams were successfully passed by 61.7% of those taking them in 2001 and 68.9% in 2002. The legacy of apartheid's inequalities and disparities is still apparent. A pattern of regional inequality in results reflects long-term inequality of resource distribution. The best-endowed provinces (Northern Cape, Western Cape and Gauteng) performed best. Lowest pass rates were recorded in the poor provinces with huge black and rural majorities. Well-endowed private schools, on the other hand, scored an average 99% pass rate.

The bottom slot has long been occupied by the Northern Province (now Limpopo province), which usually comes in last on most lists of social indicators. In 2000, only 35.2% passed the matriculation exams, which mark students' readiness for advanced education. By 2002, the pass rate had increased to 69.5%, and the province no longer ranked at the bottom. That unenviable honor went to Eastern Cape with 51.8% passing, against 45.6% the year before. (The highest pass rate came from the Northern Cape with 89.95%.)

Gender, particularly in poorer, more rural provinces, continues to be a problem: Women are less likely to pass matrics there. In Limpopo, the pass rate for women was 7% lower than for men. In contrast, in Western Cape and Gauteng, there was virtually no gender difference.

The causes of the crisis in education are manifold, and certainly the basic material provisioning—classrooms and books—is tragically slighted. KwaZulu-Natal, for example, is currently (2003) facing a shortage of 14,000 classrooms which it is estimated will take nine years to eliminate. Beyond the physical, however, the whole delivery system—an educational bureaucracy, too many of whom are unqualified,

unprepared and unmotivated—remains a challenge. A culture of learning has yet to be cultivated, and individual classrooms remain sites of threat and intimidation against both staff and students. Those who can afford it send their children to private schools.

In comparison to other regional states, South Africa's educational results are far worse. Of 11 southern and east African countries, only Lesotho and Namibia score worse than South Africa for reading and mathematics. Many historically African schools still do not offer mathematics, science or technology, which were denied under apartheid. In 2001, only 18% of matric candidates took the higher-grade mathematics portion of the exam. Almost 60% passed, but in Eastern Cape and Limpopo, only 13% wrote higher mathematics, and only about a quarter passed. In contrast, in Western Cape and Gauteng, 22% wrote higher mathematics and 80% passed.

Eastern Cape province demonstrates the deplorable conditions in which education must function in South Africa's poorest areas. In 2000, 17% of the schools had no toilets, 45% had no electricity, and 28% no water. In 2003 the provincial legislature's standing committee on education still complained about the shortage of classrooms, dilapidated mud structures, absence of toilets, electricity, telephones and water. Worse, it found a high degree of poor discipline among both teachers and students after visiting 157 provincial schools. "Drunkenness, absenteeism, truancy and use of drugs within the school premises could be cited as most striking examples," it said.

In his 2004 state-of-the-nation speech President Mbeki promised that no children would learn outdoors by the next time he described the state of the nation. In early 2005, however, his Minister of Education, Naledi Pandor, openly wondered in a parliamentary briefing why children continued to learn under trees when the provinces had the money to build classrooms. For the government the issue is critical: education remains at the heart of its plans for social transformation. Twenty-five percent of the country's budget is spent on education, and the absence of constructed classrooms too openly displayed the government's inability to deliver services.

Minister Pandor has submitted the government's plans for reforming the education sector, including a much greater directing and controlling role on the part of the national government. At present the governing bodies of school have the power to decide on admission policies, language of instruction, the level of fees, and the appointment of teachers indepen-

# South Africa

dent of the national government. Under the new plans local autonomy would virtually disappear. Schools would, for example, present the provincial education department head a shortlist of three teachers who meet the employment criteria. That official would make the final decision. Provincial authorities would be required to coordinate better with national officials to ensure allocated funds were actually used and government policies implemented.

Perhaps the most controversial issue has been the question of language. The 2005 education reform proposal makes the teaching of English and Afrikaans optional, instead offering learners the choice of studying any two of the country's 11 official languages. According to official statistics, Zulu is the mother tongue of 23.8% of the population, followed by Xhosa, the natal tongue of 17.6%. Only about 8% of South Africans speak English as their first language. The proposal accords with the government's desire to develop the other nine official languages into media of instruction. Ultimately, the plan is to have universities teach in indigenous languages.

Although she spoke of "inadequate levels of preparedness" and of the need to phase the reforms in over time, the education minister did not present any figures on the costs for teacher training and for the preparation of curriculum materials in the additional languages.

## Truth and Reconciliation Commission

Racial tensions still exist in South Africa, but given the bitterness of past experience, it is remarkable that any harmony at all is possible. One important institution which helped advance the reconciliation process is the Truth and Reconciliation Commission (TRC) established by act of parliament in 1995. Its purpose was to investigate crimes committed during the apartheid era, and as commission chairman, President Mandela appointed Archbishop Desmond Tutu, the 1984 Nobel Peace Prize winner. Tutu had been the first black Anglican Dean of Johannesburg and had led the church in South Africa into an active struggle against apartheid.

The TRC heard some 21,300 witnesses and compiled a dossier of human rights crimes committed by all sides during the apartheid era. A 3,500-page report submitted to President Mandela in October 1998 marked the conclusion of its investigative work. There was guilt aplenty in the report. The most serious culprit was the South African State itself. The Commission's analysis of why this came about was simple and direct: Racism was at the center of state action designed to protect the power and privilege of a racial minor-

ity. As a consequence, white citizens adopted a dehumanizing attitude towards black citizens. They ceased to think of them as citizens and this "created a climate in which gross atrocities committed against them were seen as legitimate."

The commission also held the opponents of apartheid—the ANC and other liberation movements—morally and politically accountable for human rights violations. Thabo Mbeki, for example, had told the TRC that a number of ANC members—including 34 in Angola when the party was in exile—were executed by the movement's own security officials. At least one of those was wrongly executed by two ANC cadres who themselves were later put to death.

Important political figures did not escape the Commission's condemnation. Winnie Madikizela-Mandela was found accountable for crimes committed by the Mandela United Football Club (MUFC). Killing, torture, assault and arson were all MUFC activities, the Commission found, and Madikizela-Mandela herself was aware of this criminal activity, but chose not to address it.

Mangosuthu Buthelezi was held accountable as leader of the Inkatha Freedom Party for all the violence committed by its members. Between 1982 and 1994 IFP supporters caused the deaths of about 3,800 people in KwaZulu-Natal province alone, against 1,100 caused by the ANC. It was, the Commission thought, a "systematic pattern" of murder and attacks by the

IFP against its opponents, often in collusion with State security forces.

The Commission was empowered to grant amnesty to those who asked for it and a separate panel was established to hold these hearings. Applicants were required to prove their crime had a political motive or was performed acting under direct orders. They were also required to offer full disclosure of their crimes and demonstrate genuine contrition. The commission received some 7,100 applications for amnesty and granted close to 1,000. It rejected the killers of Chris Hani—not a political crime the panel said. It also rejected the amnesty application of five policemen involved in the death of Steve Biko and refused a blanket amnesty to ANC leaders, arguing that the amnesty was designed for individuals.

The legislation establishing the TRC entailed the idea that victims of state-sponsored violence should be compensated by the state for their suffering. Since the conclusion of hearings, a third of the Commission's panels have dealt with reparations to the victims.

It received some 20,000 requests for financial reparation. Of these, 17,000 claimants were awarded initial payments totaling 3.7 million dollars. But the bulk of financial reparations must be made through a special government fund. President Mbeki has announced the government will be making a one-time payment of 30,000 Rand ($3800) to the 22,000 victims of apartheid designated by the TRC.

**Township housing, Gugulethu**

Photo by Judi Iranyi

**Summary of *ANC* Activities, 1990–1994**

1990–1: *ANC* engaged in fund–raising in U.S. and other overseas locations. There was a readjustment and evaluation of possibilities and alternatives. The result was an encouragement of *ANC* and *MK* aggression against *Inkatha*–Zulus.

1991–2: Fund raising abroad, consolidation at home. Continued aggression directed against Zulus. Preliminary conferences with whites via CODESA, with posturing, walk–outs and ultimatums, some of which were impossible.

1992–3: Continued confrontation, but greater emphasis on cooperation, all without surrender of goals. Constitutional negotiations held with *Inkatha* absent, a pre-empt by virtue of numbers.

1993–4: After 23 months, a negotiated settlement on constitution and elections, to be held if necessary without *Inkatha*–Zulu participation. *ANC* went to the brink of disaster without the Zulus, but retreated at the last moment in 1994 in order to include them in the elections.

April 26–30, 1994: Elections (the voting period was extended).

## Testing Thabo

President Mbeki and his government have come under increasing scrutiny as they have confronted a number of issues and problems, many of their own making. Both the president's judgment and action on these have raised questions about his capacity to lead the nation. Part of the problem lies in the president's own style and personality.

The Mbeki style is more restrained than his predecessor's. He is seen as cool, distant and lacking a common touch. His rapport with the masses, that ineffable quality some like to call "charisma," pales beside that of more popular and populist leaders. Indeed, it is widely reported that Nelson Mandela preferred Cyril Ramaphosa, the mine workers' leader and principal negotiator of the transition from apartheid to majority rule, as his successor.

Lacking a fundamental popularity and charisma and surrounded by those who have them can, one assumes, lead to a certain nervousness. Enemies can lurk and conspiracies abound, but the organizational and ideological traditions of the ANC stress internal discipline and external solidarity. Historically the movement could enforce discipline by rough revolutionary justice justified as necessary to the achievement of its goals—an elimination of the apartheid system.

Once apartheid was ended and the movement had attained control of the apparatus of the state, divergencies over the use, direction, and speed of government action to improve the everyday life of South Africans became evident. Managing those differences, and the personalities and factions that have gathered around them, tested Thabo Mbeki's judgment and leadership.

In foreign policy, the issue of Zimbabwe has loomed large. President Mbeki claimed the efficacy of "quiet diplomacy" before critics who demanded he condemn Zimbabwe's state-sanctioned violence against its opponents. The wisdom of that approach became ever more dubious as Zimbabwe collapsed economically under an increasingly dictatorial Robert Mugabe. The ANC and President Mbeki consistently refused to condemn comrade Mugabe and his thuggish antics. In this refusal, Mbeki abandoned moral leadership and jeopardized a visionary project for African development by alienating Western governments asked to finance the project.

In many ways the refusal reflects both the personal and political that infuse the president's decision making. There is a deep sense of African pride and vestigial anti-colonialism that rejects the notion that Western states have any right to condemn what Africans do. There is also a bevy of practical political concerns that color the Zimbabwe issue, some of which touch on the sometimes-delicate relationship between the ANC and COSATU, its trade union ally in the triple alliance.

In South Africa the most obvious potential sources for an effective organized opposition to the ANC are the trade unions. As a liberation movement, the ANC and its leadership are less than keen on supporting a trade-union based opposition in Zimbabwe. The experience of Zambia, where Frederick Chiluba arose out of the union milieu to defeat Kenneth Kaunda and Zambia's liberation movement, is all too clear.

On Zimbabwe's 2005 presidential election COSATU and the ANC were in very different camps. COSATU sent fact-finding missions that exposed the Mugabe regime's paranoia and abuse of human rights and sought to organize a regional protest to campaign for free and fair elections there. Unionists were asked to picket Zimbabwean embassies in the region, a blockade of the border proposed, and a demand that elections be delayed until provisions guaranteeing honest polling were implemented was presented. For Mbeki, political and economic solidarity of the SADC (Southern African Development Community) countries is a prerequisite for economic development, so any criticism of Zimbabwe, a fellow SADC country, has to be muted. One Member of Parliament went so far as to criticize COSATU action, saying there had been no need for it because there were no human rights problems in Zimbabwe. Once the results were in a government spokesman called them a "credible reflection of the will of the people."

**Cape Town Harbor Development with Table Mountain in the background**

Photo by Rita Arendt

171

# South Africa

**Goat herding in remote Northern Cape province**                    ©IRIN

Disgusted with President Mebki's moral flaccidity and lack of leadership on the Zimbabwe issue, South Africa's Nobel-Prize winning cleric Desmond Tutu unleashed a withering criticism: Mbeki, he said "would be booed in the street" if he were ever to ask ordinary Zimbabweans what they thought about his views on their country. "The people of Zimbabwe have no respect for Mbeki. They don't know why he is supporting Mugabe. They don't understand it."

In other foreign policy areas Mbeki has had perhaps greater success and certainly less pungent criticism. He continued mediation efforts first conducted by President Mandela in Burundi, and seriously involved himself in working out an agreement to end conflict in the Democratic Republic of the Congo. The African Union called upon him to mediate between contending parties in Côte d'Ivoire and he seems to have facilitated a major break through there. And in yet another effort to create continental alliances, particularly with francophone states, Mebeki sided with Algeria and recognized the Polisario Front as the legitimate government of the Saharawi Arab Democratic Republic. Morocco of course was less than happy.

## The 2004 Elections

Over the years the ANC's democratic traditions have eroded. In the early days the national executive committee conducted lively debates on important issues, but its ultimate authority has been eclipsed by a concentration of effective power in an increasingly autocratic executive. Nothing better demonstrates presidential dominance in the South African political system than President Mbeki's decision to send an entire aircraft filled with weapons to rescue a beleagured Jean-Bertrand Aristide in Haiti. The decision was single-handed, personal, and illustrative of the system's executive dominance.

Despite acquiescent silence on Zimbabwe that plunged millions of Zimbabweans into irreversible misery, and despite obtuse obstructionism on the AIDS issue that shortened lives and increased suffering of South Africans, Thabo Mbeki was effectively master of the South African political universe as the 2004 elections approached. Re-elected ANC president in 2003, Mbeki led the party to a smashing victory—nearly 70%—in the legislative polls of 2004, surpassing the 1999 results and gaining more than a two-thirds majority in parliament. The victory assured his election to a second four-year term as president by the National Assembly.

The ANC entered the poll allied with the New National Party (NNP) of Marthinus van Schalkwyk, but it hardly needed support. It won 279 seats in the 400-seat assembly, while its erstwhile coalition partner won a mere seven. The Democratic Alliance, shorn of all connection with the NNP, gathered support as the principal voice of opposition to the ANC; it won 50 seats in the legislature, 12 more than in 1999. Its electoral partner, Chief Buthelezi's IFP, lost representation, dropping from 34 to 28 seats.

With Marthinus van Schalkwyk's self-serving alliance with the ANC, the NNP lost virtually all credibility with voters. They rejected its candidates massively, and the party emerged with nine assembly seats, down from 28 in 1999. The Freedom Front Plus party won support from the NNP's white Afrikaner support base, and colored NNP voters in Western Cape fled to the Independent Democrats (ID).

Led by Patricia de Lille, the ID was barely a year old, having been formed when she left the Pan African Congress during the assembly "floor crossings" of early 2003. De Lille's was often the most vigorous voice of critical opposition in the assembly where she combined roles of gadfly and moral conscience to devastating effect. She becomes the first woman to lead a political party in parliament and promises to be the most interesting and provocative of Thabo Mbeki's critics.

The ANC's electoral victory confirmed its conquest of South Africa's political space. It secured a majority in all but two provinces, Western Cape and KwaZulu-Natal. In each it became the dominant party, and having entered each province with a coalition partner, it emerged with a majority in the two provinces which had previously eluded it.

President Mbeki asserted his party's will over its coalition partners with no-compromise. In a display of personal confidence and power, he nominated premiers in all nine of South Africa's provinces. In the Western Cape Mbeki named Ebrahim Rasool premier after the ANC's electoral partner, the New Na-

**A Traditional Artisan at Work**
Photo courtesy KZN Tourism Authority

tional Party, was decimated and its leader, Marthinus van Schalkwyk, gave up any claim to the office. The NNP's Western Cape vote tally was enough to create a majority coalition with the ANC; as his reward, van Schalkwyk was given a seat in the national cabinet as Minister of Environmental Affairs and Tourism.

In KwaZulu-Natal the situation was awkward: provincially the ANC was allied with the IFP, which opposed it nationally. When the final results came in the IFP was no longer the dominant party, and province would get an ANC premier—S'bu Ndebele, who led the ANC campaign to oust the IFP from power.

In the other seven provinces there was a general house cleaning. With one exception, Mbhazima Shilowa in Gauteng, ANC incumbents in the premierships were replaced. It was a firm presidential message: incompetent, corrupt or inefficient provincial governance would no longer be tolerated. Four of the nine ANC premiers would be women.

**Culture:** South Africa now has one of the highest rates of HIV infection and in terms of absolute numbers, the greatest number of HIV-positive people—around five million—in the world. Unlike Uganda where the rate is dropping, South Africa's keeps rising. The government was slow to recognize the problem and slower to respond.

The statistics are appalling: one in five people are already HIV positive. The national health ministry estimates that another 1,600 South African are infected daily. Five thousand babies are born each month infected with HIV. Patients with AIDS-related infections already occupy 70% of South African hospital beds. There were 360,000 AIDS deaths in 2001 alone, and in 2003, 600 persons a day were dying of the disease. As parents die, an estimated 700,000 AIDS orphans will be left behind by 2010. In February 2005 the government released statistics showing annual deaths in the country had risen 57% from 1997 to 2003, with common AIDS-related diseases like tuberculosis and pneumonia fueling much of the increase. The mortality spike was greatest in the 15 to 49 age category.

The impact on population growth will be significant. In 2015, South Africa's population will only reach 49 million, instead of 61 million—one-fifth less than earlier predicted because of AIDS. Life expectancy will decline accordingly. By 2010 it could be as low as 33 years in provinces like KwaZulu-Natal, which has one of the highest numbers of HIV/AIDS cases in the country. With more than 60% of new infections occurring in people 15 to 25 years old, the pandemic is expected to wipe out large segments of the very people who are needed to fight it—teachers, health professionals and government workers.

Until sued and made subject to a court order, the government refused to employ vaccines known to reduce the incidence of mother to child transmission of the HIV virus. In December 2001 the Pretoria High Court ordered the government to provide antiretrovirals (ARVs) to all HIV-pregnant women. The case had been brought by Treatment Action Campaign (TAC), a militant AIDS lobby group that has significantly ratcheted up techniques of public embarrassment for a foot-dragging regime.

When asked if the government was prepared to follow the court order in March 2002, the minister of health said "No, I think the courts and the judiciary must listen to the authorities—regulatory authorities—both from this country and the United States." Its appeal to the Constitutional court was rejected in April, with the court saying the government was violating the constitutional rights of women and their babies by not supplying Nevirapine, a drug by now long-proved to reduce mother-to-child HIV transmission.

Election line, 2004

173

# South Africa

| National Assembly Following the April 2004 Election | | |
|---|---|---|
| Party | Percentage | National Assembly Seats |
| African National Congress | 69.68 | 279 |
| Democratic Alliance | 12.37 | 50 |
| Inkatha Freedom Party | 6.97 | 28 |
| Others | 10.98 | |
| United Democratic Movement | | 9 |
| New National Party | | 7 |
| Independent Democrats | | 7 |
| African Christian Democratic Party | | 6 |
| Freedom Front Plus | | 4 |
| Pan Africanist Congress | | 3 |
| United Christian Democratic Party | | 3 |
| Minority Front | | 2 |
| Anzanian People's Organization | | 2 |
| Total | | 400 |

In the same month, the health minister rejected a grant to KwaZulu-Natal from the Global Fund to Fight AIDS, TB and Malaria, saying the province should not have approached the fund directly.

At an international conference in July 2002, South Africa's health minister, Dr. Manto Tshabala-Msimang, was quoted as saying the antiretrovirals were "poisons" killing "our people." She had also once suggested that those infected with HIV should eat beetroot and garlic.

When parliament reopened in February 2003 and the government had not yet signed on to a treatment and prevention plan formulated by business, labor and government representatives working within the National Economic Development and Labor Council (Nedlac), AIDS advocacy groups descended on it in protest. TAC volunteers engaged in civil disobedience, occupying government ministries and defying police to arrest them.

By April 2003 TAC protesters had taken their cause international, demonstrating outside South Africa's diplomatic missions abroad to demand the government supply anti-retroviral drugs to AIDS sufferers. In London they placed 600 pairs of shoes outside the High Commission (Embassy) to symbolize the number of people who die of AIDS-related illnesses every day in South Africa. Similar shoe protests were held in Los Angeles, Washington DC, and Milan. In November 2003 the government agreed to distribute ARVs to those needing them, but it took months to put the policy in action. At the time it was estimated that over 500,000 people were in need of the drugs; only 1,500 were cur-

rently receiving them, all in Western Cape province.

Finance Minister Trevor Manuel announced in February 2004 that an additional $305 million would be allocated to fighting HIV/AIDS over the next three years; the allocation included money for provincially-administered ARV treatment programs, but it was not until two weeks before the April 2004 elections that the drugs began to appear. (By November 2004 the legal costs of defending the government's policy in the courts had mounted to $6.3 million.)

Government delay on HIV/AIDS is directly attributable to President Mbeki himself. He has criticized ARVs both for their costs and their toxicity, a notion picked up from his reading of the scientific dissidents, those who refuse to admit a relationship between HIV and AIDS. His attitude only worsened the situation, for while his government delayed, people died and infections increased.

The currently accepted fashion is to describe President Mbeki's views on HIV/AIDS as "unorthodox." They go well beyond that, suggesting at times the kind of paranoia that has led to acceptance of "conspiracy" accusations in other areas. In October 2000, for example, he told a gathering of ANC officials that the CIA was part of a "conspiracy to promote the view that HIV causes AIDS."

According to South Africa's *Mail and Guardian* newspaper, Mbeki told the group the CIA was also working with big U.S. pharmaceutical manufacturers to undermine him. The reason for this, he explained, was the fear that his questioning of the HIV/AIDS link would lead to re-

duced profits in the sale of anti-retroviral treatments.

President Mbeki reappointed his fellow AIDS obstructionist, Dr. Manto Tshabala-Msimang—"Dr. No" to AIDS activists—as health minister in April 2004. She continues to urge people to follow a more healthful diet—lots of garlic and beetroot.

**Economy:** By regional standards, and even continental ones, the South African economy is huge. With a GDP close to $159.9 billion (2003) and a misleading per capita income of nearly $2780 (2003), South Africa dwarfs its neighbors and represents 40% of the entire economy of the continent. But the giant is sluggish.

Growth has been modest over the past few years (3.6% in 2002 and a disappointing 1.9% in 2003), and unemployment remains high. A March 2002 survey, partially funded by South Africa's Department of Labor and conducted by the Norwegian Institute for Applied Social Science, found a total of 45% of the population is unemployed—much higher than official figures. Three-fourths of South Africa's unemployed are black Africans, the principal constituency of the ANC. The government estimates that the economy must achieve a minimum of 6% growth to offset unemployment.

South Africa is rich in natural resources, but the mining sector is in decline. It has, for example, the world's largest reserves of manganese (80%), chromium (68%), and platinum-group metals (56%). At least 40% of the world's total recoverable gold reserves are in South Africa. South Africa's annual mineral production is worth about $12 billion.

Although the huge accumulated deficits of the United States have driven gold traders to speak of $500/oz gold, the industry is facing difficulties. Costs are rising and production is declining. Labor costs keep rising (to avoid a strike by the National Union of Mineworkers in 2003, the industry negotiated a major wage package: a 10% salary increase the first year and "inflation plus one" in the second), but remaining gold reserves lie deeper and deeper, requiring greater amounts of labor. Extraction has become less and less economic. In 2004 gold production was the lowest since 1931. Employment in the industry has dropped in the past decade from 530,000 to just 187,000. As of mid-2005, more than 8,000 jobs have been lost in the last eighteen months.

South Africa's other notable natural resource industry also faces problems. Some 13.7 million carats were produced in 2004, but De Beers, the foremost international diamond concern, reported that five of the its seven South African operations were the planned royalty tax on energy firms had been reduced to 1% to encourage offshore oil and gas exploration.

The government is also targeting the mining industry in its drive for Black Economic Empowerment (BEE). Basically part of the government's plans to transform the economy by giving black Africans a significant share of major economic sectors, initial legislative drafts caused panic selling of mining shares in October 2002 when first released. Some shares dropped by 40% when it was learned the government was proposing that 51% of mining assets should be controlled by black South Africans within ten years. Negotiation reduced the amount transferred to black shareholders to 26% of equity to be achieved by May 2014. As an incentive to the hard-pressed mining industry, empowerment requirements can be diluted to 16% if the company does enough to promote "benefaction"—increasing worker benefits. Similarly, the Financial Services Charter seeks to transfer a quarter of the sector to BEE interests by 2010.

BEE is a central goal of the Mbeki government. By 2014, it would like to see that South Africa's black majority holds major (largely unspecified) stakes in the economy. Whites, about 12% of the population, still control the economy, the mines, banks, factories and farms. Whites own more than 70% of the land and dominate the banking, manufacturing and tourism industries. According to government figures, white-run companies control 95% of the country's diamond production, 63% of platinum reserves and 51% of gold reserves. This situation must change, says the government.

As BEE deals have unfolded, however, the Mbeki empowerment model has come under increasing attack as enrichment of a few well-placed black businessmen that has done little to improve the conditions of average South Africans. In October 2004 ANC Secretary-General Kgalema Motlanthe condemned the program as "narrow based." "It seems," he said, "that certain individuals are not satisfied with a single bout of empowerment. Instead, they are the beneficiaries of repeated bouts of re-empowerment. We see the same names mentioned over and over again in one deal after another." Indeed, Cyril Ramaphosa and Mathews Phosa (a former premier of Mpumalanga province), both members of the ANC's highest decision-making body, the national executive council, have signed numerous empowerment deals, as has Tokyo Sexwale, the former Premier of Gauteng province. Ramaphosa's brother-in-law, Patrice Motsepe, became a very rich man after signing several major empowerment deals in the gold sector worth around $503.4 mil-

**Cape Point, the tip of the Cape of Good Hope, where the Indian and Atlantic Oceans meet.**

Photo by Connie Abell

loss-making, owing mainly to the strength of the rand. Nevertheless, the company reported net earnings of $498 million on a total turnover of $7 billion from all its operations. It was, said the company, "another good year for the diamond industry." The figures mask a darker reality for the company: De Beers raised prices by 14% in 2004 (and another 3% in early 2005) to account for the decline of the dollar. The company, once a virtual cartel, faces stiff competition from Russia. There Alrosa, the state diamond company which controls nearly the entire Russian production, plans to increase its output by 20% in 2005.

The government is shaping a new regulatory framework for the mining industry. In 2002 it enacted a law that formally transferred ownership of the country's resources to the state. Henceforth, companies exploiting those resources will have to pay royalties to the government. The initial percentages proposed by the government (around 3%) ran into stiff resistance. Most companies saw the proposed royalties as too high, especially since they were based on revenues rather than profits. The government backed away, and the final wording of its Mining and Petroleum Royalty Bill was still being negotiated in early 2005. At this time it looks as though

# South Africa

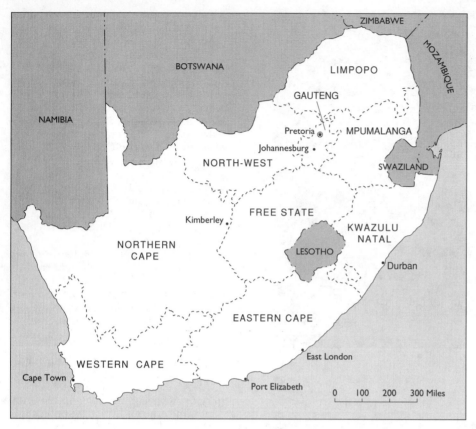

**Provinces of South Africa**

similar line of criticism has also come from Desmond Tutu, increasingly the regime's moral conscience. "We are sitting on a powder keg," the Nobel laureate said recently. While millions of South Africans live in "grueling, demeaning, dehumanizing poverty," he said, black empowerment "seems to benefit not the vast majority but an elite that tends to be recycled."

Unlike neighboring Angola, South Africa is not endowed with rich oil resources. Coal is the primary fuel produced and consumed in South Africa. Its recoverable coal reserves are estimated at 54.6 billion tons (about 5% of the world reserves). Coal is also the country's second most important foreign exchange earner, after gold, contributing 7% of export earnings.

Production is concentrated in a few regions, with Mpumalanga Province accounting for 83% of total output. Coal production was 242.7 million tons in 2002, with nearly one-third of total coal production exported—primarily to the European market. Domestically the bulk of coal resources is used to generate electricity.

Sasol, South Africa's third-largest coal producer, is active in producing oil from coal. Sasol produces about 20% of South Africa's liquid fuel requirements and is the world's largest manufacturer of oil

lion, and the opposition Democratic Alliance claims that Motsepe and Sexwale were involved in 60 percent of the $6.4 billion empowerment deals done in 2003. The benefits to BEE tycoons can be obscene, given the poverty in which most black South Africans live: When Standard Bank chose Saki Macozoma and Cyril Ramaphosa as empowerment partners, the deal netted each man around $30 million. Little wonder Secretary-General Motlanthe suggested the ANC should declare that once an individual had been empowered, he or she should no longer "be regarded as a historically advantaged person," eligible for further empowerment benefits.

Much of the BEE criticism reflects internal ANC politics. Rivals for future party leadership are more than happy to see Cyril Ramaphosa criticized. Left-wing opponents of the ANC's move to liberal economic policies still press for a re-think on the issue. The COSATU leader, Zwelinzima Vavi, has threatened to obstruct a pending $18.6 billion deal in the finance sector to bring in more black partners. It will only help, he says "a narrow group of individuals . . . already rich through transactions of this type." The banks, he argues, should use their cash to build houses for poor blacks, fund small black businesses, and subsidize black farms. A

**Ndebele women**

# South Africa

which to impose its will in any area. Thabo Mbeki combines the roles of party president and state president. As party leader he controls all provincial and subordinate leadership. As state president he has concentrated enormous powers of direction and coordination in his office. In other countries single-party dominance of this sort has almost always led to a regime of patrons and clients, disconnected from the needs of those outside the networks of patronage. The real test of Thabo Mbeki's leadership will be the extent to which he avoids the pitfalls of enormous power. Given what appears to be a paranoid personality, one has a right to be uncertain.

Former South African President F.W. de Klerk (left) and African National Congress foreign policy specialist Thabo Mbeki (right) were deputy presidents in President Nelson Mandela's first cabinet.

from coal. The technology was originally developed in the 1950s to help reduce South Africa's dependence on imported oil, but the company has been privatized and the government has ended subsidies for this undertaking. Given the high cost of compliance with environmental regulations associated with coal, Sasol looked to natural gas as an alternative. The company was actively involved in the development of Mozambique's Pande and Temane gas fields, and began importing gas from Mozambique in February 2004. The gas is transported through a 536-mile pipeline, jointly owned by Sasol and the governments of South Africa and Mozambique.

According to Interpol, South Africa is the fourth-largest cannabis producer in the world. An estimated 205,000 acres yield 387.2 million pounds of the drug. First introduced into the region some 500 years ago by Arab traders, cannabis (called "dagga" locally) is widely regarded as a traditional crop in many rural areas, particularly the Eastern Cape and KwaZulu-Natal. South African cannabis is some of the most potent in the world and enormously popular as a consequence. Around a quarter of seizures worldwide involve the South African product. In some rural areas it is possible to produce up to three crops per year. While the producers are usually subsistence farmers for whom cannabis is a unique cash crop, the U.S. State Department reports that there are more than 100 drug syndicates operating in South Africa.

**The Future:** The ANC enjoys overwhelming power in South Africa. In parliament it commands a two-thirds majority with

**A spectacular mountain landscape, KwaZulu-Natal**

KZN Tourism Authority

177

# The Kingdom of Swaziland

**King Mswati III**

**Area:** 17,364 sq. km. = 6,705 sq. mi. (about the size of Hawaii).

**Population:** 1,173,900 (July 2005 est.)

**Capital Cities:** Mbabane (Pop. 40,000, estimated—administrative); Lobamba (Pop. 23,500, estimated—legislative).

**Climate:** Temperate, with chilly nights during the winter months.

**Neighboring Countries:** Mozambique (Northeast); Republic of South Africa (North, West, South).

**Official Languages:** siSwati, English.

**Other Principal Languages:** Zulu, Afrikaans.

**Ethnic Groups:** Swazi, a small number of other Bantu groups; European.

**Principal Religions:** Christian 60%, indigenous beliefs 40%.

**Chief Commercial Products:** Sugar asbestos, wood and forest products, citrus, cotton, iron ore.

**GNI per capita:** $1,350 (2003)

**Currency:** Emalangeni (at par with the South African Rand).

**Former Colonial Status:** Under South African protection (1894–1906); British Protectorate (1906–1968).

**Chief of State:** King Mswati III (b. 1966).

**Independence Date:** September 6, 1968.

**National Flag:** Horizontal stripes of dark blue, red and dark blue, divided by thin yellow bands. A shield and spear design is in the center of the red stripe.

High plateaus and forested mountains are found in western Swaziland, gradually descending from a maximum of 4,500 feet to a central region to an average height of 2800 feet. These highlands give way to a lowland in the East, and the Lubombo Mountains rise at the easternmost border. The temperate climate is warm enough to permit large quantities of sugar cane to grow, but at the same time it is ideally suited for forest growth of excellent hardwoods.

**History:** Swaziland was thinly inhabited by a variety of Bantu groups in the 18th century. The Swazis migrated to the area from what is now Mozambique about 1750. The British–Boer competition in the last two decades of the 19th century resulted in Swaziland becoming a British protectorate. For details of early and colonial history, see *Historical Background* and *The British in Africa.*

The British granted independence to Swaziland on September 6, 1968, which was done in formal ceremonies in Mbabane. Many foreign representatives were present, along with King Sobhuza's 112 wives.

All 24 seats of the National Assembly were held initially by King Sobhuza's National Movement. Reigning since 1921 until his death in 1982, he was the world's oldest ruling monarch. Elections in 1972 reduced the party to 21 seats; Dr. Ambrose Zwane's National Liberatory Congress Party won three seats and six additional members were appointed by the King. Within weeks the King abolished the constitution, dismissed the Assembly, and announced he would rule the old-fashioned way—by decree. Later, in 1979, a new bicameral parliament was opened consisting of a 50-member lower house and a 20-member upper house. Ten of each were chosen directly by the King.

King Sobhuza died in August 1982. Intrigue and plotting among the wives and 70 sons of the dead monarch began before he was buried. The struggles revolved around (1) The Queen Regent, (2) the *Liqoqo* (National Council), (3) the "Authorized Person" (4) The Prime Minister and (5) The House of Assembly and the Senate.

The young Crown Prince, the second–youngest son (and 67th child) of the late king, studied in Britain until 1986, when he reached the age of 18; his coronation was held on April 25, 1986. The young king quickly moved to assert his power, reshuffling the cabinet, dismissing the *Liqoqo*, and replacing the Prime Minister.

The Swazi King is one of the world's last absolute monarchs. While the country has a bicameral legislature, the king appoints a number of its members, has the power to dissolve it, and can rule by decree. Political parties have been banned in Swaziland since 1973, and it is the king who appoints the cabinet.

Legislative elections were held in September and October 1998. As a result of the ban on political parties, parliamentary candidates emerged through the three-tiered *Tinkundla* system. Tinkundlas, or traditional assemblies, nominate candidates—generally conservative and loyal to the king—in all the chiefdoms of Swaziland. These hopefuls are pared down in primary elections, with the remaining candidates vying in secondaries for 55 seats in the House of Assembly. Candidates run as individuals and cannot run on a party platform. The king appoints a further 10 members of the assembly.

From the assembly, the king appoints his government, the cabinet. In 1998 King Mswati III re-appointed his Prime Minister, Sibususo Dlamini. Of the 16 members of the cabinet, only 3 had been elected. All the others had been appointed to the assembly by the King. Electoral accountability is irrelevant in an absolute monarchy.

The Swazi senate has 30 members, none of whom is directly elected. Twenty members are royal appointees. The remaining 10 are selected by the assembly. The whole system is designed to keep the King and his relatives in positions of power.

The Swaziland Federation of Trade Unions (SFTU) and the unofficial opposition, the Swaziland Democratic Alliance, remain the most vocal opponents of Swaziland's absolute monarchy. With their leadership subject to arrest and intimidation, however, the groups have not yet been able to turn the monarchy to a more open and pluralist political system.

The SFTU did pressure authorities to create a commission on a new constitution in 1994, but royalists and traditionalists make up the bulk of committee members. Actual work did not begin until 1996, and the commission was to have completed its work in 1998, but the King, finding it easier to rule by decree, postponed the commission's deadline indefinitely.

In December 2001, the hearings having concluded, Mswati appointed a team to draft the new constitution within the next 18 months. By May 2003, after more than seven years (and costs of $43 million), the drafting process had not yet been completed. Pressure built up, and Mswati announced in March 2004 that the country would have a constitution by the end of the year.

A traditional "Peoples Parliament" was summoned in September at the royal cattle kraal to discuss the work of the constitutional drafting committees, and the King announced that all debate must end, including parliament's review and passage, by mid-November. The calendar was strictly followed; the Senate approved the palace-authored document in mid-November, completing the process. The new constitution affirmed the King's absolute authority—over the legislature, security forces, and other institutions of government. The ban on political parties, in force for over thirty years, was retained. In one notable concession to democratic participation, the constitution allowed for the popular recall of members of parliament. An umbrella group of human rights, labor, and religious organizations announced they would challenge the constitution in Swaziland's High Court.

In recent years Swazi absolutism has lurched from crisis to crisis, and from one public relations disaster to another. In November 2002 the prime minister said the government would ignore a Court of Appeal ruling that denied the King's power to issue laws by decree. A second decision by the court was also rejected, provoking a rule of law crisis: All six South African judges (on loan to Swaziland) who make up the Court of Appeal—the country's highest court—resigned to protest the government's decision to ignore their rulings.

The King found himself the object of legal action when the mother of a teenager he had chosen to be his tenth wife sued for the return of her daughter. The Attorney General went to the judge hearing the case and threatened to have him fired if he did not drop the case. The judge refused and soon resigned, presumably under great pressure.

Even Swaziland's parliament, filled with royal relatives, decided to resist the King. It refused to approve purchase of a $48 million luxury plane for his majesty, proving once again how much easier it is to rule by degree. The debate was intense, and one MP (Marwick Khumalo, the king's cousin) noted the Kingdom could ill-afford such extravagance while 140,000

of the King's one million subjects were currently starving.

An absolute monarch does take lightly such personal rebukes. In March 2004 Mswati refused to open parliament until its Speaker, Marwick Khumalo (who had criticized the royal request for jet transportation two years before) quit. "I was called to the royal residence," said Khumalo, and formally told that the King had instructed that I should resign." It was feared, he told a French news agency, that he would overwhelm the parliament with his "unpopular political influence."

In political parlance, Mswati II is tone deaf. While his countrymen faced drought-induced starvation, the King asked parliament for money to build palaces for his (now) eleven wives in January 2004. The request amounted to $15 million—almost as much as the country's 2002 health budget. Two more wives have since been added to the royal seraglio.

In April 2004, the King celebrated his 36th birthday with a profligate expenditure of more than $612,000. Ten thousand guests gathered in the national football stadium to devour a portion of the national treasury. Included in the festivity's costs were 10 new BMWs. By December, these proved insufficient to royal need, and the King purchased a luxury vehicle for a princely half million dollars. Among the car's creature comforts: a TV receiver, 21-speaker surround sound system, refrigerator, telephone, heated steering wheel, interior pollen and dust filter, golf bag and silver champagne flutes. Pictures

of the vehicle have been prohibited, by royal decree.

**Culture:** About 80% of Swazis live as peasant farmers on Swazi national land, "king's land," distributed through local chiefs. Deeply conservative, rural Swazi are fully aware that had not foreign ideologies been resisted by kings past, there would be no Swazi nation today. Modern urbanites talking of human rights and democracy are in many ways out of touch with Swazi reality.

The King, by custom the father of all his subjects and the embodiment of the nation, has stated that he would never recognize "anyone who comes to me saying he represents other Swazis." It's a statement that dramatizes the tensions between tradition and modernity that bedevil the Kingdom.

Lacking the age and stature of his father, Mswati seems to have been unable to resist the pressures of royals and traditionalists. Many increasingly wonder if he has the internal resources to provide the leadership Swaziland needs. King Mswati seems no Alexander the Great, capable of cutting the Gordian knot of Swazi politics and leading his people into the 21st century.

Statistics describe the terrifying advance of AIDS among Swazis. With Botswana claiming to have reduced its infection rate to 37.5%, Swaziland, with an infection rate pegged at 40% now has the dubious distinction of the world's highest adult HIV/AIDS infection rate. More than 380,000 Swazis are already living with HIV/AIDS, and 20,000 people develop full-blown AIDS every year. At least five skilled workers in Swaziland's manufacturing sector die weekly, and the death of farm laborers and bread-winners has exacerbated the nation's food shortage, which threatens a quarter of the population. A decade ago life expectancy was 61. Now it is just 42.5 (2003).

King Mswati III has declared HIV/AIDS a "national disaster," but enlightenment on the subject is not necessarily found among his advisors. One described HIV/AIDS sufferers as "bad potatoes" and said they must be removed from society lest "all will go rotten." His solution was an isolation camp for victims of the disease.

Since HIV testing is not mandatory, most Swazi do not even know they are infected. To deal with the crisis, the government plans to roll out a seven-point program in 2004. Testing centers (still voluntary) will be increased; mother-to-child transmission will be targeted, and extended to the mother's male partner. Antiretroviral drugs will be aggressively distributed, lifting the number receiving

**An Outdoor Laundry**                    Photo by Rita Arendt

# Swaziland

them from 1,500 in 2003 to no less than 10,000 by the end of 2005. That will represent almost 50% of those eligible for treatment—a higher percentage than most countries.

AIDS orphans pose an especially critical problem. Child-headed households proliferate; at least 10% of Swazi households are "sibling families." The government estimates there will be 120,000 orphans by 2010—between ten and fifteen percent of the total population. The National Emergency Response Council on HIV/AIDS (NERCHA) has proposed establishing a corps of 10,000 women to act as surrogate parents for AIDS orphans.

Because these surrogates are already full-time mothers and will be asked to somehow find several hours a day to care for the orphans, NERCHA is requesting funding to pay the women for the additional work they do. The monies requested would provide a very modest stipend—about $40 a month, but in a tra-

ditional society, such a stipend would represent a revolutionary recognition of the economic value of women's domestic labor.

**Economy:** Swaziland's economy has been anemic for years, with a growth rate between two and three percent. In 2001, however, real economic growth slumped to 1.5%—an all-time low. The economy's prospects are not very promising. Persistent drought has damaged the agricultural sector and in September 2002 the governor of Swaziland's central bank described the economic slowdown as "exceptionally deep and broad, with no evidence that the downward spiral that began two years ago will see recovery."

Against an average population growth rate of 2.4% (1997-2003), there is little hope the average Swazi's standard of living will improve. High unemployment rates (40%) persist, and direct foreign investment is negligible. The Swazi economy is highly

dependent on neighboring South Africa, which surrounds it on three sides. Its currency is pegged to the South African Rand; all its oil is imported from South Africa, as is nearly all its electricity and 85% of its consumer goods.

Fifty percent of government revenue currently comes from customs receipts from the Southern African Customs Union (SACU), but these will be lost when the union is dissolved as part of a larger regional trade reform. To compensate for the loss, the government has embarked on an ambitious program to develop transportation and tourism. A new international airport, international conference center, new highways, luxury hotels, an industrial park and an amusement park, were launched in mid-2000 as part of King Mswati's Millennium Projects initiative.

One relative bright spot, until recently, has been Swaziland's principal export, sugar. The country is one of the world's lowest cost producers of sugar, and the industry is its biggest employer, creating an annual turnover of $1.5 billion and generating more than $637 million in export revenues. The whole industry has been artificially subsidized by the European Union, which purchased an annual quota for more than the international market price for sugar. With EU plans to slash its subsidies, the industry faces an unwanted threat.

Because cotton requires little water, unlike sugar, the government has recently contemplated resuscitation of local cotton production as a cash crop. Some 16,000 farmers were growing the crop in the 1990s, but by 2004, that number had dropped to 4,500. Ideally, any increased production could be bought by the textile factories that have opened as a consequence of America's African Growth and Opportunities Act (AGOA). Almost exclusively owned and operated by Taiwanese interests, the textile factories added some 28,000 new jobs to the Swazi economy. Even these are threatened with the removal of import quotas on textiles as of January 2005; nothing can compete, it seems, with cheap Chinese labor costs. The Swazi government estimates that a third of all industry jobs will be lost by mid-2005.

Swaziland's mountainous northern region is one of Southern Africa's prime marijuana growing areas, and the crop has been a real money-earner for Swazi farmers. Most of the buyers are South African drug-traffickers from Johannesburg and Durban who ship the bulk of their purchases to Europe.

King Sobhuza II, father of His Majesty Mswati III, became King of Swaziland in 1921 at the age of twenty-two. He ruled the country until his death in August of 1982.

**The Future:** It's difficult to see much of a future for absolute monarchy, even in such a deeply traditional society as Swaziland.

# The Republic of Zambia

**Victoria Falls**

Photo by Joe Joyner

**Area:** 745,920 sq. km. = 288,000 sq. mi. (The size of Nebraska, South Dakota, Iowa and Minnesota combined.)

**Population:** 11,261,795 (July 2005 est.)

**Capital City:** Lusaka (Pop. 1.2 million, estimated).

**Climate:** Temperate, because of its altitude, although Zambia lies close to the Equator. There is a wet season (October–April) and a dry season (May–September).

**Neighboring Countries:** Angola (West); Congo-Kinshasa (Northwest); Tanzania (Northeast); Malawi (East); Mozambique (Southeast); Zimbabwe and Botswana (South).

**Official Language:** English

**Other Principal Languages:** Over 30, including Bemba, Kaonde, Lamba, Lozi, Lunda, Luvale, Mwanga, Nsenga, Nyanja Nyiha, Tonga, and Tumbuka.

**Ethnic groups:** African 98.7%, European 1.1%, other 0.2%.

**Principal Religions:** Christian 50%–75%, Muslim and Hindu 24%–49%, indigenous beliefs 1%.

**Chief Commercial Products:** Copper, cobalt, zinc, lead, and tobacco.

**Per capita GNI:** $380 (2003).

**Currency:** 1 Zambian Kwacha (ZK) = 100 ngwee.

**Former Colonial Status:** British South Africa Company administration (1895–1923); British Colony (1924–1964).

**Independence Date:** October 24, 1964.

**Chief of State:** Levy Mwanawasa, President (since December 27, 2001)

**National Flag:** Green, with an orange eagle in flight over a square block of three vertical stripes, red, black and red, on the right side.

The Republic of Zambia is located in south central Africa, stretching 750 miles west from the mountains of the great Western Rift. This is a high plateau country with an average elevation of 3,500 feet above sea level, which modifies its otherwise equatorial climate. It is only in the low river valleys that any oppressive heat and humidity are encountered.

The gently rolling country alternates between the waving grasses of the plains and forests of widely spaced trees. Great numbers of wildlife are supported by the vegetation which grows rapidly during the rainy season of the year. The country is drained by two major river systems: the tributaries flowing north to the Congo River, and the Zambezi River, which flows southeast through Mozambique to the Indian Ocean. One of the greatest sheets of flowing water in the world is found at incomparable Victoria Falls, near Livingstone in the South. Swampy Lake Banguelu spreads its great width in the north–central part of the country; the deep blue sparkling waters of Lake Mweru and Lake Tanganyika are found in the North.

**History:** Like many of the adjacent countries, Zambia was probably inhabited in early times by pygmies and other groups. The great wave of Bantu migration over a period of several centuries virtually took over this country, and very few indications remain of earlier civilizations. For details of early and colonial history, see *Historical Background* and *The British in Africa*.

Northern Rhodesia became fully independent in 1964, taking the name Zambia from the Zambezi River. A republican form of government was established with a single legislative house initially composed of 75 members, but later increased in size. Until 1969, ten seats were reserved for white voters. The president is chosen by direct election; Kenneth Kaunda was selected as the first president in 1964.

Initially there were two major parties— the United National Independence Party (UNIP), led by Kaunda and the African National Congress (ANC), led by Harry Nkumbula (who died in 1984 in neighboring Zimbabwe). After winning a large majority in 1968, Kaunda abolished the opposition party in the name of "national unity."

Racial, religious and tribal frictions have been frequent in Zambia since independence. Political repression added to dissatisfaction with Kaunda by many. Massive nationalization of every major enterprise was started in late 1970. A system of state–owned and managed businesses and marketing facilities was instituted. Because of poor planning and lack of technical skills, the economy, particularly in the agricultural sector, suffered.

In the early 1970s, Kaunda silenced all organized political opposition. Zambia was officially made a one-party state, with UNIP the sole party. The Assembly was dissolved in 1973 and new elections were set. A "primary" election was first held; before a successful candidate could run in the general election he had to have the approval of the UNIP Central Committee; several who won in the primary were eliminated in this way. Twenty candidates were announced as "official candidates" of the party, insuring their election.

In order to receive desperately needed funds from the International Monetary Fund and the World Bank, austerity programs were instituted in the 1980s. Unpopular, they failed to improve economic conditions. Zambia broke with the IMF in May 1987 and decreed that only 10% of its export earnings would be used to repay and service external debt. This led to a freeze on outside assistance at a time when the country was again gripped by drought.

Unopposed, President Kaunda was re-elected to a sixth five–year term in 1988. Voter turnout was substantially lower than in prior elections, indicating increasing dissatisfaction with the government.

By 1990 the pressures for change had reached a breaking point. UNIP continued to endorse the single–party system, but increased food prices provoked riots and an attempted coup. Bowing to intense dissatisfaction, President Kaunda announced multi–party elections would be permitted.

On October 31, 1991, Zambians voted to decide the fate of one of Africa's most senior statesmen in the first multiparty elec-

181

# Zambia

tions in 23 years. The campaign was hard–fought. Kaunda was accused of being out of touch with the people and failing to control and economy which had produced an annual inflation rate of 400%. His opponent, Frederick Chiluba, a labor leader and head of the Movement for Multi–Party Democracy (MMD), stressed the need to eliminate almost universal corruption and theft in the government.

Kaunda, who had been in power for 27 years, was soundly defeated. Chiluba's party gained 125 of the 150 legislative seats. During his first term President Chiluba managed to reverse socialist patterns by privatizing 140 state–owned, unprofitable industries. The government monopoly on foodstuffs was ended, resulting in higher prices for commodities, but he high external debt was lowered by $2 billion.

Old problems—inflation and currency devaluation—continued. Corruption within an overstaffed bureaucracy was notorious. As November 1996 elections drew near, it became apparent that Kenneth Kaunda ("KK") would attempt a comeback. President Chiluba averted this by pushing through two constitutional amendments specifically designed to eliminate Kaunda. The first required that both parents of a candidate be Zambian. (Kaunda's parents were both from Malawi.) The second removed the requirement that a candidate win more than half the ballots to be declared president, making it possible to be elected president with a plurality of votes. Furious but helpless, Kaunda's followers boycotted the election.

Despite this the turnout was 40%; Chiluba and his Movement for Multiparty Democracy (MMD) won, gaining 131 seats in the legislature. Kaunda threatened continued civil disobedience and strikes, but was muted by a threat of criminal prosecution.

In many ways it is regrettable Kenneth Kaunda did not depart the field of political combat with greater grace. Gracious retirement is always becoming, especially in Africa where its appearance is so infrequent. The departure from power of Senegal's Leopold Senghor, Tanzania's Julius Nyerere and Ketumile Masire of Botswana has given luster to their reputations. This will not be so with Kaunda. In the bitterness of rejection and defeat he became intemperate and hostile. With rhetorical excess he warned Zambians of an "explosion" soon to come if the MMD refused to dialogue with opposition parties, i.e., Kenneth Kaunda. "Something big will come," he said, "and of course MMD will blame UNIP for that. But it won't be UNIP," he continued, "it will be the people of Zambia who are going to act."

Local elections in 1998 produced a massive victory for candidates of President Chiluba's MMD. Some 16 parties and over 400 independent candidates participated in the elections for 1,286 municipal seats. A potentially strong new party, the United Party for National Development (UPND) emerged in the election. Led by Anderson Mazoka, the outgoing head of the Anglo-American Corporation's East African operations, UPND stressed poverty alleviation as its goal. It committed itself to reduce Zambia's poverty from its 50% level to below 20%. Kenneth Kaunda campaigned widely for UNIP candidates, but to little avail. When the final results came in—from abysmally low participation—MMD had won 880 seats and UNIP 234. The new kid on the block, UPND, won 28 seats.

Events in Zambia seem to prove the adage that power is an aphrodisiac capable of generating passionate lust for itself. President Chiluba, elected to office as a reformer and committed to term limits, spent most of 2000 and 2001 seeking ways to secure himself a third term. Teams of lawyers and parliamentarians were sent to Namibia to see how it had been done there. MMD members were prohibited from announcing candidacy for the 2001 elections, and when one cabinet member, Ben Mwila, violated the edict, he was summarily dismissed.

President Chiluba coyly refrained from expressing any public desire for a third term, but everywhere his minions busily pursued the president's ambition. It was an aspiration that divided cabinet, party, and country. Those who opposed a third term were ruthlessly dispatched. Political frustration was ventilated in the streets. Violent protests erupted, and police had to intervene with tear gas. Finally, President Chiluba listened. In early May 2001 he announced that he would not seek a third term.

Thwarted but undaunted, Chiluba handpicked his successor, plucking a former vice-president, Levy Mwanawasa, out of political retirement to be the MMD presidential candidate. (Mwanawasa had switched parties to join the ruling Movement for Multiparty Democracy only a day before his appointment, angering MMD heavyweights who sought the job for themselves.) One of Zambia's leading lawyers, Mwanawasa had once served as solicitor general in the government of Kenneth Kaunda and had been the first MMD vice president in 1991. He resigned the office in 1994, criticizing the MMD's tolerance of corruption and drug trafficking, gaining a reputation as a man of integrity. It was something President Chiluba and the MMD sorely needed, but the way candidate Mwanawasa had been chosen made it appear he was little more than Chiluba's puppet.

The December 2001 presidential and parliamentary elections were overtly rigged by the Chiluba government; the EU's chief official observer described the results as both untrue and unreliable. The Electoral Commission of Zambia (ECZ) nevertheless declared the MMD's Levy Mwanawasa the victor after he won 28% of the ballots against the UPND's Anderson Mazoka, who got 27%. Nine other candidates split the remaining votes.

In parliamentary elections the MMD won 66 seats in the 158-member National Assembly. UNIP won 11 seats, while the Forum for Democracy and Development (FDD) took nine, and the Heritage Party took four. The remaining seats were attributed to minor parties.

The opposition quickly launched a series of legal challenges to the elections with Zambia's Supreme Court. The court annulled results in four district elections and stripped the MMD of its deputies, reducing the President's majority in parlia-

**President Levy Mwanawasa**

ment to a slender three votes. President Mwanawasa said he would resign as president if the court invalidated the election results, but that proved unnecessary when the court finally rejected the challenge in February 2005. It noted that the voting was flawed, but the errors did not affect the final result.

In the two and a half years he has been president, Mwanawasa has gained some popularity by the vigor with which he has pursued an anti-corruption campaign. Mwanawasa appointed a special Task Force to investigate and prosecute corrupt officials, and the biggest fish netted thus far have been ex-President Chiluba and numerous officials from his regime. The task force has identified office buildings and houses which the suspects owned in Britain, Belgium and other countries and announced it planned to seize those believed to have been purchased with state funds.

The indictment of ex-president Chiluba has deeply divided the MMD, weakening President Mwanawasa's base of support. Northern loyalists (the north voted solidly for Mwanawasa) can no longer be depended on, and Mwanawasa seems to have admitted this. The president has reshuffled his cabinet, bringing in politicians from traditional opposition areas in the south. The new cabinet (besides expanding significantly) broadened ethnic and regional representation in the government, but also threw the opposition into disarray.

Since taking office President Mwanawasa has been hammered from every side. Ex-president Chiluba, determined to play the spoiler, has backed the formation of a new party (the Party for Unity, Democracy and Development with its somewhat

infelicitous acronym PUDD) which continues to weaken Mwanawasa's support in the MMD. He has fired two vice-presidents and has had to face impeachment proceedings, charging him with violating the constitution by appointment a vice president who was not a member of parliament.

He survived the impeachment threat, but has had to face paralyzing strikes by government workers. The IMF withheld $100 million in aid when the government could not control its budget overruns. Western donors followed suit, leaving the government with nothing to offer its angry workers but future installment payments.

The government was under enormous pressure to get its financial house in order. Budgetary deficits prevented Zambia from moving forward in the Highly Indebted Poor Countries initiative (HIPC) which would significantly reduce crippling debt service costs. The consequence had devastating impact on its ability to provide social services: in 2004, for example, it would spend $156 million more on debt repayment than it would on education.

An austerity budget was presented in February 2004. The government would increase revenues by increasing taxes and cut costs by freezing the salaries of public service workers, a move that set off immediate protests. (According to the Zambian Central Statistics Office, more than 70% of government workers earn less than $100 a month.) The political gamble paid off. In early 2005 Zambia attained the HIPC completion point, and in April the World Bank approved a $3.8 billion debt relief package. Twenty to fifty million dollars a year in debt-servicing payments will be freed up to bolster the country's social services.

Civil society NGOs and opposition groups continue to pressure President Mwanawasa for major constitutional changes, i.e. a new constitution. A 41-member Constitutional Review Commission was appointed in May 2003. It's an exercise Zambians are familiar with: the original independence constitution has been replaced three times in the past 40 years. One technical committee of the commission's has already made several recommendations: eliminate the requirement that both parents of a presidential candidate be Zambian by birth; repeal restrictions on traditional chiefs from participating in elections; and require that the president be elected by a majority of all voters, requiring a run-off election if necessary between the top two candidates. The president has said he doesn't think the new constitution will be ready until May 2008 while opposition groups are demanding it be finished by December 2005, in time to apply to the 2006 elections.

The constant conflict and criticism has taken its toll on the president; he has survived, but seems exhausted. "Sometimes," he was quoted as saying, "I ponder to myself and say why is it that I have never enjoyed being president. I am tired of being criticized. I can't stand it any more."

**Culture:** Zambians tend to be conservative and closely knit within their communities—the majority are Christian, particularly in the more densely populated South and West, but many in the rural section of the North retain their traditional beliefs.

In March 1999 the ministry of health reported that 73% of Zambia's estimated 9 million people were infected with tuberculosis, and 30% of that was related to the HIV/AIDS pandemic. Some 21.5% of all adults are HIV positive and 200 a day die of the disease. As a consequence of the epidemic, life expectancy has dropped to 36.5 years (2003)—among the lowest in the world.

The northern town of Livingston has a 28% rate, making it the most afflicted town in Zambia. The cost of AIDS treatment has risen uncontrollably and continues to do so. Zambia's Central Health Board has said the budgetary costs of treating AIDS patients will rise from $1.7 million in 1990 to $21 million in 2005.

In early 2002, the Zambian youth ministry announced that there were an estimated 700,000 (the World Food Program estimates 572,000) AIDS orphans in the country. Many wind up on the streets of Zambia's cities, especially the capital, Lusaka. There, females are exploited and treated as sex objects, often raped, abused, and abandoned. Street boys tend

**Modern Lusaka**                    ©IRIN

# Zambia

to live in groups and survive by forming a gang to protect themselves. Though they don't get raped, there is a good deal of "compassionate sex" among themselves, which produces the inevitable sexually transmitted diseases.

The World Bank pledged $42 million to assist Zambia's anti-AIDS campaign, but disbursement of the funds was dependent on legislation guaranteeing the provision of antiretroviral drugs to people who need them. In 2003 the government introduced heavily-subsidized antiretrovirals (ARV) for 10,000 HIV-positive people at around eight dollars a month—a significant reduction from the regular $250 a month cost. Greater availability and treatment success have led to additional problems.

With insufficient awareness that ARV-treatment is life-long, patients have gone off the drug once feeling better. Zambian health officials are now warning of the emergence of strains of HIV that are resistant to current drug treatment. In August 2004 the government announced that it had begun the manufacture of cheap generic antiretroviral (ARV) drugs with Cuban assistance. In May 2005 it was reported that over 22,000 people have been on ARV treatment since the first of the year.

A good deal of thinking about AIDS in Zambia is influenced by religion. Safe-sex messages are often worded in moral terms. One AIDS mural proclaims "One Zambia. One Nation. One Husband. One Wife," suggesting that the disease can be prevented by marital fidelity. Sentiment is trumped by reality however. In Zambia many women become the property of their husband's relatives when the husband dies, helping the virus to spread.

**Economy:** Zambia is one of sub-Saharan Africa's most urbanized countries. Nearly one-half the population is concentrated in a few urban zones, and rural areas are under-populated. While agriculture supports half the population, with corn the principal food crop and money earner, it is copper that dominates the Zambian economy.

Zambia has long been copper-dependent. The metal traditionally produced 80% of national export revenues, and one mining company, Zambia Consolidated Copper Mines (ZCCM), contributed 25% of GDP. Socialist-style planning and administration during the Kaunda years did not help the industry develop. Two decades of under funding and a shortage of capital investment in new mines dragged copper production from its peak of 720,000 tons in 1969 to 320,000 in 1996.

The economy deteriorated rapidly as copper revenues sank. State enterprises, already bureaucratically inefficient, became heavily indebted. Deficit budgeting

increased debt and inflation. Goods and services were in short supply. Business confidence disappeared and consumer frustration mounted. The pressures forced the authoritarian Kaunda to open the political system to competitive multiparty elections. Given a voice, electors tossed him out in 1991.

The Chiluba government introduced far-reaching, market-oriented reforms. Markets were liberalized so prices were determined in the market place, not the bureaucratic office. More than 300 state enterprises were privatized, and about 82% of them were sold to Zambians, most of them well within the ambit of Zambia's governing party.

Economic reform has not meant improvement in the lives of most Zambians.

At least 73% live below the poverty line of less than a dollar per day, according to the World Bank. Formal employment has declined from 537,300 in 1990 to 200,000 in 2000. Less that ten per cent of working age Zambians work full time in the formal sector; thousands have taken to selling whatever they can find in petty-retailing markets. Prostitution, a good indicator of social breakdown, has skyrocketed since 1992.

The state mining conglomerate, ZCCM, was broken up and its constituent parts sold off after much hesitancy and delay on the part of the government. This only diminished the value of what was being sold. New management and capitalization failed to halt production declines in copper. The industry produced 256,000 tons of copper in 2000, slightly down from the 260,300 tons produced in 1999. In January 2002 the new owners of the Konkola Copper Mines (KCM) announced they were pulling out, unable to make the mines profitable with current low commodity prices. The mines remained closed for almost a year while the government sought a new buyer. (Konkola reported a loss of $159 million in 2002.) In August 2003 India's Vedanta Resources purchased 51% of KCM shares for a rock-bottom price of $25 million. With good prices on the international market, Zambian copper earnings in 2005 are expected to reach $1.3 billion.

There are signs of promising diversity, allowing Zambia to move away from its copper dependence. The country annually earns $20.3 million from the sale of gemstones, mostly emeralds. Zambia now produces 20% of the world's emeralds, and one geologist believes that with modern technology and management annual gemstone earnings could rise to $250 million. In addition to high-quality emeralds, Zambia is also endowed with rich deposits of amethysts, aquamarines, and red garnets.

China has had a long-term interest in Zambia, establishing diplomatic relations only five days after independence. It has offered assistance in a variety of areas, ranging from telecommunications, medicine, education, and tourism (designating Zambia, along with seven other African countries "Approved Destination Status" for Chinese tourists) to infrastructure improvement. It helped construct the Tanzania, Zambia Railway (TAZARA), while Sinohydro Corporation signed an agreement with Zambia Electricity Corporation (Zesco) to develop a power station on the Lower Kafue Gorge costing upwards of $600 million; when fully operational the station will have a capacity of 660 MW. Chinese investment in the country now totals over $268 million.

**The Future:** Daunting.

# The Republic of Zimbabwe

**Lake Kariba, formed by damming the Zambezi River**

**Area:** 391.090 sq. km. = 151,000 sq. mi. (slightly larger than Montana)

**Population:** 12,746,990 (July 2005 est.)

**Capital City:** Harare (Pop. 1.5 million)

**Climate:** Hot and humid in the southern Limpopo and Sabi River regions; temperate in the central and northern highlands. A rainy season normally lasts from October to April and there is a dry season from May to September. Drought conditions prevailed from 1981 to 1984.

**Neighboring Countries:** Zambia (North); Namibia (South–West Africa, West); Botswana (Southwest); Republic of South Africa (South); Mozambique (East).

**Official Language:** English.

**Other Principal Languages:** Shona, Sindebele (the language of the Ndebele, sometimes called Ndebele).

**Ethnic groups:** Shona 82%, Ndebele 14%, other African 2%, mixed and Asian 1%, white less than 1%.

**Principal Religions:** Syncretic (part Christian, part indigenous beliefs) 50%, Christian 25%, indigenous beliefs 24%, Muslim and other 1%.

**Chief Commercial Products:** Tobacco, gold, ferroalloys, and cotton.

**GDP per capita (**constant 1995 US$): $520 (2003)

**Currency:** Zimbabwean Dollar.

**Former Colonial Status:** Administered by the British South Africa Company (1889–1923); Autonomous state within the British Commonwealth (1923–1965); unilateral independence as *Rhodesia* (1965–1980), recognized independence (1980).

**Chief of State:** Robert Mugabe, President.

**Independence Date:** April 18, 1980.

**National Flag:** Seven horizontal stripes (top to bottom) of green, gold, red, black, red, gold, green. A white triangle at the staff contains a red star in which is centered the gold Zimbabwean bird.

Zimbabwe is hot and humid in the southern river basin areas. Cluttered forests of hardwood predominate in these lowlands, with both teak and mahogany towering above the scrub vegetation that is the breeding ground of the tsetse fly, carrier of dreaded sleeping sickness.

In the central areas the altitude rises in a series of fertile plateaus, with corresponding modification of the tropical climate. During the winter, the land sometimes gives off enough heat at night to allow the intrusion of a thin frost by dawn. The land that is not forested by tall trees, growing in a less densely vegetated woodland, is under cultivation.

Victoria Falls, located on the Zambezi River is one of the greatest sights of Africa—they are more than twice as high as Niagara Falls and have a width of about one mile. The sparkling waters of Lake Kariba, downstream from the Falls, stretch narrowly to the northeast, held back by the 420–foot–high walls of the Kariba Dam that provides electric power to both Zimbabwe and Zambia.

**History:** There were successive waves of Bantu migration into Zimbabwe which may have started as early as about the 4th century A.D. The Zimbabwe ruins, the only pre-European remnant of architecture found below the Sahara in Africa, is attributed to people known as the Monoma and are dated sometime between the 9th and 13th centuries, A.D. The Shona settled at an unknown time in the region; the Zulu and Barotse passed through during their migration to the south, and the Ndebele eventually came to dominate both the Shona and the region. For details of earlier history, see *Historical Background* and *The British in Africa*.

By 1923 white settlers had gained self-rule for Rhodesia. This was confirmed in 1923 when white electors rejected the possibility of joining South Africa. Instead

# Zimbabwe

Rhodesia became an autonomous member of the British Commonwealth. Although Britain reserved authority in the areas of foreign relations and military defense, that authority was never in fact exercised. A parliament of British settlers was chosen; Africans could not, with very few exceptions, pass the educational tests required to gain voting rights.

White control was further solidified in 1931 with the passage of the Land Apportionment Act. About 150,000 settlers were given exclusive rights to roughly one-half of the choicest land; 3,000,000 Africans were relegated to the remainder. Land would always be central to Zimbabwean politics.

In 1953 Southern Rhodesia was joined with Northern Rhodesia and Nyasaland to make the Central African Federation. The federation was dissolved in 1963, and Northern Rhodesia and Nyasaland were given independence as Zambia and Malawi respectively. Fearing a similar development, white Southern Rhodesians rejected the governing United Federal Party and replaced it with the more conservative Rhodesian Front (RF). By 1964 the RF was led by Ian Douglas Smith. Smith's Rhodesian Front swept the elections of 1965 and after several attempts to persuade Britain to grant independence, his government announced the Unilateral Declaration of Independence (UDI) on 11 November 1965.

## After UDI

African nationalist organizations began to flourish after 1953, a development greeted with hostility by colonial officials. The first commanding nationalist figure was Joshua Nkomo. In 1961, Nkomo (an Ndebele) joined with Robert Mugabe (a Shona), and Reverend Ndabiningi Sithole (an Ndau) to form the Zimbabwe People's Union (ZAPU). By 1963, however, Sithole, Mugabe and other Shona intellectuals, disappointed with his leadership, split from Nkomo and formed the Zimbabwe African National Union (ZANU). The split shattered what had been a multiethnic and multiregional anti-colonial movement. It shaped political rivalries well into the post-independence period. Two movements claiming nationalist goals would each become ethnically specific and regionally localized. At the declaration of UDI, African anti-colonial forces were thus divided.

UN resolutions condemned white rule in Rhodesia, and one forbade any member nation to trade with Rhodesia. Since Rhodesia was one of the very few sources outside the U.S.S.R. of chrome ore vital to the manufacture of hard steel, the U.S. Congress allowed the resumption of Rhodesian chrome purchases in 1971, in-

furiating Black African nations. Faced with international sanctions, Rhodesia turned to the development of import-substitution industries, ironically providing the basis for one of Zimbabwe's greatest economic strengths: a richly diversified economy.

Negotiations with the Smith regime came to naught. Within Rhodesia Smith allowed the creation of a third nationalist movement, the United African National Council (UANC) led by Abel Muzorewa, a bishop of the American United Methodist Church. Anxious to deal with moderate nationalist elements, Smith opened talks with Bishop Muzorewa and two other black leaders, Chief Jeremiah Chirau and Reverend Sithole, who had lost out in a ZANU leadership struggle with Robert Mugabe. Both Britain and the U.S. urged that ZAPU and ZANU be included in the talks, but this plea was ignored. Both groups had already established themselves in neighboring Zambia and had launched minor guerrilla attacks against the regime since 1965.

All-out guerrilla war began in 1972 against isolated white farmers in northeastern Rhodesia. With the collapse of Portuguese authority in 1974, ZANU guerrilla forces found a permanent base of operations in Mozambique under Robert Mugabe. Joshua Nkomo and his ZAPU supporters raised their own guerrilla army, largely Ndebele speakers from southwestern Rhodesia, and opened a second front in the guerrilla war. ZAPU guerrilla activities continued to operate out of Zambia. Both Mozambique and Zambia suffered terribly as targets of Rhodesian retaliation. By 1976 Mozambique and Zambia pressured the two guerrilla movements to fight the Smith regime jointly. This resulted in the creation of the Patriotic Front of Zimbabwe.

When the guerrilla war took on serious economic consequences in 1978, and whites began to flee the country at the rate of 1,000 per month, Prime Minister Smith signed an "internal settlement" with Muzorewa, Sithole and Chirau providing for qualified majority rule and elections with universal suffrage. Mugabe and Nkomo scoffed at this internal settlement and branded the other Black leaders as "Uncle Toms." Even when total amnesty was offered to Patriotic Front guerrillas, their leaders rejected it. In the parliamentary elections of 1979, Muzorewa's UANC won 51 of the 72 seats allotted to African candidates, beating the ZANU splinter led by Reverend Sithole, which won only 12 seats. Muzorewa became Rhodesia's first black prime minister, but Whites retained key positions within the government and the army.

The guerrilla war continued and sanctions were not lifted. Britain decided to

end the crisis by creating a government which included all nationalist elements. The Lancaster House Conference began in London in September 1979 with Muzorewa, Nkomo and Mugabe. After endless weeks of fruitless discussions against a background of continuous fighting back home—an average of 100 lives were lost each day—the white minority finally consented to hold multiracial elections, supervised by the British, in 1980. These, it was agreed, would lead to independence for Zimbabwe.

The Lancaster House constitution would operate from 1980 to 1990, guaranteeing whites representation in parliament and protecting white economic interests. A bicameral legislature was established, with reserved seats for Whites in both houses. Compulsory land acquisition was prohibited, as was the establishment of a one-party state, before 1990. The draft constitution was accepted by the three leaders and a total of nine political parties prepared for the upcoming elections. Both elements of the Patriotic Front, Nkomo's PF-ZAPU, Mugabe's ZANU-PF, ran separate candidates, as did the Muzorewa and Sithole organizations.

The election resulted in a stunning triumph for Mugabe. ZANU won 57 of 80 Black seats in the House of Assembly. Nkomo's ZAPU was successful in 20 contests, mostly in Matabeleland, while Bishop Muzorewa was sent to humiliating defeat with only three victories. The white minority was badly frightened at the prospect of having the Marxist Mugabe as Prime Minister, but acting with conciliation he assured them they would be treated as all other Zimbabweans. With representatives of 100 nations on hand, Zimbabwe achieved recognized independence on April 18, 1980.

## Post-Independence Period

President Mugabe's politics of practical reconciliation was initially successful. Nkomo was appointed to a high-ranking cabinet position. Two prominent white Zimbabweans were also included. The new government's tasks were enormous. It had to integrate what were essentially three armies—the guerrilla forces of ZAPU and ZANU and the Rhodesian Defense Forces. It had to re-establish social services and education in the rural areas, and resettle a million refugees, displaced by nearly 15 years of civil conflict. Mugabe adopted a cautious approach to socializing the economy. Farmers were placated when prices for cash crops were raised. Despite populist pressures for land reform, he assured white farmers that their property would not be confiscated. These incentives produced surpluses that allowed Zimbabwe to weather draught-

# Zimbabwe

caused crop failures of 1982-84 better than most of her neighbors.

Fissures within the Patriotic Front soon developed. A cache of arms was allegedly found on Nkomo's farm and he, along with his closest aides, was accused of trying to overthrow the government. They were expelled from the cabinet in 1981. Nkomo's followers began a loosely organized campaign of dissidence against the government. Centered in Matabeleland, the dissidence involved attacks on both white farmers and government targets.

The government responded with the full force of emergency powers first granted the Smith regime and renewed annually ever since. Sweeping raids were conducted in Matabeleland after 1981. A strict curfew was imposed on the area and food shipments were withheld to starve the area into submission. In 1983 the notorious Fifth Brigade, trained by North Korea, was sent in to suppress the dissidence. The brigade, known as Gukurahundi, or "storm that destroys everything" accomplished its goal with ghastly violence. According to the Catholic Commission for Justice and Peace it was responsible for the death of an estimated 20,000 people between 1983 and 1987. The Matabele campaign demonstrated the regime's willingness to use violence and terror against its own people to consolidate its power.

In the 1985 general election, held at the height of the Matabeleland conflict, ZANU increased its parliamentary majority by eight seats and garnered 76% of the vote. Two years later Parliament elimi-

nated seats reserved for Whites. In November, the constitution was again amended to create the post of executive president with enhanced powers, combining the roles of head of state and head of government. Mugabe was then elected to the new presidency for a term of 6 years.

In the same month the two main political parties agreed to unify. Nkomo's ZAPU was absorbed into the ruling party, ZANU-PF. It marked the triumph of the Shona branch of Zimbabwean nationalism and the creation of a de facto single-party state. The constitution was later amended to provide a second vice-presidency to which Nkomo was appointed. ZANU-PF asserted it would "seek to establish a socialist society, on the guidance of Marxist-Leninist principles, and to establish a one-party state."

Despite state repression of political opposition, four opposition parties contested the March 1990 general election. Mugabe won 78% of the vote. The Catholic Commission for Justice and Peace claimed that pre-election violence and intimidation had been so great that it was "calling into question the freedom and fairness of the general election." Voter turn out was low—54%.

President Mugabe proved out of touch with his own party when he proposed to institutionalize the one-party state later that year. The proposal was strongly opposed by churches, trade unions and students, and led to strains within the party. Ultimately a majority of the Politburo rejected the Mugabe plan. With the collapse of the Soviet Union and the decline of

communist ideology in Eastern Europe, enthusiasm for Marxist-Leninist doctrine and rhetoric declined in Zimbabwe. In June, 1991 ZANU-PF's central committee decided to drop references to "Marxism-Leninism" and "scientific socialism" from the party's constitution.

Economic issues dominated Zimbabwean politics in the 1990s. With the expiration of the Lancaster House prohibition on forced land purchases, President Mugabe announced that the government would amend the constitution to speed up land redistribution. The Land Acquisition Act, finally passed in 1992, allowed for the compulsory purchase of 13,585,000 acres of predominantly white-owned land. The commercial farming community fiercely opposed the plan and its implementation was delayed. A regional drought in 1992 brought great suffering, and the Mugabe government, blamed for inadequate planning for the anticipated crop failure, became increasingly unpopular.

With popular discontent rising, fear of the regime diminished. As it seemed to weaken in popular support, the government returned to one of Zimbabwe's genuine hot-button issues: land redistribution. It published a list of farms to be purchased in May of 1993. Seventy farms, some of them the most productive in the country, amounting to 469,300 acres, were scheduled for compulsory purchase. A year later it was revealed that the first farm seized under the Land Acquisition Act had been leased to a government-minister. Many came to believe the government was more concerned with self-enrichment than the needs of its constituents.

The general parliamentary election in April 1995 did nothing to change the political landscape. ZANU-PF won its fourth successive electoral victory, winning 118 out of 120 seats. Zimbabwe was, to all intents, a single-party state.

Mugabe was overwhelmingly reelected for another 6-year term in March 1996, but less than one-third of the electorate bothered to vote. A seeming triumph, the figures suggested ZANU's diminishing legitimacy. Emboldened by the example of President Mandela's moral leadership to the South, legislators reacted vigorously to a series of corruption scandals that tainted the government. Looting of the veterans' compensation fund by high ZANU officials was exposed; 100 ZANU-PF legislators called for an official audit of the fund. Legislators also rejected a contract for a new terminal at the Harare International Airport when it was awarded to an inexperienced Cypriot company with close ties to President Mugabe's nephew.

Public demonstrations against the regime rose. Civil servants, railway work-

**Sorting tobacco**

Photo by David Johns

187

# Zimbabwe

ers, doctors and nurses, among others, protested wages and work conditions. Veterans of the liberation struggle, mostly poorly educated peasant farmers living in poverty, demanded payment and pensions for service. Food riots in January 1998 forced the government to send in the army when the police could no longer control the situation. The regime seemed to be unraveling.

## A Regime of Personal Rule

By 1998 Robert Mugabe's control over party and state in Zimbabwe had little credible and effective opposition. Authority had been concentrated in his hands by every constitutional amendment, and there were no checks to assure accountability. Zimbabwe was henceforth subjected to a regime of personal rule, and suffered the consequences.

Mugabe's economic mismanagement resulted in an economic meltdown. The value of the Zimbabwe dollar plummeted. Inflation soared. Prices on basic commodities rose beyond the capacity of most people to afford them. Mass "stay-aways" organized by the unions almost paralyzed the nation. The government acquiesced to populist demand. Fuel price increases were rescinded, and price controls were introduced on basic commodities. With government control over the economy accentuated, the International Monetary Fund withdrew its support.

Intensifying the domestic political crisis was President Mugabe's personal decision to intervene on behalf of Laurent Kabila when the Congo was convulsed by a second rebellion in August 1998. Mugabe's claim to be supporting a "legitimate" leader was pure sophistry, but then, one of the victims in any war is language. It was the case of one authoritarian coming to the rescue of another. It also demonstrated just how unaccountable leadership in Zimbabwe had become. The government went on an arms-buying spree. China, Zimbabwe's main arms supplier, became the source of fighter aircraft; Swiss-designed cluster bombs were added to the arsenal. Defense costs skyrocketed.

Polls indicated that 70% of the citizenry opposed Zimbabwe's presence in the Congo. Faced with criticism, President Mugabe abused his critics left, right and center. Zimbabwe's few independent newspapers were subjected to ferocious criticism and threats of much closer control. Labor unions, which had led demands for political reforms and articulated public anger over economic hardship, were subjected to a six-month ban on strikes as Mugabe cracked down on his critics.

Since 1999 Zimbabwe has continued its downward spiral into economic collapse

and political chaos, driven by the ambitions of one man: Robert Mugabe. Whenever there were problems, Mugabe found a scapegoat. When fuel shortages occurred, he accused white industrialists and farmers of hoarding it. In reality, the fuel crisis reflected all the ills of twenty years of authoritarian rule. Economic mismanagement was everywhere evident. Corruption and cronyism were rampant, and unilateral decision-making disastrous.

President Mugabe's decision to assist Laurent Kabila was a major factor in the country's tale of economic woe. The daily tab for keeping 11,000 troops in Congo was $1 million. Despite acute shortages and massive lines at the gas pumps, the National Oil Company of Zimbabwe (NOCZIM) continued shipping available fuel to support the war. To pay for its costs, Zimbabwe signed a variety of deals that tended to treat the Congo as a neo-colony, rich in exploitable resources. The deals suggested less public policy to amortize war costs, than a means to engage the loyalty of the army and provide enrichment opportunities for officers, cronies, and supporters.

In one remarkable deal, Zimbabwe's army—technically the Zimbabwe Defense Forces (ZDF)—created a company called Osleg to operate parallel to Comiex, a private company owned by the Democratic Republic of the Congo (DRC) army. The two companies were granted licenses to buy and sell diamonds and gold. Among others, Osleg directors included the permanent secretary of the Ministry of Defense and the ZDF commander, General Vitalis Zvinavashe.

Perhaps the most outrageous concession Zimbabwe secured from the Kabila government was the one to log some 84 million acres of Congo's rain forest—fifteen per cent of the Congo's territory. The concession was granted to Socebo (the French acronym for Congolese Society for the Exploitation of Timber), a company which was part of a web of ZANU-PF companies controlled by Robert Mugabe's right-hand man in financial matters, Emmerson Mnangagwa—Zimbabwe's parliamentary speaker. Though intended to generate and protect revenue streams for the country's political elite, Zimbabwe's Congo ventures failed miserably without the requisite expertise. In mid-2003 the army announced it was not involved in any commercial activity in the DRC.

Ineptitude, loss, and mismanagement in the Congo mirrored the general deterioration at home. Foreign exchange nearly disappeared. Inflation soared, as did the unemployment rate. Interest rates rose and the Zimbabwe dollar declined. Over 60% of the population lived below the poverty

**President Mugabe (early photo)**

line. This was the legacy of Robert Mugabe. Worsening conditions gave rise to two major political movements.

In September 1999 the Zimbabwe Confederation of Trade Unions (ZCTU) launched a new political party, the Movement for Democratic Change (MDC). The confederation's dynamic and effective secretary-general, Morgan Tsvangirai, was designated party leader. In the months to come the MDC would provide the kind of opposition the Mugabe regime had never seen before. Its capacity to mobilize opposition was facilitated by the pre-existent structure of grassroots union organizations.

The second movement sparked by deteriorating conditions was one to amend Zimbabwe's constitution. President Mugabe appointed an official Constitutional Commission to recommend changes. It held hearings and learned that Zimbabweans overwhelmingly wanted Mugabe's power to be limited.

The whole process ended in farce. A draft, which actually strengthened and consolidated the president's powers and allowed the confiscation of white-owned farms without compensation, was swept through the final meeting of the 400-member constitutional commission. No vote was taken. To delegates' roars of "No", Judge Godfrey Chidyausiku, the chairman, declared, "the draft is adopted by acclamation."

The MDC and commercial farmers organized a "No" campaign in the February 2002 referendum on new constitutional amendments. The government, which had never lost an election in twenty years, used its power to make its opponents' lives as miserable as possible. State print and broadcast media rejected all opposition advertising and virtually all statements critical of the draft constitution.

Despite governmental intimidation, the opposition handed President Mugabe his first defeat since independence. Fifty-five percent of those voting rejected the proposed amendments. Even the promise of white lands for Africans could not silence a populace suffering twenty years of misrule.

Like the wounded and cornered lion he was, Mugabe lashed out with special ferocity, unleashing a storm of violence that reduced Zimbabwe to governance by thuggery and fear. The country witnessed seemingly "spontaneous" invasions of white-owned farms by self-styled "war veterans," "disillusioned," they said, by rejection of the constitutional amendment allowing confiscation and redistribution of lands. The reality was somewhat different.

Many of the so-called "war veterans" were far too young to have ever served. They were in fact part of the mass of urban unemployed, carefully organized and dispersed throughout the country with logistical precision. The farm invasions began within a week of Mugabe's referendum defeat in February and ultimately involved 50,000 squatters invading up to 1,400 farms. London's *Sunday Telegraph* reported the man coordinating the land seizures and organizing food and transport for squatters was none other than General Perence Shiri.

The head of Zimbabwe's air force, General Shiri had also commanded the Fifth Brigade massacres in Matabeleland in the Eighties—probably the most notorious example of the state employing coercion against its own citizens. General Shiri's name also appeared on a list of 28 senior government and military figures given farms seized from white farmers.

The campaign was, quite simply, a program of state-sponsored terrorism. Its victims were initially white farmers who had been active in the campaign against the referendum and their black employees. Whites were humiliated and killed. Black farm workers had their homes and property destroyed and were forced to participate in the depredations of the next farm to be invaded. A state of law ceased, replaced by fear, intimidation, and violence.

In this environment the June 2000 parliamentary elections were held. They were less about "landless veterans" than about ZANU-PF maintaining power. Fearful of losing power and perquisites—a whole network of ZANU-controlled corporations, for example—Mugabe and his minions resorted to force and terror to silence

**Human rights demonstration**            ©IRIN

rural supporters of the Movement for Democratic Change.

Zimbabwe's electoral geography explained the rural strategy. Rural parliamentary seats outnumber those in urban districts where opposition is greatest. Every rural victim of the regime's terror campaign became a living reminder of ZANU-PF's ability to destroy those who did not support it—a crude but effective way to rally party supporters in party strongholds.

Government-sponsored violence resulted in the death of some 30 people. Thousands were beaten, raped and intimidated, but MDC voters courageously made their way to the polls and handed ZANU-PF the surprise of its life. Out of 120 seats available through the election, the MDC won a remarkable 57; ZANU-PF won 62; the remaining seat went to Rev. Sithole's ZANU-Ndonga.

It was the best showing by any opposition party in Zimbabwe's history. Several ZANU-PF bigwigs were defeated, including Mugabe's right-hand man, Emmerson Mnangagwa. Zimbabwe's constitution allows the president to appoint an additional 30 members to parliament, and using this option Mugabe returned Mnangagwa to the House of Assembly, where he was elected Speaker.

The EU characterized the election as neither fair nor free, and the MDC challenged nearly 40 results in court. Justices annulled election results that had been compromised by violence and intimidation, adding fuel to President Mugabe's

sustained attack on the judiciary. That first started when courts ordered black squatters to end their illegal occupations of white-owned farms. War veterans, who had become the regime's storm troopers, invaded judicial premises and threatened judges. The police did nothing, and the regime informed the justices that it was unable to protect them or their families.

The chief justice of Zimbabwe's supreme court was forced to retire early, and Mugabe appointed one of his cronies, Judge Godfrey Chidyausiku, to fill the vacancy. (Judge Chidyausiku had chaired the notorious constitutional commission that had proposed constitutional amendments to increase, once again, President Mugabe's authority and allow confiscation of white-owned farms without compensation.)

## Mugabe and the Media

The regime's intimidation of judges was part of a campaign to destroy its opponents and those who abetted them in any way. The media, especially the *Daily News*—Zimbabwe's only independent newspaper and an outspoken critic of the Mugabe regime—were targeted for harassment and intimidation.

War veterans, now the regime's enforcers, assaulted *Daily News* journalists, fired steel bolts into its offices, and set up road blocks outside Harare to confiscate copies of the newspaper and prevent its distribution to outlying areas—where seventy per cent of the population lives. In January 2001, Chenjerai Hunzvi, the vet-

# Zimbabwe

erans' leader, declared that he would "ban" the paper. Within days the paper's printing works were blown up with such force that the explosion rattled houses fives miles away. Five of the *Daily News's* six presses were shattered, and the roof of the warehouse was blown off.

Investigators later determined the destruction had been caused by five anti-tank land mines, manufactured in the former Soviet Union and favored for their ability to toss a ten-ton tank into the air. Those who set them off knew how to place them for maximum effect. In other words, this was not an affair of street-crazies with a few pipe bombs.

When the government disliked the coverage it got, reporters were expelled, as has happened to most of the reporters working for foreign newspapers. Local reporters could fare worse, including torture at the local police station.

The Media Institute of Southern Africa (MISA) consistently ranks Zimbabwe as the worst offender of media freedom in the region. In May 2005 it went even further, castigating oppressive media laws as inimical to independence and democracy. Almost simultaneously, the Committee to Protect Journalists (CPJ), an international media watch-dog group, classified Zimbabwe as one of the three most dangerous environments in the world for journalists, right behind Iraq and Cuba.

Radio, far cheaper than newspapers and more effective in reaching a rural audience, has been a major concern of the regime since Zimbabwe's supreme court declared the state's broadcasting monopoly unconstitutional in September 2000. Since independence in 1980, there has been no private broadcasting station in the country. Shortly after the court's decision, Capital Radio, financed by foreign charities, started operations broadcasting music, but its life was brief. Within days armed police swept into the station's office, seized its equipment, and accused it of being a "pirate" station.

Averse to alternative voices, President Mugabe has used ZANU-PF majorities in parliament to pass a range of legislation designed to destroy free expression. A broadcasting act was rushed through parliament in April 2001 with little debate, even after it was criticized as unconstitutional by one parliamentary committee.

The bill required broadcasters to have a license, but licenses would be severely limited, and radio stations could not be owned if financed by foreign interests. Broadcast content was mandated: at least 75% of the programs broadcast must have Zimbabwean content and be produced within Zimbabwe. For commercial broadcasters, at least 50% of the music broadcast must be produced within Zimbabwe,

and at least 10% of the non-Zimbabwean music must be African.

The government retained the power to shut down broadcasters if they did anything which is, in the words of the legislation, "prejudicial to the defense, public safety, public order, public morality or public health of Zimbabwe." That's the minister's license to kill independent broadcasters, and there should be no doubt the license will be used. Zimbabwe's then information minister, Jonathan Moyo, made the government's position clear: "If there is a court which allows [independent broadcasting] in Zimbabwe, we [the government] will not allow it. It compromises our national security." So much for the rule of law.

One provision of the broadcast act prevents political parties from owning radio stations. It was a direct attack on the MDC's ability to mobilize its constituency. Equally draconian is the Political Parties Act passed at the same time. It prevents political parties or candidates from accepting foreign funding either directly from a donor or indirectly from a third party.

In the spring of 2001 Chenjerai Hunzvi and his "war vets" brought their circus of chaos to the cities. Businesses and charitable institutions were subject to veterans' raids, which amounted to little more than an excuse to steal, kidnap, and extort. When they threatened to invade embassies, the outcry was so great the plug was finally pulled on their depredations, but the regime's point had been made: it could destroy the source of support for the MDC within the business community. For Hunzvi it was a last hurrah of sorts. He died in early June, reportedly of malaria of the brain.

President Mugabe's assault on courts, media, and opposition following the referendum defeat of 2000 was part of a deliberate strategy to avoid losing the presidential election of March 2002. Police, army, and youth militia were all mobilized to intimidate and terrorize a hapless population. According to official figures, nearly three million ballots were cast, with Mugabe winning 56% of the vote. Morgan Tsvangirai, his most formidable opponent ever, won only 42%, with three minor candidates taking the remainder. ZANU-PF spokesmen claimed Mugabe won because people supported his seizure of white-owned land and saw the MDC and Tsvangirai as the stooges of white colonialists.

In reality the election was won through massive fraud, manipulation, and terror. Beforehand, suspected MDC supporters were brutally beaten, bullied and robbed of their voter registration cards to prevent them from voting. This was often done while police looked on. The Public Order

**Morgan Tsvangirai, MDC Leader**

and Security Act was used to prohibit MDC rallies and even the use of loudspeakers at those few permitted. Electoral rolls were finagled to reduce urban voters and augment rural electors. In the cities the usual number of polling places was halved; zealous officials at the stations that did open meticulously lengthened the wait of voters who were forced to stand in the hot sun for hours, or go home without voting. The lines became so long the courts had to order an additional day of voting in the urban centers.

Rural districts, in contrast, had an over-abundance of polling stations. In areas suspected of being sympathetic to the MDC, ZANU-PF militia camps were set up near polling stations to better threaten potential voters. The government rejected the use of see-through ballot boxes and prevented election monitors from even getting near polling stations. Widespread disparities in various voting reports further de-legitimized the election. In its petition to the courts to invalidate the election, for example, the MDC showed there were nearly 186,000 "missing" votes and perhaps as many as 246,000 "additional" votes.

The results provoked differing reactions. The OAU, proving its irrelevance, called the elections "transparent, credible, free and fair," a position essentially adopted by South African and SADC observers. The Crisis in Zimbabwe Coalition—a consortium of Zimbabwean NGOs—concluded that the "process of the presidential elections has not enabled the will of the people to be expressed freely and fairly." It was a consensus opinion shared by every Zimbabwean civil society group charged with assessing or supporting the electoral process. The European Parliament urged the EU "not to recognize the legitimacy" of the vote, and the Commonwealth, deeply divided, ultimately suspended Zimbabwe from its ranks on the grounds that the election was neither free nor fair.

Comrade Mugabe has turned Zimbabwe into a police state to assure his political survival. State security officers are omnipresent. Police, army, and militia forces intimidate both opposition and general citizenry by arrest, torture, rape, and maiming. Economic mismanagement has produced extraordinary suffering in the population, and that suffering has been politicized. Food distribution has become a political tool: those who support the regime eat; those who do not, starve. In Zimbabwe, human rights and economic rationality are subordinated to political survival.

## The Politics of Survival

Zimbabwe under Robert Mugabe is a handbook for those whose single goal is political survival. First, decapitate opposition leadership. Morgan Tsvangirai and two other pro-democracy leaders, Welshman Ncube and Renson Gasela, are currently on trial for treason. The charge: concocting a plot to assassinate President Mugabe. The evidence: a four-hour fuzzy, often inaudible, secretly-videotaped meeting between Tsvangirai and Ari ben Menashe, an international fraudster who admits to receiving $100,000 from the Mugabe regime as a "retainer fee." The judge: Paddington Garwe, a Mugabe appointee, installed after Mugabe had purged the higher courts of judges who had ruled that seizures of white-owned farms were illegal. Judge Garwe has taken possession of one of those farms. The possible sentence: if convicted, the three face the death penalty. Mugabe has had more than 60 people hanged during his 22 years in power. The decision: In October 2004 Judge Garwe cleared Tsvangirai of the treason charges, saying the State had failed to prove its case against him. The follow up: in early December, the State appealed Judge Garwe's decision, and in May 2005, it reinstated a second treason charge over Tsvangirai's call for mass protests in June 2003.

Second: maintain a semblance of democratic form by holding "elections," but win them by force, violence, and fraud. There were at least nine parliamentary by-elections (to replace a member who had died, or in one case, an opposition MP who fled the country in fear of his life). Each was bitterly fought and violently conducted. For ZANU-PF, the stakes were high: If it could reduce the MDC's representation below 50, it would regain a two-thirds majority, necessary to make any constitutional change it desires. The first

seven ended in victories for Mugabe's ZANU-PF after violent campaigns. The MDC's parliamentary delegation was reduced to fifty.

Two urban elections occurred at the end of March 2003. The level of violence was extraordinary. Arrests, beatings, and intimidation—mainly of opposition members, including lawmakers—were frequent, but despite a prevailing fear, over 30% of the electorate had the courage to vote, giving victory to both MDC candidates.

Third, if the opposition should elect a candidate to local executive office, appoint someone over him to render him ineffective and powerless. Zimbabwe's two largest cities, Harare and Bulawayo, were both run by elected MDC mayors until Mugabe appointed new governors to run them. The mayors were henceforth required to report to the governors, effectively reducing the MDC's authority and political activity.

To avoid any future opposition victories in mayoral elections, the government announced it would gerrymander the cities' boundaries, folding districts part of urban Harare or Bulawayo into rural areas, traditionally ZANU strongholds.

Fourth, reward and punish supporters and opponents with all means available. Torture and arbitrary imprisonment are routine for regime opponents, but even those who remain silent are brutalized. As political misrule, economic mismanagement, corruption, and drought combined to create catastrophic food shortages in early 2003, more than half Zimbabwe's 12 million people were at risk of starvation. The government used its monopoly of grain imports to channel food to friends and supporters and interfered with international food aid that might be distributed to others. MDC supporters were turned away from bread lines at ZANU-controlled shopping centers, and in the countryside, people gathered wild plants, the traditional meal in times of hardship. (Some people put principle aside and bought ZANU-PF cards in order to eat.)

And lest one have any doubt that starvation was policy, listen to Didymus Mutasa, ZANU-PF's organizing secretary, speaking at an August 2002 rally: "we would be better off with only six million people, with our own people who support the liberation struggle. We don't want all these extra people."

Fifth, muzzle and silence the press—there should be no witnesses. Since the presidential election, both local and foreign reporters have been intimidated, beaten, jailed or deported, and the government has tried to destroy the *Daily News* financially (by prohibiting all government advertising on its pages). The government forcibly deported a corre-

spondent for the British newspaper, *The Guardian,* despite court orders prohibiting his deportation. Chillingly, the government celebrated World Press Freedom Day (May 3, 2003) with the slogan "The media we have is not the media we need."

Sixth, intimidate members of the judiciary to accord their judgments with regime policy, and when they don't, ignore them—law serves the state exclusively. Despite the regime's "indigenization" of the judiciary, men of principle still, but infrequently, deliver independent rulings.

Judge Benjamin Paradza, a black judge on Zimbabwe's High Court, was such an independent voice. A former fighter in Mugabe's guerrilla army, Paradza had been warned when appointed to the bench, "not to embarrass the government with his court rulings." In mid-February 2003, he was arrested (despite constitutional prohibitions against the arrest of sitting jurists) and subjected to a campaign of personal vilification.

At his arrest Paradza said he was told: "You have been appointed to look after the government's interests, but you have embarrassed the government and now we are going to embarrass you." It was Judge Paradza who had overturned state eviction notices against white farmers whose land the government was trying to seize.

After ethnic cleansing, Zimbabwe's Supreme Court is now dominated by hard-line Mugabe supporters. The court has not issued a single ruling against the government since its appointment.

This strategy functioned to entrench Robert Mugabe and exhaust the opposition. The MDC's leadership, kept busy in court, was disorganized and dispirited, its supporters disappointed and disillusioned as Zimbabwe's March 2005 parliamentary elections approached. The MDC leadership seemed unable to consolidate previous gains, and its support base was threatened with starvation by a regime relentless in its pursuit of survival and power.

A year before the election the government announced a bumper harvest of maize and told the international donor community it would not need emergency food, but it refused to let United Nations staff assess the state of the country's crops and food stocks. The food production figures were universally dismissed and the Catholic archbishop of Bulawayo went so far as to say the government was "not telling the truth," noting that much land was lying fallow.

The run-up to the March 2005 legislative elections was characterized by a great deal of nervous politicking among ZANU bigwigs jockeying to succeed Zimbabwe's aging dictator. In March 2004 Kenya's *East African Standard* newspaper quoted Mu-

# Zimbabwe

gabe, now eighty years old, as saying he was tired of politics and wanted to write. "I have had enough," he said. "I am a writer and would like to concentrate on writing after this term of office is over." His term expires in 2008, when he will be 85 years old.

As the succession competition heated up ZANU-PF's internal politics got down and dirty in late 2004. Political guns aimed at the front runner, Emmerson Mnangagwa, the Speaker of Parliament and long Mugabe's link to ZANU-PF's's economic empire, after he seemed to have sowed up the support of provincial leaders in the race for party vice president. His enemies in the politburo convoked an emergency meeting, and a faction led by the influential former defense chief, General Solomon Mujuru, bulldozed through a resolution calling for a woman to fill the vice-presidency position. The obvious candidate was Water Resources and Infrastructural Development Minister Joyce Mujuru, wife of General Solomon Mujuru.

Because the contest for the vice president's post was generally seen as putting the victor in line to succeed President Mugabe, ZANU's internal battle was apparently bloody and no prisoners were taken. Mugabe himself threatened dissidents, saying he would crack down on "divisive elements" within the party.

Information Minister Jonathan Moyo, who had tried to rally provincial leaders to Mnangagwa, was reprimanded for opposing Mujuru, dropped from his party position, and ultimately denied the party's nomination in the March 2005 elections. He would successfully run as an independent, suggesting ZANU continued in deep disarray.

The parliamentary election of March 2005 conformed to the usual Zimbabwean standards: victory was achieved through fraud, intimidation, ballot-stuffing, and the active participation of the dead. Official results gave ZANU-PF 78 of 120 contested seats; MDC managed to eke out 41 seats, and one lonely independent—Jonathan Moyo—would take his seat in the next parliament. There was never any doubt about the election outcome. As one commentatator in the *Financial Gazette* expressed it: "Yes, a resounding victory for ZANU-PF because it is so serious when it comes to elections that it does not leave anything to chance . . ."

Rural villagers were threatened, cajoled, and denied food if there were any possibility they might support the MDC. The Catholic Archibishop of Bulawayo, Pius Ncube, condemned the "evil and systematic denial of food to hungry people," and called for civil disobedience. Well before the election the government was predicting "an above-average national harvest,"

**Artists at Shona Sculpture Park near Harare with sculpture of an AIDS victim.**

Photo by David Johns

even a bumper harvest of 2.75 million tons of maize. It was all posturing and prevarication. Zimbabwe had been dependent on international food aid over the past several years; in 2003 the World Food Program alone had provided food to nearly six million people.

By May 2005, official lies would no longer suffice; five million Zimbabweans were in urgent need of food aid. "The majority of farming households will harvest nothing and are already dependent on the market for their food requirements," wrote the Famine Early Warning Systems Network (FEWS NET). Its report classified Zimbabwe's food situation as an "emergency."

With the thirty seats President Mugabe is allowed to appoint to The House of Assembly, ZANU-PF has a two-thirds majority in parliament and can now change the constitution at will. In late May 2005, a spokesman announced government plans to introduce a constitutional amendment to nationalize all farmland; rights to private ownership of land will be abolished, a move which will no doubt plummet the economy further into the abyss. Another constitutional proposal was floated: the creation of an upper house of parliament, empowered to ap-

point a successor in case the an incumbant president's death—a proposal designed to insure Joyce Mujuru's succession as Zimbabwe's first female president.

**Culture:** AIDS rages throughout Zimbabwe and takes its horrific toll. In less than 15 years AIDS has gone from isolated occurrence to pandemic. UNAIDS estimates that 2.3 million Zimbabweans are living with HIV/AIDS (2001) and the country has the third highest infection rate (33.7%) in the world, just below Swaziland and Botswana. A new study looking at more recent statistics, conducted by the Health Ministry and the United States Centers for Disease Control and Prevention, reports that about 35% of the country's adults are now infected. At least 3,000 individuals a week are dying because of HIV/AIDS, and life expectancy has fallen from 44.5 years in 1997 to 39 in 2003; it is projected to fall to 35 in 2010 because of the disease.

One telling vignette: there are almost no traffic signs left in Zimbabwe. They've all been stolen and melted down to make coffin handles.

The HIV/AIDS pandemic is expected to worsen as a consequence of Zimbabwe's government-sponsored political violence.

Hundreds of girls and women were allegedly raped at bases set up by ZANU-PF militias in the run-up to the presidential election.

The social consequences are devastating. Zimbabwe is well on its way to losing an entire generation. Left behind are the orphans—an estimated one million since the 1980s—deprived of traditional family support and often abandoned to life on the streets of the country's larger cities. There they turn to the only life available: begging and crime. In the rural areas elderly people are increasingly having to care for the country's AIDS orphans. UNICEF estimates that one Zimbabwean child out of five will be an orphan by 2010, 80% of them because of AIDS.

Zimbabwe's social and political problems, like the spread of AIDS, have long been the subject of song by Zimbabwe's foremost musician, Thomas Mapfumo. Born in colonial Rhodesia in 1945, Mapfumo has a personal history that reads like a biography of Zimbabwe. Early recognizing how Africans were exploited in their own land, he sympathized with those fighting against white rule and wrote songs in his native Shona that uplifted the hearts and sustained the action of Zimbabwe's guerilla forces.

It was *chimurenga* music, or music of the struggle. It articulated the concerns of those who had no voice, or as Mapfumo says, it gave voice to the voiceless. Inclusion of the sounds of the *mbira*, a traditional Shona thumb piano, provided a deceptively innocent packaging for revolutionary songs of justice and freedom.

Since the heady days of the liberation struggle, the musician has become increasingly disenchanted with Zimbabwe under Robert Mugabe. His music still gives voice to those who suffer most, but it now criticizes the regime that betrayed their hopes for a better life. "Too many of my people," he says, "are still poor, hungry and without jobs, homes or land. As long as that's the case I have no choice to speak out for them."

"Chaunorwa" criticized Zimbabwe's pervasive corruption under Mugabe, and was duly banned from state-controlled airwaves. Other songs have criticized the farm invasions and Zimbabwe's involvement in the Congo War. *Chimurenga Explosion* (aNOym reCOrds, 2000) had at least one of its cuts, "Disaster," denied airtime. "Disaster" is Thomas Mapfumo's description of Zimbabwe under Robert Mugabe. "I'm very disappointed," he says. "After all our struggle, I never expected our own black government was going to destroy our country." Mapfumo has moved his family to the United States and vows not to return to Zimbabwe while President Mugabe remains in office.

**Economy:** Traditionally, Zimbabwe has gained its chief income from agricultural exports. Tobacco is the principal commercial export, but mineral resources, like gold and various ferroalloys, make a significant contribution. The economy is in free fall as a consequence of both government action and inaction. Social violence orchestrated by ZANU-PF has disrupted the agricultural sector, especially food and tobacco. The government's confiscation of commercial farms for distribution to the landless has destroyed the most vibrant component of a desperate economy. The big farms not only keep Zimbabwe fed, but produced 30% of its total exports. Tobacco alone was the single biggest earner of foreign exchange—about 35%—and traditionally contributed at least 15% of Zimbabwe's GDP.

The effects of the regime's disastrous economic policies can easily been seen in tobacco exports, Zimbabwe's principal source of foreign exchange. Despite a sharp rise in the number of tobacco growers, export earnings from tobacco have plummeted 57% since 2001. In 2001 tobacco brought in $584 million, but by 2004, earnings had fallen to $240 million; from contributing 35% of all foreign exchange earnings in 2001, tobacco contributed only 20% in 2004. Tonnage fell from 198,219 tons in 2001 to 80,000 tons in 2004. In 2004 Zimbabwe accounted for 4% of global exports of the highest quality flue-cured tobacco. Five years previously, it accounted for 20% and was second only to Brazil as a tobacco exporter.

Zimbabwe's assault on commercial farmers has redounded to the benefit of its neighbors. More than 340 commercial farmers have decamped for better opportunities in Zambia, Mozambique, Malawi, and Tanzania. In neighboring Zambia, tobacco production has more than tripled in the past four years as a consequence.

Gold has traditionally been Zimbabwe's second most important source of export earnings, but is generally declining. According to the Chamber of Mines, 2004 production was around 19.7 metric tons. The figure represents a 57% increase over 2003's production of 12.6 metric tons, but is still well below the all-time record of 28 tons in 1999. The increased production is explained by the Reserve Bank of Zimbabwe's (RBZ) increase in the price paid for gold in late 2003. Official production in 2003 would have actually been closer to 10 tons, about two-thirds below maximum production, had not the RBZ raised the amount paid small-scale miners. With prices increased to close to black market levels, there was a surge of gold deposits with the bank in the last two months of the year.

Platinum has emerged as one of the country's major foreign exchange earners and is poised to replace tobacco and gold as the country's top source of foreign currency. Zimbabwe's Great Dyke contains huge platinum reserves and the country is the world's second largest producer of platinum after South Africa. With expectations of robust growth in the industry—11.6% in 2004 and 7.5% in 2005—the government introduced an Enhanced Platinum Sector Regime (EPSR) to take effect in 2005. Henceforth, marketing of all platinum will be handled through the Reserve Bank of Zimbabwe, as is gold currently. The move gives the government greater control over desperately needed foreign exchange.

The government has introduced new mining legislation that calls for 20% of all projects to be turned over to black entrepreneurs ("historically disadvantaged persons") in the first two years, then 25% after five years, and finally 30% after a decade. The legislation is likely to pass but unlikely to increase foreign investment in the mining sector.

Tourism, another source of foreign exchange, has also been hard hit by the general deterioration of the economy. The industry's slump has been spectacular. In the late 1990s more than 2.1 million tourists visited Zimbabwe in a year; in 2004 only 1.27 visited from January to September. The arrival of international tourists (those who stay longest and spend the most) has dropped by 40%; that has been partially compensated for by an increase in the number of tourists from neighboring countries, particularly South Africa. Most were taking advantage of cheap prices occasioned by the collapse of the Zimbabwe dollar.

As part of President Mugabe's "Look East" policy the government has turned its attention to Asian, and particularly Chinese, tourists. China, which is now Zimbabwe's biggest investor, has granted it "Approved Destination" status for Chinese tourists. Some 24,500 intrepid Chinese visitors made the trip in the first nine months of 2004—hardly the flood of tourists promised by officials when Air Zimbabwe launched a twice-weekly round trip flight to China. Most press reports indicate the flights are nearly empty. So too were the flights to Dubai inaugurated in May 2005.

With virtually all sectors spiraling downwards, Zimbabwe is in economic free fall. The economy has contracted for three years in a row (–13.1% in 2003) and the IMF foresaw another contraction in 2004, producing a cumulative decline since 1999 of a staggering 45%. Inflation hit a record 632% in 2004 and was 129% in April 2005 alone. Some 75% to 80% of the population lives below the poverty line of less than one dollar a day. Central to Zimbabwe's economic implosion is the fact that the centerpiece of its

# Zimbabwe

economic program, fast-track land resettlement, has been an abject failure. President Mugabe has said his often-violent land reform program would stimulate economic growth, but the opposite is true. First, the corruption of the program: Top government officials and well-connected people—the ZANU-PF elite—grabbed some of the best and richest farmland at the expense of the landless poor. Second, the decline in production: Some 300,000 to 350,000 families have been resettled, but without adequate experience, equipment or resources (to buy fertilizer, for example), only a small percentage of the land listed, 40%, was being cultivated in the 2002/2003 season, and that in rudimentary circumstances. Third, the decline in farm employment: some 150,000 jobs, black farm workers for the most part—have been lost.

The government has consistently spent more than it takes in; by 2003 it had accumulated an external debt of $4.44 billion.

Much of this comes as a consequence of the regime's system of patronage and pre-electoral pay-off. Party faithful are rewarded with lucrative appointments in state corporations, which almost inevitably lose money. Tough elections are usually preceded by unbudgeted spending sprees. For the June 2000 parliamentary elections the government doubled the pay and allowances of MPs, increased civil servants' salaries by 90%, and boosted payments to rural leaders.

In all political systems some are more equal than others, but President Mugabe seems especially privileged. In March 2004 his salary was increased by a staggering 436%—from the twenty million Zimbabwe dollars he was receiving in January to $Z87.2 million (including a broad range of allowances). That will help pay for his retirement cottage: a three-story palace currently under construction on 42 acres in Harare's most affluent sub-

urb. It has 25 rooms, an apartment for each of Mr. Mugabe's three children, swimming pools, Jacuzzis, and servants' quarters. Sensors to warn of poison or germ attack and radiation detectors are part of palace security, and at least 50 full-time riot police will be stationed in luxury barracks on the grounds.

There is little in Zimbabwe to inspire investor confidence. Net capital inflows from investors were $502 million in 1995; the net outflow in 2002 alone was estimated at $347 million. Without investment new jobs are not being created, and old ones are being lost as business shrinks. Inflation has destroyed domestic savings as a possible source of investment. In these circumstances, the Mugabe regime has increasingly relied on Chinese assistance, generally divorced from any political or human rights concerns.

**The Future:** Bleak.

**The sophisticated architecture of ancient Zimbabwe**

Photo by David Johns

194

# EAST AFRICAN ISLAND NATIONS

The Grande Mosque, Moroni

©IRIN

## The Union of the Comoros

**Land area and terrain:** 2,170 sq. km. = 838 sq. mi. The Comoro group consists of four mountainous islands lying between Tanzania and the northern coast of Madagascar: Grand Comore (also known as Njazidja), Anjouan (Nzwani), Mohéli (Mwali) and Mayotte. The latter, with a substantial Christian minority, opposed joining the other three and, although claimed by the Union, remains a dependency of France.

**Climate:** Tropical marine; rainy season (November to May); cyclones possible during rainy season.

**Population:** 671,247 (July 2005 est.) An estimated 150,000 persons of Comorian origin also reside in France.

**Capital City:** Moroni (on Grande Comore, pop. 32, 000, estimated).

**Ethnic groups:** Antalote, Cafre, Makoa, Oimatsaha, Sakalava.

**Principal Religions:** Sunni Muslim 98%, Roman Catholic 2%.

**Official Languages:** Arabic, French

**Other Principal Languages:** Comoran (a blend of Swahili and Arabic).

**Chief Commercial Products:** Vanilla, ylang-ylang, cloves, perfume oil, and copra.

**GNI per capita**: $450 (2003)

**Currency:** Comoran franc

**Independence Date:** 6 July 1975 (from France).

**Chief of State:** Colonel Azali Assoumani.

**National Flag:** From the pole as its base, a green triangle, containing a crescent pointing right with four stars (one for each of the islands, plus one for Mayotte), arranged vertically, between the crescent tips. This lies on a field of four equal horizontal stripes, from the top: yellow, white, red, and blue.

**Political History:** The islands were first settled by Arab seafarers about 1,000 years ago. The Arabs brought in slaves from Africa and established a series of small sultanates on the different islands. It was not until 1527 that the Portuguese cartographer Diego Ribero depicted the Comoros islands on a European map. France colonized Mayotte in 1843 and extended its influence to the whole archipelago. In 1912 the four Comoros islands formally became a French colony administered from Madagascar.

Grand Comore and its capital, Moroni, are dominated by the Karthala, one of the

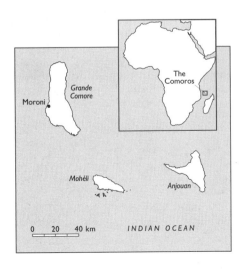

195

# Comoros

President Azali Assoumani

world's largest active volcanoes that irrupted as recently as April 2005. Referred to by the French as Anjouan, and by early English visitors as Johanna, Nzwani has been called the "pearl" of the Indian Ocean. With forested hillsides and rivers tumbling to the sea it is a beautiful island. It is essentially a triangle with approximately 31 miles on each side and a total area of 164 square miles.

Anjouan is the most densely populated island in the Comoro archipelago (over 1,280 persons per square mile). Most live in small communities found throughout the island. The major towns are Mutsamudu on the western side, the present capital, and Domoni on the eastern side, an ancient capital and seaport.

Its volcanic peak, Mount Ntingi, 1,575 meters high, is covered with vegetation, including large ferns, tropical mahoganies, and wild orchids, in contrast with the three points of the triangle, which are less luxuriant due to centuries of cultivation. Anjouan (Nzwani) is the premiere producer of essential oils including ylang-ylang, jasmine, cassis, basilic, palmarosa, and orange flower.

In 1975, Nzwani was one of the three islands to make up the newly formed independent republic of the Comoro Islands. The first president of the independent country, Ahmed Abdallah, was from Nzwani and his shrine is in his hometown of Domoni. The third president, Said Mohamed Djohar, was also a resident of Domoni and a schoolmate of Ahmed Abdallah.

After WWII the islands became Overseas French Territories and were represented in the French National Assembly. Agreement was reached in 1973 to grant independence in 1978, but on July 6, 1975, the Comoran parliament declared unilateral independence. Deputies from Mayotte abstained from this vote, and as a result the Comoran government had effective control over only Grand Comore, Anjouan, and Mohéli. Mayotte remains under French jurisdiction to this day.

The government of President Mohamed Taki Abdoulkarim, a deeply religious Sunni Muslim, was elected in 1996 following a mercenary-led coup which deposed then-president Djohar Said Mohamed. He went on to establish Islam as the basis of law: the death penalty, restrictions on the consumption of alcohol and censuring women who wore mini-skirts were all announced. In October 1996, Taki amended the constitution, strengthening the powers of the presidency and sharply eroding the powers of individual islands—the source of much future disturbance.

Taki's government directed little development money to Anjouan and Mohéli; unemployment there rose to 90%. Islanders also thought themselves unfairly taxed in indirect ways. They had, for example, to make an expensive trip across the 50-mile straits to the capital to obtain any official documents. And always there was the nearby example of Mayotte. By remaining with France, the citizens of Mayotte enjoyed free education, health benefits and a minimum wage. Rebuffed

by France when reunion with the former colonial power was proposed, Anjouan and Mohéli declared unilateral independence in August 1997.

A February 1998 referendum adopted a new independence constitution, but economic reality argued against the case for independence. Both Anjouan and Mohéli are volcanic islands with few exports, poor economies, and a population problem; there was little likelihood they could go it alone.

President Taki died suddenly of natural causes in November 1998. His death left the Islamic federation leaderless while facing the political impasse of secession. Tadjiddine Ben Said Massounde, the elderly president of the Comoros high court, was persuaded to accept an interim presidency. The opposition leader Abbas Djoussouf was appointed prime minister in an effort to create a government of national unity. France, the OAU, South Africa and other island states pressured to resolve the crisis. Ultimately representatives of the three islands agreed to attend a reconciliation conference on the island of Madagascar in April 1999.

The Madagascar conference produced agreement on the tentative outlines of a new Comoran state. The Federal Islamic Republic would become the Union of Comoran Islands. The islands would have greater autonomy. Each would have its local executive and parliament after a one-year transition. To the central government would be reserved defense, foreign affairs, the issuance of currency, higher education and research. The federal presidency, elected by the National Assembly, would be rotated between the three islands every three years.

On Grand Comore, anti-Anjouan riots broke out when the details of the agreement were announced. The government accused opposition politicians of fomenting the troubles and sent in heavily armed troops to restore order. Since the best order to a military mind is martial order, the Comoran army effected the nation's 18th coup d'état, avoiding what seemed to be a slide into chaos and anarchy.

The army commander, Colonel Azali Assoumani, told his countrymen that the army had assumed "its role as the last bastion in the survival of our nation and state." The army, he said, would remain in power for a year. That year came and went in April 2000, and little had changed. There was no return to civilian government, and no one had been able to put Comoros together again. Anjouan continued its separatist ways under Lt. Col. Said Abeid, who organized a series of farcical "elections" to legitimize Anjouan independence.

Colonels Azali and Abeid met in August 2000 and agreed on a looser relationship among the islands, but the arrangement was roundly condemned by the political class as too concessionary to secessionists and destructive of national unity. Finally, after months of torturous negotiations facilitated by both the OAU and La Francophonie, a Comoran national reconciliation forum met at Fomboni, Mohéli's capital, in February 2001.

In the agreement which emerged, known as the Fomboni Accord, Anjouan agreed to return to the federal fold, but with considerable autonomy. The island's return was eased when a military coup overthrew the secessionist regime of Col. Abeid in August 2001. The island's new military leader, Major Mohamad Bacar, openly favored rejoining the Comoros.

Details of the new institutional arrangements were painfully worked, and a new constitution, under which the islands would be governed as "autonomous entities freely managing their own affairs," was approved by referendum in December 2001. Under the new arrangements the Federal Islamic Republic of the Comoros would be replaced with a new Comoran Union whose mandate would be limited to affairs of religion and nationality, currency, foreign, and defense policy.

A series of elections in March and April 2002 began to implement the new dispensation. Voters on each island were also asked to approve a separate island constitution, elect an island president and the president of the new Union of the Comoros.

This being the Comoros, the elections were not without complaint and criticism. Opposition was expressed by Islamic parties, upset that the Islamic nature of the state had not been affirmed. Voters on the main island, Grande Comore, rejected their new constitution in a March referendum, forcing revision and delay of presidential elections there.

On Anjouan, Colonel Mohamed Bacar was elected to a five-year presidential term. Mohamed Said Fazul—appointed governor of Mohéli by Colonel Azali Assoumani in March 2001—won the island's presidency in second-round elections. Colonel Azali himself won the Union presidency, an office that would be rotated among the islands every four years.

After ratifying a revised constitution, Grande Comore chose a former opposition MP, Abdou Soule Elbak, as president. Tensions and mutual recriminations between presidents Azali and Elbak have kept Grande Comore at the brink of chaos ever since.

Exploiting constitutional ambiguities Elbak called for equal control over Grande Comore's financial sector, pitting his government against the Union government and putting the business community in an administrative quandary. In early 2003 businesses received separate mailings from the two governments' finance ministries. Both presented themselves as the appropriate authority for the collection of fees, licenses, and taxes. Many businesses refused to become an arbiter between the contending regimes and pronounced a plague on both their houses: they announced a freeze on tax payments until the conflict was resolved.

Diplomatic efforts by South Africa and the African Union, produced an agreement on control of security forces and tax collection in August. Island presidents would administer the police forces (the gendarmerie) stationed on their islands, while the Union president would control the country's army. A further reconciliation accord was signed in December 2003, defining agreements on the management of customs revenues, the transitional budget, and various security provisions. The revenue-sharing formula allocated 28% to the Union; 32.5% to Ngazidja; 30.5% for Anjouan, and 9% for Moheli. This paved the way for legislative elections in early 2004.

Held in March 2004, elections for local assemblies on each of the country's three islands were a smashing victory for the supporters of island autonomy; supporters of Union president Azali only managed to win 10 seats out of a total of 55. They did no better in April elections to the federal assembly, winning only six of eighteen elected seats. Since each island president appoints five additional members to the federal body, Azali's supporters (6) do not have a sufficient number to block potential constitutional changes proposed by the supporters of greater island autonomy (27).

With some degree of institutional stability, no matter how tenuous, established, President Azali focused on the Union's desperate economic situation, seeking to gain access to credit from the IMF, World Bank, and disillusioned donors, headed by France. Given Comoran claims on Mayotte, relations between the islands and France have remained chilly at best. A Franco-Corman joint commission last met in 1992, and President Azali is the only leader of a French-speaking country that has not been received by a French President.

A thaw occurred at the end of January 2005 when French President Jacques Chirac received Azali Assoumani on an official state visit. It was, of course, increasingly in France's interest to restore aid and kick-start development plans: Mayotte was experiencing significantly increased illegal migration from the impoverished Comoros.

There will be elections for the Union's rotating presidency in 2006 when President Azali's four-year term ends. Already a number of Anjouan politicians are jockeying for position in the race. Efforts to secure President Azali a second term as Union president seemed to have been quashed.

**Culture:** The people of the Comoros are a blend of Arab, African and Indian Ocean heritage. They speak Cormoran, closely related to the Swahili of East Africa, which is written in Arabic script. The language

**Ylang-Ylang flower**

Photo by Powell Harrison

# Comoros

is enriched with borrowings from the many cultures that have made contact with the islands. Indian, Persian, Arabic, Portuguese, English, and French words have all been added to the basic African vocabulary. Given island isolation, there are four distinct dialects of Comoran spoken, each specific to one of the four islands.

The dominant religion in the islands is Islam, and islanders are predominantly Sunni Muslims. Traditional Islam tended to incorporate local African belief and customs, like a belief in malevolent djinns and the importance of lavish weddings to secure social status. Surviving African traditions can also be detected in the property rights Comoran women enjoy. Islamic law tends to recognize only male ownership and inheritance of land, but in the Comoros, certain property, called *magnahouli*, is controlled by women and inherited through the female line, suggesting a surviving African matriarchal tradition.

Comoran marriages, especially among social elites, are often a prearranged union between an older man and a younger woman and are celebrated by a grand wedding, especially if they are a first marriage. Before the marriage the groom is expected to provide a lavish dowry for his bride, including expensive clothing, gold and jewelry, which she is entitled to keep if they divorce. As further proof of his status within the community, the groom must also pay for a party of several days to which the entire village and friends and relatives from around the country are invited. Food, drink, and accommodation are all at his expense.

The festivities of the grand marriage extend over several days, but as compensation, the groom is allowed to wear a special sash signifying his status as a grand noble. Among those who can afford it, marriage tends to be polygynous and matrilocal—the husband moves into the home of his wife. The practice reflects the survival of African matrilineal traditions, as well as the practice of merchant traders who established families in more than one community.

In a deeply conservative Muslim society, women dress modestly, favoring colorful saris, but do not cover their faces. Against the fierce Comoran sun women protect themselves with a yellowish facial cream, called *m'sidzanou*. Made of ground sandalwood and perfumed oils like ylang-ylang or jasmine, it is applied to the face as either a full mask or in a dappled pattern.

The traditionally open and tolerant version of Comoran Islam is under intense pressure with the rise of Islamic fundamentalism in the islands. The radical strain of Islam has been introduced with missionary zeal by young Comorans who have studied abroad. Lacking funds or blocked by immigration laws from studying in France, many seeking higher education were easily recruited by Islamic centers in Sudan and Saudi Arabia where Wahhabite fundamentalism prevailed. Comoros' chronic poverty and instability proved fertile recruiting grounds for the fundamentalists.

One recruit was Fazul Abdullah Mohammed, described by the FBI as a computer whiz fluent in several languages, including French, Arabic and English. Born in the Comoros, he is said to have trained with Osama bin Laden in Afghanistan and spent time in Somalia. He is charged by the U.S. in the 1998 terror attack on its Embassy in Nairobi, Kenya, and is on the FBI's list of 22 "most-wanted" terrorists. Investigators have since named him the mastermind behind the November 28, 2002, suicide attack on the ill-named Paradise Hotel in Mombassa, Kenya. Al-Qaeda claimed responsibility for the bombing, which was part of coordinated attacks on Israeli interests. In addition, there were to have been simultaneous missile attacks on an Israeli jetliner as it took off from Mombasa airport.

**Economy:** The Comoros islands are one of the poorest countries in the world. Some 80% of the population is involved in the agricultural sector, but still the islands must import a significant portion of their foodstuffs. Rice is the country's main staple and accounts for 90% of Comoran imports.

In many ways, the islands are caught in a poverty spiral. GDP grew by a modest 2.5% in 2002 and 2003, woefully inadequate to improve the life circumstances of a population that was growing rapidly—about 2.4% annually.

Endemic political instability is exacerbated by the government's regular revenue shortfall. Foreign investors have shied away; international lenders have remained hesitant, and donors, many involved in continuing mediation between conflicting actors in the Comoran political theater, evince demonstrable fatigue. External debt remains high—estimated at $290 million (2004)—only slightly less than the country's total GDP ($322.7 million in 2003).

Since early 2005, the Union has been under a surveillance program signed with the IMF as a prerequisite for assistance in reducing its external debt. Conditions involve infinitely greater control of budget deficits, particularly establishing precise objectives for a ceiling on the public payroll. At every level, political support has been traditionally secured by the distribution of government jobs. Further efforts to liberalize the economy are also expected: privatizations of government businesses, an end to the government monopoly on rice imports, greater competition in the banking sector. Once these goals have been achieved the islands can be considered for admission to debt reduction programs.

The Comoran export economy is based on vanilla, cloves, and ylang-ylang, an essence popular in perfume making. Traditionally, Comoros has generated about 200 tons of processed vanilla per year, but the 2002 harvest was only 130 tons, while the 2002-2003 harvest produced only 112 tons of dried vanilla. The decline has been attributed to aging vines, bad weather, and farmers discouraged by previous poor sales. Prices paid the farmers rise and fall according to international conditions.

An increase in demand for cloves may have had longer-term negative consequences. When planters harvested 2,500 tons of cloves to take advantage of high sale prices, rapid picking damaged many trees; future harvests were compromised.

The Comoros have long been the world's leading producer of the essence of ylang-ylang, an oil widely used in the perfume industry. Production is localized on Anjouan Island. Indeed, it was the island's feeling that it was not being given its fair share of ylang-ylang revenues that led to its secession efforts.

Less exotic are the islands' fish resources, a sector still largely underdeveloped. The government signed a three-year agreement with the EU that began in February 2001. A sizeable amount of money will be spent on developing the fisheries sector, while 65 EU ships are allowed to catch tuna. Annual compensation is expected to be about $311,000. Longer term, the sector faces the very real problem of over-fishing in the Indian Ocean and a growing problem of household and other wastes in its waters.

The stunning natural landscapes of the islands are an obvious area for future touristic development. But for the moment, political instability remains dissuasive.

**Future:** Difficult. The situation remains volatile as tensions between island and federal authorities persist.

# The Republic of Madagascar

**Area:** 595,000 sq. km. = 229,730 sq. mi. (somewhat smaller than Texas).

**Population:** 18,040,341 (July 2005 est.)

**Capital City:** Antananarivo (pop. 2 million est.); Pronounced Tah-nah-nah-reev.

**Climate:** Interior–warm and rainy (November–April); cool and dry (May–October); the southern portion of the island is semi–arid. The coastal areas are uniformly hotter than the inland altitudes. The east coast has a heavy, almost year–around rainfall brought by Indian Ocean trade winds and monsoons.

**Neighboring Countries:** The closest neighbor of this island republic is Mozambique, 300 miles west on the African mainland.

**Official Language:** Malagasy and French.

**Other Principal Languages:** Malagasy is universally understood and spoken by the people although there are several dialects, particularly in the coastal areas.

**Ethnic groups:** Malayo-Indonesian (Merina and related Betsileo), Cotiers (mixed African, Malayo-Indonesian, and Arab ancestry—Betsimisaraka, Tsimihety, Antaisaka, Sakalava), French, Indian, Creole, Comoran.

**Principal Religions:** Indigenous beliefs 52%, Christian 41%, Muslim 7%.

**Chief Commercial Products:** Prawns, coffee, vanilla, cotton, sugar and cloves and petroleum products.

**GNP per capita:** $290 (2003)

**Currency:** Ariary, made up of five subdivisions called Iraimbilanja. The Ariary, introduced in mid-2003, is worth five of the former Malagasy Francs, which remained legal tender until the end of November, 2003 and exchangeable until the end of 2009.

**Former Colonial Status:** French Protectorate (1894–1960).

**Independence Date:** June 26, 1960.

**Chief of State:** Marc Ravalomanana (since December 2001 election, validated by High Constitutional Court in April 2002).

**National Flag:** A vertical stripe of white closest to the pole with two horizontal stripes of red and green.

The Republic of Madagascar, the fourth-largest island of the world and larger than France, Netherlands, Belgium and Luxembourg combined, is situated in the Indian Ocean off the southeastern part of Africa. It split from the African continent 165 million years ago and has been isolated from all other land by deep water for some 88 million years. As a consequence some 100 unique terrestrial mammal species are found on the island.

The west coast, facing the Mozambique Channel, is a low, tropically wet and dry region, particularly in the extreme South. A series of broad plateaus rise from the coast to increasing heights of 2,300 to 4,500 feet. More abundant rainfall occurs here, and the altitude tempers the otherwise hot climate. Almost daily rains fall during the summer; the weather from May to October is cooler when temperatures in the higher altitudes drop as low as the freezing point. Several mountain ranges rise above this plateau land—Mount Tsaratanana majestically looms to a height of 9,450 feet.

The eastern shore is a narrow strip between the sea and the steep sides of the mountains. Washed by the warm waters of the Indian Ocean, and visited by the trade winds and monsoons, this coastal strip is almost uniformly hot and humid,

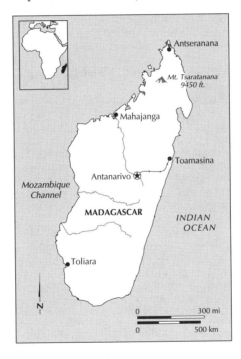

with an annual rainfall exceeding 110 inches.

**History:** The Indonesian, Arab and African heritage of the people of Madagascar gives some indication of its early history. From the time of the Christian era, there were successive waves of immigration to the island by people from what are now Indonesia and Malaysia. For early and colonial history, see *Historical Background* and *The French in Africa.*

Philibert Tsiranana (*Feel*-eh-bear Tsear-ah-*nah;* the last vowel in Malagasy names is not pronounced), a moderate, was the first president after independence in 1960. His health gradually failed, and he was unable to deal effectively with a Maoist uprising in the South in 1971. All power was given to the military in 1972, eventu-

ally headed by Lt. Commander Didier Ratsiraka (*Deed-*year Rot-see-rakh) as President of the Supreme Council of the Revolution.

Known as the Red Admiral, even issuing his only little red book of thoughts in emulation of Chairman Mao, Ratsiraka was the instigator of the Malagasy socialist revolution of 1975. The Malagasy Republic was replaced by the Democratic Republic of Madagascar. Government control of the economy under Ratsiraka rose dramatically. Just as dramatically, the economy declined. Backed by the military, Ratsiraka was reelected to successive seven-year terms in 1982 and 1989. Violence marked the regime in early the 1990's, when Ratsiraka used the military to resist a pro-democracy movement. The blackest day was 10 August 1991 when he ordered troops to fire on a huge crowd of protesters surging around the presidential palace. Fourteen people were killed and hundreds wounded. IMF economic support was suspended.

In 1991, a High Authority for State Transition, presided over by Albert Zafy, was instituted following large-scale protests. A new constitution creating a parliamentary democracy was adopted in 1992, and in 1993, Zafy won the presidential election after a long battle for multi-party democracy. It soon became apparent that constitutional democracy did not guarantee governmental stability. In less than five years following its adoption, there would be six changes of government, three changes of Prime Ministers, two motions of censure and a presidential impeachment. Recognizing the weakness of executive authority confronted with a boisterously fragmented parliament, legislators revised the constitution to reinforce presidential powers. In 1996, after a long-running battle with parliament, President Zafy was impeached and ultimately deposed when the High Constitutional Court confirmed his impeachment by the National Assembly.

Presidential elections in December 1997 resulted in the return of the Red Admiral, Didier Ratsiraka, from political desert to presidential palace. A reformed Marxist, Ratsiraka spoke of decentralization and economic liberalism. He quickly called a referendum to decentralize governmental authority to six semi-autonomous provinces in March 1998. These would be run by provincial councils elected by universal suffrage. In turn, provincial councils would elect a provincial governor and exercise control over economic and social programs. That provincial councils could be dissolved by the president gave a clue to the real purposes of the constitutional referendum: the reinforcement of presidential power.

# Madagascar

**President Marc Ravalomana taking the oath of office**

Additional constitutional provisions included in the referendum also significantly enhanced presidential authority. He would have the power to nominate the prime minister with no obligation to chose him from the political majority in parliament. The president would also have the power to dissolve parliament and nominate the most important magistrates of an "independent judiciary." Presidential impeachment would be more difficult. The goal of these provisions, said proponents, was to end the permanent political instability created by the 1992 constitution.

Voters were confronted with a single, not particularly informative question: "Do you accept the project to amend the constitution to give greater dimension to the development of all regions and to reinforce national unity?" In a country where only 50% of the population is literate, only 50,000 copies of the revised constitutional text were distributed, and those in French, not Malagasy. The opposition called for a boycott of the election, saying it would be a return to a totalitarian regime. When final results were tabulated, only 34% of registered voters managed to bring themselves to the polls, and the referendum passed by the thinnest of margins: 50.62%.

The new regional assemblies marked a slight shift of thinking on the part of the government. Previous regimes had emphasized national unity by concentrating authority at the center. Antananarivo, the capital, was privileged politically and economically, to the detriment of distant regions. The new assemblies were to be granted limited taxing abilities to fund regional programs. Money would still flow from the center for obvious reasons: Antananarivo accounts for three fifths of the state's tax collection.

Demonstrating high political skepticism, sixty to seventy per cent of registered voters boycotted the December 2000 regional elections. When the final results were in, President Ratsiraka's AREMA (*L'Avant-Garde du Renouveau de Madagascar*) party, or "independents" associated with it, captured most of the 336 regional assembly seats. Only in the capital were President Ratsiraka's supporters beaten.

The election of provincial councilors allowed the election of parliament's upper house. Members of the Senate are chosen by an electoral college of "grand electors"—members of parliament, regional councilors, and mayors. Two-thirds of Senate members are appointed by the electoral college, and the remainder are nominated by the president. Senators serve a term of four years, and half of them will be elected or appointed every two years.

In the Senate elections of February 2001, the governing AREMA party, which already had a majority of supporters among the grand electors, easily grabbed a majority of senatorships—49 out of 60. With AREMA dominating both center and periphery, President Ratisraka seemed well-positioned to call the shots in Madagascar's presidential election.

Held in December 2001, the election pitted President Ratsiraka, one of Africa's political dinosaurs—aged, ill, and tainted with corruption—against a self-made millionaire businessman, Marc Ravalomanana, the youthful, dynamic, and popular mayor of the capital, Antananarivo. The election set capital against provinces, newly empowered by decentralization, with devastating consequences for the country. Official results—later annulled—gave Ravalomanana a clear lead, but not the absolute majority needed to win the election outright—46.49% of the vote to Ratsiraka's 40.64%.

The incumbent president called for a second-round run-off, but Ravalomanana, accusing his opponent of fraud and vote rigging, claimed outright victory. He accused election officials of falsifying results and insisted that tally sheets drawn up by

his own agents showed he won 52% of the vote, rather than the 46% claimed by the interior ministry. In January 2002 Ravalomanana supporters organized a general strike, and tens of thousands closed the capital down; daily protests continued for weeks, with no concession from Ratsiraka. Representatives of the OAU sought to mediate, but were unsuccessful.

In February 2002 Ravalomanana declared himself president, staged an inauguration surrounded by judges and officers of the Ratsiraka regime, and appointed a prime minister. Ratsiraka loyalists withdrew to the coastal city of Toamasina and made it an alternative capital. After Ravalomanana announced his own cabinet, the island essentially had two governments, with every post duplicated, including the governor of the central bank.

Ratsiraka decreed martial law in Antananarivo, but the army, deeply divided, remained neutral. His supporters resorted to direct action. The pro-Ratsiraka governor of Toamasina installed roadblocks on the main route to the capital, preventing movement of food or fuel to the capital. At least six bridges linking the inland capital to coastal ports were destroyed in an effort to strangle the city economically.

Amid increasing violence, Madagascar's Supreme Court annulled first-round election results in April and ordered a recount by the High Constitutional Court (HCC). After the recount, the HCC reported Ravalomanana had won an overall majority—51% to 36% for his rival. On 6 May, he formally assumed the presidency and stepped up military action against Ratsiraka forces. Success brought recognition by the United States at the end

**Rice-paddy farming**

of June, quickly followed by France. The OAU, unsuccessful at diplomacy, saw its unity dissolve when Senegal endorsed President Ravalomanana on 4 July. Fearing the precedent of self-proclaimed presidents, it persisted in obtuseness, declaring Ravalomanana's win had not been "legally constituted." (Indeed, Madagascar would not regain its seat until July 2003, when the African Union, the OAU's successor, finally recognized the Ravalomanana government.) Three days later, on 7 July 2002, ex-president Ratsiraka flew to France and exile.

To give proof of President Ravalomanana's support and legitimacy, Western donors pressured the new government to hold early parliamentary elections. The "carrot" as they say in such cases, was the early release of the first portion of $2.3 billion they had pledged to help reconstruct the country over the next four years.

The elections were held in December, and though 40 parties vied for 160 National Assembly seats, President Ravalomanana's *Tiako i Madagasikara* (TiM: I Love Madagascar party) won an overwhelming victory: an absolute majority of 102 seats. With National Solidarity, the wider coalition of parties supporting the president, pro-Ravalomanana forces controlled 132 legislative seats.

The new government has rejected efforts by the AREMA-dominated Senate to pass an amnesty bill for all those involved in the 2002 events. *In absentia*, former president Ratsiraka has been sentenced to five years in prison for his role in the crisis, as was daughter Sophie, found guilty of blowing up a bridge during the civil conflict.

Local elections in November 2003 suggest one reason why the political establishment opposes a general amnesty. Though the president's *Tiako I Magasikara* party was generally successful, winning 29 out of the 45 cities that have municipal governments, it clearly dominated the north and the region of the capital, but appeared much weaker in other outlying areas. Madagascar's second city, the port of Toamasina, remained, for example, in AREMA control. Given this center-periphery disconnect, it is easy to see why some might fear a general amnesty might lead to the return of political exiles who could destabilize the regime.

Government efforts to decentralize authority more broadly than ever before, and put more decision-making in the hands of local people, came to fruition in September 2005 when Madagascar officially replaced its six provinces with 22 "Regions." Their leaders were named by President Ravalomanana.

**Culture:** The diversity in the heritage of the people of this great island is modified by the fact that all speak or understand the highly developed language called Malagasy, which—like the Malagasy themselves—is a synthesis of Indonesian, Polynesian, African, Arab and European influences. As in most pre-literate cultures, traditional Malagasy oratory is replete with the unhurried telling of ancestral proverbs, metaphors, and riddles, often in a participatory dialogue of call and response. It is communication that is neither fast nor direct, and, for its proponents, it is fiercely threatened by modern cell phones, whose costly charges induce brevity, speed and avoidance of ancestral wisdom.

Although about 41% of the people are Christian, most have joined traditional beliefs with ancestor worship of Hindu origin—a religious combination of east and west. During the *Famadihana* ceremony, for example, the dead are exhumed and feted as guests just returned from an extended absence. They are entertained, danced with, regaled with stories of recent family events, turned to for advice, and then reburied with fine new shrouds and presents. It placates the ancestors, who can bless or curse the activities of the living.

The capital of Antananarivo is located on the site of the old capital city of the Merina Kingdom in the high plateau region. Its population of nearly two million consists largely of Merina people. Of Indonesian origins, the Merina are physically distinct from the more African coastal peoples, having lighter features and straighter hair.

Rural poverty has generated a migration to the cities, especially Antananarivo. Now surrounded by shantytowns, the city is a microcosm of the island's problems: malnutrition, unhealthy living conditions, street children, traffic congestion, contaminated water, pollution, underemployment and insecurity. Life expectancy is just 55 years.

**Economy:** The economic balance sheet of the initial Ratsiraka years was an unmitigated disaster. Sixteen years of socialism, from 1974 to 1991, produced unprecedented decline. Key sectors of the economy were nationalized. Banks and insurance companies, export-import businesses, oil companies, and the principal firms in energy, mines, construction and navel repairs all became state agencies. Expatriate businessmen left the country, usually without indemnification, and there was nothing to attract new investors. By 1985 only 10% of total investments were private.

Under the socialist regime industry represented only 15% of the GDP and employed a mere 1% of active workers. Factories operated at only 30% to 40% of their capacity and a massive state investment program produced only white elephants—huge factories built at enormous cost that were never able to function.

**Scenic coastline near Fort Dauphine**　　　　　Photo by Ruth Evans

# Madagascar

In agriculture, farmers soon lost confidence in the regime's cooperatives, returning to subsistence agriculture. With the deterioration of roads, provisioning cities with food became a problem and Madagascar, once a food exporting country, began to import foodstuffs, especially rice. By 1989 the annual average income fell below $210.

When he returned to power in 1997, President Ratsiraka was forced to make a 180-degree turn—to put in place, under the guidance of the World Bank and IMF, a market economy. Action to disengage the state through privatization of its large companies was slow, hesitant, and often indecisive. By the time he left office in 2002, definitively but reluctantly, there had been some improvement: Average annual income rose to $250—where it had been ten years before—and economic growth was around 6%. Most benefits from economic liberalization went to a minority of urban dwellers employed in the textile industry, the country's largest export earner.

The political crisis following the December 2001 elections vitiated much of the country's economic improvement. Particularly hard hit were textile companies operating in economic development zones around Antananarivo. Unable to import fabric, factories had to close and send their workers home.

Overall, industrial output fell between 70% and 90%, and tourism virtually ceased, with revenues falling 95%. Commercial properties lost 50% to 60% of their tenants, and the World Bank estimated the dispute cost the country $12 million to $14 million a day. Economic growth for 2002 was a negative 12%.

In response, the Ravalomanana government instituted business-friendly economic and financial policies and opened the economy to foreign investment. For the first time since 1960, foreigners are permitted to buy real estate—no more than 7.9 acres and only if they have at least $500,000 backup. With stability and liberalization, Madagascar's economy rose by 9.8% in 2003, bringing GDP nearly back to its 2001 level. To mark a symbolic break with the past, the government replaced the Malagasy franc with a pre-colonial currency, the Ariary. Some 71% of the population still lives on less than a dollar a day.

One of the government's highest priorities is the agricultural sector. It dominates the Madagascan economy, employing some 85% of the working population and contributing a third of GDP. The sector is dominated by small-scale farms that produce both export and food crops. To improve production, various taxes and duties on fertilizers and machinery have been reduced. To improve distribution and commercialization, the government has made road development its highest priority. The first $100 million U.S. Millennium Challenge grant to Madagascar was made in March 2005 and focused on rural populations. Funds are to help make it easier to secure formal property rights, improve a weak banking system in which checks take 45 days to clear, to make financial services available in rural areas, to help rural Malagasy identify investment opportunities, and to provide business skills to rural farmers and entrepreneurs.

Rice is Madagascar's main food crop, with production averaging around 2.5 million tons annually. This is not enough to satisfy internal consumption needs and the country must import additional quantities. In October 2003 thirty Vietnamese experts and technicians arrived to provide advice on increasing rice production. (In 20 years Vietnamese rice production increased 300%; in the same period Malagasy production rose by only 25%.)

Maize, bananas, sweet potatoes, groundnuts, pineapples, coconuts, and sugar are also grown for local consumption. The economy's dependence on agriculture makes it subject to the caprice of a frequently hostile Mother Nature. Drought, locusts, and cyclones visit Madagascar nearly every year.

Vanilla used to be the number one export crop, but natural calamities, governmental inefficiencies in marketing, and high local taxes reduced production at the same time Mexico and Indonesia were increasing theirs. Madagascar produces nearly 60% to 65% of the world's vanilla supply. Some 70,000 vanilla farmers produce between 4,500 and 5,500 tons of green vanilla in a good year. After drying and processing, some 1,500 tons are available for export and can bring in $200 million or more to the economy.

Eyeing the huge Japanese market for prawns—Japan consumes some 300,000 tons of shrimps and prawns a year; imports make up 90% of this—the Ratsiraka government encouraged the development of crustacean fisheries. The export of prawns remains an important source of foreign exchange, with some 15,000 tons, worth $130 million, exported in 2002.

Madagascar is rich in mineral resources, including a variety of precious and semi-precious gemstones such as garnets, emeralds, rubies and sapphires. Southern Madagascar has seen the influx of thousands of miners, hot in pursuit of gem quality sapphires. What appeared an anomaly in 1995—the discovery of a huge 40-pound sapphire, nine times the size of the world's largest cut sapphire—had turned, by November 1998, into a treasure trove of easily accessible gemstones. The Ministry of Energy and Mines estimated that 200 new prospectors arrived daily. Despite the boom in the mining business, however, the government says it has earned little from the sapphire rush due to illegal exportations.

The sapphire business was starting to lose some of its early momentum in 2001. Miners and buyers shifted their attention to a new ruby strike in the eastern province of Toamasina. An estimated $40 million worth of rubies have already been exported to Thailand for cutting. Much of this was exported illegally by unscrupulous traders.

Feasibility studies are currently underway to develop nickel-cobalt deposits at Ambatovy, 80 miles east of the capital. The project, a joint venture between Phelps Dodge and the Canadian firm Dynatec, is expected to produce 50,000 tons of nickel and 4,000 tons of cobalt annually. Operating costs would be among the lowest in the world because the ore lies just under the surface and requires no major digging to extract it. Total cost of the project is estimated at between $400 and $500 million and production is expected to begin in 2007.

President Ravalomanana has aggressively sought out foreign investment, and Madagascar's offshore waters have attracted the interest of international oil companies. In December 2004 ExxonMobil paid $25 million for exploration rights in 36,000 square kilometers of coastal waters. China has long maintained a presence in the country, sending some 14 medical teams since 1975 to treat millions of Malagasy. President Ravalomanana visited China in 2004 and produced agreements from his hosts to construct an international conference center and a cement factory, as well as investments in the country's mineral resources.

The World Bank and IMF have recognized Madagascar's extreme poverty. In December 2000, Madagascar qualified for the Heavily Indebted Poor Countries Initiative (HIPC). A March 2004 IMF review noted that "Madagascar's economy rebounded in 2003 following the 2002 slump, and prospects for 2004 are for continued strong economic growth and low inflation." In October it reached a completion point in the program and qualified for debt relief of $1.9 billion—a little over 40% of its external debt of $4.59 billion (2003).

**The Future:** The opening line of the 2003 finance law exemplifies the new spirit in Madagascar: it proclaims that a new page in the country's history has been turned. With that spirit, coupled with international goodwill and commitment, the government may just reach its goal of a 7.8% growth rate.

# The Republic of Mauritius

**President Anerood Jugnauth**

**Area:** 1,856 sq. km. = 717 sq. mi., about the size of Rhode Island.

**Dependencies:** Rodrigues Island, the Agalega Islands and Cargados Carajos Shoals; Mauritius also claims sovereignty over the Chagos Archipelago, part of the British Indian Ocean Territory, where U.S. Naval Base Diego Garcia is located.

**Population:** 1,230,602 (July 2005 est.)

**Capital City:** Port Louis (pop. 146,319)

**Climate:** Tropically hot and humid, with slightly cooler temperatures in the highlands of Mauritius which rise as high as 2,500 feet.

**Neighboring Countries:** Mauritius is located 550 miles east of Madagascar; Rodrigues is 350 miles northeast of Mauritius.

**Official Language:** English.

**Other Principal Languages:** Creole (spoken by 70% of the population), Bojpoori (from Bihar, India), French, Hindi, Urdu, and Hakka.

**Ethnic Background:** Indo-Mauritian 68%, Creole 27%, Sino-Mauritian 3%, Franco-Mauritian 2%.

**Principal Religions:** Hindu 52%, Christian 28.3% (Roman Catholic 26%, Protestant 2.3%), Muslim 16.6%, and other 3.1%.

**Principal Commercial Products:** Clothing and textiles, sugar.

**GNI per capita:** $4,090 (2003)

**Currency:** Mauritius Rupee.

**Former Colonial Status:** French possession (1715–1810); British possession (1810–1968).

**Independence Date:** March 12, 1968.

**Chief of State:** Anerood Jugnauth, President. Since October 2003.

**Head of Government:** Navin Ramgoolam, Prime Minister. Since July 2005.

**National Flag:** Red, blue, gold and green horizontal stripes.

The land mass that is now the island of Mauritius is the result of volcanic activity that occurred thousands of years ago. The craggy, hardened lava, covered with fine ash and silt was in turn covered with a carpet of green vegetation, growing swiftly in the tropical sun. The island is a series of plateaus and interesting variations caused by small streams, waterfalls, crevices and coastal indentations. The island of Rodrigues is a dependency of Mauritius.

**History:** The Dutch arrived at this island, uninhabited by man prior to the time, in 1598, naming it after a prince of Holland. They remained for a century and started sugar production at the time the last clumsy dodo birds walked upon the island. Concluding that the island offered no profit, they withdrew, and the French arrived in 1715. The small group of settlers was augmented by African slaves, who worked the sugar plantations that came to dominate the island.

There was some intermarriage between French and Africans resulting in the evolution of a stable group of people now known as Creoles. The British seized the island in 1810 during the Napoleonic wars. Once slavery had been abolished, a program of importing large numbers of Indian workers to perform the strenuous plantation labor commenced.

Following World War II, the worldwide surge of nationalism gradually entered Mauritius, particularly among those of Indian descent who had become a majority of the population. When Great Britain announced the withdrawal "east of the Suez" in 1966, Mauritius was intended to be a part of this plan. Ethnic diversity was the biggest problem—the Indian majority favored independence, but the Creoles were opposed.

To placate the Creoles, a complicated plan was devised to apportion the seats of the legislature among the ethnic groups, and elections were held. Hindu Indians were able to win a parliamentary majority; Creoles became the minority. Muslim Indians were unable to elect a single representative.

For about 41 years until 1982, Sir Seewoosagur Ramgoolam and his Labor Party dominated the political scene. The party was challenged in the June 1982 elections by a French Mauritian, Paul Bérenger. The vote was so split along party and ethnic lines that a coalition government emerged, headed by Anerood Jugnauth with Bérenger as finance minister. A second collapse in the government in mid-1983 led to a second election. To compete more effectively, Jugnauth organized the Mauritian Socialist Movement (MSM), which defeated Bérenger's Mauritian Militant Movement (MMM). Jugnauth continued in power until late 1995 when he erred politically, proposing a constitutional amendment to incorporate vernacular languages (Hindi, Urdu, Tamil, Marathi, Telegu, Mandarin and Arabic) into primary education. His principal associates in the coalition resigned, and the amendment failed. The assembly had to be dissolved and new elections called.

An opposition alliance won all 60 seats in the 20 island districts. Navin Ramgoolam, son of Sir Seewoosagur, became the new prime minister, but no basic changes in government economic development policies resulted.

The language issue highlights the multiracial, multilingual and multireligious nature of Mauritian society. Unlike many former British colonies, Mauritius retained the Westminster model, but without winner-take-all provisions. Each communal group constituting the Mauritian nation obtains representation in the National Assembly, but communal tensions can and do arise. In early 1998, Prime Minister Ramgoolam ordered a holiday to celebrate the Hindu festival, which drew the criticism of opposition leaders fearful of the economic consequences of too many sectarian holidays.

Communal, age and class tensions surfaced dramatically in February 1999 when Mauritius experienced its worst riots in 30 years. They were sparked by the death, in police custody, of Joseph Topize, alias Kaya. A Creole singer and creator of "seggae"—a mixture of Jamaican reggae with the lilting Mauritian dance rhythm known as "sega," Topize had been arrested for smoking marijuana at a rally to decriminalize the drug. His death, under mysterious circumstances, set off three days of rioting by mostly young Creoles.

Class differences are sharp on Mauritius. Seventeen white Franco-Mauritian families own over half the island's cultivated land. They control not only agricul-

**MAURITIUS**

Poudre D'Or

Port Louis

Beau Bassin
Quatre Bornes
Curepipe

INDIAN
OCEAN

Souillac

0          30 km
0          30 mi

# Mauritius

Prime Minister Navin Ramgoolam

ture but industry too. At the other end of the socio-economic scale are the Creoles who often have no school certificates or vocational training. They frequently end up working as laborers, disaffected from a system in which they share so little—an urban poor, dangerous and volatile. Kaya was their idol.

For the fall 2000 elections Bérenger and Jugnauth formed an electoral alliance. In a pre-election pact the two agreed that if they won, MSM chief Sir Anerood Jugnauth, a Hindu, would serve as prime minister for the first three years; after that MMM leader Paul Bérenger, a Franco-Mauritian, would rule for the next three, becoming the nation's first non-Hindu leader since independence from Britain in 1968.

Discontent with the state of the economy and dissatisfaction with the handling of communal tensions lay at the heart of the campaign. Despite 43 parties fielding candidates, the election was a straightforward fight between the alliance and former Prime Minister Ramgoolam's Labor Party-led coalition. When the final tallies were in, the alliance won a smashing victory: 54 out of 62 seats in assembly.

Since then the government has made an effort to make parliament more representative of minority interests. It announced in March 2002 that the National Assembly would be increased in size, from 62 to 92 members. The additional 30 members would be proportionally chosen from parties that received more than 10% of the vote.

The power-sharing agreement between Jugnauth and Bérenger was implemented in September 2003. President Offmann resigned and was replaced by Prime Minister Jugnauth who left his position, making way for Paul Bérenger to become the

first non-Hindu Prime Minister of Mauritius since independence.

Bitterness from Britain's 1968 removal of the Chagos archipelago from the administrative control of Mauritius still lingers. The archipelago, which includes the island of Diego Garcia, was cleared of nearly 5,000 inhabitants and leased to the United States for use as a military and nuclear base. In return the British reportedly were able to obtain Trident submarines on favorable terms. The military base, originally intended to counter the Soviet threat, has proved its utility in both the 1991 Gulf war and the 2003 Iraqi campaign when allied bombing missions took off from its 12,000-foot runway. The lease expires in 2016.

**Culture:** Its population is culturally diverse, reflecting the island's colonial history. Europeans brought in both Indians and Africans to work the sugar plantations. Today, about 63% of the population is Indian and overwhelmingly Hindu (52%). Thirty percent of the population is African-Creole, 5% Chinese and 2% European. The various ethnic groups tend to have limited interaction with each other. The government has managed to increase literacy from 60% to 100% in a mere three years, largely by making education free. University education remains élitist, restricted to a select few. Only 3% of Mauritians obtain university degrees. This impacts the government's efforts to attract high-tech companies.

**Economy:** Mauritius has transformed its economy since independence when it was essentially dependent on the export of sugar to Great Britain. In the 1960s sugar accounted for nearly 80% of agricultural production and 86% of export earnings. Sugar is still king, but in the thirty years since independence, Mauritius has diversified its economy to create strong supports in light manufacturing, particularly textiles, and tourism. The amount of land devoted to sugar has decreased by at least 20,000 acres and converted to other, more productive uses.

The sugar industry, which employs some 24,000 people, currently accounts for 18% of export earnings, but only 6% of GDP. Natural calamities, drought and cyclones, regularly play havoc with Mauritius' sugar production. Annual average production is around 550,000 tons, making the country the world's seventh largest sugar exporter.

With production costs rising, however, the industry is facing difficult times. Some sugar producers have already shifted their interest to Mozambique where they have committed themselves to rehabilitating

Mozambican refineries and hope to produce 300,000 tons of sugar there. Sugar investments in Mozambique already amount to $110 million. The sugar industry is threatened by Australian and Brazilian initiatives at the World Trade Organization, which challenge the special subsidies given former colonial states by the European Union.

Light manufacturing, dominated by textiles, accounts for 23% of GDP. At one time there were more than 500 textile factories concentrated in Mauritius' Economic Processing Zone. They employed close to 90,000 workers, and they made Mauritius the world's second-largest exporter of woolen knits. Since the late 1990s, however, thousands of Mauritians have been cast out of the textile factories as they closed or downsized. Following September 11, exports to the U.S. fell by 15%, following a 17% growth in 2000. The economy faces even greater challenges with the ending of textile quotas beginning in 2005. Textiles firms are leaving in droves for Asian nations like China and India, which can now export unlimited amounts of clothing to Western nations. The government faces massive unemployment in the sector just at the moment of a national election.

Tourism accounts for 5% of GDP and represents one of the greatest potential growth areas. Following the decline of international travel after the events of 9/11, however, Mauritius' tourism sector has only slowly regrown since then. Tourism in Mauritius is the economy's third pillar, but recent arrival figures suggest the industry may have reached a plateau.

Recognizing the need to diversify the economy, Paul Bérenger announced government plans to make Mauritius "a knowledge island." The plan involves creating "cyber cities" that will provide a world-class telecommunications network via satellite and fiber-optic cable. (There is a fiber-optic cable that runs by the island on its way from Europe to southern India's high-tech corridor.) The first, 15 minutes outside the capital, Port Louis, is in the final stages of construction on former cane fields near the University of Mauritius. Undertaken with the help of an $800 million loan from India, the "cybercity" will be an industrial park for information-technology companies, providing computing on demand, data backup, and servers for web-hosting, e-commerce and financial transactions.

The project will require skilled workers, and in these, Mauritius is deficient. Despite doubling the size of the computer engineering department at the University, the country still only produces 500 to 600 qualified information technology specialists a year. In collaboration with the Massachusetts Institute of Technology, the university has set up a virtual learning center that gives Mauritian students access to course materials used at MIT.

The government is investing heavily in education to produce the manpower needed for its future cyber-cities. The island's educational system has been entirely overhauled. School hours will be extended 45 minutes, and nine compulsory subjects—including languages, mathematics, science and information technology—have been inserted in the curriculum. For the non-traditional student—housewives, children, the unemployed, and disabled—a "Cyber Caravan" has been fitted out for visiting the island's remoter villages. A converted bus, it is now a mobile classroom for computer studies.

The government's diversification and development plans face practical difficul-ties. Mauritius carries a sizeable budgetary deficit, running around 6.5% of GDP, which significantly limits government investment. Given the special relationship it has with India, however, this has not been a problem as Indian loans have continued. A fast growth rate could help reduce this deficit, but growth has faltered, reaching only 4.4% in 2002 and declining to 3.2% in 2003. Unemployment is increasing and stood at 10.3% (2003).

**Future:** Both the sugar industry and garment manufacturing are severely impacted by the withdrawal of preferential access to markets currently provided by international agreements. With the golden age of sugar and now textiles over, Mauritius faces its greatest economic challenge. It is unlikely job creation in cyber services will match job losses in the textile sector.

In the July 2005 parliamentary elections opposition leader Navin Ramgoolam successfully exploited both issues. Leading the Social Alliance (SA), Ramgoolam criticized the Bérenger government for failing to prepare the island for the end of textile quotas and the elimination of EU sugar subsidies. The SA won 38 of 62 contested parliamentary seats and Ramgoolam was designated the island's new Prime Minister.

Ramgoolam, 57, a doctor and lawyer who is the son of the first post-independence prime minister, returns to the job he held between 1995 and 2000. The job hasn't gotten any easier. Rising inflation and unemployment have fuelled discontent among the poor; bolstering the country's ailing sugar and textile industries, said the new prime minister, would be his highest priority.

**Meeting in the Oval Office June 26, 2003, President Bush thanked Prime Minister Jugnauth of Mauritius for hosting the Africa Growth and Opportunity Act Forum in January 2003.**

Photo by Susan Sterner, courtesy the White House

# The Republic of the Seychelles (*Say–shells*)

**Presidential Palace**

Photo by Powell Harrison

**Land area and terrain:** 100 sq. mi., about 1,000 miles off the east coast of Kenya in the Indian Ocean, consisting of some 92 islands, half of which are mountainous and very scenic. The others are little more than coral atolls.

**Population:** 81,188 (July 2005 est.)

**Capital City:** Victoria (on Mahe, pronounced Mah-*hay*, pop. 27,000 estimated.)

**Climate:** tropical marine; humid; cooler season during southeast monsoon (late May to September); warmer season during northwest monsoon (March to May).

**Official Languages:** English, French

**Other Principal Languages:** Seselwa, a French-based Creole

**Ethnic groups:** Seychellois (mixture of Asians, Africans, and Europeans).

**Religions:** Roman Catholic 86.6%, Anglican 6.8%, other Christian 2.5%, other 4.1%.

**Chief Commercial Products:** Processed fish (tuna), prawns, cinnamon bark, copra, tea and vanilla.

**GNI per capita:** $7480 (2003)

**Independence Date:** 29 June 1976 (from UK).

**Chief of State:** James Alix Michel, President (since April 2004)

**National Flag:** Five oblique bands of blue (hoist side), yellow, red, white, and

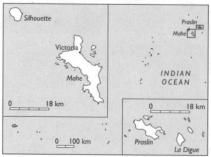

green (bottom) radiating from the bottom of the hoist side.

Located in the western Indian Ocean, 1,000 miles off the coast of East Africa, the Seychelles comprises 115 islands, spread over 154,000 square miles of the Indian Ocean. Lying just below the Equator, the islands have been dubbed a "Garden of Eden" because of the lushness and diversity of their scenery. The main archipelago consists of 42 granitic islands—thrown up by volcanic action to heights of a half mile above sea level—and some 73 coral atolls, low, flat and only a few feet above the sea. Mahé, with its lush hills and luxurious beaches, is the largest and most populated of the islands, with almost 90% of the nation's total population of 80,000. Praslin, and La Digue are the other major islands. Others, like Denis Island, a coral atoll, Sainte Anne, Bird Island, and Cousine, the smallest of the granite islands, are privately owned nature reserves usually associated with an up-scale resort. Fregate, only one-square mile in size, was named after a bird and

# Seychelles

**President James Michel of The Seychelles**

is now the home of tens of thousands of them.

**History:** The first recorded landfall on the islands was made by an expedition of the British East India company in 1609. France colonized the islands in the 18th century, but lost them to Britain as a consequence of the Napoleonic wars. French colonists established plantations worked by African slaves, but the abolition of slavery in the 1830s forced a shift away from cotton to smaller-scale agricultural cultivation. The nineteenth century saw an influx of Asians —Chinese, Indians, and Malays. Over the years the populations intermarried, producing the islands' present mixed population. The descendants of former slaves have tended to remain an underclass.

The British colony was granted self-government in 1975 and independence in 1976. James R. Mancham, the islands' first president, was overthrown in 1977 by a leftist *coup d'état* led by his prime minister, France Albert René. In 1979 René revised the constitution and created a one-party socialist state controlled by his Seychelles People's Progressive Front (SPPF).

In good Leninist fashion, a multiparty political system was not permitted until 1991, and Seychelles' first democratic multiparty elections were held in 1993. René triumphed over former president James Mancham, and the SPPF retained control of the National Assembly.

In March 1997 elections, President René was returned to power with 66.65% of the votes. James Mancham, leader of the opposition Democratic Party (DP), was the big loser, receiving only 14% of the vote, down from the 35% he had won in 1993. Reverend Wavel Ramkalawan, leader of the United Opposition (UO), drew 20% of presidential ballots, and his party replaced the DP as official opposition by winning 26% of the votes cast in legislative elections. Still, in Seychelles' mixed system of single member districts and proportional representation, that only

earned the party 3 seats in the National Assembly. Once again, the SPPF swept the legislative elections, winning 30 seats. Mancham's DP saw its parliamentary representation drop from five seats to one.

Snap presidential elections were called in September 2001, well before the expiration of the president's term of office in 2003 and well before the country's increasingly difficult economic circumstances really began to hurt. With a bit of vote-buying, charged the opposition, René secured 54% of the vote, beating off a vigorous challenge from the Seychelles National Party's Wavel Ramkalawan, who won 45% of the votes.

Seychelles' opposition leader, Reverend Ramkalawan, has proved much less conciliatory than his predecessor and much more formidable. As such he became the object of a smear campaign by the SPPF-controlled press before the legislative election of 2002. (Despite its total dominance, the SPPF made few concessions to its opposition.)

Seychelles' one daily newspaper and single radio and television service are government controlled. Coverage of the political opposition is highly restricted. President René filed several lawsuits against *Regar,* an opposition weekly, and *Vizyon,* an information bulletin of the SNP claiming defamation. In a situation where René appointed all the judges, the papers had little protection in the courts. In February 2002, *Regar* was found guilty of "libel" against the country's Vice-President and ordered to pay nearly a half million dollars. It was the latest of several sentences whose fines totaled approximately $2,648,000. This was part of René's policy of crushing any voice of opposition, even if it only has a print run of 3,000.

President René called early parliamentary elections in December 2002, well before the normal expiration of the Assembly's mandate, and presumably before the impact of a declining economy would be felt by too many voters. Once again René did all he could to prevent an opposition victory. Typically, opposition SNP candidates and supporters were intimidated: Police were generally in attendance at all its meetings, but looked away when gangs of SPPF partisans menaced the opposition. To divide the opposition, James Mancham's Democratic Party, moribund since its disastrous defeat in 1998, seemed to have been given financing by the government. Tacitly admitting the country's economic slowdown, the SPPF made "Things Can Only Get Better" its campaign slogan.

When all the ballots were counted, René's SPPF won handily, but saw its massive majority eroded, down from 30 to 24. Reverend Ramkalawan's SNP took the remaining 11 seats in the National Assem-

bly. Once again The Democratic Party was the biggest loser. Polling a miniscule 3.1% of the votes, the party failed to achieve the minimum 10% required to earn a seat by proportional representation.

Having secured his last hurray, President René retired from office in April 2004; he was succeeded by Vice-President James Michel, but maintained his position as head of the Seychelles People's Progressive Front.

**Culture:** The population of the Seychelles is relatively homogenous, the result of frequent intermarriage between the island's original French settlers and Africans who settled after the islands were ceded to Britain in the early 1800s. Small Indian and Chinese minorities also exist. Most of the population is Roman Catholic, and almost everyone speaks Creole.

Upon assuming leadership in 1977, President René invited his fellow citizens to "create the new man, with his roots." The "root" of this new Seychellois identity would be its "créolité"—its "creoleness." Since then government policy has affirmed and cultivated a common culture based on Creole roots. The language has become the first spoken and written language of everyone (English and French are the second and third languages), and the world's only Creole Institute can be found on Mahe. Each October Victoria hosts the world's largest Creole festival, featuring artists and writers from the diverse Creole world—Mauritius, Reunion, the French Caribbean islands, Guyana, etc.

In April 2002 the SPPF government celebrated 25 years of rule since the coup (or "liberation" as party stalwarts prefer to call it) that brought it to power. The government describes itself as "paternalistic,"—a fusion of socialism and capitalism, and in many ways its achievements are striking. Gone are the days when thirty families—the *grands blancs*—controlled wealth and property on the islands. Free access to education and health, a right to housing, and guaranteed employment have created a costly social security system unequaled on the African continent. Seychellois have the highest per capita income of all the African states.

Fish and rice are the basic staples of Seychelles cuisine. Islanders eat some 165 pounds of fish annually and face reduced catches from the sea. The 1998 catch was down some 60%, attributable to increased temperatures of the Indian Ocean waters. Fish are migrating to cooler waters.

The islands boast two UNESCO World Heritage Sites. The first, Aldabra, is the world's largest raised atoll, and hosts the world's largest colony of giant tortoises (150,000 of them) along with the last re-

# Seychelles

maining flightless birds in the Indian Ocean. The second is the Vallée de Mai on Praslin, the only place on earth where one finds the black parrot and the rare palm trees that bear the giant Coco de Mer or sea coconut, the world's largest and heaviest seed, perhaps better known for a voluptuous shape that reminds the erotically susceptible of portions of the female anatomy.

**Economy:** Isolated in the vast Indian Ocean, the Seychelles promote themselves as an idyllic tourist location. Some 130,000 people visit the islands annually and account for 70% of their hard currency. It's up-scale tourism only, and until recently charter flights were not permitted. The fear was that budget passengers would lower the tone of the island and not spend enough money. The number of visitors is limited to 150,000 a year, and no more than 4,500 are permitted at any one time. The government also controls the quantity and quality of hotels and does not permit camping. Accommodations are correspondingly pricey. Comrade workers will find no rest and recreation in this socialist Garden of Eden.

Post-September 11 declines in international travel affected an already declining market. In the later part of 2002 the government permitted charter flights to revivify a softening industry. In December alone there were 12 charter flights, one even a Boeing 747 carrying 400 mass-market travelers. Perhaps as a consequence the islands recorded a modest increase of 2% in the number of tourists—132,246 for all of 2002. The market continued to decline in 2003, however, falling off by eight percent. Tourism has always been the country's largest foreign exchange earner, but the diminishing number of visitors in recent years has had an impact of the country's Gross Domestic Product (GDP).

Seychelles has one of the highest living standards in Africa with a remarkable per capita Gross National Income (GNI) of more than $6,000, but the economy has constricted for the past three years. World Bank figures show GDP falling by 5.4% in 2000, 8.1% in 2001, and by a more modest 2.4% in 2002. GNI has fallen accordingly, dropping from $7,300 in 1998 to $6,780 in 2002. The IMF blames excessive government involvement in the economy, including price controls, foreign exchange allocation, restrictive import licensing, and many government-owned monopolies in manufacturing and distribution.

In December 2000, the International Monetary Fund reported that the Seychelles' net international reserves were depleted and that government debt had grown alarmingly. The foreign currency shortage resulted in empty shelves in the shops, inflation, and a black market where a dollar cost ten rupees compared to the official rate of five. By mid-2001 the government was forcing foreign tourists to pay all their bills in foreign currency rather than local rupees. Passengers at the island's international airport were reportedly searched for travelers' checks. To generate extra revenue, the authorities plan to increase the usual visitors' tax from $40 to $50 beginning in October 2003.

Because of its cash crunch, the government has defaulted on its bonds, taking its place with other financial deadbeats like Liberia and Zimbabwe—all of whom are barred from borrowing from multilateral lenders. Its accumulated debt rose from $265 million in 2001 to $408 million in 2002.

Seychelles takes advantage of its greatest natural resource, fish. Its exclusive economic zone gives it control of more than 386 thousand sq. miles of Indian Ocean, abundant in rich fishing grounds. A fleet of patrol boats enforces the exclusion zone, and all fishing vessels must stop in Victoria port, register their catch, and pay the appropriate fees. The European Union sends the most vessels to the zone, with more than 40 ships working its waters. The government is fully committed to setting up a Seychellois-owned tuna fishing fleet.

Fishing licenses and fees bring in about $7million annually, but the government decided that added value could be better achieved by processing the catch locally. In 1995, it joined with Heinz to build the new cannery on reclaimed land in Victoria harbor. The factory has a capacity of 400 tons a day. The factory generated about $100 million in 1999, almost as much as Seychelles tourism.

The great Asian tsunami of December 2004 struck the Seychelles, and while it killed only two people, 900 families were displaced and public infrastructure such as roads and bridges were damaged. The government estimated total damage at about $30 million, but both the principal pillars of the economy, fishing and tourism, were badly hit.

The country's declining economic fortunes result from excessive government involvement in the economy. According to a recent EU study, government expenditures account for 62% of GDP over the last six years. The economy is dominated by the Seychelles Marketing Board (SMB), the islands' largest employer. SMB possesses a variety of import and export monopolies and has a share of almost every enterprise.

A good socialist at heart, René claimed SMB saved the islands from dishonest merchants who imported low-quality products to make maximum profits and could not assure regular supplies to a population largely dependent on imported foodstuffs. Critics note that SMB's monopolies have not prevented shortages in a wide variety of products, but have run up a foreign debt of $ 80 million.

The IMF and EU offer a simple prescription for Seychelles' welfare-state woes: privatize government monopolies, eliminate price controls, devalue the rupee, permit foreign investment and drop controls on foreign exchange. Locally, Reverend Ramkalawan argues that the only way to regain investors' confidence and revitalize the economy is to liberalize it. If nothing changes, he says, "we will go under."

President René would hear none of it. He rejected recommendations by the International Monetary Fund (IMF), claiming they would "cripple" his country. "As soon as we liberalize our economy," he has said, "we will put all our farmers and meat producers in danger. They will never survive the price competition from other countries. Most of our factories will close down for the same reasons. And then we will know the full meaning of unemployment and suffering in the household . . ."

By July 2003 President René and his heir apparent, vice-president and finance minister James Michel, were forced to introduce a new Macro-Economic Reform Program (MERP) that suggested the government's policy would henceforth emphasize austerity and strictness. Ten months later, however, the president of the Seychelles Chamber of Commerce and Industry lamented that nothing had changed, despite the government's promise to introduce free-market reforms.

**The Future:** Obdurate before change, former President René was unwilling to liberalize the Seychelles economy. Even after the introduction of MERP, the Seychelles Marketing Board monopolies remained in place, even expanding, despite the recommendations of the IMF, the World Bank, the European Union and the local private sector. His successor, James Michel, faces the consequences. The government desperately needs to reschedule its debt ($557 million as of 2003), but its reform intransigence leaves it with few sympathetic ears.

# EASTERN AFRICA

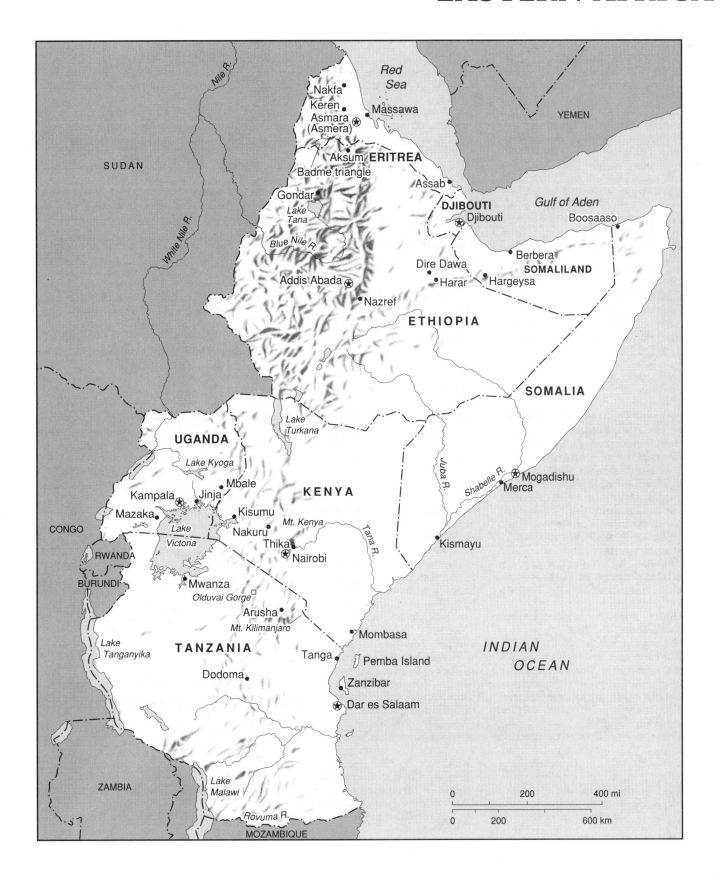

209

# The Republic of Djibouti    (pronounced Gee-booty)

**Area:** 23,000 sq. km = 9,000 sq. mi. (slightly larger than Massachusetts).

**Population:** 476,703 (July 2005 est.)

**Capital City:** Djibouti.

**Neighboring Countries:** Ethiopia (North, West, South); Somali Republic (Southeast).

**Official Language:** Arabic, French.

**Other Principal Languages:** Somali, Afar (Danakil), Arabic.

**Ethnic groups:** Somali 60%, Afar 35%, French, Arab, Ethiopian, and Italian 5%.

**Principal Religions:** Muslim 94%, Christian 6%.

**Chief Commercial Products:** Hides and skins, and coffee (in transit).

**GNI per capita:** $910 (2003).

**Currency:** Djibouti Franc.

**Former Colonial Status:** French Territory (1896–1977).

**Independence Date:** June 27, 1977.

**Chief of State:** Ismail Omar Guelleh, President (since April 1999).

**National Flag:** Two equal horizontal bands of light blue (top) and light green with a white isosceles triangle based on the hoist side bearing a red five-pointed star in the center.

The Republic of Djibouti is a tiny, sun–blistered pocket of land strategically located at the entrance to the Red Sea. The only reason for its separate existence as a colony was the deep, natural harbor at the city of Djibouti, through which Ethiopian exports and imports traveled overland since the beginning of the century. The desert country of the interior is parched and bleak, an irregular landscape seen infrequently by other than the nomadic herdsmen who pass through. It has been said that this area is even too hot for the devil.

**History:** The Republic of Djibouti was undoubtedly a focal point of African– Asian migration and travel for centuries. For details of early and colonial history, see *Historical Background* and *The French in Africa.*

France, after granting all of its remaining African colonies independence in 1960 did not concern itself with this remaining African territory until 1966. De Gaulle's August 1966 visit was marked by two days of public demonstrations by Somalis demanding independence. France conducted a referendum in March 1967 in which 60% chose to remain associated with France. In July of that year, the name French Somaliland formally changed to the French Territory of Afars and Issas to avoid any encouragement to expansionist ambitions in Somalia.

Hassan Gouled Aptidon, an Issa, easily won the ensuing presidential elections and an inter-ethnic government was formed with an Afar, Ahmed Dini, serving as Prime Minister. Successive elections in 1981 and 1986 returned the unopposed President with majorities of over 90% and affirmed Issa domination of Djibouti politics.

In November 1991 a devastating civil war erupted between the Issa-led government and a predominantly Afar rebel group which termed itself the Front for the Restoration of Unity and Democracy (FRUD). Responding to criticisms of its monopoly of political power, President Aptidon's government decided to permit multi-party politics and allowed the registration of four political parties in 1992. Only two, Aptidon's People's Rally for Progress (RPP)—the only legal party in Djibouti from 1981 to 1992—and the Party for Democratic Renewal (PRD*)* contested the national assembly election. Claiming there were too many opportunities for electoral fraud, the PRD withdrew its candidates. The RPP won all 65 assembly seats with a turnout of only 50%.

In 1994 a moderate faction of the FRUD signed a peace agreement with the government, ending three years of civil war. In this accord the government agreed to recognize FRUD as a legitimate political party and named two FRUD leaders, Afars, to cabinet positions in 1995. In December 1997 elections the ruling RPP-FRUD coalition won all 65 legislative seats.

At the age of 83, elderly and frail, President Aptidon announced that he would not stand for re–election in 1999. In April Djibouti conducted its second multiparty presidential elections and the overwhelming victory went to Aptidon's nephew, *Chef de Cabinet,* and long–time director of security services, Ismail Omar Guelleh. His campaign was slick and well-financed. Colored posters covered the walls of Djibouti; thousands of green T–shirts and hats bearing his name were distributed to Djibouti's numerous unemployed. His opponent was the seasoned politician Moussa Ahmed Idriss, a leader in the campaign for independence who served in the French parliament from 1962 until 1967. Much less well–financed, Idriss received about a quarter of the votes cast. It was an election in which both wings of FRUD participated rather than boycotted. Those who had reconciled themselves to the government supported Ismail Omar Guelleh; those who remained in armed opposition urged support of Idriss.

The usual severity of the regime to its critics continues under President Guelleh, who seems little tolerant of criticism. The government, which owns the principal newspaper, *La Nation,* has particularly little patience with the opposition press. Charges of "distributing false informa-tion" can land an editor in jail and earn the newspaper a lengthy banning. The government also owns the radio and television stations. Neither is a source of critical judgment against the government.

In February 2000 Ahmed Dini's unreconciled wing of FRUD signed an agreement on "reform and civil harmony" with the Djibouti government, seeming to bring closure to the Afar rebellion. The agreement called for rehabilitation of zones devastated by the civil war, compensation of victims of the conflict, and "real devolution, granting a wide degree of autonomy to the regions concerned."

A section of the agreement on democratization suggested FRUD's sense of exclusion from Djibouti politics. It referred to the need for "equitable representation" and an administration within which "the various national communities are equally represented." The reality of political power in Djibouti is that the Issa, the dominant Somali clan, control the ruling party and are disproportionately represented in bureaucratic and military ranks. Among the Issa, the president's subclan, the Mamassan, predominates.

Negotiations between the government and representatives of FRUD's armed faction on the specifics of the agreement began in April 2000. They ultimately concluded with a peace accord signed in May 2001, and the demobilization of FRUD fighters went smoothly. Of 1,074 disbanded troops, some 300 were integrated into the government's forces and 700 returned to their villages.

The peace agreement allowed the FRUD-Armé to be authorized as a political party when a multiparty system was approved in September 2002; as a legal party it is known as the *Alliance Républicaine pour le Développement* (ARD). Legislative elections scheduled for late 2002 were postponed to allow the numerous parties registered to organize and campaign effectively. They were ultimately held in January 2003.

In Djibouti's first multiparty elections, two coalitions competed for seats in the country's 65-seat legislature. On the government side, the *Union pour la majorité présidentielle's* (UMP) list was dominated by nominees of President Guelleh's RPP (two-thirds) and FRUD-legal (one-third). Two smaller parties were allocated 2 positions each on the list. The opposition rallied under the banner of the *Union pour l'alternance démocratique* (UAD: Union for Democratic Change) which was dominated by candidates of Ahmed Dini's ARD.

With a winner-take-all district system, election results distorted opposition strength. UMP parties supporting President Guelleh won 62.2% of the votes, against 36.9% for the opposition, but took every legislative seat. For the first time, six women are represented in parliament. Ahmed Dini, who led the Union for a Democratic Alternative, said, not without justification, the poll had been rigged and claimed his group had won at least 22 seats.

Even the government was willing to admit the voter lists were hopelessly out of date. In an interview, the Minister of the Interior said they went back to the colonial period. "There are many dead people on the lists because our citizens do not normally report deaths," he said. "We have people who are 120 years old or more on the lists."

After the terrorist attacks of September 11, 2001, Djibouti became the hub of Western anti-terrorist activity. In addition to having France's largest military contingent, Djibouti has allowed U.S. and European forces (notably German, but also Spanish, British and Italian) to use its airport facilities. For Americans the main goal is to put American forces in position to strike cells of Al Qaeda in Yemen or East Africa. Indeed, it was CIA operatives in Djibouti who directed the launch of a Hellfire missile that struck a car carrying the mastermind of the attack on the USS Cole in Yemen's port of Aden—an attack which killed 17 U.S. Navy sailors. Qaed Salim Sinan al-Harethi, a close ally of Osama bin Laden, and five others traveling in the car were killed.

Djibouti's April 2005 presidential election went off without a hitch (by local standards) and without an opposition candidate. Long-time opponent Ahmed Dini Ahmed had died the preceding September, at age 72, and the only other candidate, Mohamed Daoud Chehem, withdrew in March citing difficulties in raising campaign funds. Opposition parties called a boycott and the police had to use teargas to disperse hundred of protesters who blocked the streets with burning tires, but President Guelleh was re-elected to a second six-year term.

**Culture:** The city of Djibouti is distinctly French in atmosphere; about 24,000 Europeans live in the capital, including the French military—actually foreign legionnaires—who wander through the town in tight khaki shorts and white "kepi" hats. Soldiers with shaved heads and tattoos nightly pack the bars and restaurants the police once tried to close down as offensive to "good morals in a Muslim country." The French are joined by some of the 1,000 German soldiers now on duty in Djibouti.

The price of pleasure is high in Djibouti. A beer in town costs $6, a pizza $17. The prices, and cultural sensitivity, have helped keep U.S. servicemen off the streets and largely confined to a camp that brings in its own supplies and contributes almost nothing to the economy. When they do come to town, Americans tend to come in the afternoon and wear civilian clothes.

A widespread practice is the use of *khat* (or *qat*), a stimulant common throughout the Horn of Africa. Much of Djibouti's business activity grinds to a halt at midday, partly because of the heat and partly because this is when the daily plane from Ethiopia arrives bringing about 12 tons of the drug. It is a social drug that is never swallowed, only chewed as the user moves from stimulation to contemplative stupor. Women are discouraged from chewing *khat* and if they do it must be done in seclusion.

Female Genital Mutilation (FGM) is common in Djibouti. A 2002 survey of 1,000 women by Djibouti's health ministry concluded that 98 percent of them had been circumcised. Infibulation, one of the most brutal forms of FGM, is the most prevalent in Djibouti. The inner labia and clitoris are first cut away, then the remaining lips are sewn together, leaving only a small hole for urination and menstruation. The practice is a major contributor to Djibouti's relatively high maternal mortality rate: 69 deaths for each 10,000 live births.

Article 333 of Djibouti's *Penal Code* outlaws the practice of FGM, but few people have ever been arrested. In February 2005 the government signed the African Union's Maputo Protocol on FGM which requires member states to ban the practice. In a conference explaining the protocol, Djibouti's prime minister indicated the government was confronted with a real health problem and it was up to them to ensure that ratification of the protocol "does not end up like other documents." The Maputo Protocol is remarkable in declaring that there is "irrefutable evidence that there is no religious basis in the Qur'an—as well as in other revealed religions (Christianity and Judaism)—to justify the perpetuation of FGM."

**Economy:** The 1991–94 civil war expanded the army from 3,000 men to 18,000, devastated infrastructure and bankrupted the state. The national debt is estimated to be around $366 million. To pay for the war, public utilities were raided and payments were delayed to creditors and state employees. When the government proposed reducing public salaries, which account for nearly 80% of the budget, a general strike was declared, and the government had to suspend planned reforms. Salary arrears to government workers continue to plague the government, and it remains dependent on the generosity of friends to make up budgetary shortfalls.

With less than 1% of its soil arable and with virtually no industry, Djibouti remained an impoverished backwater. Aside from livestock, its one traditional resource was salt, mined from a "lake" of salt deposits over 1800 ft deep. From time immemorial, Afar nomads have brought their camels to Assal, loaded them with salt and led them to Ethiopia, where their cargo is exchanged for cereal and other goods. Large-scale exploitation of Assal's salt began in 1998 and increasingly trucks have replaced the traditional miner and his camel.

President Guelleh's campaign poster

# Djibouti

**Djibouti Nomads** ©IRIN

bridges, and replacing its communication system. With improvements the line will have the capacity to carry one million metric tons of freight annually.

Significant income is derived from the presence of foreign troops in Djibouti. France maintains a force of 2,800 strong there, making it France's largest foreign military base. The United States has made Djibouti a center for its war on terrorism, and some 1,500 American soldiers are stationed there. The country also hosts an additional 800 German and 50 Spanish troops.

The U.S. government has committed an additional $2 million to renovate state-run Radio Djibouti, along with $100,000 in annual rent, in exchange for a strategic transmission station the U.S. is building. The targeted audience: Yemen and the southern regions of Saudi Arabia.

**The Future:** President Guelleh has few resources with which to confront Djibouti's crippling poverty so his openness to Western military forces is understandable. Given a moderate version of Islam in the country, he is unlikely to suffer any severe consequences from the presence of these troops.

Today Djibouti is dependent on its strategic location on one of the busiest sea lanes of the world. Modernized to receive container cargoes, port facilities are the heart of the Djibouti economy. Border conflict between neighboring Ethiopia and Eritrea significantly increased activities at Djibouti port as Ethiopia diverted its trade from the Eritrean ports of Assab and Massawa. Eighty percent of all goods handled by the port are now destined for landlocked Ethiopia. As a consequence of significantly increased usage, the port has become so congested the government sought funding for a new and much larger facility at Doraleh, about five miles east of the current port.

The new facilities are being built in two phases—first an oil terminal and then a container area and free trade zone. The estimated cost of the project is some $400 million, and the government hopes it will have a major positive economic impact on the local economy, but the IMF has evinced major doubts: "Djibouti's experienced in the 1990s," said a recent IMF report, "showed that large public investment programs did not necessarily lead to sustained economic growth." The Doraleh oil terminal will become operational in July 2005.

Strenuous efforts have been made to improve rail and road connections between the port and Ethiopia to speed the transfer of imports. The 500-mile Djibouti to Addis railroad, constructed by France in 1897, suffers from dilapidated equipment more than 50 years old. The EU has granted a $40 million loan to upgrade the line. This includes enlarging its rails to accommodate the most modern locomotives, reinforcing viaducts and metal

Marine infantrymen from A Company, 1st Battalion, 24th marine Regiment stand on line during civil disturbance training at Camp Lemonier, Djibouti, March 29. The Marines, here in support of Combined Joint Task Force–Horn of Africa, are learning the tactics, techniques and procedures of riot control in case a hostile crowd were to threaten personnel here.

Photo by Cpl. Paula M. Fitzgerald, courtesy U.S. Marine Corps.

# The State of Eritrea

**Downtown Asmara**

Photo by Veronica Rentmeesters

**Area:** 93,679 sq. km. = 40,800 sq. mi. (larger than Maine).

**Population:** 4,561,599 (July 2005 est.)

**Capital City:** Asmara (est. pop. 435,000.)

**Climate:** Generally dry, moderate to chilly in the central highlands; hot and dry in the desert regions, hot and humid along the coastline.

**Neighboring Countries:** Sudan (North and East); Ethiopia (South); Djibouti (Southeast).

**Official Languages:** None, though Arabic and English are often used on official letterheads.

**Other Principal Languages:** Afar, Amharic, Arabic, Tigre and Kunama, and Tigrinya.

**Ethnic groups:** Tigrinya 50%, Tigre and Kunama 40%, Afar 4%, Saho (Red Sea coast dwellers) 3%, other 3%

**Principal Religions:** Muslim, Coptic Christian, Roman Catholic, Protestant

**Chief Commercial Products:** Livestock, sorghum, textiles, food, and small manufactures.

**GNI per capita:** $190 (2003)

**Currency:** Nakfa.

**Former Colonial Status:** Italian colony (1890–1941); British trusteeship (1941–1952); absorbed by Ethiopia 1962–1991, (defeat of Ethiopian forces), referendum in April 1993 resulted in total independence.

**Independence Date:** May 24, 1991.

**Chief of State:** Isaias Afwerki, President (April 1993).

**National Flag:** A red triangle at the pole divides a green field at the top, from a blue one at the bottom. A gold wreath encircling a gold olive branch is centered on the pole side of the red triangle

Geological evidence indicates that Eritrea was a relatively flat plateau of green trees and grass prior to the arrival of modern mankind. At an known time, massive earthquakes caused the land to change into a terrain of sharp peaks accentuated by smoldering, active volcanoes which spewed their lava freely. Although the volcanoes are now dead, the peaks remain, often rising to more than 14,000 feet, with a craggy appearance caused by lava rock formations. Except for the coastal areas, the climate is moderate, with frost appearing above 11,000 feet. Variation in temperature from noon to midnight may be as much as 60 degrees.

Eritrea is semi-arid at best, and rainfall is irregular. This, combined with the rugged terrain which dominates all but the coast along the Red Sea, makes the land somewhat inhospitable and generally incapable of producing field crops. Rainfall depends upon prevailing wind direction. If the currents aloft are from southwest to northeast, moisture capable of generating rainfall arrives from central Africa's vast rain forest area. But if the prevailing pattern is from the northwest to the southeast, the hot winds of the Sahara and sub-Sahara arrive and roast any crops that are planted.

**History:** The Coptic Christian Church established outposts in Ethiopia and Eritrea in the 4th century, and Islam arrived most probably as a result of continued contact with Arabs by the first part of the 8th century. Today, the people are almost evenly divided between Christianity and Islam. Eritreans continued to live a life of localized independence until swept into the maelstrom of events set off by two contending forces in the late 19th century: Italian efforts to colonize the area and efforts of Menelik II, King of Ethiopia, to assemble, by conquest, modern Ethiopia. For details of early history, see *Historical Background.*

The Italian conquest of Eritrea and later of Ethiopia effectively created a separate

213

# Eritrea

identity for each. After the Italians were expelled in 1941, the British assumed control over the territory. Under pressure from the British and Ethiopia, the UN adopted a plan for federation of Eritrea and Ethiopia in 1950. This was intended to protect Eritrean autonomy, but almost immediately after the federation went into effect, Eritrean rights were abridged or violated by the Ethiopian imperial government. Political parties were banned in 1955, followed by the banning of trade unions in 1958. In 1959 the name "Eritrean Government" was changed to "Eritrean Administration," and Ethiopian law was imposed. Resistance to this administrative subordination was manifested by the creation of the Eritrean Liberation Front (ELF) in 1958.

Increasing pressure on Eritreans from Addis Ababa to renounce their autonomy was ultimately successful in November 1962. A compliant Eritrean Assembly voted unanimously for the abolition of Eritrea's federal status, reducing Eritrea to a simple province of the Ethiopian empire. The liberation struggle began in earnest at the same time.

In 1974 the Ethiopian monarchy collapsed and power was seized by the military. Lt. Col. Mengistu Haile Mariam assumed power as head of state and Chairman of the governing military council known as the Derg. The regime was totalitarian in style, financed by the Soviet Union and Eastern block, and assisted by Cuba in a massive militarization of the country. War against the Eritrean rebels continued through the late 1980's. When the Soviet Union, otherwise occupied in Afghanistan, announced that it would not renew its defense and cooperation agreement with Ethiopia, army morale plummeted. The Eritrean People's Liberation Front (EPLF) joined with internal opposition to the Derg, advanced on Ethiopian positions, and ultimately drove Mengistu into exile in 1991.

The EPLF established a provisional government in May 1991 with its leader Isaias Afwerki as its head. Independence was overwhelmingly ratified in a UN-monitored referendum in April 1993. Freely-contested elections chose a National Assembly which in turn appointed Afwerki as President of the Provisional Government of Eritrea (PGE). The EPLF renamed itself the People's Front for Democracy and Justice (PFDJ) in early 1994 and became the country's only political party.

The new government faced enormous challenges. A constitution had to be written, a judiciary created, a school system reconstructed, refugees reintegrated and ex-guerrillas demobilized. Underlying all was the need to rehabilitate a badly damaged infrastructure and reform the collapsed institutions of a centrally planned economy. In March 1994 the National Assembly established a constitutional commission and members traveled throughout the country and to Eritrean communities abroad, holding meetings to explain constitutional options and solicit input. The new constitution that resulted from this broad consultative process was ratified by the constituent assembly on May 24, 1997. Elections to implement the constitution were postponed; they have yet to be held.

A full judiciary system has yet to be installed. Given an absence of legally trained personnel, the Ministry of Justice has been unable to process a large volume of civilian corruption cases. These were handled by the Ministry of Defense and in 1997 some 2,314 civilians were tried by special military courts.

At its peak fighting strength the EPLF army grew to nearly 110,000 fighters—nearly 3% of the total population. Since a fragile peacetime economy could not support such numbers, the government began to demobilize 50% to 60% of the army in 1993. Those who had served longest and had the fewest civilian skills were given higher compensation, more intensive training and more psychological counseling. Special attention was given to women fighters who made up 30% of the EPLF's combat forces. By 1998 the army had shrunk to 47,000, but then, the country went to war again with Ethiopia.

Eritrean law obliges every citizen between the ages of 18 and 40 to do national service, but national service in war took on a new meaning. Hostilities with Ethiopia broke out in May 1998. In April 1999 the government conducted evening raids across the country, rounding up young people who might have skipped out on national service. Unless they could iden-

**President Isaias Afwerki**

tify themselves as a mother, pregnant or a veteran, young Eritreans were put on buses and taken off to a police station for questioning.

At issue in the conflict with Ethiopia was an obscure triangle of land, 155 square miles of rocky barrenness called the Badme Triangle. Unlocatable on most maps, the triangle became the focus of national pride on both sides of the border. Both Presidents Afwerki and Meles found themselves in a situation from which it was difficult to retreat. Pride and personality, on both sides, generated a cultivated knack for stubbornness. Negotiations had, by May 2000, brought no resolution to the conflict. As soon as the last negotiators left, Ethiopia launched another massive attack. A surprise advance against a presumably impregnable pass brought crushing victory in nineteen days, after which Ethiopia announced its war aims achieved.

A ceasefire was announced in June 2000 and actually lasted through the conclusion of December peace negotiations conducted in Algiers. The Algiers Agreement called for a pull back of troops and creation of a demilitarized zone manned by several thousand UN peacekeepers. A five-member Eritrea-Ethiopia Boundary Commission (EEBC) was established to demarcate the disputed border. Overall, the war had mobilized 200,000 fighters into the army. It cost the lives of 19,000 Eritreans, displaced tens of thousands, and set back development plans for decades.

The Boundary Commission rendered its decision in April, 2002. The language of the 125-page decision was sufficiently obscure to allow both countries to claim victory: Badme, for example, was not explicitly mentioned in the text. Both countries launched a propaganda campaign seeking to convince its citizens that the sacrifices of war had not been in vain.

Tensions between the two countries spiked as demarcation approached in Spring 2003. In March the EEBC affirmed that Badme, the *causa belli* of recent conflict, was part of Eritrea. The Ethiopian Prime Minister rejected the decision, calling it "a blatant miscarriage of justice," as well as "illegal, unjust and irresponsible." Beating the drums and sounding the trumpets, he warned the decision could lead to "another round of war."

No one seemed to know what to do or had the will to do anything. The AU, one of the guarantors of the Algiers Agreement, was deafeningly silent, causing Eritrea to recall its ambassador from the organization. The UN could only offer more mediation and extended its peacekeeping mission. In February 2004 it appointed a former Canadian Foreign Minister, Lloyd Axworthy, as its special envoy to help defuse the tensions. By November, Ethiopia had accepted the decision "in principle," but engaged in provocative troop movements near the border soon after.

The Eritrean government continues to insist the border ruling be implemented, and it has also moved troops to the border area. Relations with Ethiopia are stretched to the breaking point. In March 2005 the UN Security Council extended the mandate of its peacekeeping force patrolling the demilitarized zone for another six months, but the peacekeepers feel increasingly insecure. Understating the obvious, a spokesman from the Eritrean president's office said in April 2005: "What is clear is that the present scenario is not sustainable." If there were no light at the end of the tunnel, he went on, "obviously that will set in motion a different set of factors."

Relations with Sudan are no better than those with Ethiopia. As the only country on the Red Sea, aside from Israel, that is not majority Muslim, Eritrea has good rea-

son to be obsessed with threats to its sovereignty. Sudan has supported the extremist Eritrean group known as the Eritrean Islamic Jihad (EIJ) and permitted opponents of the government, organized under the Alliance of Eritrean National Forces (AENF), to operate out of Sudan. In response Asmara has continued to arm and train Sudanese opposition forces and allowed Sudan's principal opposition group, the NDA, to have offices in Asmara. The government accused Sudan, Ethiopia and Yemen of forming an "Axis of Belligerence" that sought its overthrow.

Equally prickly has been President Afwerki's relationship with his domestic opposition. When fifteen members of the Central Council and National Assembly protested Afwerki's alleged "dominant and illegal" handling of party and state affairs and asked for greater democracy, authorities accused them of being involved in illegal activities which endangered the nation. In its clampdown on pro-democracy campaigners, the government closed

the private press and arrested dissidents, journalists and prominent Eritreans, all of whom were held without charge.

Safe in cyberspace, the dissidents organized a new political party—the Eritrean People's Liberation Front Democratic Party, or EPLFDP, to challenge the "autocratic and incorrigible" EPLF regime. As the first opposition party to emerge from within the EPLF, the new Democratic Party has more credibility than external opposition groups backed by Ethiopia and Sudan. Even more worrisome for the Afwerki regime, the Democratic Party has agreed on a common set of objective with two older parties.

The government takes a continual bashing for its less than sterling human rights record. The European Parliament has said President Afwerki ruled the country "with an iron grip," and expressed concern over the country's "authoritarian trend." The U.S. State Department is no more charitable, particularly in the realm of religious toleration, asserting the regime has ha-

**Italian Art Deco architecture of Asmara**

# Eritrea

rassed, arrested, and detained members of minority sects. Amnesty International calls torture, arbitrary detention, and political arrests "widespread."

**Culture:** Asmara, Eritrea's capital, is a delightful Italian–style city, sometimes called a "second Milan." Its main street is lined with palm trees, and many of its 400,000 inhabitants can often be found sipping expresso at sidewalk cafes. Its best restaurant is Italian and service there is provided by courtly and elderly Italian–speaking waiters. Eritrea's favorite drink is cappuccino, and like Italians, Eritreans share a national passion for cycle racing.

The Italian occupiers who built up Asmara in the 1930s left a legacy of experimentation in modern architectural styles. Among others, European Art Deco and Italian Futurism both found expression in colonial construction, and the city is known to architectural historians as one of the best concentrations of modernism in the world. To preserve this heritage, Asmara has established an historical district of one and a half square miles in the heart of the city; alterations to any significant buildings there are restricted.

Women are honored and possess an equality undreamed of elsewhere on the continent. During the war of liberation at least a third of the 100,000–strong rebel force was composed of women. After the war, new laws made women fully equal to men with rights to own land, to choose their own mates and even divorce them.

Much remains to do to change the status of women at home more completely. The National Union of Eritrean Women estimates that 90% of women are illiterate. They have thus far organized literacy classes for over 26,000 women.

There is still a stigma attached to HIV/AIDS in Eritrea. People do not talk about it openly, and figures on its penetration into the population are sketchy. The health ministry's AIDS control program estimates that there may be as many as 70,000 HIV-positive people in the country—about 2% of the population. More ominously, the ministry suggests the infection rate may be doubling every 18 months.

AIDS awareness programs have recently been taken to refugee camps. Between various entertainments, talks on the risks and dangers of the disease are given, the use of condoms demonstrated and prophylactics distributed. The World Bank has provided a $40 million credit to assist the government awareness programs.

**Economy:** In the 1930s Eritrea was an exporting nation, and when World War II disrupted East African imports from Europe, Eritrea supplied the markets. Postwar demand shrank in the 1950s, and in the 1960s, as a province of Ethiopia, the economy was starved of investment and began to deteriorate. With the installation of the Mengistu regime in 1974, Ethiopia adopted a command economy and economic decisions were made by *apparatchiks* working in the capital. Most private assets were nationalized, drying up foreign investment. Recurrent drought, famine and nearly three decades of armed struggle intensified the destructive effects of centrally directed policies.

At its liberation in 1991, Eritrea inherited an economy neglected, isolated and virtually destroyed by war. When independence was achieved in 1993, the government, turning its back on its own Marxist background, began a remarkable effort to rebuild infrastructure, liberalize the economy and aggressively seek foreign investment.

Those efforts were effectively ended by the 1998–99 war with neighboring Ethiopia. By Spring 1999, Eritrea had virtually ceased to produce anything. It had to accommodate and bear the costs of at least 40,000 refugees, driven out of Ethiopia. It had also gone on an expensive shopping spree for armaments. Top of the line fighter planes, MiG–29s, too sophisticated for the experience of Eritrean pilots, were purchased with scarce resources. Eastern European pilots had to fly them. Because of the war, the achievements of years were lost in months; reconstruction costs are estimated at $800 million.

Eritrea is no longer a bright and shining model of development. The economy has slowed. After a three-year decline, GDP grew by 8.7% during 2001, but was only 0.7% in 2002 following the worst drought in more than a decade. Grain production alone was down 75%, and some 90% of the country's food needs had to be appealed for, with disappointing response rates. Growth in 2003 was a modest 3%, made more modest by population growth of 2.2%.

The cessation of hostilities has provided opportunity for economic improvement. Defense spending, which topped off at 38% of GDP during the war with Ethiopia, is scheduled to fall, freeing up resources for development. Still, the consequences of war represent an enormous drag on the economy. Demobilization and reintegration efforts are costly, and some

48,000 people who were internally displaced, either by war or drought, still remain in camps. Five successive years of inadequate rainfall have made two-thirds of the population dependent on food assistance for survival.

Much of the cost of war was financed by the Eritrean diaspora. At the height of the war crisis in May 2000, when it was uncertain if Ethiopia would march on Asmara, 3,000 Eritreans living abroad bought land in the capital where they could ultimately build homes. These sales brought in a total of $29 million to the treasury. Throughout the war the government sold bonds and raised some $200 million in contributions from Eritreans who had emigrated abroad.

Plans for renovation of the seaport of Assab are in abeyance. Ethiopia's president once promised to turn Assab into a watering hole for camels and there is little likelihood Ethiopia will be using the port, having shifted its imports to the port of Djibouti. U.S. military officials reportedly visited Assab to assess its value as a staging point for U.S. troops, but apparently no action was taken out of fear of giving credibility to an increasingly authoritarian government.

Israel has developed relatively cordial relations with the Afwerki government. Massawa and Assab, the only non-Arab ports on the Red Sea, are immensely attractive to Israel as the only refuges where Israeli vessels could berth in an emergency. Israelis have also shown considerable interest in the country's offshore islands. The vast coral reef of Dahlek, perhaps the finest diving site in the Red Sea, has been considered a possible area for Israeli investment in tourism development.

One potential bright spot has been the announcement by a Canadian mining company that it discovered high grade gold at Bisha, less than 100 miles west of Asmara; exploratory drilling began in April 2005. The company noted the property has "excellent port facilities on the Red Sea."

**The Future:** Grim. Pressures on the regime are enormous. Demobilization and reintegration of 200,000 soldiers into a devastated economy will remain the first priority. More than a million Eritreans will require humanitarian assistance in 2005 as a result of war, poverty and continuing drought. The border demarcation with Ethiopia remains unsettled and volatile, and internal political repression verges on the explosive.

# The Federal Democratic Republic of Ethiopia

**Blue Nile Falls**

Photo by Judi Iranyi

**Area:** 1,178,450 sq. km.= 455,000 sq. mi. (larger than Texas and New Mexico).

**Population:** 73,053,286 (July 2005 est.)

**Capital City:** Addis Ababa (Pop. 4 million, est.)

**Climate:** Hot in the lowlands, cool and invigorating in the plateau highland. There are normally two wet seasons (June–September and February–April).

**Neighboring Countries:** Kenya (Southwest); The Sudan (West); Somali Republic, Djibouti (East, Southeast), Eritrea (Northwest).

**Official Languages:** Amharic, English.

**Other Principal Languages:** Tigrinya, Orominga, Guaraginga, Somali, and Arabic.

**Ethnic groups:** Amhara, Gurage, Oromo, Sidamo Shankella, Somali Afar, and Tigrean.

**Principal Religions:** Muslim 45%–50%, Ethiopian Orthodox 35%–40%, animist 12%, other 3%–8%.

**Chief Commercial Products:** Coffee, leather products, gold, oilseeds, beeswax and honey.

**GNI per capita:** $90 (2003)

**Currency:** Birr.

**Former Colonial Status:** Ethiopia has never been a colony in its history of almost 4,500 years. It was briefly occupied by the Italians (1936–1941).

**National Holiday:** National Revolution Day, September 12 (1974).

**Chief of State:** Girma Wolde-Giorgis, President, since October 2001.

**Head of Government:** Meles Zenawi, Prime Minister.

**National Flag:** Three equal horizontal bands of green (top), yellow, and red with a yellow pentagram and single yellow rays emanating from the angles between the points on a light blue disk centered on the three bands. Ethiopia is the oldest independent country in Africa, and the colors of her flag were so often adopted by other African countries upon independence that they became known as the pan-African colors.

Many centuries before the advent of modern mankind, Ethiopia was a relatively flat land of green grass and trees. Severe earthquakes occurred, causing fiery volcanos to push skyward, spewing molten lava throughout the land.

Today, Ethiopia is a land of sharp mountains rising to more than 15,000 feet. Their rough appearance is produced by volcanic rock formations. The Rift depression enters the country in the Southeast, and the

majestic peaks on either side of the gorge march in parallel formation towards the Red Sea. Slightly above Addis Ababa, the mountains separate and those on the left hand proceed north to the Red Sea at Asmara in Eritrea; the right hand peaks extend towards the Somali Republic.

The rugged terrain is one of the most isolated in the world. Surrounded by desert and arid land on all sides, the mountains rise so swiftly that they are almost impenetrable. The Blue Nile, originating from the cool waters of Lake Tana, flows through a gorge more magnificent that the Grand Canyon of Arizona. This river channel, more than a mile deep and 20 miles across in places, is bordered by slopes of deep green vegetation.

The climate of the highland plateaus and mountains is temperate and invigorating. Frost occurs regularly above 11,000 feet, where the daily range in temperature may span as much as 80° from noon to midnight.

**History:** For details of earlier periods, see *Historical Background* and *The Italians in Africa*.

Haile Selassie became emperor in 1930 and within a year promulgated a constitution that provided for a two–chamber legislature. In reality, he retained absolute power over the affairs of Ethiopia. A short time later, the Italians invaded and conquered the country.

Following the return of the emperor in 1941, increasing emphasis was placed on modernization of the country. The constitution was amended in 1955, providing for a Chamber of Deputies elected by uni-

217

# Ethiopia

versal suffrage to four–year terms, and a Senate, selected by the emperor from among distinguished Ethiopians to serve for six years. Another state institution was the Crown Council, a traditional institution, which included the crown prince and the Archbishop of the Ethiopian Coptic Church, as well as other dignitaries drawn from the ruling class; it assisted in forming basic policy and was convened at the call of the monarch.

Eritrea was joined with Ethiopia in 1962, but the Eritrean Liberation Front, formed in 1958, organized an armed resistance that would ultimately achieve independence after three decades of struggle.

Ethiopia remained a deeply conservative nation ruled by an elite of wealthy landowners. The beginning of the end of this system began in the 1970s with a series of natural and man–made disasters. Drought gripped the nation in 1972; rising prices and unemployment brought hordes of refugees to the cities from the parched countryside. The military, reacting to high prices, demanded higher salaries and started a limited military rebellion. Emperor Haile Selassie, aged and shaken, granted a partial increase. In the south, there were riots caused by an absence of land reform; peasants seized productive plantation land owned by absentee landlords.

Civil unrest led to the deposition of the aging Haile Selassie on September 12, 1974. A provisional administrative council of soldiers, known as the Derg ("committee"), seized power and installed a socialist military dictatorship. Beginning what would become standard practice, the Derg summarily executed 50 members of the royal family, ministers, generals and dignitaries of the imperial government. The Emperor himself was strangled to death on August 22, 1975.

Lt. Col. Mengistu Haile Mariam assumed leadership of the Derg in February 1977, after having his two predecessors killed. Mengistu turned Ethiopia into a totalitarian state and a communist killing field. From 1977 through early 1978 thousands of suspected enemies of the Derg were tortured and killed in a purge known as the "red terror." Communism was officially adopted, a Soviet-style constitution promulgated, and the Workers Party of Ethiopia created, complete with a hammer and sickle flag. Resistance, equally inspired by Marxist-Leninist thinking and practice, developed in all the major regions of the country.

To deprive the rebels of popular support, the government resorted to "resettlement" and "villagization." The first resettled people from the often-arid north to the rainier southern regions. Rejecting forced resettlement, peasants fled to Sudan and Somalia, creating huge refugee camps there. Many were shot—in the back—while fleeing. In the squalor of the refugee camps, thousands died. The second program was designed to control rural peoples so they would be unable to support rebel movements. It also was intended to make the collectivization of agriculture easier. The government did not hesitate to use foreign aid, including food, to lure people into these programs.

Sensing Ethiopia's weakened condition, the Somali Republic unleashed a band of rebels (and later regular army troops) to seize the Ogaden Desert region, where most of the people were ethnic Somalis. By mid-1977 they had penetrated as far as Dire Dawa. Mengistu's Soviet supporters sent massive quantities of arms and tech-

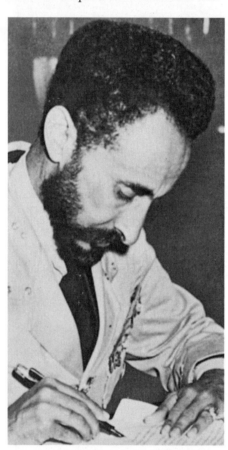

**Former Emperor Haile Selassie**

nical personnel to Ethiopia, placing the USSR in the embarrassing position of being patron and supporter of both sides of a war in which neither party had any interest in compromise. This was brief; the Somalis ejected the Soviets from their nation and turned to the United States for support.

The war was short. Soviet arms were followed by a wave of Cuban troops—flown from Angola—to support the fledgling communist regime. By early 1978 the Somalis had been routed, but the Ogaden remains unstable even today.

Incapable of dealing with drought and famine, the Derg's military dictatorship soon faced regional insurrections against its repression, particularly in the northern regions of Tigray and Eritrea. Officially created in February 1975, the Tigrayan Peoples Liberation Front (TPLF) announced its goal was "the establishment of an Independent Democratic Republic of Tigray." Allied with the Eritrean People's Liberation Front (EPLF), the TPLF waged incessant guerrilla warfare against the Derg. In 1989, the TPLF, representing a minority of only 7% of the Ethiopian population, merged with other ethnically-based opposition groups to form the Ethiopian People's Revolutionary Democratic Front (EPRDF). By May 1991, EPRDF forces were advancing on Addis Ababa; Mengistu fled to Zimbabwe where he was granted asylum by President Mugabe. On May 27 EPRDF troops took control of the capital, and a transitional government under the leadership of Meles Zenawi, head of the TPLF, was formed.

Meles Zenawi was born Legesse Zenawi, the third and youngest child of a member of the lower Tigrayan nobility. He saw himself, as did other Tigrayan students, a victim of discrimination by the Amhara, who had dominated Ethiopian political life since the rule of Emperor Menelik. After two years as a pre-medical student, he dropped out of school to join the nationalist struggle in Tigray. It was at this point that he adopted his *nom de guerre* of Meles Zenawi, honoring Meles Tekle, a Tigrayan nationalist student killed in 1974. In 1985, Meles founded the Marxist-Leninist League of Tigray (MLLT) as a "vanguard party" within the TPLF. His intellectual model at the time was Envar Hoxha, the repressive ruler of Albania. Meles took over the leadership of the TPLF in 1989, linked with other opposition groups, and brought about the downfall of the Derg's military dictatorship.

The transitional government of 1991 included the Oromo Liberation Front (OLF) and members of the Southern Ethiopia People's Democratic Coalition (SEPDC). By 1993, both had left the government and gone into opposition. The Eritrean People's Liberation Front had already established a separate provincial government in the province in May 1991, and in April 1993, Eritreans voted for independence from Ethiopia.

In December 1994 the constituent assembly completed the new constitution of a Federal Democratic Republic of Ethiopia. The constitution established a federal state and emphasized decentralized administration based on ten essentially ethnically defined regions. Regions are granted broad powers for social and economic development, the right to raise and spend their own revenues and, most remarkably, the right, in theory, to secede from the Ethiopian state. For the Tigrayan leadership at the core the EPRDF, the constitution was a means of redressing the grievances of Ethiopia's various "nationalities" against the Amhara. It is a revolutionary break with the highly centralized structures of the Empire and its Marxist successor.

In reality, political power in Ethiopia is relatively centralized around Meles Zenawi, the TPLF, and its allies within the EPRDF. Elections for Ethiopia's first popularly chosen parliament and regional legislatures were held in May and June 1995. Most opposition parties boycotted the elections, resulting in a landslide for the EPRDF. As head of the dominant force within the EPRDF, Meles was appointed to a five-year term as prime minister.

With its ethnic and regional emphasis, the new system spawned a plethora of new political parties—65 in all are registered, but most were created by or are satellites of the EPRDF, itself dominated by the Tigrayan Peoples Liberation Front (TPLF). The EPRDF links the TPLF, the Amhara National Democratic Movement (ANDM), Oromo People's Democratic Organization (OPDO), and the Southern Ethiopian Peoples Democratic Front (SEPDF)—which itself consists of members from some 20 ethnic parties. Meles Zenawi combines a variety of functions that emphasize his centrality: he is chairman of the TPLF, chairman of the EPRDF and prime minister.

Centrifugal forces, reflecting Ethiopia's origins as a conquest state, tear at the heart of the new Ethiopia. Members of the Oromo Liberation Front have resorted to urban terror and earned a repressive response from the government. Afar separatists shuttle back and forth across the border with Djibouti, and Islamist Somali separatists continue to convulse the Ogaden. The model for each is the province of Eritrea, which gained its independence constitutionally.

Despite the constitution's commitment to regional and ethnic rights, the government seems more willing to repress than share power. People unwilling to join the EPRDF are castigated as "narrow nationalists," harassed and imprisoned. In the Oromia and Somali regions, human rights groups have documented hundreds of "disappearances." Ethiopia held elections for a federal parliament, nine regional assemblies and city council members for the capital, Addis Ababa, and the eastern city of Dire Dawa in May 2000. It was only the second time that nationwide elections had been held in the country. The opposition

was given an unprecedented opportunity to air its grievances in a series of public debates. Largely attended, the debates were rebroadcast on state-run radio and television, but everywhere it was an uphill battle for the opposition.

Not a single opposition candidate managed to secure the 500 signatures necessary for nomination in the northern Tigray region. Elsewhere the EPRDF's satellite and creature parties dominated the electoral process. In the Amhara region, the opposition All-Amhara People's Organization could only sign up one candidate each for the federal parliament and the regional assembly. In the Oromiya region, the Oromo People's Democratic Organization, another Front member, nominated

**Lt. Col. Mengistu Haile Mariam**

176 candidates for parliament and 531 for the regional assembly. The opposition Oromo National Congress could only offer 28 candidates for parliament and 38 for the regional assembly. An estimated 54% of Ethiopia's population are Oromo, 24% are Amhara and only 5% are from Tigray.

Prime Minister Meles' four-party coalition won overwhelmingly: 479 of the 547 parliamentary seats. When parliament convened in October, it reelected Meles to another five-year term. Local elections were held in February and March 2001 with a similar preponderance in favor of the EPRDF.

Much to the surprise of the world community, minor hostilities occurred between Ethiopia and Eritrea in May 1998, escalating to major warfare in early June. At issue in the conflict was an obscure triangle of land, 155 square miles of rocky

barrenness called the Badme Triangle. Unlocatable on most maps, the triangle became the focus of national pride on both sides of the border. Both Prime Minister Meles and President Afwerki found themselves in a situation from which it was difficult to retreat. The internal pressures on Meles were particularly intense. Amhara imperialists had never accepted the loss of what they considered the Eritrean province, and the loss of the Red Sea ports rankled deeply, even among the Oromo majority. Galling too was the perception that the TPLF leadership had conceded too much by letting Eritrea secede and assume no share of the national debt.

Pride and personality generated stubbornness, on both sides. Negotiations had, by early May 2000, brought no resolution to the conflict. As soon as the last negotiators left, Ethiopia launched another massive attack. A surprise advance against a presumably impregnable pass brought crushing victory in nineteen days, after which Ethiopia announced its war aims achieved.

A ceasefire was announced in June 2000 and actually lasted through the conclusion of December peace negotiations conducted in Algiers. The Algiers Agreement called for a pull back of troops and creation of a demilitarized zone manned by several thousand UN peacekeepers. A five-member Eritrea-Ethiopia Boundary Commission (EEBC) was established to demarcate the disputed border. Overall, the war had cost the government $397 million and increased its military expenditures by 8.2% per year during the war. Damages were calculated in the billions of dollars.

The Boundary Commission rendered its decision in April 2002. The language of the 125-page decision was sufficiently obscure to allow both countries to claim victory: Badme, for example, was not explicitly mentioned in the text. Both countries launched a propaganda campaign seeking to convince its citizens that the sacrifices of war had not been in vain.

Tensions between the two countries spiked as demarcation approached in spring 2003. In March the EEBC affirmed that Badme, the *causa belli* of recent conflict, was part of Eritrea. The Ethiopian Prime Minister rejected the decision, calling it "a blatant miscarriage of justice," as well as "illegal, unjust and irresponsible." Beating the drums and sounding the trumpets, he warned the decision could lead to "another round of war."

No one seemed to know what to do or had the will to do anything. The AU, one of the guarantors of the Algiers Agreement, was deafeningly silent, causing Eritrea to recall its ambassador from the organization. The UN could only offer more

# Ethiopia

mediation and extended its peacekeeping mission. In February 2004 it appointed a former Canadian Foreign Minister, Lloyd Axworthy, as its special envoy to help defuse the tensions. By November, Ethiopia had accepted the decision "in principle," but it engaged in provocative troop movements near the border soon after. With an election coming up in less than six months, this was not the time to seem soft on Eritrea.

The Eritrean government continues to insist the border ruling be implemented, and it has also moved troops to the border area. Relations between the two countries are stretched to the breaking point. In March 2005 the UN Security Council extended the mandate of its 3,800-strong peacekeeping force for another six months, but the peacekeepers feel increasingly insecure. Understating the obvious, a spokesman from the Eritrean president's office said in April 2005: "What is clear is that the present scenario is not sustainable." If there were no light at the end of the tunnel, he went on, "obviously that will set in motion a different set of factors."

### Post-War Dissidence

The war and its resolution provoked dissent and impacted the leadership in both Ethiopia and Eritrea. In March 2001, twelve members of the TPLF central committee openly opposed Meles. The dissidents were narrowly defeated, removed from their party positions, and subjected to corruption charges that would keep them busy in the courts. Supporters of the

**Prime Minister Meles Zenawi**

dissidents in the army and administration were also purged from their positions.

The purges ramified to other individuals and organizations. Ethiopia's President Negasso Gidada, nearing the end of his term of office, spoke out in favor of the dissidents, describing Meles as ruthless as the former dictator Mengistu Haile Mariam. The president soon found himself forced to resign, and parliament quickly elected a new president, Girma Wolde-Giorgis, in October 2001.

In general, the regime neither understands nor appreciates dissent of any kind. A peaceful demonstration by Addis Ababa University students in April 2001 was violently broken up by the police. Two days of rioting ensued, resulting in the deaths of at least 31 people and injuries to hundreds of others. Thousands were interned without charges, and prominent human rights defenders were arrested as "instigators" of the riots.

Anti-government dissent by Oromo students at both high school and university levels has been robustly repressed by Oromiya state police, which regularly employ violence to disperse peaceful marches protesting regional governmental policies. Oromiya, the largest and most populous Ethiopian state, is dominated by Oromos, Ethiopia's largest ethnic group. Federal and regional governments tend to view all forms of protest as instigated by the rebel Oromo Liberation Front (OLF), which has led a decade-long armed struggle for regional autonomy for Oromiya.

Ethnic fighting has flared up in the western region of Gambella. Bordering on Sudan, Gambella is a swampy, malaria-infested lowland area largely inhabited by Sudanese peoples—Nuer and Anyuak—who distinguish inhabitants belonging to other Ethiopian tribes—Amhara, Oromo, and Tigray—as "highlanders." The central government has ruled the area through local parties, but real power, both political and economic, is in the hands of highlanders.

Parliamentary elections were held in May 2005 against this background of ethnic tension and political repression. The EPRDF faced two new electoral coalitions. One, the Coalition for Unity and Democracy (CUD) was made up of four parties and had at its core the All Amhara People's Organization. It called for liberalization of the economy and private ownership of land, and it gave voice to the Amhara imperial vision of Ethiopia by opposing the constitution's emphasis on ethnic federalism. Instead, it called for more power for the central government and greater emphasis on being "Ethiopian" rather than being from a particular ethnic group. The second coalition, the United Ethiopian Democratic Forces (UEDF), linked fourteen parties (five inside Ethiopia and nine based abroad) with the Oromo National Congress as its dominant core. In contrast to CUD, the UEDF demanded greater regional autonomy.

When provisional election results were announced in late May it was clear the government would have a majority in parliament, but the opposition had cut deeply into its preponderance. The ruling EPRDF coalition won 269 seats, mostly in rural areas, while smaller parties allied to it secured another 14, giving it a majority in the 547-seat body. CUD won a landslide victory in the capital, defeating the city's mayor and several ministers and taking all 23 seats representing the city. Nationally it captured at least 110 seats. In the previous legislature the opposition had held only 12 seats. Election officials had complaints of electoral fraud in more than 200 constituencies that had to be resolved before results would be official. With a working,

**Rock-carved Church of St. George, Lalibela**

Photo by Judi Iranyi

**The Annunciation**　　　　Photo by Judi Iranyi

but severely reduced, majority, Meles Zenawi was likely once again to become Ethiopia's Prime Minister.

**Culture:** The Ethiopian Orthodox Church is one of the world's oldest, Christianity having become the state religion around the same time the Emperor Constantine converted to Christianity. Tradition has it that the first Christian to be baptized was an Ethiopian noble, a top treasury official to Queen Candace who was on his way home from a pilgrimage to Jerusalem when he met the Apostle Philip. Baptism scenes are a recurring motif in Ethiopian art.

An extraordinary feature of the Ethiopian Church is its historic connection to the Old Testament and Jerusalem. Ethiopians celebrated the Sabbath on Saturday for over a millennium. Most Ethiopian churches are consecrated with a symbolic Ark of the Covenant, and tradition has it that the original Ark was brought to Ethiopia by Menelik I, son of the Queen of Sheba, following a visit to his father, King Solomon. The story of Soloman and the Queen is a popular motif in Ethiopian religious art. The original Ark is claimed by some to be in the Church of St. Mary of Zion in Aksum.

Lalibela, in a mountainous region some 400 miles north of Addis Ababa, was a "New Jerusalem" for Ethiopian Christians in the 13th century. Eleven medieval churches were carved out of solid rock there. They have been declared World Heritage sites by UNESCO and are a principal tourist attraction for Ethiopian visitors.

Ethiopia's many churches, with their rich collection of manuscripts and artifacts, have been objects of plunder over the years. The government is making strenuous efforts to recover this cultural patrimony.

The government has made less strenuous efforts to deal with the AIDS pandemic. Years of half-hearted AIDS public awareness campaigns have proved ineffective. In April 2000 President Negaso Gidada publicly admitted that the AIDS pandemic had spread to rural areas. Official figures are ominous. About three million people are living with HIV/AIDS, and the health ministry estimates that another 1000 people are infected daily. The infection kills at least 600 every day and has already orphaned five million children. Caring for orphans costs $115 million a month in a country with an annual health budget of only $140 million.

The figures indicate the AIDS crisis is greater than the periodic famines which receive much greater international attention. Ethiopia has the third largest population of people living with HIV/AIDS in the world. The HIV infection rate has reached the critical level of 10% of the sexually active population—those between the ages of 15 and 49. At that point economic growth begins to be impacted. The disease has already contributed to lowering life expectancy in Ethiopia—from 45 years in 1990 to 42 years in 2003.

Infection rates are particularly high in areas where soldiers are based, and the virus is spread as soldiers return to their hometowns or villages. In March 2003 the U.S. announced it would donate about $325,000 to fight the spread of HIV/AIDS in the military. The five-year prevention and control program will be carried out by the U.S. Centers for Disease Control and Prevention, working alongside the National Defense Forces of Ethiopia (NDFE).

Following years of drought and rural famine, Ethiopia is facing an explosion of urban growth as rural families migrate to cities. Urban expansion is increasing at around six percent a year and Addis Ababa, the capital, now has a population of some four million, making it one of the largest cities in sub-Saharan Africa.

**Economy:** Despite its Marxist origins, or perhaps because of them (Hoxha's Albania was hardly an economic success story), the government has embarked on a program of economic reform, including privatization of state enterprises. Progress

# Ethiopia

is slow: most of the manufacturing sector remains under state control.

Liberalization of the economy is seen as essential for attracting foreign investment, and the project is not without its success: the economy grew a striking 12.4% in 1996. That was, of course, before the war with Eritrea. The economy shrank by 1.9% in 1998 after the war began, and has been erratic since then, as Ethiopia experienced periodic regional drought and famine. Real GDP growth in 2001 was 7.7%, but only reached a modest 1.2% in 2002; in 2003 GDP declined by 3.7%.

At these levels economic growth has had little impact because of the country's fast-growing population—averaging around 2.3% per year. According to some estimates, Ethiopia produces about two million people every year; the population has essentially doubled in twenty years.

Necessitously, industrial development has been agriculture-driven. Small-scale agriculture involves 85% of the population, generates 80% of Ethiopian exports and contributes 45% to the GDP. Only 10.9% of Ethiopia's total land surface is under intense agricultural cultivation. There has much criticism of the government's agriculture-based industrial development policies. Seeking greater liberalization, critics have called for private land ownership, which, they believe, would help farmers secure bank loans and adopt modern agricultural techniques. Prime Minister Zenawi has quashed any move in this direction: Land would remain, he has said, state property.

A strong argument can be made that land tenure is the central issue in Ethiopian development. Peasants have no right to own land; they have no security of land tenure and little incentive to produce above mere subsistence levels. The consequence is the persistence of famine, whether under Imperial, Derg, or EPRDF governments. Under the Emperor, peasants were deprived of their production by a feudal system; under the Derg and EPRDF, state ownership was substituted, continuing the disincentive to produce. (The government argues that if land were privatized before industrial growth has occurred, peasants would sell their holdings and move to the cities where they would be unable to find employment.)

Ethiopian economic development focuses on the necessity of increasing agricultural production. More than a million people died of starvation between 1984 and 1990. Since 1992 the government has established a series of grain storehouses to be better prepared when drought and famine occur. Without this advanced planning, the death toll from reoccurring drought and famine would be signifi-

cantly greater. Though most Ethiopians usually produce enough food to support themselves, distributing and commercializing any excess faces difficulties. Most farmers live at least a half a day from a usable road.

Transportation inefficiencies, storage, and handling costs make product delivery in state-controlled agriculture slow and costly. It takes, for example, 20 to 30 days for a sack of grain to go from producer to consumer, instead of the 2 to 3 days it takes to cover the distance. Transaction costs are such that it is often cheaper for food aid organizations to import food from the world market than to procure it locally.

As part of a food security program, the government has plans for major infrastructure developments of both transportation and dams. The World Bank is providing financing and at least 12 international construction firms, many of them Chinese, have bid on the projects that will focus on farm-to-market or feeder roads.

The government also has ambitious plans to develop irrigation agriculture. Since water management and increased electricity are so essential for both agricultural and industrial development, the government plans to complete seven hydroelectric dams on the Blue Nile in the next five years. The dams would increase the present 340 megawatts electric-generating capacity of the country to 713 megawatts. Such proposals are viewed by Egypt, well down stream, but utterly dependent on the flow of Nile waters from the Ethiopian highlands, with the greatest concern.

On a more modest (and less controversial) scale, the Kassem-Tendaho project involves two dams on the Awash River in Afar state. When completed in June 2006 the dams will help irrigate over 222,000 acres of land. The development of new farming lands will require resettlement of farmers from less-productive areas and of course restrict access to former grazing lands of local pastoralists who choose not to settle down into an agro-pastoral existence.

The birthplace of coffee, Ethiopia is Africa's leading coffee exporter. The crop once accounted for 65% of the country's foreign exchange earnings. (Nearly one million families are dependent on coffee for their income. Another 15 million households benefit indirectly from coffee sales.) The international coffee market is glutted as a consequence of new entrants into the market, however, and prices have plummeted 70% since 1997.

Little wonder coffee farmers are turning to growing *khat*, a shrub whose leaves have a psychotropic effect when chewed.

Already a valuable traditional export to neighboring Djibouti and Somalia, the rewards of *khat* production are lucrative. Income from *khat* is often five times higher than coffee, and it can be harvested twice a year. Oxfam, the British NGO, has warned that within ten years Ethiopia's coffee growing areas may be fully converted to fields of *khat* to meet the massive demand for the drug in East Africa and the Middle East.

Ethiopia is estimated to have 75 million head of livestock, the largest concentration in Africa. Its pastoralists face multiple afflictions. Regional diseases, like Rift Valley fever, can completely shut down a market when traditional buyers, like Saudi Arabia and the Gulf states, prohibit import of East African livestock. Persistent cycles of drought decimate herds, while those animals that survive bring less than optimal prices. Hides and skins remain important export items for Ethiopia, second only to coffee.

Despite drought, famine, and border warfare, about 200,000 tourists still come to Ethiopia every year, so attractive are its landscape and cultural treasures. The country has seven UNESCO World Heritage sites, and its paleontological remains are probably the most famous in the world. China has made Ethiopia one of eight African countries "approved" as a destination for Chinese tourists—little surprising since the country is one of its principal points of penetration into the continent.

Since 1998, when an agreement to foster investment relations between the two countries was signed, the government has been unrelenting in its efforts to attract Chinese investment. More than 70 companies have been granted operating licenses. Manufacturers are producing goods ranging from pharmaceuticals to construction materials like iron and cement. Chinese businesses are involved in textiles, electricity, and mining, as well as major infrastructure projects from roads to hydroelectric dams and their associated irrigation projects.

**The Future:** Tense. The regime seems incapable of accommodating dissent, and political tensions, often ethnically based, are likely to increase. The recent election highlighted the huge rural-urban gulf that exists and the deep divisions over the nature of the country's national identity. Future growth prospects are limited by weak infrastructure, HIV/AIDS, and the continuing possibility of food shortages occasioned by drought and poor farming techniques.

The Badme issue remains volatile and dangerously alive.

# The Republic of Kenya

**Modern Nairobi**                    Photo by Bev Klein

**Area:** 582,750 sq. km = 225,000 sq. mi. (larger than twice the size of Nevada).

**Population:** 33,829,590 (July 2005 est.)

**Capital City:** Nairobi (pop. 2.1 million estimated).

**Climate:** Hot and dry in the area from the Tana River to the north and northeast; hot and dry, but with a short rainy season in the southeast area below the Tana River; temperate and usually moist in the central highlands and southwestern grassy plains, with two wet seasons.

**Neighboring Countries:** Tanzania (South, Southwest); Uganda (West); Sudan (Northwest); Ethiopia (North); Somali Republic (Northeast).

**Official Languages:** KiSwahili, English.

**Other Principal Languages:** More than 60 languages are spoken. Prominently: Borana, Digo, Duruma, Embu, Gikuyu, Giryama, Gusii, Kalenjin, Kamba, Logooli, Luo, Luyia, Maasai, Meru, Pökoot, Saamia, Taita, Teso, and Turkana.

**Ethnic groups:** Kikuyu 22%, Luhya 14%, Luo 13%, Kalenjin 12%, Kamba 11%, Kisii 6%, Meru 6%, and other African 15%. Non-African (Asian, European, and Arab) 1%.

**Principal Religions:** Protestant 45%, Roman Catholic 33%, indigenous beliefs 10%, Muslim 10%, other 2%.

**Chief Commercial Products:** Tea, flowers, coffee, and refined petroleum products.

**GNI per capita:** $390 (2003)

**Currency:** Kenya Shilling.

**Former Colonial Status:** British Protectorate (1895–1963).

**Independence Date:** December 12, 1963.

**Chief of State:** Mwai Kibaki President. (Since December 2002)

**National Flag:** Three horizontal stripes of black, red and green separated by narrow white stripes; a shield with two crossed spears is in the center.

Lying immediately below the heart of Africa on the east coast, Kenya extends from the Indian Ocean to the lake region of East Africa. North of the winding Tana River, there is an arid countryside which slowly rises to the southern mountains of Ethiopia. About seventy-five percent of the country is arid or semi-arid, similar to the type of land found in the Somali Republic. Nomadic pastoralists, like the Pokot, tend their herds in the eastern regions and make frequent cross border raids into Uganda.

South of the Tana River, the coastline is hot and oppressively humid—this is the only part of Kenya that is truly tropical. This gives way immediately to a thorn bush country of gently rising land extending about 175 miles from the coast.

The south central portion of Kenya is a beautiful land of high plateaus stretching between the mountains. Mount Kenya, in this area, reaches a height of 17,040 feet 80 miles north of Nairobi. The Gregory Rift, extending in an almost straight line to the south from Lake Rudolf, is an immense trench almost 3,000 feet lower than the mountains which enclose it.

From the western side of these rift formations, the land slowly descends to the shores of Lake Victoria. The cool climate of the southeastern and south central areas is invigorating—though the Equator divides these regions from northern Kenya, the climate is temperate because of the altitude. These are normally fertile lands; it is frequently possible in many sections to harvest two crops each year. Intermittent droughts, however, affect both productivity and hydroelectric potential. Given the limited availability of arable land, those droughts have also caused significant migration from the countryside to urban centers.

**History:** Arab traders working along the Kenya coast established a community in the 8th century, which remains to this day. Portuguese mariners landed in Kenya as early as 1498, seeking a sea route to the Far East. In the nineteenth century, Arab and Swahili caravans in search of ivory and slaves penetrated the interior. Colonial activity in the area was first initiated by Germans, followed by the British.

From the mid-nineteenth century, British interest in the region grew and in 1895 Kenya was declared a protectorate. Railroad construction from the port of Mombassa to Lake Victoria encouraged development of trade and settlement, and in 1920 Kenya became a crown colony administered by a British governor.

Africans were not permitted representation on the colony's legislative council, so developed their own pressure groups. Most active in these developments were members of the Kikuyu tribe, who supplied the bulk of labor used on European farms. By the 1930s there were several organizations to represent the tribe's grievances, among which were low wages and exclusion from profitable coffee growing.

In 1944 Kenya became the first East African colony to include an African on its legislative council. At almost the same time the Kenyan African Union (KAU) was created to campaign for better lands and independence for Africans. In 1947 the group chose as its leader Jomo Kenyatta, a prominent Kikuyu activist who had recently returned from a long residence in Europe.

223

# Kenya

A Kikuyu-led secret society, the Mau Mau, launched a guerrilla campaign against white farmers in 1952. The revolt had its origins in the land issue and was specifically directed against European land ownership. When Kenya became a British crown colony, Africans were dispossessed from their lands, leaseholds were restricted to white settlers, and a "white-highlands" policy herded the Kikuyu onto overcrowded reserves. The Mau Mau insurgency terrorized Kenya for nearly five years. During the "emergency" declared by the government, defense forces killed over 13,500 Africans, mostly Kikuyu; the Mau Mau killed some 100 Europeans.

Suspected of directing the Mau Mau, Jomo Kenyatta and nearly 100 other Africans were arrested immediately after the proclamation of the state of emergency. KAU was banned and its leaders charged with causing disorder or inciting other persons to cause disorder. In April 1953 Kenyatta was sentenced to a seven-year imprisonment for "managing the Mau Mau terrorist organization."

Following suppression of the Mau Mau insurgency in 1956, the British government gradually steered the country toward African majority rule. African membership on the legislative council was increased, and Africans were offered ministerial posts. In 1960 the principle of one man-one vote was conceded, and KAU, which had done so much to move Kenya to independence, split along largely ethnic lines. Tom Mboya and Oginga Odinga formed the Kenya African National Union (KANU) with a strong Kikuyu and Luo membership. In opposition to the Kikuyu/Luo grouping, Kenya African Democratic Union (KADU) was created to represent smaller tribes—Luhya and others—who feared domination by larger ones. Ethnic division would be a continuing characteristic of Kenyan politics.

KANU elected Kenyatta (still detained even after having completed his sentence) its president *in absentia*. He was finally released in August 1961 and negotiated the arrangements that led to Kenya's independence in 1963. May 1963 elections resulted in an overwhelming victory for Kenyatta and KANU. As part of Kenyatta's ethnic balancing, Oginga Odinga, a Luo, became vice-president. A year later, following intense political lobbying and negotiation, KANU and KADU merged.

Odinga, very much to the political left, became increasingly disillusioned with the KANU government, which, he felt, had abandoned the socialist principles that had brought it to power. He advocated a ceiling on the amount of land that could be owned by any one individual—500 acres, but this unsettled white farm-

ers and KANU elites who had begun to accumulate property. The party closed ranks to divest itself of a troublesome critic. The assault was organized by a fellow Luo and founder of KANU, Tom Mboya. Odinga resigned the vice-presidency, talking darkly of "international forces concerned with the ideological colonization of the country." The government's guiding star, he asserted, had become "personal gain."

The ideological rift led to Odinga's expulsion from KANU and his formation of a left-wing opposition party, the Kenya Peoples' Union (KPU). Elections in 1966 gave an overwhelming majority to KANU; the Kenya People's Union led by Oginga Odinga, won only a handful of seats. Kenyatta's KANU government nevertheless did all in its power to suppress the KPU. Its opportunity came in 1969 when the most prominent Luo in the government, Tom Mboya, was assassinated on the verge of presidential and parliamentary elections.

On a visit to the Luo heartland, President Kenyatta encountered crowds of anti-government demonstrators. When his bodyguards shot on hostile, but scarcely violent, Luo demonstrators, several were killed and many wounded. Odinga was blamed, his KPU party banned, and he himself placed under house arrest.

With Odinga out of the picture, there was no one to oppose Kenyatta. He was re-elected unopposed. The 1969 General Election also gave birth to the single-chamber legislature in which KANU held

overwhelming dominance. Kenya had become a *de facto* single-party state.

Kenyatta was re-elected again in 1974 and died in office in 1978, when he was succeeded by his vice-president, Daniel arap Moi (pronounced moy). President Moi won his own term of office in the 1979 elections, and KANU officially made Kenya a single-party state in 1982. An attempted air force coup in August the same year was quickly suppressed, but strong Luo involvement further marginalized Odinga and his Luo supporters. Odinga's son, Raila, was detained for alleged involvement in the plot. President Moi disbanded the air force and closed the University in Nairobi where student supporters of the coup were numerous.

Early elections were called by KANU and held in September 1983. Unopposed, Moi was re-elected president. He proceeded to govern an ethnically divided Kenya with authoritarian firmness. Urban Kikuyus of Nairobi charged him with cronyism as he appointed fellow Kalenjin tribesmen to lucrative government positions. The secret ballot was abolished in favor of a "queuing" system where people have to publicly line up according to their political preferences. This led to intimidation and widespread election fraud; in some districts there was only a 20% turnout in 1988, down from the former 90%.

The International Monetary Fund indicated that Kenyans owned $2.62 billion in overseas bank accounts, a mere hint of Kenya's massive corruption. Corruption charges resulted not in reform, but rather

**Maasai woman seated before a traditional plastered structure**

Photo by Lance Fuchs

224

**Kenya's high birthrate limits development**

Photo by Mary Ellen Grabski

in a crackdown on dissent. Many government critics fled the country. In 1990 six opposition leaders, including an aging Oginga Odinga, formed the Forum for the Restoration of Democracy (FORD) to lobby for democratic change. FORD brought together Luo, Kikuyu and Luhya in common opposition to KANU's single party monopoly. A massive demonstration in Nairobi in late 1991, punctuated with cries of "peace" and "democracy" was met with tear gas and riot batons. The government dismissed the participants as agitators and anarchists.

Further protest came from international aid agencies—the International Monetary Fund, the World Bank and several creditor nations—all of which cut off money destined for Kenya. This was more than the Moi regime could stand; quietly, provisions for multi–party elections in 1992 were made. Parliament repealed the one-party section of the constitution, several new parties were allowed to form, and multi-party elections were scheduled for December 1992.

To protect KANU and his own tenure, Moi immediately embarked on a course intended to divide (and conquer). The opposition carefully split among themselves; this included a division in the ranks of FORD, which had initially transcended traditional tribal rivalries. In August 1992 it split into two factions: FORD-Asili, led by a Kikuyu, Kenneth Matiba, and FORD-Kenya, led by Odinga, a Luo.

The election period was characterized by widespread ethnic tension and violence, deliberately manipulated by politi-

cians. It was particularly virulent in the Rift Valley province. Hundreds were killed and thousands of potential voters were disenfranchised when forced to flee their homes. Young Kalenjin and Maasai were recruited into gangs to terrorize suspected supporters of the opposition—primarily members of the Kikuyu, Luhya and Kamba tribes. Their property was looted, their homes set afire, and if they did not flee, their lives were forfeit. Their lands were subsequently occupied by government supporters—the wages of violence.

Moi campaigned vigorously. For added insurance, his people in the legislature pushed through a constitutional amendment providing that a presidential candidate, to be elected, must win at least 25% of the vote in five of the seven districts. Since he and his Kalenjin tribesmen controlled the western mountain district and other significant areas through political patronage, this virtually assured that none of his three principal opponents stood a chance. When the votes were tallied, Moi won a mere 36% of the vote, but earned another five-year term.

In the legislature, things were more realistic. KANU elected 95 delegates to 88 for the opposition. Riots broke out on opening day in 1993; Moi simply dissolved the legislature rather than face such vocal opposition, the first in a decade. The International Monetary Fund, infuriated by the printing of special shillings to finance KANU's effort in the election, imposed more rigid conditions on future loans.

The regime's severest critic, Oginga Odinga, died in 1994. His son, Raila, lost the struggle for leadership of FORD-Kenya, left the party and formed the National Democratic Party (NDP). A year later, Richard Leakey, a noted white conservationist, spoke out against the Moi regime and formed a new party (Safina) to oppose government corruption. The president denounced him as a racist and colonialist and arranged his public beating by a mob as police looked on.

The December 1997 elections reproduced the whole dreary cycle of violence, conflict, repression, and lost opportunities. Candidates and human rights workers were harassed and intimidated. Members of the thuggish KANU youth wing and security forces blocked meetings and rallies. Once again opposition parties failed to unite behind a single candidate—another continuing feature of Kenyan politics; their appeals were tribal rather than national. Moi was re-elected by winning a mere 40% of the popular vote and the required 25% of the votes cast in five of the eight provinces. His majority in parliament was razor thin. KANU emerged with only 109 out of 222 seats.

The 1997 elections were held in an environment of uncertainty. In July the International Monetary Fund (IMF) refused to lend any longer to Kenya, largely because corruption was so blatant it was constricting economic growth. Confirming the IMF's concern, the Commissioner-General of Kenya's Revenue Authority stunned the nation by disclosing that the country lost $1.68 billion annually through corruption.

President Moi responded by declaring war on corruption and creating the Kenya Anti-Corruption Authority (KACA). Corrupt bureaucrats were reportedly gripped by panic, but remained calm enough to bring legal action against KACA. In December 2000 a three-judge constitutional court ruled the Authority illegal, setting off alarm bells within the donor community, which already knew the judiciary to be one of the most corrupt of Kenya's numerous corrupt institutions.

As part of a calculated set of responses to impress the IMF, Moi also appointed Richard Leakey, a well-known critic of the ways things are done in Kenya, to head its civil service. Leakey, part of the world-famous paleontology family, was a long-time friend of World Bank President James Wolfensohn, and his appointment achieved its desired goal. The IMF resumed lending to Kenya in July 2000, but with the strictest of conditions.

These required enactment of anti-corruption and economic crimes bills, and ethics legislation requiring public officials to declare their wealth and liabilities. An-

# Kenya

**The Hon. Mwai Kibaki,
President of Kenya**

other condition required weekly IMF inspections of the Central Bank of Kenya accounts. The conditions were humiliating, but, given the pervasive depth of corruption in Kenya, essential.

Leakey's tenure as head of Kenya's civil service was brief—less than two years—but long enough to ruffle lots of feathers. He resigned in March 2001, and almost simultaneously the IMF stopped its lending to Kenya, citing "serious setbacks" to the fight against corruption.

President Moi announced that he would step down at the end of his term in 2002 and made a number of changes to prepare KANU for the next set of elections. Talking of the need for "new blood," he appointed the opposition leader Raila Odinga (Oginga Odinga's son) to his cabinet, forming Kenya's first coalition government in June 2001. Odinga had been imprisoned without trial by Moi for eight years following the attempted coup in 1982. In October, the president appointed Jomo Kenyatta's son, Uhuru Kenyatta to parliament; this was rapidly followed by a cabinet post for Kenyatta.

KANU voted to absorb the smaller National Democratic Party (NDP) in March 2002, revolutionizing Kenyan politics by co-opting the opposition. The NDP leader, Raila Odinga, was unanimously chosen the new party's general-secretary. Party mastodons were moved closer to discontented oblivion by the election of four so-called Young Turks as vice-presidents. The most prominent was Uhuru Kenyatta, clearly President Moi's chosen favorite. The "elections," it should be noted, were not by secret ballot, but rather by acclamation, a process designed to ratify leadership decisions. President Moi was named chairman of KANU, with extraordinary powers that made him a virtual one-man party.

The president then forced the selection of his chosen successor: Uhuru Kenyatta, a young and politically inexperienced businessman, but a Kikuyu and bearer of a name worth its weight in political gold. Kenyatta's selection was an olive branch to Kenya's largest tribe, largely marginalized over the past twenty-four years. Whatever electoral advantage might have come of this, however, was offset by the divisions the decision created in KANU.

Party barons and stalwarts defected in droves and marched into opposition. Led by Raila Odinga, they formed the "Rainbow Coalition" to incorporate all shades and hues of opposition. In October Rainbow merged with the Liberal Democratic Party (LDP), while thirteen other opposition parties, representing a variety of regions and all Kenya's major tribes, coalesced to form the National Alliance Party of Kenya (NAK). In short order NAK merged with LDP to form a super-alliance known as the National Rainbow Coalition (NARC). United, they agreed on a single candidate to oppose KANU's Kenyatta: Mwai Kibaki, also a Kikuyu.

At 71, Kibaki had already had a long political career. A founder of KANU, he had spent the last decade trying to drive it from office. An economist, he served as finance minister for both Jomo Kenyatta and Daniel Moi (1969-1982), and then as Moi's vice-president, until removed in 1988. Three years later he formed his own party and unsuccessfully ran for President in the shamefully violent and rigged elections of 1992 and 1997. The third time would prove the charm.

In December 2002 KANU faced a virtually united opposition. (There were three other minor candidates.) Voters gave Mwai Kibaki a convincing victory: 62.2% of the vote to Kenyatta's 31.3%. If anything sustained coalitions and motivated voters, it was a common hostility to Daniel arap Moi and his family and friends, many of whom had richly profited from his long tenure in office. Candidate Kibaki had made corruption and economic revitalization principal planks in his campaign.

Kibaki's National Rainbow Coalition (NARC) won 125 of the 210 elected seats in parliament against KANU's 64. The new government moved quickly to deal with the weightiest of its dossiers, corruption. A government audit showed that public land, including cemeteries, fire stations, and even hospitals had been "irregularly allocated." (The plunder of public land had been the principal means by which KANU's patronage networks had been kept oiled and greased.) Parliament moved to nullify all illegal allocations of public land to individuals and businessmen who had links to the previous KANU regime.

President Kibaki also appointed an anti-graft czar, John Githongo, a young journalist who had long campaigned against corruption as a newspaper columnist. A number of anti-corruption commissions were organized, with quick results. Kenya's Chief Justice resigned after a tribune had been set up to investigate his alleged misconduct. By the end of 2003 half of Kenya's most senior judges—twenty-three in all—had been suspended after an anti-corruption commission had gathered evidence against them. Shortly after their suspension, the judges were stripped of their privileges—asked to surrender their

**Nairobi slums, overrun with plastic bags**

government cars and vacate government houses—which to some parliamentarians seemed to breech constitutional provisions guaranteeing security of tenure.

As that suggests, the whole anti-corruption effort is beset with legal entanglement and political manipulation. Foreign donors have become increasingly frustrated that no key figure from either the past or current regime has been convicted of corruption, despite glaring evidence. In May 2004 five diplomatic missions, representing substantial donor funding, demanded the sacking of cabinet ministers linked to corruption before financial assistance would be released. "Sacking one corrupt Cabinet minister," said one diplomat, "will scare the hell out of all corrupt police officers. Sacking a police officer will never scare a minister."

President Kibaki's National Rainbow Coalition (NARC), an ungainly assemblage of opportunists and idealists has unraveled. The government's most pressing tasks, developing a new constitution and curbing corruption, have fallen victim to ambition and rivalry. Kenyans are disappointed and disillusioned; donors are dubious.

Wrangling over a new constitution has been going on for over five years. President Kibaki promised a document within 100 days of his election and that deadline has long passed. At stake are interests that focus on efforts to curtail presidential powers and create the office of Prime Minister. Kibaki loyalists, among them a cabal of fellow Kikuyus, want the presidency to retain its enormous powers. Supporters of Raila Odinga are furious that the President and his minions have reneged on an alleged pre-campaign pact that promised the premiership to Oginga.

The issue has split the NARC coalition, with Kibaki's National Alliance Party (NAP) and Odinga's Liberal Democratic Party (LDP) pulling in different directions. The cabinet is permanently divided; Kenyans have taken to the streets to protest delay with such vehemence that riot police have had to intervene with tear gas and batons to control (and create) violence. Even the opposition party, KANU has split. The new party president, Uhuru Kenyatta—with an eye to his own electoral ambitions—supports a strong presidency, and KANU's secretary-general, the liberal parliamentarian William Ruto, favors proposals to limit presidential powers.

To dispatch their erstwhile LDP partners, President Kibaki and his NAP faction have sought to create a government of national unity, bringing in dissident members of KANU. Most prominently mentioned is one of the most powerful men in the former KANU regime, Nicholas Biwott. One of Kenya's wealthiest men, Biwott has been identified as a prime suspect in the 1990 murder of Kenya's Foreign Minister, Robert Ouko. For its part, the U.S. government has refused him a visa on the grounds of unspecified corruption charges. Little wonder Mr. Odinga rages about an "exclusive" club of rich elites who want to impose their constitution on Kenyans.

The courts have ruled the new constitution cannot be simply adopted by parliament, but requires a referendum. That has been set for October. At least on this issue there appears to be a end point. One cannot say the same for corruption.

In July 2004 the British High Commissioner to Kenya, the United Kingdom's highest ranking diplomat, used utterly undiplomatic language to articulate the international community's concern and contempt for the slow pace of Kenya's anti-corruption campaign. Speaking to a group of British businessmen, Ambassador Edward Clay said that corruption had cost Kenya some $188 million just since President Kibaki took office in December 2002. Corrupt ministers, he went on, were "eating like gluttons" and "vomiting on the shoes of donors." Over all, he noted, corruption accounted for about 8% of Kenya's total GDP.

**Culture:** Kenyans felt a leap of pride in October 2004 when the Norwegian parliament awarded the Nobel Peace Prize to environmentalist and human rights campaigner Wangari Maathai. She became the first African woman to win the prize since it was initiated in 1901, and only one of six from the continent to be so honored.

(Albert Schweitzer: 1952; Albert Lutuli: 1960; Desmond Tutu: 1984; Nelson Mandela and Fredrik de Klerk: 1993 preceded her.)

From the late 1970s she led the "Green Belt Movement" which mobilized poor women throughout the continent to replant millions of trees to slow deforestation and desertification. In Kenya, she was long a political activist who challenged the regime of Daniel arap Moi when its policies, often saturated with corrupt practices, threatened Kenya's natural resources of parks and animals and forests. For her labors she was frequently beaten and jailed.

The AIDS pandemic began its terrifying march through Kenyan society in 1990. Cultural patterns and behaviors long facilitated rather than hindered its progress, but new political leadership has been key to reducing the secrecy and stigma that once surrounded the disease. In November 1999 President Moi declared the disease a "national disaster," but three years later so little had been done UNICEF called it a "national crisis" and made desperate appeals to politicians to make AIDS part of the election agenda.

The Kibaki government has adopted a more public and activist stance. The president himself has described AIDS as the "greatest threat" to the country and urged all Kenyans to be tested for the HIV virus. His government has made AIDS education compulsory, even at primary school level; a shift in attitude and practice seems to have occurred. In December 2004 the government optimistically announced that the HIV/AIDs infection rate had dropped from 14 percent to about seven

**A class in Nairobi**

# Kenya

Wangari Maathai, Noble Peace Prize winner

percent, and that public awareness of the disease had increased to an estimated 90 percent nationwide.

From one of the world's highest HIV/AIDS infection rates notable declines have begun to be seen. There were about 2.5 million people living with the disease in 2000; four years later it was 1.4 million. About ten percent of the reported cases occurred in children, the result of mother-child transmission; an estimated 200,000 infants and children were living with the virus.

The death toll, once staggering, has begun to slow. Well over 1.5 million Kenyans had already died of AIDS by the end of 2004. Their deaths have left roughly 1.8 million AIDS orphans. Gender disparities in the infection's distribution are staggering: twice as many women as men suffer the disease. To make matters worse, in the 15 to 24-year old category, the number of infected women is four times that of men.

The rapid progress of AIDS among Kenya's women reflects fundamental economic and cultural realities. Rural poverty has driven young girls, children really, to the cities where the best job they can find is child care. Their salary is $10 to $15 a month. Since this is insufficient to provide for family needs at home, many turn to prostitution. In Kisumu, a tourist site on the shores of Lake Victoria, for example, girls can find customers day and night—receiving less than a dollar for each transaction. Statistics from Kenya's National AIDS STD Control Programme (NASCOP) indicate that a third of girls aged 15 to 19 years in Kisumu are HIV-positive.

Wife inheritance is a cultural practice that contributes to the spread of HIV/AIDS. Here, a widow becomes the property of her late husband's brother. There is often little choice for the woman. Alone, she is unable to provide adequate care, food, clothing and school fees for her

children. If she does not agree to be "inherited," she is barred from entering her husband's family compound; her brothers-in-law are prohibited by custom from even digging her grave.

It is encouraging to note that several Nairobi pharmaceutical companies are now producing high quality generic AIDS drugs, and the Ministry of Health has begun to place orders. The government planned to provide anti-retroviral (ARVs) medication to more than 180,000 AIDS sufferers by 2005, and 250,000 by 2010. Pregnant women, rape victims, and hospital in-patients have first priority.

For most tourists, the most memorable people in Kenya are the Maasai. They have profited greatly from the tourist trade, but they remain essentially a cattle people. Cows are the most important animal in Maasai culture. Their milk and blood are used for food, their hide is made into mattresses, and their dung is plastered on the walls of their homes.

Although officially outlawed in 2001, Female Genital Mutilation (FGM) remains deeply embedded in traditional cultures, including the Maasai. According to a 1998 survey, 38% of women between the ages of 15 and 49 were estimated to have undergone FGM. In the most basic form of circumcision the covering of the clitoris is removed. Among the Maasai, circumcision involves cutting away the entire clitoris, together with the labia majora and labia minora. A Maasai girl is traditionally circumcised before she is married, which can be quite young. A rite of passage marking the transition from childhood to adult status, the operation is expected to be endured in silence. To cry would be a sign of childish weakness.

**Economy:** Having meager mineral resources, the economy of Kenya has traditionally rested on agriculture and tourism.

Prior to 1979, contrasted with neighboring countries, Kenya was relatively prosperous—at least for the clique of politicians and businessmen who controlled the nation's wealth. A series of economic shocks—a spike in oil prices, drought, crop failure, and famine—increased borrowing and aid dependency. Government corruption siphoned off far too much of what was received, and the economy declined for years.

International donors insistently pressured President Moi to introduce economic liberalization, end corruption, and begin greater transparency in government. In July 1997, when the government refused to meet reform commitments made earlier, the IMF refused any further loans.

The IMF suspension sent the mismanaged economy into steep decline, from which it has made little improvement. Growth was a minimal 1.1% in 2002 and only 1.8% in 2003. The deterioration of life expectations in Kenya has been made more acute by a relatively high birth rate—2.3% on average from 1997 to 2003.

In 2002, the planning minister explained another reason for such a lackluster showing: corruption. The price tag on the country's corruption in 2002 was a staggering 68 billion shillings—about $932 million, or a quarter of annual government spending.

Social statistics all indicate that Kenyans are worse off today than they were at independence. The majority of them (55% in 2003) live below the poverty line and average annual income is about $1 per day. Infant mortality for under-five-year-olds rose from 74 per thousand in 1992 to 123 in 2003. The UN's Development Program Index ranked Kenya 148th out of 177 countries in 2004; at the end of the 1980s, it placed 90th.

Kenya remains fundamentally an agricultural country. It is the major source of income for the bulk of the population, employing well over 80% of rural inhabitants. Despite its scale, agriculture contributes only around 16% of GDP (2003). About 50% of agricultural workers are engaged in subsistence farming, and food security is a continuing concern. An acute shortage of arable land, and uneven distribution of that which is, has meant that most farmers work plots of less than five acres.

In 2000, land shortages prompted one cabinet minister to call for the seizure of white-owned farms, and one MP went so far as to set up the "Pan-African Movement Over Ancestral Land" to carry this out. President Moi dismissed his campaign as "cheap and outdated politics" and had him promptly arrested for "incitement." It's not an issue the government wants to discuss, given the fact the KANU elite profited so handsomely from land acquisitions and that Kenya has one of the world's highest inequality rankings. The richest 10% of households in Kenya control more than 42% of incomes; the poorest 10% control a mere 0.76%.

Tea has been one focus of the government's attention; fortunately for the industry, that attention has provided support without interference. It's one of the economy's success stories. Kenya is now the world's second largest exporter of black tea. Liberalization of the market and favorable climatic conditions have produced bumper crops: 294,000 tons in 2001, 287,000 tons in 2002, and 322,886 tons in 2003. The tea sector employs over two million people across the country.

Like many commodities, tea prices have declined recently and one simple explanation is offered: Internationally, tea consumption has been increasing by 1% annually while production has grown by 2%. Small farmers, who produce 62% of Kenya's tea, are having difficulties making ends meet.

Kenya's coffee industry has been similarly impacted by expanded coffee production in Asia, but the industry is much more highly regulated than tea and has suffered more. Small producers are forced to be members of "co-operative societies" in order to be able to sell the produce and these have suffered chronic mismanagement and corruption. The result has been that farmers have often not been paid for their produce.

Flower growing is the fastest growing part of Kenya's agricultural sector, in part because it has less government regulation and interference. Since the early 1990s flower exports have increased around 20% per year. Kenya is now the EU's biggest source of cut flower imports—principally roses (74%) and carnations. In 2001 cut flower sales brought 8% of export earnings. Flower growing now surpasses coffee and probably tourism as a source of foreign exchange, and is only second to tea as an income producer.

Most flower farms are located in rural areas and thus have considerable impact on both the local population and environment. Cultivation is relatively labor intensive, requiring about 200 workers for 15 acres. The workers, mostly women, earn about $1.50 per day, and the industry indirectly supports an estimated 500,000 people. There is increasing concern about the impact of fertilizers and agricultural chemicals used by the industry on local water supplies.

With beautiful beaches, abundant wildlife and a well-organized system of national parks, Kenya has long been a favorite tourist destination. Contributing about 12% of the economy, spending by tourists is one of Kenya's most important foreign exchange earners. The industry directly employs a reported 300,000 people, while another 200,000 work in sectors which benefit from it. Since 1998, however, the industry has been savagely undermined by Islamic terrorism.

In 1998 the U.S. embassies in both Kenya and Tanzania were simultaneously bombed in al-Qaeda attacks, killing 224 people. On November 28, 2002, an Israeli-owned hotel near the port city of Mombasa was bombed by a group of suicide attackers only a few minutes after an Israeli airliner escaped two missiles fired as it was taking off from Mombasa airport. In each case Kenya's hotels and resorts subsequently experienced huge cancellations of reservations.

A decided pall hangs over Kenyan tourism. The American Embassy in Nairobi has warned American tourists of "the continuing threat posed by terrorism in East Africa and the capacity of terrorist groups to carry out attacks." In Mombasa, a leading Imam, Sheikh Ali Shee, explicitly warned American and Israeli tourists to stay away. "There is an undeclared war between their countries and the Muslim world," he said. "It is not good for them to come until the [Palestinian] problem is solved." It will be a while before the industry achieves its goal of bringing two million tourists a year to Kenya.

**The Future:** In-fighting within the governing coalition is a looming concern and threatens investment possibilities. The war against endemic corruption is sluggish at best.

**High above the plain**  Photo by Bev Klein

# The Somali Democratic Republic

**The National People's Assembly, Mogadishu**

Photo by Ali Abdi Addaue

**Area:** 637,140 sq. km. = 246,000 sq. mi. (slightly larger than Texas).

**Population:** 8,591,629 of which an estimated 2–3 million in Somaliland. (July 2004 est.)

**Capital City:** Mogadishu (population 980,000 in 1998)

**Climate:** Hot, with scarce and irregular rainfall and frequent droughts.

**Neighboring Countries:** Djibouti (Northwest); Ethiopia (West); Kenya (Southwest).

**Official Language:** Somali, Arabic.

**Other Principal Languages:** Italian, English.

**Ethnic Background**: Darod (North–Northeast); Hawiya (central area); Rahanwein (South); Ishaak (North Central area); all of the foregoing are collectively referred to as Somali (85%); Bantu and other non-Somali 15% (including Arabs 30,000).

**Principal Religion:** Sunni Muslim

**Chief Commercial Products:** Livestock, bananas, hides, and fish.

**GNI per capita:** NA

**Currency:** 1 Somali Shilling (So. Sh.) = 100 cents.

**Former Colonial Status:** The North was a British Protectorate (1897–1960); the South was an Italian Colony (1892–1941); British administration (1941–1949); Italian Trust Territory (1949–1960).

**Independence Date:** July 1, 1960.

**Chief of State:** Abdullahi Yusuf Ahmed (since 14 October 2004), selected by the Transitional Federal Government created in October 2004.

**National Flag:** A five–pointed white star on an azure blue background.

The Somali Republic, the easternmost nation of Africa, covers an area often referred to as the *Horn of Africa*; it has a 1700–mile coastline on the tropical waters of the Gulf of Aden and the Indian Ocean. Although the northern part of the country is hilly, reaching altitudes of 4,000 feet, the larger portion to the south is a flat, semi–arid land which is uniformly hot. During the "dry season" there is utterly no vegetation, and both man and beast wait for the cool of the evening to travel and hunt.

Acacia trees, with their roots reaching far into the land to obtain precious water, spread their umbrella–like foliage, shading portions of the otherwise shadeless, vacant countryside. Goats and antelope must stand on their hind legs to reach their precious food from these trees.

**History:** Although tradition holds that the ancestors of the Somali people, of Cushitic origins, lived in this region of Africa more than 2,000 years ago, the earliest traces of people date to the 7th century A.D. The Koreishite Kingdom was established at that time by a group of people from nearby Yemen. For details of early and colonial history, see *Historical Background, The Italians in Africa* and *The British in Africa*.

Modern Somalia is the result of the merger of fish and fowl: former British Somaliland and *Somalia Italiana* in 1960. Each came with a different colonial history and experience and those differences are at the heart of modern Somalia's present situation. British Somaliland became independent on June 26, 1960; five days later, on July 1, it joined Italian Somalia to form the Somali Republic. At independence there was no common administrative language. English was spoken in the former British protectorate, Italian in the larger *Somalia Italiana*. Somali, though spoken by all, did not exist as a written language until the 1970s.

The British interest in Somaliland was purely strategic: control of the entrance to the Red Sea and cheap provisions for Aden, its garrison at the tip of the Arabian peninsula. As a consequence, indirect rule was administratively appropriate. Northern Somalis were left to follow their own customs; traditional procedures for resolving conflicts among nomadic clan groups remained in place. Italy's treatment of Somalia was much different. Southern Somalis were forced to adopt Italian law, and nomad customs, especially traditional mechanisms for conflict resolution between clans, were abolished. Resistance was intense and military confrontation continued to the late 1920s.

From British Somaliland emerged a well–educated élite, the very best of which had been trained in British universities. Italy introduced mass education in the south, but at a relatively low level, cre-

ating a mass of very nationalistic semi–intellectuals. At unification, then, there was little in common between the two partners save a vague sense of "Somali" identity. To preserve the union which gave expression to that identity, Northerners gave up much. The capital was located in the southern city of Mogadishu. Most of the technical positions in the new government were filled by better–trained Northerners, but the bulk of political appointments went to Southerners. Political parties proliferated, reflecting the fragmentary nature of Somali clan politics, and at one point Somalia had more parties per capita than any democratic state aside from Israel. (In the last multiparty elections held, March 1969, more than 60 parties competed.)

This multitude of parties also expressed substantial differences in political style and orientation. With a dominant position in parliament, Southern nationalists, pro–Arab and militantly pan–Somali, pushed the idea of a "greater Somalia"—a claim on Somali–inhabited areas of neighboring Kenya and Ethiopia. "Modernists," mostly Northerners, stressed economic and social development and urged improved relations with other African states. Out of this welter of conflicting tendencies, the Somali Youth League gradually assumed a dominant position, successfully cutting across regional and clan loyalties. And under the leadership of Prime Minister Mohamed Ibrahim Egal (1967–69), a Northerner educated at English public schools from Exeter to London, Somalia significantly improved its relations with Kenya and Ethiopia, but its fledgling constitutional democracy was brought to an end in October 1969, when the army and police, led by Maj. General Mohamed Siyad Barré, seized power in a bloodless coup. Prime Minister Egal was thrown in jail where he remained for 12 years.

Siyad Barré was born in the Ogaden area of Ethiopia, an area once part of Italian East Africa but returned by the British to Ethiopia in 1948. Nicknamed "Afweyne" or "Mighty Mouth" by his fellow herdboys, Siyad later traveled to Mogadishu for what formal education he had and ultimately became a member of the *Polizia Africana Italiana*. He rose within police ranks to become the first Somali commissioned as a full police officer, and by 1960, when Somalia became independent, Siyad had won accelerated promotion to the rank of Brigadier–General of Police. With the formation of the Somali National Army in April 1960, Siyad transferred from Police to Army as one of its deputy commanders. He was promoted Commander–in–Chief in 1965.

Siyad moved quickly to eliminate the institutions and personnel of Somalia's democracy. Important political figures like Prime Minster Egal were detained, the constitution suspended, national assembly closed, parties banned, and Supreme Court abolished. Notwithstanding this destruction of institutions, the country was renamed the Somali Democratic Republic. The coup–makers designated themselves the Supreme Revolutionary Council (SRC) and assumed full executive and legislative power, concentrated in the hands of Siyad Barré himself. Major–General Mohamed Siyad Barré became head of state and chairman of the SRC, its politburo, the cabinet, and the committees for defense, security, and judicial matters. His models were Nasser and Kim Il Sung, and like them, a cult of personality soon emerged. "Afweyne" would ultimately be touted as "The Father of Wisdom."

Sweeping changes were introduced into Somali life. Clan and kinship ties were officially banned and the new regime promised to root out all references to clanship. To replace traditional Somali private justice—blood vengeance or blood money payments between groups—the government introduced the death sentence for those convicted of homicide. In what is probably its most enduring achievement,

the regime introduced a Latin script to make Somali a written language and aggressively pursued literacy in the new script.

In 1974, Siyad signed a treaty of cooperation with the Soviet Union. The institutional trappings of a Marxist dictatorship were gradually set in place. The regime opted for "Scientific Socialism" and in a few years most sectors of the economy were brought under state control. Banks, insurance companies, electrical power production, petroleum distribution, sugar estates and refineries were all nationalized. One exception to this nationalization program were the large banana plantations which represented significant foreign investment. State corporations were created and given absolute monopolies as the foundation of a socialist economy. Private traders were prohibited from importing, storing, purchasing or distributing food items.

The usual apparatus of state repression also emerged: The National Security Service (NNS), answerable to Siyad Barré himself, began to create its own interrogation and detention centers. Courts for the trial of those caught within its web were created and, of course, more prisons to

Somali nomads, who let their hair grow until married (left) and have it cut when married.

# Somalia

**The Somali eagle**

Photo by Ahmed in Burco

hold the guilty were built. A vast propaganda machine emerged (obviously helped by literacy in the new script) and countless posters, poems, songs and speeches were generated to praise the "father of the revolution."

Resources were lavished on an expansion of Somali military forces much to the consternation of neighboring countries, especially those with significant Somali minorities. For years Somalia had secretly assisted Somali, Oromo, Eritrean and other nationalities opposed to the central governments of Kenya and Ethiopia, but in June 1977, when the Ethiopian regime seemed weakened by drought and politically vulnerable, the policy of clandestine support ended. The army was authorized to intervene directly in Ethiopia to assist the Western Somali Liberation Front fighting for the return of the Ogaden to Greater Somalia. The Somali army entered the Ogaden in July and overran it.

Expansionist excess was severely punished, however. The Soviet Union, with alliances to both Ethiopia and Somalia, turned against the unorthodox Siyad Barré. War materiel was airlifted to Ethiopia, and a Russian–directed Ethiopian army, with Cuban regiments in support, defeated Somali forces and sent their remnants scurrying back across the border. The army was humiliated and lost its legitimacy as the guardian of pan-Somali nationalism. The country was stunned, and soon overwhelmed by an influx of refugees fleeing the re–imposition of

Ethiopian authority in the Ogaden. By 1979 there were officially 1.3 million refugees in the country, more than half of whom were located in the North. The regime's limited resources and even more limited capacity to deliver services increased tensions between it and the Northern clans.

Clan–based opposition grew, but was brutally repressed. Siyad Barré became increasingly dependent on his own clan and family, to whom went the majority of appointments and the greatest opportunities for corruption. Alliances shifted, with the regime signing on with the Americans after the debacle of the Ogaden war. "Scientific Socialism" was abandoned and U.S. forces gained access to Somali military facilities, many of which were up–graded. Somali officers were given training in U.S. military schools, and America came to the country's aid when invaded by Ethiopia in 1982.

Regime incapacity, economic mismanagement and human rights abuses moved Somalis from disillusionment to anger. Opposition increased. A few senior officers who escaped a bungled coup attempt in 1978 fled to Ethiopia and created the first opposition movement: the Somali Salvation Democratic Front (SSDF). In 1981 a second opposition movement, the Somali National Movement (SNM) was created in London by disgruntled businessmen, religious leaders, intellectuals and army officers, mostly from the Northern Isaaq clan. SNM organized guerrilla

operations out of Ethiopia against the regime, and by 1988 an all-out civil war developed. Siyad Barré focused his wrath, and American-supported military might, against his Northern opposition.

Hargeisa, Somalia's second city and the former capital of British Somaliland, was bombed, strafed and rocketed. Some 50,000 people are believed to have lost their lives there as a result of summary executions, aerial bombardments and ground attacks. The city itself was destroyed. Streams of refugees fleeing the devastation were not spared by government planes. The term "genocide" came to be used more and more frequently by human rights observers.

The northern economy was assaulted. Market centers throughout the northwest were destroyed; transport routes were mined and rendered unusable. Wells, on which nomadic pastoralists are dependent, were poisoned. Trade closed down and the Northern economy collapsed with the closure of Berbera port to animal exports from 1989 to 1991. Economic stress strained traditional kinship obligations of support to the maximum. Social stress was intensified when a major drought hit the area in 1991–92 at the height of the civil war. Famine killed between 300,000 to 500,000 and affected millions more.

Civil strife gradually expanded throughout Somalia, leading to the formation of other opposition movements. The United Somali Congress (USC) was formed in 1987 by largely Hawiye-clan exiles in Italy. The USC quickly divided into two rival factions based on different sub-clans. One faction, led by General Aideed, allied with the Somali National Movement, which provided arms. An Ogadeni-led Somali Patriotic Movement (SPM) was formed in 1989 when the highest ranking Ogadeni in the government, the Minister of Defense, was arrested.

Siyad Barré was increasingly isolated, defended by only his heavily armed presidential guard, drawn exclusively from his Marehan clan. As 1990 drew to a close, rebel forces entered Mogadishu, and early the next year Siyad Barré and his loyalists fled the city. By then, little was left of Somalia.

The army fractured into slivers of dedication focused on rival clan leaders who became warlords intent on control of territory and whatever resources remained that would sustain their power. The war in the south had produced major population dislocations. A third of the population became internal refugees, and at least a quarter of a million migrated to Mogadishu. When fighting in the capital intensified, there was a similar outflow of people.

232

The humanitarian disaster brought about Operation Restore Hope, launched in 1992 under UN auspices. The Somalia project was well–intended, but vague and shifting in direction. It was started to protect the delivery of humanitarian aid. It then refocused on creating a secure environment, which logically entailed demobilization of warlord factions. These, of course, had little interest in losing the source of their power and resisted. When General Aideed was identified as the chief trouble–maker, the project again refocused on his capture. When the wily general's forces shot down an American helicopter and killed several American troops in a pitched gun battle, the U.S. withdrew. The project yet again refocused, now seeking negotiation with the very General Aideed it had sought to capture. TV images of a dead American soldier dragged triumphantly through the streets of Mogadishu soured the American public on such foreign adventures and left policy makers with a residual horror of committing American ground troops anywhere in the world.

The international humanitarian effort in Somalia was budgeted at 1.5 billion dollars a year. It was the most expensive humanitarian effort ever undertaken, and in virtually every way it was a failure. By early 2000, four warlords still contended over divided Mogadishu. General Aideed, who was killed in a gun battle with rivals in 1996, was replaced as faction leader by his son, a young man who somewhat ironically held American citizenship and once had served in the U.S. Marine Corps. Various negotiations between southern faction leaders conducted in Egypt, Kenya, Ethiopia or Libya achieved nothing.

Front and back of the Somali Shilling

**Transitional Federal President Abdullahi Yusuf Ahmed**

Djibouti's president, Ismail Omar Guelleh, convened the 13th Somali national reconciliation conference in May 2000. The conference brought together clan elders, religious leaders, academics, businessmen and, for the first time, a group of women. Over two thousand Somali met for over three months at Arta, Djibouti, to thrash out new institutions for the Somali state. The contending warlords were, for the most part, excluded—by intention and choice.

The largest and most broadly representative of any conference, Arta proved the most sensitive to the segmentary nature of Somali society and thus had some success, at least in Djibouti. A Transitional National Assembly was selected, which then proceeded to elect a transitional head of state. Abdulkassim Salat Hassan, a former interior minister of the Siyad Barré regime, won out over some twenty rivals for the new office of transitional president. His term of office was set at three years, during which time the Transition National Government (TNG) he headed was to establish the procedures for creating permanent institutions for the renovated state.

The leadership of Somaliland and Puntland rejected the Arta results, complaining particularly about the predominance of individuals prominent in the Siyad Barré regime, a government which had done so much to destroy the north. The warlords treated Arta as simply another faction, and suggested that the transitional president would have to negotiate with them to bring lasting peace to Somalia.

An overly-optimistic international community awarded the Arta TNG Somalia's seats at the United Nations, the Organization of African Unity and the Arab League. None of these designations improved the TNG's capacity to govern, or its acceptance by those it sought to govern. By the time its mandate ran out in 2003 it was little more than another Mogadishu faction.

Ethiopia did much to undermine the TNG. In early 2001 it gathered the major warlords in Addis Ababa in what was nothing more than an anti-Arta conference. In March, claiming to be "leaders and representatives of the overwhelming majority of the political forces in Somalia," they announced creation of a Somali Reconciliation and Restoration Council (SRRC). Given post-9/11 concerns about Somalia as a refuge for terrorists, the U.S. encouraged President Moi of Kenya to use his good offices to reconcile the SRRC and the TNG.

In May 2002 Kenya, Ethiopia and Djibouti were designated by the principal regional organization—the Inter-

# Somalia

**Somaliland President
Dahir Riyale Kahin**

Governmental Authority for Development (IGAD)—to persuade Somalia's faction leaders, clan leaders and members of civil society to attend yet another peace conference. After more than two years of lengthy discussion, the conference made a breakthrough in August 2004. A 275-person transitional federal parliament was selected. By early October they had agreed on an interim president, Colonel Abdullahi Yusuf Ahmed, Puntland's warlord chief, and in December President Yusuf appointed Ali Mohammed Ghedi as prime minister. Ghedi's cabinet, consisting of some 79 individuals, reflected the delicacy of distributing employment possibilities.

Somalia's new Interim-President, a 69-year-old former military officer, will be called upon to display political and diplomatic skills that may be alien to his traditional practice, characterized by a quick resort to force. When his term of office as President of self-declared autonomous Puntland came to an end in 2001, and Puntland elders chose not to renew his mandate, Yusuf attempted to stay in office and had to be ousted by local militias in August. In November he militarily attacked the new Puntland leader, Jama Ali Jama, after Jama had been elected by elders and civic leaders. He has also used force against two regions of Somaliland.

Yusuf's challenges are great. He must install the new made-in-Kenya regime on Somali territory. Its capital is still largely controlled by warlords of the Hawiye clan, traditional rivals of his Darood clan, and it is deemed too unsafe for relocation by the transitional federal parliament. Appeals to the African Union (AU) for troops to protect the new government have not been received with eagerness by the Mogadishu warlords. And certainly a contingent of Ethiopian troops protecting the president himself would be resisted.

He must also deal with Islamists, some of whom may have ties with al-Qaeda and other terrorist organizations, and he has not endeared himself to the faithful by condemning traditional polgamy. On the issue of Somaliland, however, he will be able to rally both relgious advocates and clan warlords, all of whom view Somaliland independence as unacceptable.

Most outsiders remain hopeful, with fingers crossed, that the results of Somalia's fourteenth peace conference may draw a conclusion to the county's anarchy, strife, and statelessness. Fourteen years of civil conflict have claimed the lives of about one million Somali, while another two million have fled the country. The costs of restoration are staggering: estimates begin at $5 billion.

**Culture:** In many ways the supreme cultural achievement of Somalia can be found in its poetry. Oral verse is central to the Somali way of life. It is a means of mass communication, preserving history and shaping contemporary events, expressing personal and public sentiment and experience. Travelers invariably comment on the Somali love of harmonious sound, elaborate image, and alliterative arabesque. A poem could be as precious as a jewel; a great poet was a sage, a wise man an elder, even if not old.

Distinguished poets were heard by huge audiences of national radio and showcased by the BBC's Africa Service. Their allusive and metaphoric language could confound the foreign censor and stimulate the nationalist cause. The Somali poetic tradition remains today, not entirely muted by the thunder of arms, not entirely destroyed by political repression. So embedded in Somali consciousness is poetry that it is part of the texture and discourse of clan reconciliation meetings, the bedrock of Somali politics.

**View of Mogadishu and the ocean**

For Westerners, access to the power of Somali oral verse is indirect. One intimation of that power is the voice and music of the country's most famous musician, its first female pop star, Maryam Mursal. Her story is the story of Somalia. Mursal was a star in the 1970s singing what was called locally "Somali jazz." It combined traditional African song and Arabic sound with influences derived from Western performers like Ray Charles and Etta James. As the oppression of the Siyad Barré regime increased, so did Mursal's political engagement. Her songs became more political, more critical. "When we have a president that oppresses us," she sang, "what president or what person should we turn to in order to get help?" The regime reacted quickly. The song was banned and Mursal fired.

As the violence of civil war exploded in the 1990s, Mursal fled Somalia, trekking for some seven months through Kenya and Ethiopia and finally to Djibouti where she sought asylum at the Danish Embassy. That finally granted, she wound up with her family in a Danish refugee camp singing for her fellow escapees. She was heard by a record producer and contracted to Real World records.

Two CDs showcase her musical range and diversity. Waaberi is a compendium of traditional–style Somali songs, while The Journey transports Mursal's Somali melodies into the eclecticism of World Music. Traditional strings and percussion are replaced by keyboard bass, guitars and horns, muted trumpet, violins and accordion.

**Economy:** Livestock and bananas were Somalia's most profitable sectors. As with Somaliland, however, the Gulf states stopped buying Somali meat after another outbreak of RVF, and that source of foreign exchange was curtailed. An active cross-border cattle trading system prevails on the Kenyan border however.

In the south the most important commercial crop comes from banana plantations. The plantations, controlled by two major firms, one Italian and the other American (Dole), represent the only examples of modern agricultural techniques in the country—irrigation system and modern farm machinery. Export duties through the southern ports seem to represent the most important source of income for the Hawiye faction of Hussein Aideed.

Coastal waters off northern Somalia contain rich fishing grounds, but the absence of any governmental control of its waters encouraged illegal plundering by a variety of fishing fleets. Using the newest and most destructive of fishing techniques—drift nets and dynamiting to break up coral reefs where lobsters and other highly prized catch live—these mechanized fishermen destroy the habitats and livelihood of local fishermen.

Traditionally, Somali fishermen used nets only between September and April. In the hot season between May and August, indigenous fishermen use only hooks to catch their prey. To industrialized fishing operations which know no such limitations, the profits are enormous. Within 75 days of fishing, each ship gets up to 420 tons of fish out of Somali waters. The catch is worth $6.3 million.

To stop illegal fishing, locals have begun to arm themselves and their boats and to keep watch on the coast. When they capture a foreign fishing vessel, its occupants are forced to pay a cash fine for the illegal practice. Taiwanese and Ukrainian ships have recently been captured, but the pirates are heavily armed, and it is likely that violence will increase until the government develops a capacity to patrol its shores. Already several local fishermen and their boats are unaccounted for and presumed lost in the fishing wars.

The U.S. Treasury Department included the Al-Barakaat company, which wired money from diaspora Somalis to relatives living in Somalia, on a list of companies that funneled money to Osama bin Laden's al-Qaeda network. In Somalia, Al-Barakaat was the country's largest employer, running its biggest bank, phone system and only water purification plant.

When Al Barakaat's assets were frozen in late 2001, the company was crippled. Some 700 employees lost their jobs. Thousands lost their deposits, and those awaiting money from relatives in Europe and the United States were cut off. Remittances from diaspora Somali are a huge source of local income. The United Nations estimates that Somalia received $750

**At the Burco, Somaliland market even satellite dishes are available**

Photo by Ahmed in Burco

# Somalia

million in remittances a year; foreign aid from the West, in contrast, amounts to about $25 million a year.

The fund-transfer system that Al Barakaat exemplified, called *Hawala* in Arabic, operates on the basis of trust and can quickly shift of hundreds of thousands of dollars around the globe. To improve the industry's tainted image, Somali fund-transfer companies, aided by the UN Development Program and an international accounting firm (KPMG East Africa), launched a Somali Financial Services Association (SFSA) in December 2003. The new professional association's goal to is ensure industry self-regulation.

To a large extent, money, international trade and investment survive, indeed, thrive in Somalia—without a state. Those interested in the phenomenon can do no better than read Peter Little's *Somalia: Economy Without State.*

**The Future:** Somalia's future depends on both internal and external consensus. Regional powers need to agree on a common approach to Somali re-unification. Internal actors, be they supporters of the now-defunct TNG, obdurate warlords, or the recalcitrant mini-states of Somaliland and Puntland, need to agree on the minimum amount of authority to be granted any central government. Neither seems particularly likely very soon.

———— • ————

**Republic of Somaliland:**
**Area:** About the size of Tennessee
**Population:** 3,500,000 (est. 2003)
**Capital City:** Hargeisa (est. population: 500,000)
**Currency:** Somaliland Shilling
**Independence Date:** May 18, 1991
**Chief of State:** Dahir Riyale Kahin
**National Flag:** three horizontal, parallel, stripes and equal sections (green, white, red from top), with top section inscribed in white Arabic characters "There is no God but Allah and Mohammad was his prophet" and a five-pointed black star centered in the middle section.

In northwest Somalia, where British indirect rule did not destroy traditional Somali-systems of conflict resolution, leaders have opted for reconciliation rather than rivalry. Somali-style peace conferences, large-scale regional gatherings lasting anywhere from two to six months, managed to stabilize clan relationships. At a grand *shir*, or council, which concluded in February 1991, Isaaq clans representing 80% of the population of former British Somaliland reached an amnesty with other clans. Independence was declared in the same year with the rallying cry "No More Mogadishu."

There have been at least three of these grand councils, called "national conferences," to work out the form and structure of the state. Two elected assemblies have been created. One is essentially a small lower parliamentary house. The other is a council of elders, larger than the first and consisting of clan representatives. This chamber of elders cannot be dissolved by the president, and those who replace members who have died, been recalled or incapacitated must come from the same clan or sub-clan. The system was ratified in a constitution approved by two-thirds of the representatives in February 1997. Submitted to a referendum, the constitution received overwhelming approval from Somalilanders in May 2001.

In 1993 elders and citizens chose Muhammed Ibrahim Egal, the last prime minister of democratic Somalia, as President of the "Republic of Somaliland." He was re-elected to a five-year term as president in 1997, died in May 2002 and was immediately succeeded by Somaliland's vice-president, Dahir Riyale Kahin.

Denied recognition as a sovereign state by an international community fixated on re-creating a unitary state for Somalia, Somaliland has made remarkable progress on its own. Heavy weapons were surrendered voluntarily and often stored unguarded. State controls on the economy were virtually eliminated, and trade and commerce began to thrive. Even more remarkable has been the emergence of a stable and democratic political system operating under the rule of law. A constitution provides Somaliland's legal framework and under its provisions for presidential succession, the country made a smooth transition following the death of President Egal.

President Kahin presided over the next stage of Somaliland's political development—the preparation for presidential and parliamentary elections in 2003. Political parties were legalized and participated in municipal elections held in December 2002. Of six parties participating, three emerged with sufficient support to be allowed to run candidates in the April 2003 presidential elections: UDUB, the governing party founded by President Egal; KULMIYE, led by Ahmed Muhammad Silanyo, who had chaired the Somali National Movement during its fight against the Siyad Barré regime; and the Justice and Welfare Party (UCID), founded by Faisal Ali Warabe, a civil engineer who emphasized the notion of good governance in his campaigning.

In an important decision seen limiting the role of clan identity, the Supreme Court disallowed independent candidacies in the presidential elections. Each of the three candidates was forced to seek support among a broad range of clans and subclans. In January 2003 an article appeared in Hargeisa's English-language weekly condemning President Dahir Riyale Kahin as "unqualified and unfit to rule," citing educational deficiencies, administrative incompetence, and former membership in Siyad Barré's dreaded secret police, the National Security Service. Illustrative of Somaliland's developing political culture, the government did not ban the paper nor imprison the article's author. The loud and raucous debate that followed, covered by a local press which avoided sensationalism, heightened an appreciation of both press and presidential achievement.

When the results were tabulated, the election turned out to be a real squeaker. By a mere 80 votes, President Dahir Riyale Kahin defeated his closest rival, Ahmed Mohamed Silanyo. Clan elders headed off a potentially volatile situation by convincing Silanyo to accept the results. That he did, and that Somaliland avoided the post-electoral violence so common elsewhere in Africa, attests to the political maturity of a young democracy.

Somaliland has many of the attributes of a fully functioning state. It has its own flag and currency, its citizen drive with national license plates. It has a constitution, which allowed it to weather a succession crisis after President Egal suddenly died, and, perhaps most remarkably, in a deeply traditional society it has effectively moved from clan voting to individual voting in a multi-party democracy. It has, for the most part, seen peace and prosperity, having chosen politics over violence. None of this, however, has brought international recognition of its statehood.

Somaliland's appeals for recognition have been severely tested by a series of murders targeting foreign aid workers. The series began in October 2003 with the shooting death of an Italian doctor, Annalena Tonelli, who was killed outside the hospital she had founded in Borama. This was followed by the murder of two British teachers the same month, unsettling aid workers and expatriates. When two German aid workers were ambushed and killed in March 2004, NGOs and international aid agencies decided to withdraw their personnel from Somaliland for security reasons.

While it investigates the murders, the government offers two possible explanations. One sees the murders as the work of Islamic fundamentalists, commandos linked to Al Qaeda and coming from Mogadishu. The other sees them as part of a politically motivated plot to undermine Somaliland's bid for international recognition and force it to participate in Somalia re-unification talks.

**Culture:** Like men in Kenya and Ethiopia, Somalilanders enjoy the stimulation that comes from chewing *khat*, a shrub whose leaves have a psychotropic effect when chewed. The leaves are imported from Kenya daily and can cost the user up to five dollars a day. For importers, the profits of the *khat* trade are lucrative, and a number of luxurious homes going up in Hargeisa, the capital, belong to *khat* traders.

It is estimated that more than 90% of the women undergo a form of Female Genital Mutilation (FGM) in childhood, as young as five. Hargeisa was one of three sites chosen to launch a campaign against FGM in April 2004. (The other two were Mogadishu and Boosaaso, the commercial capital of the self-declared autonomous region of Puntland.) Campaigners estimate that 98% of Somali women who have undergone FGM have experienced the most drastic form—the clitoris is cut out and the vagina sewn up, without anesthetic—and are prone to urinary tract infections and obstetric complications in later life.

**Economy**: The Somaliland government has an annual budget of around $18 million. Employing something like 26,000 people, it spends 70% of its revenues on salaries. Revenues are mostly derived from port duties at Berbera where activity has recently increased. UN agencies have used it for transporting food relief to Ethiopia, and the Ethiopian government has turned to it in a search for alternatives to the Eritrean port of Asab.

Ethiopian Airlines has recently begun twice-weekly flights to Hargeisa, Somaliland's capital. International flights from the Gulf states, East Africa and Europe already land at Hargeisa and Berbera airports, generating about $1.5 million in revenues for the government. As of 2001, Somaliland businessmen began to pay income and profit taxes, which increased government revenues.

Wealth and profits are largely based on livestock trade, meat and hide exports. Some 1.5 million head of sheep and livestock were exported in 2000, while in 1999 about 2 million head had been exported. A new skin and hide factory has been opened to produce export-quality leather.

In 2000, Somaliland would normally have expected to export two to two and a half million head of sheep to Saudi Arabia, as well as 100,000 head of cattle to Yemen, but the states imposed a livestock ban in October after an outbreak of Rift Valley Fever (RVF). UN agencies have since found no traces of the disease in Somaliland cattle, but Saudi officials have kept the ban in place, despite lifting it for Ethiopian livestock. In normal years the country expects to earn between $150 to $200 million in foreign exchange from the livestock trade. This would normally earn the government some $8-9 million in taxes, over 30% of its total budget. Cut-off of the trade has meant a budgetary downsizing for the government.

While the livestock ban is in effect, Somaliland is largely dependent on overseas remittances by diaspora Somali, estimated at $500 million a year. Given the absence of international assistance, contributions by the Soma-

liland diaspora have been crucial in the country's development. Somaliland now has two universities and several vocational colleges whose construction was greatly aided by diaspora remittances.

The entrepreneurial spirit abounds in Somaliland. Businessmen there have created one of the cheapest telephone systems in Africa: International calls are $1.50 a minute in the day and only 80 cents at night. Traders are working to export frankincense and myrrh, and exploration has begun for oil and gemstones. A recently discovered reef of high-quality emeralds—several miles long—holds much promise as an alternative source of income.

**Future:** The best the government can hope for in its campaign for international recognition is observer status at the UN, like the Palestinian Authority, and a similar status at the AU, but even that is likely to be denied by an international community eager to see a united Somalia. With a traditional foe as President of Somalia for the next five years, Somaliland will come under increasing pressure to accommodate its desires for independence to Somali desires for national unity.

**A Somali nomad and his camels**

Photo by Ahmed in Burco

# The United Republic of Tanzania

Olduvai Gorge

Photo by Gwen Benson

**Area:** 939,652 sq. km = 362,800 sq. mi. (includes the islands of Zanzibar and Pemba; as large as Texas and most of New Mexico.

**Population:** 36,766,356 (July 2005 est.)

**Capital City:** Dar es Salaam (pop. 2.8 million, est.). Some government offices have been moved to Dodoma, which is to be the new capital at an undetermined time.

**Climate:** Tropically hot and humid in the coastal area, hot and dry in the central plateau and semi–temperate in the highlands where cooler weather prevails as the altitude increases.

**Neighboring Countries:** Mozambique (Southeast); Malawi, Zambia (Southwest); Congo (Kinshasa), Burundi, Rwanda (West); Uganda (Northwest); (Kenya (Northeast).

**Official Languages:** KiSwahili, English.

**Other Principal Languages:** Arabic (widely spoken in Zanzibar). Kiswahili (Swahili) is the mother tongue of the Bantu people living in Zanzibar and nearby coastal Tanzania; although Kiswahili is Bantu in structure and origin, its vocabulary draws on a variety of sources, including Arabic and English, and it has become the lingua franca of central and eastern Africa; the first language of most people is one of the local languages. Prominent among these are Bena, Chagga, Gogo, Ha, Haya, Maasai, Makonde, Nilamba, Nyakyusa, Nyamwezi, Nyaturu, Ruguru, Shambala, Sukuma, and Yao.

**Ethnic groups:** Mainland—native African 99% (of which 95% are Bantu consisting of more than 130 tribes), other 1% (consisting of Asian, European, and Arab); Zanzibar—Arab, native African, mixed Arab and native African.

**Principal Religions:** Mainland—Christian 30%, Muslim 35%, indigenous beliefs 35%; Zanzibar—more than 99% Muslim.

**Chief Commercial Products:** Gold, coffee, manufactured goods, cotton, cashew nuts, minerals, tobacco, and sisal.

**GNI per capita:** $290 (2003)

**Currency:** Tanzania Shilling.

**Former Colonial Status:** German Colony (1885–1917); British Mandate under the League of Nations and Trustee-ship under the United Nations (1919–1961).

**Independence Date:** 26 April 1964. Tanganyika became independent 9 December 1961 (from UK-administered UN trusteeship); Zanzibar became independent 19 December 1963 (from UK); Tanganyika united with Zanzibar 26 April 1964 to form the United Republic of Tanganyika and Zanzibar; renamed United Republic of Tanzania 29 October 1964.

**Chief of State:** Benjamin Mkapa, President (since 1995).

**National Flag:** A triangle of green in the upper left corner; a triangle of blue in the lower right–hand corner with a broad band of black between the two. These three colors are separated by narrow yellow bands.

Tanzania is a large, picturesque country lying just south of the Equator, extending between the great lakes of Central Africa and the Indian Ocean, with a 500–mile coastline. A fertile plain of up to 40 miles in width stretches along the coastline; the land slowly rises in the interior to a large central plateau averaging 4,000 feet in altitude. A mountain range of moderate height in the middle of Tanzania extends from north to south.

At the north end of these peaks, Mount Kilimanjaro rises in majestic splendor to the height of 19,340 feet—the tallest peak in Africa, which, though only three degrees south of the Equator, is capped by snow and icy glaciers year around.

Farther to the northwest, immense, fresh water Lake Victoria spreads its sparkling breadth across the semi–arid plain.

A chain of towering mountains extends along the length of the entire western border, sharply descending to Lake Tanganyika which is 2,534 feet deep. This long, narrow body of water was created centuries ago when an immense fault of land descended sharply, creating an earthquake of immeasurable proportions, and forming what is now called the Great Western Rift Valley. The large East African lakes contribute an area of 20,000 square miles of inland water to the area of Tanzania. Abundant rainfall supports dense vegetation in the coastal area, but the central plateau, hot and dry, has an average of 25 inches of rainfall per year.

In the higher elevations, cooler weather prevails and there is more abundant rainfall, produced by the rush of warm air up the high slopes of the mountains.

**History:** Centuries ago, Persian, Arabic, Indian and Portuguese traders engaged in lively trade with various coastal peoples. The country had been settled long before by large numbers of Bantus and smaller groups of Nilotic people. For details of early and colonial history, see *Historical Background, The Germans in Africa* and *The British in Africa*.

As a result of pre-independence elections in 1960, the Tanganyika African National Union (TANU), energetically led by its founder, Julius Nyerere, was installed in power. Nyerere, the son of a minor chief of the small Zanaki tribe, had been sent to a Catholic mission school as a boy. He later trained as a teacher at Makerere University College in Uganda and, with Catholic assistance, went on to Edinburgh University, where he received a master's degree in 1949. When he returned home in 1953, he was one of only two Tanganyikans trained in foreign universities, and a year later he formed TANU to agitate against British rule. Under Nyerere's leadership, TANU effectively mobilized African sentiment and led the country to independence. Granted independence by Great Britain on December 9, 1961, Tanganyika was a de facto single-party state. Nyerere became the country's first president.

In 1964 Nyerere proceeded to institutionalize the one-party system. Following eastern European models, TANU would be the sole means of organizing political expression in the country. Meanwhile, the neighboring island nation of Zanzibar, independent in 1963, experienced a destabilizing revolution that would ultimately link it to Tanganyika.

### Zanzibar

Before the 1964 revolution, Zanzibar—a collective noun which refers to both Zanzibar and Pemba islands and their volcanic neighbors—was a highly stratified society. A majority of the population, 76%, was African; Arabs made up 16%, but monopolized political power and controlled the economy of clove plantations. Trade was dominated by a smaller Indian population. After World War II, the racial structure of Zanzibar society was increasingly challenged by the majority African population. They experienced economic and social discrimination and limited opportunities. Symptomatically, initial judicial hearings were conducted in Arabic rather than the more widely used KiSwahili.

Political parties were first organized in the 1950s and reflected Zanzibar's racial divide. The Zanzibar Nationalist Party

**Former President Nyerere**

**President Benjamin William Mkapa**

(ZNP) was largely Arab and Arabized Africans; the supporters of the Afro-Shirazi Party (ASP) were Africans, often descendants of a long mixture of Arab, Persian and African heritage. In June 1963 Zanzibar gained internal self-government. A ZNP-led coalition emerged victorious in July elections, with Sultan Jamsid ibn Abdullah becoming head of state and Prime Minister Hamadi, an Arab, becoming government leader. Zanzibar was declared independent on December 10, 1963, but a month later on January 13, 1964, the Arab-dominated government was overthrown in a bloody revolution. Thousands of Arabs and Indians were massacred, the Sultan deposed, and a Republic declared, under the control of a 32-man Zanzibar Revolutionary Council led by Abeid Karume of the ASP.

Marxist-Leninist thinking was used to legitimize a tropical tyranny. The ASP monopolized political power as Zanzibar's sole legal party. All land was nationalized, political opponents thrown in jail and murdered, and a massive exodus of Arabs and Asians began amid continuing disorder. Karume appealed to neighboring Tanganyika for aid in maintaining law and order. Nyerere's government, fearing the consequences of continuing instability, dispatched Tanganyikan police forces, and in April 1964 Zanzibar and Tanganyika formed a union, later formally designated the United Republic of Tanzania. The governing parties of each partner shared a similar outlook and had long cooperated with each other. Though Nyerere's socialism was more moderate than Karume's, the union strengthened left-radical pressures on TANU.

### Tanzania

In 1964 TANU also faced instability on the mainland. Economic discontent had been fomented by trade unions and the army had mutinied in various parts of the country as soldiers protested low pay and the slow pace of Africanization of the lower officer grades. Nervous about a professional army, the government disbanded it and replaced it by a highly politicized Tanzanian People's Defense Force. The emulation of "popular democracies" was intensified following Nyerere's visit to China in 1965.

The Chinese told him that farmers were the most conservative members of society and must be uprooted from the land if socialism were to be built. Nyerere had used the KiSwahili term *ujamaa*, meaning "familyhood," to describe the ideal of communal cooperation he sought to develop, but this was given a more conventional socialist definition in TANU's Arusha Declaration of 1967. The government was asked to nationalize all means of production and to prepare development plans that did not rely on foreign assistance. Planned villages, as in China, resulted. Peasants were forcibly transferred to new villages without consultation and without compensation for the loss of their houses and farms. Unremarkably, production declined.

In 1977 Tanzania adopted a new constitution which explicitly subordinated all organs of state to the party. At the same time, TANU and the Afro-Shirazi Party merged to form a single party known as the Chama cha Mapinduzi—the Revolutionary Party, or CCM for short. Within the union, Zanzibar has considerable autonomy—its own president, who serves as Tanzanian vice-president, and chief minister, responsible for most affairs aside from defense and international relations. Under the constitution, Tanzanian's lawmaking body, the National Assembly, consists of 228 members, of whom 118 are elected from mainland constituencies and 50 from Zanzibar. Additional members are appointed by government and various "mass organizations." Given the leading role of the CCM and its monopoly of

# Tanzania

power, however, the legislature was relatively meaningless.

To reinvigorate a complacent party, an interesting variant on the one-party theme was introduced in the mid-1980s: CCM would approve two candidates for most constituencies, providing some illusion of democratic choice. Indeed, some government ministers were defeated in this manner.

President Nyerere was confirmed in office by plebiscites (it can hardly be called an election when only one candidate is running) held in 1965, 1970, 1975 and 1985. In that year he retired from the presidency, but retained the post of CCM chairman. His chosen successor was Ali Hassan Mwinyi, the former president of Zanzibar. It was during Mwinyi's two terms in office that the socialist chickens came home to roost.

The economy was bankrupt and its intellectual model proved equally bankrupt with the collapse of the Soviet Union. Plans were made to privatize some state companies and open the economic door a crack. Courageously, the government introduced the notion of competitive democracy and the constitution was amended to make Tanzania a multiparty state in 1992. Ben Mkapa was elected President in Tanzania's first competitive election held in 1995.

The elections, characterized by administrative ineptitude, were chaotic. The situation in the capital was so bad—election officials absent, ballots lost, polls opening late, if at all—that the whole thing had to be re-done after being declared null and void. Opposition parties claimed it was all a CCM plot and withdrew, but when the dust settled, on the mainland at least, 30 years of single party rule had given way to actual party competition. Chama cha Mapinduzi continued to control parliament, winning 186 of 232 elective seats; as CCM's candidate, Mkapa beat three opponents, winning a total of 61.8% of ballots cast.

The 2000 elections in many ways seemed a repeat of those held in 1995. President Mkapa overwhelmed his opposition with nearly 75% of the vote, and CCM continued its dominance in parliament, holding 244 of 274 seats.

Turmoil reigned in Zanzibar however. The CCM organization there—always more authoritarian than its mainland counterpart—made life much tougher for its Civic United Front (CUF) opponents. Government security forces and CCM toughs harassed and intimidated CUF candidates and supporters on both Pemba and Zanzibar. On election day, ballots and registration lists conveniently failed to arrive on time in opposition strongholds.

The situation on Pemba was such a disaster the Zanzibar Electoral Commission

**Cloth market, Zanzibar**          Photo by Beverly Ingram

(ZEC) nullified the results and re-ran the elections. CUF boycotted the re-runs, with the expected result: The ZEC announced that CCM's Amani Abeid Karume won the Zanzibar presidency with 67%, beating the CUF's Seif Shariff Hamad, who took 33%.

The European Union, the OAU and the United States all criticized the conduct of the election, but Amani Karume, the former minister of communication and transport and eldest son of Zanzibar's first president, Abeid Karume, seemed little inclined to make concessions to the opposition.

CUF protests continued, and in January 2001, an opposition meeting protesting October's elections was violently broken up by Tanzanian security forces, resulting in the death of at least thirty-three people. Several thousand CUF supporters fled to Kenya in fear for their lives.

After seven and a half months of arduous negotiations, the CCM and CUF signed a broad reconciliation accord in October 2001 to end the dispute. The government agreed to set up a commission to investigate the January killings. CUF dropped its demand to have the 2000 elections re-run and agreed to return to parliament, which it had been boycotting. Political detainees were to be released immediately, and the CUF leader, Seif Shariff Hamad, who had been Zanzibar's chief minister in the 1980s, would be granted the privileges to which he was entitled, heretofore refused by the CCM government—a pension, car, security, treatment abroad, electricity, an office and house servants. An independent electoral

commission was also created to guarantee future elections would be credible and free of controversy.

Perhaps most importantly, the accord, known by its Swahili name, *Muafaka*, provided for the creation of a joint commission to oversee its implementation. It was not until April 2002 that differences over the commission's structure and duties were resolved, and constitutional amendments implementing the accord were finally passed.

The question of greater autonomy for Zanzibar remains on the front burner of Tanzanian politics. Stretching the notion of "union" to its natural limits, the Zanzibar government has announced that the island would have its own flag. Zanzibar's separation is certainly nothing President Mkapa envisions. At Julius Nyerere's funeral, he made his position clear: Anyone, he said, "dreaming about breaking the unity of Tanzania . . . will be dealt with ruthlessly and their activities curtailed."

Tanzania's next presidential and legislative elections are scheduled for October 2005. In May 2005, Chama Cha Mapinduzi's national congress chose Foreign Affairs Minister Jakaya Mrisho Kikwete as its standard bearer. Zanzibar will simultaneously elect its president, and the island's CCM branch acted with authoritarian dispatch to eliminate the candidacy of Dr. Mohammed Gharib Bilal against the incumbent, President Amani Abeid Karume.

**Culture:** One of President Nyerere's greatest achievements was improving education and literacy in Tanzania. Primary education was made universally accessible with a primary school in every village. When challenged with his policy failures by World Bank officials, the president is reported to have responded that "The British Empire left us a country with 85% illiterates, two engineers and twelve doctors. When I left office, we had nine per cent illiterates and thousands of engineers and doctors."

Since those ebullient days investment in education went into decline, and literacy fell to 63% by 1990. Concentrated international assistance and effort have begun to effect a change: literacy was up to 79% in 2003. A quarter of Tanzanian adults still have no education, and women are twice as likely as men to miss out. By 2000, only 55% of seven-year-olds were enrolling in primary schools, most of which lacked teachers and were in sorely dilapidated condition. In Dar es Salaam, the capital, the average class size is 145 children per classroom. A UNICEF report highlighted the key problems in Tanzania's educational system; these included a serious shortage of books and teachers who are poorly trained and unmotivated. The report also criticized teaching methods, and characterized the overall school environment as one of fear and boredom rather than interaction and real learning.

Secondary education has languished. While primary education was universalized, there was no concomitant expansion of public education at the secondary level. As a consequence Tanzania has the lowest rate of public secondary education in the world—just under 7%. Some 43% of parents send their children to private secondary schools. The Ministry of Education has set the target of a 50% net enrollment rate by 2010.

KiSwahili is more and more becoming the national language and is credited with instilling a national pride in Tanzanians. Where most former colonies still use a European language as their official language, Tanzania is an exception, having two official languages. While KiSwahili has been a major factor in unifying the Tanzanian people, English is still the "international" language, and many Tanzanians are concerned the country will lose certain economic advantages by slowly "burying" the other official language.

The present capital, Dar-es-Salaam (Haven of Peace), has become a densely congested city, suffering the consequences of urban growth. Among other things, cesspits are polluting water tables and at least 60% of the city's solid waste goes uncollected or is disposed of inappropriately.

To "open up" the interior regions of the country and escape the congestion of the capital, centrally-located Dodoma has been selected as the new capital city. Actual relocation of government functions will probably stretch over a period of ten years because of limited funds.

**Economy:** Julius Nyerere knew little of economics, and his socialist program devastated an already poor country. Tanzanian policies emphasized government control over all aspects of the nation's economic life, with heavy spending on education and health services. Inspired by the Chinese experience, the government resettled peasant farmers in planned villages. This facilitated the distribution of services, but had disastrous effects on agricultural production, which plummeted. Government owned industries and businesses were costly failures and a drain on national resources. As agricultural production diminished and the expenses of nationalized companies rose, national income fell, foreign debt increased and Tanzania became increasingly dependent on the generosity of international donors.

In 1986 the government finally launched a comprehensive economic reform and President Mkapa has continued his predecessor's efforts to liberalize the economy. Agricultural marketing was liberalized to allow some play of market forces. Privatization of state-owned enterprises has been undertaken, exchange rates have been freed, and red tape reduced. Stubborn resistance and ingrained practices have slowed transformation.

Corruption is pandemic in Tanzania ("In my country," said former Prime Minister Joseph Warioba, the chairman of Mkapa's anti-corruption commission, "you have to pay a bribe for everything.") The very public anti-corruption campaign which followed the Warioba Report resulted in hundreds of state bureaucrats being fired, but there have been few prosecutions, and none have yet been completed. Corruption remains. On Transparency International's 2004 *Corruption Perceptions Index*, Tanzania is tied for 90th place, equal with Russia and Mozambique, but well above Nigeria's dismal ranking of 144 out of 145 nations charted.

Economic growth has been sluggish for the past several years, barely enough to keep up with population growth. In 2003 it was 7.1% barely adequate for a country whose population grew at the rate of 2.3% the same year. Agriculture accounts for 45% of GDP (2003), employs 80% of the work force and contributes over 75% of foreign exchange earnings. Like an unloved child of nature, Tanzania was subjected to meteorological extremes of drought and flooding with what seems to be cyclical regularity. Prices for most of its main agricultural products—coffee, sisal, cotton, tobacco, cashew nuts and tea—have declined. Even the much-vaunted liberalization of agriculture has failed to produce its promised benefits.

Most farmers are small-scale, say four acres of land, and remain at virtually subsistence level. Agricultural practice and inputs need improvement, but land legislation—rewritten in 1999—still makes it difficult for farmers to mortgage their land and find credit to develop their agriculture. Local roads also need to be improved to provide farmers access to markets, but even where there is access, liberalization has not raised the prices paid to farmers. Certainly commodity prices have fallen generally, but in Tanzania, buyers have formed cartels which function to keep prices down even more.

Government taxes and license fees are extensive. There are, for example, 26 different taxes, levies and licenses imposed on the coffee industry, Tanzania's third biggest foreign exchange earner. A recent study found Tanzania's taxes to be the highest of five peer coffee-producing

**Tea harvest**                    Photo by Beverly Ingram

241

# Tanzania

countries (Uganda, Ethiopia, Costa Rica, Guatemala and Tanzania).

Overall taxes represent 21% of the average price received by arabica coffee producers, and with falling market prices farmers are no longer able to cover their costs. To add insult to injury, few of the tax revenues collected by the government are reinvested in the coffee industry.

The heavy hand of taxes and regulation has impacted small coffee farmers, who account for 95% of the country's total output. They have the lowest yields in the region. Tanzanian coffee farmers average an estimated 152 pounds and acre, while Kenya's turn out 625 per acre, for example. Coffee production continues to decline.

The island of Pemba, part of Zanzibar, produces 80% of the country's clove crop. Always a bit of a socialist laggard, the Zanzibar government has been slow to liberalize the island's agricultural policy. There is only a single buyer for cloves—the Zanzibar State Trading Corporation (ZSTC). The company has traditionally offered such low prices to producers that they have usually preferred to smuggle their crops to neighboring Kenya.

Tourism, which had replaced cloves as Zanzibar's principal source of foreign exchange, has plummeted with the rise of Islamist terrorism in the region. When western nations warned their citizens of possible terrorist attacks in the islands in 2003, hotels almost immediately suffered 50% cancellation rates.

An upsurge of Islamist moralism on Zanzibar could threaten the tourist industry even more. During the 2003 Ramadan season, young Islamic toughs beat up a number of Muslim women whom they considered inappropriately dressed. In March 2004, police had to use tear gas to disperse hundreds of demonstrators from the Islamic Awareness Society agitating for government adoption of Islamic (Sharia) law.

With greater stability and an abundance of wild animal parks, mainland Tanzania remains a premier tourist attraction for the adventurous. In the 2003–2004 season the government reported 576,198 tourists visited the country, earning it $731 million.

While tourism has become sensitive to international politics, mining has become the fastest growing sector of Tanzania's economy, led by rising gold sales. As the sector was opened to private investment, mineral sales rose from $15 million in 1996 to over $400 million in 2002. Tanzania has become the third largest African gold producer (after South Africa and Ghana).

Tanzania also possesses considerable deposits of gemstones—green tourmaline, sapphires, garnets, diamonds, rubies and emeralds. The country earned $8.1 million from gemstone exports in 1998, compared with only $200,000 eleven years before when large quantities were smuggled out of the country. Smuggling remains a problem as the example of tanzanite indicates. Tanzanite is a precious blue stone found only in Tanzania southwest of Mount Kilimanjaro. Strangely, Kenya became the world's largest exporter of this unique product.

The Tanzanite market virtually collapsed in late 2001 after the *Wall Street Journal* claimed tanzanite sales were financing Osama bin Ladin's terrorist network. Tiffany, QVC and the Zale Corporation all stopped sales. In response, industry representatives and Tanzanian officials drew up the "Tucson Tanzanite Protocols." The Tanzanian government pledged to ensure that the gem is legally mined and exported. Government certificates would follow each parcel of tanzanite from mine to market, guaranteeing a buyer that the stones are terror-free. Zale recommended sales of the blue stone in May 2002, and in December the American Gem Trade Association named Tanzanite an additional birthstone for the month of December. This was the first time a birthstone has been added to the existing list since 1912.

For any type of mining venture in Tanzania, infrastructure is a problem. Roads are inadequate and in disrepair. Availability of water and electricity is often problematic.

At 17 million head, the national cattle herd is the third largest in Africa—after Ethiopia and Sudan—but conditions are so rudimentary the export of cattle, beef, and related products earned only $4 million last year. Processing plants can barely handle local demand. Transportation to the port of Dar es Salam is handicapped by hopelessly inadequate roads made impassable by seasonal rains. Bovine diseases cannot be controlled where 80% of the country's 1,998 cattle dips are malfunctioning and veterinary drugs are either too expensive or unavailable.

The greatest drag on the Tanzanian economy remains its international debt. As of 2003 it was 7.5 billion dollars. The World Bank evaluates debt burden by a ratio of debt to exports. In severely indebted countries, the ratio of debt to exports is put at 220% or more. A debt burden in that range coupled with a debt service of 20-25% of annual exports can qualify a country for Heavily Indebted Poor Country (HIPC) relief. Tanzania qualified on both counts and was admitted to the HIPC initiative in November 2001. As a consequence, Tanzania will see its external debt drop by 54% over the long term.

**The Future:** Political and religious tensions persist on Zanzibar where the opposition continues to be treated with force and violence. The question of greater autonomy for the island, indeed, whether it should become a separate state, will become ever more salient, especially in an election year. Investments in the mining sector have revitalized a dormant industry, but conflicts between artisanal miners and giant international mining concerns could continue to be disruptive. The industry poses enormous environmental concerns. Islamic fundamentalists are becoming more assertive.

**Mass production of sculpture for the tourist trade**

Photo by Jude Barnes

242

# The Republic of Uganda

**Former Colonial Status:** British Protectorate (1894–1962).
**Independence Date:** October 9, 1962.
**Chief of State:** Yoweri Museveni. (b. 1941), President.
**National Flag:** Six bands of black, yellow and red (repeated) with a silver circle in the center enclosing a crested crane.

This fertile expanse of highland bestrides the Equator in central East Africa between the Eastern and Western Rift formations. Uganda, dotted with lakes, and with immense Lake Victoria on the South, lies at an altitude of between 3,000 and 6,000 feet. If this country were at a lower altitude, its climate would be hot, moist and oppressive, but it is quite pleasantly temperate with ample rainfall to support intense cultivation. In the extreme Northeast, the climate is dry and prone to drought.

Approximately 15% of the country is covered by fresh water. The Ruwenzori Mountains to the west divide Uganda from the Democratic Republic of the Congo, having altitudes of almost 17,000 feet. In the southwest, close to Rwanda, the Virunga range of active volcanoes reaches skyward. In the East, Mount Elgon rises to a height of 14,000 feet, prominent among its neighbors of the Eastern Rift Mountains.

The Victoria Nile originates from the banks of Lake Victoria, heavily populated with hippopotomi and crocodiles, and flows to Lake Kyoga, an irregularly shaped body of water with large swamps. From there the Nile flows north and west through immense mountains to empty into Lake Albert. The Albert Nile flows northward, leaving Uganda at the Sudanese border to continue its journey of more than 4,000 miles to the Mediterranean Sea.

Lagoro refugee camp near Kitgum, northern Uganda

**Area:** 235,690 sq. km. = 91,080 sq. mi.
**Population:** 27,269,482 (July 2005 est.).
**Capital City:** Kampala (Pop. 1.3 million, estimated).
**Climate:** Temperate, though equatorial, because of altitudes averaging 4,500 feet with ample rainfall in most years (except in the semi–arid northwest) interrupted by two short dry seasons.
**Neighboring Countries:** Rwanda, Tanzania (Southwest); Congo-Kinshasa (West); The Sudan (North); Kenya (Northeast).
**Official Language:** English is taught in grade schools, used in courts of law and by most newspapers and some radio broadcasts. Ganda (or Luganda) is preferred for native-language publications in the capital.

**Other Principal Languages:** Over forty. Prominently: Acholi, Alur, Chiga, Ganda, Karamojong, Kenyi, Lango, Masaba, Nyankore Nyoro, Rwanda, Sogo, Teso, Tooro.
**Ethnic groups:** Baganda, Karamojong, Basogo, Iteso, Langi, Rwanda, Bagisu, Acholi, Lugbara, Bunyoro, Batobo, non-African (European, Asian, Arab).
**Principal Religions:** Roman Catholic 33%, Protestant 33%, Muslim 16%, indigenous beliefs 18%.
**Chief Commercial Products:** Coffee, fish and fish products, flowers, tobacco, electricity, cotton, and tea.
**GNI per capita:** $240 (2003)
**Currency:** Uganda Shilling.

# Uganda

**History**: It is difficult to trace the migrations of the Bantu people whose descendants live in Uganda today. The last Kabaka (King) of Buganda claimed to be the 37th member of an uninterrupted line of monarchs. It is not possible to determine the exact time when the Nilotic groups came to northern Uganda. For details of early and colonial history, see *Historical Background* and *The British in Africa*.

The United Kingdom of Uganda was granted internal autonomy on March 1, 1962, becoming fully independent on October 9 of that year. The government initially consisted of a federation of the kingdoms of Buganda, Busoga, Butoro and Bunyoro, which retained local autonomy, while the rest of the country was governed by the central government. Sir Edward Frederick Mutesa II, Kabaka of Buganda, became the first president and Sir William W. Nadiope, King of Bunyoro, was the first Vice-President. Prime Minister Milton Obote wielded considerable power within the central government. The cabinet was selected by a coalition of Obote's People's Congress Party and the Buganda KabakaYekka Party; the formerly dominant Democratic Party was in the minority.

The post independence era was dominated by two figures who reduced Uganda to a grisly shambles, replete with starvation and widespread deaths. Milton Obote was the first (1963-1971, 1980-1985) and the second was a military figure, Idi Amin (1971-1979).

Charging Kabaka Mutesa with making personal profits from the supply of arms in connection with a rebellion in neighboring Zaïre, Obote dismissed him and seized the government. The hereditary king barely escaped when the army stormed the presidential palace; he lived in exiled poverty until his death in 1969.

**Milton Obote**

(His remains were ceremoniously returned to Uganda in 1971.)

Obote abolished the old constitution and the traditional kingdoms; his PCP became the sole party, and he steered Uganda sharply to a socialist economy. As he appointed more and more of his fellow tribesmen to public offices, tensions mounted and political instability increased. Finally the army revolted, uniting behind Idi Amin in January 1971.

General Amin, who had once been the Ugandan heavyweight boxing champion, was initially popular, but he wasted no time alienating just about everyone. Some 70,000 Asians, mainly Indians and Pakistanis, were expelled in 1972 with little thought of their importance to the economy as merchants and traders. The expulsion won Amin immense support from those to whom he gave property and merchandise seized from Asian merchants. Controversial and damaging though the expulsion was, the ultimate consequence was that Uganda today has one of the biggest black middle classes in Africa.

Initial admiration of Field Marshall Amin quickly turned to fear. Educated Ugandans began to leave the country to escape his whims. He expelled African clergy and missionaries, claiming they were foreign agents, and outlawed some Christian denominations like the Jehovah's Witnesses. Brutality became the order of the day by 1974. Secret executions, massacres and torture were among his favorite methods, and he personally participated in some of these grisly acts.

Military efforts to oust him failed, and perpetrators were executed on the spot. The economy all but disappeared by 1978, and the country seethed with unrest. Amin tried to distract attention from his failures by claiming that Tanzania had invaded Uganda; he "responded" by having his troops invade Tanzania. They captured about 710 square miles before withdrawing.

President Julius Nyerere of Tanzania used the invasion as an excuse to get rid of Amin. Tanzanian troops, augmented by Ugandan exiles, mounted a swift invasion. Amin's forces, demoralized by his behavior, crumbled after fierce fighting had claimed the lives of many.

The conquering army entered Kampala in April 1979 and was greeted jubilantly. In the confusion, Amin escaped. Yusufu Lule was installed as president, but he was quickly replaced by Godfrey Binaisa, whose term of office was equally short lived. Obote supporters plotted Binaisa's overthrow, and Obote returned to Uganda in May 1980.

December 1980 elections were outrageously stolen by Obote, driving his political rivals into rebellion. One of those

**Idi Amin**

was Yoweri Museveni, who had contributed significantly to the military overthrow of Amin. Refusing to accept the fraudulent election results, he formed a guerrilla group and "went to the bush with only 26 guns and organized the National Resistance Army (NRA) to oppose the tyranny that Obote's regime had unleashed upon the population," as his website describes it. There ensued five years of strife in which an estimated one million fled and 300,000 lost their lives.

In January 1986 Museveni's rebel band, which now called itself the National Resistance Army (NRA), shot its way into Kampala and seized control of the country. In victory the NRA became the first guerrilla army to oust an incumbent African regime. Museveni became president as the head of the National Resistance Movement (NRM) and began the difficult task of rebuilding Uganda. He was determined to break the cycle of violence that had destroyed Uganda, restore democracy and foster economic development. Those goals required an entire rethinking of the institutions and practices that had bedeviled and destroyed the country.

Chief among the objects of his criticism were the traditional political parties, which he castigated as "sectarian and divisive," responsible for the country's political and economic ills. Political parties were prohibited, and political participation was organized within the framework of the broad-based National Revolutionary Movement (NRM). All would belong, and candidates would stand for office on personal merit rather than party platform. This was the beginning of what would come to be known as the non-party movement system.

Since the regime had come to power by force of arms promising to restore democracy and individual liberties, one of its first projects was a constitutional commission which could develop the framework which restored the rule of law. Once in existence, the commission toured the entire country and consulted broadly. The hearings resulted in the publication of *Guidelines on Constitutional Issues*, which formed the basis of continuing dialogue.

The whole process demonstrated a remarkable shift from the tradition of constitutions created on high and presented to the people. Here, people would actually participate in the development of the document that would shape their lives and futures. The process was designed to assure the new constitution would receive the respect and legitimacy of the Ugandan people. Additionally, Museveni's democratic engagement also aimed at securing legitimacy for his NRM.

The transition from anarchy to constitutionalism was lengthy; the constitutional commission's draft was debated and ratified by a popularly elected constituent assembly on July 12, 1995, and promulgated by President Museveni on October 8. The constitution that emerged from this process was equally lengthy. In its final form, the constitution weighed in with 287 articles and seven addenda, making the Uganda Constitution ten times longer than that of the United States. Fundamen-

**President Museveni**

tally, it incorporated President Museveni's ideological vision, particularly on the issue of political parties.

The constitution outlaws traditional political party activities, including branch offices, delegate conferences, staging political rallies, and sponsoring candidates for election. For Museveni, a country like Uganda, divided along ethnic and religious fault lines, simply could not afford the divisiveness of party competition. Parliament was constitutionally prohibited, however, from establishing a single-party state. After five years experience with the movement system, the constitution promised voters an opportunity to assess the system in a referendum.

President Museveni's personal rule was legitimized by May 1996 elections held in

**Northern Uganda, site of LRA activity**

accordance with the new constitution. His election slogan was "No Change," and he campaigned on his record: He had ended Uganda's cycle of blood and dictatorship, boosted security through the army and built economic success that saw the gross domestic product grow by 10% in 1994. He won handily, beating two opposition candidates. It was the first free and open presidential vote in 30 years.

Parliamentary elections followed in July 1996. There are 214 directly elected members and a number of indirectly elected seats for representatives of women (39), youth (5), workers (3), the disabled (5) and the army (10).

Uganda's economic rehabilitation was a high priority for Museveni. He had inherited a wasteland of human devastation in 1986. Piles of skulls remained at crossroads, remainders of the grisly days since independence. The economy was stagnant. Transportation and communication systems had been destroyed by war, production disrupted. The state was bankrupt; revenue from taxation was virtually nonexistent. To change course, agreements were made with the IMF. The economy was liberalized to include producer incentives, loans were secured to rehabilitate infrastructure, and the economy (starting from virtually nothing) responded with eye-catching growth rates.

### Rebels and Regional Conflicts

Although economic vibrancy returned to Uganda, not all its citizens shared in its changed conditions. In border areas to the west and north, the Uganda Peoples Defense Force (UPDF) faces on-going resistance and rebellion from those marginalized economically and politically. In the north, the Lord's Resistance Army (LRA), supported by Khartoum's meddlesome anti-Museveni regime, has waged war for years. Led by a former Roman Catholic altar boy, Joseph Kony, the LRA recruits its soldiers by kidnapping children (30,839 between 1986 and 2001 according to UNICEF), male and female, and sending them off to Sudanese camps for military training or sexual service. Those who flee or disobey—and disobedience includes riding a bicycle—have been maimed or murdered. Kony's stated goal is to overthrow Museveni and rule Uganda in accordance with the Ten Commandments.

The rebels—Museveni calls them terrorists—have killed thousands, destroyed homes and property, and prevented the distribution of social services or development projects in an already dirt-poor region. More than 1.2 million people have been forced to leave their homes. At least 300,000 of them live in "protected villages" organized by the army to prevent

# Uganda

the enemy from getting food and assistance from fellow Acholi tribesmen.

Because of its support of the LRA, and two other rebel groups—the Allied Democratic Forces and the West Nile Bank Front, active on Uganda's western border—Sudan constitutes a bulky dossier in Ugandan foreign relations. Sudanese support for these destabilizing elements is a tit-for-tat response. President Museveni shared with his colleagues in Eritrea and Ethiopia a common hostility to Sudan's Islamist regime and has long supported John Garang's SPLA in its resistance to the government in Khartoum.

A successful guerrilla commander, Museveni has shown sympathy for more than Sudanese rebels. Uganda was the training ground for members of the Tutsi-led Rwandan Patriotic Front that invaded and defeated the genocidal regime installed in Kigali. Museveni was also a central figure in organizing the forces that overthrew the Mobutu regime in Zaïre. It all represented an enormously self-confident foreign policy, distinctly at odds with the OAU traditions of non-intervention and respect for borders.

The impact of Uganda's involvement in the Democratic Republic of the Congo (ex-Zaïre) continues today. Shared security concerns with Rwanda brought initial cooperation between the two countries, but ultimately differing aims and visions brought tension and conflict between the two. Uganda's support of the anti-Kabila rebels raised fundamental questions about how a country as poor as Uganda could afford the increased defense expenditures necessary to conduct these operations. In part, the answer is simple: the war was self-financed through exploitation of Congo's rich resources. The war effort was early dominated by the question of resource extraction. Congo's wealth would corrupt all who came near and tarnish the reputations of the Ugandan army and its officers.

Corruption permeated the entire army operation. Timber prices in Uganda fell sharply because Ugandan troops in the Congo had flooded the market with cheap wood smuggled from the war zone. The tentacles of corruption spread throughout the region as ports in Kenya and Tanzania served as points of transshipment for timber, coffee and minerals headed for Asian markets.

Corruption, already notable in Uganda, became all pervasive and inched closer to President Museveni himself. His half-brother, Major-General Salim Saleh, who seemed to shuttle back and forth between the private and public sectors, was everywhere touched by the taint of corruption.

Uganda's joint support with Rwanda of the anti-Kabila coalition unraveled in 1999. In 2000 each country massed troops on its respective borders and seemed near war. Charges of supporting and training hostile forces were made by both parties, but diplomacy prevailed. Confidence-building measures—like exchanging military inspection teams—were created in 2002, but little confidence was built. Verbal sniping between the two countries continues and tensions remain.

The terrorist attacks on New York and Washington in September 2001 helped to transform Uganda's relations with Sudan. The UN placed the LRA on a list of terrorist organizations and, eager to be counted amongst the anti-terrorists, Sudan gave permission for the Ugandan army to pursue Joseph Kony's forces into Sudanese territory.

Using heavy artillery, the Uganda People's Democratic Army (UPDA) launched operation "Iron Fist," against the LRA's Sudanese bases in March 2002. No prisoners were taken and UN humanitarian organizations lamented that any hostage children had probably died under the bombs of the Ugandan army. The rebels responded by multiplying their attacks against Ugandan civilians in the north in ways that were, if possible, even more violent, vicious and destructive than previous efforts. Hostages were taken, children kidnapped to replace fallen rebels, women raped and men castrated and left to bleed to death. The effort seemed two-fold. One goal was to terrify local inhabitants and keep them from providing valuable intelligence on rebel locations and movements to the army. The other was to delegitimize the Museveni regime by proving the army's incapacity to protect local inhabitants. For them, army operations only killed the children whose abduction the army had failed to prevent.

Despite army press releases, the UPDA has not defeated the LRA. A new offensive began in April 2005 when President Museveni ordered the UPDF to hunt down and neutralize Kony and his brigands. Forces have been deployed in southern Sudan to destroy all LRA suspected hideouts.

Conditions in Northern Uganda, probably the least developed area of the country, continue to spiral downward. Insecurity prevails, and the army seems more predator than protector. The rains have failed for several years in a row. The landscape is dry, dusty and cropless. Schools are deserted and market stalls are empty and abandoned. Granaries are empty and underfed cattle, the pride of northern pastoralists, no longer provide the milk and blood of traditional sustenance. The word "akoro," meaning "hunger," is heard everywhere: In some areas people are living on one bowl of boiled leaves a day. UN officials have called it the world's worst forgotten humanitarian crisis.

Those displaced by LRA violence have become dependent on food handouts, because it is simply too dangerous to live in villages and farm the land—even if the rains come. Insecurity has created the phenomenon of "night commuters"; every night as many as 20,000 children walk miles from their villages to the relative safety of cities where they spend the night in public buildings or on the streets.

Northern pastoralists, like the Karamojong, are subject to cross-border raids from cattle-rustling peoples in Sudan or

**Ugandan army searching for LRA in northern Uganda**   ©IRIN

Kenya. Against these the army has offered insufficient protection. Worse, it has sought to disarm them, depriving the Karamajong of some defense against such raids. The area is awash in small arms, first introduced in the late 19th century by ivory hunters and traders. With the fall of the Amin government, however, their availability became widespread. Military weapons were traded, sold or lost by fleeing soldiers and local tribesmen found easy access to abandoned weapons depots. The number of machine guns circulating in the area, for example, is estimated at 40,000 to 80,000. Efforts by the army to forcibly disarm pastoralists have only increased hostility to the regime.

### The Movement and Multipartyism

In June 2000 Ugandans were asked to voice their opinions on the "movement system." A referendum asked if the movement system be maintained, or should the country adopt a multiparty system of democracy. The campaign became personalized—a referendum for or against Yoweri Museveni. Sensing the mood of a country relatively satisfied with Museveni's tenure, the opposition decided to boycott the vote. More than 90% of those who voted chose to retain the Movement system.

There was little interest in Uganda's presidential election, scheduled for March 2001, until Kizza Besigye entered the race. Suddenly there was the possibility of genuine competition. Dr. Besigye was no ordinary challenger. He was one of the original NRA fighters and Museveni's personal physician during the long bush war; he had also served as a minister in Museveni's NRM government. He knew, in other words, the regime from the inside. What he saw disillusioned him and formed the basis of his campaign against his old comrade in arms.

Corruption and nepotism were criticized, as was Uganda's involvement in the Congo war. He accused the president of becoming increasingly autocratic and of turning the ruling movement into a party intolerant of competition. The president and his supporters experienced a sense of betrayal. The campaign became unnecessarily violent and ramified regionally.

Tensions with Rwanda were magnified. Kigali was accused of contributing large sums to the Besigye campaign. Dr. Besigye's wife, a member of parliament, added to heightened suspicion between the two countries by accusing the Museveni government of aiding the *Interahamwe*, one of Rwanda's greatest *bêtes noirs*.

When all the votes were counted, President Museveni won by a huge margin, receiving 69.3% of the vote. Dr. Besigye, who ran second with 27.8% of the vote, refused to accept the results, charging fraud and intimidation. The victory may have been sweet for President Museveni, but the campaign damaged his reputation.

Equally damaging was the April 2001 report of a panel of experts to the UN Security Council on "Illegal Exploitation of Natural Resources and Other Forms of Wealth in the Democratic Republic of the Congo." Names were named, and they came very near the president himself. The panel specifically singled out the president's half-brother, Major-General Salim Saleh and his wife Jovia Akandwanaho, as being "at the core of the illegal exploitation of natural resources in areas controlled by Uganda."

The panel's judgment on President Museveni was no less harsh. He had "put himself in the position of accomplice," said the panel, by choosing not to act when information on corrupt practices was brought to his attention. Denials were, of course, issued, but the accumulation of wealth by the president's family is a major factor in a growing opposition to Museveni and his no-party regime.

Parliamentary elections in June 2001 provided some small hint of discontent. Since there are no parties, candidates were either for or against the government, and President Museveni was faced with the defeat of 12 cabinet ministers. Only two, it should be said, were replaced by individuals who actually opposed the government.

The president himself campaigned extensively, and his most painful defeat no doubt came with the election of Winnie Byanyima, the outspoken wife of his presidential opponent, Kizza Besigye. She won by less than 100 votes. Since then the government has not made life easy for her. She has faced charges of treason and illegal possession of a weapon, and as recently as April 2003, she has been accused of having connections with the People's Redemption Army (PRA) led by dissident Ugandan army officers. (The PRA, which operates out of eastern Congo, has been identified by the government as the military front of exiled presidential candidate Kizza Besigye. It also claims the PRA receives the support of Rwanda. Besigye himself lives in self-imposed exile in Pretoria, South Africa.)

With the approach of presidential elections in 2006, Uganda's parties have chafed under their legal restrictions and have become increasingly vocal in demanding a return to multipartyism. A new law regulating political parties went into effect in June 2002 and was promptly challenged in court by opposition groups, led by the Democratic Party. Their complaint was that the *Political Parties and Organisations Act (2002)* imposed unfair restrictions on traditional political parties, which were not equally applied to The Movement, Uganda's ruling party.

International donors, who subsidize a good half of Uganda's annual budget, pressured President Museveni to permit full political competition, and he seized the opportunity to spiffy up his image by becoming a born-again democrat. In late February 2003, Ugandans learned their president, long the advocate of "no-party democracy," had decided to allow parties after all. Subsequent epiphanies abounded.

By the end of March, the ruling Movement announced concurrence, and just to make things legal, Uganda's constitutional court announced its decision on the challenge to the *Political Parties and Organisations Act*. Siding with the opposition, it declared those parts of the law, which forbid political parties from carrying out their activities, unconstitutional. The decision liberated parties and transformed Uganda's political space. By early 2004 fifty political parties had applied for registration in preparation for the next elections in 2006.

President Museveni's government continues to balk and has scheduled a referendum for June 30, 2005 to decide if the country should return to multiparty politics. The United Kingdom has responded by canceling some $10 million in aid to Uganda, saying the country has not done enough to establish fair multi-party politics. The government is also continuing a project to amend the constitution to repeal provisions limiting a president to two five-year terms. This would allow President Museveni to seek re-election in next year's polls. Constitutionally, the repeal of term limits could be adopted by a two-thirds majority vote in parliament.

The Constitutional Review Commission rejects amendment by legislative vote and wants such a change submitted to referendum. Movement leadership has fractured over the issue, and long-time Museveni supporters have defected to the opposition. Uganda's Catholic bishops have warned against trying to remove the constitutional ban on a third term, and even U.S. President George Bush is reported to have told Museveni to forget a third term.

At this point it seems likely that President Museveni will seek a third term, and it is unlikely the Americans will really pressure him out of the race; Uganda is too important to U.S. anti-terrorist efforts in East Africa, which some fear might become the next base for Al-Qaeda. The U.S already has military logistics personnel at the Entebbe airport, seen as a cargo hub for possible multinational military and humanitarian actions.

# Uganda

**Culture:** Living in Uganda's northeast corner are the Karamojong, a pastoralist minority of some 100,000 people. The Karamojong are Nilotic, while the bulk of Ugandans are Bantus. Among them the cow is supreme. Milk and blood (drawn during the dry season when the animal produces no milk) provide the principal sources of Karamojong protein. Wealth, power and status are all based on cattle ownership.

The Karamojong illustrate all the problems of Uganda's underdeveloped and wretchedly poor north. Persistent drought has diminished their livestock and impoverished them further. Poverty, and the easy availability of arms, has increased banditry and insecurity. Unemployment is high. Literacy is a mere six per cent (compared with a national average of seventy per cent), diseases and child mortality are the highest in the country, and only one percent of them has ever used a telephone.

Official figures indicate that Uganda is, by a large majority, a Christian nation. The two major immigrant religions, Islam and Christianity, far exceed indigenous religions, but these figures are misleading. Most Ugandans, even after converting to Islam or Christianity, do not abandon their traditional beliefs altogether but blend them with their adopted faiths.

Uganda is fertile ground for the foundation and growth of new sects and one, The Movement for the Restoration of the Ten Commandments of God, came forcefully to attention with widely publicized stories of mass murder. Over the last decade, East Africa has been a particular focus for cult groups led by charismatic figures. Students of such movements suggest they are the response of people overwhelmed by realities they neither understand nor control. Famines, ethnic genocide of unimaginable proportions, and a devastating AIDS epidemic have left people confused and traumatized. In these circumstances communities have turned to charismatic preachers whose doomsday scenarios provide a reasonable explanation of the irrational and hold out hope of a better world to come. Such, it seems, was what the Ten Commandments Movement offered its victims.

Uganda's HIV/AIDS program has come to be viewed as a model for states affected by the pandemic. A decade ago, more than 18 percent of Ugandan adults were living with HIV/AIDS. The death of a young and productive breadwinner left many families in poverty. AIDS orphans epitomized the problem. Innocent, they suffered. Most had no access to education, labor skills, and employment. They became street kids, an urban poor; alienated and unemployed, they became a potential

**Murchison Falls**
Photo by Virginia Grady

threat to social stability. The problem was recognized early and a commitment was made to deal with it.

In many ways the program's success reflects the political culture of President Museveni's regime. Museveni has been as inclusive as possible, encouraging different actors to contribute in whatever way they could. He appointed a bishop for example, as one of the leaders of the Uganda AIDS Commission, but all the major sectarian communities participated. For its part, the Islamic Medical Association of Uganda worked with Imams to incorporate HIV/AIDS prevention information into their spiritual teachings.

Openness of discussion and commitment to education, characteristics of Museveni's rebel insurgency from the beginning, have also characterized the country's approach to AIDS. In 1988 Uganda's most famous popular singer, Philly Lutaaya, returned from Sweden after four years of political exile. In April 1989 he shocked his fans and fellow Ugandans by announcing he had AIDS. For the next eight months he led a personal crusade against AIDS. Then, at the age of 38, he died. The admission and death of so public a figure elevated HIV/AIDS to public discussion from the dark recesses of shame. Once there, action was possible.

The Uganda AIDS program is reputed to be one of the most aggressive. It features education and testing, counseling

and condoms. By far the most striking feature of Uganda's success is the drastic reduction in multiple partnering by Ugandan adults. Among women aged 15 and above, the number reporting multiple sexual partners fell from 18.4% in 1989 to 2.5% in 2000. The program is open to trials of new drugs, and indeed, nevirapine studies in Uganda showed the transmission of HIV from mother to child was reduced to about 13%.

Overall the HIV/AIDS prevalence rate in adults has declined significantly, from 18.5% in the early 1990s to 6.2% in 2003. Despite the good news, the problem remains enormous. At least 900,000 people have died of HIV/AIDS since the onset of the pandemic in the 1980s. An estimated 1.9 million Ugandans carry the HIV virus, and according to government figures released in early 2002, Uganda has an estimated 1.7 million orphans, the highest number in the world. The number is expected to rise to 3.5 million by 2010. The average life expectancy for Ugandans— just 43.2 years—is anticipated to decline to 35 in the next 10 years.

The government committed itself to offering free antiretroviral (ARV) treatment to those in urgent need as of January 2004. Between 100,000 and 120,000 patients are expected to access the drugs, with initial preference given to orphans and pregnant mothers to prevent child transmission.

Ongoing civil conflict in northern Uganda may reverse the gains made so far. As rape has increasingly become an instrument of war, high HIV infection rates among rebels and government soldiers have been found. UNICEF and government officials have reported 90% of children rescued from Lords Resistance Army rebels are HIV-positive. According to the NGO World Vision International, AIDS is killing three times more people than the ongoing war against the LRA.

**Economy:** By the time President Museveni assumed power in 1986, Uganda had become one of the poorest countries in the world. Socialist planning meant state intervention in nearly all sectors of the economy. Social services had collapsed and infrastructure had crumbled. Under President Museveni Uganda liberalized its economy and became the poster child of international lending agencies: Real GDP growth has averaged 6.7% since 1995 and was 4.7% in 2003.

Uganda's economic picture is not, however, entirely rosy. Eighteen years of warfare in the north is estimated to have cost the country 3% of its GDP and the war continues to be a drag on the economy. The government has proposed increasing defense expenditures by 19% in its 2004–05 budget, after a 48% increase over the past two years. Donors say too much is being spent already and the funds need to be allocated to poverty reduction, putting them on a collision course with the government. Economic growth is also being eroded by the effects of population growth, estimated at 3.4% a year in 2004.

Uganda's economy is agriculture based. The sector employs over 80% of the work force, and contributes about 32.4% of GDP (2003). Coffee has traditionally been the country's biggest export earner. In 1996 Uganda exported 4.15 million bags of coffee, which accounted for 65% of its export income. The expansion of coffee plantations in Asia over the past few years, however, has produced a glut of coffee on international markets and severely reduced prices. Export earnings from coffee have fallen by 80% in the last seven years—from $433 million in 1995 to a low of $84 million in 2002. Coffee now accounts for less than 30% of export earnings.

Significant efforts have been made to diversify the economy, once almost totally reliant on coffee exports. Tea remains important, though struggling to regain its former status. In 1972, Uganda produced 23,000 metric tons of tea, but by 1991, after years of neglect by the Idi Amin regime, only 8,800 tons were produced. Since then strenuous efforts have been made to reclaim some 42,000 acres that had returned to bush, and in 2002 Ugandan farmers produced 33,800 tons of tea. Tea is now Uganda's third leading export, after coffee and fish.

The government seeks to boost tea production to 40,000 metric tons by 2005, but marketing conditions are extremely difficult and the project is doubtful. The high cost of Ugandan electricity puts tea growers at a competitive disadvantage; its erratic supply also discourages investors from opening new areas for tea production. Transportation costs are also high. In March 2003 the Uganda Tea Association reported that most producers received less than they spent on production and transportation—on average about 23% less.

Another aspect of economic diversification, flowers, contributed something like $25 million to the Ugandan economy in 2002. About 5000 tons of roses, chrysanthemums and other potted plants are exported to Europe. A year-round growing season allows exporters to ship short-stemmed roses, the most popular item, to European supermarkets where they are sold in pre-made bouquets; the flowers are shipped as buds and open once they reach their final destination. Given capital start-up costs, the industry is thus far dominated by bigger companies. According to the Uganda Flower Exporters' Association, however, the real cost of starting a rose farm has declined more than 25% in the past four years, broadening industry participation to smaller-scale farmers.

Fishing and fish processing have increasing importance among Uganda's exports, especially since the EU lifted its ban (because of sanitation and pesticide concerns) on imports in 2000. In 2001 Uganda exported 28,627 tons of fish, earning about $80 million. With demand increasing among consumers trying to avoid the health risks of red meat, the country earned more in 2002—$87.5 million—from less tonnage—25,159 tons.

The fishing industry still faces many challenges. Pesticide poisoning of lakes is related to a longer range but potentially even more damaging problem: the water hyacinth. Probably brought in by Belgians as an ornamental plant, the hyacinth has no known natural predators and, like a cancer, grows with amazing rapidity. The whole of Lake Victoria, the world's second largest fresh-water lake, is threatened. Once colonized, the plant impedes fishing boats and can ultimately kill off the entire fish stock.

Already, 70,000 tons of hyacinth press against the outer walls of Uganda's Owen Falls hydroelectric dam, 80 km east of Kampala, which supplies electricity to Kenya and Tanzania. Engineers wonder how much weight it can take. Thus far spraying aquatic herbicides directly onto the plants has been the most effective method of reducing weed infestation quickly.

There are plans afoot to construct a $530 million hydroelectric dam that would drown Bujagali Falls near the source of the Nile River. The World Bank approved financial assistance up to $225 million in later 2001, and by May 2004 the government had a short list of five bidders on the project. Environmentalists have argued mightily against the dam, arguing the site supports the growing whitewater tourism industry and long term is a serious "hydrological risk," given the potential for

serious drought due to global climate change.

Two areas of potential growth should be mentioned: honey and oil. The first shipments of Ugandan honey, really little more than samples, have already reached markets in the Middle East and Europe. High quality and untainted by the antibiotics that got Chinese honey banned from Europe, Ugandan honey should have little trouble passing the EU's strict organic requirements. The product is far from being commercialized however.

In early April 2003, the Canadian firm, Heritage Oil, announced that its explorations suggested Uganda had a potential oil reserve of "several billion barrels." Test drilling has yet to occur.

In April 1998 Uganda's stellar economic performance was recognized by the World Bank and International Monetary Fund. The country was the first to qualify for the Bank's Highly Indebted Poor Countries (HIPC) project, and the lending institutions agreed to cut Uganda's $3.4 billion debt by about one fifth. By 2001, however, the proposed benefits of the HIPC debt cancellation had to be questioned. By 2002 it was clear the project had failed.

A survey conducted by the Uganda National Bureau of Statistics between August 1999 and August 2000 indicated that the number of Ugandans living in absolute poverty had fallen 9%, from 44% of the population to 35%. Urban areas experienced a much larger drop than rural areas, and there were regional variations. In the North, poverty levels *increased* from 60% in 1997/98 to 65%.

Even more striking a challenge to proposed HIPC benefits was the growth of Uganda's debt stock. When included in the HIPC program, Uganda's debt was recorded at $3.4 billion. In 2002, after the program's cancellation of more than $1 billion of indebtedness, Uganda's debt stock had risen to $4.1 billion. Little wonder civil society was lobbying for greater input into how the program would operate. By 2003 debt stock had dropped to $3.938 billion.

**The Future:** A bit rocky. Uganda's economic development is still dependent on external aid, and lender hesitancy, if not refusal, will persist until political pluralism becomes an operative reality. A Museveni candidacy for the presidency in 2006 could heighten tensions and increase investor uncertainty. Success for his Movement in a multiparty environment will largely depend on the president's ability to curb corruption, diminish civil strife and contain regional conflict. Restructuring and re-professionalizing Uganda's army will be a major element in each of these.

**Coffee berries**

# SOUTH SAHARA AFRICA

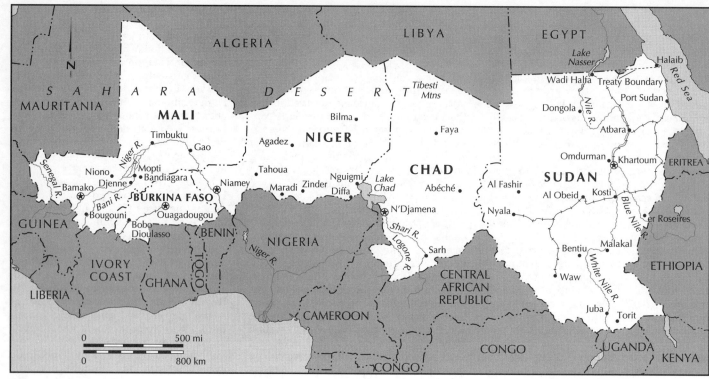

# Burkina Faso

**Area:** 274,540 sq. km. = 106,000 sq. mi. (slightly larger than Colorado).

**Population:** 13,925,313 (July 2005 est.)

**Capital City:** Ouagadougou. Pronounced Wah-gah-doo-goo.

**Climate:** Cooler and drier (November–March); warm and dry (March–May); warm with variable rainfall (June–October).

**Neighboring Countries:** Mali (West and North); Niger (East); Benin (Southeast); Togo, Ghana, Côte d'Ivoire (South).

**Official Language:** French.

**Other Principal Languages:** Bissa, Bobo, Fulfulde, Gourmanchéma, Jula, Lobi, Mòoré, Tamajek.

**Ethnic groups:** Mossi about 47%, Gurunsi, Senufo, Lobi, Bobo, Mande, Fulani, Tuareg.

**Principal Religions:** Indigenous beliefs 40%, Muslim 50%, Christian (mainly Roman Catholic) 10%.

**Chief Commercial Products:** cotton, animal products, gold.

**GNI per capita:** $300 (2003)

**Currency:** CFA Franc (no longer tied to the French franc).

**Former Colonial Status:** French Colony (1896–1932); part of Ivory Coast, Niger and French Soudan (1932–1957); French Overseas Territory (1958–1960).

**Independence Date:** August 5, 1960.

**Chief of State:** Blaise Compaoré, President.

**National Flag:** Horizontal red and green stripes with a yellow five–pointed star in center.

This country of gently rolling hills, north of the hot, steamy equatorial zone, with an average altitude of 800 feet, has a comparatively pleasant climate. The tall grass of the plains and the green forest grow rapidly during the usual wet season from May to November in years of normal rainfall. Almost daily rains are usually short thunderstorms—the rest of the day during these months is warm and sunny.

Toward the end of November, the rains become less frequent and finally almost cease altogether. The grasses of the plains which have risen to heights of six feet turn brown, waiting to be consumed by localized brush fires.

A drier area is found in the North and Northwest, which is a transition zone between the plains and the hot Sahara further north. It is from this great desert that the *harmattan* (the hot wind of the dry season) comes, covering the whole country. The rivers of Burkina Faso, the Black, Red and White Voltas, and the tributaries of the Niger in the East—are not navigable. Travel to and from land–locked Burkina Faso is principally over the railway from Ouagadougou through Bobo–Dioulasso to Abidjan in Côte d'Ivoire.

**History:** More than 800 years ago, great numbers of conquering horsemen, the Mossi, penetrated a small region in the southeast of Burkina Faso, subduing the passive farmers of the plateau. They established a feudalistic system based on collective leadership.

The Mende and Bobo, related groups, have been in this country for centuries. Legend does not indicate the time of origin of the several other groups of Burkina Faso.

Although the Mossi became peaceful farmers through the centuries, they were able to forcefully defeat efforts of the Islamic people of the North to conquer them and convert them to Islam. The Arab Berbers, however, presented a continuing threat. For details of early and colonial history, see *Historical Background* and *The French in Africa*.

A treaty was signed in 1960 granting what was then Upper Volta independence from France. A new constitution was adopted, taking effect in that year. Upper Volta was governed by a president elected for a five–year term, and a 75–member National Assembly, both elected by universal suffrage. The constitution provided for a separate judiciary. Maurice Yaméogo's Volta Democratic Union captured all the seats of the Assembly and he became the first president. Although quite popular, a combination of corruption and adverse economic conditions, including high unemployment, led to his downfall. Col. Sangoulé Lamizana assumed charge; Yaméogo was tried and imprisoned in 1969, but was released in 1971.

Col. Lamizana was a burly, imposing figure with tribal scars on his cheeks. A devout Muslim, he made a pilgrimage to the city of Mecca. He appeared to be making progress toward restoring civilian rule, but in 1970 a constitution was adopted providing that he serve for a transition period of four years; thereafter the president would be elected.

When 1974 arrived, president Lamizana dissolved the legislature, appointed himself to the additional positions of prime minister and army chief of staff, and declared Upper Volta a single–party state. In 1977 Upper Voltans voted to return to civilian rule—and for political parties to be allowed to resume their activities. Unsurprisingly, General Lamizana was elected to a seven–year term of office.

During the next two years Upper Volta plunged to economic depths. Corruption was rampant, and persistent drought impoverished the populace further. Opposition parties were squeezed out of existence, but a powerful labor movement remained. Massive strikes paralyzed the country in 1980. The military looked on with increasing alarm as the government floundered and finally intervened, placing the president under house arrest.

The leader of the bloodless coup was Lamizana's former foreign minister, Colonel Saye Zerbo, who was immediately proclaimed President of the Military Committee for Reformation and National Progress—and chief of state. Rivalries within the army produced two further coups, one in 1982 and one in August 1983 when Capt. Thomas Sankara became President of the National Council for the Revolution (CNR).

Committees for the Defense of the Revolution (CDRs) were organized to implement the CNR's Marxist-Leninist programs. Sankara himself adopted romantic austerity and self-denial as a central part of his self-image. Virtually his only possessions were his guitar and his used car, a tiny Renault 5, which he chose as the official vehicle for his whole government. By word and deed the charismatic Sankara sought to lead and mobilize, but personal revolutionary idealism alone was insufficient. The CDRs, organized as popular mass organizations, deteriorated into gangs of armed thugs and clashed with several trade unions. Revolutionary People's Courts too often resembled a Robespierrean reign of terror. Fear and resistance grew. On October 15, 1987, Sankara was assassinated, in an action directed by his friend and colleague, Blaise Compaoré. The man who had created modern Burkina Faso was unceremoniously buried in a common grave in Ouagadougou. Only later were his remains moved and the grave given a proper headstone. Years afterwards followers regularly leave flowers, and Sankara has become an icon for youthful Africans who have dubbed him "Che Sankara." Like the famous Che poster, Sankara's thin, mustachioed features grace stickers that appear on motorcycles, taxis and trucks throughout West Africa.

Compaoré, along with two other members of the CNR, Jean-Baptiste Boukary Lengani and Henri Zongo, formed the Popular Front (FP) to continue the revolution; its principal constituent was the leftist Organization for Popular Democracy/ Labor Movement (ODP/MT). Recognizing the discontent aroused by the more extreme of Sankara's policies, Compaoré moderated them and opened the Front to non-Marxist organizations. In September 1989, while he was returning from an Asian trip, Lengani and Zongo were accused of plotting the overthrow of the Popular Front. Arrested, they were summarily executed the same night.

The Popular Front drafted a new constitution, that of Burkina Faso's Fourth Republic, in 1990; it was ratified by referendum in 1991. Compaoré resigned from the army to contest December's presidential elections. He was elected without opposition, but nearly 75% of eligible voters simply stayed home on election day. The ODP/MT won a majority of legislative seats in 1992 elections, and in February 1996, it merged with several smaller opposition groups to form the Congress of Democracy and Progress (CDP).

In early 1997 the CDP used its parliamentary majority to amend the constitu-

**Ouagadougou's monument to film makers**       Photo by Andy Trimlett

251

# Burkina Faso

**President Blaise Compaoré**

tion, eliminating the provision that limited Burkina Faso's president to two terms. The opposition futilely protested the amendment would institute lifelong political power. The deposit required of presidential candidates was also increased, from two million CFA francs ($4,000) to five million CFA francs—about $10,000. Parliament also recognized world changes following the collapse of the Soviet Union by purging the constitution of such Sankara-era terminology as "the people," and "the toiling masses."

Legislative elections held in 1997 resulted in a huge CDP majority—101 out of 111 seats, but only 44% of voters responded to the electoral call. The October 1998 presidential elections posed few problems for President Compaoré, who was easily returned to office. The opposition boycotted the elections, and the only question was really about how many voters would even bother. President Compaoré needed a big enough turnout to retain his credibility, especially after the dismal participation rate seven years previously. When the results came in, Compaoré won nearly 88% of the vote. According to official figures, 56% of registered voters participated.

## Two deaths that shook the nation

President Compaoré's inauguration in December was darkened by the mysterious death of Burkina Faso's most prominent journalist, Norbert Zongo, the managing editor of the weekly *Independent*. Celebrated for his hard–hitting critiques of the regime, Zongo (actually the pen name of Henri Segbo) was known as "the Incorruptible." His charred body was found, along with three others, in the burned out wreckage of an automobile. The exterior of the auto showed no signs of fire damage; the victims had been shot with 12-caliber bullets and given a *coup de*

*grace* with a 357 Magnum. Zongo's death rocked the nation, prompting a wave of violent protests which continued through the spring. The president was forced to create an independent national commission of inquiry to examine the more-than-suspicious death. Places on the commission were reserved for representatives of the international press, human rights organizations, and members of the victims' families. Representatives of the ministries of Security, Defense and Justice joined them. Even before the work of the Commission was completed the details began to leak out confirming the widespread belief that Zongo was the victim of a political assassination. Noting "contradictions and incoherence" in the testimony of members of the Presidential Guard, the commission pointed to them as "serious suspects" in the case.

The commission's report linked Zongo's assassination to his exposé of the earlier murder of a chauffeur assigned to President Compaoré's younger brother, François. The evidence indicated that David Ouédraogo, the chauffeur, had been involved with three others in the theft of money from the younger Compaoré's wife. All four had been taken, on the order of François Compaoré, to a security prison and subjected to the most grotesque of tortures, both psychological and physical. They were then taken out and forced to dig their own graves, lined up before a firing squad, and subjected to the terror of mock execution. Ouédraogo himself reportedly died of the effects of torture, which included being roasted alive.

Norbert Zongo's reporting and demand for justice made him a popular hero, and an enemy of the state. His assassination exposed the dark side of the Compaoré regime and generated vociferous demands that "impunity" for killers not be tolerated.

The controversy forced a presidential transformation. The president seemed to look inward and developed a kinder, gentler image. Two weeks after the commission of inquiry's report was issued, the president appointed a College of Sages to

**Mosque, Bobo-Dioulasso**

Photo by Andy Trimlett

recommend action to end the political crisis. The sixteen-member council was headed by the Bishop of Bobo-Dioulasso and consisted of three former heads of state, eight religious and traditional leaders and three "resource persons." Acting with dispatch, the group asked for the arrest of all those implicated in the death of David Ouédraogo. The next day, three members of the presidential guard close to President Compaoré were detained in Ouagadougou and charged for murder of François Compaoré's driver.

In August 2000, a military tribunal met to hear the case against five members of the *Régiment de la sécurité présidentielle* (Presidential Guard) charged with David Ouédraogo's murder. Three, including the Guard's former head, Marcel Kafando, were quickly found guilty and sentenced to long jail terms. In addition, the three were ordered to pay a staggering fine of 200 million CFA in damages to the Ouédraogo family—nearly $270,000. Outside the courtroom, more than three thousand people gathered to denounce the trial as a miscarriage of justice, given the absence of the principal suspect, Francois Compaoré.

In early February 2001 the government acted to quell continuing unrest over the Zongo affair. Burkina Faso's attorney general announced the indictment of Marcel Kafando, the former head of the Presidential Guard, for murder and arson in the journalist's death, but there was little movement on the case until October 2003, when a number of soldiers were arrested for attempting a *coup d'état*. One of them, Sergeant Naon Babou of the presidential security regiment, reported that two others had been contacted to participate in Zongo's murder, but refused. As of early 2005 the investigation is "continuing."

To deal with on-going agitation over the murder, the government orchestrated a "national day of forgiveness" in late March 2001. The event had been recommended by the College of Sages to assuage years of public anger. By any standard of evaluation, it was a remarkable event.

Standing before a crowd of 30,000 Burkinabé in a local stadium, President Compaoré delivered an unprecedented apology for crimes against the populace. "I ask for pardon," he said, "and express deep regret for tortures, crimes, injustices, bullying and other wrongs."

The new mood in Burkinabé politics was manifest in the parliamentary elections of May 2002. They were organized by an Independent National Electoral Commission (CENI), a first for the country. The government agreed to finance political parties, and electoral law was changed to elect members of the legislature by pro-

portional representation. For the first time a single ballot listing all the competing parties was employed, with color photographs. To ensure electoral honesty, transparent ballot boxes, some of which had to be borrowed from neighboring Benin, were used. The CENI also hired 2,000 observers to supervise the election. The cost of all this was a hefty $9.2 million.

The inducements to electoral participation worked. Some 1,740 candidates, representing 30 political parties, entered the competition. Given a fair chance, the opposition scored strongly against the incumbent party. President Compaoré's ruling Congress for Democracy and Progress (CDP) dropped from 101 seats to 57 in Burkina Faso's 111-member parliament.

Of the 54 seats won by the opposition, Hermann Yaméogo's Alliance for Democracy and Federation/African Democratic Rally (ADF/RDA) obtained 17, while the Party for Democracy and Progress/Socialist Party (PDP/PS) of Joseph Ki-Zerbo won 10. The remaining 27 seats went to 10 other opposition parties—seven of them to "Sankarist" parties which claimed to uphold the revolutionary ideals of the young army captain.

If the 2002 elections pointed to a more difficult time for President Compaoré, the September rebellion in neighboring Côte d'Ivoire that year changed the president's political fortunes even more. He proved an effective manager of the economic crisis that followed the closing of rail connections between the two countries. Successful appeals were made to international donors, and the return of over 300,000 Burkinabé, violently driven from their homes and despoiled of their property in a frenzy of Ivoirian xenophobia, was adroitly handled.

Offended honor produced patriotic sentiment, and Burkinabé rallied around their president. Internal opponents were silenced, and the president emerged more firmly in charge of the domestic scene than he had been in several years.

His active leadership of poor cotton-producing countries, opposing subsidies to American and EU cotton farmers that impoverished African growers, restored him to the good graces of his regional colleagues. Forgotten were memories of his involvement in the lethal exchange of arms for diamonds that fueled destructive conflict in West Africa and Angola. With those wars ended, an intransigent Laurent Gbagbo, Côte d'Ivoire's president, seemed the greater threat to regional stability.

Although there has been no official announcement of his candidacy, President Compaoré will no doubt be a candidate to succeed himself in the November 2005 presidential elections. By mid-year at least seven opposition candidates had an-

nounced their intentions to run. Twelve Burkinabé opposition parties have grouped themselves into a loose alliance called *Alternance 2005*. The alliance is putting up three candidates: Hermann Yaméogo, of the National Union for Democracy and Development (UNDD); Bénéwendé Sankara, of the Union for Rebirth/Sankaraist Movement (UNIR/MS); and Philippe Ouédraogo of the African Party for Independence (PAI). Its primary objective is to force a run-off election. If that were to occur, the two candidates who had the least votes would ask their supporters to vote for the most successful of the three.

**Culture:** Since 1969 Burkina Faso has taken the art of film to heart with gusto and enthusiasm. Indeed, it's probably the only country that's given film-makers their own public monument. Ouagadougou, Burkina's capital and largest city, is the site of the important biennial Pan-African Festival of African Cinema and Television, more simply known as Fespaco. The 19th festival was held in early 2005 and exhibited 170 films to eager viewers. This year the South African director Zola Maseko won the festival's top prize—the Yennenga Stallion, worth about $20,000—for his film *Drum*. Set amid the jazz clubs and bars of Johannesburg in the 1950s, *Drum* centers on a determined reporter and his clashes with South Africa's apartheid regime.

The Burkinabé architect Diébédo Francis Kéré won the prestigious Aga Khan Award for Architecture in 2004 for his design of a primary school in Gando. While an architecture student in Berlin Kéré set up a fund-raising association to ensure a school for his natal village. Local government agencies provided funding to train brickmakers in working with compressed stabilized earth, and actual construction of the school was carried out by the village's men, women, and children. The building was honored for designing climatic comfort with low-cost construction, making the most of local materials and the potential of the local community, and adapting technology from the industrialized world to local conditions.

The United Nations estimates that anywhere from 2.7% to 6.5% of adults in Burkina Faso are infected with the AIDS virus (2003), the highest rate in West Africa. Infection rates are much higher in urban centers, and combating the disease is government priority. At the high end there are an estimated 370,000 AIDS orphans; 42% of all rural households and 45% of all urban ones include an orphan. Life expectancy was only 42.9 years in 2003, but inevitably it would push lower as a consequence of HIV/AIDS.

# Burkina Faso

Burkina Faso is one of 16 African countries that have outlawed Female Genital Mutilation (FGM). Anyone removing a girl's clitoris risks a fine of $1,800 and a prison term of three years; if a victim dies as a result of the operation, the prison term can rise to 10 years. The government has established a national telephone hotline in the fight the procedure and points with pride to statistical results in the ten-year battle: when the anti-FGM law first went into effect, around two-thirds of Burkinabé girls were being circumcised; now only 35 percent to 40 percent are victimized.

**Economy:** Following the assassination of Thomas Sankara, the government began a slow liberalization of a socialist economy. Cumbersome regulations, price controls and widespread government involvement in productive sectors, all of which were a brake on private investment, were eliminated. Some state companies have been privatized and the economy is now more open to market forces. It remains, however, dependent on agricultural production, which represents some 31% of GDP (2003). Over 80% of the population is engaged in subsistence agriculture completely dependent on weather conditions. In 2004 the annual grain harvest was reduced by 90% in some places because of a severe locust outbreak and poor rains.

Cotton remains the most important money earner, traditionally accounting for as much as 60% to 70% of export revenues. Around 700,000 people are actively engaged in cotton growing; their work directly sustains some 2.5 million people, about one out of five Burkinabé.

There is much concern over the effects of the 2002 U.S. Farm Act that protects American farmers from depressed international market prices. With these protections uneconomic farms can dump raw and ginned cotton onto world markets with impunity, leaving key African producers like Burkina Faso with little market demand and lowered prices. President Compaoré led the public assault on rich-country cotton subsidies at world trade meetings in Geneva and Cancun, Mexico, in 2003.

The country remains desperately poor, ranking 175 out of 177 countries on the UN's 2004 *Human Development Index* (just above Niger and Sierra Leone). It has long been an important labor reserve for neighboring countries. Burkina Faso's migrant workers, who annually fan out across West Africa in search of employment, traditionally send back remittances that contribute about 5% to GDP, but were reduced by the crisis in Côte d'Ivoire.

Overall, some 3 million Burkinabé lived at one time in Côte d'Ivoire, but recently several thousand have fallen victim to rising anti-foreigner sentiment there. Countless Burkinabé homes were destroyed, and Ouagadougou has announced that over 300,000 of its citizens have returned home since 19 September 2002, when a rebel war broke out there. The economic impact of Ivoirian xenophobia has been significant for Burkina's economy.

The country's commerce was deeply affected. Landlocked, Burkina Faso is dependent on Côte d'Ivoire's ports for 80% of its exports and 60% to 70% of its imports. All basic items such as soap, salt, cooking oil and rice, either imported from or produced in Côte d'Ivoire, transit through the port of Abidjan. When the crisis broke out Burkinabé imports blocked at Abidjan port had to be rerouted to Lomé, Tema, and Cotonou, adding increased transports costs. Prices rose, shortages of raw materials appeared, and exports to Côte d'Ivoire ceased.

With the border closure Burkina Faso lost its largest market for beef, goats and sheep—the second pillar of its economy. Sixty per cent of the country's cattle used to be sold in Côte d'Ivoire. The cattle industry claimed it had lost about $17 million between September and December 2002. The government estimated the country had lost more than $30 million in revenues and customs duties during the same period.

The country is rich in gold reserves and a new mining code, adopted in May 2003, is designed to make investment in the sector more attractive. A number of mining projects are still in the planning stages and could become operating mines within the next five years, or sooner, given the recent spike in gold prices.

Burkinabé industry is rudimentary, consisting mainly of cotton and agricultural product transformation. Any industrial development is utterly dependent on electricity, water, and good roads, all of which are in short supply. Bobo Dioulasso, the country's second city, has long been its economic capital, but 100% of Bobo's electricity comes from Côte d'Ivoire. It was the only product not affected by the crisis. There are plans to connect Bobo and Ouagadougou and send any surplus energy to the capital after 2005. Similarly, there are plans to connect Burkina with Ghana's electrical grid by a 127-mile line, but that's not expected to be in operation before 2012.

With its population expanding exponentially, Ouagadougou experiences regular water shortages. The government is preparing a storage dam at Ziga, some 32 miles northeast of the city. The reservoir, originally planned in 1998, will hold 200 million cubic meters of water. When completed in 2006, the dam's capacity will already have been outstripped by urban needs.

In April 2002 Burkina Faso was certified by the IMF and World Bank as having completed the requirements for admission to the Heavily Indebted Poor Countries (HIPC) initiative. It means debt relief for about 50% of the country's stock of debt over the long term. As of 2003 that debt amounted to $1.845 billion.

**Future:** President Compaoré is well situated to succeed himself in the 2005 elections. His management of the country's economic crisis, coupled with the remarkable flexibility of its citizens, has limited its negative impact and rallied popular sentiment in his favor. The opposition is divided and is likely to provide little effective competition.

**Primary school, Gando. Designed by Diébédo Francis Kéré winner of the Aga Khan Award for Architecture in 2004.**
Photo courtesy AKDN

# The Republic of Chad

**Tibesti Region, Northern Chad**

**Area:** 1,284,640 sq. km. = 496,000 sq. mi. (the size of Texas, New Mexico and Arizona).

**Population:** 9,826,419 (July 2005 est.)

**Capital City:** N'Djaména

**Climate:** Dry desert in the North varies from 10° to 122°F.; the central and southern areas are warm with increasing rainfall and humidity in the South, where there is a six-month dry season.

**Neighboring Countries:** Cameroon (South-west); Niger and Nigeria (West); Libya (North); The Sudan (East); Central African Republic (Southeast and South).

**Official Languages:** French and Arabic.

**Other Principal Languages:** Over 100, including Gulay, Kanuri, Karanda, Maba, Marba, Marfa, Masana, Mundang, Musey, Ngambay, Sango (a Creole trade language), and Sar.

**Ethnic groups:** Muslims: (Arabs, Toubou, Hadjerai, Fulbe, Kotoko, Kanembou, Baguirmi, Boulala, Zaghawa, and Maba). Non-Muslims: (Sara, Ngambaye, Mbaye, Goulaye, Moundang, Moussei, Massa). Nonindigenous: 150,000 (of whom an estimated 1,000 are French).

**Principal Religions:** Muslim 51%, Christian 35%, animist 7%, other 7%.

**Chief Commercial Products:** Cotton, cattle, and textiles.

**GNI per capita:** $250 (2003)

**Currency:** CFA franc (no longer tied to the French franc).

**Former Colonial Status:** French Colony (1910–1960).

**Independence Date:** August 11, 1960.

**Chief of State:** Idriss Déby, President.

**National Flag:** Three vertical stripes of blue, gold and red.

Landlocked Chad, more than 1,500 miles from any seaport, lies almost in the center of Africa and is one of the transitional nations between the desert to the north and the fertile southern area of the continent. For centuries it has been the crossroads of traders going back and forth between the Sahara-Mediterranean Sea region and the tropical areas of West Africa. Contact with Muslim traders may explain the conversion of some populations living in the Sahel region to Islam as early as the 9th century, before the arrival of nomadic Arab tribes.

Although Chad resembles a shallow basin in which Lake Chad, a former inland sea, occupies the "drain" position to the west, topographically it has three distinct regions. The Chadian Sahara in the North is a land of dry desert sand dunes gently rising to a height of 12,000 feet above sea level in the Tibesti Mountains. Only 1.2% of the population of Chad, mostly tribal nomads, inhabits this area. The endless expanse of desert, scorching by day, sinks to below freezing levels at night.

The central portion is a semi-arid land of treeless plains; this section traditionally has received just enough rainfall to support cattle raising, but experiences periodic devastating droughts. The green southern area, with more ample rainfall, supports 45% of the country's population, who engage in cotton cultivation.

The Lake Chad Basin is shared by five countries. Fed by the Shari and Logone Rivers in the southwest corner of the nation, Lake Chad was once one of Africa's largest lakes. The area of this immense lake has been drying up and is now a mere fraction of its former size.

**History:** There is evidence of settlements by Negroid peoples as early as Neolithic times. These populations were gradually modified by migrations of nomadic people, increasingly Arabized, from the north. Various Muslim kingdoms successively established control over the area, including, in the 18th century, the Arab dynasty of Ouaddaï. The prosperity of these Muslim states was largely based on slave raiding among animist populations living in the south. Captured slaves were transported to Egypt and the East.

France became active in the area in the late nineteenth century, and Chad became part of the federation of French Equatorial Africa in 1910. Under provisions of the constitution of the French Fifth Republic, Chad became an autonomous republic within the French Community in November 1958. Full independence was achieved in August 1960. For details of early and colonial history, see *Historical Background* and *The French in Africa*.

At independence, the country was deeply divided between the black and often Christian populations of the more fertile and economically developed southwest, and the Arabized Muslim populations of the north. The south was more receptive to colonial rule; French language and culture were introduced. The north rejected any education that did not include the teaching of Arabic and the Koran. Similarly, Christian missionaries made numerous converts in the south, increased educational opportunities, and improved healthcare. Cotton cultivation was introduced and the south became economically successful, leading the colonizer to call the south "useful." Content to look backward, the north experienced stagnation; its economy evolved little and the colonizer came to think of it as "useless."

At independence, the country's first president was a southerner, François (later Ngarta) Tombalbaye, a teacher and trade union leader. In 1963, Tombalbaye dissolved all political parties except his own *Parti progressiste tchadien* (PPT) and increasingly repressed both his fellow southerners and northerners. Northern Muslims coalesced behind the Chadian National Liberation Front (Frolinat) and rebelled against the central government. What started as reaction against the banning of political parties in 1963 turned into civil war by 1966.

Frolinat operated primarily in the north with the support of Libya, where it maintained bases. It advocated closer ties with the Arab states of North Africa and a reduction of French influence in Chad. French military forces stationed in Chad were brought in to suppress the revolt in 1973, but Frolinat continued its guer-

# Chad

rilla operations with the help of Libyan weapons.

Tombalbaye accused the French of trying to unseat him in July 1973, and, in reaction, pursued an "Africanization" program. The single party was renamed National Movement for Cultural and Social Revolution; the use of Christian forenames was abolished (the president dropping "François" for Ngarta) as was the use of French names for streets and places—except for Avenue Charles de Gaulle in the capital Fort Lamy (renamed N'Djaména). Economic conditions worsened and dissatisfaction increased, especially among the military.

In 1975 President Tombalbaye was killed by his own southern officers and replaced by another southerner, Colonel Félix Malloum. By this time Frolinat had split (a continuing tradition among northern groups) into two factions, one willing to accept support from Libya under Goukouni Oueddeï, (pronounced Weh-day), and an anti-Libyan faction headed by Hissène Habré (pronounced Ah-bray). To unify a divided country, Col. Malloum agreed to share power with Habré, but the coalition was short-lived.

Malloum and Habré soon split, and, after losing a violent power struggle, Malloum was forced to flee N'Djaména in 1979. Northern faction leaders formed a coalition government headed Goukouni Oueddeï, with Hissène Habré as prime minister. From this point Chad's civil conflict became less between north and south than a struggle among northern warlords.

French forces were asked to leave the country in May 1980; most Europeans went with them, and the U.S. Embassy was closed. The streets of N'Djaména became a no-man's land as the armies of Oueddeï and Habré struggled for supremacy. Libya offered military help to Oueddeï's beleaguered forces, and from December 1980 to November 1981 Libya occupied most of the country. Habré's rebels, unable to compete with well-equipped Libyans, faded into eastern Chad to await a better opportunity to seize power.

Oueddeï asked Libyan forces to leave in late 1981, and when they had gone, Habré saw his chance. Within days his troops had seized a large part of the country, and he was on his way to an easy victory over Oueddeï. OAU peace-keeping forces moved into Chad and checked the rebel advance, driving Habré back to eastern Chad.

Life in N'Djaména temporarily returned to a semblance of order, but in mid-1982 Habré swept out of eastern Chad and, amid bitter fighting, seized the capital. The OAU troops remained neutral, Oueddeï escaped to Cameroon, and Hissène Habré declared himself president. The OAU recognized Habré's government, and its troops withdrew by the end of June. Brought to power by violence, Habré would rule with cruelty and terror. Neither brought stability.

With Libyan help, Oueddeï continued to resist the N'Djaména government, while France and Zaïre supported Habré. With destructive forces evenly balanced, fighting became sporadic after early 1984. Diplomatic mediation remained fruitless given Chad's endemic factionalism.

When Libyan forces began building an airfield at Ouadi (Wadi) Doum in the northern desert, the French responded. The airfield was hit, and N'Djaména was bombed by a Libyan plane the next day. Then came the surprise: Oueddeï announced his resignation as head of the rebels, and declared his solidarity with Hissène Habré. Libya promptly placed him under arrest in Tripoli. This left Col. Qadhafi the sponsor of a revolution without a leader. Ouaddeï's rebels simply deserted the cause. With French assistance, the Chadian army struck Libyan units in northern Chad with devastating effect. By 1987 Libya had been forced out of the entire northern region, apart from the Aouzou strip and parts of Tibesti. (The International Court of Justice finally awarded the Aouzou Strip to Chad in 1994 and all Libyan forces withdrew from the territory a few months later.) About $1 billion in Soviet armaments was abandoned by the fleeing army. Habré regained control of N'Djaména in November 1988, but proved unable to master the country's divisive factionalism.

In April 1989, Idriss Déby, one of Habré's leading generals, defected and fled to Sudan, from whence he invaded the country in November 1990. On December 2, his troops entered war-exhausted N'Djaména without battle, President Habré and the forces loyal to him having fled. A national charter was approved by Déby's Patriotic Salvation Movement (MPS) in February 1991, and Déby became the latest Chadian president. Since then President Déby has maintained a fragile, always intermittent, peace. Armed rebels have been offered amnesty and integration into the national armed forces; opposition political parties have been co-opted and their leaders given ministerial appointments. But as soon as one group reconciles with the government, a discontented faction hives off, or another group seems to spring up.

One could see the absence of Chadian unity in terms of a north/south division. Northerners are Arabized pastoralists with a long warrior tradition. Southerners are sedentary and Christianized, long subject to slaving raids by their northern neighbors. In reality, Chad's conflicts have as much to do with a vision of power and the nature of the state. Once lodged in N'Djaména, the group in power imposes a centralized view of the state and its authority, snuffing out resistance and denying individuality. In a situation where there are over 200 different ethnic groups to be satisfied, a more reasonable course might involve greater decentralization and localized autonomy. But the central government has usually rejected federalism, seeing it as a loss of power and control over the meager resources available.

**Cattle herding**   ©Photographie Michel Hasson

256

The country's first free, multiparty presidential elections were held in June 1996. Idriss Déby won nearly 70% of the vote in a run-off election in July, vigorously protested by the 14 other candidates who had run against him. In the 1997 legislative elections, Déby's MPS fell short of an outright majority, winning only 55 of 125 seats. The Union for Renewal and Democracy (URD)—the party of his southern presidential rival General Wadal Abdelkader Kamougué—won 31. Kamougué rallied to the government and was elected speaker of the National Assembly. As part of the calculus of coalition, Déby also appointed a southerner as prime minister.

The south remained restive, and by 1997 there was a resurgence of factional resistance. At issue was the development of a major oil field, and, once again, the question of who controls resources and how they will be used. To highlight demands for greater participation in making those decisions, groups resorted to kidnapping Europeans.

Once President Déby had resolved things with southerners, one saw an upsurge of kidnappings in the North. By October 1998, it was apparent that there was yet another northern rebel movement to deal with. Led by a former defense minister, Youssouf Togoïmi, the *Mouvement pour la démocratie et la justice au Tchad* (MDJT) was centered in the sparsely populated Tibesti region—a mountainous, semi-desert area ideal for guerrilla warfare. It is also one of the most heavily mined areas in the world, with thousands of anti-tank and anti-personnel mines left over from the days of Chad's war with Libya.

The war continued through 2001 at considerable cost to the government. Libya offered mediation and ultimately got the two sides to sign peace deal ending three years of conflict. The accord provided for an immediate ceasefire, release of prisoners, rebel integration into the national army, and "government jobs" for MDJT leaders.

Tactically, the accord gave the MDJT, reportedly suffering from major re-supply difficulties, a badly needed breathing space. The government, needing political stability to assure financing of the Doba oil project and smooth spring parliamentary elections, fulfilled its obligations. Parliament voted an amnesty bill for the rebels in February and political prisoners were released. The country looked as though it were heading for its spring parliamentary elections in an atmosphere of uncharacteristic calm.

Things broke down in discussions on the specifics of those "government jobs." Youssouf Togoïmi demanded nothing less than the premiership, a position rejected by the government as "unconstitutional." The rebels themselves seemed to be divided. Intransigents supported Togoïmi in rejecting the agreement, but his deputy, Adoum Togoi, a former ambassador to Libya and reputedly close to the Libyans, argued for it. For his troubles, Togoi was briefly jailed.

In September 2002, Togoïmi died in a Libyan hospital after having been badly mauled in a landmine explosion. With its leader dead, the MDJT remains divided, split between a military high command hostile to President Déby and a political branch in exile more willing to negotiate. Each in turn has vexed the government.

The MDJT military wing asserted its awkward presence in the Spring of 2004 when it announced it had captured fleeing members of an Algerian terrorist group. Known in French as *Groupe armé salafiste pour la prédication et le combat* (GSPC), the terrorists were part of an Algerian Islamist organization wanted in connection with the kidnapping of several European tourists the year before.

As part of a State Department-sponsored program called the Pan-Sahel Initiative, the U.S. military was working with local security forces in Algeria, Chad, Mali, Niger, Mauritania to capture or kill members of the Salafist group. GSPC members were detected at the Niger-Chad border and engaged by the Chadian army, which killed several. Those who survived fled to rugged mountains of Tibesti where they were captured by MDJT soldiers.

The capture posed delicate diplomatic and logistical problems for the governments wanting the Salafists: to deal directly with the MDJT would insult Chadian authorities, who had identified them as terrorists; to accept them from the MDJT, without government approval, would violate international law. No diplomat wanted to enter the area anyway, so unsafe was it. When asked to bring their captives to the Niger border, even the MDJT admitted the territory was so dangerous even they could not provide security. A resolution came when Libya successfully negotiated with the MDJT to hand over Ammari Saifi (aka Abderezak El Para) the Salafist leader. He was extradited to Algeria in October 2004 and there awaits trial.

The MDJT conflict is one example of Chad's highly fragmented political culture and the inability of N'Djaména to project its authority throughout the country. These problems were background to two important elections. In May 2001 presidential balloting, Déby won a controversial first round victory over six opponents. Chad's Constitutional Council verified the final results: Déby, 67.17% of the votes. His nearest competitor, long-time

**President Idriss Déby**

critic and opponent Ngarlejy Yorongar, only polled 16.35%.

EU observers regretted the "numerous defects and irregularities" that were observed. The government had restricted campaigning, used force to prevent demonstrations, and violently (but briefly) arrested opposition candidates. Threat, intimidation, and violence also characterized the April 2002 legislative elections, with similar success. President Déby's ruling Patriotic Salvation Movement (MPS) took 112 of the 155 seats, assuring him of a solid legislative majority and enough to amend Chad's constitution.

The elections suggested President Déby was a man firmly in power, but power is often illusional in Chad. When civil conflict broke out in the Darfur region of neighboring Sudan, it nearly ended the Déby regime. Sudanese efforts to suppress a rebellion by what amounted to ethnic cleansing produced an exodus of refugees into eastern Chad. Among those most affected were numerous Zaghawa people, ethnic kin of the President Déby and his inner circle.

Déby, who had himself taken refuge in Darfur and received support from Sudan's rulers when he launched his attack on Hissène Habré, sought to mediate the crisis. Zaghawa elements in his army and security forces thought direct support for persecuted ethnic kin a more appropriate response. Arms were clandestinely supplied to Sudanese Zaghawa and a mutiny against Déby organized.

The attempted coup began the evening of May 16, 2004, led by officers of some of Chad's elite forces: the Republican Guard, the Nomadic National Guard, and the Presidential Security Guard. Loyalist forces stopped the mutineers and rapidly reasserted order in the capital with no loss

# Chad

of life on either side, but the incident showed how fragile the president's grasp could be.

A more muscular support of ethnic cousins in Sudan was not the only issue causing dissidence within the presidential clan. In parliament, Déby's Patriotic Salvation Movement pushed through a controversial constitutional amendment allowing the president to seek a third term in office. The president's crackdown on army corruption, most notably salary payments to "ghost soldiers" had ruffled numerous feathers. The constitutional changes must be approved by a popular referendum, scheduled for June 2005, but that's a mere formality in Idriss Déby's Chad.

Overhanging everything is the state of the president's health and the question of possible succession. Ngarlejy Yorongar, the president's most implacable opponent, somewhat maliciously describes Déby's illness as "an incurable malady which generates other opportunistic diseases," and says the president "only lives thanks to the modern technology of the twenty-first century." The president has reportedly made several trips to Paris in the past year for medical checkups, but this is denied by presidential spokesmen.

**Culture:** In July 2002 the French paleoanthropologist Michel Brunet presented a skull, unearthed in the Chadian north, which could be as old as seven million years old. Named "Toumai," the skull reveals both ape and human features. The skull could be the oldest example of a pre-human ancestor that walked upright. Scientists suspect Toumai is the closet specimen yet to the evolutionary split between humans and apes. Justifiably excited by the discovery, older than any such fossil remain found in the Rift Valley, Brunet told a Chadian audience that "the cradle of humanity is in Chad. Toumai is your ancestor."

**Economy:** Chad is one of the poorest countries in the world, ranking 167th out of 177 on the UN's 2003 *Human Development Index*. Its social statistics are grim: Out of every 1,000 children born, 117 will die at birth, and life expectancy is only 48 years (2003). Forty-five percent of Chadian men are illiterate and 62.5% of its women are unable to read or write; only 63% of those eligible to attend school are actually enrolled, and gender discrimination keeps female enrollment low.

More than 72% of the population is engaged in farming, and the sector con-

**Darfur children in a Chadian refugee camp** ©IRIN

tributes about 31% of GDP. Cotton and livestock have traditionally been the country's principal moneymakers, but economic development has been irregular and inconsistent, characterized by alternations of growth and decline brought on by drought, civil war, and continuing political instability.

Cotton is the main export crop and, until 2002, Chad's most lucrative source of income. Cotton fields cover 10% of Chad's cultivated land. Annual production varies between 150,000-200,000 tons, but the value of cotton exports has declined significantly. In 1999 cotton represented 43% of exports, but dropped to 28% in 2002.

Livestock overtook cotton as the country's major source of income in 2002. There are some 14 million head of livestock in Chad, including six million cattle, more than seven million sheep and goats, and over a million camels. Nearly 40% of the population is engaged in the livestock sector, which contributes about 20% of Chad's GDP. Cross-border smugglers, it is estimated, deprive the Chadian economy of close to two thirds of its potential livestock taxes.

Economic development and poverty alleviation in Chad rest on oil production from southern oil fields at Doba. Reserves are estimated at 900 million barrels, and peak production is projected to be around 225,000 to 250,000 barrels per day. Crude oil from some 315 wells will be transported through a 650-mile pipeline to an offshore marine terminal near Kribi, Cameroon. Total investments in the project were estimated to be near $3.5 billion. Despite stiff opposition from environmentalists, the project received backing from the World Bank, and a consortium of major oil companies—ExxonMobil, Petronas (the Malaysian National Oil Company) and Chevron—undertook the project.

An aggressive construction schedule sped the project to early completion. Official opening ceremonies were held in October 2003, and over the next 25 years an estimated 900 million barrels of oil are expected to flow from Doba to Kribi. Oil revenues are expected to reach at least $80 million a year—a potential godsend for Chad's population, whose average income is less than a dollar day.

Fearing oil income would be siphoned off by corruption or diverted from poverty alleviation projects, the World Bank, as the price of its participation, forced strict revenue controls. Chad passed a law in January 1999 creating an oversight body to monitor the management of oil revenues.

The law mandates that 85% of the oil earnings be dedicated to national health, education, agricultural and infrastructure projects; 5% will go to the producing region of Doba, and another 10% will be deposited directly in an offshore account as savings for future generations. The World Bank has also established its own watchdog panel to see if the government sticks to those commitments.

Whole kennels of watchdogs will be needed. In May 2000, the government spent $4 million of a $25 million "bonus" paid by the oil companies on the purchase of arms to fight its northern rebels. By February 2005 the IMF decided Chad had made "substantial progress" in finalizing arrangements for the "transparent management of oil resources" and approved a three-year grant to facilitate the government's poverty reduction program. A key objective of the program is to ensure that oil revenues are effectively used to support lasting poverty reduction. Key emphases will be on an expansion of the non-oil sector, particularly cotton. The government plans to disengage the state by privatizing CotonTchad which is 75%-owned by the state. Created in 1971, CotonTchad has exclusive rights to collect, purchase, prepare, ship and sell Chadian cotton production.

Economic growth figures suggest happy prospects for Chadians: GDP grew by 9.9% in 2002, 11.3% in 2003 and 39.5% in 2004. Unfortunately, nearly all that growth has occurred in the oil sector; in 2004 growth in the non-oil sector, which involves the vast bulk of Chadians, reached no more than 2%. That's insufficient to reduce poverty when annual population growth is 3%.

**The Future:** Rocky at best, and fragile as the president's health.

# The Republic of Mali

**The Great Mosque of Niono, Niono, Mali**

**Area:** 1,204,350 sq. km. = 545,190 sq. mi. (more than four times the size of Nevada).
**Population:** 12,291,529 (July 2005 est.)
**Capital City:** Bamako
**Climate:** Hot and dry in the northern two thirds of the country; increasing rainfall and more temperate in the southern third. Two short rainy seasons have watered the South, but high temperatures cause rapid evaporation.
**Neighboring Countries:** Senegal (Southwest); Mauritania (North, Northwest); Algeria (Northeast); Niger (East, Southeast); Burkina Faso, Côte d'Ivoire, Guinea (South).
**Official Language:** French.
**Other Principal Languages:** Bambara (spoken by 80% of the population). Bomu, Boso, Dogon, Fulfuldé, Kassonké, Malinké, Senoufo, Songai, Soninké, Tamajeq, Tamashek.
**Ethnic groups:** Mandé 50% (Bambara, Malinké, Sarakolé), Peul 17%, Voltaic 12%, Songhai 6%, Tuareg and Moor 10%, other 5%.
**Principal Religions:** Muslim 90%, indigenous beliefs 9%, Christian 1%.
**Chief Commercial Products:** Gold, cotton, and livestock.

**GNI per capita:** $290 (2003)
**Currency:** CFA franc.
**Former Colonial Status:** Part of French West Africa (1890–1960).
**Independence Date:** September 22, 1960.
**Chief of State:** Amadou Toumani Touré. Elected May 2002.
**National Flag:** Three vertical stripes of green, yellow and red.

Some sixty percent of landlocked Mali is covered by the Sahara Desert. This empty land, inhabited by descendants of the Berber tribes who live a nomadic, pastoral life, has virtually no rain. The otherwise flat terrain is broken occasionally by rocky hills. The country becomes more hospitable to the south of fabled Timbuktu, an important emporium on an ancient caravan route of Arab merchants. The Niger River flows north, making a great bend to the south near Timbuktu and continuing to its eventual meeting with the Atlantic in Nigeria. With its tributary, the Bani River, it forms an inland delta, the rich farming heartland of Mali.

The country becomes slightly more temperate south of the Niger, receiving greater rainfall in average years. This section is part of the so–called Guinea Savanna, a brush and low tree belt stretching from the Atlantic coast 3,000 miles inland to the east.

**History:** The fame of Mali dates back to the 13th century when Sundiata succeeded in establishing his authority over the area and creating the basis of the Empire of Mali. For details of early and colo-

# Mali

nial history, see *Historical Background* and *The French in Africa*.

Known as French Soudan, Mali became part of the French Community in 1958, with almost complete internal autonomy. With French permission, Soudan and Senegal joined in 1959 to form the Mali Federation, but this was dissolved in 1960 when Senegal dropped out. After achieving independence in 1960, the government headed by Modibo Keita withdrew from the French Community, which had evolved into a post–independence economic union of former French colonies in association with France.

Keita, announcing that Mali was a socialist nation, sought assistance from the Soviet Union and later from communist China. Russian aircraft and weapons were received, and the Chinese sent technical assistance and limited financial aid. The result was a gradual decline in the limited economy of Mali during the ensuing years. The ruling Soudanese Union Party, which also controlled the press, labor unions, and state youth organizations, gradually splintered into two groups. One favored a total socialist commitment, while the other saw advantages in economic cooperation with the former French colonies and with France itself.

By 1967 the economy was in disarray and the government bankrupt. It was clear the socialist model had failed. The pro-French faction prevailed, and in 1967 Mali rejoined the Franc Zone. This had the effect of halving the income of the small segment of Malians who were engaged in the wage economy. Unrest resulted, and Keita dissolved the Political Bureau of the state party because "it ceased to enjoy the confidence of the people."

In this unstable situation a group of young army officers seized control. President Keita was shipped off to prison in distant, desolate Kidal deep in the Sahara, and a Military Committee for National Liberation (CMLN) was established. Lt. Moussa Traoré became its president and dominant figure. The new military leaders renounced socialism and attempted economic reform, but were debilitated by internal political struggles and a disastrous drought. Ultimately corrupt and repressive, the Traoré regime sustained itself in power for years and had no interest in returning Mali to civilian rule. A new constitution created a single-party state in 1974, and in 1976 Traoré created a new party, the Democratic Union of the Malian People (UDPM). He led the party in sham elections in 1979, winning 99% of the vote. Challenges to his power, by students or from within the military, were brutally suppressed.

Desperate to improve the economy, the government approved plans for economic liberalization and signed an agreement with the IMF. By 1990, the austerity demanded of such plans had begun to pinch all but the ruling clique. The Soviet Union's collapse encouraged demands for multiparty democracy, something Traoré was unwilling to concede. In early 1991, student-led anti-government demonstrations broke out. In four days of bloody street rioting an estimated 200 people were killed by government forces. On March 26 a military *coup d'état* overthrew the president, suspended the constitution, and set in motion the process by which Mali would return to civilian rule.

A new National Reconciliation Council was headed by Lt. Col. Amadou Toumani Touré, who promised democratic reforms, lived simply, and kept his word. He governed for 14 months, during which he established the processes for multiparty democracy and then stepped down. From January to April 1992 Malians enthusiastically participated in presidential, legislative, and local elections. Twenty-one political parties participated, with eleven of them winning seats in parliament. Alpha Oumar Konaré, an archeologist, defeated nine other candidates for the presidency, and his Association for Democracy in Mali (ADEMA) secured a parliamentary majority.

During his first five-year term Konaré won plaudits for devolution of more governing powers to local authorities. Political expression flourished: some 40 independent newspapers and journals, in French, Arabic, and local languages appeared, often criticizing the government. Fifteen radio stations, a more important source of news in a largely illiterate population, blossomed in Bamako alone; 40 others broadcast elsewhere in the country. For Western states, Mali became a showcase for democracy.

In 1995 Konaré ended the long-term Tuareg rebellion which had ravaged the north. There, Tuareg nomads, pastoralists whose flocks had been decimated, whose water holes had dried up, and whose people were on the brink of starvation, had been driven to revolt by a callous and corrupt regime. They took up arms against the military dictatorship of Moussa Traoré in 1990, after thousands of tons of food destined for starving nomads had been stolen by the army. When the army proved ineffective in limiting Tuareg raids on farmers along the Niger River, the farmers themselves organized a militia, which they called *Ghanda Koy*—Masters of the Land—to strike back at nomads. Both groups rallied to Konaré's peace and reconciliation program in 1995. The armies were disarmed, some 9,000 fighters were paid $210, and efforts were made to integrate some of them into the army—always a difficult task given the preference of Tuaregs to speak Arabic rather than French. In March 1996, President Konaré symbolically set fire to several thousand weapons to seal the peace.

A committed democrat and a man of the most humane instincts—he commuted death sentences meted out to Moussa Traoré and several of his cronies to life imprisonment and closed the terrifying prison at Kidal—President Konaré had no trouble in his search for a second five-year term in 1997. Unfortunately, the 1997 presidential and legislative elections proved a disaster. Poorly administered and producing such dubious results that a court threw them out, they had to be repeated. The opposition—and there were some 62 parties in Mali, many organized around a single personality—screamed foul and took to the streets. Security forces had to use tear gas to control mobs. The second round of elections were boycotted by the opposition, and, given the circumstances, thousands stayed away from the polls fearful for their personal safety. Konaré and ADEMA won handily, but their mandate was weakened by events.

This electoral fiasco produced a permanent political tension in Mali. Municipal elections had to be postponed again and again. As a way out of this impasse, President Konaré proposed a National Political Forum to examine Mali's governing legislation. Regional forums met in December 1998 and discussed constitutional revisions, the organization of future elections, party financing, and the power of the Independent National Electoral Commission (CENI).

At the end of these regional consultations, official delegates met in Bamako in January 1999 to make final recommendations. The final document, 200 pages in length, was called "A Summary of the National Political Forum." Included, at the suggestion of Konaré himself, was a constitutional provision that explicitly limits

**President Amadou Toumani Touré**

a president to no more than two terms. The state agreed to find the necessary funding for any political party playing a positive civic role and agreed that journalists should no longer be imprisoned for offending press laws.

For the presidential elections of April 2002 twenty-four candidates presented themselves to the electorate, but only 38% of eligible voters took the elections seriously enough to participate. The election was held against a backdrop of worsening economic conditions. The cotton sector was in crisis, and export income had fallen nearly 50%. Family incomes shrank while gas and electricity prices soared. Women took to the streets with their pots and pans to complain about the high cost of living, more interested in survival than politics.

ADEMA splintered, divided by disputes between reforming young Turks and others. The "Turks" rejected the presidential ambitions of former Prime Minister Ibrahim Boubakar Keïta and drove him from the Party. To pursue his own presidential candidacy, IBK, as he is known, formed a new party, the Rally for Mali (*Rassemblement Pour Mali*: RPM), which became the 74th party to be registered in Mali.

ADEMA formally endorsed the candidacy of the brilliant and very rich Soumaila Cissé, a former finance minister. When this was done, the incumbent Prime Minister Mandé Sidibé resigned to run as an independent. Having spawned three candidacies from its ranks, ADEMA stood little chance of winning the election.

The favorite was General Amadou Toumani Touré (ATT to his friends), who ran without party affiliation, but was backed by a coalition of some twenty-eight parties. The man who overthrew the dictatorship of Moussa Traoré had developed an enormous popular following since he returned power to civilian authorities in 1992. With twenty-four candidates, a run-off was inevitable. General Touré led the vote with 28.7%, followed by the ADEMA candidate Soumaila Cissé with nearly 21.3%—enough to make the run-off. IBK, who had received the backing of Bamako's Imams during their pre-electoral Friday sermons, arrived in third place, a mere 4,000 votes behind Cissé, with 21.03%. He protested, claimed fraud, and ultimately accepted the Constitutional Court's results, urging his followers to vote for General Touré.

In the run-off General Touré won a crushing victory, defeating his rival 65% to 35%. Having run without his own party, and having declared he would not create one, ATT promised to work closely with whatever parliamentary majority emerged from Mali's 2002 legislative elections.

The elections gave RPM and ADEMA dominant positions in the National Assembly, but neither achieved a clear majority. Ibrahim Boubakar Keita was, however, overwhelmingly chosen as the parliamentary Speaker.

To form a new government, President Touré chose a Tuareg, Ahmed Mohamed Ag Hamani, as Prime Minister. A technician (a trained statistician) and former ambassador, Ag Hamani, like President Touré, had no party affiliation and formed a cabinet of national unity, including representatives from a broad range of Malian parties. With two non-party leaders at the helm, Mali seems to have entered a period of politics by consensus rather than confrontation.

In early 2004 Mali's desolate northern region became one of the latest international terrorist sites. Algerian Islamists, known in French as the *Groupe armé salafiste pour la prédication and le combat* (GSPC: Salafist Group for Preaching and Combat) had kidnapped 32 European tourists near the Libyan-Algerian border the year before and transported some of them to Northern Mali. To free its citizens, Germany paid a ransom of nearly $6 million, instantly making the GSPC leader, Ammari Saifi, the most powerful Islamic militant in the region.

Saifi, once an Algeria Special Forces paratrooper, used his hostage booty to buy arms and recruits in Northern Mali. His movements were monitored by American and Algerian intelligence, and when notified of his whereabouts, Malian troops forced him into Niger, from whence he was chased into Chad, where 43 of his men were killed or captured.

American Special Forces have trained some 300 Malian troops as part of the State Department-sponsored Pan-Sahel Initiative. The program is designed to furnish training and equipment (especially communications materials) to permit rapid response to terrorist threats in the four Sahel countries of Mauritania, Mali, Niger and Chad. Eastern Mali has long been a lawless area plagued by banditry, smuggling and kidnapping. This became particularly noticeable after the 1992 peace agreement with Tuaregs when the government withdrew it security forces from the area. The presence of large numbers of fundamentalist Pakistani preachers has also heightened concerns that the area might become a sanctuary and training ground for terrorists.

**Culture:** Much of Lassiné Minta's lifetime career as a master stonemason has been devoted to the transformation of a small local mosque into a monument of Islam—the Great Mosque in Niono. Commissioned by a Committee of Elders, and assisted by his sons with the support of the entire community, the structure is elegantly beautiful. He received the 1983 Aga Khan Award for Architecture for his achievement.

In 2004 UNESCO classified the Tomb of the Askia in Gao a World Heritage site. The 55-foot high pyramidal structure was built in 1495 by the first of the Emperors of Songhai, the Askia Mohamed, and is one of the finest examples of the monumental mud-building traditions of the West African Sahel.

Mali's musical traditions are among the most distinguished in West Africa. Traditionally the preserve of craft specialists called *griots*, music has breached the

The tomb of the Askia in Gao. Named a UNESCO World Heritage site in 2004.

# Mali

boundaries of caste in the modern era. One of Mali's greatest musical stars is Salif Keita. Born in 1949, Salif was an albino in a culture where albinos are believed cursed. Ostracized by his father, Keita and his mother were only allowed to return to his village when the local Imam predicted great things for him. Limited by sensitive skin and poor eyesight, Keita was unable to become a teacher and when he decided to become a professional musician he was practically disowned. Today he is one of the luminaries of World Music, capable of touching audiences throughout the world.

Mali's, and indeed Africa's, most distinguished scientist is the astrophysicist Cheikh Modibo Diarra. Dr. Diarra worked for NASA and was the mastermind of the Pathfinder mission to Mars. In 1998 he was appointed as the UNESCO Goodwill Ambassador to Africa—the first African and the first scientist to hold that post.

Excision—the removal of the female clitoris—is currently practiced by all of Mali's ethnic groups, with the exception of some Tamashek, Songhai and Dogon groups. A national Demographic and Health Survey conducted in 1996 indicated that 94% of all Malian women had been excised. The same survey concluded that overall, 75% of Malian women were in favor of continuing the practice. Urban women were less supportive than rural, and the more educated the women, the less likely they were to support the practice. In the desert north and east, where Islam has been less influenced by traditional animist belief, FGM is much less common. A 2002 health survey found that only 17% of women in Timbuktu, Gao and Kidal had been subjected o FGM.

**Economy:** As with other Sahel states, Mali's economy is agriculture based and subject to meteorological caprice. Cotton is the principal cash crop, and it supports nearly a quarter of the population directly or indirectly. It has traditionally accounted for half of Malian export earnings, but those earnings are utterly dependent on local climatic conditions and world market prices.

The cotton sector is plagued by exogenous difficulties. Both China and the United States, the world's biggest cotton producers and exporters, privilege their cotton farmers. The 2002 U.S. Farm Act protects American farmers from depressed international market prices, allowing otherwise uneconomic farms to dump cotton onto world markets at prices that undercut those of Malian farmers.

Oxfam, the British NGO, says that every acre of American cotton receives subsidies of $230, while China provides annual subsidies to its cotton farmers estimated to amount to some $1.2 billion. Mali has joined Burkina Faso, Benin, and Chad in highlighting the devastating effects of rich-country subsidies on African cotton farmers in various world trade meetings.

Conflict in Côte d'Ivoire shut down Ivoirian ports and increased transportation costs for cotton shippers. In better times, 70% of Mali's imports and exports transited through Abidjan. Now shippers must use Ghanaian ports or Lomé, Togo. According to Malian officials, the new export routes will cost an extra 130 million dollars. Conakry, Guinea is the nearest port, but roads need significant improvement to make transport there cost effective.

Regional road links, like all-weather road links between Mali and Gambia, have high government priority. In late

2004 the governments of Burkina Faso, Mali and Ghana instituted an axle load control system for trucks using the important Bamako-Ouagadougou-Accra route. Between 70% and 90% of all vehicles using the route were found to surpass weight limits. This overloading accelerated road deterioration and raised maintenance costs to unacceptable levels.

Gold has replaced cotton as Mali's biggest income producer since 2000. The Sadiola Hill mine has brought Mali to the top ranks of West African gold producers. Run by Canadian and South African mining interests, Sadiola is one of the largest industrial projects ever undertaken in Mali. Annual gold production is projected to be 10 tons a year over 13 years. Mali is the third largest gold producer in Africa after South Africa and Ghana.

Important, but relatively small in comparison to gold and cotton, are Mali livestock exports. The national livestock herd amounts to some six million cattle and 16 million sheep, but price plummeted in 2002-2003 when the market, with no outlet to Côte d'Ivoire, became saturated. Mali exported some 276,819 head of cattle in 2001, of which 70% to 80% went to Cote d'Ivoire.

Important for the economy are remittances sent home by some 120,000 Malians who live in France. Diaspora Malians transferred around $73 million to their families in Mali in 2002—about the amount France offered in development aid to the country.

In early 2003 the IMF announced that Mali is to benefit from debt relief amounting to approximately $675 million under the enhanced Heavily Indebted Poor Countries (HIPC) initiative. Anything will help: its accumulated external debt is $3.229 billion (2003). Mali remains one of the poorest countries in the world, 174th of 177 ranked on the UN's *Human Development Index* for 2004.

Seeking foreign investment in his country, President Touré made his first visit to China in 2004. Relations between the two countries go back nearly fifty years. Diplomatic relations began in 1960 and in 1968 China began sending medical teams once every two years. Over the years China has provided cooperation in agriculture, industry, culture, education, sports and defense. The football stadiums of Bamako, Ségou, Sikasso, Mopti, and Kayes—all used when Mali hosted the African Nations Cup in 2002—were all Chinese projects.

In his public discussions, President Touré emphasized how Chinese enterprises were particularly welcome in the cotton sector, for purchase and local planting.

Presidential palace, Koulouba

**The Future:** Difficult.

# The Republic of Niger    (pronounced Nee–*zhair*)

**President Tandja Mamadou**

area which briefly turn into ponds during the "winter."

A narrow belt of territory in the south stretches along the entire width of the country and is the only fertile region. This area of trees and shrubs, interspersed with cultivated land supported by irrigation or wells, gives way quickly to a transition zone where the trees become smaller, and the lack of moisture supports only sporadic grazing by nomads' animals. In the northern two–thirds of the territory, the shifting sands of the hot desert render human life impossible except in the region of uranium mines, and only sparse, rudimentary animal life is found.

Little more than 2% of the land area is under cultivation, most of which is gathered around the 185–mile–long portion of the Niger River within the country's boundaries. The river floods from June to September, helping to provide moisture for the surrounding vegetation. The climate is exceedingly hot and dry during eight months of the year.

**History:** For details of early and colonial history, see *Historical Background* and *The French in Africa*.

Niger became an autonomous member of the French Community in 1958, but opted for independence in 1960. Diori Hamani was chosen the country's first president. Under the first post–independence constitution, the president held office for a term of five years and was elected by universal suffrage. The National Assembly of 60 members, elected in the same manner, sat for five years. The government could be ousted and the Assembly dissolved either by a motion of censure requiring a two-thirds majority or a vote of no confidence by a simple majority.

After independence, Diori's Niger Progressive Party held all seats of the National Assembly and dominated the government. In 1974 the single-party regime was overthrown in a military coup led by Lt-Col Seyni Kountché. Kountché ruled as military dictator until 1987 when he died in Paris of AIDS. He was succeeded by his cousin, Col. Ali Saibou, as chief of state. President Saibou grudgingly agreed to a new constitution, which was approved in 1992. It greatly curtailed the power of the military and mandated multiparty elections, which were held in 1993. A 43–year–old economist, Mahamane Ousmane, of the *Convention Démocratique et Sociale* (CDS: Social Democratic Convention) won a majority.

He quickly alienated most of the National Assembly, and government came to a virtual standstill. The military, led by Brig. Gen. Ibrahim Maïnassara, staged a coup in January 1996, arresting the presi-

**Area:** 1,266,510 sq. km = 489,000 sq. mi. (three times the size of California).
**Population:** 11,665,937 (July 2005 est.)
**Capital City:** Niamey (pop. approx. 748,000)
**Climate:** Hot and dry desert in the North; semi–arid and warm in the South with a wet season from June to September producing 9 to 30 inches of rainfall in normal years.
**Neighboring Countries:** Burkina Faso (Southwest); Mali (West); Algeria (Northwest); Libya (North); Chad (East); Nigeria and Benin (South).
**Official Language:** French.
**Other Principal Languages:** Arabic, Fulfuldé, Hausa, Kanuri, Songai, Tamajek, and Zarma.
**Ethnic groups:** Hausa 56%, Djerma 22%, Fula 8.5%, Tuareg 8%, Beri Beri (Kanouri) 4.3%, Arab, Toubou, and Gourmantché 1.2%, about 1,200 French expatriates.
**Principal Religions:** Muslim 80%, remainder indigenous beliefs and Christians.

**Chief Commercial Products:** Uranium ore, livestock products, cowpeas, onions.
**GNI per capita:** $200 (2003)
**Currency:** CFA franc (pegged to the euro)
**Former Colonial Status:** French Colony (1921–1960).
**Independence Date:** August 3, 1960.
**Chief of State:** Tandja Mamadou, President, elected 1999.
**National Flag:** Three horizontal stripes of orange, white and emerald green. There is an orange globe in the middle of the white stripe.

The Republic of Niger covers an immense area in north central Africa. It is one of the most thinly populated nations of the continent. A huge plateau, the country is desolate but diversified, sometimes rocky and sometimes sandy, furrowed in many places by fossilized beds of ancient Sahara rivers. Hot and dry, it is pockmarked with small basins in the southern

# Niger

dent and prime minister. A new constitution was adopted, and elections were held in July. Maïnassara, running as an independent, won. The opposition contested the results, and the crisis deepened four months later when the eight main opposition parties boycotted legislative elections. Pro-government parties and sympathizers claimed all 80 seats in the National Assembly.

On a more positive note, the government achieved a resolution of rebellion of Tuareg and Toubou peoples, both of which felt marginalized and excluded from Nigerien society. Two main rebel movements (at one time there were some 15 rebel groups in Niger), the Organization of Armed Resistance (ORA) and the Coordination of Armed Resistance (CRA), signed a peace agreement in April 1995. It called for reintegration of these former rebels into Nigerien society. Some would be integrated into the army or paramilitary ranks, but this process was painfully slow. Parliament finally voted amnesty for all desert guerrilla groups in March 1998. Shortly afterwards, the two main rebel fronts handed over their arsenals of heavy machine guns, rocket-launchers, anti-tank mines, and ammunition. Tuaregs are now regularly appointed by the Prime Minister as members of the Cabinet.

From that highpoint General Maïnassara's difficulties increased. The country was wracked by a continuing series of strikes, protests, mutinies, and rebellions. Salaries to soldiers and civil servants and scholarships to students went unpaid for months. The political opposition found the streets a comfortable place for political theater.

Niger's long political instability reached a climax in early 1999. Local elections were held for the first time, and when early results showed the opposition winning handily, armed men appeared in those polling areas where it seemed most successful. Ballots and official tabulation reports were destroyed, the vote disrupted. The opposition was justifiably outraged. Supporters were called to the streets to protest and widespread unrest ensued; a day later they called upon the President-General to resign.

The next day, April 9, 1999, the President's own security command shot him to death as he was preparing to leave the Niamey airport. With Orwellian glibness the commander of the Presidential Guard, Major Daouda Mallam Wanke, emphasized to reporters that Maïnassara's death was totally unpremeditated, merely an "unfortunate accident." Eyewitnesses reported that Presidential Guard members repeatedly shot the President with a truck-mounted large-caliber machine gun, nearly severing his body in two.

**Ex–President Ibrahim Mainassara Barre**

Very quickly the National Assembly and Supreme Court were dissolved, the constitution and political parties suspended, and a National Council for Reconciliation (CRN) put in place. Major Wanke was chosen as President and head of the CRN, which consisted of 14 junior officers.

Expressions of outrage were heard from every part, and France (on whom the Niger economy is largely dependent) suspended all military aid and economic assistance. With the Japanese—major trading partners with Niger—announcing they would re-examine their economic cooperation unless democracy were restored, the new regime had to respond quickly. Major Wanke went on radio and television to announce that the junta would return the country to civilian rule by the end of the year. Elections would be held in November and the new president would be sworn in on 31 December. Members of the military and security forces were specifically banned from standing for election. The major also indicated that there would be a referendum on a new constitution in June. The junta's timetable was scrupulously followed.

The new constitution designed a parliamentary regime with a relatively strong president. There would be a single house legislature with executive power shared between the president and the prime minister. The president must name the prime minister from a list of three candidates proposed by the parliamentary majority. Article 141 of the new constitution provided amnesty to those responsible for "the *coups d'état* of 27 January 1996 and 9 April 1999."

The constitution of the Fifth Republic was approved by a nearly 90% majority, a figure made less impressive by the fact that only a little over 30% of the electorate participated. As promised by Major

Wanke, multiparty presidential and parliamentary elections followed in October and November.

Seven candidates competed for the presidency. In the runoffs, Tandja Mamadou, the candidate of the National Movement for a Developing Society (MNSD), beat Mahamadou Issoufou, the candidate of the Niger Party for Democracy and Socialism (PNDS) by a margin of nearly 60% to 40%.

Tandja, a retired military officer, had first become prominent when he helped oust Niger's first president, Diori Hamani, in 1974. He served as interior minister for both presidents Kountché and Ali Saibou. Under the latter, he was responsible for the bloody repression of Tuaregs in 1990. An ethnic Kanouri, Tandja profited by a runoff alliance with Mahamane Ousmane, a member of Niger's influential Hausa majority, leader of the *Convention Démocratique et Sociale* (CDS) and the country's last democratically elected president. His younger Hausa opponent, Mahamadou Issoufou spent lavishly and campaigned vigorously in what Nigerien commentators called "an American style."

In elections for the National Assembly, Tandja's MNSD and CDS alliance won an absolute majority of 55 out of 83 seats. Much to the relief of many, the electoral system eliminated minor parties. Only three other parties would be represented in the new parliament. Issoufou's PNDS won 16 seats, and the Rally for Democracy and Progress (RDP) of former president Maïnassara won eight. The remaining four seats were won by the *Alliance nigérienne pour la démocratie et le progrès* (ANDP).

President Mamadou Tandja faced military mutinies in 2002 (privates earn about $35 a month, equivalent to the price of a 200 pound bag of millet), but as his term of office drew to an end in 2004, it was clear he had brought both stability and credibility to Nigerien democracy. With Prime Minister Hama Amadou, the president had maintained civil peace, achieved a number of rural development projects that made rural voters happy, and saw to it that urban civil servants were regularly paid.

Tandja was a candidate to succeed himself in the October 2004 presidential elections and he faced five opponents. His principal rivals from 1999, Mahamadou Issoufou of the PNDS, and Mahamane Ousmane of the CDS headed the opposition, while Moumouni Djermakoye, Cheiffou Amadou, and Hamid Algabid played secondary roles. In first-round balloting President Tandja failed to secure a majority, winning only 40.67% of the votes; his nearest competitor was Mahamadou Issoufou who received 24.6%. The losers urged their voters to support

# Niger

the outgoing president, and in November runoffs, Tandja triumphed convincingly: 65.5% of the vote to his challenger's 34.5%. He became the first elected leader of Niger to have completed his term of office without being assassinated or ousted by coup. Niger's fragile democracy seemed to have matured.

In parliamentary elections, Tandja's National Movement for a Developing Society (MNSD) elected 47 deputies, while five other parties supporting the president brought the presidential majority to a comfortable 88 seats. Mahamadou Issoufou's PNDS affirmed its role as the principal opposition party with 25 seats.

Niger's sparsely populated northern region remains a security problem for the government. It has been the scene of banditry and tourist kidnappings that have forced trans-Saharan traffic to travel in convoys protected by heavily armed soldiers. Just who the attackers are is often uncertain. Some may simply reflect the frustration of a northern population that feels itself largely marginalized.

In October 2004 after the Tuareg leader Rhissa Ag Boula had been dismissed from his cabinet position and later jailed for alleged involvement in the murder of a local northern politician, his brother launched a series of attacks on government forces. The government designated him a "bandit," but Mohamed Ag Boula claimed to be defending the rights of northern nomads. "The current government has not implemented the 1995 accords," he told a French interviewer. He specifically demanded the release of "all members of the ex-rebellion currently in detention," which, of course, included his brother. In February 2005, four Nigerien soldiers who had been held captive for five months by the group were freed "for humanitarian reasons" with the help of Libyan negotiators. A month later Rhissa Ag Boula was released from jail.

The presence of armed Islamist radicals, members of the Algerian *Groupe salafiste*

*pour la prédication et le combat* (GSPC: Salafist Group for Preaching and Combat) in the same geographical area, has complicated the security situation. In March 2004 one Salafist band, involved in kidnapping over 30 European tourists in Algeria, engaged Nigerien forces and was chased into neighboring Chad, where it was badly mauled by Chadian troops.

Niger is part of the U.S. State Department-sponsored Pan-Sahel Initiative to track and destroy Islamic fundamentalists operating in the region. The program furnishes training and equipment (especially communications materials) to permit rapid response to terrorist threats in the four Sahel countries of Mauritania, Mali, Niger and Chad. American surveillance provided the intelligence on the GSPC whereabouts in Niger where the group had been working hand-in-hand with armed bandits, using hideouts and caches left over from the 1990s rebellion by Tuareg nomads.

**Culture:** A *National Geographic*-financed expedition into the Niger desert discovered extraordinary rock carvings—huge giraffes carved into desert sandstone 9,000 years ago. The largest stands over 20 feet tall; its proportions are meticulously accurate and its reticulation beautifully created in low relief. Wavy lines come from the mouths of these giraffes and to them are attached small human figures. No one is sure what they mean, but their artistic achievement is undeniable. For preservation purposes the actual site of this Sistine Chapel of rock art remains hidden. Casts will allow worldwide audiences to appreciate the consummate skill of their unknown creators.

For much of Niger's archeological heritage it is already too late. Sites are regularly plundered and even though a 1997 law imposes a $16,000 penalty and up to two years in jail for theft of artifacts, the government simply does not have the means to enforce the penalties.

Like Mauritania, Niger is challenged by the persistence of traditional slavery among its nomadic peoples. Although banned by law, slavery is still practiced. New anti-slavery provisions have been included in the country's penal code to discourage the practice. These provide prison terms of 10 to 30 years and fines of one million to five million CFA francs (about $1921 to $9605) for those found guilty of enslavement. "*Timidria*," which means "freedom" in the Tamajek language of the Tuaregs, is an NGO dedicated to fighting the practice and aiding its victims.

Female Genital Mutilation (FGM) is practiced by a third of the country's population. The practice was outlawed in 2001, but it remains widespread and no one has ever been prosecuted for performing the operation. For many, the removal of the clitoris reduces a woman's sex drive and guarantees marital fidelity. The government is concerned the practice damages girls' health and fuels the spread of HIV/AIDS through the use of non-sterilized blades.

**Economy:** President Tandja inherited a shattered economy. The UN Development Program (UNDP) ranks Niger as the second poorest country in the world—just above war-ravaged Sierra Leone. Its predicament is illustrated by 2002 statistics: GDP growth was just 3%, as was its population growth—one of the highest rates in the world. In other words, everything was steady state. Annual per capita income is estimated at $200 (2003) and over 60% of the population survives on less than $1 per day.

Niger's women bear particular burdens. They have the highest fertility rate in the world, averaging eight children per woman, and suffer one of the world's highest infant mortality rates: out of every 1,000 live births, 154 die. Only 9.3% of them are literate (2003), and only 20% of girls eligible for primary school are actually enrolled.

Niger is the world's third largest uranium producer (after Canada and Australia), extracting around 3,000 tons a year; most of this is sold to France and Japan. The uranium is mined in the region of Arlit, some 620 miles north of Niamey, by two companies (Cominak and Somaïr) employing around 1,600 persons.

For years Niger's main source of export revenues, uranium accounted for 80% of the national budget in the 1980s. Proven reserves total 280,000 tons, but production peaked at 4,360 tons in 1981. Since then, diminished demand and reduced prices have seriously affected government revenues. In 2002, uranium generated $90 million in export revenues.

**Presidential palace, Niamey**

# Niger

With heightened concern about nuclear proliferation, there was a mini-tempest about Niger allegedly selling uranium to Iraq, but the documents on which the claim was based turned out to be forgeries. Prime Minister Hama Amadou went on record as saying his country had never sold to Iraq, "although," he added, "in the 1980s when Iraq was not facing sanctions from the great powers, it tried to buy uranium under the aegis of bilateral cooperation."

Gold seems the most promising alternative in a desperate effort to diversify away from an uncertain reliance on uranium. Canadian and Moroccan interests are currently developing two neighboring gold mines—Samira Hill and Libiri. Production began at an expected annual rate of 135,000 ounces in 2004.

Surrounded by oil-producing states—Algeria, Libya, and Chad—Niger maintains some hope of productive oil discoveries. Exploration has been going on since 1958 and one reserve of some 300 million barrels has been identified in a permit area operated by Exxon Mobil. In 2004 Petronas, the Malaysian oil giant, began three exploratory wells at Nguigmi in eastern Niger, close to the Chad frontier. Given Niger's landlocked geography, the investment necessary to export the oil is simply too great. To be profitable, reserves of at least a billion barrels are necessary.

With its tremendous energy needs, China seems less concerned with commercial reality and may be willing to invest in the difficult and hard to transport. Niger has already granted exploration rights in its Tenere Block to the China National Petroleum Company. That's the same company that built an oil pipeline in Sudan to transport non-optimally located oil to port refineries on the Red Sea.

Niger's 6.7 million-head national livestock herd is an important economic resource, and cattle are the second most profitable export after uranium. Around 95% of the national production of leather and hides is exported and accounts for around 24% of export earnings.

Desertification, which continues at an alarming pace, affects both livestock and agriculture. Some 95% of Niger's 10.6 million people depend on firewood as their main source of household fuel and usage is increasing. In 1996, 153,000 tons of wood were transported to Niamey for household use. By 2002, the amount had increased to 188,000 tons. Niger's three main towns Niamey, Maradi and Zinder, used a total of 254,000 tons of wood in 2002.

Niger has qualified for participation in the Highly Indebted Poor Countries (HIPC) program, and in December 2000 the World Bank and IMF signed debt reduction agreements with the government. These have freed up about $40 million per year to help implement government health, education and rural infrastructure plans. Debt service as a percentage of government revenue will drop from nearly 44% in 1999 to 10.9% in 2003 and average 4.3% during 2010-2019. As of 2003, its external debt was still huge: $1.8 billion.

Niger remains dependent on external assistance. Nearly 50% of the government's budget, including 80% of its capital budget, derives from donor sources.

As a profoundly poor state, Niger represents all the social and medical consequences of devastating poverty. The country has been spending three times more on debt payments than on health and education. The consequence is seen in raw statistics: in Niger, more than 26% of children will die before they are five years old. Their deaths result from long-term starvation diets that weaken the immune system and allow children to be killed by measles, malaria, meningitis and diarrhea. The most horrifying of the child killers is Noma. It starts as a small black spot on the face and progresses by devouring facial tissue, muscle, and bone.

**The Future:** Economic problems are crushing, with little prospect for improvement. President Tandja will emphasize the development of Niger's agricultural sector, but even here, the problems are staggering. Irrigated agriculture is still in experimental stages, but it holds some promise for future development. Realistically, it is unlikely that foreign aid can ever arrive in amounts sufficient to cope with Niger's multiple problems.

A slave boy draws water for his master. More than 43,000 individuals are estimated to belong to the slave caste in Niger.
©IRIN/G. Cranston

# The Republic of the Sudan

**Death in Darfur: A Janjaweed militiaman.**

AFP/Getty Images

**Area:** 2,504,530 sq. km = 967,000 sq. mi. (An area as large as the U.S. east of the Mississippi joined by Louisiana, Arkansas and Missouri).

**Population:** 40,187,486 (July 2005 est.)

**Capital City:** Khartoum (Pop. 7.7 million, estimated, including the city of Omdurman and surrounding areas filled with squatter camps).

**Climate:** The northern half is arid desert, the middle and southern areas are temperate and semi–arid; the southwest is hot with a six month rainy season.

**Neighboring Countries:** Congo-Kinshasa and Central African Republic (Southwest); Chad (West); Libya (Northwest); Kenya and Uganda (Southeast).

**Official Language:** Arabic.

**Other Principal Languages:** Acholi, Bari, Bedawi, Dinka, Fulfulde, Fur, Hausa, Kanuri, Kenuzi-Dongola, Masalit, Nobiin, Nuer, Otuho , Shilluk, Toposa.

**Ethnic groups:** Black 52% (prominently including Acholi, Dinka, Nuer, Shilluk), Arab 39%, Beja 6%, foreigners 2%, other 1%.

**Principal Religions:** Sunni Muslim 70% (in north), indigenous beliefs 25%, Christian 5% (mostly in south and Khartoum).

**Chief Commercial Products:** Oil, cotton, sesame, livestock/meat, and gum Arabic.

**GNI per capita:** $460 (2003)

**Currency:** 1 Sudanese Pound (£Sd) = 100 piastres.

**Former Colonial Status:** Egyptian (1821–1885); British–Egyptian (1899–1956).

**Independence Date:** January 1, 1956.

**Chief of State:** Brig. Gen. Omar Hassan Ahmed el–Bashir, Chairman of the Revolutionary Council (b. 1947).

**National Flag:** Three horizontal stripes of red, white and black with a green isosceles triangle at the pole.

Sudan is the largest nation of Africa, covering an area of almost one million square miles. The vast Sahara Desert lies in the northern sector and is succeeded by a semi–arid plains country in the region near Khartoum, the capital city. This gently rolling territory is succeeded in the south by tropical plains land with more abundant rainfall; in the extreme south, the land becomes choked by dense jungle growth. The historic Nile River, the longest in the world, virtually divides the country and is the main route of north–south communication and travel between the Mediterranean Sea and the lower part of the African continent. The river has two points of origin—the waters of Lake Victoria flow into a portion known as the Victoria Nile. After a short distance, the river becomes lost in the Sudd swamp region of southern Sudan, which covers an immense area of land. The stream emerges again to flow northward through central Sudan. The Blue Nile originates to the east near Lake Tana in the mountains of Ethiopia. The two rivers join at Khartoum to form the main Nile, which, as it proceeds through northern Sudan, has a slight downward slope, interrupted periodically by rough cataracts. As it nears Wadi Halfa on the Egyptian border, the Nile shapes it-self into an almost perfect "S" curve. Were it not for the predominantly muddy waters of this river, much of Sudan and Egypt would be empty and desolate.

High mountains rise in the extreme east of Sudan, close to the Ethiopian border and along the Red Sea coast. Other mountains are found to the west on the Chad border, and in the South.

**History:** The ancient history of Sudan, one of the oldest civilizations in the world, revolves around the Pharaohs of Egypt and the Nubian people in central Sudan. Gigantic formations of stone in the Nile area to the north furnished the material from

# Sudan

which many of the picturesque temples and burial grounds of ancient Egypt were craved and built. In the eighth century BC Kushite kings from Nubia, now northern Sudan, conquered Egypt and created the 25th Dynasty. At the beginning of the Christian era, Sudan split into a collection of small, independent states. There were some conversions of people to Christianity in the 6th century, but much of the country remained pagan until there was a widespread adoption of Islam, primarily in the North, at the end of the 13th century. For details of early and colonial history, see Historical Background and *The British in Africa*.

Sudan has been riven by internal conflict for most of its history. That conflict has usually been referred to a one between a Muslim North and a Christian South, but that description is highly misleading. Conflict in Sudan is neither exclusively regional nor exclusively religious given the country's enormous complexity. Indeed, Sudanese themselves refer to the country as *laham ras* (literally "head-meat"), a term which refers to the highly divergent taste, texture and appearance of parts of cooked sheep's head, a popular Sudanese dish.

In this culturally complex situation, a central problem facing the state is defining its identity. Contemporary conflict is fueled by vastly divergent historical identities. For Sudan there is no unifying identity; diversity is division. Northern Sudan was conquered and unified by the Egyptian viceroy of the Ottoman Sultan in

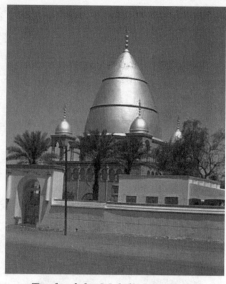

**Tomb of the Mahdi, Khartoum**

1821. Egyptian rulers claimed southern Sudan, but were unable to establish effective control over its fragmented animist populations. Access to the south was not possible until after 1839, and from that point both the Ottoman rulers and their Arab Sudanese subjects saw the south only as a source of manpower. Slavers from both groups aggressively raided southern peoples.

Not until the 1880s was a sense of Sudanese identity articulated in opposition to the Egyptian conquerors. In 1881 a religious leader proclaimed himself the Mahdi or "expected one" and began to unify peoples in western and central Sudan. Drawing upon discontent with Ottoman-Egyptian exploitation, the Mahdi led a nationalist revolt culminating in the fall of Khartoum in 1885. The Mahdi died shortly afterwards, but his state survived until destroyed by an Anglo-Egyptian army under Lord Kitchener in 1889. Sudan was proclaimed a condominium in 1899, and governed by a joint British-Egyptian administration until 1956. Northern Arab Muslims were privileged by the condominium administration and in turn, looked down on the black African animists of the south. For black Africans of southern Sudan, the memory of slave raids meant that any pale-skinned person was a potential slaver.

Though one speaks of northern Muslim populations and southern animists, neither of these populations is in any way monolithic. Sudanese Muslims are divided by affiliation with rival religious brotherhoods. The Mahdi's followers called themselves *ansars*, and the Ansar sect today is the largest of the Sudanese Muslim brotherhoods. During the period of Ottoman-Egyptian rule, Turkish-Egyp-

**Sudan States**

268

# Sudan

tians developed close relations with another Muslin brotherhood, known as the Khatmiyya. The second most important brotherhood today, the Khatmiyya retains its original pro-Egyptian, anti-Mahdist identity. Each of these two rival brotherhoods is associated with a separate political party. Mahdists are the core of the Umma Party, while the Khatmiyya forms the core of the Democratic Unionist Party (DUP). The leader of the Umma Party, Dr. Sadiq al-Mahdi, is a descendent of the first Mahdi. Smaller than either the Ansar or Khatmiyya is the more militant and fundamentalist Muslim brotherhood led by Hassan al-Turabi and very much the core of the National Islamic Front (NIF). These sectarian groupings also have their secular opponents in the North, Muslims and non-Muslims whose vision of Sudanese identity is not based on political Islam.

Southern black African animists (and today a small number of Christians) are even more divided. Symptomatically, over a hundred languages are spoken in Sudan, most of them in the south. The two major southern ethnic groups, the Dinka and Nuer, are segmentary societies with no traditions of overarching leadership and governance. Both are cattle raising people. Both were traditional rivals for pasturage and objects of mutual cattle raids. Khartoum governments, dominated by northerners, have traditionally exploited such rivalries. Within each group segments vie with each other for scarce resources and produce intra-ethnic rivalries that can be exploited by the Khartoum government. Similarly, historical antagonisms between cattle pastoralists like the Nuer or Dinka and settled farming peoples create fissures that work against southern political unity.

These cultural diversities help explain Sudan's continuing history of political instability and conflict. At independence in 1956, a civilian regime, deeply divided between its Muslim partners, was incapacitated by internal division and overthrown by a military coup in 1958. The military in turn, reneging on its promises to restore civilian government, was driven from office and succeeded by another coalition government. Power sharing between Umma and Unionist parties could not overcome problems of factionalism, economic stagnation and ethnic dissidence in the south. Espousing pan-Arab-Nationalism and professing pro-Soviet sentiments, General Jaafar Nimeri took advantage of dissatisfaction with this civilian regime and overthrew it in 1969. Soviet arms poured into Sudan. But only two years later disputes between Marxist and non-Marxist elements within the ruling military coalition resulted in an abortive communist coup. Anti-Marxist elements

quickly restored Nimeri, who, seeing the light, did a political about face and sought aid from the United States.

In 1972 the government reached a peace agreement with southern rebels. Signed at Addis Ababa, the accord made the south a self-governing region, but ultimately offered only a brief respite to Sudan's endemic conflict. After Emperor Haile Selassie was overthrown in neighboring Ethiopia by a Marxist military coup in 1974, Sudan was seen as a bulwark against Communism in the region. American arms poured into the country, and Sudan became another pawn on the chessboard of cold war politics.

Secure with American arms and support, General Nimeri began an Islamization campaign in 1983. Traditional Islamic punishments drawn from the *Sharia* were incorporated into the penal code. Ampu-

**Dr. Sadiq al–Mahdi**

tations for theft and public lashings for alcohol possession became common. When religious leaders like Sadiq al-Mahdi questioned the general's credentials for creating an Islamic state, they were thrown in jail. Civil liberties were suspended and a state of emergency declared. Rights granted southerners for a degree of autonomy were curtailed and two army battalions mutinied under the leadership of a southern Dinka, Colonel John Garang, in 1984. This began Sudan's present on-going civil war. General Nimeri himself fell in a bloodless coup a year later and was ultimately replaced by a civilian coalition again headed by Sadiq al-Mahdi.

The Southern People's Liberation Army (SPLA), founded by Garang, found a ready supply of arms from Marxist Ethiopia and by 1987, Soviet tanks and artillery supplied to the SPLA allowed it to fight positional battles and capture population centers. Subject to government bombardment and raids by its militias, massive numbers of southerners were displaced from their homes or fled to neighboring countries. The civilian government in Khartoum remained faction ridden and indecisive, incapable of winning the war. At the very moment negotiations with the rebels seemed on the verge of success, the regime was overthrown by General Omar Hassan al-Bashir in 1989.

The new military regime came to power with the backing of the militant National Islamic Front (NIF) party headed by Hassan al-Turabi. It quickly abolished the constitution, all political parties (except the NIF), and trade unions. Press freedoms were curtailed, and strict dress and behavior codes imposed on women. More than 78,000 people were purged from the army, police and civil administration to make way for those of more militant Muslim faith. Support for the new regime came from Iran, enabling the government to make massive purchases of arms from China and the former Soviet republics. These were used to step up the war against the south. In addition to an ideology of militant Islam, the discovery of huge southern oil reserves in the 1970s also fueled the desire of Khartoum to control its southern provinces. Emptying the oil producing regions of their black African animist populations became a deliberate government goal, even at the price of massive destruction and loss of life.

The overthrow in 1991 of Ethiopia's Marxist regime and questions about continued arms supply led to a factional breakup of the SPLA. Under the leadership of Riek Machar, a Nuer faction broke off and proclaimed its goal of independence from Sudan. John Garang remained head of the now, largely Dinka, SPLA and claimed his goal a unified, secular Sudan. The clash of these three visions of Sudanese identity—an Arab-Muslim Sudan, a Sudan divided into two separate states, or a unified secular Sudan—continues to the present. Fluid loyalties and deliberately divisive strategies by the Khartoum regime have led to a bewildering and complex set of shifting alliances and coalitions, few of which can be identified with much more than a desire to overthrow the present regime.

By 1995 northern and southern opponents of the regime had joined forces in the National Democratic Alliance (NDA), and by January 1997 the NDA could mount an offensive on three fronts in Eastern Sudan.

# Sudan

Troops involved came from all the members of the Alliance. The main spearhead came from the Sudan People's Liberation Army commanded by Colonel John Garang, but also included elements from the Beja Congress and northern groups such as Sadiq al-Mahdi's Umma and Mohamed Osman al-Mirghani's Democratic Unionist Party (DUP). The strategic objective was the capture of ed-Damazin, the provincial capital and site of the Roseires hydroelectric dam that supplies Khartoum with 80% of its electricity. Even more threatening for the government was the possibility that these forces, with bases in Ethiopia and Eritrea, would link up with SPLA forces in the south with bases in Uganda.

In response, Khartoum rallied Southern dissidents and signed a peace agreement with Riek Machar and other breakaway SPLA faction leaders in April 1997. Progovernment southerners were linked together under the name of the United Democratic Salvation Front (UDSF) headed by Machar; about 25 of their militias came together in the South Sudan Defense Force (SSDF) generously supported by Khartoum. In the months to come Machar was rewarded an impressive series of titles—President of the Coordinating Council of the Southern States and Assistant of the President of the Republic—and made a member of President Bashir's cabinet.

NDA forces demonstrated their capacity to inflict damage by conducting raids against the Roseires hydroelectric dam and at least twice blowing up the pipeline that transports oil from the south to refineries on the Red Sea. Khartoum's infrastructure looked increasingly vulnerable.

In February and March 1999 a seemingly successful series of reconciliation meetings between Dinka and Nuer leaders were held. More than 300 Dinka and Nuer chiefs and community leaders, local administrators, church leaders, and representatives of women and youth signed the covenant ending the seven-and-half-year conflict between the Dinka and Nuer of the West Bank of the Nile.

The Wunlit Covenant demonstrated the vitality of traditional conflict resolution procedures. Agreements were reached through consensus. Rituals surrounding the agreement stamped it with the mark of tradition. The slaughter of a large white bull by traditional spiritual leaders of both communities symbolized peace and an end to the conflict.

President Bashir had to face not only the growing unity of his Southern enemies, but also a growing threat to his authority from within the National Congress Party (NCP), the renamed National Islamic Front. His approach was twofold. A peace agreement was signed with Sadiq al-Mahdi, driving a wedge in the NDA and rallying a leading Muslim cleric to his

side in preparation for his struggle with Hassan al-Turabi. Turabi, speaker of parliament and also al-Mahdi's brother-in-law, seemed to be on the verge of reducing the president's position in both party and state. Bashir's response amounted to an internal coup. In late 1999 he acted decisively to curtail al-Turabi. Parliament was dissolved and a state of emergency declared, allowing the President to rule by decree.

In May 2000 al-Turabi was suspended as secretary-general of the National Congress Party and accused of plotting against the government. Formally expelled from the party in June, he announced creation of a new political party, the Popular National Congress (PNC), better known now as simply the Popular Congress (PC).

With the principal spokesman for political Islam sidetracked, President Bashir wooed, and won, the return of some of the northern political elite, including former president Numeiry and Sadiq al-Mahdi, who returned to lead his popular Umma Party. Ahmad al- Mirghani, a senior leader of the Democratic Unionist Party (DUP), has also returned, after 12 years of exile.

Relations with formerly hostile neighbors were improved. To buff his anti-terrorist credentials, al-Bashir allowed Ugandan army troops to pursue members of Joseph Kony's Lord's Resistence Army, to their Sudanese hideouts. Internally, however, he continued to terrorize civilians living around the disputed Bentiu oil fields. Fugitives from the offensive reported that troops—backed by tanks, helicopter gunships and aerial bombardments—were torturing, slaughtering and burning men, women and children in a drive to evict all non-Arabs from oil-producing areas.

When al-Bashir called presidential and legislative elections for December 2000, few were interested and few participated. No elections could be held in the south for security reasons, and where they were held in the north, they were actively boycotted by the major opposition parties. Official reports indicated 63% of eligible voters went to the polls, a figure that produced hoots of derision from the opposition who claimed not more than 7% had participated. Bashir and the NCP won, overwhelmingly.

In February 2001, Hassan al-Turabi was arrested and jailed after his PNC had signed a memorandum of understanding with Sudan People's Liberation Army (SPLA). The linkage between Turabi and his arch foe, John Garang, was unexpected, unprecedented, and to many of his followers, inexplicable, unless, that is, one accepts the infinite mutability of Sudanese politicians. Hassan al-Turabi re-

John Garang shakes hands with President Omar Hassan el-Bashir as President Kibaki of Kenya looks on.

**President Omar Hassan al–Bashir**

mained under house arrest, a prisoner of the state he helped to create, until freed in October 2003 while the Bashir government was negotiating a peace settlement with its southern opponents.

Sudan and its civil war rose high on Washington's list of priorities after the September 11 attacks. This was, after all, where Osama bin Laden had lived from 1991 until he was expelled in 1996. Even before those events, however, pressure from Christian and African-American constituencies, especially on the issue of slavery, had prompted President George W. Bush to reconsider American policy towards Sudan. The House of Representatives had already passed the Sudan Peace Act in June 2001 by 422 to 2. The act would "punish those who trade in blood oil," said its sponsors, by imposing capital market sanctions on companies investing in Sudan. It would also provide $10 million to Sudanese opposition forces.

To push the Sudanese peace process forward, the president appointed former senator John Danforth, an Episcopal minister, as Special Envoy for Peace in the Sudan. U.S. re-engagement in the Sudanese peace process galvanized regional efforts. With Kenyan leadership, IGAD (the Inter-Governmental Authority on Development consisting of Kenya, Eritrea, Ethiopia, Djibouti, Sudan, Somalia and Uganda) brought the government of Sudan and the SPLA together at Machakos, Kenya and, to the surprise of many, produced a framework for peace in July 2002. Both sides made concessions. The government agreed to a referendum on self-determina-

tion for southern Sudan—after six and a half years—and the SPLA accepted the application of *Sharia* law in the North.

The Machakos Protocol provided the framework and momentum for negotiation on several important issues: wealth-sharing, power-sharing, application of *Sharia* in Khartoum, and defining the border between north and south. These negotiations went on, intermittently, through all of 2003 and half of 2004. They were given added weight by face-to-face meetings in the Kenyan town of Naivasha between John Garang, the SPLA leader, and Sudanese First Vice-President Ali Uthman Muhammad Taha.

Wealth-sharing agreements came first, aided by experts from the World Bank and IMF who brought ideas and experience from other similar situations. Oil revenues will be split, after deducting 2% to go to oil-producing areas, fifty-fifty.

A power-sharing agreement creates a separate Government of Southern Sudan, which will receive a "significant devolution of powers" from the National Government. President al-Bashir will remain in office until national elections can be held, and Sudan will have two vice-presidents (appointed by the president). John Garang will be first vice-president of the National Government and president of the Government of Southern Sudan.

The parties also agreed to a bicameral legislature. The majority of the National Assembly's seats will be apportioned to the National Congress Party (52%), while the SPLM will be allocated 28%. Other northern political forces will receive 14%, with the remaining 6% going to additional southern forces. The upper house, or Council of States, will have two representatives from each of Sudan's states. A census will be held by the second year of the interim period and general elections by the end of the third year.

On the application of *Sharia* law in Khartoum, it was agreed that non-Muslims would not be subject to its provisions in the capital, but that doesn't mean you're likely to see any non-Muslim southerner opening a tavern there any time soon. Rights of non-Muslims are to be protected by a special commission appointed by the president.

The Naivasha discussions created the Comprehensive Peace Agreement (CPA) which was officially signed in January 2005, ending twenty years of civil conflict between north and south. Even as the government made peace with southerners, however, President al-Bashir faced resistance, rebellion, and insurgency elsewhere. Some northern peoples, like the Beja and the Nubians, felt as marginalized as Garang's southerners and resentful at the exclusivity of Naivasha. More omi-

nously, new groups emerged in Darfur (Sudan's Wild West) to press their demands during the Kenyan negotiations, and the government's response created a humanitarian disaster.

The Sudan Liberation Army (SLA) took up arms against the government in February 2003, accusing it of ignoring the Darfur region and demanding a place at the negotiating table. Shortly afterwards a second armed group—the Justice and Equality Movement (JEM)—emerged to make the same claims. Both rebel groups recruited from the region's African (and largely Muslim) populations—notably Fur, Zaghawa and Massaleit peoples—all of whom had historical conflicts with Arab pastoralists over water and grazing rights. In the 1980s these traditional tensions had been intensified by the central government, which took to arming Arab militia groups to disrupt and destabilize black African communities that might be sympathetic to John Garang's SPLA.

With the emergence of the SLA and JEM, Khartoum saw the hands of its enemies everywhere and resorted to the same tactics. Arab militias were armed and given a free hand to target civilian populations suspected of supporting the rebellion. The most notorious of the militias were the *Janjaweed*. Supplied with horses, camels, and AK-47s, the *Janjaweed* attacked, burned, looted and raped. They branded those they raped on their hands to make them permanent outcasts from their society. Fields, orchards, granaries, and villages were destroyed. Attacks were frequently supported by government shelling, followed by the use of regular government troops.

An estimated 2.5 million people have been displaced; upwards of 400,000 have died of disease, malnutrition and violence. Food is everywhere in limited supply as humanitarian agencies are frequently prohibited from entering the area. The UN has identified Darfur as the world's greatest humanitarian crisis.

Meaningful sanctions against the al-Bashir regime from the UN Security Council are unlikely. As a permanent member of the Council, China can veto anything that would jeopardize its oil investments in Sudan, and both China and Russia are major arms suppliers to the Khartoum regime, a lucrative trade neither wishes to end. Even the Bush administration has resisted calls for stronger action, pleased with the intelligence co-operation Khartoum has thus far offered in the war on terrorism. At best, it is likely the United States will offer logistical and communications support to the pitifully inadequate African Union force stationed in Darfur. By mid-2005, the AU had stationed a nominal 2,200 observers in Darfur, a region as large

# Sudan

as France; it hoped to increase force size to 7,700 by September.

In April 2005 the Security Council voted to refer war crimes suspects in the Darfur conflict to the International Criminal Court (ICC) in The Hague. The resolution passed when the United States, traditionally opposed to the ICC, abstained from voting. The practical utility of the resolution is dubious: the Sudanese government has made clear it refuses to permit any of its citizens to appear before the court.

Meanwhile a variety of African peacemakers has worked to little success. The predations of the *Janjaweed* and other militias continue against the Dafuri people. Khartoum seems to lack the will or ability to control the forces it deliberately armed, uniformed and unleashed.

One can only recall the words of President al-Bashir as he showed off a munitions factory in September 2002: "We manufacture weapons and arm ourselves, not for war but for imposing peace." In Dafur the regime is likely to create a wasteland devoid of people and call it peace.

**Culture:** The issue of slavery in the Sudan highlights the age-old relationship between expansive Arab nomads in the North and sedentary animist or Christian farmers in the South. In January 1999 Christian Solidarity International (CSI), a Swiss-based human rights group, announced its redemption of 1,050 slaves in the Sudan, the largest number ever liber-

ated at one time. The group accused Sudanese armed forces of capturing and using Christian and animist black Africans as slaves and war booty. It was, the group said, "one of the most potent instruments of its declared jihad (holy war) against communities that resist its totalitarian policies of forced Islamization and Arabization."

Sudan has the highest prevalence of female genital mutilation (FGM) in the world. Almost 90% of the female population in the north endure clitorectomy, in many cases in its most extreme form, infibulation. The labia are stitched together to cover the urethra and most of the vagina. Only a small opening, tiny as a matchstick or large as a small fingertip, is left to pass urine and menstrual blood. In September 2003 the Minister of Health expressed his government's commitment to eradicate FGM.

UNESCO designated Gebel Barkel and four other Nubian locations as World Heritage sites in 2003. The sites contain tombs, temples, pyramids, living complexes, and palaces that testify to the importance of the ancient cultures of Napata, Meroë, and Kush. The eighth-century rulers of Kush conquered and ruled Egypt as the twenty-fifth dynasty. Non-recognition of Nubia's pharaonic heritage is one of the complaints this northern people lodges against Khartoum's Islamist regime.

**Economy:** War, continuous and only diminished in recent months, has sapped

Sudan's capacity for growth, development, or improved life for its citizens. It cost the government half of its budget annually, President Omar al-Bashir once admitted. Oil from Sudan's southern oil fields has helped reduce budgetary deficits, but not arms purchases. Sudan produced 342,000 barrels per day (bll/d) in 2004 and expected to raise production levels to 500,000 bll/d in 2005. Oil sales bring in about $5 billion annually, allowing the government to purchase modern weapons systems from suppliers like China and Russia. Proven oil reserves stand at 563 million barrels and the Sudanese Energy Ministry optimistically believes that future exploration will raise reserves to five billion barrels.

Sudan's crude oil exports began in August 1999 when a 1,000-mile pipeline from southern Sudan to the Red Sea was opened. The pipeline was built by the Greater Nile Petroleum Operating Company (GNPOC), a consortium dominated by the state oil firms of China, Malaysia, and Sudan. China's assistance in the pipeline construction is being paid off in oil, and Khartoum is the biggest supplier of African crude to China's energy-hungry economy; Sudan accounts for 10 percent of Chinese oil imports.

Sudan's oil resources were at the heart of the struggle between the SPLA and Khartoum's Islamist regime. Two-fifths of the country's known reserves are located in rebel-controlled territory, which provided stimulus to producing the Comprehensive Peace Agreement (CPA) signed in early 2005. The CPA calls for a 50/50 sharing of oil revenues. Ambiguities and uncertainties remain about whether or not the autonomous southern government will be able to issue exploration permits.

Before the advent of oil production, Sudan's economy was traditionally dependent on agriculture and pastoral activity. About 65% of the population makes its living through crop growing or animal grazing. Principal food crops consist of millet, sorghum, rice, cassava, wheat, peanuts, beans and bananas. Exports are primarily cotton, livestock and gum Arabic.

Sudanese cotton production began in the 18th century and became commercially important in 1925 following the development of Al-Jazirah (Gezira), one of the largest irrigation projects in the world. The Gezira project distributes the waters of the Blue Nile captured by the Sennar and Roseires dams through a 2,700-mile network of canals and ditches to irrigate fields growing cotton and other cash crops. Constructed by the British, Gezira was originally developed to supply cotton for the textile factories of Lancashire. The irrigation project made Al-Jazirah the most

**Darfur refugees, victimized by Janjaweed and government forces.**  ©IRIN

272

productive agricultural area of Sudan. It takes up about half the country's total irrigated area and is, in effect, a 2 million-acre cooperative farm.

Gum Arabic is a substance obtained by tapping the *Acacia Senegal* tree. It is produced commercially in areas on the southern periphery of the Sahara desert and is widely used by U.S. candy, cosmetics and medical industries. More than 80 per cent of the world gum Arabic supplies come from Sudan, but one major harvesting area is Darfur and many of the producing trees have been destroyed by warfare there.

In the south, agricultural activity is mainly pastoral, with the main domestic livestock being cattle. Sheep, goats, camels and chickens are also reared. Sudan is an important supplier of sheep meat to the Arab world and is building new slaughterhouses in order to service this huge market.

While fresh meat and live animal exports produce the most income from the livestock sector, the leather industry is an important adjunct. It consists of two main branches—raw hide processing and footwear manufacturing. The domestic footwear industry has a capacity to produce 18 million pairs of leather shoes and 60 million pairs of other types of shoes.

At the Giad industrial complex, some 30 miles south of Khartoum, Sudan has a significant arms manufacturing capacity. Rocket-propelled grenades, machine-guns and mortars are already produced there and the government looks to an expansion of arms manufacture. It has signed an oil-for-manufactures agreement with Tartarstan, bartering oil for KamAZ trucks and various high tech products, and would like the Tartars to set up an assembly line at Giad to produce the trucks locally. On a visit to the Tartar capital, Kazan, the Sudanese delegation was particularly interested in Tu-214 aircraft, Mi-17 helicopters and military optical sighting devices.

Despite its oil wealth, Sudan is still a "Heavily Indebted Poor Country." Its external debt was projected at about $24.2 billion in 2004. Most of that is in arrears. Sudan has been the world's largest debtor to the World Bank and IMF since 1993, when the IMF suspended its voting rights and the World Bank suspended its rights to make withdrawals. Its relationship to the institutions has yet to be rehabilitated.

Rehabilitation of war-ravaged Southern Sudan will be a gargantuan task, physically and financially. The CPA's six-year transition period will allow the regional government to construct and rehabilitate basic infrastructure. The size of Kenya and Uganda put together, southern Sudan has never had an inch of tarmac roads. The Garang government plans to tarmac twelve key roads to integrate the region with northern Sudan, the Greater Horn of Africa, and Great lakes areas, creating a market space of some 300 million people. Two railroad linkages, one from Juba—the southern regional capital—to Mombasa and the other to Kisangani in the Democratic Republic of the Congo, are also envisioned. Another key element of the regional government's development plans is a hydroelectric dam at Fulla or Bedden Falls south of Juba.

**The Future:** The country seems delicately poised between triumph and tragedy. The CPA ends the long North-South war and establishes a "one country two systems" model for the next six years, but the very process that led to its signing has engendered additional conflict and resentment. Those excluded from the bargaining table had only a model of armed struggle leading to negotiated success before them. The result has been rebellion in Darfur. The government's response—ethnic cleansing in Darfur—has the potential of destabilizing the entire region. One cannot be sanguine about short-term prospects.

The Pyramids of Nubia, Northern Sudan

# NORTH AFRICA

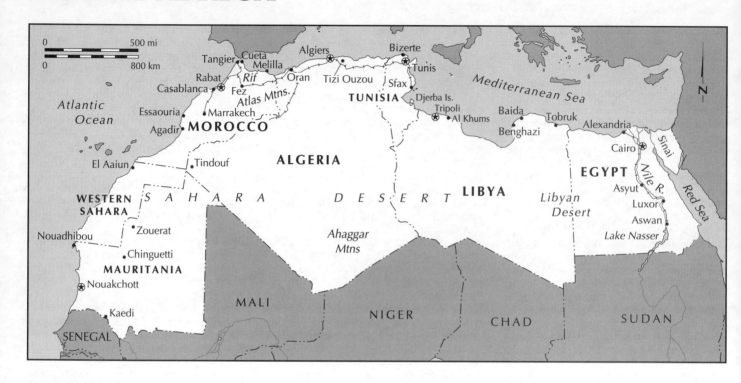

# The Democratic and Popular Republic of Algeria

**Area:** 2,460,500 sq. km. = 950,000 sq. mi. (Almost as large as the U.S. east of the Mississippi River).

**Population:** 32,531,853 (July 2005 est.)

**Capital City:** Algiers (Pop. 4.2 million, estimated).

**Climate:** In the coastal region, temperate Mediterranean weather prevails. Inland, it is temperate and cooler in the high altitudes of the mountains. South, in the Sahara Desert, it is hot and dry.

**Neighboring Countries:** Morocco (Northwest); Tunisia and Libya (East); Niger (Southeast); Mali, Mauritania (Southwest).

**Official Language:** Arabic.

**Other Principal Languages:** Berber languages, including Kabyle, Tamazight, Taznatit, Tumzabt; Tamahaq, spoken by Tuaregs, and French.

**Ethnic groups:** Arab-Berber 99%, European less than 1%.

**Principal Religions:** Sunni Muslim (state religion) 99%, Christian and Jewish 1%.

**Principal Commercial Products:** Petroleum and natural gas 97%.

**GNI per capita:** $1,920 (2003)

**Currency:** Algerian Dinar.

**Former Colonial Status:** French Colony (1831–1870); integral part of France (1870–1962).

**National Day:** Revolution Day, November 1st.

**Chief of State:** Abdelaziz Bouteflika, President (since March 1999).

**National Flag:** Two vertical stripes, green and white, with a red crescent enclosing a five–pointed star in the center.

Algeria was a seat of civilization long before recorded history. Its ports and commerce were the lifeblood of early times. The dazzling white city of Algiers, founded about 1,000 years ago, is a cosmopolitan crossroads of the East and West, climbing the Atlas Mountains from the blue Mediterranean. South of the fertile coastal regions and the mountainous areas stretches the vast Sahara Desert, where caravans still cross the arid wastelands. Gleaming modern highways now lead to green oases and oil fields.

Algeria has a 620–mile coastline on the Mediterranean. Two Atlas Mountain chains cross the country horizontally, dividing Algeria into three geographic zones: the northern Mediterranean zone, the high arid plateau between the ranges, and the Sahara. The northern zone, known as the Tell, is a sun–bathed coastal area where vineyards, orange, fig, and olive trees flourish in the valleys and hillsides. The high plateau is primarily the home of grazing herds of goats, sheep, and camels. South of the Sahara, the immense Ahaggar Mountains are the territory of the Tuaregs, a Berber group with singular customs—the men, not the women, are veiled.

**History:** Some of the earliest traces of human culture are found in the mountain ranges of the southern Sahara, including Neolithic frescoes and carvings. The people who have lived the longest in Algeria are the Berbers, thought to be descendants of ancient Numidians who lived during the Roman Empire. For details of early and colonial history, see *Historical Background* and *The French in Africa*.

After a bitter eight–year struggle against Arab nationalists from 1954 to 1962, France granted independence to Algeria four months after a cease–fire had been negotiated. More than one million

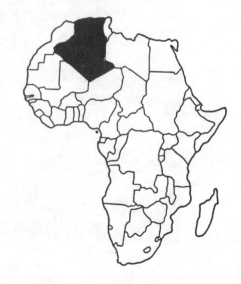

274

**A workman with wire for new railway signal lines**

French citizens and other European residents had fled the country.

Ahmed Ben Bella, a prominent member of the National Liberation Front (FLN), which had led the fight for independence, headed the new government. A wide range of reforms was undertaken, including the redistribution of land. Closer ties were established with the European communist–bloc nations. Internal tensions within the FLN led to the quiet removal of Ben Bella in 1965. He was placed under house arrest, but was never charged or tried for any crime.

Colonel Houari Boumedienne was installed as chief of state with widespread support of the party leadership. Boumedienne, the former defense minister, estab-

# Algeria

lished a 26–man Revolutionary Council to assist in governing the nation. He continued in power, weathering a 1967 attempt to oust him and a 1968 assassination plot.

In 1967, the Algerian government began creating new political institutions, beginning with communal and provincial assemblies. A new constitution, openly Marxist, was adopted in late 1976, and President Boumdienne was reelected with a 99% majority. A new National Assembly was elected in 1977. The 261 members were selected from a list of 783 candidates, all of whom were FLN members. President Boumedienne died in late December 1978, the victim of a rare blood disease. In early 1979 elections were held in which there was but one candidate: Colonel Chadli Bendjedid, a former commander and informal coordinator of defense during Boumedienne's illness. He also became Secretary General of the FLN, the two positions being closely interwoven in the one-party governmental structure.

In early 1980 Algeria was shaken by riots led by Muslim fundamentalists who sacked hotels, cafes and restaurants where alcohol—a violation of Islamic teachings—was served. Algeria had always been one of the most secular nations of the Arab world, keeping religion *strictly* out of government, but the successful Islamic revolution in Iran sparked a wave of back-to-Koranic-basics movements throughout Islamic lands. The rioters also attacked several "pleasure houses" provided for Algerian troops stationed near the border with Tunisia.

President Chadli was elected to a third five-year term in 1989. But in a decade, Algeria had changed drastically, as the consequences of lavish, but nonproductive spending by the FLN finally hit home. Algeria's external debt was impossibly high—$28 billion—and required 80% of export earnings to pay principal and interest on it. There was little left for social services and productive investment.

The FLN leadership had squandered oil royalties in "window-dressing" projects that sustained its popularity (at least on the surface), but failed to produce economic development. Widespread corruption in the government added insult to injury. By the 1990s the unemployment rate of skilled people exceeded 30%. Young people, raised with expectations of a better life, faced a bleak prospect. With their dreams shattered, they had one of two alternatives: emigration, or Islamic fundamentalism. The first choice was unavailable.

Islamic fundamentalism offered an alternative to the FLN, and *any* alternative would be better, they reasoned. The message of Islamic fundamentalists throughout North Africa and the Middle East was

quite simple: anti-Westernism. This program would bring Algeria's fundamentalists into violent conflict with the secular and westernizing elements of the FLN regime.

In response to external and internal pressures, President Chadli legalized political parties in 1989, and the first to register was the Islamic Salvation Front (FIS). It had already been clandestinely exploiting discontent among young people. As the movement gathered steam, President Chadli firmly warned against "all attempts to return Islam to the era of charlatanism and political opportunism," but it didn't work. FIS candidates won clear majorities in municipal and provincial elections in 1990, and set the stage for an energetic campaign in the forthcoming parliamentary elections.

The government declared a state of siege, arrested and jailed two FIS leaders—Abassi Madani and Ali Belhadj—and postponed the elections. When the elections were finally held in December 1991, the first round produced a striking victory for the FIS. It won 188 seats outright, and seemed virtually certain to obtain an absolute majority in the second round.

Before the run-offs could take place in January 1992, however, President Bendjedid resigned and the army intervened to cancel the elections. A five-member Higher State Council, chaired by Mohamed Boudiaf, imposed military rule. Street gatherings were banned, producing violent clashes between FIS supporters and state security forces. The regime declared a state of emergency, disbanded the FIS and dissolved all 411 FIS-controlled local authorities. On June 29 President Boudiaf was assassinated by a member of his own bodyguard with alleged links with Islamists. Violence increased and Algeria descended into civil war. The Armed Islamic Group (GIA: *Groupe Islamique Armé*) was identified as the main group behind the violence.

Brig. Gen. Liamine Zéroual was subsequently chosen as interim president. Murder, massacre, and destruction became common. Armed fundamentalist forces, principally the GIA and the Islamic Salvation Army (AIS: *Armée Islamique du Salut*), were well-equipped with modern weaponry supplied by Iraq and Iran via Sudan.

The military embarked on an anti-terrorist campaign in 1994–5. Violent rebels were interned in camps in the remote desert where they burned by day and froze by night. In rural areas, informal militias were armed as self-defense forces. To legitimize military rule, General Zéroual held presidential elections in 1995, and won a comfortable majority of 64.5%. According to official figures,

75% of the electorate turned out for the election.

The victorious military proposed a new constitution in November 1996. Even though it proclaimed Islam as the state religion, it provided that no party or candidate could have a religious affiliation as a basis for candidacy. Infuriated Islamists opposed it, and the GIA vowed to slit the throat of any person who left home to vote. The government mustered some 300,000 military and police to safeguard the election, and 85% of the electorate approved the proposed changes.

The first parliamentary elections under the new constitution were held in 1997 and resulted in Algeria's first multiparty legislature. A new party to support President Zéroual was created. Benefiting from massive administrative support, the National Democratic Rally (RND: *Rassemblement National et Démocratique*) was the big winner, taking 156 seats (out of 380) with 38% of the vote. Coming in a distant second was the moderate Islamic party, Movement of Society for Peace (MSP), which won 69 seats. The FLN, once Algeria's only party, came in third, taking 64 seats. Two rival secular Berber-based parties, the Socialist Forces Front (FFS) of Hocine Aït-Ahmed and the Rally for Culture and Democracy (RCD) of anti-Islamist Saïd Sadi, each won 19 seats. Some 300,000 security forces were again deployed around the country to guard against attacks by Islamist militants.

The brutal, unspeakably horrible massacres of the innocents continued into 1998. Savagery was not murder alone. When GIA roving bands swept into villages on their killing rampages they would often carry off young women to their mountain hideaways. Estimates vary, but up to 1600 young women between the ages of 13 and 20 were ab-

**President Abdelaziz Bouteflika**

ducted. Many who escaped were pregnant and, given an absolute ban on abortion in the country, were forced to bear the consequences of political violence.

Despite comfortable majorities in parliament and in the government, President Zéroual surprised his countrymen by resigning his office in September 1998, effective with the selection of a successor in April 1999 elections.

In the shadowy world of Algerian politics, characterized more by opacity than transparency, Zéroual had lost the confidence of Algeria's real rulers, the army. With the president's resignation, hopes that new elections could help national reconciliation and move Algeria beyond its current impasse abounded. The army's top officer, Lieutenant-General Mohamed Lamari, announced that "access to power through free election will be an irreversible practice." Zéroual himself had promised free and fair elections, but they were not to be.

By January 1999 it was clear the army had rallied to a consensus candidate, the former Foreign Minister Abdelaziz Bouteflika. In March, seven candidates were in the running, but when President Zéroual refused to meet with them to discuss charges of electoral fraud, six withdrew, leaving Abdelaziz Bouteflika the sole candidate. The election was held; Bouteflika was "elected," and once again Algerian hopes were dashed.

Given the dubious nature of his election, President Bouteflika needed to prove he was more than a creature of the generals. In July he launched a "civil concord" initiative, putting his credibility on the line almost immediately. To achieve stability he offered amnesty to all but the worst offenders in Algeria's eight-year civil war. They would have to lay down their arms by mid-January 2000; if not they would be wiped out.

The results of the amnesty are debatable at best. The government formalized a deal with the Islamic Salvation Army (AIS), the largest rebel group and military wing of the banned Islamic Salvation Front (FIS), but in fact, AIS had been observing a cease-fire since 1997. The two most notorious armed movements—the Armed Islamic Group (GIA) and the Salafist Group for Preaching and Combat (GSPC)—rejected the amnesty and stepped up their attacks. Nine thousand more Algerians were killed in 2000. Organized into small cells, the militants proved difficult to eradicate. Violence remained as intractable as ever, though, for the most part, significantly diminished.

Given the critical importance of the army, President Bouteflika appointed retired General Labri Belkheir, long a heavyweight within the army and government,

**Berber cultural claims sometimes erupt in violence**

as head of the presidential office. Despite this relations with the army remained tense, and relations with the parties that formed a governing coalition worsened.

In early 2001 the coalition, which included the National Liberation Front (FLN), National Democratic Rally (RND), Rally for Culture and Democracy (RCD), Movement of Society for Peace (MSP), National Republican Alliance (ANR), and the Ennahda (Renaissance) Movement, criticized the president for failing to deal with the nation's social and economic crises. Almost 40% of Algeria's 30 million people lived below the poverty line, and the gap between rich and poor steadily increased. Official figures put unemployment at 40%. Housing stock was inadequate, and there had been riots over the government's allocation of apartments.

The disillusionment and discontent felt by average Algerians burst into ugly anti-regime violence in the Spring of 2001. Riots in Kabylia, the Berber heartland, showed the disaffection of Berber youth. Their shouted slogans laid bare Algeria's social and economic crisis: "You cannot kill us," they screamed at the national police, "we are already dead." "Give us work and housing and hope and there will be calm." The targets of their destructive rage were the symbols of government presence and occupation.

Violence in Kabylia persisted through the legislative elections of 2002. By then,

security forces had killed more than 100 young people; the regime seemed utterly incapable of resolving the crisis. In March 2002 President Bouteflika announced that Tamazight, the Berber language, would be recognized as a national language and in April the National Assembly amended the constitution to this effect.

The gesture was symbolic and partial, a palliative that did not placate. It did, however, bring out the darker side of Berber nationalism: intransigence, inflexibility, and a totalitarian willingness to use violence to impose uniformity of action. Berber leaders noted the language was only "national," not "official" and thus not the equivalent of Arabic. They rejected the government's offer and called on Berbers to boycott the May elections.

Both Kabyle-based parties, Saïd Sadi's Rally for Culture and Democracy (RCD) and Hocine Aït-Ahmed's Socialist Forces Front (FFS), boycotted the elections in deference to local opinion. Activists closed virtually every polling place in Kabylia, and where that was impossible, physically prevented the few people who wanted to vote from getting to the polls. In the administrative region of Tizi Ouzou, the Berber capital, voter turn out was 1.8%.

The biggest winner was the FLN, which won 199 seats—an absolute majority—in the National Assembly, but achieved with only 35% of the vote. Much of the credit for bringing the party back from the

# Algeria

wilderness went to Prime Minister Ali Benflis, the party's new secretary-general. He had campaigned vigorously and suggested both the party's capacity to reform itself and his own desire to do so. During the campaign he openly denounced the party's old guard, declaring they barred younger people from participating and believed in keeping women at home.

The largest party in the outgoing legislature, the RND, suffered the greatest loss. It dropped to 47 seats from 155. Two moderate Islamist parties that had participated in the government coalition lost ground, while the National Reform Movement (MRN), which had remained in opposition, became the leading Islamist party with 43 seats. On the far left, the Workers Party raised its representation from 5 to 21 members.

The election revealed Algeria's fundamental political pattern of three main ideological blocs. About a third of the electorate could be described as nationalist, supporting the FLN or other government-endorsed party like the RND. An Islamist bloc (MRN), MSP, Ennahda) attracts the loyalty of 15% to 20%, while a Berber bloc (FFS, RCD) can secure the support of 10% to 15%. Given this distribution of sentiment, coalition governments will remain a constant feature of the political system.

The principal task of the Algerian legislature is to prove the institution matters. Most citizens would not argue it does. Formal authority tends to be concentrated in the hands of the executive, while genuine power seems diffused through the opaque relations that prevail between president and army. Constitutionally ministers are nominated by the prime minister, but appointed by the president. They owe their political survival, as a consequence, to the executive rather than the legislature.

Prime Minister Benflis, whose commitment to reform appeared genuine and whose popularity seemed to be growing, was fired by President Bouteflika in early May 2003. The sacking splintered the FLN. When Benflis supporters moved to make the dynamic young leader the party's presidential nominee, Bouteflika loyalists immobilized them in the courts with the acquiescence of compliant jurists.

In the April 2004 election, President Bouteflika ran for a second term against five opponents: Ali Benflis; an Islamist candidate, Abdallah Djaballah of the National Reform Movement (MRN); a Berber—Saïd Sadi—of the Rally for Culture and Democracy (RCD); a human rights campaigner, Ali-Fawazi Rebaïne, and Algeria's first female presidential candidate, Louisa Hanoune, representing the extreme left Workers' Party.

The army promised to remain loyal, but it appears to have encouraged all and backed one. Defying expectations, the race was anything but close. President Bouteflika won by a landslide, taking 84.99% of the votes cast. His nearest opponent, Ali Benflis, the man who many thought stood a chance of beating the incumbent, receiving a humiliating 6.42%. The least skeptical analysis of the results is that Algerians supported a man whose policy of national reconciliation had reduced political violence.

"Reduced" is the operative word; Islamist terror groups continue to take their toll. The most violent of these is the Salafist Group for Prayer and Combat (GSPC), which has pledged its loyalty to al-Qaeda. The group gained international notoriety in 2003 by kidnapping some 32 European tourists in the Algerian Sahara. The army managed to free 17, but the remaining 15, held by a different GPSC cell, were ransomed by the German government for a reported six million dollars.

The sum made the kidnappers' leader, Amari Saïfi, the most powerful regional terrorist and the major buyer of arms from local smugglers and bandits. In the spring of 2004, Saïfi's group became the object of coordinated international action when he shipped a convoy of arms north. With American surveillance intelligence, Saïfi's group was flushed from its Algerian sanctuary into Niger, where the Nigerien army pursued remnants of the group into northern Chad.

Battered by Chadian forces, a GSPC remnant finally fell into the hands of Movement for Justice and Democracy in Chad (MDJT) rebels in their Tibesti stronghold. One of the survivors was Saïfi, whom the MDJT seems to have auctioned off to the highest bidder. Libya, ever generous with lubricating funds, won the auction and delivered Saïfi to Algerian authorities in October 2004.

The incident proved the growing importance of the Sahel region—from Mauritania to Djibouti—as a potential terrorist training ground. Closer to home, the government seems to feel it's winning the war against terrorists, now reduced, its spokesman has indicated, to fewer than 500 members. It has floated the notion of a general amnesty for all involved in the long civil war. In February 2005 President Bouteflika tallied up the cost of that conflict: 150,000 dead and $30 billion of damage to the country's infrastructure.

**Culture:** The conflict between the army and Islamists in Algeria is a struggle to define the country's identity and future. The army, francophone and secular, is adamantly opposed to Arab-speaking Islamists who advocate an Arab and Mus-

**Lounès Matoub**

lim identity for Algeria. President Bouteflika treds a narrow path between the two poles of identity.

This was no better illustrated than in his support for an amended Family Code. The original 1984 Code, based in Sharia law, was fundamentally hostile to women. They needed permission of a male tutor in order to marry, and could only divorce if they could prove their husband crazy, incarcerated at least five years, or disappeared for at least ten. If a divorce were granted, the family home went to the husband. The consequence was a growing number of women forced to live on Algerian streets and rummage through garbage for food and cardboard for housing.

The amended Family Code of 2005, strongly supported by President Bouteflika, remains rooted in Islamic law. The noxious provision that requires a woman to have permission from a male *wali*, or tutor, to marry is maintained, though slightly softened by granting a woman the right to chose her own *wali*. Polygamy remains, but a man must henceforth seek the approval of his wives, whose testimony must be verified by a judge, before taking another wife. In a divorce, the mother will keep the family dwelling if she is awarded custody of the children. Proxy marriages, whereby a woman could be married without even knowing it, are prohibited in the new text.

Struggling to maintain its own language and identity is Algeria's Berber-speaking minority. Representing 20% to 30% of the population, Berbers are the original inhabitants of North Africa. They fled to the mountains to resist successive waves of invaders—Romans, Arabs, Turks and French—and preserved both language (*tamazight*) and customs despite conversion to Islam. Berber women, for example, go without the veil.

# Algeria

Algeria's Kabyle mountains, the Berber heartland, remain a focal point of opposition to the government. Kabylia is one of the country's poorest and most populous regions. Unemployment is rife, and Berber youth have few future expectations beyond present misery. People there complain of a lack of government assistance and claim they must survive on remittances from relatives who have emigrated to France.

The singer Lounès Matoub, who was assassinated in an ambush in 1998, gave musical voice to Berber nationalism.

**Economy:** Oil production started in 1957 at Hassi Messouad and Ejelek; it was quickly expanded through pipelines, refineries and additional wells made possible by the investment of foreign oil companies. Since that time oil has come to dominate Algeria's economy. It has about 11.8 billion barrels of proven reserves, but these are likely to increase with new exploration and discovery. The hydrocarbon industry accounts for over 95% of Algeria's export earnings. Some 1.93 million barrels per day (bll/d) were pumped during 2004, well above its OPEC quota of 862,000 bll/d.

Algeria has 160 trillion cubic feet of proven natural gas reserves and is Europe's most important supplier of natural gas after Russia. Two important pipelines, with an export capacity of 1.15 trillion cubic feet per year, transport the gas to Europe. The 667-mile Trans-Mediterranean line carries 847.6 billion cubic feet to Italy and ultimately to Slovenia. The Maghreb-Europe Gas line, 1,013 miles long, carries 300.2 billion cubic feet of gas to Spain, Portugal and beyond. Additional pipelines are under consideration, and the government has set a goal of exporting three trillion cubic feet of natural gas a year by 2010.

With the rise of oil prices, the country has had an income windfall. The state's coffers have been amply replenished, but there is little evidence conditions for the bulk of Algeria's population have improved in any way. Fifty-eight per cent of the population is younger than 25, and unemployment stands at 60% among those aged between 20 and 25. More than 200,000 enter the job market every year, but there is insufficient growth to generate the jobs needed for those entering the labor market.

The safety valve for Algeria's un- or underemployed is the underground economy. A lively trade and commerce based on smuggling and bribery sustains many. The system is oiled by "*tchipa*," a bribe to police and customs officers. One gets rich in Algeria, said one trader, not by knowing a general, but by knowing a customs officer. Nowadays, the dream of every young Algerian is to work for the customs service.

Besides the pervasive corruption of the black economy, there are two other indicators of social malaise worth mentioning. Suicide and attempted suicide rates have been increasing for the last four or five years (though they remain much lower than European or American rates), and crime has become the biggest worry for Algerians. A May 2003 report by the National Economic and Social Council (CNES) highlighted the emergence of organized gangs specializing in extortion, drug trafficking, and prostitution. Police statistics indicate that in the first quarter of 2003 crime was 35% higher than the previous year. Authorities saw crime rising by more than 100% during 2004-05.

For the most part these figures should be seen against a background of stagnant economic growth. Economic growth in 2001 was 2.6% and 4.1% in 2002, hardly enough to reduce growing unemployment. GDP growth in 2003 reached an exceptional 6.8%, the highest rate in five years, but this was caused by higher oil production and prices, plus an exceptionally good year for agricultural production brought on by good weather.

Agriculture makes up about 17% of the economy (2003) and consists mainly of grains, fruits, cattle, vegetables and poultry. A once-thriving wine industry was allowed to decline and is only now beginning to receive investment to rectify dilapidation. The government's National Office for the Commercialization of Wine (ONCV) plans to replant some 37,000 acres by 2007.

**The Future:** President Bouteflika's greatest burden, and threat, is Algeria's economy, whose sluggish growth has denied improved living conditions and stifled hope for Algerians of all ages, but especially its young people. Corruption and impunity remain highly sensitive issues, but the criticism of young Berbers—that the regime is corrupt, nepotistic and repressive—has resonance throughout the land. Achieving reconciliation with alienated Berber communities remains a volatile project at best, and while many Islamists seem to support the president, armed Islamist splinter groups still wage a terror campaign against the regime.

The Sahara's ever–shifting sand dunes hide a tiny fresh–water oasis

**In the Valley of the Kings . . . the Pharaohs gaze into Eternity**

# The Arab Republic of Egypt

**Captain Abdul guides his *falooka* along the Nile**     Photo by Rodney McNabb

**Area:** 1,000,258 sq. km. = 386,200 sq. mi. (The size of Texas and New Mexico).

**Population:** 77,505,756 (July 2005 est.)

**Capital City:** Cairo (Pop. 16 million, estimated, including numerous suburbs).

**Climate:** Dry, semi–tropical and hot. Temperatures are lower in the north during winter.

**Neighboring Countries:** Libya (West); Israel (Northeast); The Sudan (South).

**Official Language:** Arabic.

**Other Principal Languages:** Armenian, Domari, (spoken by Muslim Gypsies), Kenuzi-Dongola, and Nobiin. English and French are widely understood by educated classes.

**Ethnic groups:** Egyptians, Bedouins, and Berbers 99%, Greek, Nubian, Armenian, other European, primarily Italian and French 1%.

**Principal Religions:** Muslim (mostly Sunni) 94% (official estimate), Coptic Christian and other 6% (official estimate).

**Chief Commercial Products:** Crude oil and petroleum products, cotton yarn, raw cotton, textiles, metal products, and chemicals.

**GNI per capita:** $1,390 (2003)

**Currency:** Egyptian Pound.

**Former Colonial Status:** British Protectorate (1914–1922); British exercised domination in various forms over Egypt from 1882 to 1952.

**Independence Date:** July 23, 1952.

**Chief of State:** Hosni Mubarak, President.

**National Flag:** Three horizontal stripes of red, white and black with the national emblem, a shield superimposed on a golden eagle facing the hoist side above a scroll bearing the name of the country in Arabic, centered on the white stripe. The bird is the golden Eagle of Saladin, Sultan of Egypt and Syria, who expelled the crusaders from Jerusalem in 1187.

Strategically occupying the northeast corner of Africa, the land route between Africa and Asia, and commanding the sea route between the Mediterranean and Indian Ocean via the Suez Canal, Egypt is fundamentally a rainless expanse of desert. The habitable portion of this country has historically been only about 4% of its area. The remainder, within the great Sahara Desert, is a hot, endless landscape of sand dunes dotted with occasional green oases. Only 2.85% of the land, mostly the narrow fringe on either side of the Nile River, is arable, though irrigation projects are slowly transforming desert wasteland into fertile ground in areas near the Nile. From 1960 to 2000 the amount of habitable and cultivatable land rose from 6.1 million to 7.3 million acres, but during the same period total population catapulted from 25 million to 66 million people. As a consequence, Egypt has some of the highest population density in the world, in places well over 4,000 inhabitants per square mile. In the urban megalopolis of Cairo, the figure is a staggering 23,310 per square mile.

The Nile, some 3470 miles long, is the lifeblood of Egypt, providing water for irrigation and (in former years) fertile silt for the farmlands. Given demographic pressure to create new lands through irrigation, control and use of the Nile and its waters is a central aspect of Egyptian domestic and foreign policy.

A number of peaks in the Red Sea Hills rise to more than 6,000 feet, but Egypt's highest mountains are found in southern Sinai. Of them the highest is Mount Catherine with an elevation of 8,668 feet.

**History:** Egypt is the oldest cohesive nation in the world, its history dating back before 3,000 B.C. Unlike other Middle Eastern and African countries, it has a clear sense of national identity, but part of that identity comes from long periods of subordination to foreign powers. Persia, Macedonia, Rome, Muslim Arabia, Ottoman Turkey, France and England successively exercised dominion. Indeed, fol-

# Egypt

part of the Ottoman Empire. The dynasty he founded would rule Egypt from his death in 1849 to the middle of the twentieth century.

His successors' desires to modernize the country, coupled with personal profligacy, bankrupted the state. Two of them are remembered for overseeing the creation of the Suez Canal. In 1858, Said Pasha granted a canal concession to a French engineer, Ferdinand de Lesseps, and the project was completed under Ismail Pasha in 1869. Inaugurated with much fanfare amid bevies of European aristocrats, including the Empress of France, Eugenie, the canal cut 7,250 miles from the London to Bombay journey and heightened Egypt's strategic importance for Europe.

Ismail, who obtained the hereditary title of Khedive from the Ottoman sultan in 1867, borrowed so much money from European financiers that the state could not repay its debts. To protect the creditors' interests, an Anglo-French commission took charge of Egyptian finances in 1876 and the sultan was pressured to depose his Egyptian viceroy. This was effected in 1879. His son and successor, Tawfik Pasha, had little popular support and his weakness before the European powers roused the ire and contempt of a group of young nationalist army officers led by Ahmad Urabi Pasha.

Born of peasant stock, Urabi was educated at al-Azhar in Cairo, the Middle East's pre-eminent institution of Islamic learning. Conscripted into the army, he rose to the rank of colonel, early asserting his nationalist credentials by seeking to eliminate the foreigners who monopolized the army's top ranks. In 1881 he led a revolt against that dominance and a year later was named Minister of War by Tawfik Pasha. His slogan of "Egypt for Egyptians" expressed Egyptians' near universal discontent with foreign domination and terrified both the Khedive and the British.

Fearing Urabi's growing popularity, Twafik requested British and French assistance. A demonstration of naval power in the bay of Alexandria led to riots in the city. In response, the British bombarded Alexandria in July 1882, a senseless act which only increased Urabi's popular support. In what appeared a revolutionary context, Tawfik fled in fear to British protection. Urabi, calling the Khedive a traitor, organized resistance, but his army was defeated, and he was captured, tried, and ultimately exiled to Ceylon. In suppressing the Urabi rebellion, Britain became the master of Egypt. Urabi himself became a nationalist hero and model for successor officers.

When he came to power in 1892, Tawfik Pasha's successor, Abbas II, opposed

lowing his assumption of power in the 1950s, Gamal Abdel Nasser liked to describe himself as the first Egyptian to rule Egypt since the pharaohs.

The modern Egyptian state begins with the rule of Muhammad Ali, an Albanian soldier in the employ of the Ottoman Sultan. Part of the army sent to reassert Ottoman authority following Napoleon's invasion of Egypt in 1798, Muhammad Ali combined forces with the English, defeated the French, and was made governor of Egypt by a grateful Sultan in 1805. Ruthless and effective, he set the foundations of the modern state. Remnants of the former Mamluk ruling class were eliminated (slaughtered when they came as invited dinner guests), peasant rebellions were crushed, merchants and Bedouins were controlled, and members of the religious class were made pensioners of the state. Few social forces remained to oppose his innovations.

Landowners were expropriated, and by 1815 most arable land had become state property. Irrigation projects nearly doubled the amount of arable land. Cotton was introduced to supply European textile mills and the profits accrued to the

state, but these were subject to price fluctuations on the world market.

The army was modernized. Previously a mercenary force, it became a conscript army, emphasizing its national aspect, even though its officers were usually Turks or other foreigners. Western style schools were created to train personnel needed for army and state, while educational missions were sent to Europe to learn the latest in training techniques and employ foreign experts.

Egyptian forces were initially important in defending Ottoman processions. Rebellion in Arabia was suppressed, and Egyptian forces fought the Greek struggle for independence until European powers intervened and defeated the Ottoman/Egyptian fleet at the battle of Navarino in 1827. Increasingly, however, Muhammad Ali sought greater autonomy from his Turkish suzerain. Parts of the province of Syria were conquered, and more seemed possible until, once again, European powers intervened. In July 1840 Great Britain, Russia, Austria, and Prussia agreed to end Egyptian rule in Syria. In compensation, Ali and his family were granted hereditary rights to rule Egypt, which remained

# Egypt

vinced the British government to issue a unilateral declaration of (limited) independence in February 1922. Britain retained responsibility for the security of the Suez Canal and the defense of Egypt, as well as the protection of foreign interests and minorities.

In 1923 a constitutional monarchy was established with Sultan Fuad as king. Saad Zaghlul, who had once again been sent to island exile, this time to the Seychelles, was released to participate in the first elections under the new constitution. The *Wafd*, now a political party, won overwhelmingly. In January 1924 Zaghlul became prime minister, but the forces he had unleashed were ill-contained. Nationalist extremists murdered British officials and Egyptian "collaborators," and in November 1924, the British commander of the Egyptian army was assassinated. Under pressure from the British, Zaghlul resigned from office. In subsequent elections his party still found support, but aged 70, he chose not to lead the new government, opting instead to lead the Chamber of Deputies. Here he was able to exercise some control of the more extreme wing of his party until his death in 1927.

This era of heightened nationalist agitation against British hegemony, and the general disorder that accompanied it, is the background for the formation, in 1928, of the Muslim Brotherhood. Founded by Hassan al-Banna, a charismatic school teacher determined to rid Egypt of British occupation, the Brotherhood (in Arabic, *Al-ikhwan Al-muslimun*) was the first and most important of what would come to be known as Islamic fundamentalist, or Islamist, groups. It advocated a return to the Koran and sayings of the Prophet Mohammad as the foundation of a modern Islamic society and took as its slogan "The Koran is our constitution."

From the late 1920s to the military coup of 1952, little positive change occurred. King Farouk succeeded to the Egyptian throne in 1936, but provided neither vision nor leadership. British influence waned, and in the same year, the Anglo-Egyptian treaty, restricting British military presence to the Suez Canal zone, was signed. The Wafd became increasingly corrupt and bickered with both King and rival parties, all the while bickering within itself. The Muslim Brotherhood became increasingly politicized, rejecting westernization, secularization, and modernization as baleful destroyers of Islamic purity. By the mid-1940s it had organized a terrorist wing and increasingly threatened both the monarchy and the Wafd as politics passed into the hands of a more radical generation.

By the end of World War II in which Egypt was neutral, restiveness of the lower classes rose to feverish heights. The

**Hieroglyphs, Karnac, Upper Egypt**            Photo by David Johns

British power but could do little against the reality of British hegemony. When he called on Egyptians to support Germany in World War I, Britain promptly declared Egypt a protectorate, deposed the Khedive and suppressed the title, appointing his uncle as Sultan of Egypt.

The peace negotiations which followed the allied victory resonated with rhetorical idealism. Wilsonian values of "self-determination" gave rise to another powerful expression of Egyptian nationalism in the formation of the *Wafd*. The term, in Arabic, means "delegation," and originated when a delegation of three prominent Egyptian politicians, led by Saad Zaghlul approached the British High Commissioner on November 13, 1918. They demanded the protectorate be abolished and replaced by a treaty of alliance,

and that they be allowed to travel to London to negotiate such a treaty directly with the British government.

Rejection of these demands resulted in widespread rioting, organized by clandestine *Wafd* cells throughout the country. When Zaghlul and three of his compatriots were arrested in March 1919 and deported to Malta, the disorders only increased. Zughlul was released as a concession to public opinion and he promptly departed for Paris, to present the Egyptian case to the victorious allies meeting to shape the post-war peace. He made little headway there, but in Egypt he became a national hero. For the next couple of years nationalist agitation by Zaghlul and the *Wafd* movement made Egypt virtually ungovernable. Exasperated, General Allenby, the British high commissioner, con-

283

# Egypt

people were governed and exploited by King Farouk and a number of wealthy landowners who controlled almost all the wealth and spent long periods of their time in Europe. Street demonstrations organized by militant nationalists and Islamists became more frequent and more violent, making governance more and more difficult. Concern over the fate of Palestine broadened the scope of Egyptian nationalism, previously focused almost exclusively on domestic concerns. In 1948 Egypt joined with Syria, Jordan and Iraq to dislodge the newly-created state of Israel militarily. Defeat in the first Arab-Israeli war revealed the ineptitude of the regime and further eroded what little legitimacy it retained. A group of disillusioned army officers, secretly organized by Gamal Abdel Nasser into the Free Officers Movement, plotted regime change, as they call it nowadays.

## The Nasser Years

On July 23, 1952, Nasser led the Free Officers in the *coup d'état* that forced King Farouk to abdicate in favor of his infant son, Fuad II. Major General Mohammed Naguib was chosen head of the government, while Nasser was appointed to the offices of deputy premier and minister of the interior. This situation did not last long. By 1953, the monarchy was ended and a Republic proclaimed. In the spring of 1954, power struggles within the ruling military junta were resolved in Nasser's favor: General Naguib was deposed and placed under house arrest. In the same year British troops finally left Egypt following the signing of an evacuation treaty. With an alien dynasty and foreign occupation both ended, there remained only the Palestinian issue to bedevil Egyptian foreign policy.

An assassination attempt by a member of the Muslim Brotherhood in 1954 allowed Nasser to crack down on this element of domestic opposition. Scores of Brotherhood leaders were executed or jailed. Another fundamentalist plot discovered in 1965 proved the Brotherhood had successfully infiltrated both the army and the police, two pillars of Nasser's regime. More arrests and executions followed, the most important of which was Sayyid Qutb, the ideological father of modern Islamic militancy, who was sent to the gallows in 1966.

Nasser declared Egypt a Muslim socialist republic, but Leninist practice and socialist economic doctrine tended to prevail. Political parties were eliminated and a single mass organization instituted, initially called the National Union, and later the Arab Socialist Union. He promulgated a constitution making Egypt a single-party socialist Arab state with Islam as the

**A busy Cairo street**

official religion in January 1956. In June 99.8% of the electorate approved it and 99.948% marked their ballots for Nasser, the only candidate, as president.

One month later, United States and Britain, suspicious of an arms deal Nasser had signed with Czechoslovakia, refused to finance a high dam at Aswan on the Nile River, a key element in Nasser's plans for developing Egypt. In reaction, Nasser defiantly nationalized the Suez Canal Company, declaring its tolls would be used to build the dam. In October Israel invaded the Sinai, destroying Egyptian bases and virtually the entire Egyptian air force. Britain and France soon joined in, flooding the canal zone with thousands of troops. The international community roundly condemned the invasion, and a ceasefire was declared in November. The invaders withdrew and UN emergency forces (UNEF) were sent in to man the tense Egyptian-Israeli border. Seen as the victim of neocolonialist aggression, Nasser emerged from the brief war with undiminished prestige throughout the Arab world. This encouraged a robust foreign policy engagement with Arab neighbors.

As a first step in creating Arab unity, Nasser joined Egypt with Syria to form the United Arab Republic in 1958. By 1961, however, bitterness had developed between the partners and Syria withdrew. Nasser blamed Syrian "reactionaries" and pushed the Egyptian revolution further to the left. Domestically, "scientific socialism" defined state economic policy, and in 1962, he intervened on the side of republicans fighting to overthrow the monarchy in Yemen. The move antagonized Saudi

Arabia, which supported Yemeni royalists, and the United States, which cut off its aid to Egypt in the mid 1960s.

With Egyptian troops bogged down in Yeman, pressures built on Nasser to re-engage the issue of Palestine. A decade of relative peace had been established by the presence of UNEF troops on the border with Israel and Nasser had consistently argued restraint at Arab summit meetings. By 1966, however, Palestinian incursions against Israel were being launched with increasing frequency from bases in Jordan, Lebanon, and Syria. When Israel retaliated, Nasser was taunted with failing the cause of Arab unity and hiding behind the protection of UNEF.

In sympathy with the Syrian government, which was loudly protesting possible Israeli aggression, in 1967 Nasser demanded withdrawal of UN forces stationed along the Israeli border, supposedly to enable Egypt to assist Syria (if necessary). UN Secretary General U Thant ordered the immediate withdrawal of the forces without consulting the Security Council or the General Assembly. Nasser's forces quickly occupied the heights of Sharm-al-Sheikh, a strategic overlook commanding the entrance to the Gulf of Aqaba and announced that all shipping to or from Israel was barred. Al Ahram, the semi-official newspaper of Cairo, published an editorial gleefully declaring that Israel had no choice but to fight if it wished to have access to the Red Sea.

Surrounded and fearing an imminent attack, Israel launched pre-emptive air strikes against Egypt on June 5, followed by a quick ground offensive against

Egyptian, Jordanian and Syrian forces. Iraqi airfields were also bombed to eliminate air assistance from that country. The initial air assault on Egypt was from the *west*, catching almost all Egyptian aircraft (supplied by the Soviets) on the ground. In the ensuing five days of battle, the Arab forces were completely routed. An estimated 10,000 Egyptians died and the Israeli army pushed to the Suez Canal. A UN-imposed cease-fire established an uneasy peace, which continued in effect until the fighting gradually escalated in 1970-1971, requiring another informal cease-fire agreement.

The Six-Day War, as the conflict came to be known, resulted in Israeli control of Sinai, the Golan Heights, the Gaza Strip, East Jerusalem and the West Bank. Both Egyptian arms and the Arab cause were crushed. Nasser resigned from office, but a popular outpouring of support "forced" him to rescind the resignation. To replace $5 billion in lost arms, the USSR supplied almost $7 billion in equipment after 1967, but the radical phase of the Egyptian revolution, with its dependence on Eastern European notions and support, was ended

Nasser died unexpectedly in 1970 from a reported heart attack; Egypt and the Arab world were plunged into mourning. There was a dramatic funeral for the fallen leader. He had stimulated Egyptian and Arab pride, but all his foreign policy adventures had essentially ended in failure. Domestically, his development plans had increased the industrial sector from 10% of

**Anwar Sadat**

GDP in 1950 to 21% in 1970, but any benefits from that were eroded by rapid population growth. (In deference to Muslim demands, the government did not push birth control policies.) A socialist economy also produced a huge state bureaucracy—the employer of first resort—and an army of state companies that soon became sluggish, cumbersome, and corrupt.

### The Sadat Years

Nasser was succeeded by his vice president, Anwar Sadat, another member of the Free Officers. He was thought to be a weak figurehead, but things turned out

otherwise. He quickly ousted his rivals and made frequent and dramatic threats to "invade" and "crush" Israel, but until 1973 he did nothing in that direction. When the Soviets criticized Egyptian military prowess, Sadat sent all 20,000 Soviet military advisors packing in 1972, accusing the Soviets of failing to furnish the modern weaponry needed to conquer Israel.

Israeli control in the Sinai tightened after the 1967 war; there were Israeli settlements, and oil wells appeared. In an effort to wrest occupied areas from Israel, Egypt and Syria launched a two-front attack in October 1973; they had the military and financial support of Arab states and the USSR. The move, made during the Jewish religious festival of *Yom Kippur,* took Israel completely by surprise, and it appeared that Egypt might well be successful in the initial days of conflict.

Israel responded by first driving the Syrians back within shell range of their capital, Damascus, then turned to the Egyptian front. After the largest tank battle in history, the Israelis made daring crossings of the Suez Canal, launching a "pincer" attack which threatened to surround the Egyptians. Within hours the tide of battle had shifted and Cairo itself was threatened.

With Russia threatening intervention, a cease-fire strong-armed the Israelis into giving up all territory west of the canal and enough territory in the Sinai Peninsula to salvage Sadat's reputation; despite defeat, he emerged a modest hero. Additional Sinai territory, including the Abu Rudeis oil field, was ceded to Egypt in late 1976. With U.S. assistance the Suez Canal, closed since the 1967 strife, was back in operation by mid-1975.

While establishing his bona fides on Israel, Sadat changed many of his predecessor's policies. Russian military assistance had already been dispatched before the war, but to lure foreign investment, socialism was also abandoned. Egypt shifted from Soviet support to contributions from Arab oil states (principally Saudi Arabia) and the United States. The monopoly of political space by Egypt's single party was ended, and political parties were permitted to organize and operate. Sadat also reordered the relationship between the state and the Muslim faithful.

Calling himself the "Believer President," Sadat introduced Sharia law in the constitution (as one of the "sources of Egyptian legislation"), lifted restrictions on Muslim fundamentalist organizations, and permitted the proliferation of private mosques which escaped state supervision and control. This would ultimately facilitate the large-scale introduction of Wahhabi fundamentalism, financed by Saudi

**Abu Simbel, Upper Egypt**                                                                 Photo by David Johns

# Egypt

Arabia, into Egypt's more mainstream Islam. To counterbalance the weight of the Nasserite left, Sadat encouraged the growing influence of *al-Gama'a al-Islamiyya*, or Islamic Group, which had emerged around 1973 on university campuses where it violently opposed the student left. (Its spiritual leader was Omar Abdel-Rahman, currently in jail in the USA for the 1993 bombing of New York's World Trade Center.)

Elections in 1976 resulted in an overwhelming victory for Sadat's Arab Socialist Party. The victory gave the president a large political space in which to maneuver, and he proceeded to tackle the major impediment to Egyptian economic reconstruction: peace with Israel. On November 19, 1977, Sadat undertook the most controversial move of his career: he flew to Jerusalem to address a session of the Israeli Knesset. Israelis were stunned and excited at this "breakthrough." Sadat delivered an impassioned plea for a just and lasting peace, but held fast to the proposition that Israel must withdraw from occupied Arab territory and grant Palestinians "their rights." Israeli Prime Minister Begin countered with the Israeli position: we are willing to negotiate, but your price is too high. He insisted that Israel must have "defensible borders."

After much "shuttle diplomacy" and a September 1978 meeting between Sadat, Menachem Begin, the Israeli Prime Minister, and Jimmy Carter at the presidential retreat of Camp David, a peace treaty between the two countries was signed at the White House on March 26, 1979. When each nation was assured it would be protected from surprise attack, the treaty boiled down to these key points: (1) Israel agreed to withdraw all its armed forces and civilians from the Sinai Peninsula within a period of three years; (2) Egypt guaranteed passage of Israeli ships and cargoes through the Suez Canal; (3) both nations pledged full diplomatic, cultural, and economic relations, and (4) there would be a free movement of people and goods between the two countries. A vast American economic aid program would make Egypt second only to Israel as the recipient of American largess. The Nasserian revolution was virtually turned on its head.

Arab reaction to the treaty was not positive. Islamic fundamentalists declared it an act of treason. Financial aid from the Gulf States and Saudi Arabia was cut, and Egypt was expelled from the Arab League. (It did not rejoin the League until 1989.) At home, a parlous economic situation made Sadat's support fragile at best. In January 1977, well before the dramatic flight to Israel, bread riots had broken out in Egypt's major cities. Some 79 persons were killed, 1,000 wounded and another 1,250 arrested.

Sadat's liberalization of Egyptian economic and political life, limited as it was, ultimately undermined his regime. In August 1981 an alleged plot linking communists and Muslim extremists was discovered; more than 1,500 opponents of the regime, both right and left, were arrested. The Russian ambassador, accused of complicity, was expelled, and a state of emergency was declared. One month later, while reviewing a military parade, Sadat was gunned down by rebel soldiers belonging to al-Jihad (Islamic Jihad or "Holy War"), a clandestine fundamentalist group run by Ayman al-Zawahri, who later went on to become Osama Bin Laden's right-hand man. It was the group's spiritual guide, Omar Abdel-Rahman, who reportedly issued the fatwa (decree) authorizing Sadat's assassination.

Eight days after the slaying and one day after an overwhelming nationwide referendum, Vice-President Hosni Mubarak took the oath as Egypt's fourth president, pledging to continue the policies of the fallen leader. A former bomber pilot and air force chief of staff, Mubarak had been named to the largely honorific post of Vice President by Anwar Sadat as a concession to the army, whose "heroes" of the 1973 campaign he had successfully sidetracked. It confirmed the army's continuing political importance as a principal pillar of the regime.

Indeed, the army is a pampered institution, treated with kid gloves. Sadat's economic liberalization allowed the army to enter the economic field where it became an essential though discreet actor. It owns agricultural land and farm equipment businesses. It controls pharmaceutical businesses as well as construction firms, and at least 20% of Cairo's bread comes from Army bakeries. It controls the free trade zones at Port Said and Suez, and benefits from tax exemptions on the import of various goods and equipment. Its businesses are also exempt from labor legislation, which gives them a significant competitive advantage. Egypt's arms industry is army-controlled, producing mines, light arms and even Abrams tanks under American license. Retired generals sit on the boards of state corporations and members of the armed forces have access to reserved housing, commissary subsidies, and special vacation sites and opportunities.

## The Mubarak Years

The principal challenge faced by President Mubarak has been the threat to state and institutions posed by political Islam—those groups dedicated to overthrowing the regime by violence in the name of Islam. While the assassination of President Sadat is their most notable act of violence, Coptic Christians, secular intellectuals, police and army officials, as well as politicians and cabinet ministers have been targeted by Muslim extremists. In 1995 an attempt was made on the life of President Mubarak while he was attending a meeting in Addis Ababa. *Al-Gama'a al-Islamiyya* even attacked the economic underpinnings of the regime by its bloody assault on Western tourists, the worst of which came in 1997 when 58 tourists, mostly Swiss, were massacred at Luxor.

President Mubarak has diminished Islamist violence through a combination of savage repression and indulgence. After the Sadat assassination, hundreds of militant Islamists were arrested and the regime encouraged their departure to Afghanistan (via Saudi Arabia) where they could fight alongside the Afghan *mujahadin*. The Muslim Brotherhood was even permitted to participate in the elections of 1984 and 1987, but the explosion of Islamic violence in the 1990s required firmer action.

In 1993 Islamic Jihad launched attacks against both the interior minister and the prime minister. Both were unsuccessful, but in the latter attack, the bomb missed its target, injured twenty-one people and killed a twelve-year-old schoolgirl. Her death outraged Egyptians, and when her coffin was carried through the streets of Cairo people cried, "Terrorism is the enemy of God!" In the war against terrorists, mass arrests, torture, extra-judicial execu-

**Egyptian Charm**

tions, and the use of military courts to try civilians have all prompted criticism of the regime's human rights violations.

Given the reality of Islamist terrorism, Egypt complained for years about the absence of cooperation it received from its Arab and Western partners. Only after the Luxor massacre did attitudes change, and after the bombings of American embassies in Kenya and Tanzania by al-Qaeda operatives, the CIA began to work closely with its Egyptian counterparts. Since then, Egypt has obtained the extradition of a number of important militants from places like Albania, Bulgaria, Kuwait, Yemen and even Latin America. Domestically, too, the Luxor massacre changed things. Middle class opinion was appropriately horrified and turned against militant extremism to such an extent that *Gama'a al-Islamiyya's* military wing declared a unilateral cease-fire in 1999, though some cells refused the call. In 2001 the group published four books explaining its abandonment of *jihad* and the armed struggle.

Despite the seeming success of repression, the whole dreary cycle seemed to repeat itself in October 2004, when six years of relative calm were shattered by bloody attacks on tourist sites in Sinai. Terrorists struck the Taba Hilton Hotel and two tourist camps, killing 34 people and wounding 105. The government claimed the car bombings were the work of a small, isolated group of Palestinian and Egyptian terrorists who died in the attack, but it continued to track down remnants of the group which took refuge in the mountainous Bedouin area of the Sinai well into 2005. As many as 2,400 people were arrested and held without charges months after the attack.

The Egyptian political system has many of the trappings of a multiparty democracy, but they remain more decorative than real. Before legislative elections in 1984, Mubarak legalized political parties and guaranteed them freedom of the press. In the elections, somewhat less than half of the 12.4 million registered voters cast ballots, but, with an assist from administrative manipulation, they gave an overwhelming vote of confidence to Mubarak's National Democratic Party (NDP) which had replaced Sadat's Arab Socialist Party. It won 389 out of 448 total seats in the People's Assembly. The election also saw the participation of the Muslim Brotherhood, presumably to offer an alternative to the rigidly fundamentalist Islamic Jihad. The New Wafd Party, allied with the Muslim Brotherhood, won a total of 59 seats. In the highly disputed legislative elections of 1987, the NDP won 346 seats, while the Islamic alliance won 60, 37 of them from the Muslim Brotherhood. New

**President Hosni Mubarak**

Wafd, which supports a liberal economy domestically and is anti-Israeli internationally, secured 36 seats.

Legislative elections in 1995 were held against a background of President Mubarak's decision to widen an anti-terrorist, anti-Islamist campaign. Widespread arrests occurred, and military tribunals issued death sentences for some and prison terms for a great many more. Enthusiasm for the crackdown greatly accelerated following the attempt on the president's life while he was visiting Addis Ababa in midyear. Cynics claimed all of this was calculated to influence the elections later that year.

Held in November, they resulted in an overwhelming victory for the ruling National Democratic Party (NDP), achieved through unprecedented irregularity and fraud. The Muslim Brotherhood, many of whose candidates had been condemned by military court days before the election, was steamrolled; the other opposition parties were no more successful. The NDP carried 430 seats; New Wafd was reduced to six, and the Muslin Brotherhood managed to elect only a single candidate. In all, only 14 opposition representatives sat in the People's Assembly, hardly a glowing endorsement of effective multiparty democracy.

Elections to Egypt's upper house, the Shura (Consultative) Council, took place in mid-1998 amid general apathy and a boycott by those parties capable of fielding candidates. Two-thirds of the largely powerless body is elected directly, and half of these must be workers and farmers—a holdover from the days of Nasser's socialist orientation. The president of the republic appoints the other third—one of the few ways women and Coptic Christians can enter the legislature.

The People's Assembly election of October 2000, the first conducted with the supervision of judges to assure fairness, proved something of an embarrassment for President Mubarak's National Democratic Party. While the party nominally

holds 85% of the seats in the Assembly, most of the new MPs representing the party originally ran as independents. As a consequence, the government's control of its parliamentary majority is as sure a thing as it has been in the past. The Assembly elections also marked the return of the Muslim Brotherhood, which managed to win 17 seats despite the usual harassment by the authorities. Though the group remains officially banned, individuals affiliated with it ran successfully as "independents."

Egyptian presidential elections are also part of the democratic façade. There are no balloon-dropping political party nominating conventions in Egypt. Instead, the presidential candidate is nominated by parliament—the People's Assembly and the Shura Council—and then approved in a countrywide referendum. Unsurprisingly Hosni Mubarak was nominated to a fourth presidential term in July 1999. In September Egyptian voters marked their ballots—a green circle to approve, a black circle to disapprove—and 93.97% voted to approve Mubarak's nomination.

Given overwhelming single-party dominance of the system one can easily understand how opposition is sometimes expressed in outrageous political violence, but because of that violence, stability has been privileged over expression. As a consequence the regime is authoritarian and political life is stifled. The search for stability through silence is itself destabilizing. Denied voice in the political arena, Islamist sentiment erupts elsewhere.

The determination to control political life in the name of stability has had a corrosive effect on Egypt's political system. Power is dangerously concentrated in the hands of one man, the president. An aging generation of politicians has been ossified in place, with little intention of giving up the benefits of power. The system has become hermetically sealed off from social reality and desperately needs to be opened up. Its reinvigoration requires new blood and ideas.

Surprisingly, the man chosen to infuse new blood and ideas seems to be Mubarak—not the president, but his son, Gamal. Appointed to the NDP's 25-member secretariat in 2000, Gamal Mubarak is chairman of the party's policy committee, which, in early 2003, proposed the abolition of state security courts and the creation of a national council for human rights. The younger Mubarak has also spoken of the need "dynamize political life" by modernizing laws governing political parties.

Reform may actually come earliest in the economic sphere. In July 2004 a cabinet shuffle brought in a new NDP government, reportedly close to Gamal

# Egypt

Cairo modernizes—McDonald's arrives

Photo by David Johns

Mubarak and strongly reformist. The new Canadian-educated prime minister, Ahmed Nazif, was the youngest (at 52) and most effective member of the outgoing cabinet and a surprise appointment. Within a few weeks of taking office the new government had introduced far-reaching economic changes: customs tariffs were slashed by 40%, a new trade deal with Israel and the United States was signed, income taxes were cut by half, and many bureaucratic impediments to doing business in Egypt were swept away. The objective was to spur foreign investment and revitalize a dormant economy, and the Prime Minister expressed it succinctly: "Egypt is open for business."

### Foreign Policy Issues

Like Libya, Egypt has recently turned its attention to sub-Saharan Africa. The interest is both economic and political. Egypt joined the Common Market for Eastern and Southern Africa (COMESA) in 1998 and shortly afterwards, acceded to COMESA's free trade area. Tariffs on imports from COMESA countries have been reduced by 90%, but trade with these countries accounts for only 1.1% of exports and 1.3% of imports (2000). Far more important are strategic necessities. African states represent potential threats for Egypt on the issue of sharing and using the Nile waters. The existing Nile Water Agreement was signed in 1929, ratified in 1952, and barred states from using the waters of Lake Victoria without Egypt's permission. (Sudan and Egypt renegotiated the agree-

ment in 1959 to permit construction of Aswan High Dam.)

The agreement, which benefited only Egypt and Sudan, became outdated as other states on the river and its tributaries made plans to use the waters for their own development. Not being independent in 1929, and thus not themselves signatories to the original agreement, the other riverine states pressed for renegotiation. (When he was president of Tanzania, the late Julius Nyerere argued that all such treaties were nullified by independence.)

Ethiopian proposals to construct a series of dams on the Blue Nile galvanized action, and in June 2001 the Nile Basin Ini-

tiative (NBI) was created. It linked ten Nile Basin states: Burundi, the Democratic Republic of Congo, Egypt, Eritrea, Ethiopia, Kenya, Rwanda, Sudan, Tanzania and Uganda.

With $140 million granted by the World Bank and donor governments, seven feasibility studies were undertaken to study possible cooperative development of Nile resources, but frustrated by a lack of progress, Kenya announced its intention to disregard the treaty's provisions in late 2003. Pushing things further, Tanzania precipitated a crisis by diverting water from Lake Victoria in early 2004.

NBI crisis meetings were convened in Uganda the very next month. For Egypt, the issue is critical. Of the Nile's estimated annual allotment of 83 billion cubic meters (bcm), Egypt has been receiving 55 bcm under the 1929 treaty. Virtually its entire agricultural sector, especially irrigated developments in the south, is dependent on Nile waters, and the country has repeatedly said it would reject any proposal to lower its quota. It has searched for water alternatives for its neighbors, including financing the digging of wells in Kenya, but it is unlikely these will provide adequate replacement waters. By June 2004, while NBI experts were desperately seeking a legal solution, Egypt's Foreign Minister, Ahmed Maher, began to sound a softer note: "The Nile is a unifying element not a dividing one," he said. "There is plenty of water for all of us."

The war against Iraq brought extraordinary pressure to bear on the government in 2003. Though emergency laws ban public demonstrations, the government sanctioned huge mass rallies to show itself sensitive to popular outrage. The demonstrations have included members of the Muslim Brotherhood, and several Arab-language TV stations filmed the events—

Mediterranean rock formation, West of Alexandria

Photo by Rodney McNabb

288

an example of how controlled demonstrations provide a safety valve within a generally repressive system.

President Mubarak himself viewed the war as completely destabilizing and has deplored what he sees as its consequences: "If there is one bin Laden today, there will be 100 bin Ladens afterward." Responding to domestic pressures he has sought to activate Russia's role in the region to strike a balance against what most Arabs see as a biased U.S. position. This was the major thrust of a state visit the president made to Russia in May, 2004.

The visit was given unprecedented coverage by Russia's printed and electronic media, and Mubarak said enough to ruffle lots of feathers among U.S. policy makers. Among other things, the president invited Russia to join the Organization of the Islamic Conference (OIC). Russia had, he noted, "20 million Muslims who live in peace with Christians." Perversely overlooking the on-going conflict in Chechnya, he suggested Russian membership in the OIC would "invalidate theories about a clash of civilizations and cultures."

## Political Reform

Egypt's next presidential election is scheduled for October 2005, and the regime is under increasing pressure to open a closed political system. Demands for reform have become increasingly louder both within and outside the NDP. Even U.S. President Bush urged Egypt to "show the way toward democracy" in his State of the Union speech in February 2005. By May the NDP unveiled a tepid response to heated demands: a constitutional amendment for multiparty presidential elections in the fall. The proposal was hedged with limitations that would make genuine electoral competition difficult to achieve. Only parties already recognized by the government could put forth a candidate, and anyone wanting to run as an independent would have to secure 250 signatures from current members of parliament or local councils—most of whom are members of the ruling NDP. In the May referendum 83% of the voters approved the change, with 54% of registered voters going to the polls, despite a boycott called by opposition parties.

The only candidate likely to meet the new requirements in Ayman Nour, the founder of a new political party, Al-Ghad (Tomorrow). Nour has already tasted the bitter fruit accorded regime opponents in Egypt: after announcing he planned to run for president against Mr. Mubarak, he was jailed in early 2005 on trumped up charges of forging some 2,000 signatures to secure registration for his party in 2004. It was the first new party permitted in years. The incident prompted Secretary of State Condolezza Rice to cancel a planned trip to Egypt in February, and Mr. Nour was ultimately released on bail. Egyptian authorities have said he will be tried in June, and if convicted he would be ineligible for the October presidential campaign.

**Culture:** The Bibliotheca Alexandrina, in Alexandria, received the distinguished Aga Khan Award for Architecture in 2004. It was honored for its "innovative approach to the design and placement of a large, symbolic form on one of the most important waterfronts in the world." President Mubarak took up the project in 1988 to revive the legendary traditions of Alexandria as center of learning and to provide the city with a landmark worthy of its past. Excavations for the site began in 1995 and the building opened in October 2002.

The building is designed as a tilting disc rising from the ground; four levels lie below ground and seven above. Its main reading room seats 2,000 readers, and the facility houses six specialist libraries, three museums, seven research centres, three permanent galleries, space for temporary exhibitions, a planetarium, a public plaza, offices, and a cafeteria. The Aga Khan jury said the building was not only "groundbreaking in architectural and technological terms," but celebrated learning across all cultures.

The backbone of Egyptian society traditionally has been its peasant farmers. Closely tied to the soil, they tend to remain in the area of their ancestors. An age-old class system is now virtually extinct. Formerly termed Fellahin (plowmen), in recent years these agriculturalists, densely packed along the Nile, have begun to employ increasingly modern methods of farming, although beans and dark bread are still the staple food for millions.

There are an estimated five million Christians in Egypt, members of the Coptic Orthodox Church. Established by the Apostle Saint Mark early in the first century, the Coptic Church is one of the oldest Christian churches in existence. Its leader, officially Pope of Alexandria and Patriarch of the See of St. Mark, is selected by an electoral college composed predominantly of laymen. It selects three qualified monks, at least 50 years of age, as candidates for the office of Patriarch, and after prayer, the new Pope is chosen by lot. The church's present leader, His Holiness Pope Shenouda III, is the 117th Coptic patriarch in a line unbroken from St. Mark.

After the Arab conquest of Egypt in the 7th century, Copts ceased speaking Greek, increasing their isolation from other branches of Christianity. Today Arabic is the language of Coptic services with only a few short refrains spoken in Coptic.

Throughout its history the Coptic Church has been subject to periodic repressions. The Roman Emperor Diocletian was so brutal that his horrific executions of 284 AD mark the beginning of the Coptic calendar. Although important economically, Copts are frequently discriminated against in terms of employment. One of the country's most skilled diplomats, Boutros Boutros Ghali, was never made Foreign Minister because, as he was told, a Copt could never represent Egypt at meetings of the Organization of Islamic States. (He went on to become the UN Secretary General.) As a concession to his Coptic citizens, President Mubarak made the Coptic Christmas an official holiday for Egypt in early 2003.

Cairo, with all its suburbs, contains more than 16 million people—the largest city in Africa and the Middle East. Nearly two million automobiles clog its streets and pour asphyxiating exhausts into the atmosphere. To this cement, iron, chemical and metal factories and smelters offer their noxious contributions. Fumes from tons of daily garbage, uncollected, rise to join the smog. The city of a thousand minarets is almost always veiled in a cloak of yellow-gray haze. With too much of everything—noise, dust, heat, garbage and hawkers—Cairo ranks high among the world's urban stress zones. For the tourist, the city is a difficult stop. Noses run, eyes water. Many try to see the major sights—the pyramids, the Museum, the grand market—in a day and then move to less polluted centers.

Cairo's governor has plans for the chaotic city: extending water, sewage and telephone systems; reclaiming the banks of the Nile for public parks. Contractors have been found to haul away the 8,000 tons of garbage generated daily. Taxis, minivans and city buses are switching to compressed natural gas—a fuel system in which Cairo is now a world leader.

Egyptian women are slowly gaining legal protection and rights in a male–dominated society. The tortured course of rules governing female circumcision finally concluded at the end of 1997. In December the country's highest judicial authority, the Council of State, banned the practice of excision, even when the consent of child or parent is given. The court ruled that excision—surgical removal of the clitoris—was physical mutilation as defined in the Penal Code and was therefore punishable by the law. Although there is no Koranic sanction for the practice, female circumcision had long been practiced in Egypt. Indeed the operation has traditionally been seen as a mark of virtue and guarantor of modesty. In 1997 a detailed

# Egypt

His Holiness Pope Shenuda III, head of the Egyptian Coptic Church

demographic survey indicated that more than 97% of women and girls had been through the ordeal.

In early 1999 the government introduced a modification of law codes to give women greater divorce rights. Islamic law allows a man divorce by simple repetition of a ritual formula three times—and divorce is immediate. A woman, on the other hand, might have to go through years of litigation if her husband were unwilling to grant divorce. Every year some 20,000 women went before the courts requesting a divorce and if it was not given immediately, the woman remained under the legal tutelage of her husband who could, for example, prevent her from getting a passport.

The new code was finally approved in January 2000 after rousing heated controversy. (Hard-line Muslim clerics had described it as a threat to the stability of society.) The reforms of Egyptian family law are far-reaching. A woman will now be able to divorce her husband, with or without his assent. She is required to return any dowry or its equivalent in cash or property. And she will also be able to call on the Egyptian government to garnishee her husband's wages if he refuses to provide for her. If he disappears or cannot pay a court-ordered living allowance, she will be able to draw from a special state bank to keep her family afloat. Lost in the politics of compromise was a provision that would have allowed Egyptian women to travel abroad without the permission of their husbands.

Homosexuals are subject to severe repression in Egypt. For years the media and government have pretended homosexuality was a Western "disease" that hardly existed in Egypt. In May 2001,

however, the police raided the somewhat appositely named "Queen Boat"—a three deck floating discotheque moored on the Nile whose Thursday night parties attracted a sizable gay clientele—and arrested dozens of attendees. After releasing foreigners, the Egyptians were jailed. Then, using the detainees' address books and confiscated mobile phones, the police tracked down and arrested dozens more.

Prosecutors argued that their actions defiled Islam and constituted a risk to the state, justifying the trial of 52 gay men in the State Security Court—an institution created by emergency laws passed after Anwar Sadat's assassination in 1981. Human Rights Watch reported they were subjected to humiliating "forensic" examinations, tortured, and given long jail terms for "debauchery." Twenty-three were convicted and jailed for one to five years. There is no appeal from the State Security Court, and there was no intervention on the defendants' behalf by human rights organizations.

So stigmatized is homosexuality in Egypt that the Egyptian Organization for Human Rights, which had defended the rights of women, Copts, and prisoners, refused to intervene. Admitting that Egyptians simply had no tolerance for it, the organization's director said: "What could we do? Nothing. If we were to uphold this issue, this would be the end of what remains of the concept of human rights in Egypt."

Three Egyptian citizens have been honored as Nobel laureates. The late President Anwar Sadat was the first to receive the Nobel prize for peace; he was followed by the celebrated novelist Naguib Mahfouz, who won the prize for literature. In 1999, the Egyptian scientist, Dr Ahmed Zewail won the Nobel prize in chemistry. Dr. Zewali received his award for studies on the transition states of chemical reactions using spectroscopy.

**Economy:** Following the terrorist attacks of September 11 the Egyptian economy experienced its worst crisis in a decade, even worse than that following the local terrorist assault at Luxor in 1997. Tourism, which accounts for 12% of the economy, and 1 in 7 jobs, has been severely impacted. In 2000, 5.4 million people visited Egypt and accounted for $4.3 billion in revenues. A year later, following terror attacks in the United States and war in Afghanistan, visitors fell to 4.7 million and revenues to $3.8 million. The worst month was November 2001 when tourist visits declined by 52%. The 2004 attacks in Sinai chilled a trade that had just begun to recover.

The four main sources of hard currency for Egypt—tourism, oil, fees from the

Suez Canal, and workers' remittances—were all affected by the terrorist attacks in New York and Washington. The war in Iraq was a second shock to the Egyptian economy. Iraq was Egypt's number one trading partner, with exports exceeding $1.7 billion in 2002.

As a consequence of these external events, the economy slowed considerably: real GDP grew only 3.2% in 2002 and was no better in 2003. With a population growth of 1.8%, however, those figures suggest stagnation rather than improvement. Unofficial estimates place Egypt's unemployment in the 15% to 25% range (officially it's only 10%); the rate is highest among young job seekers, and each year some 800,000 more of them enter the job market.

Given the government's policy of admitting all high school graduates into the university system (12 government universities, with 8 affiliated braches and 20 campuses), the annual number of university graduates is around 195,200. Unfortunately the system fails to provide the skills most relevant to the job market. The market is simply unable to absorb the many university students graduating each year.

In recent years, oil revenues have represented about 40% of Egypt's foreign exchange, but oil production has been declining. The oil fields of the Gulf of Suez and Sinai are mature. Egypt's crude oil production peaked at 922,000 barrels per day (bll/d) in 1996; it averaged only around 594,000 bll/d in 2004. Egypt's last major discovery was 20 years ago in the Western Desert. Offshore exploration in the Mediterranean is under way, but to date, most discoveries off the Nile Delta have been natural gas.

Foreign oil companies began active exploration for natural gas in the early 1990s, and found significant deposits in the Nile Delta, offshore from the Nile Delta, and in the Western Desert. Over the last five years exploration has resulted in the discovery of at least 33 major fields—those whose output exceeds 100 million barrels of oil equivalent. Egypt's natural gas production nearly doubled between 1999 and 2003, and in 2004 it had reached 3.6 billion cubic feet per day (bcf/d); daily production was expected to rise to around five billion cubic feet by 2007. The government estimates Egyptian natural gas reserves at 66 trillion cubic feet (Tcf).

Given these resources, natural gas is likely to be the primary engine of growth for the Egyptian economy in the coming years. In a rare example of economic cooperation between Arab states, Egypt and Jordan inaugurated gas pipeline in July 2003, marking Egypt's first exports of natural gas. The pipeline is expected to move 600,000 tons of natural gas annually, from

Egypt to Jordan, earning $70 million in its first year of operation, with projections of $200 million in two years and $500 million in five. The pipeline is part of a longer line planned to eventually reach Turkey and the markets of Europe.

The availability of abundant natural gas has also made liquefaction feasible. One liquefied natural gas (LNG) complex at Damietta began shipments in January 2005. Another at Idku, is still under construction and a third is being contemplated. The Damietta LNG plant, which will ultimately have an annual capacity of over five million tons (t/y), is the largest single LNG plant in the world. Union Fenosa Gas of Spain is developing the project and has guaranteed the sale of 3.2 million t/y over its 25-year lifetime; the Egyptian Natural Gas Holding Company (EGAS) has guaranteed to sell the remaining 2.3 million t/y.

Prior to 1967 the economy was largely dependent on a single crop: cotton. Egyptian long staple and extra-long staple cotton is probably the best in the world. It is stronger and can be spun more finely than nearly any other variety in the world. In America it is associated with the most luxurious bed sheets; in Europe, with the finest shirts, and in India, with the thinnest, most diaphanous saris. Despite its reputation, however, the Egyptian cotton industry is dying. Cotton revenues have fallen below those supplied by petroleum.

The area devoted to cotton cultivation has gradually fallen from 1.3 million acres in 1980/81 to 780,000 acres. Almost all of this acreage is devoted to extra-long and long staple cotton, but only about a third of total production is exported. Roughly 200,000 tons goes to the domestic market, which cannot adequately process high-end cotton. When Gamal Abdel Nasser nationalized the industry in the 1950s, emphasis was placed on creating jobs and import substitution to clothe the country's poor population. Eastern European-supplied machinery could only process much coarser grades of cotton. Ready-to-wear textile manufacturers today prefer to import cheaper short-fiber cotton than use home-grown material.

Only 2.85% of Egypt's total land mass is arable, basically the narrow strip of land that borders the Nile and its delta. Agriculture, which is dominated by small landholders, contributed 16.1% to GDP in 2003 and employed about 35% of Egyptian workers. In 2001 Egypt exported 1.3 billion tons of agricultural products, including 585,000 tons of rice, 234,000 tons of citrus, 188,000 tons of onions and 170,000 tons of potatoes. According to government officials, the Egyptian wheat crop grew from 8 million metric tons in 1990 to 18.5 metric tons in 2000. Despite this, Egypt still imports more than half of its food, which includes 10 million tons of grain each year.

To sustain the agricultural sector the government has sought to open new farming lands through vast irrigation projects. In many ways they are Hosni Mubarak's Pharaonic legacy to Egypt when he leaves office: two enormous water projects, both involving Nile waters, both designed to create hundreds of thousands of acres of arable soil for land-starved Egyptian farmers, both costing billions of dollars.

In the south, the Toshka project is designed to pump 5 billion cubic meters of water a year from Lake Nasser into the Western Desert to put some 1.04 million acres of land under cultivation. Construction work on the pumping stations continues nightly to avoid Toshka's inhospitable temperatures, which can reach 125F in the summer. Water will be pumped in what has been described as the world's longest canal and distributed along four tributaries.

The Kingdom Agricultural Development Company, owned by a billionaire Saudi prince, has agreed to invest around $300 million to set up agro-industries on 100,000 acres of land. It might be tough to attract farmers here, no matter how land-hungry they may be. The nearest town is 62 miles away and has little excess labor supply.

The 200-mile long canal is estimated to cost nearly $2 billion. President Mubarak has named it the Sheikh Zaid al-Nahayan Canal, to honor the Emir of Abu Dhabi

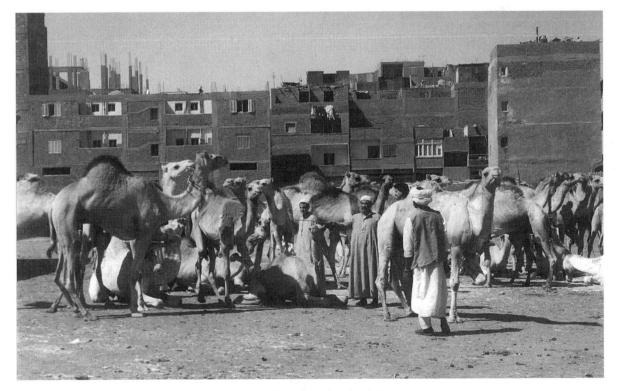

**Camel market in Cairo**

# Egypt

and recognize the sheikh's aid to earlier irrigation projects. Ethiopia, which claims to contribute over 80% of the Nile water and to use a mere 1%, has raised diplomatic storm signals over the project. Internal criticism of the project is also mounting, especially since one investment bank has recently downgraded Egypt. The *Financial Times* of London reported that the bank thought mega-projects like Toshka were "putting an unbearable strain on the government's finances, helping to create unacceptably high interest rates, a deteriorating balance of payments and putting pressure on the currency."

In the north a similar irrigation project has already started to bring water to the parched Sinai desert. The first phase of the project, which has been dubbed the "Peace Canal," was opened in late 1997. It consists of four 42-meter deep ducts that actually carry Nile waters under the Suez Canal. The project, which is designed to add 544,388 acres of arable land, will cost an estimated $1.7 billion. Financing has come mainly from the Emir of Kuwait, Sheikh Jaber al-Ahmed Al-Sabah.

High-value agricultural products offer one of the best opportunities for export expansion, but the country faces fundamental infrastructure problems even if farmers could be convinced to grow the crops. A well developed highway system to speed products to distant markets and cold storage facilities are two of the most obvious. Only recently has Cairo airport been equipped with cold storage facilities that allow perishable goods to be transported. Previously 40% were lost due to poor storage before export.

Egyptian tenant farmers, on whom the agricultural sector is dependent, have been in a state of uncertainty since 1997 when new rent control and security of tenure laws began to be implemented. The problem goes back to 1952, when one of President Nasser's first acts was to establish rent controls and give tenants an almost complete guarantee that they could pass leases on to their children in perpetuity. The policy's goal was twofold: to gain favor with peasantry and break the back of the landlord class.

By 1992 the distribution of political power had shifted. The People's Assembly was completely dominated by President Mubarak's National Democratic Party where landlords were well represented. The assembly passed new legislation that abolished rent controls and any presumptive security of tenure. Lag time was built into the legislation to give both tenants and landlords time to adjust; it was not to be implemented for five years.

Since 1997 the process of implementation has had its difficulties. Rents tripled, and tenants became dismissible at a year's notice. To break the connection between the land and its tenancy holder, some landlords forced farmers to move to another plot of land. When police were called in to enforce landlord rights, a number of regrettable incidents occurred. Skirmishes between the two parties have resulted in 87 deaths, 545 injuries and 798 arrests according to human rights groups.

Some 42,000 tenant farmers are still landless, and the government has insufficient lands to offer. In this situation one can easily understand the government's interest in its vast reclamation projects

The government hopes to create jobs by making Egypt an export-driven economy. The goals are lofty. To attain a growth of 7%, which has been targeted, exports must rise by 11% annually. Privatization, though sluggish, is envisioned as one means of increasing productivity, but perhaps there are even greater problems in finding markets for the goods produced.

Currently Egypt only exports 20% of its manufactured goods. Egyptian politicians remain wary of a trade agreement with the EU, fearing domestic manufacturers will be unable to compete with European companies in a free market. They also fear Egyptian agricultural products will find no advantage in such agreements.

**The Future:** Military and financial assistance from the U.S. will continue. The illiteracy, poverty and alienation that helped fuel the Islamist movement remain as much a presence as the pyramids. The basic illiberal nature of the regime does nothing to alleviate these concerns.

President Mubarak is reported to be growing increasingly frail, but he has never appointed a vice-president, which could complicate an eventual succession, nor, as of mid-2005, had he declared his intentions for the October presidential election. The rapid promotion of his son Gamal within the NDP—he is now one of the party's five top leaders—has suggested to some that he is being groomed as a possible successor to his father. Only 41, Gamal is seen as the leader of those younger politicians who want change and would likely encounter significant opposition from the army and older party hacks were dynastic ambitions pushed.

# Socialist People's Libyan Arab Jamahiriya

**Modern Tripoli**                Photo by Pat Crowell

**Area:** 1,758,610 sq. km = 680,000 sq. mi. (about the size of Alaska plus Arizona).

**Population:** 5,765,563 (July 2005 est.) The figure includes an estimated includes 166,510 non-nationals.

**Capital Cities:** Tripoli (Pop. 1.5 million, estimated) and Benghazi (Pop. 750,000, estimated), co–capitals; Baida is the administrative center; moves are now underway to transfer the administrative sector to Al Jofor.

**Climate:** Mediterranean, with summer and winter in a narrow 50–mile–wide band along the coast; semi–arid in the region adjoining the coastal belt, arid and hot in the remainder within the Sahara Desert.

**Neighboring Countries:** Algeria and Tunisia (West); Egypt (East); The Sudan (Southeast); Chad and Niger (South).

**Official Language:** Arabic

**Other Principal Languages:** Berber languages, including Jabal and Zuara; Tamahaq, spoken by Tuaregs; Italian, English, all widely understood in the major cities.

**Ethnic groups:** Berber and Arab 97%, Greeks, Maltese, Italians, Egyptians, Pakistanis, Turks, Indians, and Tunisians.

**Principal Religion:** Sunni Muslim 97%.

**Chief Commercial Products:** crude oil, refined petroleum products, and natural gas.

**GDP per capita:** purchasing power parity $6,400 (2003 est.)

**Currency:** Libyan Dinar.

**Former Colonial Status:** Turkish Colony (1553–1911); Italian Colony (1911–1943) British–French jurisdiction (1943–1951).

**Independence Date:** December 24, 1951.

**Chief of State:** Col. Moamer al–Qadhafi, "Leader of the Revolution."

**National Flag:** A plain green field.

Libya covers a vast area of central North Africa, most of which lies within the blistering Sahara Desert. The coastal area is fertile and populous—in reality it is a series of oases in an otherwise dry countryside. Further inland, mountains rise in plateaus to heights of up to 3,000 feet. There is irregular rainfall in the region due to the perpetual struggle between the moist winds of the Mediterranean and the dry, hot air of the desert.

A short distance inland, rainfall becomes increasingly light. Sudden showers, when they occur, fill otherwise dry river beds to overflowing, sweeping valuable topsoil to the sea. Temperatures in the winter often go below freezing, but they may rise quickly to as high as 80°F. in January because of the *Ghibli,* a hot, arid wind from the desert.

The low mountains, with scattered scrub vegetation, provide forage for the Barbary sheep which need little water to survive. The sands of the Sahara take charge about 50 miles from the sea, where temperatures may soar as high as 137°F. in the shade. In the extreme South, the land rises abruptly to heights of 10,000 feet and more in the majestic and remote Tibesti Mountains.

**History:** Libya has had a long history of being subject to foreign rule. As early as 1000 B.C. Phoenician traders established themselves along the coastline, founding what later became the city of Cyrene. Three coastal cities to the west were given the name *Tripolitania,* or *three cities,* by the Romans—Sabratha, Leptis Magna and Oea. The first two are now ruins. Oea became Tripoli. Ruins of imperial structures throughout Libya are intermixed with those of earlier temples and buildings dating back to 1000 B.C. In Tripoli, Marcus Aurelius constructed a great arch as a monument to Roman power.

After the fall of the Roman Empire, Libya was successively invaded and ruled by Vandals, Byzantines and Greeks. A massive Arab invasion from the East subdued the people in the 8th century, bringing Islam to the native Berber people. For details of early and colonial history, see *Historical Background* and *The Italians in Africa.*

By the turn of the 20th century, Libya had been historically divided into three provinces—Cyrenaica, Tripolitania and Fezzan. At the close of World War II, the allied powers, the United States, France, Great Britain and the Soviet Union, could not agree on the future of Libya. Italy had renounced all rights to the colony under the terms of the peace treaty it signed in 1947. The provinces of Cyrenaica and Tripolitania were under British control and the French administered Fezzan.

At about the same time that the so–called "Big Four" submitted the question of Libya to the UN, the British recognized Emir El Sayyid Muhammad al–Mahdi el–Senussi as head of state in Cyrenaica; he took the name King Idris. A grandson of the founder of the *Senussi* sect of Islam, he set up a government and proclaimed independence of all Libya. The UN debated for many months, and ultimately passed a resolution providing for Libyan independence by 1951. The National Constituent Assembly met and proclaimed Idris to be King of Libya; a con-

# Libya

stitution was prepared which came into effect with formal independence in 1951.

Initially a loose federation under the monarch, Libya adopted a new constitution in 1963 which provided for a central government and merged the provinces. The Kingdom had a two–chamber legislature; the Senate was appointed by the King and the Chamber of Deputies was elected by the people. There were no political parties.

Because Idris failed to ally Libya firmly enough with the Arab cause against Israel, a group of army officers, headed by 1st Lt. Moamer al–Qadhafi deposed the King in September 1969. Ironically, the King, because of illness, was prepared to announce his abdication the next day. He died in Cairo in 1983.

The government was placed in the hands of a revolutionary council and radical changes were implemented—U.S. military bases were closed and 25,000 Italians either left or were expelled, many of them leaving their property, including $25 million in bank deposits, to be confiscated.

From that point Qadhafi became the darling of the revolutionary left. He yearned for Arab unity, and he spent most of the next years financing various revolutionary movements throughout the world, using Libya's immense oil wealth. He attempted to persuade the leaders and people of virtually every Arab nation, and even tiny Malta, to enter into a union with Libya. Failure to achieve a single union produced frustration, and Qadhafi has frequently denounced the leadership of states unwilling to join his projects. In the process he increasingly distanced himself from other Arab leaders. Egypt's *El Ahram*, that nation's semi-official newspaper, once accused Qadhafi of being a "maniac and mere highwayman, even though he may own the gold of Midas."

Ever restless, Qadhafi kept Libya in turmoil through various administrative and structural reforms, while destabilizing other states through a variety of foreign adventures. In 1976 he annexed a sixty-mile wide strip of northern Chad and involved himself in the country's civil war, supporting rebel troops against the central government. The adventure ceased after Chadian troops, with French assistance, routed the Libyans in 1987, capturing about $1 billion of Soviet-manufactured military materiel. An inveterate arms-buyer, Qadhafi bought billions of dollars in military equipment during the 1970s and 1980s, more indeed, than Libya had troops to use or pilots to fly.

Relations between Libya and the United States have long been tense. In 1979 Libyan mobs sacked the U.S. Embassy. Relations between the two countries came to a standstill while the U.S. insisted Libya

take full responsibility for the attack. Qadhafi called it a "spontaneous demonstration by students," and offered neither apology or admitted responsibility. He heightened the verbal offensive against the United States in 1981 after the U.S. shot down two Libyan jets over the Gulf of Sidra. The U.S. said the incident resulted from an unprovoked attack on U.S. jets, but Qadhafi accused the U.S. of aggression.

Under Qadhafi, things in Libya are very much ad hoc and subject to change. He does not use the title of president; he prefers "Eternal Guide" or "leader of the revolution." He decreed that Libya has no central government, just a series of "Basic

**King Idris I on his 75th birthday, 1965**

People's Congresses." Their decisions are carried out by layer upon layer of committees and a General Secretariat. He made military training mandatory for both girls and boys in secondary schools. This training program, plus the formation of a "People's Army" containing school and university students, made conservative elements of the military very apprehensive. There have been several attempts on Qadhafi's life.

Terror has been an integral part of Colonel Qadhafi's foreign and domestic policy. In 1984–1986, terrorism was primarily directed at Libyan dissidents living in exile. By late 1985, Qadhafi's anti-Americanism had become virulent enough for President Ronald Reagan to urge all Americans living illegally in the country to leave. Travel visas to Libya were forbidden. In response to his anti-American rhetoric, the U.S. sent a naval task force into the Gulf of Sidra, past what

Qadhafi had labeled "the line of death," sank two Libyan patrol boats, and conducted air raids against Libyan radar and missile installations on the mainland. Shortly thereafter a bomb ripped a discotheque in West Berlin, killing two U.S. servicemen; irrefutable evidence indicated Libya was responsible. When the trial of those responsible finally took place in November 2001, a German court blamed Libya's intelligence service, and four people, including a former Libyan diplomat, were sentenced to prison terms of 12-14 years.

In April 1986 President Reagan ordered an air strike against Libya, conducted from bases in England. Among the hits made was Qadhafi's residence. An American spokesman curtly stated "We didn't know he was home." He was, and the attack visibly shook him. When he finally appeared on television about five weeks later, he was at times incoherent and appeared to be heavily sedated. For the next 18 months Qadhafi was continuously on the move, fearful of losing his life. His popularity plummeted as basic commodities disappeared from markets, but by 1988 he re-emerged and embarked, erratically, on a course to normalize Libya's relations with the rest of the world.

Recognizing the toll UN economic sanctions took, Qadhafi organized a remarkable and ultimately successful campaign to eliminate them. The sanctions had resulted from alleged Libyan complicity in terrorism against two airliners—a Pan American flight which exploded over Lockerbie, Scotland in December 1988, and a Brazzaville-to-Paris UTA flight which exploded over Niger in March 1989. In the first, 270 people had been murdered, including a number of American citizens; in the second, 170, largely French citizens, had died. When Qadhafi refused to hand over the alleged perpetrators, the UN Security Council ordered air and military embargoes in 1992.

In 1993 the sanctions were tightened to include the freezing of Libyan funds and financial resources in other countries, and a ban on the sale of equipment for oil and gas operations. Libyan sanctions never prohibited the sale of petroleum or froze petroleum investments. Unable to convince the UN on these matters, the United States imposed tougher unilateral sanctions in 1996, applying them to investments in Libya's oil or gas sectors. The lifting of the UN sanctions was conditioned on the two Libyan suspects in the Lockerbie case being turned over to the British and Americans.

By 1998 the sanctions were extracting a severe price from the Libyan economy, and at some point Colonel Qadhafi decided to eliminate these two obstacles to

# Libya

**Moamer al–Qadhafi**

Libya's reinsertion into the world community. The two cases had different velocities and followed different trajectories, both equally improbable. In the UTA case, Qadhafi allowed a French investigating judge to question some 50 members of the Libyan intelligence services in Tripoli in 1996. During this visit, the judge "found" and seized a suitcase at the intelligence service offices. Not only was the suitcase identical to the one believed to have been stuffed with explosives that brought the plane down, but somewhat miraculously, the judge also found timers and detonators similar to those used in the bombing. It was the theater of political calculation: Qadhafi abandoned his officers that the international community might abandon its isolation of Libya.

The French judge drew up charges accusing the second-in-command of the Libyan intelligence services, Abdallah Senussi—Qadhafi's own brother-in-law—of giving the order to bomb the UTA flight. Five others were also named in the indictment, and their trial *in absentia* took place in Paris in March 1999. All were found guilty and sentenced to life in prison. Libya later paid some $31 million as compensation to the victims' families.

Largely marginalized by other Arab states, Qadhafi turned increasingly to his African neighbors. Indeed, solidarity with them became the "priority of priorities" for Libya. In June 1998 the OAU voted to ignore the UN air embargo on Libya, and several African presidents flew into Tripoli to visit the Colonel. Libya downgraded its "permanent" status at the Arab League, scrapped its Arab Ministry, and changed the name of its radio from the "Voice of the Arab Nation" to "Voice of Africa." The ever-mercurial Qadhafi told an Arab delegation that "for good or worse, nothing will ever link me to

Arabs," and that he wanted "Libya's interests to be in Africa and remain there."

Some of Libya's African friends, including Nelson Mandela, facilitated a resolution of the Lockerbie case. The mechanism was unique, precedent-setting, and diplomatically complex: The two Lockerbie suspects would be tried in the Netherlands, under Scottish law. The duo was transferred in April 2000, and UN sanctions were automatically suspended.

The Lockerbie trial began in April 2000, and the panel of three Scottish judges hearing the case rendered their verdict in late January 2001. They found Abdel Basset al-Megrahi, a Libyan intelligence agent, guilty of murdering 270 people. Al-Megrahi's sentence was life imprisonment in a Scottish jail. His lawyers appealed the verdict, but a panel of Scottish judges denied it in March 2002.

The United States and the United Kingdom, however, still demanded that Libya take responsibility for the bombing and agree to a compensation package for families of the victims. Secret negotiations to this end were revealed in the spring of 2002. More than a year later, in August 2003, Libya formally took responsibility for the bombing in a letter to the UN Security Council and signed a compensation deal worth $2.7 billion with lawyers representing the families of Lockerbie victims. In September the Security Council permanently lifted its sanctions against the regime. (The French, a bit *retardataire*, saw how badly their compensation negotiations had fared and demanded they be reopened.)

Internationally, Col. Qadhafi presents himself as the new and revised edition, a rogue reformed. No longer the sponsor of terror and destabilization, the Colonel is now the sponsor and protector of stability among his African neighbors. The high point of Libya's Africa-first policy came in March 2001, when an extraordinary OAU summit met in Sirte and agreed to the creation of an African Union (AU). The AU was inaugurated in July 2002, following the last meeting of the OAU in Durban, South Africa, but Thabo Mbeki became the new formation's first president, not the dreamer of unity, Colonel Qadhafi. As part of the new African orientation, Libya has aided African states economically (oil and gasoline to Zimbabwe, food to Malawi) and militarily (troops to support President Patassé in the Central African Republic). In a strife-torn continent, there continue to be unending opportunities for The Guide to offer his services as a diplomatic broker between contending parties.

As relations with Africa warmed, relations with the Arab League chilled to the point of rupture. At an early March 2003 League summit called to discuss the situation in Iraq, Qadhafi and the Saudi Crown Prince, Abdullah Bin Abdul Aziz, traded public insults while embarrassed Egyptian TV operators desperately sought to pull the plug on live transmission. The scene was so envenomed that one Saudi paper, *Okaz,* called for Qadhafi's overthrow. The Colonel proceeded to withdraw his ambassador to the Kingdom and escalated things by demanding to withdraw from the League. To reporters he said that Libya was "above all an African country . . . the African Union is sufficient enough." The decision to leave the League definitively was announced as "irrevocable" in April 2003, but was never implemented. Colonel Qadhafi had another opportunity to offend his fellow leaders by walking out of the Arab League summit at Tunis in May 2004.

Internally, the government has faced continuing opposition, which intensified as economic conditions deteriorated. Violent clashes with militant Islamist opposition groups occurred in 1997, particularly in the Eastern region. The government tightened security measures, made hundreds of arrests and conducted military operations in the affected areas. Members and sympathizers of banned Islamic groups were closely monitored; activities at mosques were surveilled.

Colonel Qadhafi spent much of 1998 and early 1999 on crutches or in a wheel chair, the result, suggested a French news agency, of an attempted assassination. For his personal security, the Colonel travels somewhat flamboyantly, accompanied by stiletto-heeled female guards in military fatigues, a 200 motor caravan, and his desert tent rolled up in an army truck—the very model of a modern nomad officer.

To deal with its opposition, the government has frequently resorted to the use of terror. In March 1997 the Libyan General People's Congress approved a collective guilt and punishment law. By this law any group, large or small, including towns, villages, local assemblies, tribes or families can be punished in their entirety if accused by the People's Congress or a People's Committee of sympathizing, financing, or in any way helping, protecting or failing to identify perpetrators of crimes against the state. The crimes include "obstructing the people's power, instigating and practicing tribal fanaticism, possessing, trading in or smuggling unlicensed weapons, and damaging public and private institutions and property." The scope of the law is staggering.

During the heyday of socialist economics, members of so-called "Popular Committees" terrorized the bazaars of Tripoli and other cities. Formed in 1996 and made up of volunteers, often students and army

# Libya

officers, the committees were charged by Colonel Qadhafi with purifying cities of the "satanic filthiness of the West." Ambulatory peddlers, selling a few items on the streets in one of the few expressions of a free market to be found in Libya, were subject to the Committees' attention. Imported items were confiscated, sellers fined, and examples made. One Palestinian merchant was accused of "inundating the Libyan market with Israeli aphrodisiac chewing gum," proving how ever-vigilant revolutionary Puritanism needs to be. Punishment for deviance is severe: Under laws passed in 1996 any Libyan can be punished by death for speculations in food, currency, clothes or housing during a state of war or blockade—which included the UN sanctions.

Clearly those multilateral sanctions worked, and the social consequences of economic constriction were something the regime ultimately chose not to bear. Qadhafi's handling of the Lockerbie case was the clearest sign the regime had changed course. Pragmatism triumphed over ideology. The Colonel-Guide now speaks of free markets and investments, and the Revolutionary Committees have been marginalized. In September 2000 he articulated his vision of the new Libya: "Now is the era of economy, consumption, mar-

kets, and investments. This is what unites people irrespective of language, religion, and nationalities." Despite such globalist geniality, vestigial anti-Americanism remains, as does an implacable opposition to Israel.

Libya's development of a missile program, with Chinese and North Korean assistance, remained a principal U.S. security concern after the Lockerbie file had been closed. Though not part of the Bush administration's "axis of evil," Libya was accused of trying to acquire weapons of mass destruction (WMD), and the Bush administration chose not to lift American sanctions when the Security Council lifted its. Instead, it kept the issue alive and the pressure on.

The invasion of Iraq made implicit threat direct reality, and the light of war clarified the Colonel's vision on the utility and danger of WMD. Secret contacts were made with the British and Americans, negotiations conducted, and nine months later, in December 2003, the Colonel-Guide stunned the world by announcing that Libya would abandon its programs to develop weapons of mass destruction.

The programs were several: about 100 tons of mustard gas and nerve agents had been produced, and there were at least 3,000 empty bomb casings available for

the chemicals; Libya acknowledged co-operating with North Korea to develop extended range Scud missiles; a program to enrich uranium for use in nuclear weapons was in place, including high-speed centrifuge technology and, according to the UN's International Atomic Energy Agency (IAEA), evidence that Libya had produced a small amount of plutonium. Though it was insufficient to make a bomb, it was clear Libya was close to obtaining nuclear weapons capability.

In terms of nuclear intelligence, Libyan co-operation provided information on the vast procurement network operated by the Pakistani physicist, Dr. Abdul Qadeer Khan, revered as the "father" of Pakistan's nuclear bomb. In his spare time, Dr. Khan ran an international black market in nuclear-weapons materials. To enrich uranium obtained from North Korea, Libya had made some $100 million worth of purchases, primarily centrifuge technology, from the Khan network. In one small step for a less-dangerous nuclear world, the Libyan program has been dismantled and carted away.

Libya's reinsertion into the family of nations seemed nearly complete following British Prime Minister Blair's meeting with Moamar al-Qadhafi in March 2004; by the end of 2004 Gerhard Schroeder of Germany, Italian Prime Minister Silvio Berlusconi, and French President Jacques Chirac had all made official stops in Tripoli to meet with the Colonel-Guide. Full acceptance of the former pariah has yet to be achieved. Allegations that Colonel Qadhafi had approved a plan to kill Crown Prince Abdullah, Saudi Arabia's ruler, have kept Libya's name on America's list of state sponsors of terrorism.

In a tit-for-tat response, Libya withdrew half a billion dollars from a Swiss escrow account meant to be the final compensation payment to the bereaved of Lockerbie in April 2005. The payment—around $2 million per family—had been predicated on Libya's removal from the American list. Libya had already paid each family $8 million, and there was never much expectation the final payment would be made.

**Culture:** The Islamic Libyans tend to be basically conservative in their outlook. The lodges of the Islamic Senussi brotherhood have been the traditional centers of art, religious philosophy and learning, but they are gradually giving way to a system of public education based on more modern concepts and "Qadhafi ideology." Compulsory, free education greatly reduced a pre–1951 illiteracy rate of 90% to less than 50%. High schools and technical colleges emphasize the development of practical skills calculated to contribute to the growth of the economy.

**Roman Imperial theater at Sabratha**　　　Photo by Pat Crowell

**The Libyan Sahara**                                                    Photo by Pat Crowell

The cities of Tripoli and Benghazi are beautiful combinations of round, arched Arab architecture and modern skyscrapers, interspersed with the classic ruins of past civilizations and the towers of gleaming mosques. Several modern supermarkets have taken their place alongside the traditional open–air markets, and many of the comforts of European and American living are available—if you can afford them.

Libya contains a remarkable collection of sites that bear witness to the life that flourished there during prehistoric, Punic, Greek, Roman and Byzantine eras.

One rock art site alone—Tadrart Acacus on the southwest border, east of the city of Ghat—contains thousands of cave paintings in very different styles, dating from 12,000 BC to 100 AD. They catalogue the changing fauna, flora and life styles of the populations that succeeded one another in this Saharan region.

Three sites, Cyrene, Leptis Magna and Sabratha all hold enormous tourist potential.

Cyrene, founded in the seventh century BC, is one of the most complex archaeological sites in the Mediterranean region. Cyrenians built the biggest Greek Doric temple in Africa in the sixth century BC—the Sanctuary of Zeus, comparable to the Temple of Zeus at Olympia.

Leptis Magna was enlarged and embellished by Septimius Severus, who was born there and later became emperor. It was one of the most beautiful cities of the Roman Empire, with its imposing public monuments, market place, storehouses, shops and residential districts.

Sabratha, once a Phoenician trading-post that served as an outlet for the products of the African hinterland, was later Romanized and rebuilt in the 2nd and 3rd centuries AD. Its theater, victory arch and arena all bespeak the efforts of Roman city planners.

**Economy:** Libya's economy is dependent on its petroleum industry. Oil accounts for 95% of foreign earnings and 75% of government revenues, but UN sanctions hurt the economy. Libya reported estimated losses amounting to nearly $27 billion resulting from them. Economic growth became pinched. Growth of 2% was reported in 1995, but this fell to 0.7% in 1996 and 0.6% in 1997.

With the suspension of UN sanctions and higher oil prices since 1999, government oil revenues have increased dramatically—to $18.1 billion in 2004, with a 2005 forecast of $19.4 billion. Economic growth has been equally robust: 9.8 % in 2003 and 7.7% in 2004.

With sanctions curtailing investment, Libya's oil capacity remained stagnant at 1.3 million-1.4 million barrels per day (bbl/d) for a decade. Petroleum facilities and air and ground infrastructure weren't modernized in years. By 2000 oil production capacity had slipped to around 810,000 bbl/d. With only internal flights, airport maintenance and upgrading had deteriorated, and road construction languished. The lifting of sanctions opened enormous opportunities for Libya and foreign business investment.

# Libya

The Libyan prize is huge. There are about 39 billion barrels of oil reserves, and Libyan oil is extremely high-quality, low-sulfur content crude. Low production costs in Libya add incentives. Onshore costs can be as little as $5 a barrel, and given the shallowness of the Mediterranean, even offshore costs are low by world standards. Current (2004) oil production, is estimated at 1.6 million bbl/d. The government hopes to raise production levels to 2 million bll/s by 2008-2010 and to 3 million bbl/d by 2015. Exports of Libyan oil to the United States resumed in June 2004.

In 2001 the National Oil Corporation opened more than 322,000 square miles to foreign companies for exploration in production-sharing agreements. Western companies were quick to respond: Repso (Spain), OMV (Austria), Woodside (Australia), Eni (Italy), Hellenic (Greece) soon established themselves in the country. British and American firms were slower to rush in.

The Iran–Libya Sanctions Act (ILSA) of 1996 long restricted U.S. oil companies' investment in Libya. Responding to Col. Qadhafi's seeming transformation, the Bush administration eased its embargo in April 2004, clearing the way for oil firms and banks to resume commercial activities in Libya. Anticipatorily, Occidental Petroleum had already opened its office in March, and Shell, the Ango-Dutch oil giant, signed an agreement to enter Libya's oil and gas industry the same month.

When the results of the first oil exploration and production-sharing agreement auction were announced in January 2005, U.S. oil companies won 11 of the 15 concessions offered. Fifty-six international companies from 28 countries participated in the bidding. Occidental Petroleum won nine concession blocks, while Chevron-Texaco and Amerada Hess each acquired one block.

Natural gas production also has enormous potential and is a high priority for Libya. Proven reserves as of January 2005 were estimated at 52 trillion cubic feet (Tcf), though some industry experts believe them to be even higher—in the 70-100 Tcf range. Libya would like to shift to the greater use of gas rather than oil domestically, freeing up more oil for export. It also has great expectations for gas exports to Europe.

In their campaign against sanctions, Libyans have dangled the lure of huge investment prizes before the eyes of eager businessmen. Besides the petroleum industry, Libya's infrastructure needs are huge. Two railroad lines have been proposed: one would connect with the Egyptian and Tunisian frontiers; the other would connect the Fezzan to the Mediterranean. In all, 1,860 miles of track, 96 stations, 244 locomotives, and 544 bridges are envisioned. For air transportation, the government said it wanted to spend $2.5 billion to purchase 25 new and used airplanes, completely renewing the Libyan fleet, largely made up of Soviet-era Russian models. Airports at Tripoli, Benghazi, and Sabha all need modernization. By mid-2004, Boeing, the American firm, and the British aerospace group BAE Systems (which owns 20% of the airplane builder Airbus), were reportedly in talks to buy civilian aircraft.

With some 1340 miles of undeveloped coastline and remarkable architectural ruins, Libya offers enormous opportunities in tourism. The country has five UNESCO World Heritages sites (Leptis Magna, Sabratha, Cyrene, Ghadames, and the southwestern rock art sites of Tadrart Acacus), but only one five-star hotel—the Corinthia Bab Africa Hotel in Tripoli. The Corinthia, which is the first enterprise in Libya to allow customers to use credit cards, is an indication of just how nascent

the tourism industry is. Other impediments: the country remains alcohol free and has a notoriously difficult (and expensive) visa process; tourists who have Israeli visas in their passports will be denied entry to Libya.

Virtually all of the government's spare investment funds have been channeled into the Great Man-Made River Project (GMMRP). The project involves more than 2100 miles of canals to transport water from deep below the Sahara desert to the North. Northern cities would be provided better drinking water, and some 1.2 million acres of agricultural land could be developed with irrigation—part of the regime's effort to lessen its dependency on oil revenues. Under construction since 1983 and estimated to cost more than $30 billion over 50 years, the project is a massive network of water transportation and distribution systems. It will ultimately comprise 1,300 wells drilled into the Sahara Desert, pumping 8.49 million cubic yards of water per day. The five million tons of cement used to make the pipes could build a concrete road all the way from Libya to India. The reality of the project is that it may not produce water any more cheaply than desalination. More importantly, it draws down a non-renewable source of water.

Libya's transformation to a free-market economy is being overseen by Prime Minister Shukri Ghanem, a professional economist long known for his support of a liberalized economy. Besides open competition for oil exploration concessions, the government has begun a program of privatizing more than 300 government companies—selling them off to private sector and foreign investors; the banking and telecommunications sectors are already scheduled. The government has also pumped more than $5 billion into the economy in the form of soft loans and various incentives to encourage private investment. Libya is open for business.

In the short term employment may be pinched. The public sector employed more than 800,000 people who drained the state budget and offered grudging service. Private efficiencies should reduce that number, but at the same time there are a large number of Libyans who are unemployed.

**The Future:** The opening of the economy promises jobs for the unemployed—more than 30% of the population—and a chance at improved living standards. An end to the air embargo will facilitate a greater exchange of ideas and experiences for Libyans, neither of which will make Colonel Qadhafi's authoritarian regime any more comfortable.

**African Unity billboard**　　　　Photo by Pat Crowell

# The Islamic Republic of Mauritania

Crane operator at a mining site near Nouadhibou

**Area:** 1,085,210 sq. km. = 419,000 sq. mi. (One and one–half times the size of Texas).

**Population:** 3,086,859 (July 2005 est.)

**Capital City:** Nouakchott (Pop. 1.4 million estimated).

**Climate:** Hot and arid; drought conditions have existed for the last decade.

**Neighboring Countries:** Senegal (Southwest); Western Sahara (Northwest); Algeria (Northeast); Mali (East and Southeast).

**Official Languages:** Hasaniya Arabic, Wolof.

**Other Principal Languages:** Fulfulde, Soninke, Zenaga; French.

**Ethnic groups:** mixed Moor/black 40%, Moor 30%, black 30%.

**Principal Religion:** Islam.

**Chief Commercial Products:** Fish and fish products, iron ore, and gold.

**GNI per capita:** $430 (2003)

**Currency:** 1 Ouguiya (UM) = 5 khoums

**Former Colonial Status:** French Colony (1920–1960).

**Independence Date:** November 28, 1960.

**Chief of State:** Maouya Ould Sidi Ahmed Taya, President.

**National Flag:** Green with a yellow five-pointed star above a yellow, horizontal crescent; the closed side of the crescent is down; the crescent, star, and color green are traditional symbols of Islam.

Mauritania lies on the upper west coast of Africa, almost wholly within the immense Sahara Desert. The northern two-thirds of the country is totally flat and stony, with virtually no rain. Its *ergs* (huge areas of dunes) are constantly transformed by hot, dry winds, which make the implementation of road infrastructure virtually impossible. Thunderstorms occasionally intrude and brief but heavy rainfall collects into streams and rivers within a few minutes. Two hours after the end of the storm, there is no sign of moisture. In some places, the water descends to great depths, supporting a few green oases which stand out in the otherwise empty landscape. Southern regions are subject to sporadic torrential rain showers that can wreak much damage.

A narrow band of semi–arid land stretches from west to east in the southern region of the country. Its rainfall of about four inches per year supports low, sparse scrub vegetation. The most heavily populated area of the country lies along the Senegal River. The rich soil is periodically flooded during normal years by the river which, when added to the rainfall of 10 to 25 inches, permits cultivation and cattle raising.

**History:** The first inhabitants of Mauritania were West African peoples. Remains of their presence date back to the Neolithic period. In historical times, both sub-Saharan peoples and Berbers have inhabited the area. It was the Berbers who founded the austere Almoravid movement and spread its version of Islam throughout the area in the 11th century AD. An influx of Arabs, following commercial caravan routes, produced a mixed Arab-Berber culture known as Moorish. Federations of Moorish nomadic tribesmen came to dominate sedentary African farmers, many of whom adopted the Islamic faith of their conquerors. For details of early and colonial history, see *Historical Background* and *The French in Africa*.

Mauritania achieved full independence in 1960; the government adopted the presidential system, replacing the original parliamentary form. The president was elected for a five–year term by all citizens.

The first presidential elections were held in 1961 and resulted in victor for the Republic's founder, Moktar Ould Daddah.

# Mauritania

President Ould Daddah was reelected in 1966, 1971 and 1976. The unicameral National Assembly of forty members was also elected by universal suffrage. The People's Party was dominant after 1959, holding all seats in the National Assembly.

Mauritania's relations with Morocco and Algeria were quite close. In the heady days of African liberation from colonial rule, they each had an interest in Spain's holdings in Spanish Sahara—rich with billion tons of phosphate. In a flurry of diplomatic and guerrilla activity, Spain, weary of trying to appease internal and external opinion over its continued possession of a colony on the African continent, decided to surrender Spanish Sahara to literally anyone.

Mauritania joined with Morocco to exclude Algeria from the desert wasteland. The end result was a de facto partition of the former Spanish colony, with Mauritania receiving a portion in the south and Morocco receiving a larger northern area. Algeria supported the Polisario Front, Spanish Sahara's independence movement, and Mauritania soon found itself at war.

France pledged to help Mauritania against attacking Polisario guerrillas supported by Algeria in its effort to obtain economic advantage. After the guerrillas established the Saharan Arab Democratic Republic in Spanish Sahara and made forays into Mauritania, the French launched air strikes on them from bases near Dakar, Senegal.

Badly drained by a staggering military budget which had increased army strength in two years from 1,500 to 15,000 men, the economy sagged noticeably. Things worsened when the Polisario attacked the railroad moving iron ore, the country's principal money maker, to the port of Nouadhibou. In these circumstances the army intervened to topple the Ould Daddah government in mid-1978.

In 1979 Mauritania officially ended its role in the desert war over the Western Sahara. Drained by its costly struggle with Polisario guerrillas, it renounced all claims to the territory. In 1983 it officially recognized the Saharan Arab Democratic Republic.

Mauritanian politics have traditionally been dominated by the cultural and ethnic divide that separates the population. An artificial creation of the colonizer, Mauritania joins Moors, northern nomadic peoples of Arab-Berber culture, with southern, sedentary black Africans, agriculturalists concentrated in the Senegal River valley. The Moor segment of the population itself is divided into two groupings: so-called "White Moors," descended from the region's Arab-Berber

conquerors, and "Black Moors," black Africans of Arab-Berber culture, traditional servants and slaves of the conquerors. Moors speak Arabic, while the Afro-Mauritanians of the south tend to speak French in addition to their indigenous languages. Virtually all are Muslim, but Moors tend to take a single wife, while Afro-Mauritanians tend to be polygamous. This has resulted in a more rapid population increase among Afro-Mauritanians, now about one-third the population. These racial identities are the historical basis of social tensions.

At independence, White Moors held political power, while Afro-Mauritanians were more numerous within the civil administration. Founding President Moktar Ould Daddah was able to keep the tensions in check, but with the beginning of the Saharan conflict in 1978 power became increasingly concentrated, especially after Ould Daddah's overthrow in 1978, in the hands of White Moors. "Arabization" policies were pursued in schools and workplaces, to the protests of Afro-Mauritanians. Several military regimes followed until Colonel Maouya Ould Sidi Ahmed Taya took power in 1984.

Afro-Mauritanians became fearful when Moors began to invest in southern agricultural lands as early as 1983. Municipal elections of 1986 seemed to increase the power of Moors even further, just as the economic consequences of the first phase of economic liberalization began to impact Afro-Mauritanians most heavily. There was a failed *coup d'état* in 1987, the core of which was the clandestine Front for the Liberation of Africans in Mauritania (FLAM). Racial incidents in the Senegal River valley in 1989 resulted in massacres of African farmers there and retaliatory racial onslaughts against Moors in Senegal. Approximately 95,000 Afro-Mauritanians were expelled or fled from 1989 to 1991. Both Mali and Senegal, which received the bulk of those fleeing, had massive refugee problems as a consequence.

The discovery of another plot against the regime in 1991, the details of which remain obscure to this day, resulted in hundreds of Afro-Mauritanian soldiers being arrested, tortured, maimed, and executed. Parliament passed an amnesty bill in 1993 to preclude any legal pursuit of those involved and has not acknowledged responsibility or wrongdoing. It has, however, given pensions to the widows of some of those killed.

The appearance of what seemed to be racial purges, coupled with the regime's support of Iraq during the Gulf War, led to international isolation and diminished foreign aid. Col. Taya effected a turnabout by beginning the process of controlled democratization in 1991. After fourteen

years as head of the military junta, he announced that a referendum on a new constitution and general elections would be held. The new constitution was approved and legislation legalizing political parties passed shortly thereafter.

Taya's opponents coalesced to form the *Union des Forces Démocratiques* (UFD) and the outgoing regime responded by creating the *Parti Républicain et Démocratique et Social* (PRDS) which brought together Col. Taya's supporters—prominently local notables, tribal chiefs and businessmen. In the presidential elections of 1992, the UFD nominated Ahmed Ould Daddah, half-brother of Mauritania's first president, to run against Col. Taya. Taya won with 63% of the votes, but Ould Daddah's 33% was more than respectable, given the "irregularities" of the election. Refusing to accept the results of a fraudulent election, the UFD boycotted parliamentary elections later that year, allowing the PRDS to dominate the legislature.

Recognizing the failure of the boycott strategy and facing an unhappy constituency, the UFD participated in the municipal elections of 1994. With the PRDS having the full resources of the administration behind it, there was little question about the election results. The UFD took only one municipality, Kaedi in the south. Successive losses led to defections from the UFD as the pragmatic and opportunistic migrated to the PRDS. As a result of this influx of new supporters, the PRDS became the sole vehicle of meaningful political expression in Mauritania; internal clashes between factions became more im-

**A Mauritanian farmer**

©IRIN

portant than contests between rival parties in Mauritanian politics.

President Taya showed himself to be a keen political pragmatist by reversing alliances. In October 1995 the Iraqi ambassador was thrown out and Iraqi citizens loyal to the Arab nationalist *Ba'athist* movement of Saddem Hussein were accused of creating secret missions throughout Mauritania. In November, Taya's government recognized the state of Israel, definitively reorienting Mauritania's political direction.

The opposition, given a new issue with the recognition of Israel, regrouped in 1995. One part of it formed Action for Change (AC). The party was led by Messaoud Ould Boulkheir, a "Harratin," or Black Moor descended from slaves, and presented itself as the champion of the oppressed, articulating both the grievances of Black Moors and Afro-Mauritanians. Multiparty legislative elections in 1996 reinforced PRDS power; the party won 70 out of 79 seats in parliament. The AC won only a single seat, the remaining going to independents. Massive fraud on both sides was reported, with the opposition charging the government with running voters from polling station to polling station in minibuses. Still, only 30% of those registered to do so actually voted.

In advance of the presidential elections of December 1997, UFD and AC joined to create a United Opposition Front, but were no more successful than before. President Taya was re-elected to a second six-year term winning more than 90% of the vote against four opposition candidates. His main challenger, economist Ch'Bih Ould Cheikh Malainine, did particularly well in Mauritania's two major urban centers. The election was not without its usual protests from the opposition, major elements of which boycotted it. After his victory, President Taya announced that he would "wage war without mercy" on poverty, but no mention was made of the growing concentration of wealth in the hands of an emerging, but extremely narrow, middle class. During the campaign Malainine revealed that 39 Mauritanians held 70% of the country's wealth, and 27 of them were members of a single tribe, President Taya's own Smassids.

The clandestine Afro-Mauritanian political movement calling itself FLAM continues to call for the autonomy of southern Mauritania and a resolution of the issue of some 70,000 deported black Mauritanians who have been living in Senegal and Mali since 1989. FLAM accuses the regime of "Mauritanian apartheid," characterized by exclusion of Afro-Mauritanians from public affairs, generalization of Arabizing policies, and affirmation of the exclusively Arab character of the country.

**President Maouya Ould Sidi Ahmed Taya**

Igniting a firestorm of controversy within and outside the country, Mauritania agreed to establish full diplomatic relations with Israel in October 1999. With Jordan and Egypt, Mauritania became only the third Arab state to establish diplomatic relations with Israel. The al-Aqsa *intifada* that began in September 2000 brought more pressure on the government by Arab League states to sever those relations, but the government has steadfastly refused to do so. The opposition organized regular and ongoing protest demonstrations.

As always, the government's response was repression. Ahmed Ould Daddah's rechristened *Union des forces démocratiques-Ere Nouvelle* (UFD-EN) was banned in October 2000 because, said the government, it was waging a "smear campaign against the country" and calling for violence. Ch'Bih Ould Cheikh Malainine—chairman of the *Front Populaire Mauritanien* (FPM) and runner-up in the last presidential election—was arrested with two of his colleagues in April 2001 and charged with "criminal conspiracy." Security forces had to use tear gas to break up a FPM rally in Nouakchott protesting the arrests.

In June the trio was convicted and sentenced to five year's imprisonment for alleged involvement with terrorist groups and a Libyan coup plot. The trial was conducted under close police surveillance and, to avoid demonstrations, some 500 miles away from Nouakchott.

In December 2000, President Ould Taya announced a series of political reforms to give his image a more liberal sheen. Proportional representation, enhancing the opposition's chances to gain representation in parliament, was introduced for multi-member districts in the country's three largest cities—Nouakchott, Nouadhibou, and Selibaby. To strengthen political parties, the state agreed to fund them on the basis of their showing in forthcoming municipal elections and give them ac-

cess to state-controlled media. Independent candidacies would be prohibited.

The first elections to take advantage of the new provisions were the parliamentary and municipal polls of October 2001. Eighty-one National Assembly seats were up for grabs. Only President Taya's PRDS presented candidates in each of the 45 electoral districts. The Rally of Democratic Forces (RFD: *Rassemblement des forces démocratiques*), which had emerged from the remains of Ahmed Ould Daddah's UFD-EN after it was banned in October 2000, competed in only 20; Messaoud Ould Boulkheir's Action for Change (AC) presented candidates in just 15. Along with the two major opposition parties, 13 others competed in the election.

As additional confidence-building measures, the government issued new tamper-proof identity cards, published voter lists on the Internet, and employed transparent ballot boxes. Participation was up considerably—50% of those registered—from 30% in the 1996 legislative elections.

When the results were tallied, Taya's PRDS won 64 out of 81 seats; six additional seats went to small parties backing the presidential majority. The opposition garnered 11 seats, with four of them going to Action for Change and three to the Rally of Democratic Forces; Cheikh Malainine's FPM won a single seat. The PRDS also dominated municipal elections, winning control of 184 out of 216 municipalities across the country.

The EU praised the conduct of the elections and called upon Mauritanian parties to maintain a constructive dialogue "so as to strengthen confidence in democratic institutions and create an environment in which all shades of opinion can be freely expressed." President Taya is not, however, a man who has much appreciation for diversity of opinion, especially when it is critical and when presidential elections are approaching.

In January 2002 the government banned Action for Change, accusing it of inciting violence and racial tension. The decision followed a debate on government policy in 2002, during which opposition members repeatedly questioned officials on what would be done to improve race relations and end slavery. AC's leader, Messaoud Ould Boulkheir—himself a descendant of slaves—reacted by succinctly describing the Taya regime: "It is a military government, an undemocratic government that cannot accept a dissenting view, a government that is ready to trample on all rights in order to achieve its objectives."

Despite numerous political parties, Mauritania remains more authoritarian than democratic. President Taya rules with an iron fist and any velvet glove is

# Mauritania

pretty threadbare. Opposition parties that push too hard are banned, their leaders subject to imprisonment; the press is systematically censured and unions are prohibited from public demonstrations. The PRDS is now a smooth functioning political machine for winning elections and distributing the political loaves and fishes—access to political positions and the resources they control. Factional disputes within the party are largely tribal, ethnic, and regional. White Moors from Adrar (President Ould Taya's native region) and Brakna are highly influential; the majority of the Black Moor elite is to be found within the party, along with leading Afro-Mauritanian figures. To control the democratization process the regime has placed its allies in positions that allow them to obtain the support of their respective tribes and ethnic groups. Frequent ministerial reshufflings allow an efficient redistribution of spoils to reflect any necessary change or tweaking of influence within the party.

Of all the tribal factions within the PRDS it is President Ould Taya's Smassids who take a lion's share of the spoils. They constitute a virtual financial cartel with significant interests in every economic sector. Thus Ch'Bih Ould Cheikh Malainine's comment that 39 Mauritanians held 70% of the country's wealth, and 27 of them were members of a single tribe. Thus, too, the finding of the UN's Development Program that wealth in Mauritania is very unequally distributed: the richest 20% control 44% of the nation's wealth; the poorest 20% control a mere 6.4%.

Inequality, exclusion, and political repression keep tensions high in Mauritania. The regime's recognition of Israel provides focus for incendiary comment by Arab nationalists and Islamic fundamentalists, and the combustibility of the situation was revealed in June 2003, when elements of the armed forces attempted a violent overthrow of the Ould Taya government. The rebels were led by a former colonel, Salah Ould Hanenna, and though the motivations remain unclear, most observers thought they involved family and clan rivalries as much as differences over the president's political agenda. Rebels overran the presidential compound, but Ould Taya rallied his personal guard, shot his way out to nearby police headquarters and sustained a 36-hour siege. Loyalist army forces, directed by President Taya himself, suppressed the attempted coup, but it was a close call.

Three consequences of the coup were soon manifest. Security measures were significantly heightened in Nouakchott, with military check points across the city to search cars and check identity papers. Many of Ould Hanenna's relatives were purged from their government positions, including the head of the Supreme Court and the mayor of Nouadhibou.

With his vulnerability obvious (and opposition politicians lamenting the coup's failure) Ould Taya decided not to postpone presidential elections scheduled for November. Instead, he boldly appointed a black Moor, justice minister Sghaïer Ould Mbareck, his new Prime Minister, the first Harratin to occupy the office.

The appointment was not without its political implications. Ould Mbareck hailed from Mauritania's far eastern province of Hodh el-Chargui, where many of the rebels had their family roots.

In the November elections, five opposition candidates challenged Ould Taya's bid for a fresh six-year term. His most formidable opponent was Mohamad Khouna Ould Haidalla, the former military ruler who had been overthrown by Ould Taya in 1984. Haidalla attracted a heterogeneous group of opportunists to his campaign: liberal reformers, Arab nationalists, and Islamic fundamentalists—all united by a common distaste for the incumbent. When the results were tabulated, President Taya won 67% of the ballots; Ould Haidalla placed second with about 19% of the vote. The opposition rolled out its usual litany of fraud complaints, but hard-to-fake voter cards and transparent ballot boxes did much to undermine the credibility of such charges.

Haidalla himself was arrested on the eve of the elections and charged with planning a *coup d'état* at the very time he was participating in the election. He was quickly brought to trial for threatening state security. While lawyers complained about procedure inside the courtroom, police outside had to use their batons and lob teargas at hundreds of the former colonel's supporters as they battled to gain entrance. By the end of December the court handed down a five-year suspended sentence for plotting to overthrow the government; Ould Haidalla was freed from jail, but the sentence, which strips him of his civic rights, effectively bars him from participating in politics.

The government announced it had derailed two further attempts to overthrow the regime, one in August 2004 and one a month later. The interior minister called it a "vast plan of destabilization and sabotage." Arrests in September netted Saleh Ould Hanenna and a supply of Libyan arms; the plot, said a government spokesman, had been orchestrated by Ould Hanenna while a fugitive living in Burkina Faso. Relations between Mauritania and the two countries remain tense.

After the 9/11 terror attacks in New York, President Taya committed himself to the war on terror, and Mauritania, with its little-patrolled desert crossings, alleged al-Qaeda cells, and large segments of its Muslim population sympathetic to Osama bin Laden and Saddam Hussein, has received special attention from U.S. planners. The country is one of four initially part of the Pan-Sahel Initiative, designed to train and prepared local armed forces to combat terrorist groups that seek to make the Sahara a new Afghanistan.

As part of the government's on-going struggle with Islamist opposition, police conducted extensive raids against suspected terror cells, including mosques, in April and May 2005. They accused al-Qaeda of pouring vast sums into mosques and Islamic schools to recruit insurgents and send them to the front lines of holy wars in Iraq and Afghanistan. Seven alleged members of the Algerian-based GSPC (Salafist Group for Preaching Combat) were charged with plotting acts of terror.

**Culture:** At independence in 1960, some 83% of the population was nomadic. Today that figure is about 5%, the consequence of devastating droughts in the 1970s and their periodic reoccurrence. Animal herds were decimated, and traditional family life and the rural economy were virtually destroyed. The result was a massive migration to the principal urban centers. Nouakchott and the port Nouadhibou are among the fastest-growing cities in the world. In the space of 40 years the capital's population grew from 40,000 to today's 1.4 million. Eighty per cent of the country' urban population lives in the two cities of Nouadhibou and Nouakchott.

Surrounding both Nouakchott and Nouadhibou today are encampments of the impoverished, mud-built shanty towns from which the poor can view the privileged position of the ruling class. Forty percent of the country's entire population lives in and around the capital. Most live from odd jobs, and their homes have neither electricity nor running water.

The Mauritanian film writer and director, Abderrahmane Sissako, dealt with issues of social change gently and beautifully in his 2002 film *Hermakono*, or *Waiting for Happiness*. Happiness, it turns out, is leaving the country. Abdallah, the film's central character, returns to his mother's native fishing village to wait until he finds passage to Europe and a better life. The rhythms of time are slow as he waits, and Sissako uses the rusting hulks of ships in Nouadhibou harbor as visual metaphor of waiting time. Indeed, the fastest tempo seen is when crowds clamber aboard the train—a train that also takes them away.

Desert oases, once thriving commercial and cultural centers, are now prey to an advancing Sahara. Chinguetti, the legendary seventh holiest city in Islam, once boasted a population of 3,000; 30,000 camels annually drank its waters. Today it is almost a ghost town. UNESCO has named it part of the world's patrimony in recognition of its spiritual and cultural importance. In Chinguetti eight families guard its greatest treasures: thousands of manuscripts—verses of the *Koran*, treatises on religion, astronomy and traditional medicine, works of poetry. The oldest go back to the 12th century. None have been translated and almost all are in advanced stages of deterioration.

Mauritania's other great treasure is the *Parc National du Banc d'Arguin* (PNBA) which UNESCO made a World Heritage site in 1989. Located on the Atlantic coast, the park provides a unique example of the transition zone between the Sahara Desert and the Atlantic Ocean. It covers an area as large as Lebanon, equally distributed between land and sea and was founded in 1976 mainly for its bird life. More than two million wading birds rest there on their annual migrations, and during breeding season 45,000 pairs of aquatic birds—pelicans, flamingoes, spoonbills, herons, cormorants, and others—nest in the park.

PNBA also arbors a rich variety of mammals, including gazelles, jackals, foxes, hyenas and a sand cat (Felis margarita). Marine mammals include visiting killer whales and dolphins, and a small resident colony—about 150—of the one of the world's rarest mammals, the monk seal.

**Economy:** Mauritania emerged from the terrible draught conditions of the 70s and 80s with a few years of decent rain. Animal flocks that had been devastated were gradually reconstituted. Cattle, which had fallen to 7.6 million head in 1973, rose to 11 million head by 1999, but three consecutive years of drought devastated both food and cattle production. More than 100,000 head of cattle died and herders had to lead their herds further south in search of greener pastures. Only in August 2003 did the rains return, giving hope of abundant pasturage and removing the looming specter of drought and famine.

The agricultural sector traditionally employs 50% of the population and contributes 19.3% of the GDP (2003), but these figures have been severely affected by the absence of water. In 2002 rainfall was so inadequate peasant farmers were unable to sow sorghum and millet, the principal cereal grains grown. The farmer's life is one of constant struggle: "The land teaches us much," runs the Mauritanian proverb, "because it resists us."

An important rice-growing culture is located in the Senegal River valley, aided by irrigation dams at Diama, Senegal, and Manantali, Mali. The irrigation dams are part of the Senegal River Development Organization (OMVS) which brings together Mali, Mauritania and Senegal.

For years Mauritania's principal source of income was iron. The iron ore industry is centered on the open-pit mines of Zouerat in the North. Ores are processed and then transported by train to the coastal port of Nouadhibou, some 400 miles away. Convoys of up to 250 ore-bearing cars, pulled by four engines and extending a mile and a half in length, evacuate the desert's wealth. On their return trip, the trains bring food, water and supplies to Zouerat, a town of 40,000 built to sustain the mines.

The mines have an annual capacity of 12 million tons, generating about $200 million in earnings and employing some 4,000 workers. The industry is operated by SNIM (*Société Nationale Industrielle et Minière de Mauritanie*) which is 80% state-owned. Kuwaiti and Jordanian investors, along with the Islamic Bank, hold the remaining shares. The company operates with seriously aging infrastructure.

In addition to repair and upgrading of the rail connection to the Atlantic, major work on the loading port for iron ore at Nouadhibou will be undertaken. Built in 1963, the port is dilapidated. In 1999 French experts had already declared it might have to shut down because of its failure to comply with safety standards. Long a virtual state monopoly, SNIM's efficiency and productivity may be increased by competition. The State has allowed several Australian companies to begin prospecting. One prospect: dia-

**The SNIM train carries iron ore from the desert to the port of Nouadhibou**

# Mauritania

monds. In the Mghaitir area, some 300 miles northeast of Zouerat, diamond-bearing kimberlite was discovered in 2000, and excavations are currently underway.

Waters off the Mauritanian coast are rich fishing areas—perhaps too rich. From 200 ships harvesting the sea in 1996, more than 500 were working the waters in 1998. Increased fishing boats have resulted in reduced catch and income. The explanation lies in the devastation of fish stock by industrial-scale fishing techniques. Species like dolphins, sharks and turtles have declined dangerously.

In 1998, the government decreed a two-month "biological rest" to help fishing stocks renew themselves, but even this has proved ineffective. It has recently banned all fishing, except traditional non-motorized fishing by local communities, in the Banc d'Arguin National Park. The depletion of fishing stock resulted from the agreement signed between Mauritania and the European Union. In exchange for $600 million in cash over six years, EU ships were allowed unrestricted fishing rights. Giant Dutch factory trawlers, for example, could catch and freeze 300 tons of sardines a day.

Fishing currently accounts for about half of Mauritania's export income and contributes 10% of GDP. Japan is the biggest buyer of Mauritanian fish, and the country maintains a sizable trade surplus with the Asian country.

Mauritania renewed its EU fishing agreement in August 2001. Anxious to keep its fishing fleets afloat, the EU agreed to pay more, but will be allowed to send more ships. Some of the increased revenue is targeted for development of the Mauritanian fishing sector. There are, for example, no port facilities for processing the catch. If there are no processing facilities aboard their ships, fishermen must take their catch to the Canary Islands for processing.

There may not be much left to process. The new EU accord has been severely criticized by the local environmental group, Pechecops, which described signing the agreement as "tantamount to signing the death warrant of Mauritania's national fisheries sector."

Critical to that sector is octopus fishing, which has been devastated by commercial over-harvesting. In 1993, with some 400 pirogues, Mauritania's fisherman landed nearly 8,100 tons of octopus. By 2001, with more than 1,500 boats fishing octopus, artisanal fishermen landed less than 3,000 tons. In other words, three times as many boats landed about a third the octopus catch of 1993. In March 2002, the UN Environment Program reported the octopus catch in Mauritania had fallen by 50% in the last four years; local people employed in the traditional octopus fishing fell from 5,000 in 1996 to 1,800 in 2002.

What is striking is that the government signed, while octopus stocks were already declining precipitously, an EU accord that *increased* cephalopod fishing capacities by 30%. The average European cephalopod boat harvests about 800 tons, of which 60% is made up of octopus. The EU's 55 boats could thus harvest 26,000 tons of octopus annually. Since the maximum economic yield for octopus has been set at 24,500 tons, signing the accord puts the long-term potential of the Mauritanian fishing sector at risk. In this context, Morocco's refusal to renew its EU fishing accord seems more than rational.

Given its dependence on iron and fish, Mauritania desperately needs to diversify its economy, but diversification requires investment and there is little money available for that. International financial aid accounts for 80 percent of the country's investment budget and international lenders have justifiable concerns. Mauritania has faithfully followed structural adjustment programs; the budget is balanced (with foreign assistance) and infla-

tion is down. There has been reasonable growth but little distribution of its consequences. The staggering inequalities of Mauritanian life are suggested by a simple fact: 80% of Mauritania's value added tax is paid by a mere 12 individuals.

Mauritania is also faced with a huge foreign debt of $2.36 billion (2003). In December 2000, the country qualified for relief under provisions of the Highly Indebted Poor Countries (HIPC) initiative, which might reduce external debt by 40%.

The country remains deeply impoverished and ranks 152 (out of 177 countries) on the UN Development Program's *Human Development Index* for 2004. About half the population lives in poverty, with 13% suffering malnutrition; almost 60% are illiterate, and life expectancy barely exceeds 50 years.

One possible note of optimism: for some time international companies have been drilling for off-shore oil and the results seem encouraging. The Australian company Woodside has discovered two separate oil fields, one of which, Chinguetti, may contain 100 million barrels of oil. In May 2004 Woodside announced plans to invest some $430 million to develop Chinguetti. The company expects to extract 75,000 barrels a day, with production beginning in March 2006.

Environmentalists have already evinced concerns about balancing oil exploration and exploitation with ecological preservation. At the heart of those concerns in the Banc d'Arguin reserve, located along the coast between the political and business capitals of Nouadhibou and Nouakchott. Safeguarding the World Heritage site is a constant concern for Mauritanian authorities.

**The Future:** Tense. Oil revenues increase the stakes greatly. President Taya's Israel policy and co-operation with the United States easily lend themselves to inflammatory manipulation by hostile opponents.

**The Monk Seal, one of the world's rarest mammals**

# The Kingdom of Morocco

**The World Heritage site of Ait Benhaddou**       Photo by Jinny Lambert

**Area:** 458,730 sq. km. = 200,320 sq. mi. (larger than California; the disputed territory of Western Sahara, now actually a part of Morocco, comprises another 102,703 sq. mi.).

**Population:** 32,725,847 (July 2005 est.)

**Capital City:** Rabat (est. pop. 1.4 million).

**Climate:** Semi–tropical and moist along the coastline and inland for 125 miles. Cool, with frost and snow in the high altitudes of the Atlas Mountains. A hot, semi–arid plateau on the south side of the Atlas Mountains quickly gives way to the Sahara Desert. The dry season of the coastal regions is from April to October.

**Neighboring Countries:** Algeria (East, Southeast); Mauritania (South); Morocco claims the entire territory of Western Sahara, formerly Spanish Sahara, most of which it occupies.

**Official Language:** Arabic.

**Other Principal Languages:** Berber languages, including Ghomara, Tachelhit, Tamazight, Tarifit; French, Spanish (largely in the enclaves of Melilla and Ceuta).

**Ethnic groups:** Arab-Berber 99.1%, other 0.7%, Jewish 0.2%.

**Principal Religions:** Muslim 98.7%, Christian 1.1%, and Jewish 0.2%.

**Chief Commercial Products**: Food and beverages 30%, semiprocessed goods 23%, consumer goods 21%, and phosphates 17%.

**GNI per capita:** $1,320 (2003)

**Currency:** Dirham.

**Former Colonial Status:** French Protectorate (1912–1956).

**Independence Date:** March 2, 1956.

**Chief of State:** King Mohamed VI (since July 1999).

**National Flag:** A five–pointed star in green outline on a red background.

Situated on the northwest corner of Africa, Morocco is the African nation closest to the European continent, separated from Spain by the narrow Strait of Gibraltar.

Three ranges of the high, rugged Atlas Mountains extend through the central and eastern portions of the country for more than 500 miles. In the hinterland of Fez, the Middle Atlas meets the Rif Range, which forms a crescent of land 6,000 feet high flanking the Mediterranean. To the south, the Middle Atlas is succeeded by the High Atlas, some of whose peaks reach a height of 13,000 feet. The Atlas, stretching almost the entire length of Morocco, form a natural barrier between the

fertile coast and the dry Sahara Desert and give the country three major environmental zones: relatively well-watered coastal lowlands, the mountain highlands, and the eastern deserts.

The coastal region is fertile, with a gentle climate. When ample rainfall arrives intense cultivation of the land is possible, but precipitation is irregular and droughts are not uncommon. White beaches along the seacoast stretch for almost 1700 miles along the Atlantic Ocean and the Mediterranean Sea, providing ample opportunity for the development of tourism.

Temperatures are cool in the highlands and bitterly cold in the winter. They are often snow-capped in the summer, permitting skiing at the same time bathers relax in the sun along the coast. Rainfall is concentrated in the cooler months from October to May, while summers are dry.

**History:** Many centuries before the birth of Christ, the Phoenicians had established trading posts in what is now Morocco and settled numerous people in the land. From the 1st century B.C. until the 5th century A.D. Morocco was a Roman province, providing foodstuffs for the people of the Empire.

# Morocco

After the fall of the Roman Empire, there was a quick succession of Vandals, Visigoths, and Byzantine Greeks who conquered Morocco. In the ninth century Arab forces arrived, bringing Islam to the people whom they subdued. The Berbers of inland Morocco were readily converted to this religion. The first rulers of the country claimed to be direct descendants of the Prophet Mohammed. The next centuries were a period of strife between the Muslim-Berbers and the Arab invaders.

After achieving some degree of unity in the 12th century, Morocco began to expand. Its borders ultimately reached from the Atlantic to Egypt and as far as Timbuktu to the south. After consolidating this immense territory, the Moors (the name given to the mixture of Arab and Berber people) conquered almost all of Spain, which became a Moroccan province. There was a slow decline of this vast empire, culminating in the first part of the 16th century.

There was another period of decline in the 19th century, and at one point, Morocco requested the United States to protect it from European expansion. Because of the country's strategic position, France indicated an interest in Morocco. After the conquest of Algeria, France slowly subdued Morocco, and a joint French-Spanish administration was set up in 1906. This quickly gave way to a French Protectorate under the terms of the treaty of Fez in 1912.

When Sultan Moulay Yusuf died in 1927 the French chose his younger son, Sidi Muhammad, as sultan. Known for his retiring disposition, the prince turned into a skilled and forceful king as Muhammad V. Around him Moroccan nationalists of all stripes gathered and challenges to French rule mounted. French attempts to divide Berbers and Arabs backfired and nationalists initiated a new national day, the *Fête du Trône* or Throne Day in 1933. It accentuated the monarch's role as symbol of national unity.

Popular enthusiasm for the young king was often accompanied by anti-French demonstrations. Political parties soon emerged seeking greater Moroccan self-rule. The explicit demand for independence logically followed the country's experiences in World War II. Muhammad V urged cooperation with France when war broke out in 1939 and Moroccan troops fought valiantly to defend the colonial ruler. A defeated France shone less brightly, and Vichy's racial laws were offensive to a monarchy that had a large Jewish population. The Allies, meeting in Casablanca in 1943, expressed little enthusiasm for continued French presence in Morocco and by 1944 an Independence Party, *Hizb al-Istiqlal*, was formed.

The monarch's willingness to permit existence of the independence movement was more than annoying to French administrators. He roused further hostility by refusing to countersign decrees of the French resident general, denying them legal validity. Seeking to divide Arabs and Berbers, French administrators began to cultivate Berber leadership as a counter foil to a nationalist monarch. One of the most formidable, Thami al-Glaoui, the feudal overlord of Marrakesh, condemned Muhammad V as not being the sultan of Moroccans as much as he was the sultan of *Istiqlal*.

Together al-Glaoui and France worked to depose the Sultan, but when the French removed him from office in 1953, it made Muhammad a nationalist hero. The Algerian uprising in 1954 diverted French attentions from Morocco and under the overwhelming influence of a popular monarch and a strong nationalist party, Morocco became independent in 1956.

Power in independent Morocco was concentrated in the hands of the monarch. Sultan Muhammad V (who officially adopted the title of king in August 1957) chose his ministers personally and kept personal control of the all-important army and the police forces. He was assisted, if that be the word, by a Consultative Assembly of 60, which he himself named. His eldest son, Moulay Hassan, became chief of staff and learned the art of politics and power from a skilled practitioner. Royal absolutism was slightly modified by a royal charter issued in May 1958 creating a constitutional monarchy.

When *Istiqlal* split along generational and ideological lines in 1959, the King positioned himself as neutral arbiter, well above the political fray. *Istiqlal*'s main faction, containing older and more traditional elements, was headed by Muhammad 'Allal al-Fasi. A smaller section headed by Mehdi Ben Barka was formed of younger men, intellectuals who favored socialism and had republican leanings. To pursue these goals, they formed the National Union of Popular Forces (UNFP).

Moulay Hassan was elevated to the throne as King Hassan II upon the unexpected death of his father in 1961. He promptly drafted a new constitution providing a parliamentary government. Elections were held in 1963 and the National Assembly began to function. Both Istiqlal factions were in opposition, while a miscellany of royal supporters coalesced in the Front for the Defense of Constitutional Institutions. Political bickering led to political paralysis. The king dissolved parliament after only a year and resorted to personal rule. Over the years it was clearly Hassan II's preferred form of governance.

The king's most formidable opponent, Mehdi Ben Barka, was forced into exile. Once the king's mathematics instructor, Ben Barka later turned radical, touting a Nasserist "Arab revolution" against Morocco's "reactionary" monarch. His support of revolutionary Algeria led to subsequent charges of high treason, including allegations of plotting against the life of Hassan II. He was sentenced *in absentia* to death. From his home in Paris Ben Barka became leader of the opposition to Hassan—until, that is, he was kidnapped and disappeared in October 1965. Numerous observers have suggested that the Ben

**Rissani Suq, Tafilat**

Barka plot was managed by General Muhammad Oufkir, the king's minister of the interior.

There followed a period of constitutions and coups, none of which were successful. Army rebels attempted it in 1971, raking the king's birthday party with gunfire and killing 98 guests, one of which was the Belgian ambassador. A year later General Oufkir apparently led a second coup which almost downed the royal plane. Hassan survived, as he did some eight other attempts on his life. For the faithful, such luck meant he must be a good ruler, gifted with *baraka*—a kind of divine grace.

His opponents were less fortunate. General Oufkir died at the royal palace, supposedly by his own hand. Hundreds of suspects, including members of his family, were imprisoned. It was a tad more genteel than the fate of rebels against his father. While Crown Prince and army chief in 1958 Hassan had suppressed a rebellion in the Rif mountains. Rebellion ringleaders, so the story goes, were flown out to sea in helicopters and shoved overboard. True or not, it certainly contributed to the prince's image: fear, not love, was a more likely policy. Indeed, force seemed to be respected by Moroccans. Hassan's forceful policies to absorb Spanish Sahara increased his popularity in the mid-1970s.

Hassan turned Western Sahara into a fervent nationalist cause. Good relations with Israel and Washington provided the weaponry to defeat the Polisario Front, a guerrilla insurrection seeking independence for the area. Ultimately the war evolved to a stalemate, with Moroccans hunkering down behind massive walls of sand. Nationalist fervor over Sahara could not for long disguise the country's real social and economic and political problems.

Constitutional tinkering, and it was frequent, never threatened the king's personal rule. Royal decrees could not be debated, for that would be like challenging the will of God. It was also a crime to question the royal finances. Repressed political energy will always find a way out, and the regime faced not only plots against its ruler, but periodic riots, strikes, and other manifestations of discontent.

By the early 1980s bad harvests, a sluggish economy, and the continuing financial drain of the Sahara war increased domestic strains. Islamic fundamentalism was finessed by the king's claim of descent from the Prophet, but its growing influence among both the educated and the impoverished suggested fundamental weaknesses in the system. International lenders and human rights organizations pressed for reform.

The king responded, as always, with a combination of symbol and reality. There seemed to be a greater liberalization. Am-

**King Mohamed VI**

nesties were granted to some long imprisoned in remote places; curbs on the powers of security and police forces were announced. Another constitutional referendum was held in 1992, but its provisions were superseded by yet another constitutional change submitted to referendum in 1996. There would be a new bicameral parliament. It would consist of an indirectly–elected upper house and, for the first time since independence, a directly elected popular assembly. It was still change from above—royally-directed political reform.

The 1997 elections were Morocco's first direct elections for the lower house of parliament and an effort to spread democracy to rural areas. More than 3,000 candidates contested 325 seats under conditions of greater openness than ever before. Three main political groups took almost equal numbers of seats in the Chamber of Deputies. The *Koutla* left-wing opposition block took 102 seats. Its dominant partner, the Socialist Union of Popular Forces (USFP) won 57 seats to become the largest party in parliament. The right-wing *Wifak* block won 100 and a center-right grouping received 97. The relatively equal distribution of seats among the principal forces hinted at stalemate rather than action.

For the first time a fundamentalist religious party, the Islamist Popular Constitutional Democratic Movement (MPCD), won seats (nine) in parliament. The remaining seats in the 325-seat chamber went to a scattering of minor parties. The big loser in the elections was *Istiqlal*. It won only 32 seats, down from 43 in 1993 elections, and blamed its loss on fraud

and electoral manipulation by the Ministry of the Interior.

Though a parliamentary system, the government emerged less from parliament than from the king. Hassan II reserved the right to appoint and fire ministers. The king asked Aberrahmane Youssoufi, the 73-year old leader of the USFP, to form a government. The cabinet ultimately included representatives of five opposition parties with USFP and Istiqlal taking the majority of posts. The King retained control over two of the most important ministries. The Interior assignment went to the king's right-hand man, Driss Basri. Defense remained in the hands of the king as supreme commander of the Royal Armed Forces. Hassan had learned much from his father: meaningful power still lay in the hands of the monarch.

To Moroccans Driss Basri was the most powerful and feared of Hassan's ministers. As minister of the interior for over 20 years, Basri controlled a web of security agents and spies who informed him of the slightest hint of dissent or opposition. He controlled appointments of governors and other regional and local officials. The police were under his control and his jails were places of detention and torture. Even critical foreign-policy questions were under his purview. In many ways the interior ministry was a parallel government operating above the law and responding only to the king. Basri was Grand Vizir of the king's dark side.

After thirty-eight years of less than progressive rule King Hassan died in July 1999. He was succeeded by his unmarried elder son, Crown Prince Sidi Mohamed. Mohamed VI's first speech ignited a spark of optimism brighter than any generated by the half-hearted reforms of his father. He evoked the poverty of his people, the fate of women, and the need for change. Action followed words. Corrupt governors were fired and some 10,000 prisoners released from Moroccan prisons. Victims of human rights abuses and relatives of those who had simply "disappeared" were recognized and offered compensation by the state. Before a December 1999 deadline, the Moroccan human rights commission received 5,500 requests for compensation from victims of the former regime. In November 1999 King Mohamed confirmed his commitment to change by dismissing the much-feared interior minister, Driss Basri.

Mohamed also began the process of bringing his father's political opponents home from exile or freeing them from house arrest. The most notable of the exiles was the 73-year old Abraham Serfaty. Head of the Marxist-Leninist *Ila al-Amam* group, Serfaty had been sentenced to life

# Morocco

**An olive seller**

Photo by Jinny Lambert

in prison for making statements in favor of self-determination for the Western Sahara. After a seventeen-year incarceration, he was released from jail and expelled from Morocco after enormous international pressure. He had been living in exile for 8 years when the young king allowed him to return, a free citizen once again. The family of Mehdi Ben Barka, who "disappeared" under mysterious circumstances in 1965 while living in France, had their passports restored and were allowed to return to Morocco.

The other notable political opponent restored was the Islamist leader Sheikh Abdessalam Yassine, the most radical of King Hassan's challengers. The 72-year old Yassine was head of *al-Adl wal-Ihsane* (Justice and Charity). Active mainly on university campuses and in the poor districts of large cities, Justice and Charity is the country's biggest Muslim fundamentalist organization, and advocates the reestablishment of the Caliphate and the application of Sharia law.

Sheikh Yassine had long been a thorn in the side of King Hassan. In the 1970s he had been detained without trial for more than three years for sending a 114-page letter to the royal palace criticizing the king for copying Western values—described as barbarous, materialistic and egoistic—and demanding the application of Sharia law. Government ministers had long called for his release, but palace officials argued he should first acknowledge the religious authority of King Mohamed VI, who bears the title *Amir al-Mu'minin* or "Commander of the Faithful."

The Sheikh, seemingly an inveterate letter writer, persisted in his ways even while under house arrest. In February 2000 he addressed a 35-page letter to the king raising one of the most taboo of subjects—the royal family's wealth. It called on the king to return billions of dollars that Islamists allege his father had stashed abroad. Yassine was finally released from 10 years of house arrest in May 2000.

Despite fresh vigor and a new optimism generated by the new king, it is difficult to say that much progress has been made on Morocco's most pressing problems. There remain utterly fundamental problems about the source of policy innovation and direction between a democratically elected government and a king possessing extraordinary sources of constitutional power and traditional legitimacy. The weight of authority seems to have swung back to the monarch. It was the king who, drawing upon his religious authority as commander of the faithful, took practical action to deal with two of the country's abiding problems: illiteracy and unemployment. In August 2000 he announced that Morocco's mosques would be used to dispense literacy courses, as well as religious, civic and health education. Women—whose literacy in the rural areas is estimated to be as low as 10%—were a primary target of the program.

The 2002 legislative elections confirmed royal dominance. Certainly the fairest elections every held, the very honesty of the elections reflects royal will: the King saw the first elections to take place during his reign as a means of regaining the trust of a population grown cynical with previous electoral fraud and falsification. Free, fair, and transparent elections were the monarch's top priority, along with fulsome participation. The government organized an extensive media campaign to encourage people to vote. Perhaps it was too much to expect a population so inexperienced in the ways of genuine democratic expression to suspend skepticism: less than 52% of registered voters were mobilized to vote.

The election featured several innovations. Proportional representation, with electors voting for a party list rather than individual candidates, was employed. To assure female representation in parliament, voters also selected ten per cent of their future MPs from a national list of exclusively female candidates. Among all the Arab states, this set-aside assured Morocco of having the largest contingent of women in its legislature. For the first time also ballots featured party logos to facilitate recognition by illiterate voters. To dissuade fraud and fixing, more than 50,000 bottles of indelible ink were imported to dab the hands of voters, and prison sentences were introduced for vote-buying by candidates—a great tradition of Moroccan politics.

One obvious consequence of these changes was a greater number of political parties participating. Twenty six of them nominated 5,873 candidates (269 of them women) on 1,772 lists in 91 electoral districts. In the final results representation in parliament was more fragmented than ever: 22 parties would take seats in the new legislature where only fifteen had sat before.

The election produced no seismic change. Retiring prime minister Youssoufi's USFP claimed the largest number of seats: 50 in the 325-member House of Representatives. *Istiqlal* took second place with 48 seats, while the moderate Islamist Party of Justice and Development (PJD) made the biggest gain, winning 42 seats to its previous 14. Sheikh Yassine's fundamentalist Justice and Charity party called for an election boycott and ran no candidates, so its popularity remained untested.

Paradoxically, the new government that emerged from Morocco's cleanest, most transparent and most democratic election would not be party based. Following the election the king appointed his current interior minister, Driss Jettou, as prime minister. Unaffiliated with any political party, Jettou was a businessman—a former shoe manufacturer—who heads a team of born-again democrats. In Moroccan politics the palace remains the final arbiter. The monarch not only appoints the prime minister, but four other ministries, including defense, foreign affairs and Islamic affairs, are palace appointments. The king presides over meetings of this select cabinet, which operates in parallel with the prime minister's own cabinet, and takes most of the important policy decisions.

In 2002 Moroccan security forces dismantled an al-Qaeda sleeper cell, directed by three Saudis, with plans to blow up American and British war ships passing through the Strait of Gibraltar. A year later, al-Qaeda-linked terrorists set off five bombs near Western and Jewish targets in Casablanca, killing 43 people (including 12 terrorists) and wounding more than 100. Alawite Morocco, ruled by a descendent of the prophet, was no longer immune to international Islamic terrorism; May 16, 2003 became the country's 9/11.

Parliament reacted by passing a strict anti-terrorism law, but the King, the embodiment of official Islam, remained silent. One Rabat paper, Al-Alam, referred to a "savage terrorist aggression with foreign hands," but investigation showed the May 16 perpetrators were largely local. Indigenous Islamic fundamentalism was the major threat to Morocco's developing democracy. Symptomatically, municipal elections were postponed from June to September, giving the government more time to campaign against the possibility of a fundamentalist take-over of the country's biggest cities: Casablanca, Rabat, Fez, and Tangier.

The September elections were dominated by the two leading traditional parties: Istiqlal and the socialist USFP together won more than 30% of the vote for 23,000 local seats. The one legal Islamist party, the PJD, won less than 3% of the vote, but only because it discreetly chose to run candidates in only 20% of the constituencies. In Casablanca, Morocco's largest city, the PJD won in all eight districts where it presented candidates; had it chosen to run in the city's other eight districts, Casablanca would have had an Islamist government.

On two of Morocco's most prickly policy issues, Spain and Western Sahara, the king has provided policy initiative. In October 2001 he withdrew, without consulting his government, Morocco's ambassador to Spain, signaling the depth of tensions that had developed between the two countries. Relations had soured over Spain's continued support of the Algerian-backed Polisario Front (PF) and its claims for self-determination in Western Sahara. This was, however, only one of several issues that made the Spanish-relations dossier one of the thickest.

**Relations With Spain**
Wary of the fearsome decline of fishing stocks in its Atlantic waters, Rabat has re-

fused to renew its fishing agreement with the EU. The Spanish fishing fleet was by far the worst affected. More than 300 vessels and their crews were idled by the failure to reach a new agreement, and the EU had to come up with funds to effect a reconversion of fleet and crews.

Morocco's fundamentally stagnant economy has not been characterized by significant job creation. Unemployment among the young is at 30%, forcing thousands of men, educated and uneducated, to migrate in search of employment. Spain, a ninety-minute boat ride away, is a natural first stop, and a steady stream of clandestine immigrants arrives on Spanish shores. Spain detained some 15,000 illegal immigrants in 2000, all picked up along her coastline. In many ways North Africa is to southern Europe as Mexico is to the U.S., with the threat of Islamic fundamentalism thrown in.

The jumping off spots for many of those seeking clandestine entry into Spain are the two Spanish enclaves of Ceuta (Sebta to Moroccans) and Melilla—microscopic residuals from an earlier era. Ceuta, barely seven square miles in size, is a peninsula across from Gibraltar that is, like Melilla, an autonomous region of the Spanish Kingdom. Moroccans have lived and worked and bought duty free goods in both the enclaves for years. With increased illegal migration (a profitable activity of organized crime groups), Spanish authorities heightened security measures.

They ringed both enclaves with two razor-wire fences, ten and a half feet high. The fences are six feet apart, separated by a no-man's land, constantly observed by 37 infrared cameras, 230 searchlights and 21 watchtowers. Coastal patrols have been increased, and a $120 million radar system was installed to surveil the strait.

The two countries traded hostilities at the UN General Assembly in November 2001. The Moroccan ambassador denounced Spanish occupation of the two enclaves and likened them to Gibraltar and Spanish demands it be returned to Spanish sovereignty—an equivalency, of course, rejected by the Spanish. Their retort focused on the other territorial tension between the two states: The Sahara, replied the Spanish foreign minister, is "a historical claim of Moroccan nationalism which Spain will never share."

Tensions over territorial sovereignty were ratcheted up in the summer of 2002. In July Spanish troops ejected a group of Moroccan soldiers who had occupied an uninhabited droplet of land barely large enough to be called an island off the Moroccan coast. Spain claimed it had controlled the island for centuries. Ambassadors were withdrawn, but by January

2003 the two countries announced the restoration of full diplomatic ties.

As Morocco increasingly looked to greater economic cooperation with Europe, Spain stood at a critical juncture in those relations. The EU's Euro-Mediterranean Partnership (EMP), an effort to lower tariffs and encourage trade, was an additional source of strain. Spanish farmers, for example, protested the importation of cheap Moroccan tomatoes, claiming they were destroying business.

Relatively large immigrant populations are a continuing source of tension between the two countries. Moroccans are the largest immigrant group in Spain, estimated to number around 333,000 in 2003. To service their spiritual needs, there are an estimate 1,000 mosques, functioning out of sight of outsiders in apartments, garages, or workshops with often radical preachers. From this milieu came the al-Qaeda-linked terrorists responsible for the March 11, 2004 train bombings in Madrid. They killed 191 people, wounded more than 1,500, toppled an incumbent government, and transformed relations between Morocco and Spain.

In the still-unfolding investigations, Spanish authorities have identified 14 of 18 so far charged with the bombings as Moroccans. One of the ringleaders, a Tangiers native named Jamal Zougam, had connections to two banned Moroccan groups: *Salafiya Jihadiya*, implicated in the 2003 Casablanca bombings, and the *Groupe islamiste combattant marocain* (GICM: Moroccan Islamic Combat Group), which claims to struggle for an Islamic state in the kingdom.

Zougam was a disciple of Muhammad al-Fizazi, the spiritual leader of *Salafiya Jihadiya*. Al-Fizazi, had been preaching a virulently anti-Western brand of Islam from a mosque in Tangiers until he was arrested, tried, and given a 30-year sentence of inciting violence in Morocco in 2003. Unfortunately, in the Madrid killers he found perfect translation of his exhortation to utilize portable telephones as "an arm of Islam": they converted their cell phones into detonators.

Facing a common threat from Islamist militancy, Morocco and Spain now cooperate closely in both legal and security issues concerning illegal immigration, international terror and, increasingly, its ties to drug trafficking and organized criminal networks. A new agreement, signed in May 2004, provides for a Spanish judge to be based in Rabat and a Moroccan judge in Madrid to speed up judicial procedures involving both countries.

**Western Sahara**
Western Sahara, formerly known by the names of its two former subdivisions,

# Morocco

Saguia el–Hamra and Rio de Oro, lies within one of the most oppressive parts of the immense Sahara Desert. A narrow band along the coast receives torrential thunderstorms wafted inland by the steady trade winds. The only thing that remains after the rain is more erosion—the water either spills into the short rivers emptying silt into the Atlantic Ocean, or is quickly swallowed up by the scorched land.

This thinly populated desert region became a Spanish colony when no one else wanted it during the scramble for colonies at the close of the 19th century. For details of earlier and colonial history, see *Historical Background* and *The Spanish in Africa*.

The territory, then known as Spanish Sahara, came under Moroccan–Mauritanian domination as a result of a series of diplomatic and military actions after the Spanish left in 1975.

Morocco, Algeria and Mauritania had joined together in the early 1970s to pressure Spain to relinquish the territory. Spain dragged its feet as long as possible, all the while mining the phosphate deposits which were the colony's only resource. When guerrilla activity commenced in 1974 and sabotaged phosphate extraction, Spain surrendered the territory. The question, of course, was to whom or what it should be relinquished. Morocco, Mauritania and Algeria had rival claims and positions.

The Algerians supported the Polisario Front (PF: Popular Front for the Liberation of Saguia el–Hamra and Rio de Oro)—an organization which claimed to represent the national ambitions of the people of the former colony. Morocco, then backed by Mauritania, insisted that Spain should "return" the Western Sahara as part of greater Morocco.

Seizing the initiative, King Hassan announced a "green march" into Spanish Sahara. Some 200,000 Moroccan civilians crossed the border and penetrated six miles into the territory. Spain transferred administrative responsibility to Morocco and Mauritania, and the Polisario proclaimed the existence of the "Sahrawi Democratic Arab Republic," which was immediately recognized by Algeria as the former colony's only legitimate government. Armed conflict soon broke out between the various actors.

Moroccan and Mauritanian troops quickly solidified their position in Western Sahara, while Algeria supported Polisario sabotage and violence. Initially Morocco and Mauritania seemed in firm control, but PF guerrilla activities posed substantial problems for both nations. Incursions into Mauritania by PF guerillas threatened the Mauritanian capital. A poor nation with an all but non–existent military capability, Mauritania folded in August 1978. King Hassan proclaimed Western Sahara the 37th province of Morocco, rallying his subjects to a sense of Moroccan nationalism.

Morocco now controls all but the easternmost portion of Western Sahara, which is walled by a ten–foot–high "berm" intended to keep Sahrawi "rebels" out. Since that time, rebel activity has been irregular. Most Sahrawi—more than 150,000 of them—are sheltered in camps near Tindouf, Algeria, subject to the less than tender mercies of the Polisario Front.

For thirteen years, and at the cost of half a billion dollars, the UN has been trying to hold a referendum that would allow the Sahrawi to determine their own future. Since no one can agree on just who is a Sahrawi and who should be eligible to vote in the referendum, the issue is unresolved.

Former Secretary of State James Baker, Kofi Annan's personal representative for Western Sahara, launched another drive to resolve the dispute in May 2000. In 2002, Baker, faced with consistent intransigence from all parties, submitted four proposals to the UN Security Council. The first was to proceed with referendum plans for the territory without the agreement of both parties on specifics. Second was a proposal to grant significant autonomy to the region as part of Morocco. After five years, the Sahrawi would be given a chance to vote on their status. The third proposal was to partition the territory between the contending parties, and the fourth, indicating the degree of frustration the issue has provoked, was simply to walk away, admitting the UN was unable to solve the problem.

The Security Council met in April 2002 to choose a course of action—and could not. Independence for the Sahrawi Arab Democratic Republic seems a non-starter. King Mohamed has made the Moroccan position abundantly clear on two visits to Western Sahara: "Morocco will not relinquish a single inch of the territory." Morocco opposes the partition plan, believing it would create a weak client state for Algeria, whose only interest is access to the Atlantic Ocean. Some sort of autonomy within Morocco is the most likely outcome. Whether or not the Sahrawi will be allowed a vote on that autonomy, and at what point, may be the only issue left.

There are several signs that resolution of the problem may be possible. On the Polisario side, the Front has lost its nearly mythical military commander, Lahbib Sid'Ahmed Lahbib Aouba, better known by his *nom de guerre*, Commandant Ayoub. A co-founder of the PF, Commandant Ayoub broke with PF authorities and defected to Morocco, pledging his personal allegiance to King Mohamed in September 2002.

French president Chirac has referred to Western Sahara as Morocco's "southern provinces," and France appears to be pressuring Algeria to abandon its demand for a referendum. During his historic visit to Algeria in early March 2003, Chirac asked President Bouteflika to initiate "direct talks" with Morocco—in other words, to abandon Algeria's traditional position

**A local vegetable retailer**

Photo by Taylor O'Connor

310

that any discussion must include the Polisario Front. In another sign of change, Algeria's former Defense Minister, General Khaled Nezzar, was reported as saying that "Algeria did not need a new state on its borders."

The possibility of oil off the Western Saharan coast may well be the greatest lubricant of movement on the issue. Both TotalFinaElf, France's largest oil firm, and the Oklahoma City-based Kerr McGee Corporation, have signed exploration contracts with Morocco. After several years of securing little more than frequent-flyer mileage, Ambassador Baker resigned as mediator in June 2004. In September, Morocco received its most significant diplomatic rebuke in years when South African president Thabo Mbeki extended diplomatic recognition to the self-proclaimed Sahrawi Republic. Morocco withdrew its ambassador from South Africa and went through an agonizing period of critical self-appraisal of the failure of its diplomacy.

Thirteen years after their cease fire, Morocco and the Polisario front remain without agreement. In April 2005, with little else to do, the UN Security Council extended its peacekeeping mission in Western Sahara (MINURSO) for another six months.

**Culture:** A note on royal names and titles. Moroccan princes are referred to with the title Moulay (master), unless their name is Mohamed. Since the only "Master Mohamed" is the Prophet, princes named Mohamed are addressed as Sidi (my lord). Princesses are given the title Lalla.

The historic city of Meknès, founded in the 11th century by Almoravid rulers as a military town, is a major tourist attraction. Meknès became a capital under Sultan Moulay Ismaïl (1672–1727), the founder of the Alawite dynasty. The sultan transformed the city into a impressive center of Spanish-Moorish style surrounded by high walls. Monumental entrance doors show the harmonious blending of Islamic and European styles of the 17th-century Maghreb.

The Alawite dynasty has provided the country's sultans since the mid-17th century. Like his predecessors, King Mohamed bears several titles—Commander of the Faithful, Savior, and Shadow of the Prophet on Earth—that reflect the dynasty's claim to be directly descended from the Prophet Mohammed. The claim has been the traditional means by which Moroccan kings have legitimized their rule and, more recently, checked the claims of Islamists.

Boosting the social and economic status of women was a major policy focus of the Youssoufi government. In a traditional, male-dominated society women are disadvantaged. More than 60 percent of Moroccan women are illiterate, for example, with the rate rising to 90% in poor rural areas. This limits their ability to contribute significantly to the country's economic development.

In March 1999 the government introduced a series of proposals that would alter the country's traditional Islamic marriage statutes. The plan would ban polygamy and raise the minimum age for marriage from 15 to 18. A system of legal divorce would replace the current norm of simple verbal dissolution through repudiation by the husband. Under the new proposals divorce would be in the hands of a judge. The new statutes also stipulated that a couple's assets must be shared after divorce.

After the government announced its reforms, most political and religious groups expressed passionate reactions. Fundamentalists and modernists staged dueling marches in Casablanca and Rabat. An estimated 500,000 traditionalists demonstrated in Casablanca against the project, dwarfing a demonstration by supporters of the plan, who rallied about 40,000 people in Rabat. The government stayed its hand; reform of the family code languished.

Following the bloody Casablanca bombings, Islamists kept a low profile. In the breathing space provided by quiesence, the King took up the issue of family code reform, something central to his concerns since the beginning of his reign. In October 2003 he announced a new code, "in perfect harmony with the spirit of Islam," and, exercising audacious leadership, helped push the code through parliament. (It was passed unanimously by both chambers, including the Islamic PJD.) The new code, which became effective in February 2004, recognizes the equality of the sexes, suppresses the husband's right of repudiation, raises the age of consent to 18 and renders polygamy virtually impossible to practice.

With the adoption of the *Mudawana*, or Family Code, Morocco becomes a rare exception in the Muslim world, where the status of women remains a battlefield between modernists and radical Islamists.

**Economy:** Agriculture contributes about 18.3% of Morocco's economy and accounts for about 50% of the labor force, but it is highly dependent on rainfall patterns. As a consequence, economic growth tends to be erratic, making the conditions of rural farmers difficult at best. According to government statistics, GDP grew in 1998 by 6.7%, but was stagnant in 1999 and only 0.9% in 2000, following two successive years of drought. Better rains during 2001, 2002, and 2003, brought higher economic growth (6.3%, 3.2%, and 5.5% respectively).

Morocco is considered to have the best agricultural land in North Africa and produces wheat, barley, beans sugar beets and citrus fruits. Frequent droughts and erratic rainfall in recent years have caused agricultural productivity to fall. Much of the arable land remains unused due to a lack of irrigation, one of the priorities in the government's five-year development plan.

There are no government statistics on Morocco's cannabis crop (known locally as *kif*), the amount of which, no doubt, also fluctuates with rainfall conditions. Morocco is among the world's largest producers of cannabis. Its cultivation and sale are the economic basis for much of the Rif Mountains of northern Morocco, where over 200,000 acres are devoted to its production. About two-thirds of the 800,000 people of the Rif, most of them Berbers, depend on cannabis for their income. They produce an estimated 47,400 tons of hashish a year, most of it exported to Algeria, Tunisia, and Europe—smuggled to Spain, Portugal, and France by sea, then by road to other countries in Europe. The total trade is estimated to be worth more than $13 billion, but most of the profits are taken by drug lords, most of them European criminals living on Spain's Costa del Sol.

For most Rif inhabitants, cannabis cultivation is simply a matter of survival: "It keeps us alive, not the government," said one local. The region is isolated, underdeveloped, impoverished, and alienated. Resentments still linger from the brutal repression of a Berber rebellion in 1958. After that, the central government pretty much abandoned the region to its own; infrastructure investments—roads and schools—were minimal. When an earth-

**A nesting stork**
Photo by Taylor O'Connor

# Morocco

quake hit the area in early 2004, it took several days for supplies to reach some villages because of difficult topography and poor infrastructure.

Attempts to diversify have produced a modestly mixed economy. The mining sector remains crucially important. There are about 90 mining companies producing about 20 different mineral products. Phosphates account for 92% of mineral production. Morocco has the largest phosphate reserves in the world—110 billion tons—and produces significant amounts of fertilizers and phosphoric acid. It is the world's number one phosphoric acid exporter, averaging 1.7 million tons of exports annually. Phosphates and their by-products account for 18% of Morocco's total exports. With environmental concerns about ammonium phosphate fertilizers in North America, however, export demand there has fallen since 1999, and the industry has had to search for new markets. The royal family, which is said to own about a fifth of the country's land, also controls the country's rich phosphate mines.

A fishing industry is developing, perhaps even a bit too quickly. The ocean off Morocco's Atlantic coast is one of the richest fishing grounds in the world. Over-fishing by aggressive industrial fishing fleets has severely reduced the stock of available fish, and Morocco has had to declare an occasional "biological repose" in response to overly zealous fishing. Much of that was done by European fishing fleets, and Morocco has refused to renew its fishing agreement with the EU. With nearly 900,000 tons fish taken annually, Morocco is by far the largest African producer. Unlike its neighbor to the South, Morocco has the capacity to process much of its catch—canning anchovies and freezing sardines, for example—to add significant value to the basic catch.

Tourism is of growing importance, but subject to sharp fluctuations reflecting world events. In 1999 Morocco received 2 million visitors, an increase of 18% over the previous year. A short way across the Mediterranean, however, tiny Gibraltar attracted six million visitors. The industry was dealt a deadly blow by the terrorist attacks on New York in September 2001. By December an estimated 100,000 hotel reservations had been cancelled. Overall, the number of tourists who arrived in 2002 fell 3%, with heavy declines in the cities of Marrakesh and Agadir which usually attract more than two-thirds of Morocco's tourists.

In May 2002 Prime Minister Youssoufi announced a tourism development scheme. Dubbed Plan Azur, the program aims to add 40,000-50,000 hotel rooms as part of a plan to attract 10 million tourists to the country by 2010. Five coastal sites, including the walled city of Essaouira—known for its closely-knit community of Sephardic Jews and particularly its Jewish musicians—have been selected for development. For the moment the tourism sector accounts for an average of 7% of GDP and 6% of employment, but it remains enormously vulnerable to terror attacks like those of May 2003. Indeed, it is deliberately targeted: tourism is Morocco's second largest earner of foreign exchange, after worker remittances.

Morocco's manufacturing base is expanding and currently contributes around 16.4% to the country's GDP. The U.S. and Morocco signed a Free Trade Agreement (FTA) in June 2004 after 13 months of tough negotiations. Morocco's largest exports to the U.S. are semi-conductors, minerals, and clothing, while the largest U.S. sales to Morocco are grains and civilian aircraft. What the impact of the agreement will be is uncertain. Total trade between the two countries is small: around $850 million in 2003—less that what the U.S. and Mexico do in two days.

Not endowed with the fabulous wealth of some of its neighbors, Morocco's economic growth has been modest, but opportunity has often been frittered away. A major reason, argues the World Bank, is the country's bloated and heavily unionized administration. It employs some 750,000 people, including security forces and para-military forces, under the direct control of the interior ministry. The wages of this army of civil servants devour a full 12% of Morocco's GDP, and the share is growing.

The effects are immediate and real: Morocco budgets more for education than its neighbors, but achieves less because of excessive administrative costs. One out of two children of school age do not go to school in Morocco. One in two Moroccans can neither read nor write, a literacy rate worse than India's. The rates are worse in many isolated Berber communities, which only contributes to the sense of abandonment the community already feels.

Morocco is characterized by scandalous disparities of wealth and poverty (in Morocco the richest 10% consume 14 times what the poorest 10% consume). At least 4 million Moroccans live on less than $1 a day, and the number of poor steadily increased between 1991 and 1999. Poverty remains a particularly rural phenomenon, with more that 25% of the rural population living below the poverty line, compared to just 12% of the urban population.

Ruins of the Roman city of Volubilis. Many of the city's buildings were destroyed to provide building materials to construct the palaces of Moulay Ismail in nearby Meknès.

Unemployment has also increased. In 1982, 10% of the active population was unemployed. Presently it's at least 16% and more in the urban centers—up to 25%. Among young people, unemployment figures rise to at least 30%.

The economy needs to create approximately 250,000 jobs a year to accommodate the young who enter the job market annually. Given limited opportunity, many head abroad as illegal immigrants seeking work in Europe. An estimated 100,000 to 200,000 depart every year.

Over all, Morocco's economic development hangs the debt guillotine. According to World Bank figures, Morocco's accumulated external debt is $18.82 billion—equivalent to 43% of GNP. Once debt servicing and civil service salaries are paid, there is precious little left to invest.

There are some potentialities. Morocco has stayed the course of the economic liberalization it launched in 1991, and this has brought significant foreign invest-

ment. Its privatization program has been described by the *Financial Times* as "North Africa's most advanced," but privatizations in 2002 failed to attract any buyers.

Perhaps the most important potential for the Moroccan economy lies with the discovery of oil in the Talsint region of southeast Morocco. For years Morocco has had to import virtually all of its oil and gas. To encourage exploration and development, it drastically overhauled its investment code: required participation by the state in such endeavors was reduced from 50% to 25%, and companies were offered a ten-year tax abatement once production begins.

In announcing the discovery to the nation, Mohammed VI demonstrated a keen ear for Islamic critics. These riches, he told his audience, would never be allowed "to engulf us in fatalism, indolence and consumerism, paralyzing our energy and our human and natural potentialities." Per-

haps more importantly, in terms of Morocco's economic development, he seemed to look to neighboring Algeria as a negative model: "The wealth discovered," he affirmed, "will never constitute an alternative to our agricultural heritage, but rather a tool for its enrichment."

**The Future:** Morocco's democratic political system remains fragile. The dynamic for change clearly rests more with King than parliament. Proclaimed "King of the Poor," the young monarch owes his adulation as much to reaction against the dark days of his father as to his own personality. Despite having a parliament, all major decisions still reside in the hands of the king, and the whole system seems unable to function without direction from that source.

Endemic poverty and a sense of abandonment felt by many, especially northern Berber communities, provide rich recruiting grounds for Islamic radicals.

The Basilica at the Roman site of Volubilis, north of Meknès

# The Republic of Tunisia

**A group of men discuss the day's events at the harbor of Sousse**

**Area:** 164,206 sq. km. = 63,431 sq. mi. (slightly larger than Florida).

**Population:** 10,074,951 (July 2005 est.)

**Capital City:** Tunis (Pop. 2 million estimated).

**Climate:** Warm, Mediterranean in the northern and central parts; hot and dry in the semi–Sahara south–southwest.

**Neighboring Countries:** Algeria (West); Libya (East, southeast).

**Official Language:** Arabic.

**Other Principal Languages:** French; possibly some Berber languages.

**Ethnic groups:** Arab 98%, European 1%, Jewish and other 1%.

**Principal Religions:** Muslim 98%, Christian 1%, Jewish and other 1%.

**Chief Commercial Products:** Hydrocarbons, textiles, agricultural products, phosphates and chemicals.

**GNI per capita:** $2,240 (2003)

**Currency:** Dinar.

**Former Colonial Status:** French Protectorate (1881–1956).

**Independence Date:** July 20, 1956.

**Chief of State:** Zine Abidine Ben Ali, President.

**National Flag:** A white disk bearing a red crescent and a five–pointed star centered on a red background.

Tunisia, the smallest country of North Africa, lies almost in the center of the Mediterranean Sea coastline, with a seashore almost 1,000 miles long. The coastal belt, with an average of 50 miles in width, is the site of farmland. The coastline extends horizontally for 140 miles in the North and then proceeds irregularly southward for a lineal distance of 300 miles. There are three large gulf areas of gentle warm waters which carve semi–circles. The coastal strip is succeeded by a gently rolling tableland with an average altitude of 1,600 feet—an area of grass and forestland. This, in turn, is followed by the semi–desert to the south–southwest where there is little rainfall, and shallow salt lakes. Though this sparsely settled territory is within the desert, it is not quite as bleak and hot as the central Sahara.

**History:** The early history of Tunisia includes the presence of almost every powerful empire of old. An early settlement of Phoenicians developed in the 6th century B.C. Ruins of the city of Carthage as it existed in the days of Hannibal lie today a short distance north of Tunis. Elephants undoubtedly were present in this northern area at the time Hannibal used them in his famed offensive against the Roman Republic. For details of early and colonial

314

history, see *Historical Background* and *The French in Africa.*

France recognized Tunisian independence on July 20, 1956. The old monarchy was abolished in 1957 when the Constituent Assembly established a republic, naming Habib Bourguiba president. Following adoption of a Constitution, the first elections were held in 1959 in which there was only small opposition to the New Constitution Party of President Bourguiba.

The single–chamber Assembly is elected for terms of five years. There is a separate judiciary patterned on that of France. Elections since independence uniformly resulted in overwhelming victories for the *New Constitution Party* and Bourguiba. Although aging, the President was elected to a third term in October 1969 and in late 1974 he was proclaimed president for life.

Close ties have been maintained with France after some tension caused by a delay in the withdrawal of French forces. The lands of French farmers were nationalized in 1965 and an attempt was made to organize them into collectives. This, coupled with a 1969 drought, badly damaged the economy.

During 1970–71, when Bourguiba was suffering from a liver ailment, there were increasing pressures for constitutional reform. The basic issue was whether the National Assembly should have the power to censure an administration when dissatisfied on a particular issue. Bourguiba, somewhat recovered, resisted the move, arguing that such a system was bound to result in a new government several times a year. Fully recovered in 1974, he presided over a party congress which "erased" the memory of the 1971 reform movement.

An open split between the government and trade unions occurred in 1977; they had been consistent supporters of the president. The government held a hard line, putting down strikes and refusing to negotiate with the strikers. Tunisia has been plagued since independence by widespread unemployment (20%–30%), low wages and an uneven distribution of income; these conditions have sparked many clashes. President Bourguiba continued a tough policy, even removing cabinet ministers who felt the government should assume a more moderate position.

The Tunisian constitution recognizes Islam as the state religion, but this has always been a tolerant and open society. Bourguiba, however, did many things to make the Muslim fundamentalists angry. He permitted wives to institute divorce proceedings against their husbands and encouraged women to enter all trades and professions. He also westernized the court system by abolishing most of the powers of the Muslim religious courts and rabbinical tribunals by turning their functions over to the civil courts. All distinctions between religious and public schools were abolished. He even went further in 1984, and included two women in his cabinet. Islamic fundamentalists saw these moves as cutting the tap roots of the Islamic traditions.

Islamic fundamentalists were arrested and refused permission to function as a political party; stiff prison sentences were substituted for death penalties. The straw that broke the camel's back came in June 1981 when fundamentalists raided a beach resort where Europeans, in sometimes scanty attire, lived "the good life;" the resort was all but destroyed. This was a terrible blow to Tunisia's profitable tourist industry and marked the beginning of the crackdown on the zealots.

Former President Bourguiba remained quite popular in spite of advancing years. When a dispute erupted over succession to the presidency in 1984 he quickly settled it. The Prime Minister (who wielded considerable power) would immediately become president and name a successor prime minister.

After thirty years in power, Habib Bourguiba, suffering from Parkinson's Disease, became visibly senile—he could not remember things he had done the previous day and started taking irrational actions. His persecution of Islamic fundamentalists, whose number had been swollen by migration to the cities from rural areas, reached an intolerable level. Acting

swiftly, former Prime Minister Zine Abidine Ben Ali declared Bourguiba incapable of carrying out his office and removed him on November 7, 1987, thus becoming president of Tunisia. The move had widespread support from all elements and factions within Tunisian society. Among his first moves, the new president commuted the sentences of several hundred Islamic fundamentalists and suggested he would dissolve the parliament and hold elections earlier than the scheduled date in 1991. He rescheduled them for November 1989.

When it appeared that he and his party were well ahead of any competitor, President Ben Ali advanced the contest to April 1989. His judgment was correct—the Democratic Constitutional Rally (RCD), the new name of Bourguiba's party, won more than 80% of the vote and all 141 seats in the National Assembly.

By late 1991 the Islamic fundamentalists had again bloomed and seriously threatened a tourist industry which was reaching new heights of prosperity. The government, acting through the military in 1992, brought 171 members and leaders of the outlawed *Nahda* group before the Tunis military court. Thirty–five received life sentences, 142 received sentences of 3 to 20 years, and four were acquitted.

The firmness with which the Islamists were handled sent a clear message to other political groups in Tunisia. It has become increasingly clear that President Ben Ali is not a man who is comfortable with opposition. Repression in one form or an-

**Relief from the desert heat in a cool oasis**

# Tunisia

**Habib Bourguiba**

other has been extended out from the fundamentalists. Amnesty International claims that hundreds of political prisoners are held behind bars in Tunisia. The consequence is clear: Tunisia's opposition parties are some of the most restrained in Africa. The press more often than not appears more as lap dog than watch dog.

In the 1994 presidential elections no opposition party was able to put forth a candidate. The Tunisian constitution requires potential presidential candidates to secure the nominating signatures of 30 members of parliament, but with the president's RCD in a monopoly position there, it's hard for any candidate to get his papers signed. Unopposed, Zine Abidine Ben Ali won 99.9% of the vote. In the legislative balloting of the same year, four opposition parties were only able to win 19 seats in parliament, but it was the first time the opposition would be represented there; Ben Ali's RCD won 144 seats. Tunisia remained firmly within the President's iron grip.

In the years since President Ben Ali first came to power the apparatus of surveillance and control has come to dominate Tunisian life. The number of police is four times larger than it was in 1987, and it is aided by a host of additional agencies of surveillance that have been created by authorities. The secretary-general of Amnesty International has spoken of a strategy of "interiorizing fear" within the citizenry and the International Federation for the Rights of Man has called Tunisia a "police state." Membership in the RCD is a political necessity. One's membership card is often a survival tool, the first thing shown police when stopped for questioning. Perhaps apocryphally, but suggestively, the story goes about that Tunisian children, asked to design a new symbol for their country, drew a police van.

Presidential elections were held in October 1999 with new election laws permitting the possibility of multiparty elections for the first time in Tunisian history. No longer were the signatures of 30 political grandees required. Leaders of political parties who had been in that role for five years, and whose parties were represented in parliament, were eligible to run for the office of president. Only two candidates besides the president met these requirements: Mohamed Belhaj Amor, secretary general of the *Parti de l'unité populaire* (PUP), and Abderrahmane Tlili of the *Union démocratique unioniste* (UDU).

Election results were scarcely credible: President Zine el Abidine Ben Ali was re-elected by 99.4% of the voters. It was enough to assure Tunisia a place in the Jurassic museum of retrograde political forms.

Despite a network of 132,000 policemen and 5,000 wiretaps on the telephone lines of its citizens, the regime did not anticipate the social unrest that rocked both Tunis and several southern cities in early 2000. Taxi drivers disabled the capital for three days in February, protesting a new driving code with increased fines. In the same month several Tunisian cities witnessed protests against stiff increases in the price of gasoline, transport, and food products, especially bread.

In some places the protest began in secondary schools and colleges. When students went out to protest in the streets, they clashed with police, but were supported by locals, mainly youth and mostly unemployed.

None of these events was, of course, reported in the local press. Censorship is a basic element of a security state, and the Tunisian Press Code allows the government to pre-censor and ban publications.

Any information that might be used to criticize the government is eliminated. Politically sensitive articles are sent to the interior ministry for review, and each edi-

**President Ben Ali**

tion must be registered with the ministry before publication.

On the occasion of the thirteenth anniversary of his accession to power in November 2000, President Ben Ali spoke soothing words to his critics. Stressing his "unshakeable faith in the principles of human rights," he announced the state would pay compensation to any individual unlawfully arrested and detained. This, of course, was merely days after a Paris news conference where four Tunisian students had given graphic accounts of beatings, rape, and torture they endured at the hands of Tunisian security agents. The press conference also announced publication of a 200-page report entitled "Torture in Tunisia," issued by the Committee for the Respect of Freedom and Human Rights in Tunisia (CRLDHT).

In the same November address he announced future amendments to the Press

**A stone carver**

Code to eliminate physical punishment of journalists. He specifically noted punishments for "libel of public order," a crime of infinite breadth and ambiguity the president called "rather murky" and open to "various interpretations."

One would be right to remain skeptical. In Tunisia the problem is not legislation, but its non-respect. In a security state behavioral patterns long established are difficult to change.

President Ben Ali was scheduled to end his constitutionally permitted third term in 2004. Instead, a series of constitutional amendments were proposed in 2002, the effect of which was to allow him to run for an unlimited number of terms. The constitutional age limit for candidates was also raised from 70 to 75 years. Government propaganda emphasized the second legislative house to be created and the requirement that there be run-off elections to assure a majority vote for the presidency. Less mentioned were the provisions that increased presidential powers and gave immunity from prosecution, during and after his presidency, for any official acts. Human rights organizations could only evince dismay.

The constitutional amendments easily passed the RCD-dominated legislature and were then submitted to a popular referendum—a first in Tunisian history. When the interior minister announced the results of the May 26, 2002 voting—99.56% approved—he said they would "surprise only those who do not know Tunisia." Ninety-five percent of registered voters participated—not unusual in a country where civil servants fetch in those who might have overslept on election day.

Presidential and parliamentary elections took place in October 2004, and the results were less than surprising. The opposition could not produce anything like a clear vision of where they wished to lead the country and could do little more than agree with many of the president's campaign proposals. President Ben Ali won convincingly over three opponents, taking a palindromic 94.49% of the vote; his nearest competitor, Mohamed Bouchiha of the Party of Popular Unity took a mere 3.8%.

In parliamentary elections, the president's RCD took 152 of 189 seats in the Chamber of Deputies; five parties shared the 20% of seats allocated to the opposition. The Movement of Socialist Democrats will be the largest parliamentary opposition with 14 deputies. Perhaps the most interesting result of the election is the significant resentation of women in parliament. President Ben Ali made the decision to allocate 25% of postions on the party's district slates to female candidates, and as a consequence, 43 newly-elected members of parliament are women.

**The medina in Kairouan**

The percentage of women in the Tunisian legislature—22.7%—is the highest in the Arab world, whose legislative bodies average only 6.7%. Internationally it is one of the highest in the world, ranking above the average found in European legislatures—19%—and only below the legislatures of Nordic countries which contain nearly 40% women.

**Culture:** A variety of well-maintained museums offer testimony to the diverse cultural heritage of Tunisia. The National Museum of the Bardo, located in the old palace of the Bey in a Tunis suburb, is the finest archeological museum in the Mahgreb. Its stellar attractions are the mosaic floors from the Roman cities of northern Tunisia, rich evidence of the extraordinary wealth and luxury of Rome's breadbasket province. Further evidence of Tunisia's importance to Rome is the grand amphitheater of El Jem. After the coliseums of Rome and Capua, the one at El Jem was the third largest ever built by the Romans; it accommodated some 30,000 spectators.

Near Kairouan, the sacred city of Islamic Tunisia, one can visit the national Museum of Islamic Art with its stunning collection of ceramics and calligraphy. In Mahdia, in the heart of the East Coast tourist areas and still an important weaving center, one can visit the Textile Museum of the Dar el-Himma. The museum features a fine collection of traditional Tunisian costumes, one of the principal manifestations of women's artistic creativity.

A secular state, Tunisia allows greater freedom to its women than many other Muslim countries. The 1956 personal status code declared polygamy illegal and granted the right of judicial divorce to men and women equally. President Bourguiba, who did so much to create modern secular Tunisia and liberate its women, died in April 2000.

Women have played an important role in traditional Berber culture and two of Tunisia's most heroic figures are women: Dido, or Alyssa, the Phoenician princess who founded Carthage and dallied with Aeneas, and Kahina, a warrior-queen who led the Berber resistance to the Arab invasion of the eighth century. One rarely sees a woman dress in the body-covering *chador*. In the cities younger women dress in Western attire, but increasingly one sees women wearing the Islamic scarf to cover their heads.

In addition to the increased usage of the headscarf, sociologists also note an increased and ostentatious attendance at Friday prayers. Both have seen by some psychologists as a defense mechanism or form of passive resistance against the few opportunities for political expression. President Ben Ali's allocation of female seats in the 2004 legislative elections can be understood in this light, but it is also an expression of independent Tunisia's commitment to women. In comparison to other Arab countries, Tunisia provides greater gender equality and more pro-fessional opportunity to women than anywhere else. Women constitute 27% of judges, 31% of lawyers, 40% of higher-education teachers, and 34% of all journalists.

The government pursues a policy of Arabization, the speed and fervor of which often depends on relations with France. Bilingualism is still tolerated, for it is not the intention of the government to eliminate French, but merely to readjust its place in an Arab nation. Shopkeepers

# Tunisia

have already been forced to remove signs employing the Latin alphabet and the administration is under orders to use the country's official language in all its documents by the end of 2000.

In education the problems are greater. First, it is a question of which Arabic to use. A Tunisian's mother tongue is a dialectical Arabic, spoken on a daily basis but non-written. At school, the student is introduced to written classical Arabic, the language of instruction. In the larger society an Intermediate Arabic, halfway between the two, has been developing, and for the past few years a fourth alternative has been offered by the daily presence of Arabic-language television broadcasts emanating from the Persian Gulf state of Qatar.

The private television network, Al Jazirah, is based in Qatar and is frequently referred to as the CNN of the Arab world. Tunisians watch to learn something about their own country, but at the same time the broadcasts may be leading to a homogenization of Arabic, or at least an elevation of the standards of spoken Tunisian Arabic.

Dialectical differences in Arabic suggest the second problem facing the government's Arabization program—the availability of textbooks. Given the absence of standardized terminology in some of the sciences, for example, there are no university textbooks available.

**Economy:** Historically a granary of the Mediterranean, Tunisia's agricultural sector has been eclipsed by its petroleum production. For years its biggest moneymaker has been oil, but production, from aging wells, is in decline. According to the US Department of Energy, oil production in 2003 averaged around 66,000 barrels per day (bbl/d), down nearly 45% from the country's peak output of 120,000 bbl/d between 1982 and 1984 A booming economy has meant increased energy demand, only partially compensated by increased production of natural gas. To meet these demands, the government has sought to encourage new exploration with a more liberal hydrocarbon code, but success rates have been low. The country has 2.8 trillion cubic feet of proven natural gas reserves, most of which is located offshore, and local demand was rising more rapidly than supply. To increase supplies, Tunisia and Libya are constructing a pipeline to bring gas to southern Tunisia in 2005.

Agriculture employs about 30% of the workforce and accounts for around 12% of GDP (2003). Relatively rich and productive, around 30% of the land is arable. The minister of environment has noted, however, that desertification destroys some 66,690 acres of fertile land every year, occasioning losses of $15 million. In 2002 agricultural production was hit by the most severe drought in most Tunisians' living memories, and the agricultural sector shrank.

Some 60 million olive trees occupy a third of the country's arable land, and olive oil is Tunisia's most important agricultural export. The country is the world's fourth-ranked producer, after Spain, Italy and Greece. From extensive grape vineyards, mostly in the north, Tunisia produces table grapes and over 60 types of wine.

Tourism replaced oil as Tunisia's biggest foreign exchange earner in 1999. Annual revenue from tourism amounts to $2.5 billion, around 10% of GDP, brought in by some six million tourists who visit the country annually. More than 54% of the national budget is earned through tourism.

Tourism bears the consequences of international terrorism, dropping after the 9/11 attacks, and especially after the April 2002 attack on the Ghriba synagogue on Djerba Island. Twenty people were killed, including 13 German tourists, and the attack has been linked to al-Qaeda. Built in the 1920s, Ghriba sits on the site of Africa's oldest synagogue, believed to have been built about 2,500 years ago. According to tradition, the first Jews came to Djerba in biblical times, bringing a stone from the First Temple, destroyed by the Babylonians in 586 BC. The stone is kept in a grotto at Djerba's synagogue. The thousands who make an annual *Lag Ba'omer* pilgrimage to the synagogue were down to hundreds in 2002.

The textile industry is among the most important sectors of the Tunisian economy, accounting for almost half the country's export earnings in 2002 and 18% of GDP. Expiration of multilateral textile agreements in 2005 and the opening of markets to a flood of Chinese products could impact the sector negatively.

Tunisia's GDP grew by 5.6% 2003, up from a paltry 1.7% in 2002 occasioned by climatic difficulties that year. Foreign investors, undeterred by human rights issues, have responded to the economy's stability and success. Foreign direct investment in Tunisia exceeded $1 billion for the first time in 2000. Job creation has been significant, but despite this, the unemployment rate remains at about 16%, by official figures. Unofficially, it is much higher, and job creation featured as President Ben Ali's number one priority in the 2004 election campaign.

All in all, Tunisia is an economic success story, and its citizens, 60% of whom are middle-class, seem willing to accept economic benefit at the cost of political freedom. Political control may be the price Tunisians are willing to pay for a stable and growing economy.

For the Ben Ali regime, security and stability are contingent on control. But control in Tunisia has weakened potential checks on the government. An effective secular opposition has not been allowed to develop, and Islamic fundamentalists have thrived most where no meaningful secular opposition has existed. Without a free press, corruption can flourish and the rule of law vanish. These are the kinds of concerns that face potential investors. For the Ben Ali government the tension between political control and economic liberalization will dominate the next few years.

**The Future:** Anti-terrorism will justify continued crackdowns on dissidents. Tensions between the state and civil society will continue to mount, and there will be only modest movement towards a more liberal state. The present system is based on control, and a genuine pluralist political system almost inevitably means loss of control.

**Modern interpretations of traditional architecture on the island of Djerba**

318

# WEB Sites and Selected Bibliography of Key English Language Sources

**General WEB Site:**

*Africa South of the Sahara: Selected Internet resources* http://www.sul.stanford.edu/depts/ssrg/africa/guide.html. Prepared by Karen Fung for the Information and Communication Technology Group (ICTG), African Studies Association, USA. A comprehensive introduction.

**International Governmental Agency Sources:**

UN Conference of Trade and Development http://www.unctad.org/. Statistical data on Least Developed Countries and discussion of poverty strategies.

UN Development Programme. *Human Development Reports*. http://hdr.undp.org. Provides important material on country achievement on life expectancy, educational attainment and adjusted real income.

UN Economic Commission for Africa. http://www.uneca.org/. ECA is the regional arm of the United Nations, mandated to support the economic and social development of its 53 member states. Its annual economic reports are useful.

Integrated Regional Information Networks (IRIN), part of the UN Office for the Coordination of Humanitarian Affairs (OCHA): http://www.irinnews.org/. Current news on humanitarian issues. Its focus reports and specials often contain useful political insights.

The International Monetary Fund (IMF). http://imf.org/external/country/index.htm. Useful material on country projects and debt alleviation.

World Bank in Africa. http://www.worldbank.org/afr/. Useful statistical material and poverty alleviation projects.

**U.S. Government Sources:**

Central Intelligence Agency (CIA) *The World Factbook* http://www.cia.gov/cia/publications/factbook/index.html. Basic material on land, people, government and economy for each country.

Department of Energy. Energy Information Agency. http://www.eia.doe.gov/. Country analyses provide useful material on energy resources of producing states.

**State Department:**

Bureau of African Affairs: http://www.state.gov/p/af/. Particularly useful are its *Background Notes* for individual countries.

Bureau of Democracy, Human Rights, and Labor: Annual *Human Rights Reports* for each country: http://www.state.gov/g/drl/hr/.

Annual *International Religious Freedom Reports*: http://www.state.gov/g/drl/rls/irf/.

Bureau for International Narcotics and Law Enforcement Affairs Annual *International Narcotics Control Strategy Report*: http://www.state.gov/g/inl/rls/nrcrpt/.

Counterterrorism Office. Issues the annual "Patterns of Global Terrorism" report: http://www.state.gov/s/ct/

**Non-governmental Organizations (NGOs)**

Amnesty International http://amnesty.org/. The human rights situation country by country.

Global Witness. http://globalwitness.org/. Among the many environmental groups, one of the most productive, especially on forest conservation

Human Rights Watch. http://hrw.org/. Excellent reports on a range of human rights issues.

Institute for Security Studies. http://www.iss.co.za/. A South African research institute. Excellent studies, mostly on Southern African issues.

The International Crisis Group (ICG). http://www.crisisweb.org/. An independent, non-profit, multinational think-tank. Its reports on Central, Southern, and West Africa, as well as the Horn of Africa are packed with information and insight.

Transparency International. http://www.transparency.de. A German NGO. Its annual *Global Corruption Report* is in English.

**News Agencies**

http://news.bbc.co.uk. BBC news—better than the *New York Times*, *Washington Post* or *Los Angeles Times* for major news events. North African news is often covered under its "Middle East" rubric.

http://allafrica.com/. Republishes current news stories and topical features from some 100 African newspapers and agencies. For detailed African news, the best site.

**Miscellaneous**

http://www.xe.com/ucc/. The Universal Currency Converter. For the more obscure African currencies, go to http://www.xe.com/ucc/full.shtml.

http://www.banknoteworld.com. To see what a country's currency looks like.

http://www.embassy.org/embassies/. To locate a country's embassy in Washington.

**Books: General**

Adams, William and Andrew Goudie, eds. *Physical Geography of Africa*. New York: Oxford University Press, 1999.

Adebajo, Adekeye and Ismail Rashid, eds. *West Africa's Security Challenges: Building Peace in a Troubled Region*. Boulder, CO: Lynne Rienner, 2004.

Ake, Claude. *The Feasibility of Democracy in Africa*. Dakar: Council for the Development of Social Science Research in Africa (CODESRIA), 2000.

Ali, Taisier M. and Robert O. Matthews, eds. *Civil Wars in Africa: Roots and Resolution*. Montreal: McGill-Queen's University Press, 1999.

Bayart, Jean-Francois, Stephen Ellis, and Béatrice Hibou. *The Criminalization of the State in Africa*. Oxford: James Currey, 1999.

Bayart, Jean-Francois. *The State in Africa: The Politics of the Belly*. New York: Longman, 1993.

Chabal, Patrick and Jean-Pascal Daloz. *Africa Works: Disorder as Political Instrument*. Oxford: James Currey, 1999.

Chabal, Patrick, et al. *The History of Postcolonial Lusophone Africa*. Bloomington: Indiana University Press, 2002.

Cowen, Michael and Liisa Laakso, eds. *Multi-Party Elections in Africa*. NY: Palgrave, 2002.

Deng, Francis M. and Terrence Lyons, eds. *Africa Reckoning: a Quest for Good Governance*. Washington, DC: Brookings Institution Press, 1998.

Englebert, Pierre. *State Legitimacy and Development in Africa*. Boulder, CO: Lynne Rienner, 2002.

Fietzek, Gerti. *Under Siege: Four African Cities—Freetown, Johannesburg, Kinshasa, Lagos*. Ostfildern-Ruit, Germany: Hatje Cantz, Verlag, 2002. (Distributed in USA by Art Publishers).

French, Howard W. *A Continent for the Taking: The Tragedy and Hope of Africa*. New York: Alfred A. Knopf, 2004.

Good, Kenneth. *The Liberal Model and Africa: Elites Against Democracy*. New York: Palgrave, 2002.

Gordon, April A. and Donald L. Gordon, eds. *Understanding Contemporary Africa*. Boulder, CO: Lynne Rienner, 2001.

Gyimah-Boadi, E., ed. *Democratic Reform in Africa: The Quality of Progress*. Boulder, CO: Lynne Rienner, 2004

Herbst, Jeffrey. *States and Power in Africa: Comparative Lessons in Authority and Control*. Princeton, NJ: Princeton University Press, 2000.

Howe, Herbert M. *Ambiguous Order: Military Forces in African States*. Boulder, CO: Lynne Rienner Publishers, 2000.

Hunter, Susan. *Black Death. AIDS in Africa.* NY: Palgrave, 2003.

Ishikawa, Kaoru. *Nation Building and Development Assistance in Africa: Different but Equal.* New York: Saint Martin's Press, 1999.

Kalu, Kelechi A. *Agenda Setting and Public Policy in Africa: Contemporary Perspectives on Developing Societies.* Burlington, VT: Ashgate, 2004.

Karl, Terry Lynn. *The Paradox Of Plenty: Oil Booms and Petro-States.* Berkeley: University of California Press, 1997. [Though the work focuses on Venezuela, it is abundantly relevant to Africa's petro-states.]

Keppel, Gilles. *Jihad: The Trail of Political Islam.* Cambridge, MA: Belknap Press of Harvard University Press, 2002.

Kevane, Michael. *Woman and Development in Africa: How Gender Works.* Boulder, CO: Lynne Rienner, 2004.

Larémont, Ricardo René, ed. *Borders, Nationalism, and the African State.* Boulder, CO: Lynne Rienner, 2005.

Larémont, Ricardo René, ed. *The Causes of War and the Consequences of Peacekeeping in Africa.* Portsmouth, NH: Heinemann, 2002.

Le Vine, Victor T. *Politics in Francophone Africa.* Boulder, CO: Lynne Rienner, 2004.

Lindsay, Lisa A. and Stephan F. Miescher, eds. *Men and Masculinities in Modern Africa.* Portsmouth, NH: Heinemann, 2003.

Lumumba-Kasongo, Tukumbi. *The Dynamics of Economic and Political Relations between Africa and Foreign Powers: a Study in International Relations.* Westport, CT: Greenwood Publishing Group, 1999.

Mamdani, Mahmood. *Citizen and Subject: Contemporary Africa and the Legacy of Late Colonialism.* Princeton, NJ: Princeton University Press, 1996.

McIntosh, Susan K., ed. *Beyond Chiefdoms: Pathways to Political Complexity in Africa.* New York: Cambridge University Press, 1999.

Miers, Suzanne and Martin A. Klein. *Slavery and Colonial Rule in Africa.* Portland, OR: Frank Cass Publishers, 1999.

Morris, James. *Butabu: Adobe Architecture of West Africa.* NY: Princeton Architectural Press, 2004.

Nzongola-Ntalaja, Georges and Margaret C. Lee. *The State and Democracy in Africa.* Lawrenceville, NJ: Africa World Press, 1998.

Olivier de Sardan, Jean Pierre. *Anthropology and Development: Understanding Contemporary Social Change.* London: Zed Books, 2005.

Renner, Michael. *The Anatomy of Resource Wars.* Washington, D.C.: Worldwatch Institute, 2002.

Reno, William. *Warlord Politics and African States.* Boulder, CO: Lynne Rienner Publishers, 1999.

Rosander, Eva Evers, and David Westerlund, eds. *African Islam and Islam in Africa: Encounters between Sufis and Islamists.* Athens: Ohio University Press, 1997.

Rotberg, Robert I., ed. *State Failure and State Weakness in a Time of Terror.* Washington, DC: Brookings Institution Press, 2003.

Rwomire, Apollo. *Social Problems in Africa: New Visions.* Westport, CT: Greenwood Publishing Group, 2001.

Schatzberg, Michael G. *Political Legitimacy in Middle Africa: Father, Family, Food.* Bloomington: Indiana University Press, 2001.

Schwab, Peter. *Africa: A Continent Self-Destructs.* NY: Palgrave, 2002.

Segal, Ronald. *Islam's Black Slaves: The Other Black Diaspora.* New York: Farrar, Straus and Giroux, 2001.

Singer, P. W. (Peter Warren) *Corporate Warriors: The Rise of the Privatized Military Industry.* Ithaca: Cornell University Press, 2003.

Van de Walle, Nicholas, et al. eds. *African Economies and the Politics of Permanent Crisis, 1979-1999.* Cambridge: Cambridge University Press, 2001.

Visonà, Monica Blackmun, et al. *A History of Art in Africa.* New York: Harry Abrams, Inc., 2001.

Vogel, Joseph O., ed. *The Encyclopedia of Pre-colonial Africa: Archaeology, History, Languages, Cultures, and Environment.* Walnut Creek, CA: Alta Mira Press, 1997.

Werbner, Richard and Terence Ranger. *Postcolonial Identities in Africa.* London: Zed Books, 1996.

Wesseling, H.L., trans. by Arnold J. Pomerans. *Divide and Rule: the Partition of Africa 1880–1914.* Westport, CT: Greenwood Publishing Group, 1996.

World Bank. *Breaking the Conflict Trap: Civil War and Development Policy.* New York: Oxford University Press, 2003.

World Bank. *World Development Report 1997: The State in a Changing World.* New York: Oxford University Press, 1997.

World Bank. *World Development Report 2003: Sustainable Development in a Dynamic World: Transforming Institutions, Growth, and Quality of Life.* New York: Oxford University Press, 2002.

World Bank. *World Development Report 2005: Investment Climate, Growth, and Poverty.* New York: Oxford University Press, 2004.

Young, Crawford. *The African Colonial State in Comparative Perspective.* New Haven, CT: Yale University Press, 1994.

Zartman, I. William, ed. *Collapsed States: The Disintegration and Restoration of Legitimate Authority.* Boulder: CO: Lynne Rienner, 1995.

Zeleza, Paul Tiyambe, ed. *Encyclopedia of Twentieth-Century African History.* London and New York: Routledge, 2002.

Zell, Hans. *The African Studies Companion: A Guide to Information Sources.* Third Edition. Hans Zell Publishing Consultants: Locharron, Scotland, 2003.

## Coastal West Africa

Adebajo, Adekeye. *Building Peace in West Africa: Liberia, Sierra Leone, and Guinea-Bissau.* Boulder, CO: Lynne Rienner, 2002.

Clapham, Christopher S. *African Guerrillas.* Bloomington, IN: Indiana University Press, 1998.

Clark, Andrew Francis and Lucie Colvin Phillips. *Historical Dictionary of Senegal.* Lanham, MD: Scarecrow Press, 1994.

Daniels, Morna. *Côte d'Ivoire.* Santa Barbara, CA: ABC-CLIO, 1996.

Decalo, Samuel. *Historical Dictionary of Benin.* Lanham, MD: Scarecrow Press, 1995.

Decalo, Samuel. *Historical Dictionary of Togo.* Lanham, MD: Scarecrow Press, 3rd ed. 1996.

Dunn, D. Elwood. *Historical Dictionary of Liberia.* Lanham, MD: Scarecrow Press, 2001.

Eades, J.S. and Christopher Allen. *Benin.* Santa Barbara, CA: ABC-CLIO, 1997

Forrest, Joshua B. *Lineages of State Fragility: Rural Civil Society in Guinea-Bissau.* Athens, OH: Ohio University Press, 2003.

Gellar, Sheldon. *Senegal: An African Nation Between Islam and the West.* Boulder, CO: Westview Press, 1995.

Gifford, Paul. *Ghana's New Christianity: Pentecostalism in a Globalising African Economy.* Bloomington: Indiana University Press, 2004.

Hirsch, John L. *Sierra Leone: Diamonds and the Struggle for Democracy.* Boulder, CO: Lynne Rienner, 2001.

Huband, Mark. *The Liberian Civil War.* Portland, OR: International Specialized Book Services, 1998.

Hughes, Arnold. *Historical Dictionary of The Gambia.* 3rd ed. Lanham, MD: Scarecrow Press, 1999.

Human Rights Watch. *How to Fight, How to Kill.* New York: Human Rights Watch, 2004.

Johnson, John William *Son-Jara: The Mande Epic.* Bloomington: Indian University Press, 2004.

Kourouma, Ahmadou. *Waiting for the Vote of the Wild Animals.* Translated by Carrol F. Coates. Charlottesville: University Press of Virginia, 2001.

Kulah, Arthur F. *Liberia Will Rise Again: Reflections on the Liberian Civil Crisis.* Nashville, TN: Abingdon Press, 1999.

Lobban, Richard. *Cape Verde: Crioulo Colony to Independent Nation*. Boulder CO: Westview Press, 1995.

Lobban, Richard. *Historical Dictionary of Cape Verde*. Lanham MD: Scarecrow Press, 3rd ed. 1995.

Mundt, Robert J. *Historical Dictionary of Côte d'Ivoire (the Ivory Coast)*. Lanham, MD: Scarecrow Press, 1995.

Richards, Paul. *Fighting for the Rainforest: War, Youth and Resources in Sierra Leone*. Portsmouth, NH: Heinemann, 1996.

Söderling, Ludwig and J. Clark Leith. *Ghana-Long Term Growth, Atrophy and Stunted Recovery: Research Report No. 125*. Uppsala, Sweden: The Nordic Africa Institute, 2003.

**Central West Africa**

Achebe, Chinua. *Home and Exile*. Oxford: Oxford University Press, 2000.

Amadi, L.O. *Dictionary of Nigerian History: from Aba to Zazzau*. Bethesda, MD: International Scholars Publications, 1998.

Bocquené, Henri. *Memoirs of a Mbororo: The Life of Ndudi Umaru: Fulani Nomad of Cameroon*. New York: Berghahn Books, 2002.

DeLancey, Mark W. *Historical Dictionary of the Republic of Cameroon*. Lanham, MD: Scarecrow Press, 3rd. ed. 2000.

Dibie, Robert A. *The Military-Bureaucracy Relationship in Nigeria: Public Policy Making and Implementation*. Westport, CT: Greenwood Publishing Group, 2000.

Falola, Toyin. *The History of Nigeria*. Westport, CT: Greenwood Publishing Group, 1999.

Fegley, Randall. *Equatorial Guinea*. Santa Barbara, CA: ABC-CLIO, 1992.

Gross, Jean-Germain, ed. *Cameroon. Politics and Society in Critical Perspectives*. Lanham, MD: University Press of America, 2003.

Human Rights Watch. *The Price of Oil: Corporate Responsibility and Human Rights Violations in Nigeria's Oil Producing Communities*. New York: Human Rights Watch, 1999.

Human Rights Watch. *The Warri Crisis: Fueling Violence*. New York: Human Rights Watch, 2003.

Kalck, Pierre and Thomas O'Toole. *Historical Dictionary of the Central African Republic*. Lanham, MD: Scarecrow Press, 2nd ed. 1992.

Liniger-Goumaz, Max. *Historical Dictionary of Equatorial Guinea*. Lanham, MD: Scarecrow Press, 1998.

Liniger-Goumaz, Max. *Small Is Not Always Beautiful : The Story of Equatorial Guinea*. London: Hurst, 1988.

Maier, Karl. *This House Has Fallen: A Journey Through Nigeria's Heart of Darkness*. New York: Public Affairs, 2000.

Osaghae, Eghosa E. *The Crippled Giant: Nigeria since Independence*. Bloomington, IN: Indiana University Press, 1998.

Oyewole, Anthony. *Historical Dictionary of Nigeria*. Lanham, MD: Scarecrow Press, 1998.

Paden, John N. *Muslim Civic Cultures and Conflict Resolution. The Challenge of Democratic Federalism in Nigeria*. Washington: Brookings, 2005

Rotberg, Robert I., ed. *Crafting the New Nigeria: Confronting the Challenges*. Boulder, CO: Lynne Rienner, 2004.

Suberu, Rotimi T. *Federalism and Ethnic Conflict in Nigeria*. Washington, DC: United States Institute of Peace Press, 2001.

Wright, Stephen. *Nigeria: Struggle for Stability and Status*. Boulder, CO: Westview Press, 1998.

**Equatorial West Africa**

Adelman, Howard and Astri Suhrke, eds. *The Path of a Genocide: the Rwanda Crisis from Uganda to Zaire*. Piscataway, NJ: Transaction Publishers, 1998.

Ballentine, Karen and Michael Nest, eds. *The Democratic Republic of Congo: Economic Dimensions of War and Peace*. Boulder, CO: Lynne Rienner, 2005

Brittain, Victoria. *Death of Dignity: Angola's Civil War*. Trenton, NJ: Africa World Press, 1998.

Broadhead, Susan H. *Historical Dictionary of Angola*. Lanham, MD: Scarecrow Press, 1992.

Cilliers, Jakkie and Christian Dietrich, eds. *Angola's War Economy: The Role of Diamonds*. Pretoria, SA: Institute for Security Studies, 2000.

Ciment, James. *Angola and Mozambique: Post-Colonial Wars in Southern Africa*. New York: Facts on File, 1997.

Dallaire, Romeo. *Shake Hands with the Devil: The Failure of Humanity in Rwanda*. New York: Random House, 2003.

Decalo, Samuel. *Historical Dictionary of Congo*. Lanham, MD: Scarecrow Press, 1996.

De Witte, Ludo. *The Assassination of Lumumba*. Trans. Ann Wright and Renée Fenby. New York: Verso Books, 2003.

Doom, Ruddy and Jan Gorus, eds. *Politics of Identity and Economics of Conflict in the Great Lakes Region*. Brussels: VUB University Press, 2000.

Dunn, Kevin. *Imagining the Congo: The International Relations of Identity*. NY: Palgrave, 2003.

Eggers, Ellen K. *Historical Dictionary of Burundi*. Lanham, MD: Scarecrow Press, 1997.

Gourevitch, Philip. *We Wish To Inform You That Tomorrow We Will Be Killed With Our Families: Stories From Rwanda*. New York: Farrar, Straus, Giroux, 1998.

Hochschild, Adam. *King Leopold's Ghost*. New York: Houghton Mifflin Co., 1999.

Hodges, Tony. *Angola: Anatomy of An Oil State*. 2nd edition. Oxford: James Currey, 2004.

Human Rights Watch. *Leave None to Tell the Story: Genocide in Rwanda*. New York: Human Rights Watch, 1999. Reissued April 2004 with update.

Human Rights Watch. *Some Transparency, No Accountability: The Use of Oil Revenue in Angola and Its Impact on Human Rights*. New York: Human Rights Watch, 2004.

James, W. Martin. *A Political History of the Civil War in Angola, 1974–1990*. New Brunswick, NJ: Transaction, 1992.

Lemarchand, René. *Burundi: Ethnocide as Discourse and Practice*. New York: Cambridge University Press, 1994.

MacGaffey, Wyatt. *Kongo Political Culture: The Conceptual Challenge of the Particular*. Bloomington: Indiana University Press, 2000.

Mamdani, Mahmood. *When Victims Become Killers: Colonialism, Nativism and the Genocide in Rwanda*. Princeton: Princeton University Press, 2001.

Mendes, Pedro Rosa. *Bay of Tigers*. New York: Harcourt, 2003.

Melvern, Linda. *Conspiracy to Murder: The Rwanda Genocide and the International Community*. London: Verso Books, 2004.

Nzongola-Ntalaja, Georges. *The Congo. From Leopold to Kabila: A People's History*. NY: Palgrave, 2002.

Ould-Abdallah, Ahmedou. *Burundi on the Brink, 1993-95*. Herndon, VA: U.S. Institute of Peace Press, 2000.

Peterson, Dale. *Eating Apes*. California Studies in Food and Culture, 6. Berkeley: University of California Press, 2003.

Peterson, Scott. *Me against My Brother: at War in Somalia, Sudan and Rwanda*. New York: Routledge, 2000.

Pottier, Johan, et al. eds. *Re-Imagining Rwanda: Conflict, Survival and Disinformation in the Late Twentieth Century*. Cambridge: Cambridge University Press, 2002.

*Review of African Political Economy*, 29:93/94 (September/December, 2002). Special issue devoted to "State Failure in the Congo: Perceptions & Realities."

Shaw, Caroline S. *São Tomé and Principe*. Santa Barbara, CA: ABC-CLIO, 1994.

Trefon, Theodore, ed. *Reinventing Order in the Congo: How People Respond to State Failure in Kinshasa*. London: Zed Books, 2004.

Tvedten, Inge. *Angola: Struggle for Peace and Reconstruction*. Boulder, CO: Westview Press, 1997.

Walker, John Frederick. *A Certain Curve Of Horn: The Hundred-Year Quest for The Giant Sable Antelope of Angola*. New York: Atlantic Monthly Press, 2002.

Williams, Dawn Bastian, et al., *Zaïre*. Santa Barbara, CA: ABC-CLIO, 1995.

Wrong, Michela. *In the Footsteps of Mr. Kurtz: Living on the Brink of Disaster in the Congo*. New York: HarperCollins, 2001.

## Southern Africa

Azevedo, Mario Joaquim. *Historical Dictionary of Mozambique*. Lanham, MD: Scarecrow Press, 1991.

Baregu, Mwesiga and Christopher Landsberg, eds. *From Cape to Congo: Southern Africa's Evolving Security Challenges*. Boulder, CO: Lynne Rienner, 2003.

Bauer, Gretchen and Scott D. Taylor. *Politics in Southern Africa: State and Society in Transition*. Boulder, CO: Lynne Rienner, 2004.

Beck, Roger B. *The History of South Africa*. Westport, CT: Greenwood Publishing Group, 2000.

Beinart, William and Saul Dubow, eds. *Segregation and Apartheid in Twentieth Century South Africa*. New York: Routledge, 1995.

Blair, David. *Degrees in Violence: Robert Mugabe and the Struggle for Power in Zimbabwe*. London and New York: Continuum Books, 2002.

Booth, Alan R. *Historical Dictionary of Swaziland*. Lanham, MD: Scarecrow Press, 2000.

Boraine, Alex. *A Country Unmasked: Inside South Africa's Truth and Reconciliation Commission*. NY: Oxford University Press, 2000.

Bowen, Merle L. *The State Against the Peasantry: Rural Struggles in Colonial and Postcolonial Mozambique*. Charlottesville: University Press of Virginia, 2000.

Crosby, Cynthia A. *Historical Dictionary of Malawi*. Lanham, MD: Scarecrow Press, 1993.

Dale, Richard. *Botswana's Search for Autonomy in Southern Africa*. Westport, CT: Greenwood Press, 1995.

Decalo, Samuel. *Malawi*. Santa Barbara, CA: ABC-CLIO, 2nd ed. 1995.

Eades, Lindsay Michie. *The End of Apartheid in South Africa*. Westport, CT: Greenwood Publishing Group, 1999.

Elbadawi, Ibrahim and Trudi Hartzenberg. *Development Issues in South Africa*. New York: Saint Martin's Press, 2000.

Galli, Rosemary. *People's Spaces and State Spaces: Land and Governance in Mozambique*. Lanham, MD: Rowman & Littlefield Publishers, 2003.

Gillis, D. Hugh. *The Kingdom of Swaziland: Studies in Political History*. Westport, CT: Greenwood Publishing Group, 1999.

Giliomee, Hermann. *The Afrikaners: Biography of a People*. Charlottesville: University of Virginia, 2003.

Graybill, Lyn S. *Truth and Reconciliation in South Africa: Miracle or Model?* Boulder, CO: Lynne Rienner, 2002.

Grotpeter, John J. *Historical Dictionary of Zambia*. Lanham, MD: Scarecrow Press, 1998.

Hall, Margaret and Tom Young. *Confronting Leviathan: Mozambique since Independence*. Athens, OH: Ohio University Press, 1997.

Hansen, Karen Tranberg. *Salaula: the World of Secondhand Clothing and Zambia*. Chicago: University of Chicago Press, 2000.

Harrison, Graham. *The Politics of Rural Democratization in Mozambique: grassroots governance in Mecúfi*. Lewiston, NY: Edwin Mellen, 2000.

Hart, Gillian Patricia. *Disabling Globalization: Places of Power in Post-Apartheid South Africa*. Berkeley: University of California Press, 2002.

Hassan, Fareed M.A. *Lesotho: Development in a Challenging Environment: a Joint World Bank-African Development Bank Evaluation*. Abidjan: African Development Bank; Washington, D.C.: World Bank, 2002.

Human Rights Watch. *Deadly Delay: South Africa's Efforts to Prevent HIV in Survivors of Sexual Violence*. New York: Human Rights Watch, 2004.

Human Rights Watch. *Not Eligible: The Politicization of Food in Zimbabwe*. New York: Human Rights Watch, 2003.

Jackson, Ashley. *Botswana 1939–1945: an African Country at War*. New York: Oxford University Press, 1999.

Jacobs, Sean and Richard Calland, eds. *Thabo Mbeki's World. The Politics and Ideology of the South African President*. NY: Palgrave, 2003.

Johnston, Deborah. *Lesotho*. Santa Barbara, CA: ABC-CLIO, rev. ed., 1997.

Lodge, Tom. *Politics in South Africa: from Mandela to Mbeki*. Bloomington: Indiana University Press, 2003.

Lyman, Princeton N. *Partner to History. The U.S. Role in South Africa's Transition to Democracy*. Herndon, VA: U.S. Institute of Peace Press, 2002.

Meredith, Martin. *Our Votes, Our Guns: Robert Mugabe and the Tragedy of Zimbabwe*. New York: Public Affairs, 2002.

Newitt, Malyn. *A History of Mozambique*. Bloomington, IN: Indiana University Press, 1995.

Nyeko, Balam. *Swaziland*. Santa Barbara, CA: ABC-CLIO, 1994.

Pitcher, M. Anne. *Transforming Mozambique: The Politics of Privatization, 1975–2000*. Cambridge; New York, NY: Cambridge University Press, 2002.

Ross, Robert. *A Concise History of South Africa*. New York: Cambridge University Press, 1999.

Saunders, Christopher C. and Nicholas Southey. *Historical Dictionary of South Africa*. Lanham, MD: Scarecrow Press, 1999.

Schoeman, Stanley and Elna Schoeman. *Namibia*. Santa Barbara, CA: ABC-CLIO, rev. ed. 1997.

Sheldon, Kathleen E. *Pounders of Grain: A history of women, work and politics in Mozambique*. Portsmouth, NH: Heinemann, 2002.

Shea, Dorothy. *The South African Truth Commission*. Herndon, VA: U.S. Institute of Peace Press, 2000.

Sparks, Donald L. and December Green. *Namibia: The Nation After Independence*. Boulder, CO: Westview Press, 1992.

Temkin, Ben. *Buthelezi. A Biography*. Portland, OR: Frank Cass Publishers, 2003.

Terreblanche, Sampie (Solomon Johannes), *A History of Inequality in South Africa, 1652–2002*, Scottsville, SA: University of KwaZulu-Natal Press, 2003.

Vale, Peter. *Security and Politics in South Africa: The Regional Dimension*. Boulder, CO: Lynne Rienner, 2003.

Walker, Liz, et al. *Waiting to Happen: HIV/AIDS in South Africa—The Bigger Picture*. Boulder, CO: Lynne Rienner, 2004.

Woods, Anthony. *The Creation of Modern Malawi*. Boulder, CO: Westview Press, 1998.

## East Africa Island Nations

Allen, Philip M. *Madagascar: Conflicts of Authority in the Great Island*. Boulder, CO: Westview Press, 1995.

Bennett, George and Pramila Ramgulan Bennett. *Seychelles*. Santa Barbara, CA: ABC-CLIO, 1993.

Bowman, Larry W. *Mauritius: Democracy and Development in the Indian Ocean*. Boulder, CO: Westview Press, 1991.

Bradt, Hilary. *Madagascar*. Santa Barbara, CA: ABC-CLIO, 1994.

Metz, Helen Chapin, ed. *Indian Ocean: Five Island Countries*. Washington, DC: U.S. GPO, 3rd ed. 1995.

Ottenheimer, Martin and Harriet Ottenheimer. *Historical Dictionary of the Comoro Islands*. Lanham, MD: Scarecrow Press, 1994.

Scarr, Deryck. *Seychelles since 1770: History of a Slave and Post-Slave Society*. Lawrenceville, NJ: Africa World Press, 1999.

Storey, William K. *Science and Power in Colonial Mauritius*. Rochester, NY: University of Rochester Press, 1997.

## Eastern Africa

Aboubaker Alwan, Daoud. *Historical Dictionary of Djibouti*. Lanham, MD: Scarecrow Press, 2000.

Baltimore, The Walters Art Museum. *Ethiopian Art: The Walters Museum*. Lingfield, UK: Third Millennium Publishing, 2001.

Bigsten, Arne and Steve Kayizzi-Mugerwa. *Crisis, Adjustment, and Growth in Uganda: a Study of Adaptation in an African Economy.* New York: Saint Martin's Press, 1999.

Crummey, Donald. *Land and Society in the Christian Kingdom of Ethiopia: from the Thirteenth to the Twentieth Century.* Champaign, IL: University of Illinois Press, 1999.

Darch, Colin. *Tanzania.* Santa Barbara, CA: ABC-CLIO, rev. ed. 1996.

Donham, Donald L. *Marxist Modern: an Ethnographic History of the Ethiopian Revolution* Berkeley, CA: University of California Press, 1999.

Fegley, Randall. *Eritrea.* Santa Barbara, CA: ABC-CLIO, 1995.

Forster, Peter G. and Sam Maghimbi, eds. *Agrarian Economy, State, and Society in Contemporary Tanzania.* Brookfield, VT: Ashgate Publishing Company, 1999.

Fozzard, Adrian. *Djibouti.* Boulder, CO: Westview Press, 1999.

Gregory, Robert G. *South Asians in East Africa: An Economic and Social History, 1890-1980.* Boulder, CO: Westview Press, 1993.

Hansen, Holger Bernt and Michael Twaddle, eds. *Developing Uganda.* Athens, OH: Ohio University Press, 1998.

Heldman, Marilyn with Stuart C. Munro-Hay. *African Zion: The Sacred Art of Ethiopia.* New Haven: Yale University Press, 1993.

Henze, Paul B. *Layers of Time: A History of Ethiopia.* New York: Saint Martin's Press, 1999.

Henze, Paul. *Eritrea's War.* Summerset, NJ: Transaction, 2002.

Killion, Tom. *Historical Dictionary of Eritrea.* Lanham, MD: Scarecrow Press, 1998.

Levine, Donald N. *Greater Ethiopia: The Evolution of a Multiethnic Society.* Chicago: University of Chicago Press, 2000.

Little, Peter D. *Somalia: Economy Without State.* Oxford : International African Institute in association with James Currey, 2003.

Maloba, Wunyabara O. *Mau Mau and Kenya: An Analysis of a Peasant Revolt.* Bloomington, IN: Indiana University Press, 1998.

Marcus, Harold G. *A History of Ethiopia.* Berkeley, CA: University of California Press, 1994.

Maxon, Robert M. *Historical Dictionary of Kenya.* 2nd ed. Lanham, MD: Scarecrow Press, 2000.

Mukhtar, Mohamed Haji and Margaret Castagno. *Historical Dictionary of Somalia.* Revised edition. Lanham, MD: Rowman & Littlefield Publishers, 2003.

Munro-Hay, Stuart and Richard Pankhurst. *Ethiopia.* Santa Barbara, CA: ABC-CLIO, 1995.

Negash, Tekeste. *Eritrea and Ethiopia: The Federal Experience.* New Brunswick, NJ: Transaction Publishers, 1997.

Neyko, Balam. *Uganda.* Santa Barbara, CA: ABC-CLIO, rev. ed. 1996.

Ocitti, Jim. *Political Evolution and Democratic Practice in Uganda, 1952-1996.* Lewiston, NY: The Edwin Mellen Press, 2000.

Oded, Arye. *Islam and Politics in Kenya.* Boulder, CO: Lynne Rienner Publishers, 2000.

Ofcansky, Thomas P. and Robert M. Maxon. *Historical Dictionary of Kenya.* Lanham, MD: Scarecrow Press, 1999.

Ofcansky, Thomas P. and Rodger Yeager. *Historical Dictionary of Tanzania.* 2nd ed. Lanham, MD: Scarecrow Press, 1997.

Pankhurst, Barbara. *The Ethiopians.* Malden, MA: Blackwell Publishers, 1998.

Pausewang, Siegfried, et al. *Ethiopia Since the Derg. A Decade of Democratic Pretension and Performance.* NY: Palgrave, 2003.

Peterson, Scott. *Me against My Brother: At War in Somalia, Sudan and Rwanda.* New York: Routledge, 2000.

Prouty, Chris and Eugene Rosenfeld. *Historical Dictionary of Ethiopia and Eritrea.* Lanham, MD: Scarecrow Press, 2nd ed. 1994.

Schraeder, Peter J. *Djibouti.* Santa Barbara, CA: ABC-CLIO, 1991.

Tesfai, Alemseged. *Post-Conflict Eritrea: Prospects for Reconstruction and Development.* Lawrenceville, NJ: Red Sea Press, 1999.

Watson, Mary Ann, ed. *Modern Kenya: Social Issues and Perspectives.* Lanham, MD: University Press of America, 2000.

Woodward, Peter. *The Horn of Africa. Politics and International Relations.* Rev. ed. NY: Palgrave, 2003.

## South Sahara Africa

Amnesty International. *Sudan: The Human Price of Oil.* London: Amnesty International, 2000.

Azevedo, Mario. *Chad: A Nation in Search of Its Future.* Boulder, CO: Westview Press, 1997.

Burr, J. Millard and Robert O. Collins. *Africa's Thirty Years' War: Chad, Libya, and the Sudan, 1963–1993.* Boulder, CO: Westview Press, 1999.

Burr, Millard and Robert Collins. *Revolutionary Sudan: Hasan al-Turabi and the Islamist state, 1989-2000.* Leiden; Boston, MA : Brill, 2003.

Decalo, Samuel. *Historical Dictionary of Chad.* Lanham, MD: Scarecrow Press, 1997.

Decalo, Samuel. *Historical Dictionary of Niger.* Lanham, MD: Scarecrow Press, 1996.

Deng, Francis Mading. *War of Visions: Conflict of Identities in the Sudan.* Washington, DC: Brookings Institution Press, 1995.

Human Rights Watch. *Behind the Red Line: Political Repression in Sudan.* New York: Human Rights Watch, 1996.

Human Rights Watch. *Sudan, Oil, and Human Rights.* New York: Human Rights Watch, 2003.

International Crisis Group. *Darfur Rising: Sudan's New Crisis.* (Africa Report No. 76). Brussels: International Crisis Group, 25 March 2004. (http://www.crisisweb.org/)

Johnson, Douglas H. *The Root Causes of Sudan's Civil Wars.* Bloomington: Indiana University Press, 2003.

Khalid, Mansour. *War and Peace in Sudan: A Tale of Two Countries.* NY: Kegan Paul, 2003.

McFarland, Daniel M. *Historical Dictionary of Burkina Faso.* Lanham, MD: Scarecrow Press, 1998.

Mosely Lesch, Ann. *The Sudan: Contested National Identities.* Bloomington, IN: Indiana University Press, 1998.

Peterson, Scott. *Me against My Brother: At War in Somalia, Sudan, and Rwanda.* New York: Routledge, 2000.

Petterson, Donald. *Inside Sudan: Political Islam, Conflict, and Catastrophe.* Rev. ed. Boulder, CO: Westview Press, 2003.

Popenoe, Rebecca. *Feeding Desire: Fatness, Beauty, and Sexuality among a Saharan People.* New York: Routledge, 2004.

Schutyser, Sebastian. *Banco: Adobe Mosques of the Inner Niger Delta.* Milan: Five Continents Editions, 2003.

Scroggins, Deborah. *Emma's War.* New York: Pantheon, 2002.

Warburg, Gabriel. *Islam, Sectarianism, and Politics In Sudan Since the Mahdiyya.* Madison: University of Wisconsin Press, 2003.

Zamponi, Lynda F. *Niger.* Santa Barbara: ABC-CLIO, 1994.

## North Africa

Abdo, Geneive. *No God but God: Egypt and the Triumph of Islam.* New York: Oxford University Press, 2000.

Adamson, Kay. *Algeria: A Study in Competing Ideologies.* Herndon, VA: Cassell Academic, 1998.

Ahmida, Ali Abdullatif. *The Making of Modern Libya: State Formation, Colonialization, and Resistance, 1830–1932.* Albany, NY: State University of New York, 1994.

Arnold, Guy. *The Maverick State: Gaddafi and the New World Order.* Herndon, VA: Cassell Academic, 1996.

Beattie, Kirk J. *Egyptian Politics During Sadat's Presidency*. New York: Saint Martin's Press, 2000.

Borowiec, Andrew. *Tunisia: a Democratic Apprenticeship*. Westport, CT: Greenwood Publishing Group, 1998.

Burr, J. Millard and Robert O. Collins. *Africa's Thirty Years' War: Chad, Libya, and the Sudan, 1963–1993*. Boulder, CO: Wesview Press, 1999.

Calderini, Simonetta, et al., *Mauritania*. Santa Barbara, CA: ABC-CLIO, 1992.

Ciment, James. *Algeria: the Fundamentalist Challenge*. New York: Facts on File, 1997.

Daly, Martin W., ed. *Modern Egypt from 1517 to the End of the Twentieth Century*. New York: Cambridge University Press, 1999.

El-Kikhia, Mansour O. *Libya's Qaddafi: the Politics of Contradiction*. Gainesville, FL: University Press of Florida, 1997.

Findlay, Anne M., et al., *Morocco*. Santa Barbara, CA: ABC-CLIO, 1995.

Gould, St. John. *Morocco*. NY: Routledge, 2002.

Human Rights Watch. *Egypt: In a Time of Torture*. New York: Human Rights Watch, 2004.

Jensen, Erik. *Western Sahara: Anatomy of a Stalemate*. Boulder, CO: Lynne Rienner, 2004.

King, Stephen J. *Liberalization against Democracy: The Local Politics of Economic Reform in Tunisia*. Bloomington: Indiana University Press, 2003.

Lawless, Richard I. *Algeria*. Santa Barbara, CA: ABC-CLIO, 1995.

Long, David E. and Bernard Reich. *The Government and Politics of the Middle East and North Africa*. 4th ed. Boulder, CO: Westview, 2002.

Murphy, Emma C. *Economic and Political Change in Tunisia: From Bourguiba to Ben Ali*. New York: Saint Martin's Press, 1999.

Naylor, Phillip Chivages and Alf Andrew Heggoy. *Historical Dictionary of Algeria*. Lanham, MD: Scarecrow Press, 2nd ed. 1994.

Niblock, Tim. *"Pariah States" & Sanctions in the Middle East: Iraq, Libya, Sudan*. Boulder, CO: Lynne Rienner Publishers, 2001

Park, Thomas K. *Historical Dictionary of Morocco*. Lanham, MD: Scarecrow Press, 1996.

Pazzanita, Anthony G. *Historical Dictionary of Mauritania*. Lanham, MD: Scarecrow Press, 1996.

Pennell, C.R. *Morocco Since 1830: A History*. Millwood, NY: Labyrinth, 2000.

Perkins, Kenneth J. *Historical Dictionary of Tunisia*. Lanham, MD: Scarecrow Press, 1997.

Quandt, William B. *Between Ballots and Bullets: Algeria's Transition from Authoritarianism*. Washington, DC: Brookings Institution Press, 1998.

Rubin, Barry. *Islamic Fundamentalism in Egyptian Politics*. NY: Palgrave, 2002.

St. John, Ronald Bruce. *Historical Dictionary of Libya*. Lanham, MD: Scarecrow Press, 3rd ed. 1998.

Stora, Benjamin. *Algeria, 1830–2000: A Short History*. Ithaca, NY: Cornell University Press, 2001.

Sullivan, Denis J. *Islam in Contemporary Egypt: Civil Society vs. the State*. Boulder, CO: Lynne Rienner Publishers, 1999.

Takeyh, Ray. *The Origins of the Eisenhower Doctrine: The U.S., Britain and Nasser's Egypt, 1953–57*. New York: Saint Martin's Press, 2000.

Vandewalle, Dirk. *Libya since Independence: Oil and State-Building*. Ithaca, NY: Cornell University Press, 1998.

White, Gregory. *A Comparative Political Economy of Tunisia and Morocco: On the outside of Europe looking in*. Albany, NY: State University of New York Press, 2001.

Willis, Michael. *The Islamist Challenge in Algeria: A Political History*. New York: New York University Press, 1997.

Zartman, William, ed. *Tunisia: The Political Economy of Reform*. Boulder, CO: Lynne Rienner Publishers, 1991.

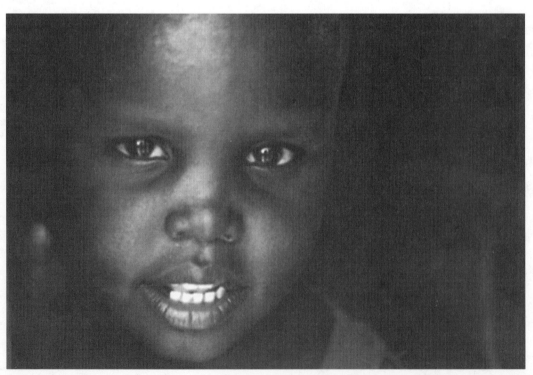

Courtesy of Wojtek Kalociński and Piotr Zaporowski